BUSINESS ACCOUNTING 2

BUSINESS ACCOUNTING 2

Eighth Edition

Frank Wood BSc (Econ), FCA
and
Alan Sangster BA, MSc, Cert TESOL, CA

FINANCIAL TIMES
PITMAN PUBLISHING

FINANCIAL TIMES
MANAGEMENT

LONDON • SAN FRANCISCO
KUALA LUMPUR • JOHANNESBURG

*Financial Times Management delivers the knowledge,
skills and understanding that enable students,
managers and organisations to achieve their ambitions,
whatever their needs, wherever they are.*

London Office:
128 Long Acre, London WC2E 9AN
Tel: +44 (0)171 447 2000
Fax: +44 (0)171 240 5771
Website: www.ftmanagement.com

A Division of Financial Times Professional Limited

Eighth edition published in Great Britain in 1999

ISBN 0 273 63743 6

British Library Cataloguing in Publication Data
A CIP catalogue record for this book can be obtained from the British Library.

10 9 8 7 6 5 4 3 2 1

Printed and bound in Great Britain by Clays Ltd, St Ives plc

The Publishers' policy is to use paper manufactured from sustainable forests.

Contents

Preface to the eighth edition

This is the second volume of the textbook. It completes the coverage of the financial accounting part of quite a few examinations in accounting. As examination syllabuses are constantly being revised, it would not make sense to be too specific as to which chapters would be needed by students taking each of the various examinations.

The examining bodies whose students will find the book of most value include:

The various Institutes of Chartered Accountants
Association of Chartered Certified Accountants
Chartered Institute of Management Accountants
Institute of Chartered Secretaries and Administrators
Association of Accounting Technicians
London Chamber of Commerce and Industry
Royal Society of Arts Examinations Board
General Certificate of Education A–Level

This volume examines all the current accounting standards (both *Statements of Standard Accounting Practice* – SSAPs – and *Financial Reporting Standards* – FRSs) in as much detail as is needed by most students at this level. However, where they represent a complete examination paper, some students will need a much more detailed knowledge of them than a textbook of this kind can provide. In this case, students would be well advised to refer to a specialist textbook on the topic, or to the standards themselves.

We wish to acknowledge the permission to use past examination papers granted by the Institute of Chartered Accountants in England and Wales; the Association of Chartered Certified Accountants; the Chartered Institute of Management Accountants; the Association of Accounting Technicians; the Institute of Chartered Secretaries and Administrators; the Edexcel Foundation, London Examinations (formerly the University of London Examinations and Assessments Council); the University of Cambridge Local Examinations Syndicate; the Associated Examining Board; and the Welsh Joint Education Committee.

As in previous editions, all answers to questions are the product of our own work and have not been supplied by any of the examining bodies. The examining bodies bear no responsibility for the example answers to questions taken from their past examination papers which are contained in this publication.

Twelve new chapters have been added to this edition. Two of these – Chapters 3 (*Container accounts*) and 18 (*Investment accounts*) – appeared in previous editions but were not included in the 7th edition. Chapter 32 (*Accounting theory*) was previously in volume 1. The other nine chapters are all new to *Frank Wood's Business Accounting* and represent a major expansion in the range of topics covered. All nine are concerned with managerial accounting and are to be found in Parts 6, 7, 8, and 9 of this book. We are indebted to the many users of *Frank Wood's Business Accounting* whose advice resulted in these changes being made. We are especially grateful to Michael Siaw Jun Choi, Muhammad Hanif Ghanghi, and Pamela Malton for their insightful suggestions. There are many others too numerous to mention to whom we are indebted, and we trust that they will not be offended by our inability to list them all here.

Frank Wood and Alan Sangster

Available free to lecturers who adopt *Business Accounting*

Business Accounting Solutions Manual (8th edn)   (0 273 64147 6)

Fully-displayed answers to all questions with the suffix 'A' in the texts, together with overhead transparency masters, are available free of charge to lecturers who recommend *Business Accounting* Volumes 1 or 2 on their course.

Multiple Choice Question Test Software *Volume 1*   (0 273 62546 2)
Multiple Choice Question Test Software *Volume 2*   (0 273 62547 0)

Other books in the Frank Wood series:

Business Accounting Multiple Choice Question Book   (0 273 64193 X)
Business Accounting *Volume 1* (8th edn)   (0 273 63742 8)

Business Accounting: Irish Edition (2nd edn)   (0 273 63153 5)
Business Accounting: Irish Edition, Multiple Choice Question Book (0 273 60832 0)

Business Accounting: South African Edition   (0 273 62126 2)

Business Accounting: Hong Kong Edition *Volume 1*   (0 273 63847 5)
Business Accounting: Hong Kong Edition *Volume 2*   (0 273 63848 3)

Book-keeping and Accounts (4th edn)   (0 273 03770 6)

A-level Accounting (2nd edn)   (0 273 63161 6)

Business Accounting NVQ Level 2 Accounting *Student's Workbook* (0 273 60188 1)
Business Accounting NVQ Level 3 Accounting *Student's Workbook* (0 273 60446 5)

Transaction Accounting for NVQ Level 2   (0 273 61349 9)

FINANCIAL TIMES
PITMAN PUBLISHING

Part 1

SPECIAL ACCOUNTS

1 Branch accounts
2 Hire purchase accounts
3 Container accounts

Introduction

This part is concerned with three items that are treated in a similar way, irrespective of the form of business involved.

1
Branch accounts

Objectives

After you have studied this chapter, you should:

- *know two methods of recording the entries relating to branch accounts*
- *be aware of the issues relating to foreign branch accounts*

1.1 Accounting records and branches

When we look at accounting records to show transactions at the branches of an organisation, we have a choice of two main methods. These are:

(*a*) the head office keeps all the accounting records, or
(*b*) each branch has its own full accounting system.

It is easier to understand branch accounts if these two main methods are dealt with separately.

1.2 If the head office maintains all the accounts

The accounts are used for three main purposes:

(*a*) to record transactions showing changes in assets, liabilities and capital;
(*b*) to ascertain the profitability of each branch;
(*c*) in addition, if possible, to check whether anyone at the branches is stealing goods or cash.

This third purpose is very important for firms that have many branches. The people who manage or work in these branches are receiving and paying out large sums of money. In addition they may be handling large amounts of stocks of goods. The branch or branches may be a considerable distance away from the head office. This may mean that the manager, or any of his staff, may think that they can steal things without being caught.

1.3 Methods for checking stock and cash

If a firm with only a few branches sells only very expensive cars, it would be easy to check on purchases and sales of the cars. The number of cars sold would not be very great. Checking that cars or money have not been stolen would be easy. However, a firm such as a store with branches selling many thousands of cheap items could not be checked so easily. To keep a check on each carton of salt or bag of flour sold would be almost impossible. Even if it could be done, such checking would cost too much. The accounting answer to this problem is to record all transactions at the branch in terms of selling prices. Then for each accounting period, it should be possible to check whether the closing stock is as it should be. For a small branch, for example, you may be given the following figures:

	£
Stock on hand at 1 January – at selling price	500
January – Goods sent to the branch by the head office – at selling price	4,000
January – Sales by the branch – obviously at selling price	3,800

The calculation of the closing stock becomes:

	£
Opening Stock 1 January (selling price)	500
Add Goods sent to the branch (selling price)	4,000
Goods which the branch had available for sale (selling price)	4,500
Less Goods sold (selling price)	3,800
Closing stock at 31 January should therefore be (selling price)	700

1.4 Allowances for deficiencies

In every business there will be:

(*a*) Wastage of goods for some reason. Goods may be damaged or broken, or they may be kept too long or somehow waste away.
(*b*) Stealing by customers, especially in the retail business.
(*c*) Thefts by employees.

No one can be certain how much stock is wasted or stolen during a period. Only experience will enable a firm to make a good estimate of these losses.

1.5 The double column system

At regular intervals, obviously at least once a year but usually more frequently, the head office may draft a trading and profit and loss account for each branch. The trading account can be shown with two columns, one in which goods sent to the branch or in stock are shown at cost price, i.e. the normal basis for any business. This column is therefore part of a normal trading account for the branch. The other column will show all trading account items at selling price. This column allows deficiencies in trading to be compared with the normal deficiency allowed for wastages, etc. It is not a part of the double entry recording; it is a memorandum column for control purposes only.

Exhibit 1.1

This is drafted from the following details for a firm which sells goods at a uniform mark-up of $33\frac{1}{3}$ per cent on cost price:

	£
Stock 1 Jan 19X8 (at cost)	1,200
Goods sent to the branch during the year (at cost)	6,000
Sales (selling price)	7,428
Stock 31 Dec 19X8 (at cost)	1,500
Expenses	1,000

Allowances for wastage, etc., 1 per cent of sales.

Branch Trading and Profit and Loss Account for the year ended 31.12.19X8					
	At selling price			At selling price	
	£	£		£	£
Stock 1 Jan 19X8	1,600	1,200	Sales	7,428	7,428
Goods from head office	8,000	6,000	Deficiency (difference)	172	
	9,600	7,200			
Less Stock 31 Dec 19X8	2,000	1,500			
	7,600	5,700			
Gross profit c/d		1,728			
	7,600	7,428		7,600	7,428
Expenses		1,000	Gross profit b/d		1,728
Net profit		728			
		1,728			1,728

As the actual deficiency of £172 exceeds the amount expected, i.e. 1 per cent of £7,428 = £74, an investigation will be made.

This method is suitable where all the sales are for cash, there being no sales on credit.

1.6 The stock and debtors system

Further adjustments are needed when there are credit sales as well as cash sales. There are two ways of making the entries. These are:

(a) using memoranda columns only to keep a check on stock, in a similar way to that shown in 1.5;
(b) building the control of stock fully into the double entry system. This is often called an integrated system.

We can now examine both of these methods.

Using the following basic data, Exhibit 1.2 shows the records when the memoranda method is used, while Exhibit 1.3 shows the records when the integrated method is in use.

Data: A branch sells all its goods at a uniform mark-up of 50 per cent on cost price. Credit customers are to pay their accounts directly to the head office.

		£
First day of the period:		
Stock (at cost)	(A)	2,000
Debtors	(B)	400
During the period:		
Goods sent to the branch (at cost)	(C)	7,000
Sales – Cash	(D)	6,000
Sales – Credit	(E)	4,800
Cash remitted by debtors to head office	(F)	4,500
At the close of the last day of the period:		
Stock (at cost)	(G)	1,800
Debtors	(H)	700

The letters A to H beside the figures have been inserted to identify the entries in Exhibit 1.3. The entries for each of the above items will have the relevant letter shown beside it.

Memoranda columns method

Exhibit 1.2

Branch Stock

	Selling price memo. only			Selling price memo. only	
	£	£		£	£
Stock b/d	3,000	2,000	Sales: Cash	6,000	6,000
Goods sent	10,500	7,000	Credit	4,800	4,800
Gross profit to			Stock c/d	2,700	1,800
profit and loss		3,600			
	13,500	12,600		13,500	12,600
Stock b/d	2,700	1,800			

Branch Debtors

	£		£
Balances b/d	400	Cash	4,500
Branch stock	4,800	Balance c/d	700
	5,200		5,200
Balance b/d	700		

Goods Sent to Branches

	£		£
Transfer to head office trading account	7,000	Branch stock	7,000

Cash Book

	£	
Branch stock – cash sales	6,000	
Branch debtors	4,500	

The branch stock account is thus in effect a trading account, and is identical to the type used in the double column system. In addition, however, a branch debtors account is in use.

The balance of the goods sent to the branches account is shown as being transferred to the head office trading account. This figure is deducted from the purchases in the head office trading account, so that goods bought for the branch can be disregarded when the gross profit earned by the head office is calculated.

The integrated system

The integrated system introduces the idea that the gross profit earned by a firm can be calculated by reference to profit margins only. A simple example illustrates this point. Assume that a self-employed travelling salesman sells all his goods at cost price plus 25 per cent for profit. At the start of a week he has £4 stock at cost, he buys goods costing £40, he sells goods for £45 (selling price) and he has goods left in stock at the end of the week which had cost him £8. A normal trading account based on this data is shown below.

Trading Account for the week ended...

	£		£
Opening stock	4	Sales	45
Add Purchases	40		
	44		
Less Closing stock	8		
Cost of goods sold	36		
Gross profit	9		
	45		45

This could, however, also be shown as:

	£
Profit made when opening stock is sold	1
Profit made when purchases are sold	10
Profit made when all goods are sold	11
But he still has left unsold goods (cost £8) on which the profit still has to be realised	2
Therefore profit realised	9

This could be expressed in account form as:

Salesman's Adjustment Account

	£		£
Gross profit	9	Unrealised profit b/d	1
Unrealised profit c/d	2	Goods bought	10
	11		11

The integrated system uses an adjustment account which is needed because goods sent to the branch are shown at cost price in a 'goods sent to branches account'. In the branch stock account these goods are shown at selling price. Obviously if one entry is made at cost price and the other at selling price, the accounts would not balance. To correct this, an extra account called a branch adjustment account is opened. The entries in this account are in respect of the profit content only of goods.

The branch stock account acts as a check upon stock deficiencies. The branch adjustment account shows the amount of gross profit earned during the period.

Exhibit 1.3 shows the accounts needed for the integrated system from the same information on pages 5–6 used to complete Exhibit 1.2. In this example a stock deficiency does not exist. The letters A to H in Exhibit 1.3 conform to the letters A to H shown against the information on page 6.

Exhibit 1.3

Branch Stock (Selling Price)

		£			£
Balance b/d	(A)	3,000	Sales: Cash	(D)	6,000
Goods sent to branch	(C)	10,500	Credit	(E)	4,800
			Balance c/d	(G)	2,700
		13,500			13,500
Balance b/d	(G)	2,700			

Branch Debtors (Selling Price)

		£			£
Balances b/d	(B)	400	Cash	(F)	4,500
Branch stock	(E)	4,800	Balances c/d	(H)	700
		5,200			5,200
Balances b/d	(H)	700			

Goods Sent to Branches (Cost Price)

		£			£
Transfer to head office trading account		7,000	Branch stock	(C)	7,000

Branch Adjustment (Profit Content)

		£			£
Gross profit to profit and loss		3,600	Unrealised profit b/d	(A)	1,000
Unrealised profit c/d	(G)	900	Branch stock – goods sent	(C)	3,500
		4,500			4,500
			Unrealised profit b/d	(G)	900

The opening and closing stocks are shown in the branch stock account at selling price. However, the balance sheet should show the stock at cost price. The previous balance sheet should therefore have shown stock at cost £2,000. This is achieved by having a compensating £1,000 credit balance brought forward in the branch adjustment account so that the debit balance of £3,000 in the branch stock account, when it comes to being shown in the balance sheet, has the £1,000 credit balance deducted to show a net figure of £2,000. Similarly, at the close of the period the balance sheet will show stock at £1,800 (branch stock debit balance £2,700 *less* branch adjustment credit balance £900).

1.7 The stock and debtors integrated system – further points

Returns

Goods may be returned:

(a) from the branch stock to the head office;
(b) from the branch debtors to the branch stock;
(c) from the branch debtors to the head office.

Exhibit 1.4

To examine the entries needed, suppose a firm sells goods at cost plus 25 per cent profit, and according to the categories stated the following goods were returned, all prices shown being selling prices: (a) £45, (b) £75, (c) £15. The entries needed are:

Branch Stock (Selling Price)

		£				£
Returns from debtors	(b)	75	Returns to head office	(a)		45

Branch Adjustment (Profit Loading)

		£
Returns from branch	(a)	9
Returns from debtors	(c)	3

Goods Sent to Branches (Cost Price)

		£
Returns from branch	(a)	36
Returns from debtors	(c)	12

Branch Debtors (Selling Price)

			£
	Returns to branch	(b)	75
	Returns to head office	(c)	15

Entries (b) both being in accounts shown at selling price were two in number, i.e. £75 Dr and £75 Cr; entries (a) and (c) each needed entries in three accounts, (a) being £45 Cr and £9 Dr and £36 Dr, (c) being £15 Cr and £12 Dr and £3 Dr.

1.8 If each branch maintains full accounting records

This method is rarely used in firms with many branches. It is more common in a firm with just one or two or a few branches, and is particularly relevant if a branch is large enough to warrant employing a separate accounting staff.

A branch cannot operate on its own without resources, and it is the firm that provides these in the first instance. The firm will want to know how much money it has invested in each branch, and from this arises the concept of branch and head office current accounts. The relationship between the branch and the head office is seen as that of a debtor/creditor. The current account shows the branch as a debtor in the head office records, while the head office is shown as a creditor in the branch records.

The current accounts are used for transactions concerned with supplying resources to the branch or in taking back resources. For such transactions full double entry records are needed both in the branch records and in the head office records, i.e. each item will be recorded twice in each set of records. Some transactions will, however, concern the branch only, and these will merely need two entries in the branch records and none in the head office records. Exhibit 1.5 shows several transactions and the records needed.

Exhibit 1.5

A firm with its head office in London opened a branch in Manchester. The following transactions took place in the first month:

(A) Opened a bank account at Manchester by transferring £1,000 from the London bank account.
(B) Bought premises in Manchester, paying by cheque drawn on the London bank account, £5,000.
(C) Manchester bought a motor van, paying by cheque £600 from its own bank account.
(D) Manchester bought fixtures on credit from A B Equipment Ltd, £900.
(E) London supplied a machine valued at £250 from its own machinery.
(F) Manchester bought goods from suppliers, paying by cheque on its own account, £270.
(G) Manchester's cash sales banked immediately in its own bank account, £3,000.
(H) Goods invoiced at cost to Manchester during the month by London (no cash or cheques being paid specifically for these goods by Manchester), £2,800.
(I) A cheque is paid to London by Manchester as general return of funds, £1,800.
(J) Goods returned to London by Manchester – at cost price, £100.

The exact dates have been deliberately omitted. It will be seen later that complications arise because of differences in the timing of transactions. Each transaction has been identified by a capital letter. The relevant letter will be shown against each entry in the accounts.

Head Office Records (in London)
Manchester Branch Current Account

		£			£
Bank	(A)	1,000	Bank	(I)	1,800
Bank – premises	(B)	5,000	Returns from Branch	(J)	100
Machinery	(E)	250			
Goods sent to Branch	(H)	2,800			

Bank

		£			£
Manchester Branch	(I)	1,800	Manchester Branch	(A)	1,000
			Manchester premises	(B)	5,000

Machinery

					£
			Manchester Branch	(E)	250

Goods sent to Branch

		£			£
Returns from Branch	(J)	100	Manchester Branch	(H)	2,800

Branch Records (in Manchester)

Head Office Current Account

		£			£
Bank	(I)	1,800	Bank	(A)	1,000
Returns	(J)	100	Premises	(B)	5,000
			Machinery	(E)	250
			Goods from Head Office	(H)	2,800

Bank

		£			£
Head Office	(A)	1,000	Motor van	(C)	600
Cash sales	(G)	3,000	Purchases	(F)	270
			Head Office	(I)	1,800

Premises

		£	
Head Office	(B)	5,000	

Motor Van

		£	
Bank	(C)	600	

Fixtures

		£	
A B Equipment Ltd	(D)	900	

A B Equipment Ltd

			£
	Fixtures	(D)	900

Machinery

		£	
Head Office	(E)	250	

Purchases

		£	
Bank	(F)	270	

Sales

			£
		Bank (G)	3,000

Goods from Head Office

		£			£
Head Office	(H)	2,800	Head Office – returns (J)		100

It can be seen that items C, D, F and G are entered only in the Manchester records. This is because these items are purely internal transactions and are not concerned with resources flowing between London and Manchester.

1.9 Profit or loss and current accounts

The profit earned by the branch (or loss incurred by it) does not belong to the branch. It belongs to the firm and must therefore be shown as such. The head office represents the central authority of the firm and profit of the branch should be credited to the Head Office Current Account, any loss being debited.

The branch will therefore draw up its own trading and profit and loss account. After agreement with the head office the net profit will then be transferred to the credit of the Head Office Current Account. The head office in its own records will then debit the Branch Current Account and credit its own profit and loss account. Taking the net profit earned in Exhibit 1.5 as £700, the two sets of books would appear thus:

Head Office Records (in London)

London Profit and Loss Account

		£
	Net profit earned by the Manchester Branch	700

Manchester Branch Current Account

	£		£
Bank	1,000	Bank	1,800
Bank: premises	5,000	Returns from Branch	100
Machinery	250		
Goods sent to Branch	2,800		
Net profit to main profit and loss account	700	Balance c/d	7,850
	9,750		9,750
Balance b/d	7,850		

Branch Records (in Manchester)

Manchester Profit and Loss Account

	£		
Net profit carried to the Head Office Current Account	700		

Head Office Current Account

	£		£
Returns to Head Office	100	Bank	1,000
Bank	1,800	Premises	5,000
		Machinery	250
		Goods from Head Office	2,800
Balance c/d	7,850	Profit and loss account	700
	9,750		9,750
		Balance b/d	7,850

1.10 The combined balance sheet

After the trading and profit and loss accounts have been drawn up a balance sheet is required for the whole firm. The branch will send its trial balance to the head office which will add the assets in its own trial balance to those in the branch trial balance to give the total for each type of asset to be shown in the balance sheet, and a similar procedure will be carried out for the liabilities.

In the trial balances the Head Office Current Account will be a debit balance while the Branch Current Account will be a credit balance, e.g. the two figures of £7,850 in the London and Manchester books. These therefore cancel out and are not shown in the combined balance sheet. This is in order, as the two balances do not in fact represent assets or liabilities, but are merely a measure of the resources at the branch.

1.11 Items in transit

It was stated earlier that the timing of transactions raised complications. Obviously a cheque sent by a Manchester branch one day would probably arrive in London the next day, while goods sent from London to Manchester, or returned from Manchester to London, could well take longer than that. Both the head office and the branch will have entered the transactions at the dates of remittance or receipt, and as the remittance from one place will occur on one day and the receipt occur at the other place on another day, then where items are in transit at the end of a financial period each set of records will not contain identical figures. This will mean that the balances on the current accounts will not be equal to one another.

It is, however, necessary to have identical amounts of balances on the current accounts so that they will cancel out when the combined balance sheet is prepared. As the two sets of records contain some figures which are different from each other they must somehow be reconciled so that the balances carried down are the same. Which set of figures are to be altered? The answer is one of expediency. It would be normal to find the most experienced accountants at the Head Office, and therefore the amendments should all be made in the Head Office books instead of leaving it to junior accountants at the branches who would be more likely to make mistakes. Also if there are several branches the problems of communicating specific instructions to several accountants some distance away make it easier for all amendments to be made at the Head Office.

Exhibit 1.6 is for a second month of the business shown in Exhibit 1.5. However, whereas there were no items in transit at the end of the first month, this does not hold true at the conclusion of the second month.

Exhibit 1.6

Head Office records (showing current accounts only)	£
Goods sent to Branch	3,700
Cheques received from Branch	2,950
Returns received from Branch	440

Branch records	
Goods received from Head Office	3,500
Cheques sent to Head Office	3,030
Returns sent to Head Office	500

It may be assumed that the net profit as shown by the profit and loss account of the branch is £800.

Branch Records (in Manchester)

Head Office Current Account

	£		£
Bank	3,030	Balance b/d	7,850
Returns to Head Office	500	Goods from Head Office	3,500
Balance c/d	8,620	Net profit	800
	12,150		12,150
		Balance b/d	8,620

Head Office Records (in London)

Manchester Branch Current Account

		£			£
Balance b/d		7,850	Bank	(B)	2,950
Goods sent to Branch	(A)	3,700	Returns received	(C)	440
Net profit		800			

At this point the following items are observed to be in transit at the end of the period (these should be confirmed to ensure that they are not merely errors in accounting records):

1 Goods sent to the branch amounting to £200 (£3,700 − £3,500).
2 Cheques sent by the branch amounting to £80 (£3,030 − £2,950).
3 Returns from the branch amounting to £60 (£500 − £440).

(A) needs amending to £3,500. This is done by crediting the account with £200.
(B) needs amending to £3,030. This is done by crediting the account with £80.
(C) needs amending to £500. This is done by crediting the account with £60.

As these are items in transit they need to be taken to the period in which they arrive, i.e. the next month. This is effected by carrying them down as balances into the next period.

The branch current account will now be completed.

It may appear at first sight to be rather strange that all the items in transit are shown as debit balances. However, it must be appreciated that goods (including returns) and money in transit are assets of the firm at the end of a financial period. That they are in transit is merely stipulating that the assets are neither at the head office nor at the branch but are somewhere else. Assets are always shown as debit balances and there is no reason why it should be different just because they have not reached their destination on a certain date.

Manchester Branch Current Account

	£		£
Balance b/d	7,850	Bank	2,950
Goods sent to branch	3,700	Returns received	440
Net profit	800	Goods in transit c/d	200
		Cheques in transit c/d	80
		Returns in transit c/d	60
		Balance c/d	8,620
	12,350		12,350
Balance b/d	8,620		
Goods in transit b/d	200		
Cheques in transit b/d	80		
Returns in transit b/d	60		

All of these four balances are shown in the trial balance. When the combined balance sheet is being prepared the balance of the two current accounts, i.e. in this case £8,620, will cancel out as it is a debit balance in one trial balance and a credit balance in the other. The goods in transit £200 and the returns in transit £60, both being goods, are added to the stock in the balance sheet. This is because stock is made up of the following items:

At the end of the second month:

	£
Stock at London	
Add Stock at Manchester	
Add Stocks in transit (£200 + £60)	260
Total stock	

Similarly, the balance for cheques or remittances in transit is added to the bank balances at London and Manchester:

	£
Bank balance at London	
Add Bank balance in Manchester	
Add Remittances in transit	80

This is rather like a man who has £14 in one pocket and £3 in another. He takes a £5 note from the pocket containing the larger amount and is transferring it to his other pocket when someone asks him to stay perfectly still and calculate the total cash in his possession. He therefore has:

	£
Pocket 1	9
Pocket 2	3
Cash in transit	5
	17

1.12 Items in transit and the balance sheet

Using the figures already given in Exhibit 1.6 but adding some further information, trial balances for London Head Office and the Manchester Branch are now shown in Exhibit 1.7 after the profit and loss accounts have been drawn up for the second month.

Exhibit 1.7

Trial Balances as at 29 February 19X8				
	London Head Office		Manchester Branch	
	Dr	Cr	Dr	Cr
	£	£	£	£
Premises	10,000		5,000	
Machinery	2,000		400	
Fixtures	3,100		1,400	
Motor vans	1,500		900	
Closing stock	3,800		700	
Debtors	1,100		800	
Bank	12,200		600	
Head Office Current Account				8,620
Branch Current Account	8,620			
Goods in transit	200			
Cheques in transit	80			
Returns in transit	60			
Creditors		1,300		1,180
Capital account as at 1 Jan 19X8		37,860		
Net profit for the two months (Branch £1,500 + Head Office £2,000)		3,500		
	42,660	42,660	9,800	9,800

The combined balance sheet can now be drawn up.

Balance Sheet as at 29 February 19X8

	£	£
Fixed assets		
Premises		15,000
Machinery		2,400
Fixtures		4,500
Motor vans		2,400
		24,300
Current assets		
Stocks	4,760	
Debtors	1,900	
Bank	12,880	
	19,540	
Less Current liabilities		
Creditors	2,480	
Working capital		17,060
		41,360

Capital
Balance at 1 January 19X8   37,860
Add Net profit:
   London   2,000
   Manchester   1,500
                                             41,360

Notes:

Stocks:		£	Bank:		£
	London	3,800		London	12,200
	Manchester	700		Manchester	600
	In transit (£200 + £60)	260	In transit		80
		4,760			12,880

1.13 Foreign branch accounts

The treatment of the accounts of foreign branches is subject to only one exception from that of branches in your own country. This is concerned with the fact that when the trial balance is drawn up by the branch then this will be stated in a foreign currency. To amalgamate these figures with your own country's figures will mean that the foreign branch figures will have to be translated into your currency.

There are rules for general guidance as to how this can be done. SSAP 20: *Foreign currency translation* gives rules for organisations to follow. These are the ones which will be shown. (Before you read further you should check whether or not this topic is part of your examination requirements.)

The amount of a particular currency which one can obtain for another currency is known as the exchange rate. Taking an imaginary country with a currency called *chips*, there might be a general agreement that the exchange rate should stay about 5 chips to equal £1. At certain times the exchange rate will exactly equal that figure, but due to all sorts of economic reasons it may well be 5.02 chips to £1 on one day and 4.97 chips to £1 several days later. In addition, some years ago there may have been an act of devaluation by one of the countries involved; the exchange rate could well have then been 3 chips to £1. To understand more about exchange rates and devaluation the reader of this book would be well advised to consult a relevant economics textbook.

It is clear, however, that all items in the trial balance should not be converted to your currency on the basis of the exchange rate ruling at the date of the trial balance. The rules in SSAP 20 have been devised in an attempt to bring about conversion into your currency so as not to distort reported trading results.

1.14 Conversion rules per SSAP 20

1 (a) Fixed assets at the exchange rate ruling when the assets were bought – the **temporal method**. If fixed assets have been bought on different dates, then different rates will have to be used for each separate purchase.
    (b) Depreciation on the fixed assets at the same rate as the fixed assets concerned.
2 Current assets and current liabilities – at the rate ruling at the date of the trial balance. This is known as the **closing method**.
3 Opening stock in the trading account – at rate ruling at previous balance sheet date.
4 Goods sent by the head office to the branch, or returns from the branch – at the actual figures shown in the Goods Sent to Branches Account in the head office books.
5 Trading and profit and loss account items, other than depreciation, opening and

closing stocks, or goods sent to or returned by the branch – at the average rate for the period covered by the accounts.

6 The Head Office Current Account – at the same figures as shown in the Branch Current Account in the Head Office books.

1.15 Conversion of trial balance figures

When the conversion of the figures into your currency is completed, the totals of the debit and credit sides of your currency trial balance will not normally be equal to one another. This is due to different exchange rates being taken for conversion purposes. A balancing figure will therefore be needed to bring about the equality of the totals. For this purpose a **difference on exchange account** will be opened and a debit entry made therein if the lesser total is on the debit side of the trial balance. When the head office redrafts the profit and loss account any debit balance on the difference on exchange account should be transferred to it as an expense. A credit balance on the difference on exchange account should be transferred to the credit of the profit and loss account as a gain.

In consolidated accounts, special rules are applied for foreign exchange conversion.

Exhibit 1.8

An example of the conversion of a trial balance into UK currency is now shown. The branch is in Flavia, and the unit of currency is the Flavian dollar. The exchange rates needed are:

(a) On 1 January 19X3, 10 dollars = £1
(b) On 1 January 19X5, 11 dollars = £1
(c) On 1 January 19X8, 17 dollars = £1
(d) On 31 December 19X8, 15 dollars = £1
(e) If no further information were given the average rate for 19X8 would have to be taken as (c) + (d) ÷ 2, i.e. 16 dollars = £1. This is not an advisable procedure in practice; the fact that the average has been calculated from only two readings could mean that the average calculated might be far different from a more accurate one calculated from a larger number of readings.

Trial Balance as on 31 December 19X8

	Dr (F$)	Cr (F$)	Exchange rates	Dr £	Cr £
Fixed assets:					
Bought 1 Jan 19X3	10,000		10 = £1	1,000	
Bought 1 Jan 19X5	8,800		11 = £1	800	
Stock 1 Jan 19X8	6,800		17 = £1	400	
Expense accounts	8,000		16 = £1	500	
Sales		32,000	16 = £1		2,000
Goods from Head Office	21,900		£ per account in Head Office books	1,490	
Head Office current account		43,000	£ per account in Head Office books		3,380
Debtors	9,000		15 = £1	600	
Creditors		4,500	15 = £1		300
Bank	15,000		15 = £1	1,000	
	79,500	79,500		5,790	5,680
Difference on exchange account					110
				5,790	5,790

The stock at 31 December 19X8 is 12,000 dollars. When the trading account is drawn up this will be converted at 15 dollars = £1, i.e. £800.

Main points to remember

1 There are two main methods used to record transactions of the branches of an organisation:
(a) all accounting records are kept by the head office.
(b) each branch has its own full accounting system.

2 Foreign branch figures need to be translated using the principles set down in SSAP 20: *Foreign currency translation*.

Review questions

1.1 Octopus Ltd, whose head office is at Cardiff, operates a branch at Swansea. All goods are purchased by head office and invoiced to and sold by the branch at cost plus 33⅓ per cent.

Other than a sales ledger kept at Swansea, all transactions are recorded in the books at Cardiff.

The following particulars are given of the transactions at the branch during the year ended 28 February 19X7.

	£
Stock on hand, 1 March 19X6, at invoice price	4,400
Debtors on 1 March 19X6	3,946
Stock on hand, 28 February 19X7, at invoice price	3,948
Goods sent from Cardiff during the year at invoice price	24,800
Credit sales	21,000
Cash sales	2,400
Returns to head office at invoice price	1,000
Invoice value of goods stolen	600
Bad debts written off	148
Cash from debtors	22,400
Normal loss at invoice price due to wastage	100
Cash discount allowed to debtors	428

You are required to write up the branch stock account and branch total debtors account for the year ended 28 February 19X7, as they would appear in the head office books.

(*Institute of Chartered Accountants*)

1.2 A Co Ltd has a branch in Everton at which a full set of books are kept. At the end of the year the following is a summary of the transactions between the branch and the head office as recorded in the latter's books:

	£
Balance due from branch 1 January	20,160
Cash received from branch	30,000
Goods supplied to branch	23,160
Goods returned by branch	400
Expenses paid on behalf of branch	6,000

At 30 June the branch profit and loss account showed a net profit of £3,500.

(a) Show the above items as they would appear in the ledger of the head office.
(b) How can any resulting balance from these figures be proved, and what does it indicate?

1.3 RST Limited is a family-controlled company which operates a chain of retail outlets specialising in motor spares and accessories.

Branch stocks are purchased by a centralised purchasing function in order to obtain the best terms from suppliers.

A 10 per cent handling charge is applied by head office to the cost of the purchases, and branches are expected to add 25 per cent to the resulting figure to arrive at normal selling prices, although branch managers are authorised to reduce normal prices in special situations. The effect of such reductions must be notified to head office.

On 1 April 19X6, a new branch was established at Derham. The following details have been recorded for the year ended 31 March 19X7:

	£
Purchase cost to head office of stock transferred to Derham	82,400
Derham branch sales: cash	89,940
credit	1,870
Stocks transferred from Derham to other branches, at normal selling prices	3,300
Authorised reductions from normal selling prices during the year	2,250

All records in respect of branch activities are maintained at head office, and the branch profit margin is dealt with through a branch stock adjustment account.

Required:
(a) Prepare:
    (i) the branch stock account (maintained at branch selling prices);
    (ii) the branch stock adjustment account.
    The *book stock* should be taken for this part of the question.
(b) List four of the possible reasons for the stock difference revealed when a physical stocktaking at the Derham branch on 31 March 19X7 showed stock valued at selling prices amounting to £14,850.
(c) State which of the following is the figure to be included in RST Limited's balance sheet at 31 March 19X7, for Derham branch stock:
    (i) £11,138
    (ii) £11,880
    (iii) £10,800
    (iv) None of these.

Justify your choice with appropriate calculations.

(*Chartered Institute of Management Accountants*)

1.4A Paper Products has a head office in London and a branch in Bristol. The following information has been extracted from the head office books of account as at 31 March 19X6:

Information relating to the branch

Balances	Opening £000	Closing £000
Branch bank account (positive balance)	3	12
Branch debtors	66	81
Branch stock (at transfer price)	75	90

Transactions during the year	£000
Bad debts written off	15
Branch general expenses (paid from bank branch account)	42
Cash received from credit customers and banked	390
Cash sales banked	120
Cash transferred from branch to head office bank account	459
Credit sales	437

Discounts allowed to credit customers	9	
Goods returned by credit customers	8	
Goods returned from branch (at transfer price from head office)		30
Goods sent to branch (at transfer price from head office)		600

Information relating to head office

Balances	Opening	Closing
	£000	£000
Stock	180	220

Transactions during the year	£000
Bad debts written off	24
Cash sales	1,500
Credit sales	2,000
Discounts allowed to credit customers	29
General expenses	410
Goods returned by credit customers	40
Purchases	2,780

Additional information:

1 Most of the accounting records relating to the branch are kept by the head office in its own books of account.

2 All purchases are made by the head office, and goods are invoiced to the branch at selling price, that is, at cost price plus 50 per cent.

Required:

(*a*) Write up the following ledger accounts for the year to 31 March 19X6, being careful to bring down any balances as at that date:

  (*i*)   branch stock account;
  (*ii*) goods sent to branch account;
  (*iii*) branch stock adjustment account;
  (*iv*) branch debtors account; and
  (*v*)   branch bank account.

(*b*) Compile Paper Products' trading, and profit and loss account for the year to 31 March 19X6.

(*c*) Examine briefly the merits and demerits of Paper Products' method of branch bookkeeping including comments on the significance of the 'balancing figure' in the branch stock account.

(*Association of Accounting Technicians*)

1.5 Packer and Stringer were in partnership as retail traders sharing profits and losses: Packer three-quarters, Stringer one-quarter. The partners were credited annually with interest at the rate of 6 per cent per annum on their fixed capitals; no interest was charged on their drawings.

Stringer was responsible for the buying department of the business. Packer managed the head office and Paper was employed as the branch manager. Packer and Paper were each entitled to a commission of 10 per cent of the net profits (after charging such commission) of the shop managed by him.

All goods were purchased by head office and goods sent to the branch were invoiced at cost.

The following was the trial balance as on 31 December 19X4.

	Head Office Books		Branch Books	
	Dr	Cr	Dr	Cr
	£	£	£	£
Drawings accounts and fixed capital accounts:				
Packer	2,500	14,000		
Stringer	1,200	4,000		
Furniture and fittings, at cost	1,500		1,100	
Furniture and fittings, provision for depreciation as at 31 December 19X3		500		350
Stock on 31 December 19X3	13,000		4,400	
Purchases	37,000			
Goods sent to branches		18,000	17,200	
Sales		39,000		26,000
Provision for doubtful debts		600		200
Branch and head office current accounts	6,800			3,600
Salaries and wages	4,500		3,200	
Paper, on account of commission			240	
Carriage and travelling expenses	2,200		960	
Administrative expenses	2,400			
Trade and general expenses	3,200		1,800	
Sundry debtors	7,000		3,000	
Sundry creditors		5,800		400
Bank balances	600			1,350
	81,900	81,900	31,900	31,900

You are given the following additional information:
(a) Stocks on 31 December 19X4, amounted to: head office £14,440, branch £6,570.
(b) Administrative expenses are to be apportioned between head office and the branch in proportion to sales.
(c) Depreciation is to be provided on furniture and fittings at 10 per cent of cost.
(d) The provision for doubtful debts is to be increased by £50 in respect of head office debtors and decreased by £20 in the case of those of the branch.
(e) On 31 December 19X4 cash amounting to £2,400, in transit from the branch to head office, has been recorded in the branch books but not in those of head office; and on that date goods invoiced at £800, in transit from head office to the branch, had been recorded in the head office books but not in the branch books.
Any adjustments necessary are to be made in the head office books.

You are required to:
(a) prepare trading and profit and loss accounts and the appropriation account for the year ended 31 December 19X4, showing the net profit of the head office and branch respectively;
(b) prepare the balance sheet as on that date; and
(c) show the closing entries in the branch current accounts giving the make-up of the closing balance.
Income tax is to be ignored.

(*Institute of Chartered Accountants*)

1.6A L R, a trader, commenced business on 1 January 19X9, with a head office and one branch.

All goods were purchased by the head office and goods sent to the branch were invoiced at a fixed selling price of 25 per cent above cost. All sales, both by the head office and the branch, were made at the fixed selling price.

The following trial balance was extracted from the books at the head office at 31 December 19X9.

Trial Balance

	£	£
Capital		52,000
Drawings	1,740	
Purchases	123,380	
Sales		83,550
Goods sent to branch (at selling price)		56,250
Branch current account	24,550	
Fixed assets	33,000	
Debtors and creditors	7,980	11,060
General expenses	8,470	
Balance at bank	3,740	
	202,860	202,860

No entries had been made in the head office books for cash in transit from the branch to head office at 31 December 19X9, £1,000.

When the balances shown below were extracted from the branch books at 31 December 19X9, no entries had been made in the books of the branch for goods in transit on that date from head office to branch, £920 (selling price).

In addition to the balances which can be deduced from the information given above, the following balances appeared in the branch books on 31 December 19X9.

	£
Fixed assets	6,000
General expenses	6,070
Debtors	7,040
Creditors (excluding head office)	1,630
Sales	51,700
Balance at bank	1,520

When stock was taken on 31 December 19X9, it was found that there was no shortage at the head office, but at the branch there were shortages amounting to £300, at selling price.

You are required to prepare trading and profit and loss accounts (*a*) for head office and (*b*) for the branch, as they would have appeared if goods sent to the branch had been invoiced at cost, and a balance sheet of the whole business as on 31 December 19X9.

Head office and branch stocks are to be valued at cost.

Ignore depreciation of fixed assets.

(*Institute of Chartered Secretaries and Administrators*)

1.7   Nion is a retail stock outlet operating from a head office in London and a branch in Brighton. The following trial balances have been extracted from the books of account as at 31 October 19X1.

	Head Office Books		Branch Books	
	Dr	Cr	Dr	Cr
	£	£	£	£
Drawings	40,000			
Fixed assets: at cost	350,000		100,000	
accumulated depreciation (at 1 November 19X0)		140,000		30,000
Stock (at 1 November 19X0)	8,000		20,000	
Provision for unrealised profit		4,000		
Purchases	914,000			
Goods sent to branch at invoiced value		380,000	375,000	
Sales		850,000		437,000
Provision for doubtful debts		9,000		2,500
Head office/branch current accounts	175,000			120,000
Distribution expenses	80,500		5,000	
Administrative expenses	200,000		16,500	
Trade debtors	60,000		60,000	
Trade creditors		50,000		
Cash and bank balances	15,500		13,000	
Capital		410,000		
	£1,843,000	£1,843,000	£589,500	£589,500

Additional information:
1   All goods are purchased by the head office. Those goods sent to the branch are invoiced at cost plus 25 per cent.
2   Stocks were valued at 31 October 19X1 as being at head office, £12,000; and at the branch, £15,000 at their invoiced price.
3   Depreciation is to be provided for the year on the fixed assets at a rate of 10 per cent on the historic cost.
4   The provision for doubtful debts is to be maintained at a rate of 5 per cent of outstanding trade debtors as at the end of the financial year.
5   As at 31 October 19X1, there was £50,000 cash in transit from the branch to the head office; this cash was received in London on 3 November 19X1. There was also £5,000 of goods in transit at invoice price from the head office to the branch; the branch received these goods on 10 November 19X1.

Required:
Prepare in adjacent columns: (*a*) the head office, and (*b*) the branch trading and profit and loss accounts for the year to 31 October 19X1; and a **combined** balance sheet for Nion as at that date.

Notes:
(*i*)   a combined trading and profit and loss account is NOT required; and
(*ii*)   separate balance sheets for the head office and the branch are also NOT required.

(*Association of Accounting Technicians*)

1.8A Star Stores has its head office and main store in Crewe, and a branch store in Leek. All goods are purchased by the head office. Goods are invoiced to the branch at cost price plus a profit loading of 20 per cent. The following trial balances have been extracted from the books of account of both the head office and the branch as at 31 December 19X9:

	Head Office Books		Branch Books	
	Dr	Cr	Dr	Cr
	£000	£000	£000	£000
Administrative expenses	380		30	
Distribution costs	157		172	
Capital (at 1 January 19X9)		550		
Cash and bank	25		2	
Creditors and accruals		176		20
Current accounts	255			180
Debtors and prepayments	130		76	
Motor vehicles:				
at cost	470		230	
accumulated depreciation at 31 December 19X9		280		120
Plant and equipment:				
at cost	250		80	
accumulated depreciation at 31 December 19X9		120		30
Proprietor's drawings during the year	64			
Provision for unrealised profit on branch stocks at 1 January 19X9		5		
Purchases	880			
Sales		1,200		570
Stocks at cost/invoiced amount at 1 January 19X9	80		30	
Transfer of goods to the branch/ from the head office		360	300	
	£2,691	£2,691	£920	£920

Additional information:
1   The stocks in hand at 31 December 19X9 were estimated to be as follows:

	£000
At head office (at cost)	100
At the branch (at invoiced price)	48

In addition, £60,000 of stocks at invoiced price had been despatched to the branch on 28 December 19X9. These goods had not been received by the branch until 5 January 19X0 and so they had not been included in the branch books of account.
2   On 31 December 19X9, the branch had transferred £15,000 of cash to the head office bank, but this was not received in Crewe until 2 January 19X0.

Required:
(*a*) Prepare in adjacent columns and using the vertical format: (*i*) the head office, and (*ii*) the branch trading and profit and loss accounts for the year to 31 December 19X9 (*note*: a combined profit and loss account is NOT required); and
(*b*) prepare in the vertical format, Star Stores' balance sheet as at 31 December 19X9 (*note*: separate balance sheets for the head office and the branch are NOT required).

(*Association of Accounting Technicians*)

1.9 EG Company Limited, a manufacturing business, exports some of its products through an overseas branch whose currency is 'florins', which carries out the final assembly operations before selling the goods.

The trial balances of the head office and branch at 30 June 19X8 were:

	Head Office £	Head Office £	Branch 'Fl.'	Branch 'Fl.'
Freehold buildings at cost	14,000		63,000	
Debtors/creditors	8,900	9,500	36,000	1,560
Sales		104,000		432,000
Authorised and issued capital		40,000		
Components sent to branch		35,000		
Head office/branch accounts	60,100			504,260
Branch cost of sales			360,000	
Depreciation provision, machinery		1,500		56,700
Head office cost of sales (including goods to branch)	59,000			
Administration costs	15,200		18,000	
Stock at 30 June 19X8	28,900		11,520	
Profit and loss account		2,000		
Machinery at cost	6,000		126,000	
Remittances		28,000	272,000	
Balance at bank	4,600		79,200	
Selling and distribution costs	23,300		28,800	
	220,000	220,000	994,520	994,520

The following adjustments are to be made:

1 The cost of sales figures include a depreciation charge of 10 per cent per annum on cost for machinery.
2 A provision of £300 for unrealised profit in branch stock is to be made.
3 On 26 June 19X8 the branch remitted 16,000 'Fl.'; these were received by the head office on 4 July and realised £1,990.
4 During May a branch customer in error paid the head office for goods supplied. The amount due was 320 'Fl.' which realised £36. It has been correctly dealt with by head office but not yet entered in the branch books.
5 A provision has to be made for a commission of 5 per cent of the net profit of the branch after charging such commission, which is due to the branch manager.

The rates of exchange were:

At 1 July 19X7	10 'Fl.' = £1
At 30 June 19X8	8 'Fl.' = £1
Average for the year	9 'Fl.' = £1
On purchase of buildings and machinery	7 'Fl.' = £1

You are required to prepare, for internal use:
(a) detailed operating accounts for the year ended 30 June 19X8;
(b) combined head office and branch balance sheet as at 30 June 19X8;
(c) the branch account in the head office books, in both sterling and currency, the opening balance on 1 July 19X7 being £25,136 (189,260 'Fl.').
Taxation is to be ignored.

(*Chartered Institute of Management Accountants*)

1.10 OTL Ltd commenced business on 1 January 19X0. The head office is in London and there is a branch in Highland. The currency unit of Highland is the Crown.

The following are the trial balances of the head office and the Highland branch as at 31 December 19X0:

	Head Office		Highland Branch	
	£	£	Crowns	Crowns
Branch account	65,280			
Balances at bank	10,560		66,000	
Creditors		21,120		92,400
Debtors	18,480		158,400	
Fixed assets (purchased 1 January 19X0)	39,600		145,200	
Head office account				316,800
Profit and loss account (net profit for year)		52,800		79,200
Issued share capital		86,400		
Stocks	26,400		118,800	
	160,320	160,320	488,400	488,400

The trial balance of the head office was prepared before any entries had been made in respect of any profits or losses of the branch.

Remittance from head office to branch and from branch to head office were recorded in the books at the actual amounts paid and received.

The rates of exchange were:

On 1 January 19X0	5 crowns = £1
Average rate for year 19X0	4.4 crowns = £1
On 31 December 19X0	4 crowns = £1

Required:

(a) The trial balance of the Highland branch as at 31 December 19X0, in sterling.

(b) The closing entries, as at 31 December 19X0, in the branch account in the books of the head office.

(c) A summary of the balance sheet of OTL Ltd as at 31 December 19X0.

Ignore depreciation of fixed assets.

Ignore taxation.

(*Institute of Chartered Secretaries and Administrators*)

1.11A Home Ltd is incorporated in the UK and rents mobile homes to holidaymakers in this country and in Carea. The company has a head office in London and a branch in Carea where the local currency is 'Mics'. The following balances are extracted from the books of the head office and its 'self-accounting' branch at 31 December 19X4.

	Head Office £	Branch Mics
Debit balances		
Fixed assets at cost	450,000	900,000
Debtors and cash	17,600	36,000
Operating costs	103,700	225,000
Branch current account	42,600	
	613,900	1,161,000
Credit balances		
Share capital	200,000	–
Retained profit, 1 January 19X4	110,800	–
Sales revenue	186,300	480,000
Creditors	9,700	25,000
Head office current account	–	420,000
Accumulated depreciation	107,100	236,000
	613,900	1,161,000

The following information is provided regarding exchange rates, some of which is relevant.

The fixed assets of the branch were acquired when there were 8 Mics to the £. Exchange rates ruling during 19X4 were:

	Mics to the £
1 January	6
Average	5
31 December	4

There are no cash or goods in transit between head office and branch at the year end.

Required:
The final accounts of Home Ltd for 19X4. The accounts should be expressed in £s sterling and, for this purpose, the conversion of Mics should be made in accordance with the temporal method of translation as specified in SSAP 20: *Foreign currency translation*.

(*Institute of Chartered Secretaries and Administrators*)

2

Hire purchase accounts

Objectives

After you have studied this chapter, you should:

- *know what distinguishes 'hire purchase' from outright purchase*
- *know what distinguishes 'hire purchase' from a lease*
- *know how to record the entries relating to hire purchase transactions*

2.1 Nature of hire purchase

Hire purchase is a means of buying assets. Instead of paying at the time of purchase, or shortly afterwards, a hire purchase contract is different. The essential differences are:

(*a*) The asset does not belong to the purchaser when it is received from the supplier. Instead it belongs to the supplier providing the hire purchase.
(*b*) The purchaser will pay for the item by instalments over a period of time. This may be for as long as two or three years, or longer.
(*c*) The hire purchase price will be higher than the price would have been if paid immediately, i.e. the cash price. The extra money paid is for interest.
(*d*) The asset does not legally belong to the purchaser until two things happen:
    (*i*) the final instalment is paid, and
    (*ii*) the purchaser agrees to a legal option to buy the asset.

If the purchaser wants to, he could stop paying the instalments. He would then have to give the asset back to the seller. He would not be able to get a refund of instalments already paid.

If the purchaser is unable to continue paying the instalments, the seller could normally repossess the asset. The seller would keep all the instalments already paid.

2.2 Law of hire purchase

The Hire Purchase Act 1964 governs all hire purchase transactions.

2.3 Interest payable on hire purchase

When each payment is made on a hire purchase contract, it will consist of the following:

(a) part of the instalment will be paying off part of the amount owing for the cash price of the asset;

(b) the other part of the instalment will be for the interest that has accrued for the period of time.

The total payment (a) + (b) made for each instalment may either be of equal amounts or unequal amounts.

Exhibit 2.1 Unequal instalments

(a) A machine is bought from A King at the start of year 1. Cash price is £2,000.
(b) Hire purchase price is £2,300.
(c) Payable in 2 annual instalments at the end of each year. Each instalment to be £1,000 plus interest accrued for that year.
(d) Rate of interest is 10 per cent per annum.

			£
Year 1:	Cash price	(A)	2,000
	Add Interest 10% of (A) £2,000		200
			2,200
	Less Instalment paid		1,200
	Owing at end of year 1	(B)	1,000
Year 2:	*Add* Interest 10% of (B) £1,000		100
			1,100
	Less Instalment paid		1,100
	Owing at end of year 2		–

Exhibit 2.2 Equal instalments

The facts are the same as in Exhibit 2.1, except that each instalment is £1,152. (Each figure of interest is rounded down to the nearest £.)

			£
Year 1:	Cash price	(A)	2,000
	Add Interest 10% of (A) £2,000		200
			2,200
	Less Instalment paid		1,152
	Owing at end of year 1	(B)	1,048
Year 2:	*Add* Interest 10% of (B) £1,048		104
			1,152
	Less Instalment paid		1,152
	Owing at end of year 2		–

The interest for year 1 is the same for both equal or unequal instalments, as the whole of the cash price is owed in both cases for a full year.

2.4 Accounting for hire purchase

Accounting treats assets bought on hire purchase as though they belonged immediately to the purchaser.

This is because businesses normally buy assets on hire purchase with the intention of paying all the instalments, so that the asset finally will belong to them. As they mean to keep the asset and legally own it on the final payment, accounting enters it as though legal ownership occurred on purchase.

This is an illustration of the use of the 'substance over form' concept. Legally the firm does not yet own the asset (form), yet for all intents and purposes it does from an economic point of view (substance).

The total purchase price is split into two parts for the accounts:

(*a*) *cash price*: this is the amount to be debited to the fixed asset account;
(*b*) *interest*: this is an expense of borrowing money and needs charging to an expense account, i.e. hire purchase interest account.

As interest accrues over time, each period should be charged only with the interest accrued for that period. This is shown in Exhibit 2.3.

Exhibit 2.3

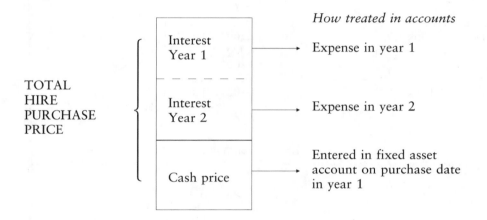

2.5 Illustrations of purchaser's accounts

The double entry needed is:

(A)	Cash price:	Debit fixed asset
		Credit supplier
(B)	Hire purchase interest:	Debit hire purchase interest
	(for each period's interest)	Credit supplier
(C)	Hire purchase instalments:	Debit supplier
		Credit cash book
(D)	Charge interest to profit and loss:	Debit profit and loss
		Credit hire purchase interest

We can now look at the accounts which would have been used to enter the facts as in Exhibit 2.1. (For simplicity, depreciation has been omitted from the example.)

Letters shown against the entries are as shown above.

Machinery

			£	
Year 1				
Jan 1 A King	(A)	2,000		

Hire Purchase Interest

		£				£
Year 1			Year 1			
Dec 31 A King	(B)	200	Dec 31 Profit and loss	(D)	200	
Year 2			Year 2			
Dec 31 A King	(B)	100	Dec 31 Profit and loss	(D)	100	

A King

		£			£
Year 1			Year 1		
Dec 31 Bank	(C)	1,200	Jan 1 Machinery	(A)	2,000
Dec 31 Balance c/d		1,000	Dec 31 HP interest	(B)	200
		2,200			2,200
Year 2			Year 2		
Dec 31 Bank	(C)	1,100	Jan 1 Balance b/d		1,000
			Dec 31 HP interest	(B)	100
		1,100			1,100

Cash Book

				£
	Year 1			
	Dec 31 A King	(C)	1,200	
	Year 2			
	Dec 31 A King	(C)	1,100	

Profit and Loss Account (Extracts)

		£
Year 1 Hire purchase interest	(D)	200
Year 2 Hire purchase interest	(D)	100

2.6 Depreciation and assets bought on hire purchase

Depreciation is based on the cash price. The interest does not enter depreciation calculations.

2.7 Balance sheets and assets bought on hire purchase

In the balance sheet for a sole trader or partnership, fixed assets being bought on hire purchase can be shown as follows:

Fixed assets	£	£
Machinery at cost		20,000
Less Owing on hire purchase	6,000	
Depreciation to date	10,000	16,000
		4,000

In Exhibit 2.1 above, if the machinery had been depreciated using the straight line method at 20 per cent, the balance sheet entries would have been:

Balance Sheet (end of year 1)

Fixed assets	£	£
Machinery at cost		2,000
Less Owing on hire purchase (*a*)	1,000	
Depreciation to date	400	1,400
		600

Note: (*a*) is balance of A King's account.

Balance Sheet (end of year 2)

Fixed assets	£	£
Machinery at cost	2,000	
Less Depreciation to date	800	1,200

Note: at the end of year 2 there was nothing owing to A King for hire purchase.

However, in company balance sheets this is *not* allowed. The Companies Acts do not permit an amount owing on a hire purchase contract to be deducted from the value of the asset in the balance sheet.

In a company's balance sheet, the entries would be:

Balance Sheet (end of year 1)

Fixed assets	£	£
Machinery at cost		2,000
Less Depreciation to date		400
		1,600
Liabilities		
Creditors (Owing on hire purchase) *(a)*		1,000

Note: (*a*) is balance of A King's account.

Balance Sheet (end of year 2)

Fixed assets	£	£
Machinery at cost	2,000	
Less Depreciation to date	800	1,200

2.8 A fully worked example

Exhibit 2.4 illustrates hire purchase more fully. It covers three years of hire purchase and shows the balance sheet figures that would appear if sole traders and partnerships adopted the first approach shown in section 2.7.

Exhibit 2.4

(*a*) A machine is bought by K Thomas for £3,618, hire purchase price, from Suppliers Ltd on 1 January 19X3.
(*b*) It is paid by 3 instalments of £1,206 on 31 December of 19X3, 19X4 and 19X5.
(*c*) The cash price is £3,000.
(*d*) Rate of interest is 10 per cent.
(*e*) Straight line depreciation of 20 per cent per annum is to be provided.

The letters (A) to (F) refer to the description of entries following the account.

Machinery

19X3			£			
Jan 1 Suppliers Ltd	(A)		3,000			

Suppliers Ltd

19X3		£	19X3		£
Dec 31 Bank	(B)	1,206	Jan 1 Machinery	(A)	3,000
„ 31 Balance c/d	(D)	2,094	Dec 31 HP interest	(C)	300
		3,300			3,300
19X4			19X4		
Dec 31 Bank	(B)	1,206	Jan 1 Balance b/d	(D)	2,094
„ 31 Balance c/d	(D)	1,097	Dec 31 HP interest	(C)	209
		2,303			2,303
19X5			19X5		
Dec 31 Bank	(B)	1,206	Jan 1 Balance b/d	(D)	1,097
			Dec 31 HP interest	(C)	109
		1,206			1,206

Hire Purchase Interest

19X3		£	19X3		£
Dec 31 Suppliers Ltd	(C)	300	Dec 31 Profit and loss	(E)	300
19X4			19X4		
Dec 31 Suppliers Ltd	(C)	209	Dec 31 Profit and loss	(E)	209
19X5			19X5		
Dec 31 Suppliers Ltd	(C)	109	Dec 31 Profit and loss	(E)	109

Provision for Depreciation: Machinery

			19X3		£
			Dec 31 Profit and loss	(F)	600
			19X4		
			Dec 31 Profit and loss	(F)	600
			19X5		
			Dec 31 Profit and loss	(F)	600

Balance Sheets as at 31 December

			£	£	£
19X3	Machinery (at cost)			3,000	
	Less Depreciation		600		
	Owing on hire purchase agreement		2,094		
				2,694	306
19X4	Machinery (at cost)			3,000	
	Less Depreciation to date		1,200		
	Owing on hire purchase agreement		1,097		
				2,297	703
19X5	Machinery (at cost)			3,000	
	Less Depreciation to date			1,800	1,200

Description of entries:

(A) When the asset is acquired the cash price is debited to the asset account and the credit is in the supplier's account.
(B) The instalments paid are credited to the bank account and debited to the supplier's account.
(C) The interest is credited to the supplier's account for each period as it accrues, and it is debited to the expense account, later to be transferred to the profit and loss account for the period (E).
(D) The balance carried down each year is the amount of the cash price still owing.
(F) Depreciation provisions are calculated on the full cash price, as the depreciation of an asset is in no way affected by whether or not it has been fully paid for.

The balance sheet consists of balance (A), the cash price, less balance (F), the amount of the cash price apportioned as depreciation. Balance (D), the amount of the cash price still owing at each balance sheet date, is shown separately under creditors.

2.9 The seller's books: apportionment of profits

There are many ways of drawing up the final accounts of a business which sells goods on hire purchase. The method used should be the one most suitable for the business.

The total profit for the seller of goods on hire purchase breaks down as follows:

	£
Profit on item sold: Cash price less cost	xxx
Profit made because of interest charged	xxx
	xxx

In Exhibit 2.4, Suppliers Ltd sold a machine to K Thomas. Assume that the machine had cost Suppliers Ltd £2,100. The total profit upon the final instalment being paid is:

			£	£
Profit on sale of machine:	Cash price		3,000	
	Cost		2,100	900
Profit earned by charging interest:	19X3		300	
	19X4		209	
	19X5		109	618
Total profit over 3 years				1,518

Apportionment of profit on sale

There are two main methods of dealing with the problem of how to split the £900 profit on sale of the machine:

(a) It is considered profit in the period in which it was first sold to the purchaser. In this case the £900 would all be shown as profit for 19X3.
(b) The profit is divided among the three years.

The ratio is calculated as follows:

$$\frac{\text{Cash received in period}}{\text{Total cash to be received}} \times \text{Profit}$$

In this case the profits will be shown as:

19X3 $\dfrac{£1,206}{£1,206 \times 3} \times £900 = \frac{1}{3} \times £900 = £300$

19X4 $\dfrac{£1,206}{£1,206 \times 3} \times £900 = \frac{1}{3} \times £900 = £300$

19X5 $\dfrac{£1,206}{£1,206 \times 3} \times £900 = \frac{1}{3} \times £900 = £300$

Total profit on sale for three years £900

This case shows equal profits because equal instalments were paid each year. Unequal payments would result in unequal profits.

Apportionment of interest to profit and loss account

The interest accrued for each period should be taken into profit calculations. As the amount owed reduces, so does the interest:

	£
Year 19X3	300
Year 19X4	209
Year 19X5	109
Total interest for the three years	618

2.10 The seller's books: accounts needed

We can now look at Exhibit 2.5 taking the details from Exhibit 2.4 as it would appear in the seller's books. Items (A) to (C) have already been shown in Exhibit 2.4.

Exhibit 2.5

(A) The machine was sold on 1 January 19X3 to K Thomas on hire purchase terms. Cash price was £3,000 plus hire purchase interest.
(B) Hire purchase interest was at a rate of 10 per cent.
(C) There are to be 3 instalments of £1,206 each, receivable on 31 December of 19X3, 19X4 and 19X5. These were paid by K Thomas on the correct dates.
(D) This was the only hire purchase sale during the 3 years.
(E) The profit on the cash price is to be shown as profits for 19X3, the year in which the sale was made.
(F) The cost of the machine to Suppliers Ltd was £2,100.

Hire Purchase Sales

19X3			£	19X3					£
Dec	31	Trading	3,000	Jan	1	K Thomas		(A)	3,000

K Thomas

19X3				£	19X3					£
Jan	1	Sales	(A)	3,000	Dec	31	Bank		(C)	1,206
Dec	31	HP interest	(B)	300	„	31	Balance c/d			2,094
				3,300						3,300
19X4					19X4					
Jan	1	Balance b/d		2,094	Dec	31	Bank		(C)	1,206
Dec	31	HP interest	(B)	209	„	31	Balance c/d			1,097
				2,303						2,303
19X5					19X5					
Jan	1	Balance b/d		1,097	Dec	31	Bank		(C)	1,206
Dec	31	HP interest	(B)	109						
				1,206						1,206

Hire Purchase Interest

19X3			£	19X3					£
Dec	31	Trading	300	Dec	31	K Thomas		(B)	300
19X4				19X4					
Dec	31	Trading	209	Dec	31	K Thomas		(B)	209
19X5				19X5					
Dec	31	Trading	109	Dec	31	K Thomas		(B)	109

Cost of Hire Purchase Goods

19X3				£	19X3			£
Jan	1	Bank	(F)	2,100	Dec	31	Trading	2,100

Cash Book

19X3				£	19X3			£
Dec	31	K Thomas	(C)	1,206	Jan	1	Hire purchase goods (F)	2,100
19X4								
Dec	31	K Thomas	(C)	1,206				
19X5								
Dec	31	K Thomas	(C)	1,206				

Trading Accounts
Year ended 31 December 19X3

	£		£
Cost of goods sold	2,100	Hire purchase sales	3,000
		Hire purchase interest	300

Year ended 31 December 19X4

		£
	Hire purchase interest	209

Year ended 31 December 19X5

		£
	Hire purchase interest	109

In Exhibit 2.5 all the profit was taken as being earned in 19X3. If we decided to take the profit as being earned when the instalments are received, then the only account which would be altered would be the trading account. All the other accounts would be exactly the same as in Exhibit 2.5.

The amendments needed are shown as Exhibit 2.6.

Exhibit 2.6

Trading Accounts
Year ended 31 December 19X3

		£			£
Cost of goods sold		2,100	Hire purchase sales		3,000
Hire purchase profit suspense			Hire purchase interest		300
profit not yet earned	(G)	600			

Year ended 31 December 19X4

			£
Hire purchase profit suspense			
profit for 19X4	(H)		300
Hire purchase interest			209

Year ended 31 December 19X5

			£
Hire purchase profit suspense			
profit for 19X5	(H)		300
Hire purchase interest			109

Hire Purchase Profit Suspense

19X4			£	19X3			£
Dec 31 Trading	(H)		300	Dec 31 Trading	(G)		600
Dec 31 Balance c/d			300				
			600				600
19X5				19X5			
Dec 31 Trading	(H)		300	Jan 1 Balance b/d			300

The double entry needed was:

(G) In year of sale: Debit trading account with profits carried to future years
                          Credit hire purchase profit suspense
(H) In following years: Debit hire purchase profit suspense with profits earned in each year
                          Credit trading account

The entries for hire purchase interest have not changed.

2.11 Repossessions

When customers stop paying their instalments before they should do, the goods can be taken away from them. This is called **repossession**. The amounts already paid by the customers will be kept by the seller.

The repossessed items should be entered in the books of the seller, as they are now part of his stock, but they will not be valued as new stock. The items must be valued as used goods.

Exhibit 2.7 shows how the accounts must be changed.
(*a*) On 1 January 19X4 we buy 15 calculators for £300 each.
(*b*) On 1 January 19X4 we sell 12 of them for a cash price of £480 plus £120 interest to be paid = £600 total.
(*c*) 24 monthly instalments are to be paid of £25 each = £600.
(*d*) Because of the difficulties of apportioning interest, each instalment is taken to include £5 interest, i.e. 24 × £5 = £120 interest.
(*e*) On 1 November 19X4, after 10 instalments have been received, a customer who bought 2 calculators cannot pay any more instalments. Both calculators are returned by him. We do not have to repay the instalments paid by him.
(*f*) The 2 calculators returned are valued at £140 each. Also in stock on 31 December 19X4 are 3 of the calculators bought on 1 January 19X4 for £300 each and still valued at that.
(*g*) Profit is to be calculated based on the number of instalments paid.

Exhibit 2.7

Trading Account for the year ended 31 December 19X4

		£			£
Purchases	(*i*)	4,500	Sales at cash price	(*ii*)	4,800
Less Stock	(*v*)	1,180	Hire purchase interest	(*iii*)	600
Cost of goods sold		3,320	Instalments received		
			on repossessions	(*iv*)	500
Provision for unrealised					
profit	(*vi*)	900			
Gross profit	(*vii*)	1,680			
		5,900			5,900

Notes: Calculations are made as follows:
(*i*)   15 × £300 each = £4,500.
(*ii*) 10 were sold (and not returned) at cash price of £480 each.
(*iii*) Interest on 10 sold (and not returned) × £5 × 12 months = £600.
(*iv*) 10 instalments paid (including interest) on 2 calculators = 10 × £25 × 2 = £500.

(*v*) Stock =

new items 3 × £300	=	£900	
repossessed items 2 × £140	=	£280	
		£1,180	

(*vi*) Profit per calculator = cash price £480 – cost £300 ... = £180
To be paid: 12 instalments out of 24 = ½ profit ... = £90
Number sold and not returned, 10 × £90 ... = £900

(*vii*)Gross profit can be checked:
Earned to date 10 × £90 ... = £900
Interest earned to date £5 × 10 × 12 months ... = £600
Profit on repossessions:
Instalments received ... £500
Loss of value on repossessions
Cost 2 × £300 ... £600
Value taken back ... £280 = £320 ... £180
... £1,680

2.12 SSAP 21: Accounting for leases and hire purchase contracts

In August 1984, when SSAP 21 was issued, the background was stated in the following terms:

Leasing and hire purchase contracts are means by which companies acquire the right to use (lease) or purchase (hire purchase) fixed assets. In the UK there is normally no provision in a lease contract for legal title to the leased asset to pass to the lessee during the term of a lease. In contrast, under a hire purchase contract the hirer may acquire legal title by exercising an option to purchase the asset upon fulfilment of certain conditions (normally the payment of an agreed number of instalments).

Lessors fall into three broad categories. They may be companies, including banks and finance houses, which provide finance under lease contracts to enable a single customer to acquire the use of an asset for the greater part of its useful life; they may operate a business which involves the renting out of assets for varying periods of time probably to more than one customer; or they may be manufacturer or dealer lessors who use leasing as a means of marketing their products, which may involve leasing a product to one customer or to several customers. As a lessor and lessee are both parties to the same transaction it is appropriate that the same definitions should be used and the accounting treatment recommended should ideally be complementary. However, this will not mean that the recorded balances in both financial statements will be the same, because the pattern of cash flows and the taxation consequences will be different.

Leases can appropriately be classified into **finance leases** and **operating leases**. The distinction between a finance lease and an operating lease will usually be evident from the substance of the contract between the lessor and the lessee. A finance lease usually involves repayment to a lessor by a lessee of the full cost of the asset together with a return on the finance provided by the lessor. As such, a lease of this type is normally non-cancellable or cancellable only under certain conditions, and the lessee enjoys substantially all the risks and rewards associated with the ownership of an asset, other than the legal title.

An operating lease involves the lessee paying a rental for the hire of an asset for a period of time which is normally substantially less than its useful economic life. The lessor retains the risks and rewards of ownership of an asset in an operating lease and normally assumes responsibility for repairs, maintenance and insurance.

Briefly, this standard requires that a finance lease should be accounted for by the lessee as if it were the purchase of the property rights in an asset with simultaneous recognition of the obligation to make future payments, in the same way that a hire purchase is normally accounted for. Under an operating lease, only the rental will be taken into account by the lessee. The standard recognises that the substance of a transaction rather than its legal form should govern the accounting treatment.

New terms

Hire purchase agreements (p. 29): These are legal agreements by which an organisation can obtain the use of an asset in exchange for payment by instalment.

Finance lease (p. 40): This is an agreement whereby the lessee enjoys substantially all the risks and rewards associated with ownership of an asset other than legal title.

Operating lease (p. 40): This is an agreement whereby the lessor retains the risks and rewards associated with ownership and normally assumes responsibility for repairs, maintenance and insurance.

Main points to remember

1   Hire purchase is a means of buying assets where:
   (a) the asset does not belong to the purchaser until the final instalment is paid *and* the purchaser agrees to a legal option to buy the asset; *but*
   (b) for accounting purposes, the asset is treated immediately as if it belonged to the purchaser.

2   Each payment made on a hire purchase contract is part interest and part payment of the cash price of the asset.

Review questions

2.1   An engineering concern purchased machines on the HP system over a period of three years, paying £846 on 1 January 19X3, and further annual payments of £2,000 due on 31 December 19X3, 19X4 and 19X5.

The cash price of the machine was £6,000, the vendor company charging interest at 8 per cent per annum on outstanding balances.

Show the appropriate ledger accounts in the purchaser's books for the three years and how the items would appear in the balance sheet at 31 December 19X5; depreciation at 10 per cent per annum on the written-down value is to be charged and interest calculated to the nearest £.

2.2A   On 1 January 19X3 J Donkins bought a machine (cash price £2,092) from CD & Co. Ltd on the following hire purchase terms. Donkins was to make an immediate payment of £600 and three annual payments of £600 on 31 December in each year. The rate of interest chargeable is 10 per cent per annum.

Donkins depreciates this machinery by 10 per cent on the diminishing balance each year.

(a)   Make the entries relating to this machine in Donkins' ledger for the years 19X3, 19X4 and 19X5. (All calculations are to be made to the nearest £.)

(b)   Show how the item machinery would appear in the balance sheet as at 31 December 19X3.

2.3   Bulwell Aggregates Ltd wish to expand their transport fleet and have purchased three heavy lorries with a list price of £18,000 each. Robert Bulwell has negotiated hire purchase finance to fund this expansion, and the company has entered into a hire purchase agreement with Granby Garages plc on 1 January 19X1. The agreement states that Bulwell Aggregates will pay a deposit of £9,000 on 1 January 19X1, and two annual instalments of £24,000 on 31 December 19X1, 19X2 and a final instalment of £20,391 on 31 December 19X3.

Interest is to be calculated at 25 per cent on the balance outstanding on 1 January each year and paid on 31 December each year.

The depreciation policy of Bulwell Aggregates Ltd is to write off the vehicles over a four-year period using the straight line method and assuming a scrap value of £1,333 for each vehicle at the end of its useful life.

The cost of the vehicles to Granby Garages is £14,400 each.

Required:
(a)   Account for the above transactions in the books of Bulwell Aggregates Ltd, showing the entries in the profit and loss account and balance sheet for the years 19X1, 19X2, 19X3 and 19X4.
(b)   Account for the above transactions in the books of Granby Garages plc, showing the entries in the hire purchase trading account for the years 19X1, 19X2, 19X3. This is the only hire purchase transaction undertaken by this company.

Calculations to the nearest £.

(*Association of Accounting Technicians*)

2.4A   J York was acquiring two cars under hire purchase agreements, details of which are as follows:

Registration number	JY 1	JY 2
Date of purchase	31 May 19X6	31 October 19X6
Cash price	£18,000	£24,000
Deposit	£3,120	£4,800
Interest (deemed to accrue evenly over the period of the agreement)	£1,920	£2,400

Both agreements provided for payment to be made in 24 monthly instalments commencing on the last day of the month following purchase.

On 1 September 19X7, vehicle JY 1 became a total loss. In full settlement on 20 September 19X7:

(a)   an insurance company paid £12,500 under a comprehensive policy; and
(b)   the hire purchase company accepted £6,000 for the termination of the agreement.

The firm prepared accounts annually to 31 December and provided depreciation on a straight line basis at a rate of 20 per cent per annum for motor vehicles, apportioned as from the date of purchase and up to the date of disposal.

All instalments were paid on due dates.

The balance on the hire purchase company account in respect of vehicle JY 1 is to be written off.

You are required to record these transactions in the following accounts, carrying down the balances as on 31 December 19X6 and 31 December 19X7:
(a)   Motor vehicles;
(b)   Depreciation;
(c)   Hire purchase company;
(d)   Assets disposal.

2.5   On 30 September 19X7, B Wright, who prepares final accounts annually to 30 September, bought a motor lorry on hire purchase from the Vehicles and Finance Co. Ltd. The cash price of the lorry was £3,081. Under the terms of the hire purchase agreement, Wright paid a deposit of £1,000 on 30 September 19X7, and two instalments of £1,199 on 30 September, 19X8 and 19X9. The hire vendor charged interest at 10 per cent per annum on the balance outstanding on 1 October each year. All payments were made on the due dates.

Wright maintained the motor lorry account at cost and accumulated the annual provision for depreciation, at 25 per cent on the diminishing balance method, in a separate account.

You are required to:
(a) prepare the following accounts as they would appear in the ledger of B Wright for the period of the contract:
(i)   Vehicles and Finance Co Ltd;
(ii) Motor lorry on hire purchase;
(iii) Provision for depreciation of motor lorry;
(iv) Hire purchase interest payable;
(b) show how the above matters would appear in the balance sheet of B Wright at 30 September 19X8.

The Vehicles and Finance Co. Ltd prepares final accounts annually to 30 September, on which date it charges B Wright with the interest due.

Make calculations to the nearest £.

2.6   S Craven started business on 1 October 19X5 selling machines of one standard type on hire purchase terms. During the year to 30 September 19X6 he purchased machines at a uniform price of £60 and sold 1,900 machines at a total price under hire purchase agreements of £100 per machine, payable by an initial deposit of £30 and 10 quarterly instalments of £7.

The following trial balance was extracted from Craven's books as at 30 September 19X6.

	£	£
Capital		76,000
Drawings	4,000	
Fixed assets	10,000	
Purchases	120,000	
Cash collected from customers		83,600
Rent, rates and insurance	4,500	
Wages	8,600	
General expenses	10,270	
Balance at bank	10,630	
Sundry trade creditors		8,400
	168,000	168,000

The personal accounts of customers are memorandum records (i.e. they are not part of the double entry system).

Craven prepares his annual accounts on the basis of taking credit for profit (including interest) in proportion to cash collected from customers.

Prepare Craven's hire purchase trading account and a profit and loss account for the year ended 30 September 19X6 and a balance sheet as at that date.

Ignore depreciation of fixed assets.

2.7   RJ commenced business on 1 January 19X8. He sells refrigerators, all of one standard type, on hire purchase terms. The total amount, including interest, payable for each refrigerator, is £300. Customers are required to pay an initial deposit of £60, followed by eight quarterly instalments of £30 each. The cost of each refrigerator to RJ is £200.

The following trial balance was extracted from RJ's books as on 31 December 19X8.

Trial Balance

	£	£
Capital		100,000
Fixed assets	10,000	
Drawings	4,000	
Bank overdraft		19,600
Creditors		16,600
Purchases	180,000	
Cash collected from customers		76,500
Bank interest	400	
Wages and salaries	12,800	
General expenses	5,500	
	£212,700	£212,700

850 machines were sold on hire purchase terms during 19X8.

The annual accounts are prepared on the basis of taking credit for profit (including interest) in proportion to the cash collected from customers.

You are required to prepare the hire purchase trading account, and the profit and loss account for the year 19X8 and balance sheet as on 31 December 19X8.

Ignore depreciation of fixed assets.

Show your calculations.

(*Institute of Chartered Secretaries and Administrators*)

2.8A   Object Limited is a retail outlet selling word processing equipment both for cash and on hire purchase terms. The following information has been extracted from the books of account as at 31 August 19X6:

	Dr £	Cr £
Authorised, issued and fully paid share capital		
(ordinary shares of £1 each)		75,000
Administration and shop expenses	130,000	
Cash at bank and in hand	6,208	
Cash received from hire purchase customers		315,468
Cash sales		71,000
Depreciation of premises and equipment (at 1 September 19X5)		45,000
Hire purchase debtors (at 1 September 19X5)	2,268	
Premises and equipment at cost	100,000	
Profit and loss account (at 1 September 19X5)		8,000
Provision for unrealised profit (at 1 September 19X5)		1,008
Purchases	342,000	
Stock (at 1 September 19X5)	15,000	
Trade creditors		80,000
	£595,476	£595,476

Additional information:

1   The company's policy is to take credit for gross profit (including interest) for hire purchase sales in proportion to the instalments collected. It does this by raising a provision against the

profit included in hire purchase debtors not yet due.

2 The cash selling price is fixed at 50 per cent and the hire purchase selling price at 80 per cent respectively above the cost of goods purchased.

3 The hire purchase contract requires an initial deposit of 20 per cent of the hire purchase selling price, the balance to be paid in four equal instalments at quarterly intervals. The first instalment is due three months after the agreement is signed.

4 Hire purchase sales for the year amounted to £540,000 (including interest).

5 In February 19X6 the company repossessed some goods which had been sold earlier in the year. These goods had been purchased for £3,000, and the unpaid instalments on them amounted to £3,240. They were then taken back into stock at a value of £2,500. Later on in the year they were sold on cash terms for £3,500.

6 Depreciation is charged on premises and equipment at a rate of 15 per cent per annum on cost.

Required:
Prepare Object Limited's trading, and profit and loss account for the year to 31 August 19X6, and a balance sheet as at that date.

    Your workings should be submitted.

(Association of Accounting Technicians)

2.9A On 1 January 19X6, F Limited commenced business selling goods on hire purchase. Under the terms of the agreements, an initial deposit of 20 per cent is payable on delivery, followed by four equal quarterly instalments, the first being due three months after the date of sale. During the year sales were made as follows:

	Cost price	HP Sales price
	£	£
10 January	150	225
8 March	350	525
12 May	90	135
6 July	200	300
20 September	70	105
15 October	190	285
21 November	160	240

The goods sold in July were returned in September and eventually sold in November for £187 cash. All other instalments are paid on the due dates.

It may be assumed that:

(*a*) gross profit and interest are credited to profit and loss account in the proportion that deposits and instalments received bear to hire purchase price, or

(*b*) the cost is deemed to be paid in full before any credit is taken for gross profit and interest.

You are to prepare for the first year of trading, a hire purchase trading account compiled firstly on assumption (*a*) and secondly on assumption (*b*) and give the relevant balance sheet entries under each assumption.

    Workings should be clearly shown.

(Chartered Institute of Management Accountants)

2.10A On 1 January 19X7, Carver bought a machine costing £20,000 on hire purchase. He paid a deposit of £6,000 on 1 January 19X7 and he also agreed to pay two annual instalments of £5,828 on 31 December in each year, and a final instalment of £5,831 on 31 December 19X9.

The implied rate of interest in the agreement was 12 per cent. This rate of interest is to be applied to the amount outstanding in the hire purchase loan account as at the beginning of the year.

The machine is to be depreciated on a straight line basis over five years on the assumption that the machine will have no residual value at the end of that time.

Required:
(*a*) Write up the following accounts for each of the three years to 31 December 19X7, 19X8 and 19X9 respectively:
 (*i*) machine account;
 (*ii*) accumulated depreciation on machine account; and
 (*iii*) hire purchase loan account; and
(*b*) show the balance sheet extracts for the year as at 31 December 19X7, 19X8 and 19X9 respectively for the following items:
 (*i*) machine at cost;
 (*ii*) accumulated depreciation on the machine;
 (*iii*) long-term liabilities: obligations under hire purchase contract; and
 (*iv*) current liabilities: obligations under hire purchase contract.

(*Association of Accounting Technicians*)

2.11 Dundas Limited purchased a machine under a hire purchase agreement on 1 January 19X8. The agreement provided for an immediate payment of £2,000, followed by five equal instalments of £3,056, each instalment to be paid on 30 June and 31 December respectively.

The cash price of the machine was £10,000. Dundas estimated that it would have a useful economic life of five years, and its residual value would then be £1,000.

In apportioning interest to respective accounting periods, the company uses the 'sum of digits'* method.

Required:
(*a*) Write up the following ledger accounts for each of the three years to 31 December 19X8, 19X9 and 19X0 respectively:
 (*i*) machine hire purchase loan account; and
 (*ii*) machine hire purchase interest account; and
(*b*) show the following balance sheet extracts relating to the machine as at 31 December 19X8, 19X9 and 19X0 respectively:
 (*i*) fixed assets: machine at net book value;
 (*ii*) creditors: amounts payable within one year – obligation under hire purchase contract; and
 (*iii*) creditors: amounts falling due after more than one year – obligation under hire purchase contract.

Note – sum of digits
This is very similar to the 'rule of 78', explained on pp. 672-3. It is explained in detail on p. 378 of the eighth edition of *Business Accounting 1*. In brief, if a machine is expected to last 4 years, you write-off the cost by weighting year 1 as 4, year 2 as 3, year 3 as 2 and year 4 as 1. The total of these weights is used as the denominator. Thus, year 1 depreciation would be 4/10 of the amount to be written-off; year 2 would be 3/10, year 3 would be 2/10 and year 4 would be 1/10.

(*Association of Accounting Technicians*)

3

Container accounts

Objectives

After you have studied this chapter, you should:

- *be able to distinguish between disposable containers and returnable containers*

- *know how to enter transactions relating to returnable containers in the journal*

3.1 The nature of containers

A container is anything in which goods are contained. This may consist of a packet containing cigarettes, a large wooden crate containing tractor parts, or a liquid gas cylinder. Some will be returnable by the purchaser after use, an obvious example being the gas cylinder, while others such as the cigarette packet will be disposed of at will by the customer. The returnable containers will often be subject to a deposit being charged to the customer, a refund being allowed when the container is returned in good condition to the supplier.

In suppliers' books it is therefore convenient to divide containers into those which are (1) not chargeable to the customers, and (2) those where a deposit charge is made to the customer.

3.2 Containers not charged to customers

Many containers will be treated as manufacturing expenses, e.g. cigarette packets, flour bags or tin cans containing foods. Theoretically they are a distribution expense if the contents and the containers are regarded as being two distinct items, and as such would be chargeable to the profit and loss account. However, in reality, the containers for such items are an integral part of the goods sold and are therefore chargeable to the manufacturing account. On the other hand, returnable cylinders in which goods are delivered would be chargeable to the profit and loss account.

There will normally be a stock of containers in hand at the end of each accounting period. Exhibit 3.1 shows an account for cartons in which salt is packed for sale.

Exhibit 3.1

	£
Stocks of containers 1 January 19X6	100
Containers bought in the year ended 31 December 19X6	2,800
Stock of containers 31 December 19X6	300

Containers

19X6		£	19X6		£
Jan 1	Stock b/d	100	Dec 31	Manufacturing account	2,600
Dec 31	Cash (bought during the year)	2,800	„ 31	Stock c/d	300
		2,900			2,900
19X7					
Jan 1	Stock b/d	300			

For returnable containers on which deposits are not charged the question of whether or not accurate statistical records would be kept would depend on the nature and value of containers.

3.3 Containers on which deposits are charged to customers

There are containers which many purchasers would not return if they were not charged with a deposit refunded only on return. These are obviously containers which require more than a marginal effort to return, or those which could be put to alternative uses. The deposit chargeable must therefore be sufficient to discourage the purchaser from keeping the containers after use, but should not be so great as to deter him from buying the goods in the first place. In some instances, a time limit is fixed within which the container is to be returned to obtain a cancellation of the deposit charged. Common sense must, however, prevail, as it would be unwise to refuse to allow returns in circumstances which could bring about a worsening in the firm's relationship with customers it wished to retain.

Accounting for containers must therefore fulfil two needs, (a) it must enable some form of check on the stock of containers, and (b) it must reveal the amount of deposit returnable to customers. This can be satisfied, for (a) a containers stock account can be kept, and for (b) a containers suspense account may be opened.

Volume 1 has already illustrated the need for the depreciation of containers to be provided normally by the revaluation method. The containers stock account will therefore provide for the depreciation element by the process of revaluing the containers at the end of each accounting period. Each container account may also include, in addition to the £ columns, further columns for quantities and for the monetary rates at which the transactions are carried out.

3.4 Comprehensive example where a deposit is chargeable

Exhibit 3.2

A new firm, IVY and Co, sells its goods in crates on which a deposit is chargeable to the customer, a credit being allowed on their return within three months.

During the year ended 31 December 19X5:

A   50 crates were bought for £3 each.

B   180 crates were sent to customers, these being charged to their accounts at £4 deposit each. (You may well wonder how 180 crates can be sent out when only 50 have been bought by IVY and Co. The figure of 180 consists of recounting the same crates, as they are sent out and returned several times each year.)

    C   150 crates were returned by customers, credits being entered in their accounts for £4 each.

    D   10 crates were kept by customers beyond the three months' limit, and they therefore forfeited their right to return them to obtain a refund of the deposit.

    E   2 crates were damaged and were sold for £1 each.

On 31 December 19X5 the following facts are relevant:

    F   There were 20 returnable crates with customers.

    G   There were 18 crates at IVY's warehouse.

The stock of crates at 31 December 19X5 are to be valued at £2 each to provide for depreciation through usage.

    The identifying letters A to G are shown against the recorded transactions in the accounts that now follow.

Containers Stock

		Rate	No.	£				Rate	No.	£	£
19X5						19X5					
Dec 31	Cash (bought during the year)	A 3	50	150		Dec 31	Containers suspense: kept by customers	D 4	10	40	
						„ 31	Cash: damaged crates	E 1	2	2	
						„ 31	Profit and loss: cost of container usage			32	
						„ 31	Stock c/d				
							In warehouse	G 2	18	36	
							At customers	F 2	20	40	
				50	150					50	150
19X6											
Jan 1	Stock b/d										
	In warehouse	G 2	18	36							
	At customers	F 2	20	40							

Containers Suspense

		Rate	No.	£				Rate	No.	£	£
19X5						19X5					
Dec 31	Sales ledger: crates credited to customers' accounts on return	C 4	150	600		Dec 31	Sales ledger: crates charged to customers' accounts	B 4	180	720	
„ 31	Containers stock: kept by customers	D 4	10	40							
„ 31	Deposits on crates returnable c/d	F 4	20	80							
			180	720							
						19X6					
						Jan 1	Deposits on crates returnable b/d	F 4	20	80	

The balance sheet will show the balances in the following manner:

IVY & Co
Balance Sheet as at 31 December 19X5

	£
Current assets	
Crates – at valuation	76
Current liabilities	
Containers suspense – deposits returnable	80

3.5 Comprehensive example where there is a true charge

Sometimes containers are charged out to customers at an initial price greater than that allowed on their return. The difference represents a hiring charge. If the same data is taken as in Exhibit 3.2 but, instead of £4 being allowed on return, it had been been restricted to £3, the accounts would have appeared as follows:

Containers Stock

			Rate	No.	£	£				Rate	No.	£	£
19X5							19X5						
Dec	31	Cash (bought during the year)	3	50		150	Dec	31	Containers suspense: kept by customers	3	10		30
„	31	Profit and loss: profit on container usage				138	„	31	Cash: damaged crates	1	2		2
							„	31	Containers suspense: Hiring charge				180
							„	31	Stock c/d				
									In warehouse	2	18		36
									At customers	2	20		40
					50	288						50	288
19X6													
Jan	1	Stock b/d											
		In warehouse	2	18		36							
		At customers	2	20		40							

Containers Suspense

			Rate	No.	£	£				Rate	No.	£	£
19X5							19X5						
Dec	31	Sales ledger: crates credited to customers' accounts on return		150		450	Dec	31	Sales ledger: crates charged to customers' accounts	4	180		720
„	31	Containers stock: kept by customers	3	10		30							
„	31	Containers stock hiring charge				180							
„	31	Deposits on crates Returnable	3	20		60							
				180		720					180		720
							19X6						
							Jan	1	Deposits on crates returnable b/d	3	20		60

The balance sheet would have appeared in the following manner:

IVY & Co

Balance Sheet as at 31 December 19X5

	£
Current assets	
Crates – at valuation	76
Current liabilities	
Containers suspense – deposits returnable	60

Main points to remember

1 Containers will either be disposable and treated as part of the cost of sales, or they will be returnable and involve the taking and returning (possibly only part) of a deposit.

2 Accounting for containers must enable some form of check on the stock of containers and must reveal the amount of returnable customer deposits held.

3 Both a container stock account and a container suspense account are used in order to record details relating to returnable containers.

Review questions

3.1 D Clark's manufactures are sold in boxes which are returnable. They are charged out to customers at £8 each and credit of £6 is given for each box returned within two months. For the purpose of the annual accounts, the value of boxes in the factory and those in customers' hands, which had been invoiced within two months, was taken as being £1.50 each. The quantities of these on 31 January 19X3 were 600 and 4,000 respectively.

The following were the transactions as regards boxes during the year ended 31 January 19X4

- Purchases – 5,000 at £2 each
- Invoiced to customers – 17,000
- Returned by customers – 14,000
- 450 could no longer be used and were sold, realising £100.

The number of boxes invoiced after 30 November 19X3 and still in customers' hands on 31 January 19X4 was 6,200.

Required:

Write up the accounts in the books of D Clark to record these transactions and to show the profit on boxes and the quantities involved.

3.2 A company makes a charge to its customers for cases in which the product is delivered. If they are returned in good condition within two months a refund is made.

At the start of the year there were 9,600 cases in stock at the company's warehouse and 6,100 in the hands of customers supplied within the previous two months. The company bought 18,000 new cases during the year and following a dispute with a supplier returned 4,000 new cases for which a credit note of £11,610 was received. At 31 December 19X6 there were still in the hands of customers 4,800 supplied during the previous two months.

During the year 19X6, 47,600 cases were sent to customers and 43,100 returned by them. The company scrapped 3,500 damaged cases and sold the timber for £55. A physical check of cases in stock in 31 December 19X6 revealed an unaccounted deficit of 420 cases.

- New cases cost £3 each
- Cases were charged out to customers at £5 each
- Customers were credited £4 on the return of each case
- Cases were valued for stocktaking at £2 each

Show the accounts in the books for 19X6 to record the above, and the balances of cases, in quantities and values at 31 December 19X6.

You are required to deduce the following missing information from the details above:
(*a*) The number of cases kept by customers over the two-month limit for returning them.
(*b*) The number of cases in the warehouse on 31 December 19X6.

3.3   S Limited delivers its product to customers in returnable containers. These are invoiced to the customer at £20 each and, if returned in good condition within six months, are credited in full. The containers are purchased for £10 each.

At 30 June 19X6, there were 2,000 containers held in S Limited's warehouse and provision was made in the 19X6 accounts for an estimated liability in respect of 5,500 containers in customers' hands. During 19X7, 1,250 new containers were purchased and 120 were scrapped.

8,750 containers were charged to customers and 9,050 containers were returned within the six-month period.

At 30 June 19X7, the physical stocktaking showed 3,390 containers in the warehouse and information derived from customers indicated that there was a potential liability in respect of 4,950 containers. The stocks of containers are valued at cost price.

Required:
Prepare the containers stock account and the containers suspense account necessary to record these transactions in the books of S Limited.

(*Chartered Institute of Management Accountants*)

3.4   Lagg Ltd sells its goods in cases. These cases are purchased by the company at £6 per case, but each case is written down to a standard book value (SBV) of £5 per case immediately it is purchased. For stocktaking purposes, all cases are valued at £5 per case irrespective of whether they are still in stock or in the hands of the customers. Cases are charged out to customers at £10 per case, but the customer is credited with £8 per case if the case is returned in good condition within three months of receipt.

The following information relates to the year to 31 March 19X7:

	Cases
1 Stock of cases at 1 April 19X6:	
In stock	1,000
In hands of customers 1 January 19X6	3,000

2 During the year, 2,000 cases were purchased.
3 25,000 cases were issued to customers.
4 23,000 cases were returned by customers within the time limit.
5 1,500 cases were not returned within the time limit and were duly paid for by the customers. Cases still in the hands of customers at 31 March 19X7 had all been invoiced since 1 January 19X7.
6 100 cases kept in stock by Lagg had been damaged and were beyond repair.
7 £1,400 had been spent on repairing some slightly damaged cases.
8 50 other damaged cases had been sold for £2 per case.

In order to keep an accurate record of its transactions in cases, Lagg maintains the following accounts:

(*i*)   a cases stock account in which cases are recorded at their standard book value;
(*ii*) a cases suspense account in which cases in the hands of customers are recorded at their return price;

(*iii*) a cases sent to customers account in which cases sent to customers are recorded at their issue price; and

(*iv*) a cases profit and loss account.

Required:

Write up the following accounts in the books of Lagg Ltd for the year to 31 March 19X7;

(*a*) cases stock account;

(*b*) cases suspense account;

(*c*) cases sent to customers account; and

(*d*) cases profit and loss account.

(*Association of Accounting Technicians*)

3.5A KRR Ltd sells goods in containers which are charged to customers at £2.00 each. Customers are credited with £1.25 for each container returned within four months.

On 31 December 19X7, there were 1,580 containers on the company's premises and 5,520 containers, the time limit for the return of which has not expired, were held by customers.

During 19X8:

(*i*) KRR Ltd purchased 8,700 containers for £1 each.

(*ii*) 26,460 containers were charged to customers.

(*iii*) 23,720 containers were returned by customers and credited to them.

On 31 December 19X8, customers held 6,000 containers, the time limit for the return of which had not expired.

For purposes of the annual accounts of KRR Ltd, all stocks of containers on the company's premises and returnable containers in the possession of customers are valued, at £1 each.

You are required to show the container stock account and the container trading account for the year 19X8. These accounts should be provided with additional memorandum columns in which quantities are to be shown.

(*Institute of Chartered Secretaries and Administrators*)

3.6A The G Company supplies gas in expensive containers which are returnable after use. These containers cost £20 each and are charged out to customers on sale or return within six months at £26 each. Provided they are returned within the six months period they are credited at £23 each. As each container is returned it is inspected and overhauled at a cost of £2.

At the end of the year the company values all returnable containers in customers' hands and containers held in stock at £16 each.

You are advised that:

	At the Beginning of the Year	At the End of theYear
Containers held by the company	2,760	3,144
Returnable containers held by customers	4,790	2,910

During the year 3,100 new containers were purchased, 20,620 were invoiced to customers and 17,960 were returned. On inspection 260 required additional repairs costing £325 and 56 had to be sold as scrap for £60.

From the information given above prepare:

(*a*) returnable containers suspense account;

(*b*) an account showing the profit or loss on dealings in containers.

(*Chartered Institute of Management Accountants*)

Part 2

COMPANIES

Introduction

This part is concerned with the accounts and financial statements of limited companies. It considers how various accounting transactions should be entered in the books and how the financial statements should be presented, including the requirements of the Companies Acts and of accounting standards.

4
Limited companies: general background

Objectives

After you have studied this chapter, you should:

- *be aware of the legal nature of limited companies*
- *be aware of the statutory framework governing limited companies*
- *be aware of some of the major characteristics of limited companies*

4.1 Preliminary study

An introduction was made to the accounts of limited companies in Volume 1. It was intended to show some of the basic outlines of the final accounts of limited companies to those people who would be finishing their studies of accounting with the completion of Volume 1. This volume now carries the study of limited companies accounting to a more advanced stage.

4.2 The Companies Acts

The Acts of Parliament now governing limited companies are the Companies Acts 1985 and 1989. The 1989 Act both adds to and amends the 1985 Act, so that both Acts have to be read together. In this volume we cannot deal with many of the complicated issues arising from the Companies Acts: these are better left until the reader has reached a more advanced stage in his/her studies.

The Companies Acts are the descendants of modern limited liability company legislation which can be traced back to the passing of the Companies Act 1862. This Act was a triumph for the development of the limited liability principle which had been severely restricted since the so-called 'Bubble Act' of 1720, this latter Act being the remedy for a multitude of spectacular frauds perpetrated behind the cloak of limited liability. Not until 1862 was general prejudice overcome, and the way paved for the general use of the limited liability principle which is now commonplace. Company law therefore consists of the Companies Acts 1985 and 1989, together with a considerable body of case law which has been built up over the years. It must be borne in mind that there are still a number of chartered companies in existence which were incorporated by Royal Charter, such as the Hudson's Bay Company, or else which were formed by special Acts of Parliament.

4.3 Changes in company law

Over the last 20 to 30 years the United Kingdom has made many changes in its company law. This has been brought about because of the obligation to observe the company law directives issued by the Council of the European Community. Such changes do not eliminate completely the differences in company law throughout the European Union, but they have considerably reduced such differences and have provided minimum standards to be observed.

The 1985 and 1989 Companies Acts lay down detailed rules of the format of the final accounts of limited companies. These will be considered later.

Banks and insurance companies do not come under the same legislation as that for other companies. A separate part of the 1989 Act deals with banks, whilst insurance companies are the subject of a special directive.

4.4 Other forms of company

The Companies Acts also cover companies with unlimited liability. These are now very rarely met in practice. Also covered are companies limited by guarantee, which may or may not have a share capital, but the Companies Act 1985 forbids the future formation of such companies, if they have a share capital. Both of these types of limited company are relatively unimportant, and therefore any future reference to a 'limited company' or merely a 'company' will be concerned with limited liability companies of the normal type.

4.5 Separate legal entity

The outstanding feature of a **limited company** is that, no matter how many individuals have bought shares in it, it is treated in its dealings with the outside world as if it were a person in its own right: it is said to be a separate 'legal entity'. Just as the law can create this separate legal person, then so also can it eliminate it, but its existence can only be terminated by using the proper legal procedures. Thus the identity of the shareholders in a large concern may be changing daily as shares are bought and sold by different people. On the other hand, a small private company may have the same shareholders from when it is incorporated (the day it legally came into being), until the date when liquidation is completed (the cessation of the company, often known also as 'winding up' or being 'wound up'). A prime example of its identity as a separate legal entity is that it may sue its own shareholders, or in turn be sued by them.

The legal formalities by which the company comes into existence can be gleaned from any textbook on company law. It is not the purpose of this book to discuss company law in any great detail; this is far better left to a later stage of one's studies. As companies must, however, comply with the law, the essential company law concerning accounting matters will be dealt with in this book as far as is necessary.

What is important is that the basic principles connected with company accounts can be seen in operation. In order that the student may not be unduly confused, points which very rarely occur, or on which the legal arguments are extremely involved and may not yet have been finally settled, will be left out completely or merely mentioned in passing. This means that some generalisations will bear closer scrutiny when accounting studies reach a more advanced stage.

4.6 Memorandum and Articles of Association

Each company is governed by two documents, known as the **Memorandum of Association** and the **Articles of Association**, generally referred to as the **memorandum** and the **articles**. The memorandum consists of five clauses for private companies, and six for public companies, which contain the following details:

1 The name of the company.
2 The part of the UK where the registered office will be situated.
3 The objects of the company.
4 A statement (if a limited liability company) that the liability of its members is limited.
5 Details of the share capital which the company is authorised to issue.
6 A public limited company will also have a clause stating that the company is a public limited company.

The memorandum is said to be the document which discloses the conditions which govern the company's relationship with the outside world.

4.7 Limited liability

The principle of limited liability underlying clause 4 has been of the utmost importance in industry and commerce. It is inconceivable that large business units, such as Imperial Chemical Industries Ltd or Great Universal Stores Ltd, could have existed except for a very few instances. The investor in a limited company, who therefore buys shares in it, is a shareholder. The most he can lose is the money he has paid for the shares, or where he has only partly paid for them, then he is also liable for the unpaid part in addition. With public companies, where their shares are dealt in on a Stock Exchange, he can easily sell them whenever he so wishes. The sale of a share in a private company is not so easily effected.

4.8 Classes of shares

The main classes of shares are **ordinary** shares and **preference** shares. Unless clearly stated in the Memorandum or Articles of Association, preference shares are assumed to be of the cumulative variety already described in Volume 1.

There are also a variety of other shares. The rights attaching to these shares are purely dependent on the skill and ingenuity of the draftsman of the Memorandum and Articles of Association. An entirely new type of share may be created provided it does not contravene the law.

The shares which carry the right to the whole of the profits remaining after the preference shares (and any other fixed dividend shares) have been paid a dividend are often known as the equity share capital or as **equities**.

Until 1981 the only type of share which could be bought back from the shareholders by the company itself were redeemable preference shares. This has changed completely, and will be considered in detail in Chapter 6.

4.9 Distributable profits

In Volume 1, Chapter 46, the calculation of dividends from profits available for distribution was described. This means that there should be some way of knowing what **distributable profits** are.

In the Companies Acts there is a definition of **realised profits** and **realised losses**. This definition also applies for the purpose of calculating a company's distributable profits. A company's realised profits and losses are defined as 'those profits and losses which are treated as realised in the accounts, in accordance with principles generally accepted with respect to the determination of realised profits and losses for accounting purposes at the time when those accounts are prepared'. In accounting, the realisation concept recognises profit or loss at the point when a contract is made in the market to buy or sell assets.

4.10 Table A

Besides the Memorandum of Association, every company must also have Articles of Association. Just as the memorandum governs the company's dealings with the outside world, the articles govern the relationships which exist between the members and the company, between one member and the other members, and other necessary regulations. The Companies Act has a model set of articles known as Table A. A company may, if it so wishes, have its articles exactly the same as Table A, commonly known as 'adopting Table A', or else adopt part of it and have some sections altered. The adoption of the major part of Table A is normal for most private companies. In accounting textbooks, unless stated to the contrary, the accounting examples shown are usually on the basis that Table A has been adopted.

Table A lays down regulations concerning the powers of the directors of the company. On the other hand, the company may draft its own regulations for the powers of directors. Any such regulations are of the utmost importance when it is realised that the legal owners of the business, the shareholders, have entrusted the running of the company to the directors. The shareholders' own rights are largely limited to attending Annual General Meetings and having voting rights thereat, although some shares do not carry voting rights. The Companies Acts make the keeping of proper sets of accounting records and the preparation of Final Accounts compulsory for every company. In addition the accounts must be audited, this being quite different from a partnership or a sole trader's business where an audit is not compulsory at all.

Companies having limited liability, whether they are private or public companies, have to send a copy of their Final Accounts, drawn up in a prescribed manner, to the Registrar of Companies. Public companies must submit Accounts within seven months of their financial year end; private companies within ten months of their year end. Chapters 12–14 are concerned with stating the accounting requirements of the Companies Acts.

4.11 Public companies and the Stock Exchange

The shares of most of the public companies are dealt in on one or other of the recognised Stock Exchanges. The shares of private companies cannot be bought and sold on any Stock Exchange, as this would contravene the requirements for the company being recognised as a 'private' company. The sale and purchase of shares on the Stock Exchanges have no effect on the accounting entries made in the company's books. The only entry made in the company's books when a shareholder sells all, or some, of his shares to someone else, is to record the change of identity of the shareholders. The price at which shares were sold on the Stock Exchange does not enter into the company's books.

While no accounting entries are necessary, the price of the shares on the Stock Exchange has repercussions on the financial policy of the company. If some new shares are to be issued, what price they are to be issued at will be largely dependent on the Stock Exchange valuation. If another firm is to be taken over by the company, part of the purchase price being by the means of shares in the company, then the Stock Exchange value will also affect the value placed upon the shares being given. A takeover bid from another firm may well be caused because the Stock Exchange value of the shares has made a takeover seem worthwhile.

It must be recognised that the Stock Exchanges are the 'second-hand market' for a company's shares. The company does not actually sell (normally called **issue**) its shares by using the Stock Exchange as a selling place. The company issues new shares directly to the people who make application to it for the shares at the time when the company has shares available for issue. The company does not sell to, or buy from, the Stock Exchanges. This means that the shares of a public company sold and bought on Stock Exchanges are passing from one shareholder to another person who will then become a shareholder. Apart from the effect upon the financial policies of the firm the double entry accounts of the company are not affected.

4.12 Stocks and shares

Later in this book you are shown the procedure whereby the shares of a company may be made into **stock**. Thus 500 ordinary shares of £1 each may be made into £500 stock. The dividends paid on the shares or the stock would be the same, and the voting powers would also be the same. Apart from administrative convenience there is really no difference between shares and stock.

New terms

Limited company (p. 57): A form of organisation established under the Companies Acts as a separate legal entity, and required to comply with the provisions of the Acts. The members of the company, known as shareholders, are only liable to pay the full price of the shares – not for any further amount, i.e. their liability is limited.

Memorandum of Association (p. 59): The document that discloses the conditions governing a company's relationship with the outside world.

Articles of Association (p. 59): The document that arranges the internal relationships, for example, between members of the company, and the duties of directors. The Companies Act gives a model known as Table A.

Main points to remember

1 Limited companies are governed by the Companies Acts.

2 Limited companies are each a separate legal entity.

3 Each company is governed by two documents:
   (a) the Memorandum of Association; and
   (b) the Articles of Association.

4 Investors in limited companies can only lose the amount they paid (plus any amount still unpaid if the shares are only part-paid) when they acquired their investment in the company, i.e. they have 'limited liability'.

5

The issue of shares and debentures

Objectives

After you have studied this chapter, you should:

- *understand the terminology relating to the issue of shares and debentures*
- *be aware of the steps in the process of issuing of shares and debentures*
- *know how to record the accounting entries relating to the issue of shares and debentures*

5.1 The issue of shares

In the case of public companies a new issue of shares can be very costly indeed, and the number of shares issued must be sufficient to make the cost worthwhile. However, for simplicity, so that the principles are not obscured by the difficulties of grappling with large amounts, the numbers of shares shown as issued in the illustrations that follow will be quite small.

Shares can be issued being payable for (*a*) immediately on application, or (*b*) by instalments. The first instances will be of shares being paid for immediately. Issues of shares may take place on the following terms connected with the price of the shares:

(*a*) Shares issued at par. This would mean that a share of £1 nominal value would be issued for £1 each.
(*b*) Shares issued at a premium. In this case a share of £1 nominal value would be issued for more than £1 each, say for £3 each.
(*c*) At one time, shares could be issued at a discount. Thus, shares each of £5 nominal value might have been issued for £3 each. However, this is no longer permitted, having been expressly forbidden in the 1980 Companies Act.

5.2 Share premiums and discounts

This will all seem rather strange at first. How can a £1 share, which states that value on the face of it, be issued for £3 each, and who would be foolish enough to buy it? The reasons for this apparently strange state of affairs stem from the Companies Act requirement that the share capital accounts always show shares at their nominal value, irrespective of how much the shares are worth or how much they are issued for. To illustrate this, the progress of two firms can be looked at, firm A and firm B. Both firms started in business on 1 January 19X1 and issued 1,000 ordinary shares each of £4 nominal value at par. Ignoring any issue expenses, the balance sheets on that date would appear:

Firms A Ltd and B Ltd

Balance Sheet as at 1 January 19X1

	£
Bank	4,000
Capital	4,000

Five years later, on 31 December 19X5, the balance sheets show that the companies have fared quite differently. It is to be assumed here, for purposes of illustration, that the balance sheet values and any other interpretation of values happen to be identical.

£4,000 capital is needed by A Ltd, and this is to be met by issuing more ordinary shares. Suppose that another 1,000 ordinary shares of £4 nominal value each are issued at par. Column (*a*) shows the balance sheet before the issue, and column (*b*) shows the balance sheet after the issue has taken place.

A Ltd Balance Sheets (Solution 1) as at 31 December 19X5

	(*a*) £	(*b*) £
Fixed and current assets (other than bank)	9,000	9,000
Bank	1,000	5,000
	10,000	14,000
Financed by:		
Ordinary share capital	4,000	8,000
Profit and loss	6,000	6,000
	10,000	14,000

Now the effect of what has happened can be appreciated. Before the new issue there were 1,000 shares. As there were £10,000 of assets and no liabilities, then each share was worth £10. After the issue there are 2,000 shares and £14,000 of assets, so that now each share is worth £7. This would be extremely disconcerting to the original shareholders who see the value of each of their shares fall immediately by £3.

On the other hand, the new shareholder who has just bought shares for £4 each sees them rise immediately to be worth £7 each. Only in one specific case would this be just, and that is where each original shareholder buys an equivalent number of new shares. Otherwise this obviously cannot be the correct solution. What is required is a price which is equitable as far as the interests of the old shareholders are concerned, and yet will attract sufficient applications to provide the capital required. As in this case the balance sheet value and the real value are the same, the answer is that each old share was worth £10 and therefore each new share should be issued for £10 each. The balance sheets will now appear:

A Ltd Balance Sheets (Solution 2) as at 31 December 19X5

	(a)\n£	(b)\n£
Fixed and current assets (other than bank)	9,000	9,000
Bank	1,000	11,000
	10,000	20,000
Financed by:		
Ordinary share capital (at nominal value)	4,000	8,000
Share premium (*see* note below)		6,000
Profit and loss	6,000	6,000
	10,000	20,000

Thus in (*a*) above 1,000 shares own between them £10,000 of assets = £10 each, while in (*b*) 2,000 shares are shown as owning £20,000 of assets = £10 each. Both the old and new shareholders are therefore satisfied with the bargain that has been made.

Note: The **share premium** shown on the capital side of the balance sheet is needed, ignoring for a moment the legal requirements to be complied with in company balance sheets, simply because the balance sheet would not balance without it. If shares are stated at nominal value, but issued at another price, the actual amount received increases the bank balance, but the share capital shown is increased by a different figure. The share premium therefore represents the excess of the cash received over the nominal value of the shares issued.

The other, B Ltd, has not fared so well. It has, in fact, lost money. The accumulated losses are reflected in a debit balance on the profit and loss appropriation account as shown in the following balance sheet at (*c*). It can be seen that there are £3,000 of assets to represent the shareholders' stake in the firm of 1,000 shares, i.e. each share is worth £3 each. If more capital was needed 1,000 more shares could be issued. From the action taken in the previous case it will now be obvious that each new share of £4 nominal value would be issued for its real value of £3 each, were it permitted to do so. The balance sheets would appear:

B Ltd Balance Sheets (correct solution) as at 31 December 19X5

	(c)	(d)
Fixed and current assets (other than bank)	2,000	2,000
Bank	1,000	4,000
Discounts on shares (*see* below)		1,000
Profit and loss – debit balance	1,000	1,000
	4,000	8,000
Ordinary share capital	4,000	8,000

Once again, as the share capital is shown at nominal value, but the shares issued at a different figure, the difference being **discounts on shares** must be shown in order that the balance sheet may balance. It is, of course, not actually an asset, it is merely a balancing figure needed because the entries already made for an increase in the ordinary share capital and the increase in the bank balance have been at different figures. The figure for discounts on shares therefore rectifies the double entry 'error'.

Although shares cannot now be issued at a discount, there will very occasionally still be items in company balance sheets for discounts on shares issued before 1980. Although not listed as an item in the balance sheet formats per the 1985 Companies Act, a separate heading will have to be inserted to accommodate the item.

For the purpose of making the foregoing explanations easier it was assumed that balance sheet values and other values were the same. This is very rarely true for all the assets, and in fact there is more than one other 'value'. A balance sheet is a historical view of the past based on records made according to the firm's interpretation and use of accounting concepts and conventions. When shares are being issued it is not the historical view of the past that is important, but the view of the future. Therefore the actual premiums and discounts on shares being issued is not merely a matter of balance sheet values, but on the issuing company's view of the future and its estimate of how the investing public will react to the price at which the shares are being offered.

It is to be noted that there are no restrictions on issuing shares at par or at a premium. The actual double entry accounts can now be seen.

5.3 Shares payable in full on application

The issue of shares in illustrations (1), (2) and (3) which follow are based on the balance sheets that have just been considered.

1 Shares issued at par

1,000 ordinary shares with a nominal value of £4 each are to be issued. Applications, together with the necessary money, are received for exactly 1,000 shares. The shares are then allotted to the applicants.

Bank

		£	
Ordinary share applicants	(A)	4,000	

Ordinary Share Applicants

		£			£
Ordinary share capital	(B)	4,000	Bank	(A)	4,000

Ordinary Share Capital

			£
	Ordinary share applicants	(B)	4,000

It may appear that the ordinary share applicants account is unnecessary, and that the only entries needed are a debit in the bank account and a credit in the ordinary share capital account. However, applicants do not always become shareholders; this is shown later. The applicant must make an offer for the shares being issued, accompanied by the necessary money: this is the application. After the applications have been vetted the allotments of shares are made by the company. This represents the acceptance of the offer by the company and it is at this point that the applicant becomes a shareholder. Therefore (A) represents the offer by the applicant, while (B) is the acceptance by the company. No entry must therefore be made in the share capital account until (B) happens, for it is not until that point that the share capital is in fact in existence. The share applicants account is therefore an intermediary account pending allotments being made.

2 Shares issued at a premium

1,000 ordinary shares with a nominal value of £4 each are to be issued for £10 each (*see* A Ltd previously). Thus a premium of £6 per share has been charged. Applications and the money are received for exactly 1,000 shares.

Bank

	£		
Balance b/d	1,000		
Ordinary share applicants	10,000		

Ordinary Share Applicants

		£			£
Ordinary share capital	(A)	4,000	Bank		10,000
Share premium	(B)	6,000			
		10,000			10,000

Share Premium

			£
	Ordinary share applicants	(B)	6,000

Ordinary Share Capital (A Ltd)

			£
	Balance b/d		4,000
	Ordinary share applicants	(A)	4,000

Note: (A) is shown as £4,000 because the share capital is shown at nominal value and not as total issued value. (B) The £6,000 share premiums must therefore be credited to a share premium account to preserve double entry balancing.

3 Shares issued at a discount (prior to 1980)

1,000 ordinary shares with a nominal value of £4 each are to be issued for £3 each (*see* B Ltd previously). Thus a discount of £1 per share is being allowed. Applications and the money are received for exactly 1,000 shares.

Bank

	£		
Balance b/d	1,000		
Ordinary share applicants	3,000		

Ordinary Share Applicants

	£		£
Ordinary share capital	4,000	Bank	3,000
		Discounts on shares	1,000
	4,000		4,000

Ordinary Share Capital

			£
	Balance b/d		4,000
	Ordinary share capital		4,000

Discounts on Shares

	£		
Ordinary share applications	1,000		

4 Oversubscription and undersubscription for shares

When a public company invites investors to apply for its shares it is obviously very rare indeed if applications for shares equal exactly the number of shares to be issued. Where more shares are applied for than are available for issue, then the issue is said to be **oversubscribed**. Where fewer shares are applied for than are available for issue, then the issue has been **undersubscribed**.

With a brand-new company, a minimum amount is fixed as being necessary to carry on any further with the running of the company. If the applications are less than the minimum stated, then the application monies must be returned to the senders. This does not apply to an established company. If therefore 1,000 shares of £1 each are available for issue, but only 875 shares are applied for, then only 875 will be issued, assuming that this is above the fixed minimum figure. The accounting entries will be in respect of 875 shares, no entries being needed for the 125 shares not applied for, as this part does not represent a transaction.

The opposite of this is where the shares are oversubscribed. In this case, some sort of rationing is applied so that the issue is restricted to the shares available for issue. The process of selecting who will get how many shares depends on the policy of the firm. Some firms favour large shareholders because this leads to lower administrative costs. Why the costs will be lower will be obvious if the cost of calling a meeting of two companies each with 20,000 shares is considered. H Ltd has 20 shareholders with an average holding of 1,000 shares each. J Ltd has 1,000 shareholders with an average holding of 20 shares each. They all have to be notified by post and given various documents including a set of the final accounts. The cost of printing and sending these is less for H Ltd with 20 shareholders than for J Ltd with 1,000 shareholders. This is only one example of the costs involved, but it will also apply with equal force to many items connected with the shares. Conversely, the directors may prefer to have more shareholders with smaller holdings, one reason being that it decreases the amount of voting power in any one individual's hands. The actual process of rationing the shares is then a simple matter once a policy has been agreed. It may consist of scaling down applications, of drawing lots or some other chance selection, but it will eventually bring the number of shares to be issued down to the number of shares available. Excess application monies will then be refunded by the company.

An issue of shares where 1,000 ordinary shares of £1 nominal value each are to be issued at par payable in full, but 1,550 shares are applied for, will appear as follows:

Bank

	£		£
Ordinary share applicants	1,550	Ordinary share applicants (refunds)	550

Ordinary Share Applicants

	£		£
Bank	550	Bank	1,550
Ordinary share capital	1,000		
	1,550		1,550

Ordinary Share Capital

			£
		Ordinary share applicants	1,000

5.4 Issue of shares payable by instalments

The shares considered so far have all been issued as paid in full on application. Conversely, many issues are made which require payment by instalments. These are probably more common with public companies than with private companies. It should be noted that a public company is now not allowed to allot a share unless there has been paid on it a sum equal to at least one-quarter of its nominal value plus the whole of any premium.

The various stages, after the initial invitation has been made to the public to buy shares by means of advertisements (if it is a public company), etc., are as follows:

(A) Applications are received together with the application monies.

(B) The applications are vetted and the shares allotted, letters of allotment being sent out.

(C) The excess application monies from wholly unsuccessful applicants, or, where the application monies received exceed both the application and allotment monies required, wholly and partly unsuccessful applicants, are returned to them. Usually, if a person has been partly unsuccessful, his excess application monies are held by the company and will reduce the amount needed to be paid by him on allotment.

(D) Allotment monies are received.

(E) The next instalment, known as the first call, is requested.

(F) The monies are received from the first call.

(G) The next instalment, known as the second call, is requested.

(H) The monies are received from the second call.

This carries on until the full number of calls have been made, although there is not usually a large number of calls to be made in an issue.

The reasons for the payments by instalments become obvious if it is realised that a company will not necessarily require the immediate use of all the money to be raised by the issue. Suppose a new company is to be formed: it is to buy land, erect a factory, equip it with machinery and then go into production. This might take two years altogether. If the total sum needed was £1,000,000, the allocation of this money could be:

Ordinary Share Capital

	£
Cost of land, payable within 1 month	300,000
Cost of buildings, payable in 1 year's time	200,000
Cost of machinery, payable in 18 months' time	200,000
Working capital required in 2 years' time	300,000
	1,000,000

The issue may therefore well be on the following terms:

	Per cent
Application money per share, payable immediately	10
Allotment money per share, payable within 1 month	20
First call, money payable in 12 months' time	20
Second call, money payable in 18 months' time	20
Third call, money payable in 24 months' time	30
	100

The entries made in the share capital account should equal the amount of money requested to that point in time. However, instead of one share applicants account, this is usually split into several accounts to represent the different instalments. For this purpose application and allotment are usually joined together in one account, the application and *allotment account*, as this cuts out the need for transfers where excess *application monies* are held over and set off against allotment monies needed. When allotment is made, and not until then, an entry of £300,000 (10 per cent + 20 per cent) would be made in the share capital account. On the first call an entry of £200,000 would be made in the share capital account, likewise £200,000 on the second call and £300,000 on the third call. The share capital account will therefore contain not the monies received, but the amount of money requested. Exhibit 5.1 now shows an instance of a share issue.

Exhibit 5.1

A company is issuing 1,000 7 per cent preference shares of £1 each, payable 10 per cent on application, 20 per cent on allotment, 40 per cent on the first call and 30 per cent on the second call. Applications are received for 1,550 shares. A refund of the money is made in respect of 50 shares, while for the remaining 1,500 applied for, an allotment is to be made on the basis of 2 shares for every 3 applied for (assume that this will not involve any fractions of shares). The excess application monies are set off against the allotment monies asked for. The remaining requested instalments are all paid in full. The letters by the side of each entry refer to the various stages outlined earlier.

Bank

		£			£
Application and allotment:			Application and		
Application monies	(A)	155	allotment refund	(C)	5
Allotment monies					
(£1,000 × 20% *less* excess					
application monies £50)	(B)	150			
First call	(F)	400			
Second call	(H)	300			

Application and Allotment

		£			£
Bank – refund of			Bank	(A)	155
application monies	(C)	5	Bank	(B)	150
Preference share capital	(B)	300			
		305			305

First Call

		£			£
Preference share capital	(E)	400	Bank	(F)	400

Second Call

		£			£
Preference share capital	(G)	<u>300</u>	Bank	(H)	<u>300</u>

7 per cent Preference Share Capital

		£			£
			Application and allotment	(B)	300
			First call	(E)	400
Balance c/d		1,000	Second call	(G)	<u>300</u>
		<u>1,000</u>			<u>1,000</u>
			Balance b/d		1,000

If more than one type of share is being issued at the same time, e.g. preference shares and ordinary shares, then separate share capital accounts and separate application and allotment accounts and call accounts should be opened.

5.5 Forfeited shares

Sometimes, although it is probably fairly rare in recent times, a shareholder fails to pay the calls requested from him. The Articles of Association of the company will probably provide that the shareholder will have his shares forfeited, provided that certain safeguards for his protection are fully observed. In this case the shares will be cancelled, and the instalments already paid by the shareholder will be lost to him.

After the forfeiture, the company may reissue the shares, unless there is a provision in the Articles of Association to prevent it. There are certain conditions as to the prices at which the shares can be reissued. These are that the amount received on reissue plus the amount received from the original shareholder should at least equal (*a*) the called-up value where the shares are not fully called up, or (*b*) the nominal value where the full amount has been called up. Any premium previously paid is disregarded in determining the minimum reissue price.

Exhibit 5.2

Take the same information as that contained in Exhibit 5.1, but instead of all the calls being paid, Allen, the holder of 100 shares, fails to pay the first and second calls. He had already paid the application and allotment monies on the required dates. The directors conform to the provisions of the Articles of Association and (A) Allen is forced to suffer the forfeiture of his shares. (B) The amount still outstanding from Allen will be written off. (C) The directors then reissue the shares at 75 per cent of nominal value to J Dougan. (D) Dougan pays for the shares.

First Call

	£			£
Preference share capital	400	Bank		360
		Forfeited shares	(B)	<u>40</u>
	<u>400</u>			<u>400</u>

Second Call

		£			£
Preference share capital		300	Bank		270
			Forfeited shares	(B)	30
		300			300

7 per cent Preference Share Capital

		£			£
Forfeited shares	(A)	100	Application and allotment		300
Balance c/d		900	First call		400
			Second call		300
		1,000			1,000
			Balance b/d		900
Balance c/d		1,000	J Dougan	(C)	100
		1,000			1,000
			Balance b/d		1,000

Forfeited Shares

		£			£
First call	(B)	40	Preference share capital	(A)	100
Second call	(B)	30			
Balance c/d		30			
		100			100
J Dougan (*see* following note)		25	Balance c/d		30
Balance c/d		5			
		30			30

Bank

		£	
First call (£900 × 40%)		360	
Second call (£900 × 30%)		270	
J Dougan	(D)	75	

J Dougan

		£			£
Preference share capital		100	Bank	(D)	75
			Forfeited shares (discount on reissue) – *see* following note		25
		100			100

Note: The transfer of £25 from the forfeited shares account to J Dougan's account is needed because the reissue was entered in the preference share capital account and Dougan's account at nominal value, i.e. following standard practice of a share capital account being concerned with nominal values, but Dougan was not to pay the full nominal price. Therefore the transfer of £25 is needed to close his account.

The balance of £5 on the forfeited shares account can be seen to be: cash received from original shareholder on application and allotment £30 + from Dougan £75 = £105. This is £5 over the nominal value so that the £5 appears as a credit balance. This is usually stated to be either transferred to a profit on reissue of forfeited shares account, but it really cannot be thought that this is followed in practice for small amounts. More normally it would be transferred to the credit of a share premium account.

5.6 Calls in advance and in arrear and the balance sheet

At the balance sheet date some shareholders will not have paid all the calls made. These are collectively known as **calls in arrear**. On the other hand, some shareholders may have paid amounts in respect of calls not made by the balance sheet date. These are **calls in advance**.

Calls in arrear, i.e. **called-up share capital not paid**, is to be shown in the balance sheet in one of the positions shown in the format per the 1985 Companies Act (*see* Chapter 13). There is no specified place for calls in advance, so this will be inserted in the balance sheet as an extra heading.

5.7 Rights issues

The costs of making a new issue of shares can be quite high. A way to reduce the costs of raising new long-term capital in the form of issuing shares may be by way of a **rights issue**. To do this the company circularises the existing shareholders, and informs them of the new issue to be made and the number of shares which each one of them is entitled to buy of the new issue. In most cases the shareholder is allowed to renounce his rights to the new shares in favour of someone else. The issue is usually pitched at a price which will make the rights capable of being sold, i.e. if the existing shareholder does not want the shares he can renounce them to A who will give him £x for the right to apply for the shares in his place, a right that A could not otherwise obtain. If any shareholder does not either buy the shares or transfer his rights, then the directors will usually have the power to dispose of such shares not taken up by issuing them in some other way.

5.8 Debentures

A **debenture** is a bond, acknowledging a loan to a company, usually under the company's seal, which bears a fixed rate of interest. Unlike shares, which normally depend on profits out of which to appropriate dividends, debenture interest is payable whether profits are made or not.

A debenture may be redeemable, i.e. repayable at or by a specified date. Conversely it may be irredeemable, redemption only taking place when the company is eventually liquidated, or in a case such as when the debenture interest is not paid within a given time limit.

People lending money to companies in the form of debentures will obviously be interested in how safe their investment will be. In the case of some debentures, the debenture holders are given the legal right that on certain happenings they will be able to take control of specific assets, or of the whole of the assets. They can then sell the assets and recoup the amount due under their debentures, or deal with the assets in ways specified in the deed under which the debentures were issued. Such debentures are known as being secured against the assets, the term **mortgage** debenture often being used. Other debentures carry no prior right to control the assets under any circumstances. These are known as **simple** or **naked** debentures.

5.9 The issue of debentures

The entries for the issue of debentures are similar to those for shares. It would, however, certainly not be the normal modern practice to issue debentures at a premium. If the word 'debentures' appears instead of 'share capital', then the entries in the accounts would be identical.

5.10 Shares of no par value

It can be seen that the idea of a fixed par value for a share can be very misleading. For anyone who has not studied accounting, it may well come as a shock to find that a share with a par value of £1 might in fact be issued for £5. If the share is dealt in on the Stock Exchange they might find a £1 share selling at £10 or even £20, or equally well it may sell for only 10p.

Another disadvantage of a par value is that it can give people entirely the wrong impression of the activities of a business. If a par value is kept to, and the dividend based on that, then with a certain degree of inflation the dividend figure can look excessive. Many trade union leaders would howl with disapproval if a dividend of 100 per cent were declared by a company. But is this so excessive? Exhibit 5.3 gives a rather different picture.

Exhibit 5.3

Allen bought a share 40 years ago for £1. At the time he was satisfied with a return of 5 per cent on his money. With a 5 per cent dividend he could buy a certain amount of goods which will be called x. Forty years later to buy that same amount of goods, x, he would need, say, 20 times as much money. Previously £5 would have bought x, now it would take £100. To keep his dividend at the same level of purchasing power he would need a dividend now of 100 per cent, as compared with the 5 per cent he was receiving 40 years ago.

In the United States of America, Canada, and Belgium, as well as other countries, no par value is attached to shares being issued. A share is issued at whatever price is suitable at the time, and the money received is credited to a share capital account.

New terms

Share premium (pp. 62–4): Where a share is issued at a price above its par, or nominal value, the excess is known as a premium.

Share discount (pp. 62–4): Where a share was issued at a price below its par, or nominal value, the shortfall was known as a discount. However, it is no longer legal under the Companies Acts to issue shares at a discount.

Rights issue (p. 72): An issue of shares to existing shareholders.

Debenture (pp. 72–3): A bond or document acknowledging a loan to a company, normally under the company's seal and carrying a fixed rate of interest.

Shares at no par value (p. 73): Shares which do not have a fixed par, or nominal value.

Main points to remember

1 Shares may be issued either:

   (*a*) at par, or nominal value – i.e. a £1 ordinary share would be issued in exchange for payment of £1, or

   (*b*) at a premium – i.e. if a £1 ordinary share were issued at a premium of 25p, it would cost the buyer £1.25 (and the 25p would be put into the issuing company's *share premium* account).

2 The accounting entries made on the issue of debentures are identical to the accounting entries made on the issue of shares.

Review questions

5.1 A limited company has a nominal capital of £120,000 divided into 120,000 ordinary shares of £1 each. The whole of the capital was issued at par on the following terms:

	Per share
Payable on application	£0.125
Payable on allotment	£0.25
First call	£0.25
Second call	£0.375

Applications were received for 160,000 shares and it was decided to allot the shares on the basis of three for every four for which applications had been made. The balance of application monies were applied to the allotment, no cash being refunded. The balance of allotment monies were paid by the members.

   The calls were made and paid in full by the members, with the exception of a member who failed to pay the first and second calls on the 800 shares allotted to him. A resolution was passed by the directors to forfeit the shares. The forfeited shares were later issued to D Regan at £0.90 each.

   Show the ledger accounts recording all the above transactions, and the relevant extracts from a balance sheet after all the transactions had been completed.

5.2 Badger Ltd has an authorised capital of £100,000 divided into 20,000 ordinary shares of £5 each. The whole of the shares were issued at par, payments being made as follows:

	£
Payable on application	0.5
Payable on allotment	1.5
First call	2.0
Second call	1.0

Applications were received for 32,600 shares. It was decided to refund application monies on 2,600 shares and to allot the shares on the basis of two for every three applied for. The excess application monies sent by the successful applicants is not to be refunded but is to be held and so reduce the amount payable on allotment.

   The calls were made and paid in full with the exception of one member holding 100 shares who paid neither the first nor the second call and another member who did not pay the second call on 20 shares. After requisite action by the directors the shares were forfeited. They were later reissued to B Mills at a price of £4 per share.

   You are to draft the ledger accounts to record the transactions.

5.3 The authorised and issued share capital of Cosy Fires Ltd was £75,000 divided into 75,000 ordinary shares of £1 each, fully paid. On 2 January 19X7, the authorised capital was increased by a further 85,000 ordinary shares of £1 each to £160,000. On the same date 40,000 ordinary shares of £1 each were offered to the public at £1.25 per share payable as to £0.60 on application (including the premium), £0.35 on allotment and £0.30 on 6 April 19X7.

The lists were closed on 10 January 19X7, and by that date applications for 65,000 shares had been received. Applications for 5,000 shares received no allotment and the cash paid in respect of such shares was returned. All shares were then allocated to the remaining applicants pro rata to their original applications, the balance of the monies received on applications being applied to the amounts due on allotment.

The balances due on allotment were received on 31 January 19X7, with the exception of one allottee of 500 shares and these were declared forfeited on 4 April 19X7. These shares were reissued as fully paid on 2 May 19X7, at £1.10 per share. The call due on 6 April 19X7 was duly paid by the other shareholders.

You are required

(a) To record the above-mentioned transactions in the appropriate ledger accounts; and

(b) To show how the balances on such accounts should appear in the company's balance sheet as on 31 May 19X7.

(*Association of Chartered Certified Accountants*)

5.4A During the year to 30 September 19X7, Kammer plc made a new offer of shares. The details of the offer were as follows:

1   100,000 ordinary shares of £1 each were issued payable in instalments as follows:

	Per share £
On application at 1 November 19X6	0.65
On allotment (including the share premium of £0.50 per share) on 1 December 19X6	0.55
On first and final call on 1 June 19X7	0.30
	£1.50

2   Applications for 200,000 shares were received, and it was decided to deal with them as follows:

(a) to return cheques for 75,000 shares;

(b) to accept in full applications for 25,000 shares; and

(c) to allot the remaining shares on the basis of three shares for every four shares applied for.

3   On the first and final call, one applicant who had been allotted 5,000 shares failed to pay the due amount, and his shares were duly declared forfeited. They were then reissued to Amber Ltd on 1 September 19X7 at a price of £0.80 per share fully paid.

Note: Kammer's issued share capital on 1 October 19X6 consisted of 500,000 ordinary shares of £1 each.

Required:

Record the above transactions in the following ledger accounts:

(a) ordinary share capital;

(b) share premium;

(c) application and allotment;

(d) first and final call;

(e) forfeited shares; and

(f) Amber Ltd's account.

(*Association of Accounting Technicians*)

5.5 M Limited has an authorised share capital of £1,500,000 divided into 1,500,000 ordinary shares of £1 each. The issued share capital at 31 March 19X7 was £500,000 which was fully paid, and had been issued at par. On 1 April 19X7, the directors, in accordance with the company's Articles, decided to increase the share capital of the company by offering a further 500,000 ordinary shares of £1 each at a price of £1.60 per share, payable as follows:

On application, including the premium	£0.85 per share
On allotment	£0.25 per share
On first and final call on 3 August 19X7	£0.50 per share

On 13 April 19X7, applications had been received for 750,000 shares and it was decided to allot the shares to applicants for 625,000 shares, on the basis of four shares for every five shares for which applications had been received. The balance of the money received on application was to be applied to the amounts due on allotment. The shares were allotted on 1 May 19X7, the unsuccessful applicants being repaid their cash on this date. The balance of the allotment money was received in full by 15 May 19X7.

With the exception of one member who failed to pay the call on the 5,000 shares allotted to him, the remainder of the call was paid in full within two weeks of the call being made.

The directors resolved to forfeit these shares on 1 September 19X7, after giving the required notice. The forfeited shares were reissued on 30 September 19X7 to another member at £0.90 per share.

You are required to write up the ledger accounts necessary to record these transactions in the books of M Limited.

(*Chartered Institute of Management Accountants*)

5.6A Applications were invited by the directors of Grobigg Ltd for 150,000 of its £1 ordinary shares at £1.15 per share payable as follows:

	Per share
On application on 1 April 19X8	£0.75
On allotment on 30 April 19X8 (including the premium of £0.15 per share)	£0.20
On first and final call on 31 May 19X8	£0.20

Applications were received for 180,000 shares and it was decided to deal with these as follows:

1 To refuse allotment to applicants for 8,000 shares.
2 To give full allotment to applicants for 22,000 shares.
3 To allot the remainder of the available shares pro rata among the other applicants.
4 To utilise the surplus received on applications in part payment of amounts due on allotment.

An applicant, to whom 400 shares had been allotted, failed to pay the amount due on the first and final call and his shares were declared forfeit on 31 July 19X8. These shares were reissued on 3 September 19X8 as fully paid at £0.90 per share.

Show how the transactions would be recorded in the company's books.

(*Association of Chartered Certified Accountants*)

6

Companies purchasing and redeeming their own shares and debentures

Objectives

After you have studied this chapter, you should:

- *understand, in the context of shares and debentures, the difference between the terms 'purchasing' and 'redeeming'*

- *be aware of the alternative ways in which a company may purchase or redeem its own shares and debentures*

- *know the difference between the purchase/redemption opportunities available to private companies, and those available to other companies*

- *know how to record the accounting entries relating to the purchase and the redemption of shares and debentures*

6.1 Purchasing and redeeming own shares

To a student the words 'purchasing' and 'redeeming' may appear to be exactly the same as far as this chapter is concerned. To all intents and purposes it is the same, for it involves an outflow of cash by the company to get back its own shares and then cancel them. However, from a rather more legal and precise point of view, 'redeeming' means the buying back of shares which were originally issued as being 'redeemable' in that the company stated when they were issued that they would be, or could be, redeemed (i.e. bought back by the company). The terms of the 'redemption' (buying back) would be stated at the time when the shares were issued. However, when shares are issued and are not stated to be 'redeemable' then, when they are bought back by the company it is then said to be the 'purchase' of its shares by the company, usually in the open market.

Until 1981 a company in the United Kingdom could not, in normal circumstances, 'purchase' its own shares. In addition 'redemption' was limited to one type of share, **redeemable preference shares**. This had not been the case in the United States and Europe for many years where companies had, with certain restrictions, been allowed to buy back their own shares. The basic reason why this was not allowed in the UK was the fear that the interests of creditors could be adversely affected if the company used its available cash to buy its own shares, thus leaving less to satisfy the claims of the creditors. The possibilities of abuse with preference shares was considered to be less than with ordinary shares, thus it was possible to have redeemable preference shares.

Now, under the Companies Acts, if it is authorised to do so by its articles of association, a company may:

(a) Issue redeemable shares of any class (preference, ordinary, etc.). Redeemable shares include those that are to be redeemed on a particular date as well as those that are merely liable to be redeemed at the discretion of the shareholder or of the company. There is an important proviso that a company can only issue redeemable shares if it has in issue shares that are *not* redeemable. Without this restriction a company could issue only redeemable shares, then later redeem all of its shares, and thus finish up without any shareholders.

(b) 'Purchase' its own shares (i.e. shares that were not issued as being redeemable shares). Again there is a proviso that the company must, *after* the purchase, have other shares in issue at least some of which are not redeemable. This again is to stop the company redeeming its whole share capital and thus ceasing to have members. The company must have, after the purchase, at least one member.

6.2 Advantages of purchase and redemption of shares

Certainly there are quite a few possible advantages of a company being able to buy back its own shares. These are strongest in the case of private companies. For public companies the main advantage is that those with surplus cash resources could find it useful to be able to return some of this surplus cash back to its shareholders by buying back some of its own shares, rather than have pressure put on them to use such cash in uneconomic ways.

For private companies the main possible advantages would appear to be overcoming snags which occur when a shareholder cannot sell his shares on the 'open market', i.e. a stock exchange. This means that:

(a) It will help shareholders who have difficulties in selling their shares to another individual to be able to realise their value when needed, for any reason.

(b) People will be more willing to buy shares from private companies. The fear of not being able to dispose of them previously led to finance being relatively difficult for private companies to obtain from people outside the original main proprietors of the company.

(c) In many 'family' companies cash is needed to pay for taxes on the death of the shareholder.

(d) Shareholders with grievances against the company can be bought out, thus contributing to the more efficient management of the company.

(e) Family-owned companies will be helped in their desire to keep control of the company when a family shareholder with a large number of shares dies or retires.

(f) Similar to public companies, as described above, the company could return unwanted cash resources back to its shareholders.

(g) For both private companies, and for public companies whose shares are not listed on a stock exchange, it may help boost share schemes for employees, as the employees would know that they could fairly easily dispose of the shares instead of being stuck with them.

6.3 Accounting entries

The accounting entries for either 'purchase' or 'redemption' of shares are exactly the same, except that the word 'redeemable' will appear as the first word in the title of the accounts for shares that are redeemable. The figures to be entered will naturally be affected by the **terms** under which shares are redeemed or purchased, but the actual type of **location** of the debits and credits to be made will be the same.

The reader will more easily understand the rather complicated entries needed if s/he understands the reasoning behind the Companies Acts. The protection of the creditor was uppermost in the minds of Parliament. The general idea is that **capital** should not be returned to the shareholders, except under certain circumstances. If capital is returned to the shareholders, thus reducing the cash and bank balances, then the creditors could lose out badly if there was not then sufficient cash/bank balances to be able to pay their claims. Thus the shareholders, seeing that things were not progressing too well in the company, could get their money out possibly at the expense of the creditors.

There are dividends which can quite legitimately be paid to the shareholders out of distributable profits, but the idea is to stop the shareholders withdrawing their capital. Included under the general heading of 'capital' for this purpose are those particular reserves which cannot be used up for the payment of cash dividends. There are special exceptions to this, namely the reduction of capital by public companies (*see* Chapter 10) and the special powers of a private company to purchase or redeem its own shares out of capital (*see* later in this chapter), but apart from these special cases the company law regulations are intended to ensure that capital figures do not fall when shares are redeemed or purchased. This general purpose is behind the accounting entries which are now to be examined.

6.4 Rules for redemption or purchase

It is important to note that in *all* cases shares can only be redeemed or purchased when they are fully paid.

The safeguards for the protection of 'capital' contained in the Companies Acts may be summarised as follows.

6.5 Nominal value

In respect of the **nominal** value of shares redeemed or purchased, either (*a*) there must be a new issue of shares to provide the funds for redemption or purchase or (*b*) sufficient distributable profits must be available (i.e. a large enough credit balance on the appropriation account) which could be diverted from being used up as dividends to being treated as used up for the purpose of redeeming or purchasing the shares. Therefore, when shares are redeemed or purchased other than out of the proceeds of a new issue, then, and only then, the amount of distributable profits treated as being used up by the nominal value of shares redeemed or purchased is debited to the appropriation account and credited to a **capital redemption reserve**. (At one time, this was called a 'capital redemption reserve fund'. However, use of the word 'fund' has now been dropped.) Thus the old share capital will equal the total of the new share capital *plus* the capital redemption reserve. The capital redemption reserve is a 'non-distributable' reserve. This means that it cannot be transferred back to the credit of the appropriation account, and so increase the profits available for distribution as cash dividends. The process of diverting profits from being usable for dividends means that the non-payment of the dividends leaves more cash in the firm against which creditors could claim if necessary.

Note: In all the examples which follow, the shares being redeemed/purchased could either be redeemable shares or those not specifically stated to be redeemable. Obviously, in a real company, the titles of the accounts would state which shares were redeemable.

To get the reader used to journal entries, and then seeing the effect on the face of the balance sheet, journal style entries will be shown first, followed by the balances for the balance sheet.

Exhibit 6.1

£2,000 preference shares are redeemed/purchased at par, a new issue of £2,000 ordinary shares at par being made for the purpose.

		Dr £	Cr £
(A1)	Bank	2,000	
(A2)	Ordinary share applicants		2,000
	Cash received from applicants		
(B1)	Ordinary share applicants	2,000	
(B2)	Ordinary share capital		2,000
	Ordinary shares allotted		
(C1)	Preference share capital	2,000	
(C2)	Preference share purchase*		2,000
	Shares to be redeemed/purchased		
(D1)	Preference share purchase*	2,000	
(D2)	Bank		2,000
	Payment made to redeem/purchase shares		

*Note: In all the examples which follow, the shares being purchased/redeemed are preference shares. In fact they could be any type of share, ordinary, preference, preferred ordinary, etc. The shares to be redeemed/purchased are transferred to a preference share purchase account. In fact if they were being redeemed it would be a preference share redemption account. It will make it easier to follow if the answers are standardised.

	Balances before £	Effect	Dr £		Cr £	Balances after £
Net assets (except bank)	7,500					7,500
Bank	2,500	(A1)	2,000	(D2)	2,000	2,500
	10,000					10,000
Ordinary share capital	5,000			(B2)	2,000	7,000
Ordinary share applicants	–	(B1)	2,000	(A2)	2,000	–
Preference share capital	2,000	(C1)	2,000			–
Preference share purchase	–	(D1)	2,000	(C2)	2,000	–
	7,000 *					7,000*
Profit and loss	3,000					3,000
	10,000					10,000

*Note: total 'capitals' remain the same.

Exhibit 6.2

£2,000 preference shares redeemed/purchased at par, with no new issue of shares to provide funds for the purpose. Therefore an amount equal to the nominal value of the shares redeemed *must* be transferred from the profit and loss appropriation account to the credit of a capital redemption reserve.

		Dr £	Cr £
(A1)	Preference share capital	2,000	
(A2)	Preference share purchase		2,000
	Shares to be redeemed/purchased		
(B1)	Preference share purchase	2,000	
(B2)	Bank		2,000
	Cash paid as purchase/redemption		
(C1)	Profit and loss appropriation	2,000	
(C2)	Capital redemption reserve		2,000
	Transfer per Companies Act 1985, Section 45		

	Balances before £		Effect Dr £		Effect Cr £	Balances after £
Net assets (except bank)	7,500					7,500
Bank	2,500			(B2)	2,000	500
	10,000					8,000
Ordinary share capital	5,000					5,000
Preference share capital	2,000	(A1)	2,000			–
Preference share purchase	–	(B1)	2,000	(A2)	2,000	–
Capital redemption reserve	–			(C2)	2,000	2,000
	7,000*					7,000*
Profit and loss	3,000	(C1)	2,000			1,000
	10,000					8,000

*Note: total 'capitals' (share capital + non-distributable reserves) remain the same at £7,000.

Exhibit 6.3

£2,000 preference shares redeemed/purchased at par, being £1,200 from issue of ordinary shares at par and partly by using appropriation account balance.

		Dr £	Cr £
(A1)	Bank	1,200	
(A2)	Ordinary share applicants		1,200
	Cash received from applicants		
(B1)	Ordinary share applicants	1,200	
(B2)	Ordinary share capital		1,200
	Ordinary shares allotted		
(C1)	Profit and loss appropriation	800	
(C2)	Capital redemption reserve		800
	Part of redemption/purchase not covered by new issue, to comply with Companies Act 1985		
(D1)	Preference share capital	2,000	
(D2)	Preference share purchase		2,000
	Shares being redeemed/purchased		
(E1)	Preference share purchase	2,000	
(E2)	Bank		2,000
	Payment made for redemption/purchase		

	Balances before £		Effect Dr £		Cr £	Balances after £
Net assets (except bank)	7,500					7,500
Bank	2,500	(A1)	1,200	(E2)	2,000	1,700
	10,000					9,200
Ordinary share capital	5,000			(B2)	1,200	6,200
Ordinary share applicants	–	(B1)	1,200	(A2)	1,200	–
Preference share capital	2,000	(D1)	2,000			–
Preference share purchase	–	(E1)	2,000	(D2)	2,000	–
Capital redemption reserve	–			(C2)	800	800
	7,000*					7,000*
Profit and loss	3,000	(C1)	800			2,200
	10,000					9,200

*Note: total 'capitals' remain the same.

6.6 Premiums

The next requirement under the Companies Acts is that when shares are being redeemed/purchased at a premium, but they were *not* originally issued at a premium, then an amount equal to the premium *must* be transferred from the appropriation account to the credit of the share purchase/redemption account. This again is to divert profits away from being distributable to being part of 'capital'.

Exhibit 6.4

£2,000 preference shares which were originally issued at par are redeemed/purchased at a premium of 20 per cent. There is no new issue of shares for the purpose. In this example the ordinary shares had been originally issued at a premium, thus the reason for the share premium account being in existence. However, it is *not* the ordinary shares which are being redeemed and therefore the share premium *cannot* be used for the premium on redemption/purchase of the preference shares.

		Dr £	Cr £
(A1)	Preference share capital	2,000	
(A2)	Preference share purchase		2,000
	Shares being redeemed/purchased		
(B1)	Profit and loss appropriation	400	
(B2)	Preference share purchase		400
	Premium on purchase/redemption of shares *not* previously issued at premium		
(C1)	Profit and loss appropriation	2,000	
(C2)	Capital redemption reserve		2,000
	Transfer because shares redeemed/purchased out of distributable profits		
(D1)	Preference share purchase	2,400	
(D2)	Bank		2,400
	Payment on purchase/redemption		

	Balances before £	Effect Dr £		Effect Cr £		Balances after £
Net assets (except bank)	7,500					7,500
Bank	2,500			(D2)	2,400	100
	10,000					7,600
Ordinary share capital	4,500					4,500
Preference share capital	2,000	(A1)	2,000			–
Preference share purchase	–	(D1)	2,400	(A2)	2,000	–
				(B2)	400	
Capital redemption reserve	–			(C2)	2,000	2,000
Share premium	500					500
	7,000*					7,000*
		(C1)	2,000			
Profit and loss	3,000	(B1)	400			600
	10,000					7,600

Note: total 'capitals' remain the same.

Under the Companies Acts, when shares are being redeemed or purchased at a premium, *and* they were originally issued at a premium, *and* a new issue of shares is being made for the purpose, then the share premium account *can* have an amount calculated as follows transferred to the credit of the share purchase/redemption account. This is shown as (E).

Share Premium Account

			£
	Balance before new issue	(A)	xxx
Add	Premium on new issue	(B)	xxx
	Balance after new issue	(C)	xxx
	Amount that *may* be transferred	(E)	
	is lesser of:		
	Premiums that were received when it first issued the shares now being redeemed/purchased (D)	xxx	
	or		
	Balance after new issue (C) above	xxx	
	Transfer to share purchase/redemption	(E)	xxx
	New balance for balance sheet (could be nil)		xxx

Where the amount being deducted (E) is *less* than the premium paid on the *current* redemption or purchase, then an amount equivalent to the difference must be transferred from the debit of the appropriation account to the credit of the share purchase/redemption account. (An instance of this is shown in Exhibit 6.5.) This again diverts profits away from being distributable.

Exhibit 6.5

£2,000 preference shares originally issued at a premium of 20 per cent now being purchased/redeemed at a premium of 25 per cent. The position can be shown in three different companies for the purpose of purchase/redemption:

- Company 1 issues 2,400 ordinary £1 shares at par;
- Company 2 issues 2,000 ordinary £1 shares at 20 per cent premium;
- Company 3 issues 1,600 ordinary £1 shares at 50 per cent premium.

Share Premium Account

		Company 1 £	Company 2 £	Company 3 £
Balance before new issue	(A)	150^1	400	400
Premium on new issue			400	800 (B)
Balance after new issue	(C)	150	800	1,200
Amount transferable to share purchase/ redemption is therefore lower of (C) or original premium on issue (£400)		150^2	400^2	400^2
New balance for balance sheet		–	400	800

Notes:
1 In Company 1 it is assumed that of the original £400 premium the sum of £250 had been used up to issue bonus shares (*see* Chapter 10 later).
2 As these figures are less than the premium of £500 *now* being paid, the differences (Company 1 £350; Companies 2 and 3 £100 each) must be transferred from the debit of the appropriation account to the credit of the preference share/purchase redemption account.

Journal entries:

	Company 1		Company 2		Company 3	
	Dr	*Cr*	*Dr*	*Cr*	*Dr*	*Cr*
	£	£	£	£	£	£
(A1) Bank	2,400		2,400		2,400	
(A2) Ordinary share applicants		2,400		2,400		2,400
Cash received from applicants						
(B1) Ordinary share applicants	2,400		2,400		2,400	
(B2) Ordinary share capital		2,400		2,000		1,600
(B3) Share premium		–		400		800
Ordinary shares allotted						
(C1) Preference share capital	2,000		2,000		2,000	
(C2) Preference share purchase		2,000		2,000		2,000
Shares being redeemed/purchased						
(D1) Share premium account	150		400		400	
(D2) Preference share purchase		150		400		400
Amount of share premium account used for redemption/purchase						
(E1) Profit and loss appropriation	350		100		100	
(E2) Preference share purchase		350		100		100
Excess of premium payable over amount of share premium account usable for the purpose						
(F1) Preference share purchase	2,500		2,500		2,500	
(F2) Bank		2,500		2,500		2,500
Amount paid on redemption/purchase						

Exhibit 6.6

The following balance sheets for the three companies of Exhibit 6.5 are given *before* the purchase/redemption. The balance sheets are then shown *after* purchase/redemption.

Balance Sheets (*before* redemption/purchase)

	Company 1	Company 2	Company 3
	£	£	£
Net assets (except bank)	7,500	7,500	7,500
Bank	2,500	2,500	2,500
	10,000	10,000	10,000
Ordinary share capital	4,850	4,600	4,600
Preference share capital	2,000	2,000	2,000
Share premium	150	400	400
	7,000	7,000	7,000
Profit and loss account	3,000	3,000	3,000
	10,000	10,000	10,000

Balance Sheets (*after* redemption/purchase)

	Company 1 £	Company 2 £	Company 3 £
Net assets (except bank)	7,500	7,500	7,500
Bank	2,400	2,400	2,400
	9,900	9,900	9,900
Ordinary share capital	7,250	6,600	6,200
Share premium	–	400	800
	7,250	7,000	7,000
Profit and loss account	2,650	2,900	2,900
	9,900	9,900	9,900

6.7 Private companies: redemption or purchase of shares out of capital

The Companies Act of 1981 introduced a *new* power for a *private* company to redeem/purchase its own shares where *either* it has insufficient distributable profits for the purpose *or* it cannot raise the amount required by a new issue. Previously it would have had to apply to the court for **capital reduction** as per Chapter 10. The 1981 legislation made it far easier to achieve the same objectives, both in terms of time and expense. This is carried on in the current Companies Acts.

A book on company law should be read for the detail of the various matters which must be dealt with. A very brief outline may be given as follows:

(*a*) The company must be authorised to do so by its Articles of Association.
(*b*) Directors must certify that, after the **permissible capital payment,** the company will be able to carry on as a going concern during the next twelve months, and be able to pay its debts immediately after the payment and also during the next twelve months.
(*c*) Auditors to make a satisfactory report.
(*d*) Permissible capital payment is the amount by which the price of redemption or purchase exceeds the aggregate of (i) the company's distributable profits and (ii) the proceeds of any new issue. This means that a private company should use its available profits and any share proceeds before making a payment out of capital.

6.8 Permissible capital payments

(*a*) Where the permissible capital payment is *less* than the nominal value of shares redeemed/purchased, the amount of the difference *shall* be transferred to the capital redemption reserve from the appropriation account (or undistributed profits).
(*b*) Where the permissible capital payment is *greater* than the nominal value of shares redeemed/purchased, *any* non-distributable reserves (e.g. share premium account, capital redemption reserve, revaluation reserve, etc.) or fully paid share capital can be reduced by the excess.

This can best be illustrated by taking two companies, R and S, with similar account balances *before* the purchase/redemption, but redeeming on different terms:

Exhibit 6.7

Company R	Before £		Dr £		Cr £	After £
Net assets (except bank)	2,500					2,500
Bank	7,500			(B2)	4,000	3,500
	10,000					6,000
Ordinary shares	1,000					1,000
Preference shares	4,000	(A1)	4,000			–
Non-distributable reserves	2,000					2,000
Capital redemption reserve				(C2)	3,000	3,000
Preference share purchase	–	(B1)	4,000	(A2)	4,000	
	7,000					
Profit and loss	3,000	(C1)	3,000			
	10,000					6,000

Preference shares redeemed at par £4,000. No new issue.

Therefore pay	£4,000
Less Profit and loss account	£3,000
Permissible capital payment	£1,000

Nominal amount shares redeemed/purchased	£4,000
Less Permissible capital payment	£1,000
Deficiency to transfer to capital redemption reserve (C1 and C2)	£3,000

(A1) and (A2) represents transfer of shares redeemed/purchased.
(B1) and (B2) represents payment to shareholders.

Company S	Before £		Dr £		Cr £	After £
Net assets (except bank)	2,500					2,500
Bank	7,500			(D2)	7,200	300
	10,000					2,800
Ordinary share capital	1,000					1,000
Preference shares	4,000	(A1)	4,000			–
⎰ Non-distributable reserves	2,000	(C1)	200			1,800
⎱ Capital redemption reserve	–					–
Preference share purchase		(D1)	7,200	(A2)	4,000	
				(B2)	3,000	
				(C2)	200	
	7,000					2,800
Profit and loss	3,000	(B1)	3,000			–
	10,000					2,800

Preference shares redeemed/purchased at premium 80%. No new issue.

Therefore pay	£7,200
Less Profit and loss account	£3,000
Permissible capital payment	£4,200
Permissible capital payment	£4,200
Less Nominal amount redeemed/purchased	£4,000
Excess from *any* of non-distributable reserves (or capital) (C1 and C2)	£200

(A1) and (A2) represents shares redeemed/purchased.
(B1) and (B2) is transfer to redemption/purchase account of part of source of funds.
(D1) and (D2) is payment to shareholders.

6.9 Cancellation of shares purchased/redeemed

All shares purchased/redeemed must be cancelled immediately. They cannot be kept in hand by the company and traded in like any other commodity.

6.10 Redemption of debentures

Unless they are stated to be irredeemable, debentures are redeemed according to the terms of the issue. The necessary funds to finance the redemption may be from:

(*a*) an issue of shares or debentures for the purpose;
(*b*) the liquid resources of the company.

As it resembles the redemption of redeemable preference shares, when the redemption is financed as in (*a*), no transfer of profits from the profit and loss appropriation account to a reserve account is needed. However, when financed as in (*b*) it is good accounting practice, although not legally necessary, to divert profits from being used as dividends by transferring an amount equal to the nominal value redeemed from the debit of the profit and loss appropriation account to the credit of a reserve account.

Redemption may be effected:

1   by annual drawings out of profits;
2   by purchase in the open market when the price is favourable, i.e. less than the price which will have to be paid if the company waited until the last date by which redemption has to be carried out;
3   in a lump sum to be provided by the accumulation of a sinking fund.

These can now be examined in more detail.

Regular annual drawings out of profits

(a) When redeemed at a premium

In this case the source of the bank funds with which the premium is paid should be taken to be (*a*) the share premium account, or if this does not exist, or the premium is in excess of the balance on the account, then any part not covered by a share premium account is deemed to come from (*b*) the profit and loss appropriation account. Exhibit 6.8 shows the effect on a balance sheet where there is no share premium account, while Exhibit 6.9 illustrates the case when a share premium account is in existence.

Exhibit 6.8

Starting with the *before* balance sheet, £400 of the debentures are redeemed at a premium of 20 per cent.

Balance Sheets

	Before	+ or –	After
	£	£	£
Other assets	12,900		12,900
Bank	3,400	– 480 (A)	2,920
	16,300		15,820
Share capital	10,000		10,000
Debenture redemption reserve	–	+ 400 (B)	400
Debentures	2,000	– 400 (A)	1,600
Profit and loss	4,300	– 400 (B)	
		– 80 (A)	3,820
	16,300		15,820

Exhibit 6.9

Starting with the *before* balance sheet, £400 of the debentures are redeemed at a premium of 20 per cent.

Balance Sheets

	Before	+ or –	After
	£	£	£
Other assets	13,500		13,500
Bank	3,400	– 480 (A)	2,920
	16,900		16,420
Share capital	10,000		10,000
Share premium	600	– 80 (A)	520
Debenture redemption reserve	–	+ 400 (B)	400
Debentures	2,000	– 400 (A)	1,600
Profit and loss	4,300	– 400 (B)	3,900
	16,900		16,420

In both Exhibits 6.8 and 6.9 the debenture redemption reserve account is built up each year by the nominal value of the debentures redeemed each year. When the whole issue of debentures has been redeemed, then the balance on the debenture redemption reserve account should be transferred to the credit of a general reserve account. It is, after all, an accumulation of undistributed profits.

(b) Redeemed – originally issued at a discount

The discount originally given was in fact to attract investors to buy the debentures, and is therefore as much a cost of borrowing as is debenture interest. The discount therefore needs to be written off during the life of the debentures. It might be more rational to write it off to the profit and loss account, but in fact accounting custom, as permitted by law, would first of all write it off against any share premium account or, secondly, against the profit and loss appropriation account.

The amounts written-off over the life of the debentures are:

(*a*) equal annual amounts over the life of the debentures; or

(*b*) in proportion to the debenture debt outstanding at the start of each year. Exhibit 6.10 shows such a situation.

Exhibit 6.10

£30,000 debentures are issued at a discount of 5 per cent. They are repayable at par over five years at the rate of £6,000 per annum.

Year	Outstanding at start of each year	Proportion written off		Amount
	£			£
1	30,000	$^{30}/_{90} \times £1,500$	=	500
2	24,000	$^{24}/_{90} \times £1,500$	=	400
3	18,000	$^{18}/_{90} \times £1,500$	=	300
4	12,000	$^{12}/_{90} \times £1,500$	=	200
5	6,000	$^{6}/_{90} \times £1,500$	=	100
	90,000			1,500

Redeemed by purchase in the open market

A sum equal to the cash actually paid on redemption should be transferred from the debit of the profit and loss appropriation account to the credit of the debenture redemption reserve account. The sum actually paid will of course have been credited to the cash book and debited to the debentures account.

Any discount (or profit) on purchase will be transferred to a reserve account. Any premium (or loss) on purchase will be deemed to come out of such a reserve account, or if no such account exists or it is insufficient, then it will be deemed to come out of the share premium account. Failing the existence of these accounts any loss must come out of the profit and loss appropriation account. It may seem that purchase would not be opportune if the debentures had to be redeemed at a premium. However, it would still be opportune if the premium paid was not as high as the premium to be paid if the final date for redemption was awaited.

Redemption of debentures by a sinking fund

Where debentures are issued which are redeemable (and most are redeemable) consideration should be given to the availability of cash funds at the time.

This method involves the investment of cash outside the business. The aim is to make a regular investment of money which, together with the accumulated interest or dividends, is sufficient to finance the redemption of the debentures at the requisite time.

Before calculations become too involved a simple proposition can be examined. As each period's interest (or dividend) is received, then that amount is immediately reinvested. Apart from the reinvestment of interest the other money taken for investment is to be an equal amount each period. This being so, if the money is to be invested at 5 per cent per annum, and the debenture is £500 to be redeemed in five years' time, then how much should be taken for investment each year? If £100 were taken each year for five years, then this would amount to more than £500 because of the interest and of the interest on the reinvested interest. Most readers will recognise this as money being invested at compound interest. Therefore something less than £100 per annum is needed. The exact amount can be calculated by the use of the compound interest formula. Chapter 46 illustrates how the amount needed can be calculated. As these calculations are left until later in the book, a summarised set of tables is now shown to help the student at this stage.

Annual sinking fund instalments to provide £1

Years	3%	3½%	4%	4½%	5%
3	0.323530	0.321933	0.320348	0.318773	0.317208
4	0.239028	0.237251	0.235490	0.233744	0.232012
5	0.188354	0.186481	0.184627	0.182792	0.180975
6	0.154597	0.152668	0.150761	0.148878	0.147017
7	0.130506	0.128544	0.126609	0.124701	0.122819
8	0.112456	0.110476	0.108527	0.106609	0.104721
9	0.098433	0.096446	0.094493	0.092574	0.090690
10	0.087230	0.085241	0.083291	0.081378	0.079504

The table gives the amount required to provide £1 at the end of the relevant number of years. To provide £1,000 multiply by 1,000; to provide for £4,986 multiply by 4,986.

6.11 Double entry records for sinking fund

When the annual instalment has been found, the double entry needed each year is:

Annual instalment:
    Dr Profit and loss appropriation
        Cr Debenture redemption reserve
Investment of 1st instalment:
    Dr Debenture sinking fund investment
        Cr Bank
Interest/dividends on sinking fund investment
    Dr Bank
        Cr Debenture redemption reserve
Investment of second and later instalments (these consist of equal annual instalment plus interest/dividend just received)
    Dr Debenture sinking fund investment
        Cr Bank

Exhibit 6.11

Debentures of £10,000 are issued on 1 January 19X1. They are redeemable five years later on 31 December 19X5 on identical terms. The company therefore decides to set aside an equal annual amount, which at an interest rate of 5 per cent will provide £10,000 on 31 December 19X5. According to the table £0.180975 invested annually will provide £1 in five years' time. Therefore £0.180975 × 10,000 will be needed annually = £1,809.75.

Profit and Loss Appropriation for years ended 31 December

(19X1) Debenture redemption reserve 1,809.75	
(19X2) Debenture redemption reserve 1,809.75	
(19X3) Debenture redemption reserve 1,809.75	
(19X4) Debenture redemption reserve 1,809.75	
(19X5) Debenture redemption reserve 1,809.75	

Debenture Redemption Reserve

	£	19X1		£
		Dec 31 Profit and loss		1,809.75
		19X2		
19X2		Dec 31 Bank interest		
Dec 31 Balance c/d	3,709.99	(5% of £1,809.75)		90.49
		Dec 31 Profit and loss		1,809.75
	3,709.99			3,709.99
		19X3		
		Jan 1 Balance b/d		3,709.99
		Dec 31 Bank interest		
19X3		(5% of £3,709.99)		185.49
Dec 31 Balance c/d	5,705.23	Dec 31 Profit and loss		1,809.75
	5,705.23			5,705.23
		19X4		
		Jan 1 Balance b/d		5,705.23
		Dec 31 Bank interest		
19X4		(5% of £5,705.23)		285.26
Dec 31 Balance c/d	7,800.24	Dec 31 Profit and loss		1,809.75
	7,800.24			7,800.24
		19X5		
		Jan 1 Balance b/d		7,800.24
		Dec 31 Bank interest		
19X5		(5% of £7,800.24)		390.01
Dec 31 Debentures now redeemed	10,000.00	Dec 31 Profit and loss		1,809.75
	10,000.00			10,000.00

Debenture Sinking Fund Investment

19X1	£		£
Dec 31 Bank	1,809.75		
19X2			
Dec 31 Bank (*see* note (*a*))	1,900.24		
19X3			
Dec 31 Bank (*see* note (*b*))	1,995.24		
19X4		19X5	
Dec 31 Bank (*see* note (*c*))	2,095.01	Dec 31 Cash: Sale of investment	7,800.24
	7,800.24		7,800.24

Notes:

Cash invested	(*a*)	(*b*)	(*c*)
	£	£	£
The yearly instalment	1,809.75	1,809.75	1,809.75
Add interest received reinvested immediately	90.49	185.49	285.26
	1,900.24	1,995.24	2,095.01

Bank (extracts)

		£			£
19X1			19X1		
Jan 1	Debentures (issued)	10,000.00	Dec 31	Debenture sinking fund investment	1,809.75
19X2			19X2		
Dec 31	Debenture redemption reserve (interest on investment)	90.49	Dec 31	Debenture sinking fund investment	1,900.24
19X3			19X3		
Dec 31	Debenture redemption reserve (interest on investment)	185.49	Dec 31	Debenture sinking fund investment	1,995.24
19X4			19X4		
Dec 31	Debenture redemption reserve (interest on investment)	285.26	Dec 31	Debenture sinking fund investment	2,095.01
19X5			19X5		
Dec 31	Debenture redemption reserve (interest on investment)	309.01	Jan 1	Debentures (redemption)	10,000.00

Debentures

		£			£
19X6			19X1		
Jan 1	Bank (redemption)	10,000.00	Jan 1	Bank	10,000.00

The instalment for 19X5 is not in fact invested, nor is the interest received on 31 December 19X5 reinvested. The money to redeem the debentures is required on 1 January 19X6, and there is not much point (even if it were possible, which would very rarely hold true) in investing money one day only to withdraw it the day afterwards. The amount required is £10,000 and is available from the following sources:

	£
Dec 31 19X5 Sale of investment	7,800.24
„ 31 19X5 Interest received but not reinvested	390.01
„ 31 19X5 The fifth year's instalment not invested	1,809.75
	10,000.00

Sometimes debentures bought in the open market are not cancelled, but are kept 'alive' and are treated as investments of the sinking fund. The annual appropriation of profits is credited to the sinking fund account, while the amount expended on the purchase of the debentures is debited to the sinking fund investment account. Interest on such debentures is debited to the profit and loss account and credited to the sinking fund account, thus the interest, as far as the sinking fund account is concerned, is treated in the same fashion as if it was cash actually received by the firm from an outside investment. The sum expended on investments will then be equal to the annual appropriation + the interest on investments actually received + the interest on debentures kept in hand.

6.12 Convertible loan stock

Particularly in periods of high inflation the attractions to lenders to provide funds at reasonable rates of interest is much reduced as they stand to lose significantly on the real value of the funds lent, since the repayment of the loan is normally fixed at its original cash value. One way of attracting lenders has been to give them the right to convert their loan into shares. The right can usually be exercised once a year over a stated number of years at a given rate of conversion from loan to shares. The value of the conversion right will depend on the performance of the shares in the market. If the shares increase in value significantly, the conversion value will increase and attract the lender to opt into shares. If the shares do badly, the lender can retain the loan stock with its higher levels of security.

The accounting entries are as previously described for the redemption of the loan. The value of the shares issued to meet the redemption will be fixed under the terms of the original agreement by reference to the market prices at specified dates.

New terms

Capital redemption reserve (p. 79): A 'non-distributable' reserve created when shares are redeemed or purchased other than from the proceeds of a fresh issue of shares.

Sinking fund (p. 88): An external fund set up to meet some future liability such as the redemption of debentures. Cash is paid into the fund at regular intervals to accumulate with compound interest to the required future sum.

Main points to remember

1 The accounting entries made on the redemption or purchase by a company of its own shares are the same, except that the word 'redeemable' will appear as the first word in the title of the accounts for shares that are redeemed.

2 In order to protect creditors, companies *must* still have irredeemable shares in issue after undertaking any purchase or redemption of its own shares.

3 A company cannot redeem or purchase its own shares unless they are fully paid.

4 The rules on reserves to use when purchasing or issuing their own shares at a premium are less strict for private companies.

5 Debentures are redeemed according to the terms of their issue.

Review questions

6.1 Exercises (*a*) to (*e*) inclusive are based on the following commencing balance sheet.

RSV Ltd

Balance Sheet

	£
Net assets (except bank)	20,000
Bank	13,000
	33,000
Preference share capital	5,000
Ordinary share capital	15,000
Share premium	2,000
	22,000
Profit and loss	11,000
	33,000

Note also that each of exercises (*a*) to (*e*) are independent of each other. They are not cumulative.

(*a*) RSV Ltd, per 6.1, redeems £5,000 preference shares at par, a new issue of £5,000 ordinary shares at par being made for the purpose. Show the balance sheet after completion of these transactions. Workings are to be shown as journal entries.

(*b*) RSV Ltd, per 6.1, redeems £5,000 preference shares at par, with no new issue of shares to provide funds. Show the balance sheet after completing the transaction. Workings: show journal entries.

(*c*) RSV Ltd, per 6.1, redeems £5,000 preference shares at par. To help finance this an issue of £1,500 ordinary shares at par is effected. Show the balance sheet after these transactions have been completed; also show the necessary journal entries.

(*d*) RSV Ltd, per 6.1, redeems £5,000 preference shares at a premium of 25 per cent. There is no new issue of shares for the purpose. In this question the share premium account is taken as being from the issue of ordinary shares some years ago. Show the balance sheet after these transactions have been completed, and the supporting journal entries.

(*e*) RSV Ltd, per 6.1, redeems £5,000 preference shares at a premium of 40 per cent. There is an issue of £7,000 ordinary shares at par for the purpose. The preference shares had originally been issued at a premium of 30 per cent. Show the balance sheet after these transactions have been completed, and also the supporting journal entries.

6.2A Exercises (a) to (e) inclusive are based on the same commencing balance sheet, as follows:

BAR Ltd
Balance Sheet

	£
Net assets (except bank)	31,000
Bank	16,000
	47,000
Preference share capital	8,000
Ordinary share capital	20,000
Share premium	4,000
	32,000
Profit and loss	15,000
	47,000

Note also that exercises (a) to (e) are independent of each other. They are not cumulative.

(a) BAR Ltd, per 6.2A, purchases £10,000 of its own ordinary share capital at par. To help finance this £7,000 preference shares are issued at par. Show the necessary journal entries and the balance sheet after the transactions have been completed.

(b) BAR Ltd, per 6.2A, purchases £12,000 of its own ordinary shares at a premium of 20 per cent. No new issue of shares is made for the purpose. It is assumed that the share premium account is in respect of the issue of preference shares some years before. Show the balance sheet after the transactions have been completed, and also the supporting journal entries.

(c) BAR Ltd, per 6.2A, purchases all the preference share capital at par. These shares were not originally redeemable preference shares. There is no new issue of shares to provide funds. Show the requisite journal entries, and the closing balance sheet when the transaction has been completed.

(d) BAR Ltd, per 6.2A, purchases £12,000 of its own ordinary shares at par, a new issue of £12,000 preference shares at par being made for the purpose. Show the journal entries needed and the balance sheet after completing these transactions.

(e) BAR Ltd, per 6.2A, purchases £6,000 ordinary shares at a premium of 50 per cent. They had originally been issued at a premium of 20 per cent. There is an issue of £10,000 preference shares at par for the purpose. Show the amended balance sheet, together with the journal entries.

6.3 A company's balance sheet appears as follows:

	£
Net assets (except bank)	12,500
Bank	13,000
	25,500
Preference share capital	5,000
Ordinary share capital	10,000
Non-distributable reserves	6,000
	21,000
Profit and loss	4,500
	25,500

Required:

(a) If £6,000 of the ordinary shares were purchased at par, there being no new issue of shares for the purpose, show the journal entries to record the transactions and the amended balance sheet.

(b) If, instead of (a), £6,000 ordinary shares were purchased at a premium of 100 per cent, there being no new issue of shares for the purpose, show the journal entries to record the transactions and the amended balance sheet.

6.4A Debentures of £30,000 are issued on 1 January 19X3. Redemption is to take place, on equal terms, four years later. The company decides to put aside an equal amount to be invested at 5 per cent which will provide £30,000 on maturity. Tables show that £0.232012 invested annually will produce £1 in four years' time.

You are required to show:

(a) debenture redemption reserve account;
(b) debenture sinking fund investment account;
(c) debentures account;
(d) profit and loss account extracts.

6.5 Some years ago M plc had issued £375,000 of 10 per cent debentures 19X6/19X0 at par. The terms of the issue allow the company the right to repurchase these debentures for cancellation at or below par, with an option to redeem, at a premium of 1 per cent, on 30 September 19X6. To exercise this option the company must give three months' notice which it duly did on 30 June 19X6 indicating its intention to redeem all the debentures outstanding at 30 September 19X6.

M plc had established a sinking fund designed to accumulate the sum of £378,750 by 30 September 19X6 and had appropriated profits annually and invested these, together with the interest from such investments and the profits made on any realisations from time to time. A special No 2 bank account was established specifically to deal with the receipts and payments relating to the debentures and the sinking fund.

By 30 June 19X6 annual contributions amounting to £334,485, together with the interest on the sinking fund investments of £39,480, had all been invested except for £2,475 which remained in the No 2 bank account at that date.

The only investments sold, prior to 30 June 19X6, had cost £144,915 and realised £147,243. This was used to repurchase debentures with a par value of £150,000.

Transactions occurring between 1 July and 30 September 19X6 were:

(i) interest received on the sinking fund investments:

7 July – £1,756

13 September – £1,455

(ii) proceeds from the sale of investments:

2 August – £73,215 (book value was £69,322)

25 September – £160,238 (remaining investments)

(iii) redemption of all the debentures, on 30 September, with the exception of £15,000 held by B Limited. The company had received notice of a garnishee order.*

(iv) M plc deposited with the W Bank plc the sum of £15,150 on 30 September 19X6.

You are to ignore debenture interest and income tax.

You are required, from the information given above, to prepare the ledger accounts (including the No 2 bank account) in the books of M plc for the period 30 June to 30 September 19X6, showing the transfer of the final balances to the appropriate accounts.

Note – Garnishee Order

This order, issued by the court, instructs M plc not to release the money owing to B Limited until directed by the court to do so.

(*Chartered Institute of Management Accountants*)

6.6A   The following information relates to White Rabbit Trading plc:

Summarised Balance Sheet as at 31 January 19X7

	£000
Fixed assets	2,400
Investments	120
Net current assets	1,880
	4,400
Financed by:	
Capital and reserves	
Ordinary shares of 50p each fully paid	2,000
Redeemable shares of £1 each (19X7/19X1)	500
Share premium	200
Revaluation surplus	400
Profit and loss account	900
	4,000
Long-term liabilities	
8% debentures (19X7/19X0)	400
	4,400

On 1 February 19X7 the company closed the list of applications for 400,000 ordinary shares at a premium of 50p. The shares were to be paid for as follows: 60p on application, 25p on allotment and 15p on the first and final call, which was to be made on 1 May 19X7. A total of £1,320,000 was received, the shares were allotted and £1,032,000 was returned to unsuccessful applicants. The call money was received by 31 May from all shareholders, with the exception of two shareholders, one of whom had been allotted 500 shares. The other subscriber for 100 shares still owed £25 for allotment in addition to the call money. Eventually both lots of shares were forfeited and reissued to an existing shareholder for a payment of £500 which was duly received.

At a board meeting on 15 February 19X7 the directors decided to make a fresh issue of 500,000 £1 redeemable shares at a premium of 60p, and to redeem all of the existing redeemable shares at a premium of 40p. The shares had originally been issued for £1.20 each. All moneys due on application were duly received by 31 March 19X7, and the redemption took place on 6 April 19X7.

In January 19X5 White Rabbit Trading plc had purchased, for cash, 80,000 25p ordinary shares in March Hares Ltd for £25,000, and this is included in investments on the balance sheet at 31 January 19X7. On 1 April 19X7 the company purchased 400,000 out of a total issue of 500,000 25p ordinary shares in March Hares Ltd, by exchanging 200,000 of its own ordinary shares.

The 8 per cent debentures were redeemed on 15 May 19X7 at a 10 per cent premium, and on the same date £500,000 7 per cent debentures (19X0/19X3) were issued at a discount of 5 per cent.

Required:
Show the full journal entries to record the above events, including cash/bank transactions, in the books of White Rabbit Trading plc.

(Association of Chartered Certified Accountants)

6.7   During the year to 30 September 19X9, Popham plc issued 100,000 £1 ordinary shares. The terms of the offer were as follows:

19X9		£
31 March	on application	0.30 (including the premium)
30 April	on allotment	0.70
30 June	first and final call	0.20

Applications were received for 200,000 shares. The directors decided to allot the shares on the basis of 1 for every 2 shares applied for and apply the excess application money received against the amount due on allotment.

All amounts due on application and allotment were received on the due dates, with the exception of one shareholder who had been allotted 10,000 shares, and who defaulted on the first and final call. These shares were forfeited on 31 July 19X9, and reissued on 31 August 19X9 at a price of £1.10 per share.

Required:

Write up the above details in the books of account of Popham plc using the following ledger accounts:

(*i*)   application and allotment;
(*ii*) first and final call; and
(*iii*) investment – own shares.

(*Association of Accounting Technicians*)

6.8A   Alas plc has an authorised share capital of 150,000 ordinary shares of £10 each. Upon incorporation, 50,000 shares were issued and fully paid. The company has decided to issue another 50,000 shares, the details of which are as follows:

	Per share
Upon:	£
Application	3
Allotment (including a premium of £5)	8
First call	2
Final call	2
	15

Additional information:

1   Applications were received for 85,000 shares out of which 10,000 shares were rejected, the cash being returned immediately to the applicants. The remaining applicants were allotted two shares for every three shares applied for, and the surplus application money was carried forward to the allotment stage.
2   The total amount due on allotment was duly received.
3   All cash due at the first call was received, but the final call resulted in 5,000 shares being forfeited. These shares were subsequently reissued at a price of £13 per share.

Required:

Compile the following ledger accounts:

(*a*)   ordinary share capital;
(*b*)   ordinary share applications;
(*c*)   ordinary share allotment;
(*d*)   share premium;
(*e*)   ordinary share first call;
(*f*)   ordinary share final call;
(*g*)   investments – own shares (originally known as the forfeited shares account).

6.9   The following information relates to Grigg plc:

1   On 1 April 19X8 the company had £100,000 10 per cent debentures in issue. The interest on these debentures is paid on 30 September and 31 March.

2   The debenture redemption fund balance (relating to the redemption of these debentures) at 1 April 19X8 was £20,000. This fund is being built up by annual appropriations of £2,000. The annual appropriation (along with any dividends or interest on the investments) is invested on 31 March.

3   Debenture redemption fund investments can be realised at any time in order to purchase debentures in the open market either at or below par value. Such debentures are then cancelled.

4   On 31 December 19X8 £10,000 of investments were sold for £11,400, and the proceeds were used to purchase debentures with a par value of £12,000.

5   Dividends and interest on redemption fund investments during the year to 31 March 19X9 amounted to £1,600.

6   The cost of dealing with the above matters and any taxation effects may be ignored.

Required:
Write up the following ledger accounts for the year to 31 March 19X9:
(*a*)   10 per cent debentures;
(*b*)   debenture redemption fund;
(*c*)   debenture redemption fund investments;
(*d*)   debenture redemption; and
(*e*)   debenture interest.

(*Note*: the debenture redemption fund is sometimes known as a **sinking fund**.)

7

Limited companies taking over other businesses

Objectives

After you have studied this chapter, you should:

- *know how to record the accounting entries relating to a limited company taking over another business*

- *be aware of the difference in the accounting treatment of takeovers by limited companies of sole traders, partnerships and limited companies*

- *be aware of the two methods whereby a limited company may take over another limited company*

- *know how to deal with pre-incorporation profits and losses*

7.1 Introduction

Limited companies will often take over other businesses which are in existence as going concerns. The purchase considerations may either be in cash, by giving the company's shares to the owners, by giving the company's debentures, or by any combination of these three factors.

It must not be thought that because the assets bought are shown in the selling firm's books at one value the purchasing company must record the assets taken over in its own books at the same value. The values shown in the purchasing company's books are those values at which the company is buying the assets, such values being frequently quite different than those shown in the selling firm's books. As an instance of this, the selling firm may have bought premises many years ago for £1,000 but they may now be worth £5,000. The company buying the premises will obviously have to pay £5,000 and it is therefore this value that is recorded in the buying company's books. Alternatively, the value at which it is recorded in the buying company's books may be less than that shown in the selling firm's books. Where the total purchase consideration exceeds the total value of the identifiable assets then such excess is the goodwill, and will need entering in a goodwill account in the purchasing company's books. Should the total purchase consideration be less than the values of the identifiable assets, then the difference would be entered in a capital reserve account.

Before the accounting entries necessary to record the purchase of a going business are looked at, it must be pointed out that such recording of the transactions is the simple end of the whole affair. The negotiations that take place before agreement is reached, and the various strategies undertaken by the various parties, are a study in themselves. The accounting entries are in effect the 'tip of the iceberg', i.e. that part of the whole affair which is seen by the eventual reader of the accounts.

7.2 Taking over a sole trader's business

It is easier to start with the takeover of the simplest sort of business unit, that of a sole trader. Some of the balance sheets shown will be deliberately simplified so that the principles involved are not hidden behind a mass of complicated calculations.

Exhibit 7.1

Earl Ltd is to buy the business of M Kearney. The purchase consideration is to be £6,000 cash, the company placing the following values on the assets taken over – Machinery £3,000, Stock £1,000. The goodwill must therefore be £2,000, because the total price of £6,000 exceeds the values of Machinery £3,000 and Stock £1,000 by the sum of £2,000. The company's balance sheets will be shown before and after the takeover, it being assumed that the transactions are all concluded immediately.

M Kearney
Balance Sheet

	£
Machinery	3,000
Stock	1,000
	4,000
Capital	4,000

Earl Ltd
Balance Sheets

	Before £	+ or – £	After £
Goodwill		+2,000	2,000
Machinery	11,000	+3,000	14,000
Stock	5,000	+1,000	6,000
Bank	9,000	–6,000	3,000
	25,000		25,000
Share capital	20,000		20,000
Profit and loss	5,000		5,000
	25,000		25,000

Exhibit 7.2

Suppose the purchase had been made instead by issuing 7,000 shares of £1 each at par to Kearney. The goodwill would then be £7,000 – assets taken over £4,000 = £3,000. The balance sheets of Earl Ltd would be:

Earl Ltd

Balance Sheets

	Before £	+ or – £	After £
Goodwill		+3,000	3,000
Machinery	11,000	+3,000	14,000
Stock	5,000	+1,000	6,000
Bank	9,000		9,000
	25,000		32,000
Share capital	20,000	+7,000	27,000
Profit and loss	5,000		5,000
	25,000		32,000

Exhibit 7.3

If the purchase had been made by issuing 5,000 shares of £1 each at a premium of 50 per cent, then the total consideration would have been worth £7,500 which, if the assets of £4,000 are deducted, leaves goodwill of £3,500. The balance sheets would then be:

Earl Ltd

Balance Sheets

	Before £	+ or – £	After £
Goodwill		+3,500	3,500
Machinery	11,000	+3,000	14,000
Stocks	5,000	+1,000	6,000
Bank	9,000		9,000
	25,000		32,500
Share capital	20,000	+5,000	25,000
Share premium		+2,500	2,500
Profit and loss	5,000		5,000
	25,000		32,500

Exhibit 7.4

Now if the purchase had been made by the issue of 1,000 shares of £1 each at a premium of 40 per cent, £3,000 worth of 7 per cent debentures at par and £4,000 in cash, then the total purchase consideration would be shares valued at £1,400, debentures valued at £3,000 and cash £4,000, making in all £8,400. The assets are valued at £4,000, the goodwill must be £4,400. The balance sheets would appear:

Earl Ltd

Balance Sheets

	Before £	+ or – £	After £
Goodwill		+4,400	4,400
Machinery	11,000	+3,000	14,000
Stocks	5,000	+1,000	6,000
Bank	9,000	–4,000	5,000
	25,000		29,400
Share capital	20,000	+1,000	21,000
Share premium		+400	400
Profit and loss	5,000		5,000
Debentures		+3,000	3,000
	25,000		29,400

In each of Exhibits 7.1 to 7.4 it has been assumed that all transactions were started and completed within a few moments. The fact is that an intermediary account would be created but then closed almost immediately when the purchase consideration was handed over. Taking Exhibit 7.3 as an example, there will be a credit in the share capital account and in the share premium account, and debits in the goodwill, machinery and stock accounts. Nevertheless, shares cannot be issued to goodwill, machinery or stocks. They have in fact, been issued to M Kearney. This means that there should have been an account for M Kearney, but that the balance on it was cancelled on the passing of the purchase consideration. The actual accounts for Exhibit 7.3 were as follows in the books of Earl Ltd:

Share Premium

			£
		M Kearney	2,500

Share Capital

Balance c/d	25,000	Balance b/d	20,000
		M Kearney	5,000
	25,000		25,000
		Balance b/d	25,000

Profit and Loss

			£
		Balance b/d	5,000

Goodwill

	£		
M Kearney	3,500		

Machinery

	£		£
Balance b/d	11,000		
M Kearney	3,000	Balance c/d	14,000
	14,000		14,000
Balance b/d	14,000		

Stock

	£		£
Balance b/d	5,000		
M Kearney	1,000	Balance c/d	6,000
	6,000		6,000
Balance c/d	6,000		

(In fact, the £1,000 would probably be entered in the purchases account. It does, however, obviously increase the actual amount of stock.)

Bank

	£	
Balance b/d	9,000	

M Kearney

	£		£
Consideration passing:		Assets taken over	
Share capital	5,000	Goodwill	3,500
Share premium	2,500	Machinery	3,000
		Stock	1,000
	7,500		7,500

Some accountants would have preferred to use a business purchase account instead of a personal account such as that of M Kearney.

Sometimes the company taking over the business of a sole trader not only pays a certain amount for the assets but also assumes responsibility for paying the creditors in addition. Take the case of a sole trader with assets valued at Premises £5,000 and Stock £4,000. To gain control of these assets the company is to pay the sole trader £11,000 in cash, and in addition the company will pay off creditors £1,000. This means that the goodwill is £3,000, calculated as follows:

			£
Paid by the company to gain control of the sole trader's assets:			
Cash to the sole trader			11,000
Cash to the sole trader's creditors			1,000
			12,000
The company receives assets:		£	
Premises		5,000	
Stock		4,000	
			9,000
Excess paid for goodwill			3,000

7.3 Partnership business taken over by a limited company

The entries are basically the same as for those of taking over a sole trader. The main difference is the distribution of the purchase consideration. In the case of a sole trader s/he gets all of it. In a partnership it has to be divided between the partners.

This means that in a partnership a realisation account will have to be drawn up to calculate the profit or loss on sale of the partnership business. The profit or loss on sale will then be shared between the partners in their profit/loss-sharing ratios.

The double entry needed in the partnership books is:

(A)   Transfer assets being disposed of to realisation account:
Dr Realisation
Cr Assets (various)

(B)   Enter purchase price:
Dr Limited company (purchaser)
Cr Realisation

(C)   If profit on sale:
Dr Realisation
Cr Partners' capitals (profit-sharing ratio)

(D)   If loss on sale:
Dr Partners' capitals (profit-sharing ratio)
Cr Realisation

(E)   Receipt purchase price:
Dr Cash
Dr Shares (if any) in limited company
Dr Debentures (if any) in limited company
Cr Limited company (purchaser)

(F)   Final settlement with partners:
Dr Partners' capital and current accounts
Cr Cash
Cr Shares (if any) in limited company
Cr Debentures (if any) in limited company

Entries for these are illustrated in Exhibit 7.5.

Exhibit 7.5

Kay and Lee were in partnership, sharing profits and losses in the ratio 2:1 respectively. The following was their balance sheet as at 31 December 19X4.

Kay and Lee

Balance Sheet as at 31 December 19X4

		£
Fixed assets:		
Buildings		30,000
Motor vehicles		15,000
		45,000
Current assets:		
Stock	8,000	
Debtors	6,000	
Bank	1,000	15,000
		60,000
Capitals: Kay	32,000	
Lee	16,000	48,000
Current accounts: Kay	3,000	
Lee	4,000	7,000
Current liabilities:		5,000
Creditors		60,000

On 1 January 19X5 Cayley Ltd was to take over the assets, other than bank. The purchase price is £80,000, payable by £60,000 in £1 shares in Cayley Ltd at par, plus

£20,000 cash. Kay and Lee will pay off their own creditors. Shares are to be divided between the partners in their profit-sharing ratio.

First we will see the closing entries in the accounts of Kay and Lee. The only asset account shown will be that of the bank account. The creditors' accounts are also not shown. The letters in brackets refer to the description of the double entry already given.

Books of Kay and Lee:

Realisation

Assets taken over:		£			£
Buildings	(A)	30,000	Cayley Ltd	(B)	80,000
Motor vehicles	(A)	15,000			
Stock	(A)	8,000			
Debtors	(A)	6,000			
Profit on realisation:					
Kay ⅔	(C) 14,000				
Lee ⅓	(C) 7,000	21,000			
		80,000			80,000

Cayley Ltd

		£			£
Realisation: sale price	(B)	80,000	Bank	(E)	20,000
			Shares in Cayley Ltd	(E)	60,000
		80,000			80,000

Shares in Cayley Ltd

		£			£
Cayley Ltd	(E)	60,000	Capitals: Kay	(F)	40,000
			Lee	(F)	20,000
		60,000			60,000

Capitals

		Kay £	Lee £			Kay £	Lee £
Shares in Cayley	(F)	40,000	20,000	Balances b/d		32,000	16,000
Bank	(F)	6,000	3,000	Profit on realisation	(C)	14,000	7,000
		46,000	23,000			46,000	23,000

Current Accounts

		Kay £	Lee £			Kay £	Lee £
Bank	(F)	3,000	4,000	Balances b/d		3,000	4,000

Bank

		£			£
Bank b/d		1,000	Creditors		5,000
Cayley Ltd	(E)	20,000	Capitals: Kay		6,000
			Lee		3,000
			Current accounts: Kay		3,000
			Lee		4,000
		21,000			21,000

Note: It would have been possible to transfer the balances of the current accounts to the capital accounts before settlement.

Assuming that Cayley values the buildings at £41,000 and stock at £7,000 its balance sheet at 1 January 19X5 would appear as (B) under. The items shown under (A) were the balances before the takeover.

Balance Sheet(s)

	(A) *Before* £	+ £	− £	(B) *After* £
Goodwill				11,000
Buildings	50,000	41,000		91,000
Motor vehicles	25,000	15,000		40,000
Stock	28,000	7,000		35,000
Debtors	17,000	6,000		23,000
Bank	30,000		20,000	10,000
	150,000	69,000	20,000	210,000
Share capital (£1 shares)	100,000	60,000		160,000
Profit and loss	40,000			40,000
Creditors	10,000			10,000
	150,000	60,000		210,000

7.4 The takeover of a limited company by another limited company

One company may take over another company by one of two methods:

1 By buying all the assets of the other company, the purchase consideration being by cash, shares or debentures. The selling company may afterwards be wound up: either the liquidators may distribute the purchasing company's shares and debentures between the shareholders of the selling company, or else the shares and debentures of the buying company may be sold and the cash distributed instead.
2 By giving its own shares and debentures in exchange for the shares and debentures of the selling company's share and debenture holders.

Exhibit 7.6 is an illustration of each of these methods.

Exhibit 7.6

The following are the balance sheets of three companies as at the same date.

Balance Sheets

	R Ltd	S Ltd	T Ltd
	£	£	£
Buildings	13,000	–	1,000
Machinery	4,000	2,000	1,000
Stock	3,000	1,000	2,000
Debtors	2,000	1,000	3,000
Bank	1,000	2,000	3,000
	23,000	6,000	10,000
Share capital (£1 shares)	18,000	3,000	5,000
Profit and loss	2,000	1,000	4,000
Current liabilities	3,000	2,000	1,000
	23,000	6,000	10,000

R takes over S by exchanging with the shareholders of S two shares in R at a premium of 10 per cent for every share they hold in S.

R takes over T by buying all the assets of T, the purchase consideration being 12,000 £1 shares in R at a premium of 10 per cent, and R will pay off T's creditors. R values T's assets at Buildings £2,000, Machinery £600, Stock £1,400, Debtors £2,500, and the Bank is £3,000, a total of £9,500.

R's deal with the shareholders of S means that R now has complete control of S Ltd, so that S Ltd becomes what is known as a subsidiary undertaking of R Ltd, and will be shown as an investment in R's balance sheet.

On the other hand, the deal with T has resulted in the ownership of the assets resting with R. These must therefore be added to R's assets in its own balance sheet. As R has given 12,000 £1 shares at a premium of 10 per cent plus taking over the responsibility for creditors £1,000, the total purchase consideration for the assets taken over is £12,000 + £1,200 (10 per cent of £12,000) + £1,000 = £14,200. Identifiable assets as already stated are valued at £9,500, therefore the goodwill is £14,200 – £9,500 = £4,700.

The distinction between the acquisition of the two going concerns can be seen to be a rather fine one. With S the shares are taken over, the possession of these in turn giving rise to the ownership of the assets. In the books of R this is regarded as an investment. With T the actual assets and liabilities are taken over so that the assets now directly belong to R. In the books of R this is therefore regarded as the acquisition of additional assets and liabilities and not as an investment (using the meaning of 'investment' which is used in the balance sheets of companies). The balance sheet of R Ltd therefore becomes:

R Ltd

Balance Sheet

	Before £		+ or – £	After £
Goodwill		+(T)	4,700	4,700
Buildings	13,000	+(T)	2,000	15,000
Machinery	4,000	+(T)	600	4,600
Investment in S at cost		+(S)	6,600	6,600
Stock	3,000	+(T)	1,400	4,400
Debtors	2,000	+(T)	2,500	4,500
Bank	1,000	+(T)	3,000	4,000
	23,000			43,800
Share capital	18,000	+(S)	6,000	
		+(T)	12,000	= 36,000
Share premium		+(S)	600	
		+(T)	1,200	= 1,800
Profit and loss	2,000			2,000
Current liabilities	3,000	+(T)	1,000	4,000
	23,000			43,800

No entry is necessary in the books of S Ltd, as it is merely the identity of the shareholders that has changed. This would be duly recorded in the register of members, but this is not really an integral part of the double entry accounting system.

If, however, T Ltd is now liquidated, then a realisation account must be drawn up and the distribution of the shares (or cash if the shares are sold) to the shareholders of T Ltd must be shown. Such accounts would appear as follows:

Books of T Ltd

Realisation

	£		£
Book values of assets disposed of:		R Ltd: Total purchase	
Buildings	1,000	consideration	14,200
Machinery	1,000		
Stock	2,000		
Debtors	3,000		
Bank	3,000		
Profit on realisation transferred			
to sundry shareholders	4,200		
	14,200		14,200

Share Capital

	£		£
Sundry shareholders	5,000	Balance b/d	5,000

Profit and Loss

	£		£
Sundry shareholders	4,000	Balance b/d	4,000

Creditors

	£		£
R Ltd – taken over	1,000	Balance b/d	1,000

R Ltd

	£		£
Realisation:		Creditors	1,000
Total consideration	14,200	Sundry shareholders: 12,000	
		£1 shares received at premium	
		of 10 per cent	13,200
	14,200		14,200

Sundry Shareholders

	£		£
R Ltd: 12,000 £1 shares at premium		Share capital	5,000
of 10 per cent	13,200	Profit and loss	4,000
		Profit on realisation	4,200
	13,200		13,200

It can be seen that the items possessed by the sundry shareholders have been transferred to an account in their name. These are (a) the share capital which obviously belongs to them, (b) the credit balance on the profit and loss account built up by withholding cash dividends from the shareholders, and (c) the profit on realisation which they, as owners of the business, are entitled to take. As there were 5,000 shares in T Ltd, and 12,000 shares have been given by R Ltd, then each holder of 5 shares in T Ltd will now be given 12 shares in R Ltd to complete the liquidation of the company.

7.5 The exchange of debentures

Sometimes the debentures in the company taking over are to be given in exchange for the debentures of the company being taken over. This may be straightforward on the basis of £100 debentures in company A in exchange for £100 debentures in company B. However, the problem often arises where the exchange is in terms of one or both sets of debentures being at a discount or at a premium. The need for such an exchange may be twofold:

(a) To persuade the debenture holders in Company B to give up their debentures some form of inducement may be needed, such as letting them have A's debentures at a discount even though they may well be worth the par value.

(b) There may be a difference in the debenture interest rates. For instance, a person with a £100 7 per cent debenture would not normally gladly part with it in exchange for a £100 6 per cent debenture in another company. The first debenture gives him/her £7 a year interest, the second one only £6 per year. Thus the debenture in the second company may be issued at a discount to redeem the debenture in the first company at a premium. As the amount of interest is only one factor – there are also others such as the certainty of the debenture holder regaining his/her money if the firm had to close down – the precise terms of the exchange cannot be based merely on arithmetical calculations of interest rates, but it is one of the measures taken when negotiating the exchange of debentures.

Exhibit 7.7

1 D Ltd is to give the necessary debentures at a discount of 10 per cent required to redeem £9,000 debentures in J Ltd at a premium of 5 per cent. The problem here is to find exactly what amount of debentures must be given by D Ltd.

> *Answer:*
> Total nominal value of debentures to be redeemed (exchanged) $\times \dfrac{\text{Redeemable value of each £100 debenture of J Ltd}}{\text{Issue value of each £100 debenture of D Ltd}}$
>
> = Total nominal value of D Ltd to be issued
>
> = £9,000 $\times \dfrac{105}{90}$ = £10,500

Thus, to satisfy the agreement, debentures of D Ltd of a total nominal value of £10,500 are issued at a discount of 10 per cent to the debenture holder of J Ltd.

2 H Ltd is to give the necessary debentures at par to redeem £5,000 debentures in M Ltd at a premium of 4 per cent.

£5,000 $\times \dfrac{104}{100}$ = Debentures of £5,200 nominal value are given by H Ltd at par.

7.6 Profit (or loss) prior to incorporation

Quite frequently companies take over businesses from a date which is actually before the company was itself incorporated. It could be that two persons enter into business and start trading with the intention of running the business as a limited company. However, it takes more than a few days to attend to all the necessary formalities before the company can be incorporated. Obviously it depends on the speed with which the formation is pushed through and the solution of any snags which crop up. When the company is in fact incorporated it may enter into a contract whereby it adopts all the transactions retrospectively to the date that the firm (i.e. with two persons it was a partnership) had started trading. This means that the company accepts all the benefits and disadvantages which have flowed from the transactions which have occurred. The example used was that of a brand-new business; it could well have been an old-established business that was taken over from a date previous to incorporation.

Legally a company cannot earn profits before it comes into existence, i.e. is incorporated, and therefore to decide what action will have to be taken, such profits will first of all have to be calculated. Any such profits are of a capital nature and must be transferred to a capital reserve account, normally titled **Pre-Incorporation Profit Account** or **Profit Prior to Incorporation Account.** That this should be so is apparent if it is realised that, though the actual date from which the transactions have been adopted falls before the date of incorporation, the price at which the business is being taken over is influenced by the values of the assets, etc., at the date when the company actually takes over, i.e. the date of incorporation. Suppose that Doolin and Kershaw start a business on 1 January 19X5 with £1,000 capital, and very shortly afterwards Davie and Parker become interested as well, and the four of them start to form a company in which they will all become directors, Davie and Parker to start active work when the company is incorporated. The company is incorporated on 1 May 19X5 and the original owners of the business, Doolin and Kershaw, are to be given shares in the new company to compensate them for handing over the business. If they know, not necessarily with precision, that the original £1,000 assets will have grown to net assets of £6,000, then they most certainly would not part with the business to the company for £1,000. Ignoring goodwill they would want £6,000 of shares. Conversely, if the net assets have shrunk to £400, would Davie and Parker be happy to see £1,000 of shares handed over? This means that the price at which the business is taken over is dependent on the expected value at the date of the company incorporation, and not on the value at the date on which the company is supposed to take over. Taking the case of the increase in net assets to £6,000 the £5,000 difference is made up of profits. If these profits could be distributed as dividends, then in effect the capital payment of £6,000 in shares is being part used up for dividend purposes. This is in direct contradiction to the normal accounting practice of retaining capital intact (the accountant's meaning of 'capital' and not the meaning given to 'capital' by the economist). The £5,000 profits must therefore be regarded as not being available for dividends. They are thus a capital reserve.

Although the profit cannot be regarded as free for use as dividends, any such loss can be taken to restrict the dividends which could be paid out of the profits made after incorporation. This is the concept of prudence once again coming into play, and if the price paid on takeover was misjudged and a high figure was paid, and it was discovered later that a loss had been made, then the restriction of dividends leads to the capital lost being replaced by assets held back within the firm. Alternatively the amount of the pre-incorporation loss could be charged to a goodwill account, as this is also another way of stating that a higher price has been paid for the assets of the firm than is represented by the value of the tangible assets taken over.

It is possible for the profits up to the date of incorporation to be calculated quite separately from those after incorporation. However, the cost of stocktaking etc. may be felt to be not worth while merely to produce accounts when in fact the accounts could be left until the normal financial year end. This is invariably the case in examination questions. Therefore when the accounts for the full financial year are being made up, they will consist of profits before and after incorporation. The accounts must therefore be split to throw up the two sets of profit (or loss), so that distinction can be made between those profits usable, and those not usable, for dividend purposes. There is no hard-and-fast rule as to how this shall be done. Known facts must prevail, and where an arbitrary apportionment must be made it should meet the test of common sense in the particular case. Exhibit 7.8 shows an attempt to calculate such profits.

Exhibit 7.8

Slack and King, partners in a firm, are to have their business taken over as from 1 January 19X4 by Monk Ltd which is incorporated on 1 April 19X4. It was agreed that all profits made from 1 January 19X4 should belong to the company, and that the vendors be entitled to interest on the purchase price from 1 January to date of payment. The purchase price was paid on 30 April 19X4, including £1,600 interest. A profit and loss account is drawn up for the year ended 31 December 19X4. This is shown as column (X). This is then split into before incorporation, shown as column (Y), and after incorporation as column (Z). The methods used to apportion the particular items are shown after the profit and loss account, the letters (A) to (I) against the items being the references to the notes. These particular methods must definitely not be used in all cases for similar expenses; they are only an indication of different methods of apportionment. The facts and the peculiarities of each firm must be taken into account, and no method should be slavishly followed. Assume for this example that all calendar months are of equal length.

Monk Ltd

Profit and Loss Account for the year ended 31 December 19X4

		(X) Full year		(Y) Pre-incorporation		(Z) After	
		£	£	£	£	£	£
Gross profit	(A)		38,000		8,000		30,000
Less:							
Partnership salaries	(B)	1,000		1,000			
Employees' remuneration	(C)	12,000		3,000		9,000	
General expenses	(C)	800		200		600	
Commission on sales	(D)	1,700		200		1,500	
Distribution expenses	(E)	1,900		400		1,500	
Bad debts	(F)	100		20		80	
Bank overdraft interest	(G)	200				200	
Directors' remuneration	(H)	5,000				5,000	
Directors' expenses	(H)	400				400	
Debenture interest	(H)	500				500	
Depreciation	(C)	1,000		250		750	
Interest paid to vendors	(I)	1,600		1,200		400	
			26,200		6,270		19,930
Net profit			11,800				
Transferred to capital reserves					1,730		
Carried down to the appropriation account							10,070

Notes:

(A) For the three months to 31 March sales amounted to £40,000, and for the remaining nine months they were £150,000. Gross profit is at a uniform rate of 20 per cent of selling price throughout the year. Therefore the gross profit is apportioned (Y) 20 per cent of £40,000 = £8,000, and (Z) 20 per cent of £150,000 = £30,000.

(B) The partnership salaries of the vendors, Slack and King, obviously belong to (Y), because that is the period of the partnership.

(C) These expenses, in this particular case, have accrued evenly throughout the year and are therefore split on the time basis of (Y) three-twelfths, (Z) nine-twelfths.

(D) Commission to the salesmen was paid at the rate of ½ per cent on sales up to 31 March, and 1 per cent thereafter. The commission figure is split:

(Y) ½ per cent of £40,000	=	200
(Z) 1 per cent of £150,000	=	1,500
		1,700

(E) In this particular case (but not always true in every case) the distribution expenses have varied directly with the value of sales. They are therefore split:

$$(Y) \quad \frac{\text{Y sales}}{\text{Total sales}} \times \text{Expenses} = \frac{40,000}{190,000} \times £1,900 = \frac{4}{19} \times £1,900 = £400$$

$$(Z) \quad \frac{\text{Z sales}}{\text{Total sales}} \times \text{Expenses} = \frac{150,000}{190,000} \times £1,900 = \frac{15}{19} \times £1,900 = £1,500$$

(F) The bad debts were two in number:

(*i*) in respect of a sale in January, the debtor dying penniless in March, £20;

(*ii*) in respect of a sale in June, the debtor being declared bankrupt in December, £80.

(G) The bank account was never overdrawn until June, so that the interest charged must be for period (Z).

(H) Only in companies are such expenses as directors' salaries, directors' expenses and debenture interest to be found. These must naturally be shown in period (Z).

(I) The interest paid to the vendors was due to the fact that the company was receiving all the benefits from 1 January but did not in fact pay any cash for the business until 30 April. This is therefore in effect loan interest which should be spread over the period it was borrowed, i.e. three months to (Y) and 1 month to (Z).

New term

Pre-incorporation profits or losses (p. 112): Profits or losses which arise immediately before a limited company is legally incorporated. Any such profits will be treated as 'capital profits' not for distribution while, for sake of prudence, any such losses will be set against post-incorporation profits.

Main points to remember

1   The basic accounting entries are the same whether a limited company takes over a sole trader or a partnership.

2   Limited companies may take over other limited companies either:
    (*a*) by buying all the assets of the other company; or
    (*b*) by giving its own shares and debentures in exchange for the shares and debentures of the company being taken over.

3   Pre-incorporation profits are not available for distribution.

Review questions

7.1 Checkers Ltd was incorporated on 1 April 19X5 and took over the business of Black and White, partners, as from 1 January 19X5. It was agreed that all profits made from 1 January should belong to the company and that the vendors should be entitled to interest on the purchase price from 1 January to date of payment. The purchase price was paid on 31 May 19X5 including £1,650 interest.

The following is the profit and loss account for the year to 31 December 19X5:

	£		£
Salaries of vendors	1,695	Gross profit	28,000
Wages and general expenses	8,640		
Rent and rates	860		
Distribution expenses	1,680		
Commission on sales	700		
Bad debts	314		
Interest paid to vendors	1,650		
Directors' remuneration	4,000		
Directors' expenses	515		
Depreciation	£		
Motors	1,900		
Machinery	575		
	2,475		
Bank interest	168		
Net profit	5,303		
	28,000		28,000

You are given the following information:

1. Sales amounted to £20,000 for the three months to 31 March 19X5 and £50,000 for the nine months to 31 December 19X5. Gross profit is at a uniform rate of 40 per cent of selling price throughout the year, and commission at a rate of 1 per cent is paid on all sales.
2. Salaries of £1,695 were paid to the vendors for their assistance in running the business up to 31 March 19X5.
3. The bad debts written off are:
   (a) a debt of £104 taken over from the vendors;
   (b) a debt of £210 in respect of goods sold in August 19X5.
4. On 1 January 19X5 motors were bought for £7,000 and machinery for £5,000. On 1 March 19X5 another motor van was bought for £3,000 and on 1 October 19X5 another machine was added for £3,000. Depreciation has been written off motors at 20 per cent per annum, and machinery 10 per cent per annum.
5. Wages and general expenses and rent and rates accrued at an even rate throughout the year.
6. The bank granted an overdraft in June 19X5.

Assuming all calendar months are of equal length:

(a) set out the profit and loss account in columnar form, so as to distinguish between the period prior to the company's incorporation and the period after incorporation;
(b) state how you would deal with the profit prior to incorporation;
(c) state how you would deal with the results prior to incorporation if they turned out to be a net loss.

7.2   On 31 December 19X6 Breeze Ltd acquired all the assets, except the investments, of Blow Ltd.

The following are the summaries of the profit and loss account of Blow Ltd for the years 19X4, 19X5 and 19X6:

	19X4	19X5	19X6		19X4	19X5	19X6
Motor expenses	1,860	1,980	2,100	Trading profits	22,050	25,780	25,590
Depreciation of plant				Investment income	290	340	480
and machinery	4,000	3,200	2,560	Rents received	940	420	–
Bank overdraft interest	180	590	740	Profit on sale of			
Wrapping expenses	840	960	1,020	property		4,800	
Preliminary expenses							
written off	–	690	–				
Net profit	16,400	23,920	19,650				
	23,280	31,340	26,070		23,280	31,340	26,070

The purchase price is to be the amount on which an estimated maintainable profit would represent a return of 25 per cent per annum.

The maintainable profit is to be taken as the average of the profits of the three years 19X4, 19X5 and 19X6, after making any necessary adjustments.

You are given the following information:
(a) The cost of the plant and machinery was £20,000. It is agreed that depreciation should have been written off at the rate of 12½ per cent per annum using the straight line method.
(b) A form of new plastic wrapping material introduced on to the market means that wrapping expenses will be halved in future.
(c) By a form of long-term rental of motor vehicles, it is estimated that motor expenses will be cut by one-third in future.
(d) Stock treated as valueless at 31 December 19X3 was sold for £1,900 in 19X5.
(e) The working capital of the new company is such that an overdraft is not contemplated.
(f) Management remuneration has been inadequate and will have to be increased by £1,500 a year in future.

You are required to set out your calculation of the purchase price. All workings must be shown. In fact, your managing director, who is not an accountant, should be able to decipher how the price was calculated.

7.3   CJK Ltd was incorporated on 15 December 19X9 with an authorised capital of 200,000 ordinary shares of £0.20 each to acquire as at 31 December 19X9 the business of CK, a sole trader, and RP Ltd, a company.

From the following information you are required to prepare:
(a)   the realisation and capital accounts in the books of CK and RP Ltd showing the winding up of these two concerns;
(b)   the journal entries to open the books of CJK Ltd, including cash transactions and the raising of finance;
(c)   the balance sheet of CJK Ltd after the transactions have been completed.

The balance sheet of CK as at 31 December 19X9 is as follows:

Balance Sheet

	£
Freehold premises	8,000
Plant	4,000
Stock	2,000
Debtors	5,000
Cash	200
	19,200
Capital	16,000
Creditors	3,200
	19,200

The assets (excluding cash) and the liabilities were taken over at the following values: freehold premises £10,000, plant £3,500, stock £2,000, debtors £5,000 less a bad debts provision of £300, goodwill £7,000, creditors £3,200 less a discount provision of £150. The purchase consideration, based on these values, was settled by the issue of shares at par.

The balance sheet of RP Ltd as at 31 December 19X9 is as follows:

Balance Sheet

	£
Freehold premises	4,500
Plant	2,000
Stock	1,600
Debtors	3,400
	11,500
Share capital: 10,000 shares at £0.40 each	4,000
Revenue surplus	2,500
Creditors	1,500
Bank overdraft	3,500
	11,500

The assets and liabilities were taken over at book value with the exception of the freehold premises which were revalued at £5,500. The purchase consideration was a cash payment of £1 and three shares in CJK Ltd at par in exchange for every two shares in RP Ltd.

   Additional working capital and the funds required to complete the purchase of RP Ltd were provided by the issue for cash of:

(i)   10,000 shares at a premium of £0.30 per share;
(ii)   £8,000 7 per cent debenture stock at 98.

The expenses of incorporating CJK Ltd were paid, amounting to £1,200.

(*Chartered Institute of Management Accountants*)

7.4A The balance sheet of Hubble Ltd as at 31 May 19X0 is shown below.

Hubble Ltd

	£	£
Fixed assets:		
Freehold premises at cost		375,000
Plant and machinery at cost		
Less Depreciation £48,765		101,235
Motor vehicles at cost		
Less Depreciation £1,695		6,775
		483,010
Current assets:		
Stock-in-trade	102,550	
Debtors	96,340	
Cash in hand	105	
		198,995
		682,005
Authorised share capital		
650,000 ordinary shares of £1 each		650,000
Issued share capital:		
400,000 ordinary shares of £1 each fully paid		400,000
Profit and loss account		180,630
		580,630
Current liabilities		
Trade creditors	63,200	
Bank overdraft	38,175	
		101,375
		682,005

Hubble Ltd agreed to purchase at this date the freehold premises, plant and machinery and stock of A Bubble at agreed valuations of £100,000, £10,000 and £55,000, respectively. The purchase price was to be fully settled by the issue to Bubble of 120,000 ordinary shares of £1 each in Hubble Ltd, and a cash payment to Bubble of £25,000. Bubble was to collect his debts and to pay his creditors.

Hubble Ltd sold one of its own premises prior to taking over Bubble for £75,000 (cost £55,000) and revalued the remainder at £400,000 (excluding those acquired from Bubble).

You are required to:
(*a*) show the journal entries, including cash items, in the books of Hubble Ltd to give effect to the above transactions; and
(*b*) show the balance sheet of Hubble Ltd after completing them.

(*Association of Chartered Certified Accountants*)

7.5A   From the following information you are required to prepare a statement apportioning the unappropriated profit between the pre-incorporation and post-incorporation periods, showing the basis of apportionment:

VU Limited was incorporated on 1 July 19X9 with an authorised share capital of 60,000 ordinary shares of £1 each, to take over the business of L and Sons as from 1 April 19X9.

The purchase consideration was agreed at £50,000 for the net tangible assets taken over, plus a further £6,000 for goodwill.

Payment was satisfied by the issue of £30,000 8 per cent debentures and 26,000 ordinary shares both at par, on 1 August 19X9. Interest at 10 per cent per annum on the purchase consideration was paid up to this date.

The company raised a further £20,000 on 1 August 19X9 by the issue of ordinary shares at a premium of £0.25 per share.

The abridged profit and loss account for the year to 31 March 19X0 was as follows:

	£	£
Sales:		
1 April 19X9 to 30 June 19X9	30,000	
1 July 19X9 to 31 March 19Y0	95,000	
		125,000
Cost of sales for the year	80,000	
Depreciation	2,220	
Directors' fees	500	
Administration salaries and expenses	8,840	
Sales commission	4,375	
Goodwill written off	1,000	
Interest on purchase consideration, gross	1,867	
Distribution costs (60 per cent variable)	6,250	
Preliminary expenses written off	1,650	
Debenture interest, gross	1,600	
Proposed dividend on ordinary shares	7,560	
		115,862
Unappropriated profit carried forward		9,138

The company sells one product only, of which the unit selling price has remained constant during the year, but due to improved buying the unit cost of sales was reduced by 10 per cent in the post-incorporation period as compared with the pre-incorporation period.

   Taxation is to be ignored.

(*Chartered Institute of Management Accountants (part (a) of question only)*)

7.6A   Rowlock Ltd was incorporated on 1 October 19X8 to acquire Rowlock's mail order business, with effect from 1 June 19X8.

The purchase consideration was agreed at £35,000 to be satisfied by the issue on 1 December 19X8 to Rowlock or his nominee of 20,000 ordinary shares of £1 each, fully paid, and £15,000 7 per cent debentures.

The entries relating to the transfer were not made in the books which were carried on without a break until 31 May 19X9.

On 31 May 19X9 the trial balance extracted from the books is:

	£	£
Sales		52,185
Purchases	38,829	
Wrapping	840	
Postage	441	
Warehouse rent and rates	921	
Packing expenses	1,890	
Office expenses	627	
Stock on 31 May 19X8	5,261	
Director's salary	1,000	
Debenture interest (gross)	525	
Fixed assets	25,000	
Current assets (other than stock)	9,745	
Current liabilities		4,162
Formation expenses	218	
Capital account – Wysocka, 31 May 19X8		29,450
Drawings account – Wysocka, 31 May 19X8	500	
	85,797	85,797

You also ascertain the following:
1   Stock on 31 May 19X9 amounted to £4,946.
2   The average monthly sales for June, July and August were one-half of those for the remaining months of the year. The gross profit margin was constant throughout the year.
3   Wrapping, postage and packing expenses varied in direct proportion to sales, whilst office expenses were constant each month.
4   Formation expenses are to be written off.

You are required to prepare the trading and profit and loss account for the year ended 31 May 19X9 apportioned between the periods before and after incorporation, and the balance sheet as at that date.

(*Chartered Institute of Management Accountants*)

8

Taxation in company financial statements

Objectives

After you have studied this chapter, you should:

- *know why profit per the profit and loss account is normally different from assessable profit for corporation tax calculations*

- *be aware of how income tax on interest affects companies and individuals*

- *understand how the 'imputation system' operates*

- *understand how and why deferred tax is relevant to capital allowances*

8.1 Introduction

This chapter is concerned with the entries made in the financial statements of firms in respect of taxation. It is not concerned with the actual calculation of the taxes. Taxation legislation is now extremely complex and contains many exceptions to the general rules applicable to companies. It is impossible in a book at this level to delve into too many of the complications, and it should therefore be appreciated that, as far as companies are concerned, though the facts in this chapter apply to the great majority of limited companies, there are some other complications in a small minority of cases.

Taxation that affects companies can be split between:

1   Direct taxes, payable to the Inland Revenue, this being the government department responsible for the calculation and collection of the taxes. For a company these taxes are corporation tax and income tax. SSAP 8 (*The treatment of taxation under the imputation system in the accounts of companies*) deals with the treatment of taxation in company financial statements, and will be adhered to in this chapter.
2   Value added tax, abbreviated as VAT. This has been dealt with in Volume 1.

8.2 Limited companies: corporation tax and income tax

The tax which limited companies suffer is known as corporation tax. It is legally an appropriation of profits, it is not an expense, and it should therefore be shown in the profit and loss appropriation account. Two law cases, many years ago, did in fact settle any arguments as to whether it was an expense or appropriation, both cases being decided in favour of the view that it was an appropriation of profits.

When a company makes profits, then such profits are assessable to corporation tax. It does not mean that corporation tax is payable on the net profits as shown in the financial statements. What it does mean is that the corporation tax is assessable on the profit calculated after certain adjustments have been made to the net profit shown according to the profit and loss account. These adjustments are not made in the actual financial statements, they are made in calculations performed quite separately from the drafting of financial statements. Suppose that K Ltd has the following profit and loss account:

K Ltd Profit and Loss Account for the year ended 31 March 19X8

	£	£
Gross profit		100,000
Less: General expenses	30,000	
Depreciation of machinery	20,000	
		50,000
Net profit		50,000

The depreciation provision for machinery is the accounting figure used for the financial statements. It is not usually the same figure as that allowed by the Inland Revenue for the depreciation of the machinery. The allowances made for depreciation by the Inland Revenue are known as **capital allowances**. These are calculated by rules which usually vary at one point or another from the methods applied by the company in determining depreciation provisions.

A detailed study of a textbook on taxation would be necessary to see exactly how capital allowances are calculated. In some fairly rare cases, hardly ever found in large or medium-sized concerns but probably more common in very small firms, the capital allowances are calculated and the financial provision for depreciation is taken at the same figure. In the case of K Ltd, assume that the capital allowances amount to £27,000, and that the rate of corporation tax is 40 per cent on assessable profits. The calculation of the corporation tax liability would be:

	£
Net profit per the financial statements	50,000
Add Depreciation provision not allowed as a deduction for corporation tax purposes	20,000
	70,000
Less Capital allowances	27,000
Adjusted profits assessable to corporation tax	43,000

As the corporation tax is assumed to be at the rate of 40 per cent of assessable profits, the corporation tax liability will be £43,000 × 40 per cent = £17,200. Sometimes the adjusted profits are greater than the net profits shown in the financial statements, but may equally well be less. This illustrates the fact that it is relatively rare for the external observer to be able to calculate the corporation tax payable merely by knowing the net profit made by the company. In fact, there are also other items besides depreciation provisions that need adjusting to find the correct assessable profits for corporation tax purposes. All that is needed here is the understanding that profit per the profit and loss account is normally different from assessable profit for corporation tax calculations.

8.3 The rate of corporation tax

The rate of corporation tax is fixed by the Chancellor of the Exchequer in his Budget, presented to Parliament each year. In the Budget, the corporation tax rates are fixed covering the period from 1 April until 31 March the year following. This rate is to be applied to the assessable profits of companies earned during this period. A company whose financial year end is not 31 March will, therefore, span two governmental financial years, and will need to apportion its taxable profits across the two periods.

Exhibit 8.1

Company T Ltd: adjusted profits for the year ended 31 December 19X8 = £160,000.

Rates of corporation tax:
For the government financial year ended 31.3.19X8, 45 per cent.
For the government financial year ended 31.3.19X9, 40 per cent.

	£
3 months' profit 1.1.19X8 to 31.3.19X8	
3/12 months × £160,000 = £40,000 × 45 per cent	18,000
9 months' profit 1.4.19X8 to 31.12.19X8	48,000
9/12 months × £160,000 = £120,000 × 40 per cent	66,000

8.4 Corporation tax – when payable

All companies have a payment date of 9 months after the end of each accounting period. For the rest of this chapter, although companies with relatively small profits can pay tax at a lower rate than companies with greater profits, unless mentioned otherwise, for the purposes of illustration, corporation tax will be assumed to be at the rate of 40 per cent.

8.5 Advance corporation tax (ACT)

In the past, when a company paid a dividend, a sum equal to a fraction of that figure had to be paid to the Inland Revenue as **advance corporation tax** (ACT). When a company was due to pay its corporation tax bill, it adjusted the amount it sent to the Inland Revenue by the amount of ACT it had paid or reclaimed during the relevant period. ACT was repealed with effect from 1999 and is not included in any of the examples or questions in this book.

8.6 Income tax

As already stated, companies do not pay income tax, instead they suffer corporation tax. In the case of a sole trader, income tax is not directly connected with the business, as the calculation of it depends on many factors including, for example, whether the sole trader is married or not and on the amount and type of other income received by him/her, etc. It should therefore be charged to the drawings account.

The income tax charged upon a partnership is also subject to the personal situation of the partners. The actual apportionment of the tax between the partners must be performed by someone who has access to the personal tax computations; it most certainly is not apportioned in the partners' profit-sharing ratios. When the apportionment has been made each partner should have the relevant amount debited to his drawings account. Sole traders and partnerships are not liable to corporation tax.

Income tax does, however, come into the financial statements of limited companies in that the company, when paying charges such as debenture interest or some types of royalty, will deduct income tax from the amount to be paid to the debenture holder or royalty owner. This figure of income tax is then payable by the company to the Inland Revenue. This means simply that the company is acting as a tax collector on behalf of the Inland Revenue.

Suppose, for example, that the company has a thousand different debenture holders. It is far easier for the Inland Revenue if the company pays only the net amount (i.e. the amount of debenture interest less income tax) due to each debenture holder and then pays the income tax deducted, in one figure, to the Inland Revenue. This saves the Inland Revenue having to trace a thousand debenture holders and then collect the money from them. It obviously cuts down on the bad debts that the Inland Revenue might suffer, it makes it more difficult to evade the payment of income tax, plus it makes it cheaper for the Inland Revenue to administer the system. This system is based on the same principles as PAYE on wages or salaries.

For clarity, throughout the rest of this chapter it will be assumed that the basic rate of income tax is 25 per cent. The real rate will obviously differ from time to time. In addition, where an individual has a high or low income he/she will pay rates of income tax which may differ from 25 per cent. However, even though individual debenture holders may have to pay income tax at higher rates, or indeed pay lower rates or no income tax at all, a company will generally deduct income tax at the basic rate.

This means that if a company had 8 per cent debentures amounting to £100,000 then, assuming that the debenture interest was payable in one amount, cheques amounting to a total of £6,000 (8 per cent of £100,000 = £8,000 less 25 per cent income tax, £2,000 = £6,000) will be paid to the debenture holders. A cheque for £2,000 will then be paid to the Inland Revenue by the company. Assume that debenture holder AB is liable on his income to income tax at the rate of 25 per cent, and that he receives interest of £75 net (i.e. £100 gross less income tax £25), on his debenture of £1,250 then he has already suffered his rightful income tax by deduction at the source. He will not get a further bill from the Inland Revenue for £25 tax, he has already suffered the full amount due by him, and the company will have paid the £25 income tax as part of the total income tax cheque of £2,000.

On the other hand, debenture holder CD may not be liable to income tax because his income is low, or he may have sufficient factors qualifying for tax relief that he is not liable to pay any income tax. If he has a debenture of £1,000 he will receive a cheque for interest amounting to £60 (i.e. £80 gross, less income tax £20). As he is not liable to income tax, but as £20 of his money has been included in the total cheque paid by the company to the Inland Revenue of £2,000, then he will be able to claim a refund of £20 from the Inland Revenue. Such a claim is made direct to the Inland Revenue, the company having nothing to do with the refund.

Another debenture holder, EF, is liable to a higher rate of income tax of 40 per cent on his income. If he has a debenture of £25,000, then the company will pay a cheque to him of £1,500 (£2,000 gross less income tax £500). In fact, he is really liable for £800 income tax (£2,000 at 40 per cent) on this income. As £500 income tax has been taken from him and handed over by the company in the total cheque of £2,000 income tax paid to the Inland Revenue, eventually the Inland Revenue will send an extra demand for income tax of £300 to EF (£800 liable less £500 already paid). The company will have nothing to do with this extra demand.

8.7 Income tax on interest

Of course, a company may well have bought debentures or may own royalties, etc., in another company. This may mean that the company not only pays charges, such as debenture interest, but also receives similar items from other companies. The company will receive such items net after income tax has been deducted. When the company both receives and pays such items, it may set off the tax already suffered by it from such interest, etc. received against the tax collected by it from its own charges, and pay the resultant net figure of income tax to the Inland Revenue.

The figures of charges to be shown as being paid or received by the company in the company's own profit and loss account are the gross charges, i.e. the same as they would have been if income tax had never been invented. An exhibit will now be used to illustrate this more clearly.

Exhibit 8.4

RST Ltd has 7 per cent debentures amounting to £10,000 and has bought a £4,000 debenture of 10 per cent in a private company, XYZ Ltd. During the year cheques amounting to £525 (£700 less 25 per cent) have been paid to debenture holders, and a cheque of £300 (£400 less 25 per cent) has been received from XYZ Ltd. Instead of paying over the £175 income tax deducted on payment of debenture interest, RST Ltd waits until the cheque is received from XYZ Ltd and then pays a cheque for £75 (£175 collected by it less £100 already suffered by deduction by XYZ Ltd) to the Inland Revenue in settlement.

Debenture Interest Payable

	£		£
Cash	525	Profit and loss	700
Income tax	175		
	700		700

Debenture Interest Receivable

	£		£
Profit and loss	400	Cash	300
		Income tax	100
	400		400

Income Tax

	£		£
Unquoted investment income	100	Debenture interest	175
Cash	75		
	175		175

It may well have been the case that although the income tax had been deducted at source from both the payment out of the company and the amount received, no cash has been paid specifically to the Inland Revenue by the company by the balance sheet date. This means that the balance of £75 owing to the Inland Revenue will be carried down as a credit balance and will be shown under current liabilities in the balance sheet.

8.8 Franked payments and franked investment income

When a dividend is paid by a company, this is done without any specific deduction of tax of any kind from the dividend payment. Previously, when a company paid a dividend, it also incurred a liability to pay ACT – *see* Section 8.5. The recipient received the dividend plus a tax credit, equal to the ACT, which could then be set against the recipient's income tax liability. When the dividend was paid to another company, the total of the dividend paid plus the tax credit was known as the **franked payment**. The total of the dividend received plus the tax credit was called **franked investment income**. With the repeal of ACT in 1999, these two terms appear unlikely to continue to be used.

8.9 Deferred taxation

It was pointed out earlier in the chapter that *profits per the financial statements* and *profits on which tax is payable* are often quite different from each other. The main reasons for this are:

(a) The figure of depreciation shown in the profit and loss account may be far different from the Inland Revenue's figure for 'capital allowances', which is *their* way of calculating allowances for depreciation.
(b) Some items of expense charged in the profit and loss account will not be allowed by the Inland Revenue as expenses. Examples are political donations, fines for illegal acts, and expenses of entertaining UK customers.

Timing differences

In the case of capital allowances under (a) above, the amount of 'depreciation' charged for an asset over the years will eventually equal the amount allowed by the Inland Revenue as 'capital allowances'. Where the difference lies is in the periods when these items will be taken into account.

For instance, let us take an asset which will be used for three years and then put out of use. It costs £4,800 and will be sold three years later for £2,025. The depreciation rate is to be 33⅓ per cent straight line. Inland Revenue capital allowances are 25 per cent reducing balance.

Years ended 5 April	19X2 £	19X3 £	19X4 £	Total £
Depreciation in accounts	925	925	925	2,775
Capital allowances in tax calculations	1,200	900	675	2,775
Timing differences	+275	–25	–250	nil

Let us suppose that profits for each year, after charging depreciation, amounted to £1,000. A comparison of profits per financial statements and profits for tax purposes becomes as follows:

Years ended 5 April	19X2 £	19X3 £	19X4 £	Total £
Profits per accounts after depreciation	1,000	1,000	1,000	3,000
Profits for tax purposes	725	1,025	1,250	3,000
Differences	–275	+25	+250	nil

As you can see, profits have in fact remained the same at £1,000; it is the timing difference of capital allowances which gives different figures for tax purposes. Taking the point of view that profits of £1,000 per year give a more sensible picture than the £725, £1,025 and £1,250 per the Inland Revenue calculations, the company's way of depreciating is probably more suitable than the Inland Revenue's method which does not vary between different companies.

You may well be asking if it matters at all. Analysts and potential investors and shareholders themselves place a great reliance on *earnings per share **after tax*** (EPS). Suppose that corporation tax was 40 per cent for each of the three years and that there were 10,000 shares. This would give the following figures:

Tax based on 'real profits', i.e. company's calculations:

	19X2 £	19X3 £	19X4 £
Profits per accounts before taxation	1,000	1,000	1,000
Less Corporation tax (40%)	400	400	400
Profit after tax	600	600	600
Earnings per share ÷ 10,000	6.0p	6.0p	6.0p

Tax based on Inland Revenue calculations:

	19X2 £	19X3 £	19X4 £
Profits per accounts before tax	1,000	1,000	1,000
Less Corporation tax:			
40% of £725	290		
40% of £1,025		410	
40% of £1,250			500
Profits after tax	710	590	500
Earnings per share ÷ 10,000	7.1p	5.9p	5.0p

In truth, each of the years has been equally as profitable as any other – this is shown by the company's calculation of 6.0p earnings per share each year. On the other hand, if no adjustment is made, the financial statements when based on actual tax paid would show 7.1p, 5.9p and 5.0p. This could confuse shareholders and would-be shareholders.

So as not to distort the picture given by financial statements, the concept of deferred taxation was brought in by accountants. This was given approval in SSAP15: *Accounting for deferred taxation*. The double entry is as follows:

1   In the years when taxation is lower than it would be on comparable accounting profits:

> Dr Profit and loss appropriation account
> Cr Deferred taxation account

with the amount of taxation understated.

2   In the years when taxation is higher than it would be on comparable accounting profits:

> Dr Deferred taxation account
> Cr Profit and loss appropriation account

with the amount of taxation overstated.

We will now look at Exhibit 8.5 to see how the profit and loss appropriation account and deferred taxation account would have been drawn up for the example given above. To make the exhibit follow the wording for published company financial statements, instead of 'Profit per financial statements before taxation' we will call it instead 'Profit on ordinary activities before taxation'.

Exhibit 8.5

Profit and Loss Appropriation Account for the years ended 5 April

	19X2		19X3		19X4	
	£	£	£	£	£	£
Profit on ordinary activities before taxation		1,000		1,000		1,000
Tax on profit on ordinary activities:						
Corporation tax	290		410		500	
Deferred taxation	110	400	(10)	400	(100)	400
Profit on ordinary activities after taxation		600		600		600

For purposes of shareholders, stock exchange analysts, would-be shareholders, etc. the profit after taxation figures on which earnings per share (EPS) would be calculated is the figure of £600 for each of the three years. The distortion has thus been removed.

Assuming that corporation tax is payable on 1 January following each accounting year end, the accounts for corporation tax and deferred tax would be as follows:

Corporation Tax

19X2			£	19X2				£
Apr	5	Balance c/d	290	Apr	5	Profit and loss appropriation		290
			290					290
19X3				19X2				
Jan	1	Bank	290	Apr	6	Balance b/d		290
				19X3				
Apr	5	Balance c/d	410	Apr	5	Profit and loss appropriation		410
			700					700
19X4				19X3				
Jan	1	Bank	410	Apr	6	Balance b/d		410
				19X4				
Apr	5	Balance c/d	500	Apr	5	Profit and loss appropriation		500
			910					910
				19X4				
				Apr	6	Balance b/d		500

Deferred Taxation

19X2			£	19X2			£
Apr	5	Balance c/d	110	Apr	5	Profit and loss appropriation	110
			110				110
19X3				19X2			
Apr	5	Profit and loss appropriation	10	Apr	6	Balance b/d	110
Apr	5	Balance c/d	100				
			110				110
19X4				19X3			
Apr	5	Profit and loss appropriation	100	Apr	6	Balance b/d	100
			100				100

The balance sheets would appear:

	19X2	19X3	19X4
	£	£	£
Creditors: amounts falling due within one year			
Corporation tax	290	410	500
Provisions for liabilities and charges			
Deferred taxation	110	100	–

Permanent differences

Differences in profits for accounts purposes and those for tax purposes because of non-allowable items such as political donations, entertaining expenses etc., are not adjusted for.

A fully worked example

Exhibit 8.6 shows the accounts in which tax will be involved for the first year of a new company, Harlow Ltd. Exhibit 8.7 follows with the second year of that company. This should make your understanding easier – to consider one year alone very often leaves students with many unanswered questions in their minds.

The tax rates used are: corporation tax 35 per cent, income tax 25 per cent.

Exhibit 8.6

Harlow Ltd has just finished its first year of trading on 31 December 19X4. Corporation tax throughout was 35 per cent, and income tax was 25 per cent. You are given the following information:

(A) Net trading profit for the year was £165,000, before adjustment for debenture interest.
(B) Debenture interest (net) of £12,000 was paid on 31 December 19X4 and (C) the income tax deducted was paid on the same date.
(D) An ordinary interim dividend of 10 per cent on the 210,000 £1 ordinary shares was paid on 1 July 19X4.
(E) A proposed final ordinary dividend of 25 per cent for the year is to be accrued.
(F) Depreciation of £12,000 has been charged before arriving at net trading profit. Capital allowances of £37,000 have been approved by the Inland Revenue. Account for timing differences.
(G) Corporation tax on the first year's trading is expected to be £38,500.

You are required to:

(*a*) show double-entry accounts (other than bank) to record the above;
(*b*) prepare extracts from the profit and loss account and balance sheet.

Exhibit 8.7 will carry on to Harlow Ltd's second year in trading.

Debenture Interest

19X4			£	19X4		£
Dec 31 Bank	(B)		12,000	Dec 31 Profit and loss		16,000
Dec 31 Income tax	(C)		4,000			
			16,000			16,000

Income Tax

19X4		£	19X4			£
Dec 31 Bank	(C)	4,000	Dec 31 Debenture interest	(C)		4,000

Ordinary Dividends

19X4			£	19X4		£
Jul 1 Bank	(D)		21,000	Dec 31 Profit and loss		73,500
Dec 31 Accrued c/d			52,500			
			73,500			73,500

Deferred Taxation

19X4	£	19X4		£
Dec 31 Balance c/d	8,750	Dec 31 Profit and loss*	(F)	8,750

*(F) allowed £37,000 but only charged £12,000
= £25,000 × 35% corporation tax deferred = £8,750.

Corporation Tax

19X4	£	19X4		£
Dec 31 Balance c/d	38,500	Dec 31 Profit and loss	(G)	38,500

Profit and Loss Account (extracts) for the year ended 31 December 19X4

		£	£
Net trading profit	(A)		165,000
Less Debenture interest	(B)		16,000
Profit on ordinary activities before taxation			149,000
Corporation tax	(G)	38,500	
Deferred taxation	(F)	8,750	47,250
Profit on ordinary activities after taxation			101,750
Less Dividends on ordinary shares:			
Interim paid 10 per cent	(D)	21,000	
Proposed final dividend 25 per cent		52,500	
			73,500

Balance Sheet (extracts) as at 31 December 19X4

Creditors: amounts falling due within one year	£
Proposed ordinary dividend	52,500
Corporation tax	38,500
Deferred tax	8,750

Exhibit 8.7

Harlow Ltd, as per Exhibit 8.6, has now finished its second year of trading. From 19X4 there will be three balances (concerned with the exhibit) to be brought forward. These accounts are:

Proposed ordinary dividend	(A)	Cr	£52,500
Corporation tax	(B)	Cr	£38,500
Deferred taxation	(C)	Cr	£8,750

The following information is given to you:

(D) The proposed ordinary dividend £52,500 was paid on 1 March 19X5.

(E) Corporation tax remains at 35 per cent and income tax remains at 25 per cent.

(F) Shares had been bought in STU Ltd and a dividend of £1,500 was received on 31 August 19X5.

(G) An interim dividend of 15 per cent on the 210,000 £1 ordinary shares was paid on 1 July 19X5.

(H) Debentures had been bought in RRR Ltd and interest (net) of £4,500 was received on 30 December 19X5.

(I) Harlow Ltd paid its own debenture interest (net) of £12,000 on 31 December 19X5, and (J) the income tax account (net) was paid on the same date.

(K) The corporation tax due for 19X4 was paid on 30 September 19X5.

(L) A final ordinary dividend for the year of 30 per cent was proposed. This will be paid in March 19X6.

(M) Corporation tax for the year ended 31 December 19X5 is expected to be £41,300.

(N) Depreciation of £28,000 has been charged in the accounts, while capital allowances amounted to £22,000.

(O) Net trading profit after deducting depreciation but before adjusting for the above was £178,000.

It would have been quite possible to open a tax on profit on ordinary activities account and transfer tax items to there, prior to closing to the profit and loss account. We will now use this method.

Ordinary Dividends

19X5			£	19X5			£
Mar	1	Bank	(D) 52,500	Jan	1	Balance b/d	(A) 52,500
Jul	1	Bank interim	(G) 31,500	Dec	31	Profit and loss	94,500
Dec	31	Accrued c/d	(L) 63,000				
			147,000				147,000

Investment Income

19X5			£	19X5			£
Dec	31	Profit and loss	1,500	Aug	31	Bank	(F) 1,500
			1,500				1,500

Debenture Interest Payable

19X5			£	19X5		£
Dec 31	Bank	(I)	12,000	Dec 31	Profit and loss	16,000
Dec 31	Income tax		4,000			
			16,000			16,000

Debenture Interest Receivable

19X5		£	19X5			£
Dec 31	Profit and loss	6,000	Dec 30	Bank	(H)	4,500
			Dec 30	Income tax		1,500
		6,000				6,000

Income Tax

19X5			£	19X5		£
Dec 30	Debenture interest receivable		1,500	Dec 31	Debenture interest payable	4,000
Dec 31	Bank	(J)	2,500			
			4,000			4,000

Deferred Taxation

19X5			£	19X5			£
Dec 31	Tax on profit on ordinary activities (6,000 × 35%)	(N)	2,100	Jan 1	Balance b/d	(C)	8,750
Dec 31	Balance c/d		6,650				
			8,750				8,750

Corporation Tax

19X5			£	19X5			£
Sep 30	Bank	(K)	38,500	Jan 1	Balance b/d	(B)	38,500
Dec 31	Accrued c/d		41,300	Dec 31	Tax on profit on ordinary activities	(M)	41,300
			79,800				79,800

Tax on Profit on Ordinary Activities

19X5			£	19X5			£
Dec 31	Corporation tax	(M)	41,300	Dec 31	Deferred taxation	(N)	2,100
				Dec 31	Profit and loss		39,200
			41,300				41,300

Profit and Loss account (extracts) for the year ended 31 December 19X5

		£	£
Net trading profit	(O)		178,000
Add Debenture interest received		6,000	
Investment income		1,500	7,500
			185,500
Less Debenture interest payable			16,000
Profit on ordinary activities before taxation			169,500
Tax on profit on ordinary activities			39,200
Profit on ordinary activities after taxation			129,700
Less Dividends on ordinary shares			
Interim paid 15 per cent		31,500	
Proposed final dividend		63,000	94,500

Balance Sheet (extracts) as at 31 December 19X5

Creditors: amounts falling due within one year	£
Proposed ordinary dividend	63,000
Corporation tax	41,300
Deferred tax	6,650

New terms

Corporation tax (p. 122): A form of direct taxation levied on the profits of companies. The rate is determined each year in the Finance Act.

Deferred taxation (p. 127): Timing differences arise between the accounting treatment of events and their taxation results. Deferred taxation accounting adjusts the differences so that the accounts are not misleading.

Main points to remember

1   Profit per the profit and loss account is normally different from assessable profit for corporation tax calculations.

2   Deferred tax eliminates the differences that arise as a result of depreciation being replaced by capital allowances when calculating corporation tax payable.

Review questions

For those taking examinations with little tax content, questions 8.5 and 8.6 will be sufficient for your purposes.

8.1   Long Acre Ltd has just finished its first year of trading to 31 December 19X3. Corporation tax throughout was 35 per cent and income tax 25 per cent. You are given the following information:

(*i*)   Net trading profit, after adjustment for (*ii*) but before other adjustments, was £220,000.

(*ii*)   Depreciation of £50,000 was charged in the accounts. Capital allowances amounted to £90,000.

(*iii*)   An interim dividend of 5 per cent on 400,000 £1 ordinary shares was paid on 1 July 19X3.

(*iv*)   Debenture interest of £9,600 (net) was paid on 31 December 19X3.

(*v*)   Income tax deducted from debenture interest was paid on 31 January 19X4.

(*vi*)   A final dividend of 7½ per cent was proposed for the year.
(*vii*) Corporation tax for the year was estimated to be £90,000.

You are required to:
(*a*) draw up the double entry accounts recording the above (except bank);
(*b*) show the relevant extracts from the profit and loss account and the balance sheet.

Note that question 8.2A is concerned with the second year of trading for Long Acre Ltd.

8.2A   Long Acre Ltd has just finished its second year of trading to 31 December 19X4. Balances per 8.1 need to be brought forward into this question. Tax rates are the same as for 19X3.
The following information is available:

(*i*)   The proposed final dividend for 19X3 (*see* 8.1) was paid on 31 January 19X4.
(*ii*)   Shares in Covent Ltd were bought on 1 January 19X4. A dividend of £2,400 was received on 30 September 19X4.
(*iii*) Debentures in Covent Ltd were bought 1 July 19X4. Debenture interest of £7,200 (net) was paid to us on 31 December 19X4.
(*iv*)   Debenture interest of £9,600 (net) was paid by us on 31 December 19X4.
(*v*)   Income tax owing to the Inland Revenue for 19X4 was not paid by us until 19X5. The 19X3 income tax had been paid on 30 January 19X4.
(*vi*)   An interim dividend of 7½ per cent on 400,000 £1 ordinary shares was paid by us on 10 July 19X4.
(*vii*) A final dividend of 17½ per cent was proposed for the year.
(*viii*) Depreciation of £70,000 was charged in the accounts. Capital allowances amounted to £96,000.
(*ix*)   Net trading profit (before taking into account (*ii*), (*iii*), and (*iv*)) was £360,000.
(*x*)   The corporation tax due for 19X3 was paid on 1 October 19X4. Corporation tax for the year to 31 December 19X4 is expected to be £95,000.

You are required to:
(*a*) Draw up the double entry accounts recording the above (except bank).
(*b*) Show the relevant extracts from the profit and loss account for the year and balance sheet at the year end.

Question 8.3 is a typical professional examination question. It is not easy. Remember to bring forward the balances from the previous year which will often have to be deduced. The letters (A) to (L) against the information will make it easier for you to check your answer against that given at the back of the book.

8.3   Corporation tax for financial years 19X1, 19X2, and 19X3 was 35 per cent and income tax for each year was 25 per cent.

(A)   Barnet Ltd's draft profit and loss account for the year ended 31 December 19X2 shows net trading profit of £560,000. This figure is before taking into account (B) and (C1) and (C2).
(B)   Debenture interest paid on 30 November 19X2 (gross) was £80,000. Ignore accruals.
(C1) Fixed rate interest received is £24,000 (net). Date received 31 October 19X2. Ignore accruals.
(C2) A dividend of £900 was received from CD Ltd on 1 September.
(D)   Depreciation, already charged before calculating net trading profit, was £50,000. This compares with £90,000 capital allowances given by the Inland Revenue. There is to be full provision for all timing differences for 19X2.
(E)   The income tax bill (net) in respect of (B) and (C1) was paid on 15 December 19X2.
(F)   Preference dividend paid on 30 June 19X2 £18,000.
(G)   Ordinary interim dividend paid 15 July 19X2 £75,000.
(H)   Proposed final ordinary dividend for 19X2 (paid in 19X3) was £120,000.
(I)   Proposed final ordinary dividend for 19X1 (paid 31 March 19X2) was £90,000.

(J) There was a credit balance on deferred taxation account on 31 December 19X1 of £67,000.

(K) Tax for 19X1 had been provided for at £115,000 but was finally agreed at £112,000 (paid on 30 September 19X2).

(L) Corporation tax for 19X2 is estimated to be £154,000.

You are required to enter up the following accounts for the year ended 31 December 19X2 for Barnet Ltd: Deferred tax; Income tax; Interest receivable; Debenture interest; Investment income; Corporation tax; Tax on profit on ordinary activities; Preference dividends; Ordinary dividends; Profit and loss account extract. Also Balance sheet extracts as at 31 December 19X2.

8.4A KK Ltd has a trading profit, before dealing with any of the undermentioned items, for the year ended 31 December 19X9 of £200,000. You are to complete the profit and loss account for the year.

(a) The standard rate of income tax is taken as being 30 per cent.

(b) KK Ltd has bought £80,000 of 10 per cent debentures in another company. KK Ltd receives its interest, less income tax, for the year on 15 December 19X9.

(c) KK has issued £150,000 of 8 per cent debentures, and pays interest, less income tax for the year on 20 December 19X9.

(d) No cheque has been paid to the Inland Revenue for income tax.

(e) KK Ltd has a liability for corporation tax, based on the year's profits for 19X9, of £97,000.

(f) KK Ltd owns 60,000 ordinary shares of £1 each in GHH Ltd, and receives a cheque for the dividend of 20 per cent in November 19X9. GHH Ltd is neither a subsidiary company nor a related company.

(g) KK Ltd proposed a dividend of 15 per cent on the 100,000 ordinary shares of £1 each, payable out of the profits for 19X9.

(h) Transfer £20,000 to general reserve.

(i) Unappropriated profits brought forward from last year amounted to £19,830.

8.5 BG Ltd has a trading profit for the year ended 31 December 19X7, before dealing with the following items, of £50,000. You are to complete the profit and loss account.

(a) The standard rate of income tax is taken as being 30 per cent.

(b) BG Ltd had £40,000 of 9 per cent debentures. It sent them cheques for debenture interest for the year less income tax, on 31 December 19X7.

(c) BG Ltd had bought £10,000 of 11 per cent debentures in another company. It received a year's interest, less income tax, on 30 December 19X7.

(d) No cheque has been paid to the Inland Revenue for income tax.

(e) BG Ltd had bought 15,000 ordinary shares of £1 each in MM Ltd. MM Ltd paid a dividend to BG Ltd of 20 per cent on 30 November 19X7. MM Ltd is a 'related company'.

(f) BG Ltd had a liability for corporation tax, based on profits for 19X7, of £24,000.

(g) BG proposed a dividend of 30 per cent on its 70,000 ordinary shares of £1 each, out of the profits for 19X7.

(h) Transfer £5,000 to general reserve.

(i) Unappropriated profits brought forward from last year amounted to £9,870.

8.6 The following information relates to Kemp plc for the year to 31 March 19X9: £m

		£m
1	Dividends	
	Proposed final ordinary dividend for the year to 31 March 19X8 paid on 31 August 19X8	28
	Interim ordinary dividend paid on 31 December 19X8	12
	Proposed final ordinary dividend for the year 31 March 19X9 to be paid on 31 July 19X9	36

2   Deferred taxation account
    Credit balance at 1 April 19X8   3
    During the year to 31 March 19X9 a transfer of £5 million was made from the
    profit and loss account to the deferred taxation account.

3   Tax rates
    Corporation tax 35 per cent
    Income tax 25 per cent

Required:

Write up the following accounts for the year to 31 March 19X9, being careful to insert the
appropriate date for each entry, and to bring down the balances as at 31 March 19X9:

(*i*)   ordinary dividends;

(*ii*)   deferred taxation.

(*Association of Accounting Technicians*)

8.7A   The following figures appeared in W Ltd's balance sheet at 31 March 19X2:

Current liability – corporation tax	£600,000
Deferred taxation	£300,000

During the year ended 31 March 19X3, W Ltd made a payment of £520,000 to the Collector of
Taxes in settlement of the company's corporation tax for the year ended 31 March 19X2. Dividend
payments totalling £60,000 were made during the year ended 31 March 19X2 and a further
dividend of £200,000 had been proposed at the year end.

Two dividend payments were made during the year ended 31 March 19X3. A payment of
£200,000 was made in respect of the final dividend for the year ended 31 March 19X2. An interim
dividend of £40,000 was paid in respect of the year ended 31 March 19X3. These payments were
made in May 19X2 and September 19X2 respectively. The directors have provided a final dividend
of £240,000 for the year ended 31 March 19X3.

W Ltd received a dividend of £12,000 from a UK quoted company. This was received in August
19X2.

W Ltd's tax advisers believe that corporation tax of £740,000 will be charged on the company's
profits for the year ended 31 March 19X3. This amount is net of the tax relief of £104,000 which
should be granted in respect of the exceptional loss which the company incurred during the year. It
has been assumed that corporation tax will be charged at a rate of 35%. The basic rate of income
tax was 25%.

It has been decided that the provision for deferred tax should be increased by £20,000. No
provision is to be made in respect of timing differences of £400,000.

You are required:

(*a*)   to prepare the note which will support the figure for the provision for corporation tax in W
        Ltd's published profit and loss account for the year ended 31 March 19X3;

(*b*)   to calculate the liability for corporation tax which will appear in W Ltd's published balance
        sheet at 31 March 19X3;

(*c*)   to prepare the deferred tax note which will support the figure for the liability which will
        appear in W Ltd's published balance sheet at 31 March 19X3.

(*Chartered Institute of Management Accountants*)

9

Provisions, reserves and liabilities

Objectives

After you have studied this chapter, you should:

- *be aware of the difference between a 'provision' and a 'liability'*
- *be aware of the difference between revenue and capital reserves*
- *know how capital reserves may be used*
- *know what normally comprises distributable profit*

9.1 Provisions

A **provision** is an amount written-off or retained by way of providing for depreciation, renewals or diminution in value of assets, or retained by way of providing for any known liability of which the amount cannot be determined with 'substantial' accuracy. This therefore covers such items as **provisions for depreciation**. A **liability** is an amount owing which can be determined with substantial accuracy.

Sometimes, therefore, the difference between a provision and a liability hinges around what is meant by 'substantial' accuracy. Rent owing at the end of a financial year would normally be known with precision; this would obviously be a liability. Legal charges for a court case which has been heard, but for which the lawyers have not yet submitted their bill, would be a provision. The need for the distinction between liabilities and provisions will not become obvious until Chapter 12, where the requirements of the Companies Acts regarding disclosures in the final accounts are examined.

9.2 Revenue reserves

A **revenue reserve** is where an amount has been voluntarily transferred from the profit and loss appropriation account by debiting it, thus reducing the amount of profits left available for cash dividend purposes, and crediting a named **reserve account**. The reserve may be for some particular purpose, such as a **foreign exchange reserve account** created just in case the firm should ever meet a situation where it would suffer loss because of devaluation of a foreign currency, or it could be a **general reserve account**.

Such transfers are, in fact, an indication to the shareholders that it would be unwise at that particular time to pay out all the available profits as dividends. The resources represented by part of the profits should more wisely and profitably be kept in the firm, at least for the time being. Revenue reserves can be called upon in future years to help swell the profits shown in the profit and loss appropriation account as being available for dividend purposes. This is effected quite simply by debiting the particular reserve account and crediting the profit and loss appropriation account.

9.3 General reserve

A general reserve may be needed because of the effect of inflation. If in the year 19X3 a firm needs a working capital of £4,000, the volume of trade remains the same for the next three years but the price level increases by 25 per cent, then the working capital requirements will now be £5,000. If all the profits are distributed, the firm will still only have £4,000 working capital which cannot possibly finance the same volume of trade as it did in 19X3. Transferring annual amounts of profits to a general reserve instead of paying them out as dividends is one way to help overcome this problem. On the other hand it may just be the convention of conservatism asserting itself, with a philosophy of 'it's better to be safe than sorry', in this case to restrict dividends because the funds they would withdraw from the business may be needed in a moment of crisis. This is sometimes overdone, with the result that the firm has excessive amounts of liquid funds being inefficiently used, whereas if they were paid out to the shareholders, who after all are the owners, then the shareholders could put the funds to better use themselves.

This then leaves the question of the balance on the profit and loss appropriation account if it is a credit balance. Is it a revenue reserve? There is no straightforward answer to this; the fact that it has not been utilised for dividend purposes could mean that it has been deliberately held back and as such could be classified as a revenue reserve. On the other hand, there may be a balance on the account just because it is inconvenient to pay dividends in fractions of percentages.

9.4 Capital reserves

A **capital reserve** is normally quite different from a revenue reserve. It is a reserve which is not available for transfer to the profit and loss appropriation account to swell the profits shown as available for cash dividend purposes. Most capital reserves can never be utilised for cash dividend purposes; notice the use of the word 'cash', as it will be seen later that bonus shares may be issued as a 'non-cash' dividend.

The ways that capital reserves are created must therefore be looked at.

Capital reserves created in accordance with the Companies Acts

The Companies Acts state that the following are capital reserves and can never be utilised for the declaration of dividends payable in cash:

(a) capital redemption reserve – see Chapter 6;
(b) share premium account – see Chapter 5;
(c) revaluation reserve – where an asset has been revalued then an increase is shown by a debit in the requisite asset account and a credit in the Revaluation Account. The recording of a reduction in value is shown by a credit in the asset account and a debit in the Revaluation Account.

Capital reserves created by case law

Distributable profits per the Companies Acts have been described earlier in this volume.

The definition includes the words 'in accordance with principles generally accepted'. As accounting develops and changes there will obviously be changes made in the 'principles generally accepted'.

There are quite a few law cases decided to establish exactly whether an item would be a distributable profit or not and therefore available for cash dividend purposes. This makes the difference as to whether an item should be transferred to a capital reserve account as not being distributable, or else to a revenue reserve account if it is distributable. These cases will have to be studied at the more advanced stages of accounting, and so will not be dealt with here.

9.5 Capital reserves put to use

These can only be used in accordance with the Companies Acts. The following description of the actions which can be taken assumes that in fact the articles of association are the same as Table A for this purpose, and that therefore there are no provisions in the articles to prohibit such actions.

Capital redemption reserve (for creation *see* Chapter 6)

(*a*) To be applied in paying up unissued shares of the company as fully paid shares. These are commonly called 'bonus shares', and are dealt with in Chapter 10.

(*b*) Can be reduced only in the manner as to reduction of share capital (*see* Chapter 10).

(*c*) Can be reduced, in the case of a private company, where the permissible capital payment is greater than the nominal value of shares redeemed/purchased (*see* Chapter 6).

Share premium account (for creation *see* Chapter 5)

(*a*) The same provision referring to bonus shares as exists with the capital redemption reserve.

(*b*) Writing off preliminary expenses.

(*c*) Writing off expenses and commission paid on the issue of shares or debentures.

(*d*) In writing off discounts on shares or debentures issued (for creation of these accounts, *see* Chapter 5).

(*e*) Providing any premium payable on redemption or purchases of shares or debentures.

Revaluation reserve

Where the directors are of the opinion that any amount standing to the credit of the revaluation reserve is no longer necessary then the reserve must be reduced accordingly. An instance of this would be where an increase in the value of an asset had been credited to the revaluation account, and there had subsequently been a fall in the value of that asset.

The revaluation reserve may also be reduced where the permissible capital payment exceeds the nominal value of the shares redeemed/purchased.

Profits prior to incorporation (for creation *see* Chapter 7)

These can be used for the issuing of bonus shares, in paying up partly paid shares, or alternatively they may be used to write down goodwill or some such similar fixed asset.

Created by case law

These can be used in the issue of bonus shares or in the paying up of partly paid shares.

9.6 Distributable profit

Distributable profits have already been defined. Accounting Standards will apply unless they come into conflict with the Companies Acts themselves.

Normally the revenue reserves, including any credit balance on the profit and loss account, would equal distributable profit.

Development costs

Under Section 269, any development costs which have been capitalised have to be deducted from distributable profits, *unless* there are special circumstances justifying the capitalisation. Normally this means that SSAP 13 (Research and development) will apply.

Depreciation on revalued assets

There is a conflict here between SSAP 12 (Depreciation) and the Companies Acts. The Companies Acts require depreciation on revalued assets to be based on the revalued amounts. However, the Companies Acts allow the extra depreciation because of the revaluation to be *added back* when calculating distributable profit.

Distributions in kind

Where a company makes a non-cash distribution, for example by giving an investment, and that item (i.e. in this case the investment) has been revalued, it could generally be said that part of the distribution was unrealised profit locked into investment. However, the Companies Acts allow this because the 'unrealised' profit is 'realised' by the distribution (from the company's viewpoint, anyway).

9.7 Distributions and auditors' reports

The Companies Acts prohibit any particular distribution if the auditor's report is qualified, with one exception. That is that if the amount involved is *not* material and the auditor agrees to this fact, then distribution of an item can take place.

If a distribution is unlawfully made, any member knowing it to be so could be made to repay it. If the company could not recover such distributions then legal proceedings could be taken against the directors.

New terms

Provision (p. 138): An amount written-off or retained by way of providing for depreciation, renewals or diminution in value of assets, or retained by way of providing for any known liability of which the amount cannot be determined with 'substantial accuracy'.

Revenue reserves (p. 138): A balance of profits retained available to pay cash dividends including an amount voluntarily transferred from the profit and loss appropriation account by debiting it, reducing the amount of profits left for cash dividend purposes, and crediting a named reserve account, such as a general reserve.

Capital reserve (p. 139): A reserve which is a balance of profit retained that can never be used for the payment of cash dividends. These are normally created specifically under the provisions of the Companies Acts. Examples include a capital redemption reserve and a share premium account.

Main points to remember

1 Provisions involve uncertainty over the precise amount involved, it being impossible to determine the amount with 'substantial' accuracy.

2 Liabilities can be determined with 'substantial' accuracy.

3 There are two main categories of reserves:
   (*a*) revenue reserves (can be freely distributed); and
   (*b*) capital reserves (subject to restrictions on their distribution).

Review question

9.1 An extract from the draft accounts of Either Ltd at 30 November 19X5 shows the following figures before allowing for any dividend which might be proposed:

	£000
Ordinary shares of £1 each	400
6% preference shares of £1 each	150
Capital redemption reserve	300
Revaluation reserve	125
General reserve	80
Profit and loss account	13
	1,068
Operating profit before taxation for the year	302
Taxation	145
	£157

Additional information includes:
(*i*) The revaluation reserve consists of an increase in the value of freehold property following a valuation in 19X3. The property concerned was one of three freehold properties owned by the company and was subsequently sold at the revalued amount.
(*ii*) It has been found that a number of stock items have been included at cost price, but were being sold after the balance sheet date at prices well below cost. To allow for this, stock at 30 November 19X5 would need to be reduced by £35,000.
(*iii*) Provision for directors' remuneration should be made in the sum of £43,000.

(*iv*) Included on the balance sheet is £250,000 of research and development expenditure carried forward.

(*v*) No dividends have yet been paid on either ordinary or preference shares for the year to 30 November 19X5, but the directors wish to pay the maximum permissible dividends for the year.

(*vi*) Since the draft accounts were produced it has been reported that a major customer of Either Ltd has gone into liquidation and is unlikely to be able to pay more than 50p in the £ to its creditors. At 30 November 19X5 this customer owed £60,000 and this has since risen to £180,000.

(*vii*) It has been decided that the depreciation rates for plant and machinery are too low but the effect of the new rates has not been taken into account in constructing the draft accounts. The following information is available:

	£
Plant and machinery	
Purchases at the commencement of the business on	
1 December 19X1 cost	100,000
Later purchases were: 1 June 19X3	25,000
29 February 19X4	28,000
31 May 19X4	45,000
1 December 19X4	50,000

In the draft financial statements depreciation has been charged at the rate of 25 per cent using the reducing balance method and charging a full year's depreciation in the year of purchase. It has been decided to change to the straight line method using the same percentage but charging only an appropriate portion of the depreciation in the year of purchase. There have been no sales of plant and machinery during the period.

Required:

(*a*) Calculate the maximum amount which the directors of Either Ltd may propose as a dividend to be paid to the ordinary shareholders whilst observing the requirements of the Companies Acts. Show all workings and state any assumptions made.

(*b*) Outline and discuss any differences which might have been made to your answer to (*a*) if the company were a public limited company.

For the purposes of this question you may take it that corporation tax is levied at the rate of 50 per cent.

(*Association of Chartered Certified Accountants*)

10

The increase and reduction of the share capital of limited companies

Objectives

After you have studied this chapter, you should:

- *be aware of the various ways in which a limited company may alter its share capital*
- *know the difference between a 'bonus' issue and a 'rights' issue of shares*
- *understand why a company may introduce a scheme for the reduction of its capital*
- *be aware of the effect upon the balance sheet of bonus issues, rights issues and schemes for the reduction of capital*

10.1 Alteration of capital

A limited company may, if so authorised by its articles, and if the correct legal formalities are observed, alter its share capital in any of the following ways.

1   Increase its share capital by new shares, e.g. increase authorised share capital from £5,000 to £15,000.
2   Consolidate and divide all or any of its share capital into shares of a larger amount than its existing shares, for instance to make 5,000 ordinary shares of £1 each into 1,000 ordinary shares of £5 each.
3   Convert all or any of its paid-up shares into stock, and reconvert that stock into shares of any denomination, e.g. 10,000 ordinary shares of £1 each made into £10,000 ordinary stock.
4   Subdivide all, or any, of its shares into shares of smaller denominations, e.g. 1,000 ordinary shares of £6 each made into 2,000 ordinary shares of £3 each, or 3,000 ordinary shares of £2 each, etc.
5   Cancel shares which have not been taken up. This is 'diminution' of capital, not to be confused with reduction of capital described later in the chapter. Thus a firm with an authorised capital of £10,000 and an issued capital of £8,000 can alter its capital to be authorised capital £8,000 and issued capital £8,000.

10.2 Bonus shares

These are shares issued to existing shareholders free of charge. An alternative name is **scrip issue**.

If the articles give the power, and the requisite legal formalities are observed, the following may be applied in the issuing of bonus shares:

1   the balance of the profit and loss appropriation account;
2   any other revenue reserve;
3   any capital reserve, e.g. share premium.

This thus comprises all of the reserves.

The reason why this should ever be needed can be illustrated by taking the somewhat exaggerated example shown in Exhibit 10.1.

Exhibit 10.1

A company, Better Price Ltd, started business 50 years ago with 1,000 ordinary shares of £1 each and £1,000 in the bank. The company has constantly had to retain a proportion of its profits to finance its operations, thus diverting them from being used for cash dividend purposes. Such a policy has conserved working capital.

The firm's balance sheet as at 31 December 19X7 is shown as:

Better Price Ltd

Balance Sheet as at 31 December 19X7
(before bonus shares are issued)

	£
Fixed assets	5,000
Current assets *less* current liabilities	5,000
	10,000
Share capital	1,000
Reserves (including profit and loss appropriation balance)	9,000
	10,000

If in fact an annual profit of £1,500 was now being made, this being 15 per cent on capital employed, and £1,000 could be paid annually as cash dividends, then the dividend declared each year would be 100 per cent, i.e. a dividend of £1,000 on shares of £1,000 nominal value. It is obvious that the dividends and the share capital have got out of step with one another. Employees and trade unions may well become quite belligerent, as owing to the lack of accounting knowledge, or even misuse of it, it might be believed that the firm was making unduly excessive profits. Customers, especially if they are members of the general public, may also be deluded into thinking that they are being charged excessive prices, or, even though this could be demonstrated not to be true because of the prices charged by competitors, they may well still have the feeling that they are somehow being duped.

In point of fact, an efficient firm in this particular industry or trade may well be only reasonably rewarded for the risks it has taken by making a profit of 15 per cent on capital employed. The figure of 100 per cent for the dividend is due to the very misleading convention in accounting in the UK of calculating dividends in relationship to the nominal amount of the share capital.

If it is considered, in fact, that £7,000 of the reserves could not be used for dividend purposes, due to the fact that the net assets should remain at £8,000, made up of fixed assets £5,000 and working capital £3,000, then besides the £1,000 share capital which cannot be returned to the shareholders there are also £7,000 reserves which cannot be rationally returned to them. Instead of this £7,000 being called reserves, it might as well be called capital, as it is needed by the business on a permanent basis.

To remedy this position, as well as some other needs less obvious, bonus shares were envisaged. The reserves are made non-returnable to the shareholders by being converted into share capital. Each holder of one ordinary share of £1 each will receive seven bonus shares (in the shape of seven ordinary shares) of £1 each. The balance sheet, if the bonus shares had been issued immediately, would then appear:

Better Price Ltd

Balance sheet as at 31 December 19X7
(after bonus shares are issued)

	£
Fixed assets	5,000
Current assets *less* current liabilities	5,000
	10,000
Share capital (£1,000 + £7,000)	8,000
Reserves (£9,000 − £7,000)	2,000
	10,000

When the dividends of £1,000 per annum are declared in the future, they will amount to:

$$\frac{£1,000}{£8,000} \times \frac{100}{1} = 12.5 \text{ per cent}$$

This will cause less disturbance in the minds of employees, trade unions and customers.

Of course the issue of bonus shares may be seen by any of the interested parties to be some form of diabolical liberty. To give seven shares of £1 each free for one previously owned may be seen as a travesty of social justice. In point of fact the shareholders have not gained at all. Before the bonus issue there were 1,000 shareholders who owned between them £10,000 of net assets. Therefore, assuming just for this purpose that the book 'value' is the same as any other 'value', each share was worth £10. After the bonus issue each previous holder now has eight shares for every one share he held before. If he had owned one share only, he now owns eight shares. He is therefore the owner of $\frac{8}{8,000}$ part of the firm, i.e. a one thousandth part. The 'value' of the net assets are £10,000, so that he owns £10 of them, so his shares are worth £10. This is exactly the same 'value' as that applying before the bonus issue was made.

It would be useful, in addition, to refer to other matters for comparison. Anyone who had owned a £1 share 50 years ago, then worth £1, would now have (if he was still living after such a long time) eight shares worth £8. A new house of a certain type 50 years ago might have cost £x; it may now cost £$8x$. The cost of a bottle of beer may now be y times greater than it was 50 years ago, a packet of cigarettes may be z times more and so on. Of course, the firm has brought a lot of trouble on itself by waiting so many years to capitalise reserves. It should have been done by several stages over the years.

This is all a very simplified, and in many ways an exaggerated version. There is, however, no doubt that misunderstanding of accounting and financial matters has caused a great deal of unnecessary friction in the past and will probably still do so in the future. Yet another very common misunderstanding is that the assumption the reader was asked to accept, namely that the balance sheet values equalled 'real values', is often one taken by the reader of a balance sheet. Thus a profit of £10,000 when the net assets' book values are £20,000 may appear to be excessive, yet in fact a more realistic value of the assets may be saleable value − in this case the value may be £100,000.

The accounting entries necessary are to debit the reserve accounts utilised, and to credit a bonus account. The shares are then issued and the entry required to record this is to credit the share capital account and to debit the bonus account. The journal entries would be:

The Journal

	Dr	Cr
	£	£
Reserve account(s) (show each account separately)	7,000	
Bonus account		7,000
Transfer of an amount equal to the bonus payable in fully paid shares		
Bonus account	7,000	
Share capital account		7,000
Allotment and issue of 7,000 shares of £1 each, in satisfaction of the bonus declared		

10.3 Rights issue

A company can also increase its share capital by making a **rights issue**. This is the issue of shares to existing shareholders at a price lower than the ruling market price of the shares.

The price at which the shares of a very profitable company are quoted on the Stock Exchange is usually higher than the nominal value of the shares. For instance, the market price of the shares of a company might be quoted at £2.50 while the nominal value per share is only £1.00. If the company has 8,000 shares of £1 each and declares a rights issue of one for every eight held at a price of £1.50 per share, it is obvious that it will be cheaper for the existing shareholders to buy the rights issue at this price instead of buying the same shares in the open market for £2.50 per share. Assume that all the rights issue were taken up, then the number of shares taken up will be 1,000 (i.e. 8,000 ÷ 8), and the amount paid for them will be £1,500. The journal entries will be:

The Journal

	Dr	Cr
	£	£
Cash	1,500	
Share capital		1,000
Share premium		500
Being the rights issue of 1 for every 8 shares held at a price of £1.50 nominal value being £1.00		

It is to be noted that because the nominal value of each share is £1.00 while £1.50 was paid, the extra 50p constitutes a share premium to the company.

Notice also that the market value of the shares will be reduced or 'diluted' by the rights issue, as was the case for bonus shares. Before the rights issue there were 8,000 shares at a price of £2.50, giving a market capitalisation of £20,000. After the issue there are 9,000 shares and the assets have increased by £1,500. The market value may therefore reduce to £2.39 [(20,000 + 1,500)/9,000)], although the precise market price at the end of the issue will have been influenced by the information given surrounding the sale about the future prospects of the company and may not be exactly the amount calculated.

10.4 Reduction of capital

Where capital is not represented by assets

Any scheme for the reduction of capital needs to go through the legal formalities via the shareholders and other interested parties, and must receive the consent of the court. It is assumed that all of this has been carried out correctly.

Capital reduction means in fact that the share capital – all of it if there is only one class such as ordinary shares, or all or part of it if there is more than one class of shares – has been subjected to a lessening of its nominal value, or of the called-up part of the nominal value. Thus:

(a) a £4 share might be made into a £3 share;
(b) a £5 share might be made into a £1 share;
(c) a £3 share, £2 called up, might be made into a £1 share fully paid up;
(d) a £5 share, £3 called up, might be made into a £3 share £1 called up;

plus any other variations.

Why should such a step be necessary? The reasons are rather like the issue of bonus shares in reverse. In this case the share capital has got out of step with the assets, in that the share capital is not fully represented by assets. Thus Robert Ltd may have a balance sheet as follows:

Robert Ltd

Balance Sheet as at 31 December 19X7

	£
Net assets	30,000
Ordinary share capital	
10,000 ordinary shares of £5 each fully paid	50,000
Less Debit balance – profit and loss account	20,000
	30,000

The net assets are shown at £30,000, it being felt in this particular firm that the book value represented a true and fair view of their 'actual value'. The company will almost certainly be precluded from paying dividends until the debit balance on the profit and loss appropriation account has been eradicated and a credit balance brought into existence. Some firms, in certain circumstances, may still pay a dividend even though there is a debit balance, but it is to be assumed that Robert Ltd is not one of them. If profits remaining after taxation are now running at the rate of £3,000 per annum, it will be more than seven years before a dividend can be paid. As the normal basic reason for buying shares is to provide income, although there may well enter another reason such as capital appreciation, the denial of income to the shareholders for this period of time is serious indeed.

A solution would be to cancel, i.e. reduce, the capital which was no longer represented by assets. In this case there is £20,000 of the share capital which can lay no claim to any assets. The share capital should therefore be reduced by £20,000. This is done by making the shares into £3 shares fully paid instead of £5 shares. The balance sheet would become:

Robert Ltd
Balance Sheet as at 31 December 19X7

	£
Net assets	30,000
	30,000
Ordinary share capital	30,000
	30,000

Now that there is no debit balance on the profit and loss appropriation account the £3,000 available profit next year can be distributed as dividends.

Of course, the firm of Robert Ltd is very much a simplified version. Very often both preference and ordinary shareholders are involved and sometimes debenture holders as well. Even creditors occasionally sacrifice part of the amount owing to them, the idea being that the increase in working capital so generated will help the firm to achieve prosperity, in which case the creditors hope to enjoy the profitable contact that they used to have with the firm. The whole of these capital reduction schemes are matters of negotiation between the various interested parties. For instance, preference shareholders may be quite content for the nominal value of their shares to be reduced if the rate of interest they receive is increased. As with any negotiation the various parties will put forward their points of view and discussions will take place, until eventually a compromise solution is arrived at. When the court's sanction has been obtained, the accounting entries are:

(a) For amounts written off assets:
>   *Debit* Capital reduction account.
>   *Credit* Various asset accounts.

(b) For reduction in liabilities (e.g. creditors):
>   *Debit* Liability accounts.
>   *Credit* Capital reduction account.

(c) The reduction in the share capital:
>   *Debit* Share capital accounts (each type).
>   *Credit* Capital reduction account.

(d) If a credit balance now exists on the capital reduction account:
>   *Debit* Capital reduction account (to close).
>   *Credit* Capital reserve.

It is very unlikely that there would ever be a debit balance on the capital reduction account, as the court would very rarely agree to any such scheme which would bring about that result.

Capital reduction schemes for private companies will be used less frequently with the advent of powers to companies to purchase their own shares. The new powers given will normally be more suitable for private companies.

Where some of the assets are no longer needed

Where some of the firm's assets are no longer needed, probably due to a contraction in the firm's activities, a company may find itself with a surplus of liquid assets. Subject to the legal formalities being observed, in this case the reduction of capital is effected by returning cash to the shareholders, i.e.:

(a) *Debit*   Share capital account (with amount returnable).
  Credit Sundry shareholders.
(b) *Debit*   Sundry shareholders.
  Credit Bank (amount actually paid).

Such a scheme could be objected to by the creditors if it affected their interests.

New terms

Bonus shares (p. 145): Shares issued to existing shareholders free of charge. (Also known as 'scrip' issues.)

Rights issue (p. 147): Shares issued to existing shareholders at a price below their current market price.

Main points to remember

1   A limited company may alter its share capital if it is authorised to do so by its Articles of Association.

2   Alterations to share capital can be made by a limited company:
   (a) issuing new shares;
   (b) consolidating all or any of its share capital into shares of a higher nominal value;
   (c) converting paid-up shares into debentures and then reconverting the debentures back into shares of another denomination;
   (d) subdividing all or any of its share capital into shares of a lower nominal value;
   (e) cancelling shares that have not been 'taken up' – the difference between the 'authorised share capital' and the 'issued share capital'.

3   Where share capital is overvalued in relation to assets, a capital reduction scheme may be adopted in order to bring the share capital into line with the underlying asset value of the business as reported in the balance sheet.

Review questions

10.1   The Merton Manufacturing Co Ltd has been in business for many years making fitted furniture and chairs. During 19X4 and 19X5 substantial losses have been sustained on the manufacture of chairs and the directors have decided to concentrate on the fitted furniture side of the business which is expected to produce a profit of a least £22,500 per annum before interest charges and taxation. A capital reduction scheme has been proposed under which:

(i)   a new ordinary share of 50p nominal value will be created;
(ii)   the £1 ordinary shares will be written off and the shareholders will be offered one new ordinary share for every six old shares held;
(iii)   the £1 6 per cent redeemable preference shares will be cancelled and the holders will be offered for every three existing preference shares, one new ordinary share and £1 of a new 8 per cent debenture;
(iv)   the existing 11½ per cent debenture will be exchanged for a new debenture yielding 8 per cent and in addition existing debenture holders will be offered one new ordinary share for every £4 of the old debenture held;
(v)   existing reserves will be written off;
(vi)   goodwill is to be written off;

(*vii*) any remaining balance of write-off which is necessary is to be achieved by writing down plant and equipment; and

(*viii*) existing ordinary shareholders will be invited to subscribe for two fully paid new ordinary shares at par for every three old shares held.

The balance sheet of the Merton Manufacturing Co Ltd immediately prior to the capital reduction is as follows:

	£	£
Fixed intangible assets		
Goodwill at cost less amounts written off		50,000
Fixed tangible assets		
Freehold land and buildings at cost		95,000
Plant and equipment at cost	275,000	
Less Depreciation to date	89,500	
		185,500
		330,500
Current assets		
Stocks	25,000	
Debtors	50,000	
	75,000	

	£		
Current liabilities			
Creditors	63,500		
Bank overdraft	15,850		
		79,350	
Excess of current liabilities			(4,350)
			326,150
Long-term loan			
11½ per cent debenture, secured on the freehold land and buildings			100,000
			226,150

	£
Share capital and reserves	
£1 ordinary shares fully paid	90,000
6 per cent £1 redeemable preference shares fully paid	150,000
Share premium account	25,000
Profit and loss account	(38,850)
	226,150

On a liquidation, freehold land and buildings are expected to produce £120,000, plant and equipment £40,000, stocks £15,000 and debtors £45,000. Goodwill has no value.

There are no termination costs associated with ceasing the manufacture of chairs.

Required:

(*a*) Assuming that the necessary approval is obtained and that the new share issue is successful, produce a balance sheet of the company showing the position immediately after the scheme has been put into effect.

(*b*) Show the effect of the scheme on the expected earnings of the old shareholders.

(*c*) Indicate the points which a preference shareholder should take into account before voting on the scheme.

Corporation tax may be taken at 33⅓ per cent.

(*Association of Chartered Certified Accountants*)

10.2 Deflation Ltd, which had experienced trading difficulties, decided to reorganise its finances.

On 31 December 19X5 a final trial balance extracted from the books showed the following position:

		£	£
Share capital, authorised and issued:			
150,000 6 per cent cumulative preference shares of £1 each			150,000
200,000 ordinary shares of £1 each			200,000
Share premium account			40,000
Profit and loss account		114,375	
Preliminary expenses		7,250	
Goodwill (at cost)		55,000	
Trade creditors			43,500
Debtors		31,200	
Bank overdraft			51,000
Leasehold property	(at cost)	80,000	
,,	(provision for depreciation)		30,000
Plant and machinery	(at cost)	210,000	
,,	(provision for depreciation)		62,500
Stock in hand		79,175	
		577,000	577,000

Approval of the Court was obtained for the following scheme for reduction of capital:

1 The preference shares to be reduced to £0.75 per share.
2 The ordinary shares to be reduced to £0.125 per share.
3 One £0.125 ordinary share to be issued for each £1 of gross preference dividend arrears; the preference dividend had not been paid for three years.
4 The balance on share premium account to be utilised.
5 Plant and machinery to be written down to £75,000.
6 The profit and loss account balance, and all intangible assets, to be written off.

At the same time as the resolution to reduce capital was passed, another resolution was approved restoring the total authorised capital to £350,000, consisting of 150,000 6 per cent cumulative preference shares of £0.75 each and the balance in ordinary shares of £0.125 each. As soon as the above resolutions had been passed 500,000 ordinary shares were issued at par, for cash, payable in full upon application.

You are required:

(a) to show the journal entries necessary to record the above transactions in the company's books; and

(b) to prepare a balance sheet of the company, after completion of the scheme.

(*Institute of Chartered Accountants*)

10.3 On 31 March 19X6 the following was the balance sheet of Finer Textiles.

Balance Sheet

	£	£
Fixed assets		
Goodwill and trade marks as valued	225,000	
Plant and machinery (at cost *less* depreciation)	214,800	
Furniture and fittings (at cost *less* depreciation)	12,600	
		452,400
Current assets:		
Stock-in-trade	170,850	
Sundry debtors	65,100	
Cash in hand	150	
		236,100
		688,500
Authorised capital:		
150,000 7 per cent preference shares of £1 each	150,000	
2,100,000 ordinary shares of £0.5 each	1,050,000	
		1,200,000
Issued and fully paid capital		
150,000 7 per cent preference shares of £1 each	150,000	
1,200,000 ordinary shares of £0.5 each	600,000	
		750,000
Capital reserve		48,000
		798,000
Deduct profit and loss account (debit balance)		183,900
		614,100
Current liabilities		
Sundry creditors		31,800
Bank overdraft		42,600
		688,500

The following scheme of capital reduction was sanctioned by the Court and agreed by the shareholders:

(*i*) Preference shares were to be reduced to £0.75 each.
(*ii*) Ordinary shares were to be reduced to £0.2 each.
(*iii*) The capital reserve was to be eliminated.
(*iv*) The reduced shares of both classes were to be consolidated into new ordinary shares of £1 each.
(*v*) An issue of £150,000 8 per cent debentures at par was to be made to provide fresh working capital.
(*vi*) The sum written off the issued capital of the company and the capital reserve to be used to write off the debit balance of the profit and loss account and to reduce fixed assets by the following amounts:

Goodwill and trade marks	£210,000
Plant and machinery	£45,000
Furniture and fittings	£6,600

(*vii*) The bank overdraft was to be paid off out of the proceeds of the debentures which were duly issued and paid in full.

A further resolution was passed to restore the authorised capital of the company to 1,200,000 ordinary shares of £1 each.

Prepare journal entries (cash transactions to be journalised) to give effect to the above scheme and draw up the balance sheet of the company after completion of the scheme.

10.4A The balance sheet of Planners Ltd on 31 March 19X6 was as follows:

Balance Sheet

	£	£
Goodwill		20,000
Fixed assets		100,000
		120,000
Current assets:		
Stock	22,000	
Work in progress	5,500	
Debtors	34,000	
Bank	17,500	
		79,000
Capital expenses:		
Formation expenses		1,000
		200,000
Issued share capital:		
120,000 ordinary shares of £1 each		120,000
50,000 6 per cent cumulative preference shares of £1 each		50,000
		170,000
Less Profit and loss account debit balance		40,000
		130,000
6 per cent debentures		50,000
Current liabilities:		
Creditors		20,000
		200,000

The dividend on the preference shares is £9,000 in arrears. A scheme of reconstruction was accepted by all parties and was completed on 1 April 19X6.

A new company was formed, Budgets Ltd, with an authorised share capital of £200,000, consisting of 200,000 ordinary shares of £1 each. This company took over all the assets of Planners Ltd. The purchase consideration was satisfied partly in cash and partly by the issue, at par, of shares and debentures by the new company in accordance with the following arrangements:

1   The creditors of the old company received, in settlement of each £10 due to them, £7 in cash and three fully paid ordinary shares in the new company.
2   The holders of preference shares in the old company received seven fully paid ordinary shares in the new company to every eight preference shares in the old company and three fully paid ordinary shares in the new company for every £5 of arrears of dividend.
3   The ordinary shareholders in the old company received one fully paid share in the new company for every five ordinary shares in the old company.
4   The holders of 6 per cent debentures in the old company received £40 cash and £60 6 per cent debentures issued at par for every £100 debenture held in the old company.
5   The balance of the authorised capital of the new company was issued at par for cash and was fully paid on 1 April 19X6.
6   Goodwill was eliminated, the stock was valued at £20,000 and the other current assets were brought into the new company's books at the amounts at which they appeared in the old company's balance sheet. The balance of the purchase consideration represented the agreed value of the fixed assets.

You are required to show:
(*a*) The closing entries in the realisation account and the sundry shareholders account in the books of Planners Ltd.
(*b*) Your calculation of:
      (*i*)   the purchase consideration for the assets; and
      (*ii*) the agreed value of the fixed assets.
(*c*) The summarised balance sheet of Budgets Ltd as on 1 April 19X6.

10.5A   The summarised balance sheet of Owens Ltd at 31 December 19X9 was as follows:

	£
Freehold premises	60,000
Plant	210,000
Stock	64,000
Debtors	70,000
Development expenditure	75,000
Cash at bank	6,000
Profit and loss account	85,000
	570,000
Issued capital:	
150,000 6 per cent preference shares of £1 each	150,000
300,000 ordinary shares of £1 each	300,000
Creditors	120,000
	570,000

A capital reduction scheme has been sanctioned under which the 150,000 preference shares are to be reduced to £0.75 each, fully paid, and the 300,000 ordinary shares are to be reduced to £0.10 each, fully paid.

Development expenditure and the debit balance on profit and loss account are to be written off, the balance remaining being used to reduce the book value of the plant.

Prepare the journal entries recording the reduction scheme and the balance sheet as it would appear immediately after the reduction. Narrations are not required in connection with journal entries.

11

Accounting Standards and related documents

Objectives

After you have studied this chapter, you should:

- *know of the measures being taken by the Accounting Standards Board to develop a framework for the preparation and presentation of financial statements*

- *be aware of the full range of accounting standards currently in issue, and of their aims and objectives*

11.1 Introduction

The external users of accounts need to be sure that reliance can be placed on the methods used by a business in calculating its profits and balance sheet values. In the late 1960s there was a general outcry that the methods used by different businesses were showing vastly different profits on similar data. In the UK, a controversy had arisen following the takeover of AEI Ltd by GEC Ltd. In fighting the takeover bid made by GEC, the AEI directors had produced a forecast, in the tenth month of their financial year, that the profit before tax for the year would be £10 million. After the takeover, the accounts of AEI for that same year showed a loss of £4.5 million. The difference was attributed to being £5 million as 'matters substantially of fact' and £9.5 million to 'adjustments which remain matters substantially of judgement'.

There was a general outcry in the financial pages of the national press against the failure of the accounting profession to lay down consistent principles for businesses to follow.

In December 1969, the Institute of Chartered Accountants in England and Wales issued a *Statement of Intent on Accounting Standards in the 1970s*. The Institute set up the Accounting Standards Steering Committee in 1970. Over the following six years, they were joined by the five other UK and Irish accountancy bodies and, in 1976, the committee became the Accounting Standards Committee (ASC). The six accountancy bodies formed the Consultative Committee of Accountancy Bodies (CCAB).

Prior to the issue of any accounting standard issued by the ASC, a great deal of preparatory work was done culminating in the publication of an exposure draft (ED). Copies of the exposure draft were then sent to those with a special interest in the topic. The journals of the CCAB also give full details of the exposure drafts. After full and proper consultation, when it was seen to be desirable, an accounting standard on the topic was issued. The Standards issued by the ASC were called Statements of Standard Accounting Practice (SSAPs).

Because the ASC had to obtain approval from its six professional accountancy body members, it did not appear to be as decisive and independent as was desired and, in 1990, a new body, the Accounting Standards Board (ASB), took over the functions of the ASC. The ASB is more independent of the accounting bodies and can issue its recommendations, known as Financial Reporting Standards (FRSs), without approval from any other body. The ASB has accepted the SSAPs in force and these will remain effective until replaced by an FRS. As with the ASC, the ASB issues exposure drafts – FREDs! – developed in a similar fashion to before.

While there is no general law compelling observation of the standards, accounting standards have had statutory recognition since the Companies Act 1989 was issued. As a result, apart from entities exempted from certain standards or sections within standards – SSAPs 13 (Research and development) and 25 (Segmental reporting), and FRS 1 (Cash flow statements), for example, all contain exemption clauses based on company size – accounting standards must be complied with when preparing financial statements intended to present a true and fair view. The Companies Acts state that failure to comply with the requirements of an accounting standard must be explained in the financial statements.

The main method of ensuring compliance with the standards has been through the professional bodies' own disciplinary procedures on their members. The ASB has, however, set up a Review Panel that has power to prosecute companies under civil law where their financial statements contain a major breach of the standards.

This book deals with the main outlines of all SSAPs and FRSs issued to November 1998. It does not deal with all the many detailed points contained in the standards and exposure drafts. It would be a far larger book if this was attempted. Students at the later stages of their professional examinations will need to get full copies of all standards and study them thoroughly [*see also* J Blake, *Accounting Standards* and A Sangster, *Workbook of Accounting Standards* (Financial Times Pitman Publishing)].

This chapter deals with all the current SSAPs, FRSs and related documents which are not covered in detail elsewhere.

11.2 International Accounting Standards

The International Accounting Standards Committee (IASC) was established in 1973. Representatives from each of the founder members, which include the UK, sit on the committee, as well as co-opted members from other countries.

The need for an IASC has been said to be mainly due to the following:

(*a*) The considerable growth in international investment means it is desirable to have similar methods the world over so that investment decisions are more compatible.
(*b*) The growth in multinational firms which have to produce accounts covering a large number of countries. Standardisation between countries makes the accounting work easier, and reduces costs.
(*c*) As quite a few countries now have their own standard setting bodies, it is desirable that their efforts should be harmonised.
(*d*) For poor countries which cannot afford to have standard setting bodies, the IASC can help by letting them use the international standards instead of setting their own standards.

In the United Kingdom the FRSs have precedence over International Accounting Standards. In fact, most of the provisions of International Accounting Standards are incorporated into existing SSAPs and FRSs. Each FRS indicates the level of compliance with the relevant IAS.

11.3 Statement of Principles

In 1991, the Accounting Standards Board proposed a statement of the principles that underlie accounting and financial reporting. In its initial parts this closely followed the IASC text *Framework for the Preparation and Presentation of Financial Statements*. The objective of the ASB draft *Statement of Principles* is to assist the ASB, and all other users of financial statements, by clarifying the concepts that underlie the preparation and presentation of such statements. The *Statement of Principles* is not, however, an accounting standard and does not override any standard.

Scope

The ASB has indicated the following topics that will be covered in relation to financial statements (balance sheets, profit and loss accounts, cash flow statements and, following the issue of FRS 3: *Reporting financial performance*, the statement of total recognised gains and losses):

1 objectives;
2 attributes necessary to fulfil purpose;
3 elements making them up;
4 when items should be recognised;
5 how net resources and performance are measured and changes in these;
6 how items can best be presented;
7 the principles underlying consolidations and related matters.

The users identified by the ASB are the same as those shown in Chapter 30, and they are not reproduced here.

Objectives

'The objective of Financial Statements is to provide information about the financial position, performance and financial adaptability of an enterprise, that is useful to a wide range of users in making economic decisions.'

It is recognised, however, that financial statements alone will not be sufficient for economic decision making since they portray past events and may not include important non-financial information.

The assessment of management stewardship is also recognised, i.e. accountability of management for resources entrusted to it.

In covering the areas of financial position, performance and cash flow the *Statement of Principles* deals with those areas included in the analysis of accounts through ratios, e.g. liquidity and profitability, and indicates that the accounts should assist such analysis.

Qualitative characteristics of financial information

Exhibit 11.1 shows in diagrammatic form the structure adopted. The numbers in each box refer to explanations given below.

Note 1

Materiality means that if omission or mis-statement of some information would influence a decision, then it is material. Information which is not material is therefore not useful and beyond the threshold for inclusion.

Exhibit 11.1

THE QUALITATIVE CHARACTERISTICS OF ACCOUNTING INFORMATION

Reproduced with the permission of the Accounting Standards Board

Note 2

To be useful, information must be relevant to the decision-taking needs of users. Relevance relates to the influence of the information on the user's evaluation of events – past, present or future. This evaluation can be influenced by the way items in accounts are presented.

Note 3

Reliability means information free from material error and bias and which can be relied on by users to conform with descriptions given.

It is clear that information may be very relevant but unreliable – e.g. a betting tip at a horse race. Reliability may not ensure relevance, e.g. reliable analysis of last year's performance may exclude very important indicators of future potential, such as new management in position. *Relevance* and *reliability* are primary characteristics of accounting information. They are broken down into further characteristics as follows:

Relevance
Note 4

Predictive value means using an analysis of current or past performance to predict a future outcome. The same information can be used to confirm whether predictions in past periods have come true.

Confirmatory value is this second part, i.e. checking past predictions.

Note 5

The term 'choice of aspect' implies that there may be significant choice for the preparer of accounts as to which aspects of transactions to represent. For example, a business might acquire a new building in a good position for trading and on which it owns the freehold. Another relevant piece of information is that the property is in an area proposed for a new motorway and could well be the subject of a compulsory purchase order. To be relevant to a user who wishes to value the business for future prospects, both aspects of the information are relevant. Note that a simple statement that the property was owned and showing its purchase price would be a valid description and measurement and therefore reliable – so far as it went.

Reliability
Note 6

Substance indicates that information should represent the events it purports to represent. Sometimes complex legal arrangements may be entered into to obscure the ownership of assets. To be reliable the true operation and ownership of the assets re the substance must be reflected in the accounts. Artificial legal transactions should not obscure the substance.

Note 7

Although the title indicates the intention, it is important to relate this aspect of reliability to Note 5 'choice of aspect'. 'Valid description and measurement' needs to be applied to the appropriate aspects of events.

Note 8

This indicates that incomplete information may make it false or misleading and thus not relevant.

Note 9

Neutrality implies freedom from bias. This indicates that accounts should not be prepared with the intention of influencing decisions in any particular way.

Note 10

Prudence is the concept already described in the earlier chapters and in relation to SSAP 2. It implies a degree of caution (anticipating losses) in the valuation of assets. In many cases this is subjective as it relates to the future, e.g. in predicting doubtful debts. This aspect should not be used to overestimate potential losses and thus misrepresent the affairs of an organisation.

In the second part of the chart, secondary characteristics which, if lacking, would limit the usefulness of the information are shown. The titles of these are self-explanatory and are not discussed further in this text.

11.4 SSAP 1: Accounting for associated companies

Except for smaller entities applying the FRSSE (*Financial reporting standard for smaller entities*, issued in November 1997), this standard was superseded by FRS 9 (*Associates and joint ventures*) issued in November 1997. Both SSAP 1 and FRS 9 are dealt with in Chapter 29 of this book.

11.5 SSAP 2: Disclosure of accounting policies

This standard, issued in 1971, does not set out to give a basic theoretical framework of accounting. It accepts the view that there may well be more than one accounting method which could be adopted in many cases, as the circumstances of different organisations will vary. Such varying practices may well be suitable in particular cases, but the users of accounting statements should be made aware of which practice has been used in each case.

SSAP 2 requires disclosure when the generally accepted accounting concepts are not complied with. The ones specifically mentioned as being generally applied are *accruals*, *consistency*, *going concern*, and *prudence*. SSAP 2 does not mention other concepts and conventions generally recognised in the academic world, described in Volume 1, although it accepts that there are other concepts than the four mentioned. This has been confirmed since SSAP 2 was first issued, a number of other concepts having been formally introduced by the Companies Acts and other accounting standards: the Companies Act 1985 introduced the concept of 'separate determination' – each item included in the financial statements must be evaluated separately before being included in the total for its class. FRS 2: *Accounting for subsidiary undertakings* introduced the 'control' concept, and FRS 5: *Reporting the substance of transactions* introduced the 'substance over form' concept.

Accounting bases are the methods which could be used in applying the concepts. It should be recognised that these are subject to limitations imposed by adherence to legislation and accounting standards. At the same time, management must exercise its own judgement in choosing the bases to apply in their particular circumstances.

Accounting policies are the accounting bases judged by management to be the most appropriate. There should be a note attached to the accounts explaining the policies chosen. Five examples are given to illustrate where judgements may easily vary:

1 methods of depreciating fixed assets;
2 the valuation of stocks and of work in progress;
3 capitalisation of development expenditure;
4 the recognition of profit on long-term contracts;
5 hire purchase or instalment transactions.

11.6 SSAP 3: Earnings per share

This standard was replaced in 1998 by FRS 14: *Earnings per share – see* Section 11.43, below.

11.7 SSAP 4: Accounting for government grants

Many different types of grant are or have been obtainable from government departments. Where these relate to revenue expenditure, e.g. subsidies on wages, they should be credited to revenue in the period when the revenue is incurred. The principle is that the grants should be recognised in the profit and loss account so as to match with the expenditure to which they are intended to contribute.

Where there are grants relating to capital expenditure, then SSAP 4 states that they should be credited to revenue *over the expected useful economic life of the asset*. This may be achieved by treating the amount of the grant as a deferred income, a portion of which is credited to the profit and loss account annually, over the life of the asset, on a basis consistent with depreciation. The amount of the deferred credit should, if material, be shown separately. It should not be shown as part of shareholders' funds.

The same effect as treating the grant as deferred income would be achieved by crediting the grant to the fixed asset account and depreciating only the net balance of the cost of the asset over its lifetime (depreciation is thus reduced by the grant). However, although this method is acceptable in principle, it is considered to be illegal under the Companies Act 1985, para. 17 of Schedule 4, which requires the balance sheet value of a fixed asset to be its purchase price or production cost.

11.8 SSAP 5: Accounting for value added tax

All that needs to be noted here is that Volume 1 of this book deals with SSAP 5. There is no need here to go into further detail.

11.9 SSAP 6: Extraordinary items and prior year adjustments

This standard has now been replaced by FRS 3 (*see* Section 12.9).

11.10 SSAP 7: Accounting for changes in the purchasing power of money

This was the original standard on inflation accounting, later replaced by SSAP 16.

11.11 SSAP 8: The treatment of taxation under the imputation system in the accounts of companies

Part of this standard is no longer relevant after the repeal with effect from 1999 of *advanced corporation tax* (ACT). Chapter 8 of this book adheres throughout to the remainder of this SSAP.

11.12 SSAP 9: Stocks and long-term contracts

Due to the many varying kinds of businesses and conditions in companies, there simply cannot be one system of valuation for stocks and work in progress. All that the standard can do is to narrow down the different methods that could be used.

Stocks should be stated at the total of the lower of cost and net realisable value of the separate items of stock or of groups of similar items. Profit should not, except in the case of long-term contracts, be recognised in advance, but immediate account should be made for anticipated losses.

In the balance sheet (or in the notes), stocks should be sub-classified so as to indicate the amounts held in each of the main categories in the standard balance sheet formats (as adapted where appropriate) of the Companies Act 1985. (These categories are *raw materials and consumables, work in progress, finished goods and goods for resale*, and *payments on account*.)

Net realisable value consists of the expected selling price less any expenses necessary to sell the product. This may be below cost because of obsolescence, deterioration and similar factors. SSAP 9 also defines 'cost' and certainly in the case of a manufacturing business it will also include overhead expenses, so that prime cost could not be used. **Cost** is defined in SSAP 9 in relation to the different categories of stocks and work in progress as being:

> that expenditure which has been incurred in the normal course of business in bringing the product or service to its present location and condition. This expenditure should include, in addition to cost of purchase [as defined later] such costs of conversion [as defined later] as are appropriate to that location and condition.

Cost of purchase comprises purchase price including import duties, transport and handling costs and any other directly attributable costs, less trade discounts, rebates and subsidies.

Cost of conversion comprises:

(a) costs which are specifically attributable to units of production, i.e. direct labour, direct expenses and subcontracted work;
(b) production overheads (as defined later);
(c) other overheads, if any, attributable in the particular circumstances of the business to bringing the product or service to its present location and condition.

Production overheads based on the normal level of activity, taking one year with another, should all be included including fixed production overheads. Obviously, neither selling nor general administration costs should be included in cost.

Notice that abnormal costs should not be included, as they should not have the effect of increasing stock valuation.

The LIFO and base stock methods should not be used, as they do not provide an up-to-date valuation. Although LIFO is not accepted by the SSAP, the Companies Act 1985 accepts its use.

The Standard does accept that replacement cost may, in certain circumstances, be acceptable and therefore the lower of replacement or net realisation value may be used since, again, this is in accord with the Companies Act 1985.

Long-term contract work

Chapter 16 of this book deals with long-term contracts.

11.13 SSAP 10: Statement of source and application of funds

This was replaced by FRS 1: *Cash flow statements*, covered in Chapter 15 of this book.

11.14 SSAP 11: Deferred tax

The original standard on deferred tax, replaced in 1978 by SSAP 15 (*see* Chapter 8).

11.15 SSAP 12: Accounting for depreciation

This standard applies to all fixed assets, except for:

1 investment properties, dealt with in SSAP 19;
2 goodwill, dealt with in SSAP 22 and FRS 10;
3 development costs, dealt with in SSAP 13;
4 investments.

First of all some terms are defined:

- **Depreciation:** is the measure of wearing out, consumption or other reduction in the useful economic life of a fixed asset whether arising from use, effluxion of time or obsolescence through technological or market changes.
- **Useful economic life:** of an asset is the period over which the present owner will derive economic benefits from its use.
- **Residual value:** is the realisable value of the asset at the end of its economic life, based on prices prevailing at the date of acquisition or revaluation, where this has taken place. Realisation costs should be deducted in arriving at residual values.
- **Recoverable amount:** is the greater of the net realisable value of an asset (at the date of the balance sheet) and where appropriate, the amount recoverable from its further use.

Depreciation should be provided in respect of all fixed assets which have a finite useful economic life. It should be provided by allocating the cost less net realisable value over the periods expected to benefit from the use of the asset being depreciated. No depreciation method is prescribed, but the method selected should be that which produces the most appropriate allocation of depreciation to each period in relation to the benefit being received in that period through use of the asset. The depreciation should be calculated on the value as shown on the balance sheet and not on any other figure. It *must* be charged against the profit and loss account, and *not* against reserves.

Useful economic lives should be reviewed on a regular basis, normally at least every five years. Where the amended asset life would materially distort future results if treated normally, it should be treated as an exceptional item as defined by FRS 3: *Reporting financial performance* and included under the same statutory format heading as the ongoing depreciation charge.

The depreciation method may only be changed when to do so will result in an improvement in the true and fair view. A change in method does not constitute a change in accounting policy. When the method is changed, the net book value should be depreciated over the remaining useful economic life of the asset, commencing with the period when the change occurred. Where a change of method occurs, the effect, if material, should be shown as a note attached to the financial statements.

Urgent Issues Task Force (UITF) Abstract 5, issued in July 1992, introduced rules relating to situations where current assets are included in the balance sheet at the lower of cost and net realisable value. Specifically, it addressed the question of an appropriate transfer value when a current asset becomes a fixed asset through its being retained for use on a continuing basis. (This could arise, for example, when a motor dealer removes a second-hand car from sale and provides it as a company car to the company secretary.) To avoid entities being able to effect transfers from current assets to fixed assets at above net realisable value and subsequently write down the value through a debit to a revaluation reserve, UITF 5 requires that all such transfers are done at the lower of cost and net realisable value, with any diminution in value at that point being charged in the profit and loss account.

Asset revaluation

Asset revaluation is recommended and if a policy of revaluation is adopted, the valuations should be kept up to date. Any permanent reduction should be written off immediately, the remainder being written off over the asset's remaining useful economic life. Such adjustments are via the profit and loss account.

Depreciation should be charged irrespective of when the asset was revalued. According to paragraph 21 of FRS 3: *Reporting financial performance*, the profit or loss on the disposal of an asset should be accounted for in the profit and loss account of the period in which the disposal occurs as the difference between the net sale proceeds and the net carrying amount, whether carried at historical cost (less any provisions made) or at a valuation.

An increased value arising from a revaluation does not mean that depreciation should not be charged. The new value is the one on which future depreciation should be based. Depreciation charged before revaluation should not be credited back to profit and loss.

Land and buildings

Freehold land

As this normally lasts forever there is no need to depreciate, unless subject to depletion or loss of value for reasons which may be applicable in certain circumstances, such as desirability of location, land erosion, extraction of minerals, dumping of toxic waste, etc.

It is rare to encounter circumstances under which freehold land should be subject to depreciation. The problem that most often occurs is the distinction between the cost/value of freehold land and the cost/value of the buildings upon it. SSAP 12 implies that the distinction should be made as only the buildings should be depreciated. Failure to separate the two elements of the cost/value will result in non-compliance with the standard.

Buildings

These should be depreciated, except that if the amount is not material and their life is expected to be very long then there will be no need to charge depreciation. If estimated residual value equals or is more than net value depreciation can be ignored.

Notes to accounts

The following should be disclosed:

1   method of depreciation used;
2   economic life or depreciation rate in use;
3   total depreciation for period;
4   depreciable assets – gross amount and accumulated depreciation.

11.16 SSAP 13: Accounting for research and development

SSAP 13 divides research and development expenditure under three headings, except for the location or exploitation of oil, gas or mineral deposits, or where all expenditure will be reimbursed by a third party. The three headings are:

(a) **pure (or basic) research:** experimental or theoretical work undertaken primarily to acquire new scientific or technical knowledge for its own sake rather than directed towards any specific aim or application;

(b) **applied research:** original or critical investigation undertaken in order to gain new scientific or technical knowledge and directed towards a specific practical aim or objective;

(c) **development:** use of scientific or technical knowledge in order to produce new or substantially improved materials, devices, products or services, to install new processes or systems prior to the commencement of commercial production or commercial applications, or to improve substantially those already produced or installed.

Expenditure incurred on pure and applied research can be regarded as part of a continuing operation required to maintain a company's business and its competitive position. In general, one particular period rather than another will not be expected to benefit and therefore it is appropriate that these costs should be written-off as they are incurred.

The development of new and improved products is, however, distinguishable from pure and applied research. Expenditure on such development is normally undertaken with a reasonable expectation of specific commercial success and of future benefits arising from the work, either from increased revenue and related profits or from reduced costs. However, development expenditure should be written-off in the year of expenditure, except in the following circumstances when it may be deferred to future periods:

1 there is a clearly defined project; and
2 the related expenditure is separately identifiable; and
3 the outcome of such a project has been assessed with reasonable certainty as to:
   (a) its technical feasibility; and
   (b) its ultimate commercial viability considered in the light of factors such as:
      (i)   likely market conditions (including competing products);
      (ii) public opinion;
      (iii) consumer and environmental legislation;
4 furthermore, a project will be of value only if:
   (a) the aggregate of the deferred development cost and any further development costs to be incurred on the same project together with related production, selling and administration costs is reasonably expected to be exceeded by related future revenues; and
   (b) adequate resources exist, or are reasonably expected to be available, to enable the project to be completed and to provide any consequential increases in working capital.

The elements of uncertainty inherent in the considerations set out in points 1 to 4 are considerable. There will be a need for different persons having differing levels of judgement to be involved in assessing the technical, commercial and financial viability of the project. Combinations of the possible different assessments which they might validly make can produce widely differing assessments of the existence and amounts of future benefits.

If these uncertainties are viewed in the context of the concept of prudence, the future benefits of most development projects would be too uncertain to justify carrying the expenditure forward. Nevertheless, in certain industries it is considered that there are numbers of major development projects that satisfy the stringent criteria set out above.

The Standard says that if the criteria are satisfied then expenditure may be deferred to the extent that its recovery can reasonably be regarded as assured. It is also required that where this policy is adopted, all projects meeting the criteria should be included.

If development costs are deferred, they should be amortised over the period of sale or use of the product.

At each accounting date the unamortised balance of development expenditure should be examined project by project to ensure that it still fulfils the criteria. Where any doubt exists as to the continuation of those circumstances the balance should be written-off.

Fixed assets may be acquired or constructed in order to provide facilities for research and/or development activities. The use of such fixed assets will usually extend over a number of accounting periods and accordingly they should be capitalised and written-off over their usual life.

The Standard requires that accounting policy on research and development expenditure should be stated and explained. The total amount of research and development expenditure charged in the profit and loss account should be disclosed, analysed between the current year's expenditure and amounts amortised from deferred expenditure. Movement on deferred expenditure and the amount carried forward at the beginning and end of the period should be disclosed. Deferred development expenditure should be disclosed under intangible fixed assets in the balance sheet.

11.17 SSAP 14: Group accounts

This Standard was replaced in 1992 by FRS 2: *Accounting for subsidiary undertakings* (*see* Chapter 29).

11.18 SSAP 15: Accounting for deferred taxation

The description of the methods of accounting for deferred taxation is given in Chapter 8. It follows SSAP 15 exactly and there is no need to repeat it here.

11.19 SSAP 16: Current cost accounting

The outlines of this outdated and suspended SSAP are given in Chapter 33 of this book.

11.20 SSAP 17: Accounting for post-balance sheet events

Quite often there will be events occurring after a balance sheet date which will provide evidence of the value of assets, or of the amounts of liabilities, as at the balance sheet date. Obviously any event up to the balance sheet date will have affected the balance sheet. Once the board of directors have formally approved the financial statements it becomes impossible to alter them. However, there is the period between these dates during which events may throw some light upon the valuation of assets or amounts of liabilities. SSAP 17 directs its attention to such events during this period.

SSAP 17 brings in two new terms – 'adjusting events' and 'non-adjusting events'.

Adjusting events

These are events which provide additional evidence relating to conditions existing at the balance sheet date. They require changes in amounts to be included in financial statements. Examples of adjusting events are now given:

(a) **Fixed assets.** The subsequent determination of the purchase price or of the proceeds of sale of assets purchased or sold before the year end.

(b) **Property.** A valuation which provides evidence of a permanent diminution in value.

(c) **Investments.** The receipt of a copy of the financial statements or other information in respect of an unlisted company which provides evidence of a permanent diminution in the value of a long-term investment.

(d) **Stocks and work in progress:**
  (i) the receipt of proceeds of sales after the balance sheet date or other evidence concerning the net realisable value of stocks;
  (ii) the receipt of evidence that the previous estimate of accrued profit on a long-term contract was materially inaccurate.

(e) **Debtors.** The renegotiation of amounts owing by debtors, or the insolvency of a debtor.

(f) **Dividends receivable.** The declaration of dividends by subsidiaries and associated companies relating to periods prior to the balance sheet date of the holding company.

(g) **Taxation.** The receipt of information regarding rates of taxation.

(h) **Claims.** Amounts received or receivable in respect of insurance claims which were in the course of renegotiation at the balance sheet date.

(i) **Discoveries.** The discovery of errors or frauds which show that the financial statements were incorrect.

Non-adjusting events

These are events which arise after the balance sheet date and concern conditions which did not exist at that time. Consequently they do not result in changes in amounts in financial statements. They may, however, be of such materiality that their disclosure is required by way of notes to ensure that financial statements are not misleading. Examples of non-adjusting events which may require disclosure are now given:

(a) **Mergers and acquisitions.**

(b) **Reconstructions** and proposed reconstructions.

(c) **Issues** of shares and debentures.

(d) **Purchases and sales of fixed assets** and investments.

(e) **Loss of fixed assets** or stocks as a result of a catastrophe such as fire or flood.

(f) **Opening new trading activities** or extending existing trading activities.

(g) **Closing a significant part** of the trading activities if this was not anticipated at the year end.

(h) **Decline in the value** of property and investments held as fixed assets, if it can be demonstrated that the decline occurred after the year end.

(i) **Changes in rates of foreign exchange.**

(j) **Government action,** such as nationalisation.

(k) **Strikes** and other labour disputes.

(l) **Augmentation of pension benefits.**

11.21 SSAP 18: Accounting for contingencies

This standard was replaced in 1998 by FRS 12: *Provisions, contingent liabilities and contingent assets* – *see* Section 11.41, below.

11.22 SSAP 19: Accounting for investment properties

Under the accounting requirements of SSAP 12: *Accounting for depreciation*, fixed assets are generally subject to annual depreciation charges to reflect on a systematic basis the wearing out, consumption or other loss of value whether arising from use, effluxion of time or obsolescence through technology and market changes. Under those requirements it is also accepted that an increase in the value of such a fixed asset does not generally remove the necessity to charge depreciation to reflect on a systematic basis the consumption of the asset.

A different treatment is, however, required where a significant proportion of the fixed assets of an enterprise is held not for consumption in the business operations but as investments, the disposal of which would not materially affect any manufacturing or trading operations of the enterprise. In such a case the current value of these investments, and changes in that current value, are of prime importance rather than a calculation of systematic annual depreciation. Consequently, for the proper appreciation of the financial position, a different accounting treatment is considered appropriate for fixed assets held as investments (called in this standard 'investment properties').

Investment properties may be held by a company which holds investments as part of its business such as an investment trust or a property investment company.

Investment properties may also be held by a company whose main business is not the holding of investments.

Where an investment property is held on a lease with a relatively short unexpired term, it is necessary to recognise the annual depreciation in the financial statements to avoid the situation whereby a short lease is amortised against the investment revaluation reserve whilst the rentals are taken to the profit and loss account.

This statement requires investment properties to be included in the balance sheet at open market value. The statement does not require the valuation to be made by qualified or independent valuers, but calls for disclosure of the names or qualifications of the valuers, the bases used by them and whether the person making the valuation is an employee or officer of the company. However, where investment properties represent a substantial proportion of the total assets of a major enterprise (e.g. a listed company) the valuation thereof would normally be carried out:

(*a*) annually by persons holding a recognised professional qualification and having recent post-qualification experience in the location and category of the properties concerned; and

(*b*) at least every five years by an external valuer.

11.23 SSAP 20: Foreign currency translation

The rules of SSAP 20 are already shown in Chapter 1 of this book. There is only need here for a few extra comments.

Hyper-inflation

If there is hyper-inflation the methods described in Chapter 1 may not give a fair view of the results. In these cases it may first of all be necessary to produce accounts adjusted for inflation. However, no guidance is provided in the standard as to how to define a 'high rate' of inflation or how to perform the adjustment to current price. UITF 9: *Accounting for operations in hyper-inflationary economies*, was issued in June 1993 in order to clarify this area.

UITF 9 confirmed that adjustments are required when the hyper-inflationary impact will affect the true and fair view. It also states that adjustments are required where the cumulative inflation rate over three years is approaching or exceeds 100 per cent – effectively a 'rule-of-thumb' definition of the term 'hyper-inflation'.

It suggested two methods that could be adopted in order to eliminate the distortions caused by hyper-inflation. (If neither was deemed suitable, the reason(s) should be stated and another method should be adopted.) Either the local currency financial statements should be adjusted to reflect current price levels before being translated, or a relatively stable currency (e.g. the US dollar or sterling) should be used as the currency of measurement (the *functional* currency) for the relevant foreign operations. In the latter case, the functional currency would effectively be the *local* currency as defined in SSAP 20; and, if the transactions are not initially recorded in the functional currency, they must be measured in that currency by applying the temporal method based on the functional currency.

Hedging against exchange losses

Losses incurred may be set off against profits made in the computation of exchange dealings.

Disclosure

The method used to translate currencies should be disclosed. Net profits/net losses on translation must be disclosed, irrespective of whether they are shown in the profit and loss account or as a movement of reserves.

11.24 SSAP 21: Accounting for leases and hire purchase contracts

Details of SSAP 21 are given in Chapter 2.

11.25 SSAP 22: Accounting for goodwill

Except for smaller entities applying the FRSSE (*Financial reporting standard for smaller entities*, issued in November 1997), this standard was superseded by FRS 10 (*Goodwill and intangible assets*) issued in December 1997 – *see* Section 11.39, below. For application to those smaller entities to which it still applies at September 1998, a brief summary of SSAP 22 is as follows:

1   No amount should be attributed to non-purchased goodwill in the balance sheet of companies or groups.

2   Where goodwill is purchased, the account should be the difference between the fair

value of the consideration given (the price paid) and the aggregate of the fair value of the net assets acquired.

3 The amount attributed to purchased goodwill should not include any value for intangible items. The amount paid for these should be included under the heading for intangible assets in the balance sheet.

4 Purchased goodwill should not remain on the balance sheet as a permanent item. It may either be:
   (*a*) written-off immediately on acquisition against reserves; or
   (*b*) amortised by charges against the profit and loss on ordinary activities over its useful economic life.

5 Where the fair value of the assets acquired exceeds the fair value of the consideration given (negative goodwill), the excess should be credited directly to reserves.

6 It should not be revalued but, if there is a permanent diminution in its value, it should be written-down immediately through the profit and loss account to its estimated recoverable amount.

Note: In the chapters dealing with consolidated financial statements, a figure for goodwill will often be calculated. It must be borne in mind that this is subject to the contents of FRS 10 (or SSAP 22, if the entity is a small enterprise applying the FRSSE) just as much as for a company simply buying the business of a sole trader or partnership.

11.26 SSAP 23: Accounting for acquisitions and mergers

This Standard was replaced by FRS 6: *Acquisitions and mergers* in 1994 (*see* Chapter 28).

11.27 SSAP 24: Accounting for pension costs

The details may have to be studied if you proceed to a higher level in accounting. Basically the objective is that the employer should recognise the expected cost of providing pensions on a 'systematic and rational basis' over the period during which he/she derives benefit from the employees' services.

11.28 SSAP 25: Segmental reporting

This Standard was introduced to help interpret the requirement of the Companies Act 1985 that the information in the accounts should be broken down (segmented) in two principal ways – by class of business and geographically. A **class of business** is a distinguishable component of an entity that provides a separate product or service. A **geographical segment** is an area comprising an individual country or group of countries in which an entity operates.

   The main provisions of the Standard can be summarised in brief as follows. If an entity has two or more classes of business and operates in two or more geographical segments, then it should report for each class and segment:

(*a*) **turnover** – split between that to external activities and that to other segments;
(*b*) **result**, i.e. profit before taxation, minority interest and extraordinary items;
(*c*) **net assets**.

11.29 Statements of Recommended Practice and UITF Consensus Pronouncements

In 1986 the Accounting Standards Committee (ASC) issued the first Statement of Recommended Practice (SORP). It is important to note that they are different from accounting standards. Provisions in standards must be carried out, unless there is sufficient and adequate evidence to prove otherwise and, in addition, any non-compliance must be clearly stated. A SORP simply sets out what is considered to be the best practice on a particular topic, in respect of which it is not considered suitable to issue a standard at that time. Companies are simply encouraged to use the SORP. No action will be taken by the accounting bodies if a SORP is not followed.

A sub-category of SORPs was introduced, called 'franked SORPs'. Generally these refer to topics which are of limited application for a specific industry and they are not included in this text.

The Accounting Standards Board will not issue its own SORPs. In the event that the ASB's own authority is required to standardise practice within a specialised industry, the ASB's preference is to issue an industry standard if the issue cannot be resolved under the existing accounting standards.

In 1991, the ASB set up a committee known as the Urgent Issues Task Force (UITF). This committee assists the ASB in areas where an accounting standard or Companies Act provision exists but where unsatisfactory or conflicting interpretations have developed or seem likely to do so. In these circumstances, the UITF issues a 'consensus pronouncement' (or 'abstract'). The ASB considers that compliance with consensus pronouncements will form an important element in detecting whether accounts give a true and fair view. Consequently, they have the same status as accounting standards and *must* be observed. As at September 1998, 22 UITF Abstracts had been issued, of which 19 were still in force (the others having been withdrawn following the issue of FRSs 3 and 4). In addition, a further UITF (UITF 3) was withdrawn by FRS 10 other than for smaller entities applying the FRSSE. Wherever appropriate, UITFs are included in this book when the topic to which they relate is being discussed.

11.30 FRS 1: Cash flow statements

See Chapter 15.

11.31 FRS 2: Accounting for subsidiary undertakings

See Chapter 29.

11.32 FRS 3: Reporting financial performance

See Chapter 12.

11.33 FRS 4: Capital instruments

FRS 4 is concerned with accounting for capital instruments by the entities that issue them.

A capital instrument is anything issued to raise finance. This includes shares, debentures, loans and debt instruments, and options and warrants that give the holder the right to subscribe for or obtain capital instruments. The term includes those issued by subsidiaries, except when held by another member of the group. Leases, warrants issued under employee share schemes, and equity shares issued as part of a business combination that is accounted for as a merger are not covered by FRS 4. Nor are investments in capital instruments issued by other entities.

The objective of FRS 4 is to ensure that financial statements provide a clear, coherent and consistent treatment of capital instruments, in particular in relation to:

- the classification of capital instruments;
- treating the costs associated with capital instruments in a manner consistent with their classification (and allocated to accounting periods on a fair basis over the period the instrument is in issue, in the case of redeemable instruments);
- ensuring that financial statements provide relevant information concerning the nature and amount of the entity's sources of finance and the associated costs, commitments and potential commitments.

All capital instruments should be accounted for in the balance sheet within one of the following categories:

- shareholders' funds;
- liabilities; or, for consolidated financial statements,
- minority interests.

Shares and warrants should be reported as part of shareholders' funds. When issued, the net proceeds should be reported in the reconciliation of movements in shareholders' funds. When repurchased or redeemed, shareholders' funds should be reduced by the value of the consideration given. The balance sheet should show the total amount of shareholders' funds, analysed between the amount attributable to non-equity interests (i.e. the aggregate of amounts relating to all classes of non-equity shares and warrants for non-equity shares) and the amount attributable to equity interests (i.e. the difference between total shareholders' funds and the total amount attributable to non-equity interests). When the entitlement to dividends in respect of non-equity shares is calculated by reference to time, the dividends should be reported as appropriations of profit and accounted for on an accruals basis except when ultimate payment is remote (for example, when profits are insufficient to justify a dividend and the dividend rights are non-cumulative). Where the finance costs of non-equity shares are not equal to the dividends, the difference should be accounted for in the profit and loss account as an appropriation of profit. The finance costs for non-equity shares should be calculated on the same basis as the finance costs for debt.

All capital instruments other than shares should be classified as liabilities if they contain an obligation to transfer economic benefits. Otherwise, they should be reported within shareholders' funds. Convertible debt should be reported separately within liabilities from non-convertible debt. Debt should be analysed on the basis of its maturity distinguishing between debt with up to one year, one to five years, and five or more years to maturity, maturity being determined on the basis of the earliest date on which the lender can require payment. The finance cost of convertible debt should be calculated on the basis that the debt will never be converted. When converted, the amount recognised in shareholders' funds in respect of the shares issued should be the amount at which the liability for the debt is stated at the date of conversion, and therefore no gain or loss should be recognised. When issued, debt should be stated at the amount of the net proceeds and its finance cost should be allocated over the term of the debt at a constant rate on the carrying amount, charged in the profit and loss account (unless the entity is an investment company, in which case it may be included in the statement of total gains and losses to the extent that it relates to capital). The carrying amount of debt should be increased by the finance cost in respect of the reporting period and reduced by payments made in respect of the debt in that period. Accrued finance costs may be included in accruals (rather than in the carrying amount of debt) to the extent that the period costs have accrued in one period and will be paid in cash in the next. However, in the event that the debt is repurchased or settled early, any such accrual should be included in the carrying amount of the debt for the purposes of calculating finance costs and gains and losses on the transaction, and any such gains or losses should be recognised in the profit and loss account in the period during which the transaction occurs.

Where subsidiaries have issued shares outside the group, those shares should be reported as minority interests, unless the group as a whole has an obligation to transfer economic benefit in connection with the shares. In such cases, they should be accounted for as liabilities within the consolidated financial statements. The amount of minority interests in the balance sheet should be split between the amounts attributable to equity and non-equity interests, the calculation of the amounts attributed to non-equity minority interests (and their associated finance costs) being calculated in the same way as those for non-equity shares. The finance costs associated with such interests should be included in minority interests in the profit and loss account.

11.34 FRS 5: Reporting the substance of transactions

The purpose of FRS 5 is to ensure that the substance of an entity's transactions is reported in its financial statements. The commercial effect of the entity's transactions, and any resulting assets, liabilities, gains or losses, should be faithfully represented in its financial statements.

The standard does not apply to:

- forward contracts and futures;
- foreign exchange and interest rate swaps;
- contracts where a net amount will be paid or received based on a movement in a price or an index;
- expenditure commitments and orders placed, until the earlier of delivery or payment;
- employment contracts.

In determining the substance of a transaction, all its aspects and implications should be identified and greater weight given to those more likely to have a commercial effect in practice. Where a group or series of transactions achieve, or are intended to achieve, an overall commercial effect, they should be viewed as a whole, not as individual transactions.

The substance of a transaction depends upon whether it has given rise to new assets or liabilities for the reporting entity, and whether it has changed the entity's existing assets and liabilities. An entity has rights or other access to benefits (and therefore has an asset) if the entity is exposed to the risks inherent in the benefits, taking into account the likelihood of those risks having a commercial effect. Evidence that an obligation to transfer benefits (i.e. a liability) exists is shown if there is some circumstance in which the entity cannot avoid, legally or commercially, an outflow of benefits.

Where an asset or a liability results from a transaction, it should be recognised in the balance sheet if there is sufficient evidence of its existence (including, where relevant, any future inflow or outflow of benefit), and if it can be measured at a monetary amount with sufficient reliability.

Where transactions have no significant effect upon either the entity's rights or other access to benefits arising from a previously recognised asset, or to the entity's exposure to the risks inherent in those benefits, the entire asset should continue to be recognised. When the transactions transfer *all* the significant rights or other access to benefits *and all* the significant exposure to risk, the entire asset should cease to be recognised. Where a stage between nil and full effect is found, and it is a significant change, the description or monetary amounts relating to an asset should be changed and a liability recognised for any obligations to transfer benefits that are assumed. However, the standard also states that this partial case arises in only three situations:

1 a transfer of only part of the item;
2 a transfer of all of the item for only part of its life;
3 a transfer of all of the item for all of its life but where the entity retains some significant right to benefits or exposure to risk.

Where a transaction is in substance a financing of a recognised asset (whether previously recognised or not) the finance should be shown deducted from the gross amount of the item it finances on the face of the balance sheet within a single asset caption of 'linked presentation'. The gross amounts of both the item and the finance should be shown on the face of the balance sheet. Profit on a linked presentation should be recognised on entering into the arrangement only to the extent that the non-returnable proceeds received exceed the previous carrying value of the item. Thereafter, any profit or loss arising should be recognised in the period in which it arises, both in the profit and loss account and in the notes.

Assets and liabilities should not be offset, except where they do not constitute separate assets and liabilities.

Where an entity has a quasi-subsidiary (i.e. a company, trust, partnership or other vehicle that is directly or indirectly controlled by the reporting entity, but that is not a subsidiary, and which gives rise to benefits for the reporting entity that are in substance no different from those that would arise were the vehicle a subsidiary) the substance of the transactions entered into by the quasi-subsidiary should be reported in the consolidated statements. The fact that a quasi-subsidiary has been included in the consolidated financial statements should be disclosed and a summary of the financial statements of the quasi-subsidiary should be provided in the notes.

Disclosure of a transaction in the financial statements should be sufficient to enable the user of those statements to understand its commercial effect. Where a transaction has resulted in the recognition of assets or liabilities whose nature differs from that of items usually included under the relevant balance sheet heading, the differences should be explained.

11.35 FRS 6: Acquisitions and mergers

See Chapter 28.

11.36 FRS 7: Fair values in acquisition accounting

See Chapter 25.

11.37 FRS 8: Related party disclosures

This FRS requires disclosure of all material related party transactions. The FRS extends the disclosure requirements contained in the Companies Acts, thus providing guidance in an area that had previously not been covered adequately by either statute or the Stock Exchange rules.

11.38 FRS 9: Associates and joint ventures

See Chapter 29.

11.39 FRS 10: Goodwill and intangible assets

FRS 10 was issued in December 1997, repealing SSAP 22 other than for smaller entities applying the FRSSE (*Financial reporting standard for smaller entities*, issued in November 1997). (For details of the contents of SSAP 22, *see* Section 11.25, above.)

Although written with a focus upon goodwill arising from the acquisition of a subsidiary undertaking by a parent company that prepares consolidated accounts, the standard also applies to reporting entities acquiring a business or an investment that is accounted for using the equity method (*see* Section 29.7).

A brief summary of the FRS is as follows:

1 Positive purchased goodwill should be capitalised as an asset on the balance sheet.

2 Internally generated goodwill should not be capitalised.

3 An intangible asset acquired as part of the acquisition of a business should be capitalised separately from goodwill, initially at its fair value. Unless the asset has a readily ascertainable market value, the fair value should be limited to an amount that does not create or increase any negative goodwill arising on the acquisition.

4 An intangible asset acquired as part of the acquisition of a business whose fair value cannot be measured reliably should be included within the amount of the purchase price attributed to goodwill.

5 An intangible asset purchased separately should be capitalised at cost.

6 An internally developed intangible asset may be capitalised only if it has a readily ascertainable market value.

7 Where goodwill and intangible assets are regarded as having limited useful economic lives, they should be amortised on a systematic basis over those lives.

8 Where goodwill and intangible assets are regarded as having indefinite useful economic lives, they should *not* be amortised. A life of longer than 20 years can only be used if the durability of the acquired business or intangible asset can be demonstrated and the goodwill or intangible asset is capable of continued measurement over the period selected. Companies legislation requires goodwill to be amortised over a finite period. When no amortisation occurs, this departure from the legislation must be justified as being required in order to provide a true and fair view.

9 The useful economic lives of goodwill and intangible assets should be reviewed at the end of each reporting period and revised if necessary.

10 The straight line method of amortisation should be adopted, unless another method can be demonstrated to better reflect the expected pattern of depletion of the goodwill or intangible asset.

11 Intangible assets may be revalued but, if one is, all others of the same class must also be revalued. Any revalued intangible assets must be subject to sufficiently frequent further revaluations to ensure that the carrying value does not differ materially from

the market value at the balance sheet date.

12 Goodwill should not be revalued, except when previous adjustments for impairment losses (that arose, for example, when part of an acquired business was held to have a lower value than had been adopted at the time of acquisition) are reversed and it causes the recoverable amount of the goodwill above its current carrying value. (The same impairment-derived adjustment rules apply to intangible assets.)

13 When the fair value of the assets acquired exceed the fair value of the consideration given, the resulting negative goodwill should be recognised and separately disclosed on the face of the balance sheet immediately below the goodwill heading, followed by a subtotal showing the net amount of positive and negative goodwill.

11.40 FRS 11: Impairment of fixed assets and goodwill

This FRS was issued in July 1998. It applies to all fixed assets and purchased goodwill that is recognised in the balance sheet except:
- fixed assets within the scope of any FRS addressing disclosures of derivatives and other financial instruments. (The ASB anticipated issuing an FRS on this topic in late 1998.)
- investment properties as defined by SSAP 19 (*see* Section 11.22, above).
- an entity's own shares held by an ESOP (employee share ownership plan) and shown as a fixed asset in the balance sheet under UITF 13 (*Accounting for ESOP trusts*), and,
- costs capitalised while a field is being appraised under the Oil Industry Accounting Committee's SORP, *Accounting for oil and gas exploration and development activities.*

Investments in subsidiary undertakings, associates, and joint ventures *do* fall within the scope of FRS 11. However, smaller entities applying the FRSSE are exempt from the FRS unless required to apply it by the FRSSE as a consequence of their preparing consolidated financial statements.

A brief summary of the FRS is as follows:

1 An impairment review should be carried out if events or changes in circumstances indicate that the carrying amount of a fixed asset or of goodwill may not be recoverable.

2 Impairment is measured by comparing the carrying value of an asset with its recoverable amount (the higher of its net realisable value and its value in use).

3 Impairment losses are recognised in the profit and loss account except that impairment losses on revalued fixed assets are shown in the *Statement of total recognised gains and losses*. Impairments on both unrevalued and revalued assets below the depreciated historical cost are recognised in the profit and loss account.

4 If the recoverable amount of a previously impaired asset or investment increases because of a change in economic conditions or in the expected use of the asset, the resulting reversal of the impairment loss should be recognised in the current period to the extent that it increases the carrying amount up to the amount that it would have been had the original impairment not occurred. The reversal should be recognised in the profit and loss account unless it arises on a previously revalued fixed asset, in which case it should be recognised in the profit and loss account to the extent that the previous impairment loss (adjusted for subsequent depreciation) was recognised in the profit and loss account, any remaining impairment reversal balance being recognised in the *Statement of total recognised gains and losses*.

11.41 FRS 12: Provisions, contingent liabilities and contingent assets

This FRS was issued in September 1998, repealing SSAP 18. FRS 12 defines a provision as:

> *a liability that is of uncertain timing or amount, to be settled by the transfer of economic benefits.*

A provision should only be recognised when it is probable that a transfer of economic benefits will have to occur and a reasonable estimate can be made of the amount involved.

It defines a contingent liability as:

> *either a possible obligation arising from past events whose existence will be confirmed only by the occurrence of one or more uncertain future events not wholly within the entity's control; or a present obligation that arises from past events but is not recognised because it is not probable that a transfer of economic benefits will be required to settle the obligation or because the amount of the obligation cannot be measured with sufficient reliability.*

It defines a contingent asset as:

> *a possible asset arising from past events whose existence will be confirmed only by the occurrence of one or more uncertain events not wholly within the entity's control.*

Neither contingent liabilities nor contingent assets should be recognised.
Smaller entities applying the FRSSE are exempt from FRS 12.

11.42 FRS 13: Derivatives and other financial instruments: disclosures

This FRS was issued in September 1998. It defines a derivative as:

> *a financial instrument that derives its value from the price or rate of some underlying item. Underlying items include equities, bonds, commodities, interest rates, exchange rates, and stock market and other indices.*

The disclosures required by the standard focus mainly upon the risks that arise in connection with financial instruments and how they have been managed. It requires a range of information to be presented concerning the risks arising from the entity's financial instruments, and its attitude and response to those risks. In effect, entities are required to publish in summary form details of their loans, investments and hedging transactions.

Smaller entities applying the FRSSE are exempt from FRS 13.

11.43 FRS 14: Earnings per share

This FRS was issued in October 1998, repealing SSAP 3. The figure for earnings per share is calculated by dividing the net profit or loss attributable to ordinary shareholders by the weighted average number of ordinary shares outstanding during the period.

The FRS prescribes how to adjust the average number of shares when events occur to change the number of ordinary shares, such as bonus issues, share splits, and share consolidations. Students taking examinations which cover FRS 14 in detail should read the actual standard. It contains many examples concerning how the adjustment to the denominator should be made.

Earnings per share (EPS) is a widely used stock market measure. The FRS tries to bring about a more consistent method to aid comparability and reduce misunderstandings.

Basically, EPS is the profit per ordinary share calculated as follows:

	£	£
Profit on ordinary activities after taxation		XXXX
Extraordinary activities (less tax)		XXXX
		XXXX
Less Minority interest (see chapters on group accounts)	XXXX	
Preference dividends	XXXX	
		XXXX
Profit available to equity shareholders		XXXX

$$EPS = \frac{\text{Profit available to equity shareholders}}{\text{Number of ordinary shares}} = \text{EPS in pence}$$

As you will see later, minority interest only exists where the company controls another undertaking, and outsiders own part of that undertaking.

11.44 FRSSE: Financial reporting standard for smaller entities

The FRSSE was issued in November 1997. It may be applied to all financial statements intended to give a true and fair view of the financial position and profit or loss (or income and expenditure) of all entities that are small companies or groups or entities (other than building societies) that would be classified as such were they incorporated under companies legislation.

Small companies are defined in the FRSSE according to the definition contained in sections 247 and 247A of the Companies Act 1985 as being those that in a year satisfy at least two of the following: turnover no greater than £2.8 million, a balance sheet total no greater than £1.4 million, an average of no more than 50 employees. Other than in the case of newly incorporated companies, the condition must have been satisfied in two of the last three years. For small groups, the threshold limits are aggregate turnover not exceeding £2.8 million 'net' (i.e. after set-offs and other adjustments required by Schedule 4A of the Companies Act 1985) or £3.6 million 'gross' (i.e. before the set-offs and adjustments); aggregate balance sheet total not exceeding £1.4 million net, £1.68 million gross; and aggregate number of employees not exceeding 50. (Companies Act 1985, Sections 248 and 249.)

Application of the FRSSE is voluntary – reporting entities may chose, instead, to apply all the other accounting standards and UITFs. Those that do apply it are exempt from complying with the other accounting standards and UITFs unless preparing consolidated financial statements, in which case certain other accounting standards and UITFs apply.

The FRSSE contains a simplified, but lengthy set of requirements derived from those included in all the other standards and UITFs. It would not be appropriate to describe these in detail here. For information concerning the precise contents of the FRSSE, reference should be made to the FRSSE itself or to a book specialising in accounting standards.

Main points to remember

1 Accounting standards have statutory recognition and must, therefore, be complied with when preparing financial statements intended to present a true and fair view.

2 As at November 1998, there were 31 Accounting Standards (16 SSAPs, 14 FRSs, and one FRSSE) and 19 UITF Abstracts in force.

3 Some of the SSAPs and UITFs, including SSAPs 1 and 22 and UITF 3, have been replaced by FRSs but remain in force for entities applying the FRSSE.

Review questions

11.1 In preparing its accounts for the year to 31 May 19X7, Whiting plc had been faced with a number of accounting problems, the details of which were as follows:

(*i*) The company had closed down its entire American operations which represented a significant part of Whiting plc's business.

(*ii*) The corporation tax for the year to 31 May 19X6 had been over-provided by £5,000.

(*iii*) Land and buildings had been revalued at an amount well in excess of the historic cost (note: the current value is to be adjusted in the accounts).

(*iv*) A trade debtor had gone into liquidation owing Whiting plc an amount equivalent to 20 per cent of Whiting's turnover for the year. It is highly unlikely that any of this debt will ever be repaid.

(*v*) During the year, the company changed its method of valuing stock. If the same method had been adopted in the previous year, the profits for that year would have been considerably less than had previously been reported.

Required:

(*a*) being careful to give your reasons, explain how each of the above matters should be treated in the financial statements of Whiting plc for the year to 31 May 19X7 if the company follows the requirements of FRS 3; and

(*b*) outline the provisions of SSAP 22 (accounting for goodwill) and FRS 10 (goodwill and intangible assets) for the treatment of both non-purchased and purchased goodwill in the balance sheets of companies and groups of companies.

(*Association of Accounting Technicians*)

11.2 The directors are preparing the published accounts of Dorman plc for the year to 31 October 19X5. The following information is provided for certain of the items which are to be included in the final accounts.

(*i*) *Stocks of raw material, monolite:*

	£
Cost	26,500
Replacement cost	48,100

(*ii*) *Stocks of finished goods:*

	Paramite £	Paraton £
Direct costs	72,600	10,200
Proportion of fixed factory overhead	15,300	4,600
Proportion of selling expenses	6,870	1,800
Net realisable value	123,500	9,520

(*iii*) *Plant and machinery.* An item of plant was shown in the 19X4 accounts at a net book value of £90,000 (£160,000 cost less accumulated depreciation £70,000). The plant was purchased on 1 November 19X2 and has been depreciated at 25 per cent reducing balance. The directors now consider the straight line basis to be more appropriate: they have estimated that at 1 November 19X4 the plant had a remaining useful life of six years and will possess zero residual value at the end of that period.

(*iv*) *Freehold property.* The company purchased a freehold property for £250,000 11 years ago, and it is estimated that the land element was worth £50,000 at that date.

The company has never charged depreciation on the property but the directors now feel that it should have done so; the building is expected to have a total useful life of forty years.

(*v*) *Research expenditure:* incurred in an attempt to discover a substitute for raw materials currently purchased from a politically sensitive area of the world amounted to £17,500 during the year.

(*vi*) *Development expenditure:* on Tercil, which is nearly ready for production, amounted to £30,000. Demand for Tercil is expected significantly to exceed supply for at least the next four years.

(*vii*) *Accident.* On 1 December 19X5 there was a fire in the warehouse which damaged stocks, other than the items referred to in (*i*) and (*ii*) above. The book value of these stocks was £92,000. The company has discovered that it was underinsured and only expects to recover £71,000 from the insurers.

(*viii*) *Investments.* Dorman purchased 30,000 ordinary shares in Lilleshall Ltd on 1 November 19X4 for £96,000, and immediately succeeded in appointing two of its directors to Lilleshall's board. The issued share capital of Lilleshall consists of 100,000 ordinary shares of £1 each. The profits of Lilleshall for the year to 31 October 19X5 amounted to £40,000. (Ignore taxation.)

Required:

Explain how each of the above items should be dealt with in the published financial statements of Dorman plc.

(*Institute of Chartered Secretaries and Administrators*)

11.3A In preparing the published financial statements of a company, briefly state the significant accounting/disclosure requirements you would have in mind in ensuring that the financial statements comply with best accounting practice as embodied in accounting standards concerning:

(*a*) Value added tax.
(*b*) Earnings per share.
(*c*) The disclosure requirements of each major class of depreciable assets.
(*d*) Research expenditure.
(*e*) Capital-based grants relating to fixed assets.
(*f*) Goodwill on consolidation.
(*g*) The disclosure requirements relating to generally accepted fundamental accounting concepts.
(*h*) The accounts of a subsidiary undertaking having similar activities to that of the parent undertaking.

(*Association of Accounting Technicians*)

11.4A Oldfield Enterprises Limited was formed on 1 January 19X5 to manufacture and sell a new type of lawn mower. The bookkeeping staff of the company have produced monthly figures for the first ten months to 31 October 19X5 and from these figures together with estimates for the remaining two months, Barry Lamb, the managing director, has drawn up a forecast profit and loss account for the year to 31 December 19X5 and a balance sheet as at that date.

These statements together with the notes are submitted to the board for comment. During the board meeting discussion centres on the treatment given to the various assets. The various opinions are summarised by Barry Lamb who brings them, with the draft accounts, to you as the company's financial adviser.

Oldfield Enterprises Ltd

Draft Profit and Loss Account for the year to 31 December 19X5

	£000s	£000s
Sales		3,000
Cost of sales		1,750
Gross profit		1,250
Administration overheads	350	
Selling and distribution overheads	530	
		880
Net profit before taxation		370

Draft Balance Sheet at 31 December 19X5

Fixed assets – tangible	Cost £000s	Depreciation and Amortisation £000s	Net £000s
Leasehold land and buildings	375	125	250
Freehold land and buildings	350	–	350
Plant and machinery	1,312	197	1,115
	2,037	322	1,715
Fixed assets – intangible			
Research and development			375
Current assets			
Stock		375	
Debtors		780	
		1,155	
Current liabilities			
Creditors	250		
Bank overdraft	125	375	
			780
			2,870
Share capital			2,500
Net profit for year			370
			2,870

Notes
(a) Administration overheads include £50,000 written-off research and development.
(b) The lease is for 15 years and cost £75,000. Buildings have been put up on the leasehold land at a cost of £300,000. Plant and machinery has been depreciated at 15 per cent. Both depreciation and amortisation are included in cost of sales.

Opinions put forward
Leasehold land and buildings:
The works director thinks that although the lease provides for a rent review after three years the buildings have a 50-year life. The buildings should therefore be depreciated over 50 years and the cost of the lease should be amortised over the period of the lease.

The managing director thinks that because of the rent review clause the whole of the cost should be depreciated over three years.

The sales director thinks it is a good idea to charge as much as the profits will allow in order to reduce the tax bill.

Freehold land and buildings:

The works director thinks that as the value of the property is going up with inflation no depreciation is necessary.

The sales director's opinion is the same as for leasehold property.

The managing director states that he has heard that if a property is always kept in good repair no depreciation is necessary. This should apply in the case of his company.

Plant and machinery:

The managing director agrees with the 15 per cent for depreciation and proposes to use the reducing balance method.

The works director wants to charge 25 per cent straight line.

Research and development:

The total spent in the year will be £425,000. Of this £250,000 is for research into the cutting characteristics of different types of grass, £100,000 is for the development of an improved drive system for lawn mowers and £75,000 is for market research to determine the ideal lawn mower characteristics for the average garden.

The managing director thinks that a small amount should be charged as an expense each year.

The works director wants to write-off all the market research and 'all this nonsense of the cutting characteristics of grass'.

The sales director thinks that, as the company has only just started, all research and development expenditure relates to future sales so all this year's expenditure should be carried forward.

Stock:

Both the managing director and the works director are of the opinion that stock should be shown at prime cost.

The sales director's view is that stocks should be shown at sales price as the stock is virtually all sold within a very short period.

Required:

(a) You are asked to comment on each opinion stating what factors should be taken into account to determine suitable depreciation and write off amounts.

(b) Indicate what amounts should, in your opinion, be charged to profit and loss and show the adjusted profit produced by your recommendations, stating clearly any assumptions you may make.

(*Association of Chartered Certified Accountants*)

11.5 The accountant of Hook, Line and Sinker, a partnership of seven people, has asked your advice in dealing with the following items in the partnership accounts for the year to 31 May 19X7.

(a) (i) Included in invoices prepared and dated in June 19X7 were £60,000 of goods despatched during the second half of May 19X7.

(ii) Stocks of components at 31 May 19X7 include parts no longer used in production. These components originally cost £50,000 but have been written-down for purposes of the accounts to £25,000. Scrap value of these items is estimated to be £1,000. Another user has expressed interest in buying these parts for £40,000.

(b) After May 19X7 a customer who accounts for 50 per cent of Hook, Line and Sinker sales suffered a serious fire which has disrupted his organisation. Payments for supplies are becoming slow and Hook, Line and Sinker sales for the current year are likely to be substantially lower than previously. This customer owed £80,000 to Hook, Line and Sinker at 31 May 19X7.

(c) During the year to 31 May Hook, Line and Sinker commenced a new advertising campaign using television and expensive magazine advertising for the first time. Sales during the year were not much higher than previous years as the partners consider that the effects of advertising will be seen in future years.

Expenditure on advertising during the year is made up of:

	£
Television	50,000
Advertisements in magazines	60,000
Advertisements in local papers	25,000

All the expenditure has been treated as expense in the accounts but the partners wish to carry forward three-quarters of the television and magazine costs as it is expected that this cost will benefit future years' profits and because this year's profits will compare unfavourably with previous years if all the expenditure is charged in the accounts.

(d) Three projects for the construction of sinkers have the following cost and revenue characteristics:

	Project A	Project B	Project C
Degree of completion	75%	50%	15%
	£	£	£
Direct costs to date	30,000	25,000	6,000
Sales price of complete project	55,000	50,000	57,500
Overheads allocated to date	4,000	2,000	500
Costs to complete – Direct	10,000	25,000	40,000
– Overheads	2,000	2,000	3,000

No profits or losses have been included in the accounts.

(e) After considerable discussion with management, the sales of a newly developed special purpose hook have been given the following probabilities:

First year of production

Sales	Probability
£	
15,000	0.2
30,000	0.5
40,000	0.3

Second year of production

Increase over first year	Probability
£	
10,000	0.1
20,000	0.5
30,000	0.4

Second year sales may be assumed independent of first year levels.
Cost-volume-profit analysis shows that the breakeven point is £50,000.

Production of the special purpose hook started prior to the end of the accounting year and stocks of the finished product are included at cost amounting to £20,000. It has been decided that if there is less than 0.7 probability of breakeven being reached in the second year then stocks should be written down by 25 per cent.

(f) During the year it was discovered that some stock sheets had been omitted from the calculations at the previous year end. The effect is that opening stock for the current year, shown as £35,000, should be £42,000. No adjustment has yet been made.

Required:
Discuss the treatment of each item with reference to relevant accounting standards and accounting concepts and conventions. Recommend the appropriate treatment for each item showing the profit effect of each recommendation made.

(*Association of Chartered Certified Accountants*)

11.6 The chief accountant of Uncertain Ltd is not sure of the appropriate accounting treatment for a number of events occurring during the year 19X5/6.

(*i*) A significant number of employees have been made redundant, giving rise to redundancy payments of £100,000 which have been included in manufacturing cost of sales.

(*ii*) One of Uncertain Ltd's three factories has been closed down. Closure costs amounted to £575,000. This amount has been deducted from reserves in the balance sheet.

(*iii*) The directors have changed the basis of charging depreciation on delivery vehicles. The difference between the old and new methods amounts to £258,800. This has been charged as a prior period adjustment.

(*iv*) During October 19X6 a fire occurred in one of the remaining factories belonging to Uncertain Ltd and caused an estimated £350,000 of additional expenses. This amount has been included in manufacturing cost of sales.

(*v*) It was discovered on 31 October 19X6 that a customer was unable to pay his debt to the company of £125,000. The £125,000 was made up of sales in the period July to September 19X6. No adjustment has been made in the draft accounts for this item.

Uncertain Ltd
Draft Profit and Loss Account for the year ended 30 September 19X6

	£	£
Sales		5,450,490
Manufacturing cost of sales		3,284,500
Gross profit		2,165,990
Administration expenses	785,420	
Selling expenses	629,800	
		1,415,220
		750,770
Corporation tax (50%)		375,385
		375,385
Proposed dividend on ordinary shares		125,000
		250,385
Prior period adjustment	258,800	
Corporation tax	129,400	
		129,400
		120,985

Required:

(*a*) Write a report to the chief accountant of Uncertain Ltd with suggestions for appropriate treatment for each of the items (*i*) to (*iv*), with explanations for your proposals.

(*b*) Amend the draft profit and loss account to take account of your proposals.

(*Association of Chartered Certified Accountants*)

11.7 With reference to SSAP 17 (Accounting for post-balance sheet events) and FRS 12 (Provisions, contingent liabilities and contingent assets):

(*a*) define the following terms:
    (*i*) post-balance sheet events;
    (*ii*) adjusting events;
    (*iii*) non-adjusting events; and
    (*iv*) contingent asset/liability;

(*b*) give FOUR examples of adjusting events, and FOUR examples of non-adjusting events; and

(*c*) state how
    (*i*) a material contingent liability, and
    (*ii*) material contingent assets should be accounted for in financial statements.

12

The final accounts of limited companies: profit and loss accounts, related statements and notes

Objectives

After you have studied this chapter, you should:

- *be aware of the alternative presentation formats available under the Companies Acts that must be used when preparing profit and loss accounts for external reporting purposes*

- *know how to present information under the most commonly used of the Companies Act formats*

- *be aware of the differences between the statutory format and formats generally adopted for internal use*

- *be aware of the FRS 3 requirements that relate to the profit and loss account concerning:*
  - *continuing operations*
  - *acquisitions*
  - *discontinued operations*
  - *sale or termination of an operation*
  - *reorganisation and restructuring costs*
  - *profits and losses on disposal of fixed assets*
  - *exceptional and extraordinary items*
  - *prior period adjustments*

- *be aware of the impact of FRS 3 upon the Companies Act format*

- *be aware of the format of the Statement of Total Recognised Gains and Losses*

- *be aware of the format of the Note of Historical Cost Profits and Losses*

12.1 Introduction

When a company draws up its own final accounts, purely for internal use by directors and the management, it can draft them in any way it wishes. Students should be aware that drawing up a trading and profit and loss account and balance sheet for the firm's own use is not necessarily the same as drawing up such accounts for examination purposes. If a firm wishes to charge something in the trading account which perhaps in theory ought to be shown in the profit and loss account, then there is nothing to prevent the firm from so doing. The examinee, on the other hand, must base his/her answers on accounting theory and not on the practice of his/her own firm.

When it comes to publication, i.e. when the final accounts are sent to the shareholder or to the Registrar of Companies, then the Companies Acts lay down the information which must be shown, and also how it should be shown. Prior to 1981, provided the necessary information was shown it was completely up to the company exactly how it did so. The provisions of the 1981 Act brought the United Kingdom into line with the Fourth Directive of the EC, and the freedom previously available to companies on how to show the information was removed. There are, however, some advantages to be gained from such standardisation.

12.2 Layout of accounts

The Companies Acts do, nevertheless, give companies the choice of two alternative formats (layouts) for balance sheets, and four alternative formats for profit and loss accounts. As the reader for this chapter will most probably be studying this for the first time, it would be inappropriate to give all the details of all the formats. Only the far more advanced student would need such details. In this book, therefore, the reader will be shown an internal profit and loss account which can easily be adapted to cover publication requirements under the Acts, along with a balance sheet.

All companies, even the very smallest, have to produce accounts for shareholders giving the full details required by the Acts. 'Small' and 'medium-sized' companies can, however, file summarised accounts with the Registrar of Companies, but they must still prepare full accounts for their shareholders. In addition, listed companies may send their shareholders summary financial statements in place of the full version, unless a shareholder specifically requests a full version. These points will be examined later.

(Currently, a 'small' company is one for which two of the following are true: turnover does not exceed £2.8 million; the balance sheet total does not exceed £1.4m; the average number of employees does not exceed 50. For 'medium-sized' companies, the equivalent limits are £11.2 million, £5.6 million, and 250 employees.)

Of the four formats which could be used, the format that will be used for the published profit and loss account in this book is Format 1. It is in a vertical style, which is much more modern and also more likely to gain extra marks from examiners and, in addition, it is much more like common UK practice before 1981. The other Formats, not shown in this book, are Format 2 (vertical style) and Formats 3 and 4 (horizontal style).

12.3 Format 1

The Companies Acts show Format 1 as in Exhibit 12.1.

Exhibit 12.1

Profit and loss account

Format 1

1 Turnover
2 Cost of sales
3 Gross profit or loss
4 Distribution costs
5 Administrative expenses
6 Other operating income
7 Income from shares in group undertakings
8 Income from participating interests
9 Income from other fixed asset investments
10 Other interest receivable and similar income
11 Amounts written off investments
12 Interest payable and similar charges
13 Tax on profit or loss on ordinary activities
14 Profit or loss on ordinary activities after taxation
15 Extraordinary income
16 Extraordinary charges
17 Extraordinary profit or loss
18 Tax on extraordinary profit or loss
19 Other taxes not shown under the above items
20 Profit or loss for the financial year

This is simply a list and it does not show where subtotals should be placed. The important point is that the items 1 to 20 have to be displayed in that order. If some items do not exist for the company in a given year, then those headings will be omitted from the published profit and loss account. Thus, if the company has no investments, items 7, 8, 9, 10, and 11 will not exist, and item 6 will be followed by item 12 in that company's published profit and loss account. The category reference numbers on the left-hand side of items do not have to be shown in the published accounts.

12.4 Accounts for internal use

Exhibit 12.2 shows a trading and profit and loss account drawn up for internal use by a company. There are no statutory rules concerning how financial statements are drawn up for internal use. However, if the internal accounts were drawn up in a completely different fashion to those needed for publication, then there would be quite a lot of work needed in order to reassemble the figures into a profit and loss account for publication. In Exhibit 12.2 the internal accounts have been drawn up in a style which makes it much easier to get the figures for the published profit and loss account. Examination questions on this topic often ask for both (a) internal and (b) published accounts and it therefore makes it simpler for students if the internal and published accounts follow a similar order of display.

Exhibit 12.2 (accounts for internal use)

Block plc

Trading and Profit and Loss Account for the year ended 31 December 19X6

	£000	£000	£000
Turnover			800
Less Cost of sales:			
Stock 1 January 19X6		100	
Add Purchases		525	
		625	
Less Stock 31 December 19X6		125	500
Gross profit			300
Distribution costs:			
Salaries and wages	30		
Motor vehicle costs: Distribution	20		
General distribution expenses	5		
Depreciation: Motors	3		
Machinery	2	60	
Administrative expenses			
Salaries and wages	25		
Motor vehicle costs: Administration	2		
General administration expenses	7		
Auditors' remuneration	2		
Depreciation: Motors	3		
Machinery	1	40	
			100
			200
Other operating income			30
			230
Income from shares in group undertakings		20	
Income from participating interests		10	
Income from shares from non-related companies		5	
Other interest receivable		15	
			50
			280
Amounts written off investments		4	
Interest payable:			
Loans repayable within five years	10		
Loans repayable in ten years' time	6		
		16	
			20
Profit on ordinary activities before taxation			260
Tax on profit on ordinary activities			95
Profit on ordinary activities after taxation			165
Retained profits brought forward from last year			60
			225
Transfer to general reserve		40	
Proposed ordinary dividend		100	
			140
Retained profits carried forward to next year			85

12.5 Accounts for publication

Note that there are no items in Exhibit 12.2 that would appear under items 15 to 19 in Companies Act Format 1. Exhibit 12.3 redrafts Exhibit 12.2 into a form suitable for publication according to Format 1. However, as before, the category reference numbers to the left-hand side of Exhibit 12.3 are for the benefit of the reader of this book – they do not have to be included.

Exhibit 12.3 (Accounts for publication presented according to Format 1)

Block plc

Profit and Loss Account for the year ending 31 December 19X6

		£000	£000
1	Turnover		800
2	Cost of sales		500
3	Gross profit		300
4	Distribution costs	60	
5	Administrative expenses	40	
			100
			200
6	Other operating income		30
			230
7	Income from shares in group undertakings	20	
8	Income from participating interests	10	
9	Income from other fixed asset investments	5	
10	Other interest receivable and similar income	15	
			50
			280
11	Amounts written off investments	4	
12	Interest payable and similar charges	16	
			20
	Profit or loss on ordinary activities before taxation		260
13	Tax on profit or loss on ordinary activities		95
14	Profit or loss on ordinary activities after taxation		165
	Transfer to reserves	40	
	Dividends paid and proposed	100	
			140
	Retained profits for the period		25

Note that the retained profits from the previous year is not shown. It would normally appear in a note to the financial statements concerning movements on the reserves.

It would be legally possible for the internal accounts, as shown in Exhibit 12.2, to be published just as they are, because all the items are shown in the correct order. This would not have been possible if the internal accounts were drafted in a different order. However, the Companies Act does not force companies to publish fully detailed accounts (for example, as detailed as Exhibit 12.2), because their competitors may thereby be given information which would lead to them being placed in a better competitive position. The law therefore states the minimum information which must be disclosed. A company can show more than the minimum should it so wish.

12.6 Definition of items in Format 1

Format Item 1

Turnover is defined as the amounts derived from the provision of goods and services falling within the company's ordinary activities, net after deduction of VAT and trade discounts.

Format Items 2, 4 and 5

The figures for cost of sales, distribution costs and administrative expenses must include any depreciation charges connected with these functions. In the case of Block plc, because of the type of business, there are depreciation charges as part of distribution costs and administration expenses, but not cost of sales.

Format Item 6

This is operating income which does not fall under Item 1. Such items as rents receivable or royalties receivable might be found under this heading.

Format Item 7

In Chapter 19 of this book the reader will be introduced to parent and subsidiary undertakings. A parent is able to exert a dominant influence (i.e. control) over the activities of the subsidiary usually, but not necessarily, as a result of its owning a majority of the voting rights in the subsidiary. The parent and all its subsidiaries are a 'group'. Any dividends received by a company from its investments in shares in any member of the 'group' have to be shown separately.

Format Item 8

The term 'participating interest' means one where the parent company has a long-term holding of shares or their equivalent in an undertaking for the purpose of securing a contribution to the investor's own activities by the exercise of control or influence arising from or related to that interest. Where the equity stake exceeds 20 per cent, there is a presumption of such influence unless the contrary is shown.

Format Item 12

This includes bank interest on loans and overdrafts, debenture interest, etc.

The profit and loss account produced will not appear precisely as presented in Exhibit 12.1. As can be seen in Exhibit 12.3, the published profit and loss account for Block plc contains no items in categories 15, 16, 17, 18, 19 or 20. In addition, after item 14, there are several more lines, those of transfer to reserves, and proposed dividends. Although the format omits them, they are required according to the detailed rules accompanying the format. This also applies to line 20 'Profit or loss for the financial year' shown in Exhibit 12.1, when that line is included.

It would also have been possible to amalgamate items, for instance 4 and 5 could have been shown together as 'Net operating expenses £100,000'. In this case, included in the notes appended to the accounts would be an item showing the composition of the figure of £100,000.

In the notes attached to the profit and loss account, the Companies Acts require that the following be shown separately:

(*a*) interest on bank loans, overdrafts and other loans:
  (*i*) repayable within 5 years from the end of the accounting period;
  (*ii*) finally repayable after 5 years from the end of the accounting period;
(*b*) amounts set aside for redemption of share capital and for redemption of loans;
(c) rents from land, if material;
(d) costs of hire of plant and machinery;
(e) auditors' remuneration, including expenses.

Where a company carries on business of two or more classes differing substantially from each other, a note is required of the amount of turnover for each class of business, and the division of the profit and loss before taxation between each class. Information also has to be given of the turnover between geographical markets.

Notes are also required concerning numbers of employees, wages and salaries, social security costs, and pension costs.

Three further disclosure requirements of the Companies Act are expanded by FRS 3:

- the effect must be stated of any amount relating to any preceding financial year included in any item in the profit and loss account;
- particulars must be given of any extraordinary income or charges arising in the financial year; and
- the effect of any transaction of exceptional size or incidence that falls within the ordinary activities of the company must be stated.

12.7 Layout of the profit and loss account

Had Block plc had items relevant to the other Format 1 categories, the profit and loss account would have been presented as shown in Exhibit 12.4. Note that the lines added have been included simply to show what the statement would look like. Where a category has no value, it would normally be omitted from the statement, as was the case in Exhibit 12.3. In addition, Exhibit 12.4 shows the extra lines that must be included, but were not shown in Format 1 in the Companies Act. It is also worthwhile noting that the four lines in Format 1 that relate to *extraordinary items* are virtually eliminated as a result of the definition of the term that was introduced in FRS 3: *Reporting financial performance*. As a result of its issuing FRS 3, the Accounting Standards Board does not expect any company to identify an item as 'extraordinary' in their financial statements and so items 15–18 are unlikely to be seen in any future published profit and loss accounts. (This will be covered in greater detail in section 12.11.)

Exhibit 12.4

Block plc

Profit and Loss Account for the year ending 31 December 19X6

		£000	£000
1	Turnover		800
2	Cost of sales		500
3	Gross profit		300
4	Distribution costs	60	
5	Administrative expenses	40	
			100
			200
6	Other operating income		30
			230
7	Income from shares in group undertakings	20	
8	Income from participating interests	10	
9	Income from fixed asset investments	5	
10	Other interest receivable and similar income	15	
			50
			280
11	Amounts written off investments	4	
12	Interest payable and similar charges	16	
			20
	Profit or loss on ordinary activities before taxation		260
13	Tax on profit or loss on ordinary activities		95
14	Profit or loss on ordinary activities after taxation		165
15	Extraordinary income	0	
16	Extraordinary charges	0	
17	Extraordinary profit or loss	0	
18	Tax on extraordinary profit or loss	0	
			0
			165
19	Other taxes not shown under the above items		0
20	Profit or loss for the year		165
	Transfer to reserves	40	
	Dividends paid and proposed	100	
			140
	Retained profits for the year		25

12.8 Allocation of expenses

It will be obvious under which heading most expenses will be shown, whether they are

(a) cost of sales; or
(b) distribution costs; or
(c) administrative expenses.

   However, as the Companies Acts do not define these terms, some items are not so easy to allocate with certainty. Some companies may choose one heading for a particular item, while another company will choose another. These items can now be examined.

1   **Discounts received.** These are for prompt payment of amounts owing by us. Where they are for payments to suppliers of goods they could be regarded as either being a

reduction in the cost of goods or, alternatively, as being a financial recompense – i.e. the reward for paying money on time. If regarded in the first way they would be deducted from cost of sales, whereas the alternative approach would be to deduct them from administrative expenses. However, these discounts are also deducted when paying bills in respect of distribution costs or administrative expenses, and it would also be necessary to deduct from these headings if the cost of sales deduction approach is used. As this raises complications in the original recording of discounts received, it would be more suitable in this book if all cash discounts received are deducted in arriving at the figure of administrative expenses.

2 **Discounts allowed.** To be consistent in dealing with discounts, this should be included in administrative expenses.

3 **Bad debts.** These could be regarded as an expense connected with sales: after all, they are sales which are not paid for. The other point of view is that for a debt to become bad, at least part of the blame must be because the proper administrative procedures in checking on customers' creditworthiness has not been thorough enough. In this book all bad debts will be taken as being part of administrative expenses.

12.9 FRS 3: Reporting financial performance

Accounting is not a static subject. Changes occur over the years as they are seen to be necessary, and also get general agreement as to their usefulness. Since the advent of SSAPs and FRSs the number of changes that practitioners and students have had to learn has increased at a very fast rate. A prime example of this is the introduction of FRS 3, which necessitates changes to the formats of profit and loss accounts when certain events have occurred.

This Standard superseded SSAP 6: *Extraordinary items and prior year adjustments*, amended SSAP 3: *Earnings per share*, and also made changes as a consequence to various other accounting standards.

Suppose that you are considering the affairs of a business over the years. The business has not changed significantly, there have been no acquisitions, no discontinued operations, no fundamental reorganisation or restructuring of the business, nor have there been any extraordinary items affecting the accounts. In these circumstances, when comparing the accounts over the years, you are comparing like with like, subject to the problem of the effect of inflation or deflation.

On the other hand, suppose that some of the things mentioned have occurred. When trying to see what the future might hold for the company, simply basing your opinions on what has happened in the past can be very confusing.

To help you to distinguish the past and the future, and to give you some idea as to what changes have occurred, FRS 3 requires that the following are highlighted in the profit and loss account if they are material in amount:

(a) *What the results of continuing operations are, including the results of acquisitions.* Obviously acquisitions affect future results, and are therefore included in continuing operations.

(b) *What the results have been of discontinued operations.* This should help distinguish the past from the future.

(c) *The profits or losses on the sale or termination of an operation, the costs of fundamental reorganisation or restructuring,* and *the profits and losses on the disposal of fixed assets.* The profits and losses concerning these matters are not going to happen again, and so this also helps us distinguish the past from the future.

We can see how FRS 3 requires (a), (b) and (c) to be shown on the face of the profit and loss account in Exhibit 12.5. Not only is the turnover split to show the figures relevant to continuing operations, acquisitions and discontinued operations, the operating profit is split in a similar fashion. In addition any profit or loss on the disposal of the discontinued operations would also be shown. Exhibit 12.5 is restricted to the first 6 categories of Format 1 as this is the part of the statement affected by these FRS 3 requirements. Once again, it uses Block plc for the example.

Exhibit 12.5

Block plc

Profit and Loss Account for the year ending 31 December 19X6 (extract)

		£000	£000
1	Turnover		
	Continuing operations	520	
	Acquisitions	110	
		630	
	Discontinued operations	170	
			800
2	Cost of sales		500
3	Gross profit		300
4	Distribution costs	60	
5	Administrative expenses	40	
			100
	Operating profit		
	Continuing operations	160	
	Acquisitions	60	
		220	
	Discontinued operations (loss)	(20)	
			200
	Profit on disposal of discontinued operations *(i)*		10
			210
6	Other operating income		20
	Profit or loss on ordinary activities before interest		230

The item marked (*i*) can be described as an exceptional item. It is material in amount, falls within the ordinary activities of the firm, and needs to be shown so that the accounts will give a 'true and fair view'.

It is exceptional in that it is not the ordinary daily occurrence, but remember that it falls within the ordinary activities of the company. FRS 3 requires that three categories of exceptional items be shown separately on the face of the profit and loss account after operating profit and before interest, and included under the appropriate heading of continued or discontinued operations:

- profits or losses on the sale or termination of an operation;
- costs of a fundamental reorganisation or restructuring having a material effect on the nature and focus of the reporting entity's operations;
- profits or losses on the disposal of fixed assets.

Other exceptional items should be credited or charged in arriving at the profit or loss on ordinary activities by inclusion under the heading to which they relate. The amount of each exceptional item should be disclosed in a note, or on the face of the profit and loss account, if necessary in order to give a true and fair view.

12.10 Other statements and notes required by FRS 3

1 Statement of total recognised gains and losses

The *statement of total recognised gains and losses* is one of two new primary statements introduced by FRS 3. It shows the extent to which shareholders' funds have increased or decreased from all the various gains and losses recognised in the period, and enables users to consider all recognised gains and losses of a reporting entity in assessing its overall performance; an example of what would be included in the statement would be unrealised gains on fixed asset revaluations. Exhibit 12.6 presents an example of the statement using the data from Block plc. (*Note*: only the profit figure can be found in the profit and loss account. The others have been inserted to demonstrate what the statement looks like. Also, as with all these statements, including the profit and loss account, comparative figures would also be shown.)

Exhibit 12.6

Block plc
Statement of Total Recognised Gains and Losses

	19X6 £000
Profit for the financial year	165
Unrealised surplus on revaluation of properties	12
Unrealised (loss)/gain on trade investment	(8)
	169
Currency translation differences on foreign currency investments	(5)
Total recognised gains and losses relating to the year	164
Prior period adjustment	(19)
Total gains and losses recognised since last annual report	145

2 Note of historical cost profits and losses

Where assets have been revalued, which obviously affects depreciation, it may have a material effect upon the results shown in the accounts using the revalued figures. If this is the case, FRS 3 requires that there should also be shown as a note what the profit and loss account would have been if the account had been shown using historical (i.e. not revalued) figures. The note should also show how the reported profit on ordinary activities (using accounts with revalued assets) can be reconciled with that calculated using historical figures, and should also show the retained profit figure for the financial year reported on the historical cost basis. The note should be presented immediately following the profit and loss account or the statement of total recognised gains and losses. An example of the note is presented in Exhibit 12.7. (*Note*: as with the statement of total recognised gains and losses, only the profit figure can be identified in the profit and loss account. Also, comparative figures should be shown.)

Exhibit 12.7

Block plc

Note of Historical Cost Profits and Losses

	19X6
	£000
Reported profit on ordinary activities before taxation	260
Realisation of property revaluation gains of previous years	12
Difference between a historical cost depreciation charge and the actual depreciation charge of the year calculated on the revalued amount	1
Historical cost profit on ordinary activities before taxation	273
Historical cost profit for the year retained after taxation, minority interests, extraordinary items and dividends (273 – 95 – 100)	78

3 Reconciliation of movements in shareholders' funds

The profit and loss account and the statement of total recognised gains and losses reflect the performance of a reporting entity in a period, but there are other changes that can occur in shareholders' funds that these two statements do not disclose, and which can be important in understanding the change in the financial position of the entity – for example, a new share issue or goodwill written-off. For this reason, FRS 3 also gave the *reconciliation of movements in shareholders' funds* the status of a primary statement, its purpose being to highlight these other changes in the financial position. When shown as a primary statement (there is an option to show it as a note), the reconciliation should be shown separately from the statement of total recognised gains and losses. Exhibit 12.8 presents an example of the statement. (*Note*: the figures can be found in the other statements except for the new share capital, the goodwill written off and the opening shareholders' funds amounts. As before, comparative figures should also be presented.)

Exhibit 12.8

Block plc

Reconciliation of Movements in Shareholders' Funds

	19X6
	£000
Profit for the financial year	165
Dividends	(100)
	65
Other recognised gains and losses relating to the year (net)	(1)
New share capital subscribed	20
Goodwill written off	(25)
Net addition to shareholders' funds	59
Opening shareholders' funds (originally £321,000 before deducting prior period adjustment of £19,000)	302
Closing shareholders' funds	361

12.11 FRS 3 and extraordinary items

You have just seen that in FRS 3 some of the exceptional items have to be highlighted on the face of the profit and loss account, whilst others can be put under appropriate headings with notes giving details being attached to the accounts.

In Exhibit 12.3 all of these exceptional items will have been dealt with by the time that item 14, profit for the year on ordinary activities after taxation, has been reached. Extraordinary items, as per Format 1, would be shown after that as items 15, 16, 17 and 18.

Before FRS 3, the distinction between what was an exceptional item and what was an extraordinary item was not as well defined as it could have been. This led to directors of companies sometimes manipulating the figures for their own ends whilst keeping within the necessary legal boundaries.

They did this because the profit per item 14 was a very well-used figure for assessing how well, or otherwise, a company was being managed. It was a vital part of calculating the earnings per share (EPS) which is a main indicator to many people of the company's performance. If a favourable item could be called an 'exceptional item' it would increase the size of the profit per 14. On the other hand, should an item be unfavourable, and therefore lower the figure of profit per 14, then perhaps it could be (and it often was) called an 'extraordinary item' instead. In this way, the profit per 14 could be shown at a higher figure than was really justified. Such actions could affect the stock exchange values of the company's shares.

FRS 3 is more strict about what is, or is not, an extraordinary item, and thus to be shown after item 14 in the profit and loss account. Extraordinary items should be:

(a) material items possessing a high degree of abnormality which arise from events or transactions that fall outside the ordinary activities of the business, and

(b) are not expected to recur, and

(c) do not include exceptional items, and

(d) do not include items relating to a prior period merely because they relate to a prior period.

Extraordinary items fall *outside* the 'ordinary' activities of a company, whereas exceptional items fall *within* them. 'Ordinary activities' are any activities undertaken by a reporting entity as part of its business and such related activities in which the reporting entity engages in furtherance of, incidental to or arising from these activities. Ordinary activities include the effects on the reporting entity of any event in the various environments in which it operates. It is little wonder that the ASB did not believe that anything could ever be described as an extraordinary item after the introduction of FRS 3.

12.12 FRS 3 and prior period adjustments

A prior period adjustment is a material adjustment applicable to prior periods arising from changes in accounting policies or from the correction of fundamental errors. They do not include normal recurring adjustments or corrections of accounting estimates made in prior periods.

They are accounted for by restating the comparative figures for the preceding period in the primary statements and notes and adjusting the opening balance of reserves for the cumulative effect. The cumulative effect of the adjustments should also be noted at the foot of the statement of total recognised gains and losses of the current period (*see* Exhibit 12.6). The effect of prior period adjustments on the results for the preceding period should be disclosed where practicable.

12.13 FRS 3 and comparative figures

Comparative figures should be shown for all items in the primary statements and the notes to the statements required by FRS 3. The comparative figures in respect of the profit and loss account should include in the continuing category only the results of those operations included in the current period's continuing operations.

Main points to remember

1 There are set formats for the preparation of published financial statements.

2 Accounts for internal use need not comply with these set formats.

3 FRS 3: *Reporting financial performance* has altered the set format for the profit and loss account by requiring further details to be disclosed concerning:
   (*a*) continuing and discontinued operations;
   (*b*) restructuring; and
   (*c*) disposal of fixed assets.

4 In addition, by defining extraordinary items out of existence, it effectively made obsolete a number of the categories contained in the set format profit and loss accounts relating to extraordinary items.

5 FRS 3 introduced two additional primary financial statements:
   (*a*) the statement of total recognised gains and losses; and
   (*b*) the reconciliation of movements in shareholders' funds (may be shown as a note).

6 It also introduced a new note – the note of historical cost profits and losses.

Advice

It is important for you to know that the published profit and loss account of a company must show certain items in a given order.

The contents of FRS 3 are likely to attract quite a lot of exam questions. In particular the definition of extraordinary items per FRS 3 will undoubtedly see quite a crop of questions. Some may come in the form of the directors of a company wanting to classify something as extraordinary, and therefore shown after item 14, 'Profit or loss on ordinary activities after taxation'.

Review questions

12.1 From the following selected balances of Rogers plc as at 31 December 19X2 draw up (*i*) a trading and profit and loss account for internal use, and (*ii*) a profit and loss account for publication.

	£
Profit and loss account as at 31 December 19X1	15,300
Stock 1 January 19X2	57,500
Purchases	164,000
Sales	288,000
Returns inwards	11,500
Returns outwards	2,000
Carriage inwards	1,300
Wages and salaries (*see* note (*b*))	8,400
Rent and rates (*see* note (*c*))	6,250
General distribution expenses	4,860
General administrative expenses	3,320
Discounts allowed	3,940
Bad debts	570
Debenture interest	2,400
Motor expenses (*see* note (*d*))	7,200
Interest received on bank deposit	770
Income from shares in undertakings in which the company has a participating interest	660
Motor vehicles at cost: Administrative	14,000
Distribution	26,000
Equipment at cost: Administrative	5,500
Distribution	3,500
Royalties receivable	1,800

Notes:
(*a*) Stock at 31 December 19X2 £64,000.
(*b*) Wages and salaries are to be apportioned: Distribution costs ⅓, Administrative expenses ⅔.
(*c*) Rent and rates are to be apportioned: Distribution costs 60 per cent, Administrative expenses 40 per cent.
(*d*) Apportion Motor expenses equally between Distribution costs and Administrative expenses.
(*e*) Depreciate Motor vehicles 25 per cent and Equipment 20 per cent on cost.
(*f*) Accrue auditors' remuneration of £500.
(*g*) Accrue corporation tax for the year on ordinary activity profits £30,700.
(*h*) A sum of £8,000 is to be transferred to general reserve.
(*i*) An ordinary dividend of £30,000 is to be proposed.

12.2 You are given the following selected balances of Federal plc as at 31 December 19X4. From them draw up (*i*) a trading and profit and loss account for the year ended 31 December 19X4 for internal use and (*ii*) a profit and loss account for publication.

	£
Stock 1 January 19X4	64,500
Sales	849,000
Purchases	510,600
Carriage inwards	4,900
Returns inwards	5,800
Returns outwards	3,300
Discounts allowed	5,780
Discounts received	6,800
Wages (putting goods into saleable condition)	11,350
Salaries and wages: Sales and distribution staff	29,110
Salaries and wages: Administrative staff	20,920
Motor expenses (*see* note (*c*))	15,600
Rent and rates (*see* note (*d*))	25,000
Investments in undertakings in which the company has a participating interest (market value £66,000)	80,000
Income from shares in undertakings in which the company has a participating interest	3,500
General distribution expenses	8,220
General administrative expenses	2,190
Bad debts	840
Interest from government securities	1,600
Haulage costs: Distribution	2,070
Debenture interest payable	3,800
Profit and loss account: 31 December 19X3	37,470
Motor vehicles at cost: Distribution and sales	75,000
Administrative	35,000
Plant and machinery at cost: Distribution and sales	80,000
Administrative	50,000
Production	15,000
Directors' remuneration	5,000

Notes:
(*a*) The production department puts goods bought into a saleable condition.
(*b*) Stock at 31 December 19X4 £82,800.
(*c*) Apportion Motor expenses: Distribution ⅔, Administrative ⅓.
(*d*) Apportion Rent and rates: Distribution 80 per cent, Administrative 20 per cent.
(*e*) Write £14,000 off the value of investments in undertakings in which the company has a participating interest.
(*f*) Depreciate Motor vehicles 20 per cent on cost, Plant and machinery 10 per cent on cost.
(*g*) Accrue auditors' remuneration £2,000.
(*h*) Accrue corporation tax on ordinary activity profits £74,000.
(*i*) A sum of £20,000 is to be transferred to debenture redemption reserve.
(*j*) An ordinary dividend of £50,000 is to be proposed.

12.3 The following information has been extracted from the books of account of Rufford plc for the year to 31 March 19X6:

	Dr £000	Cr £000
Administration expenses	97	
Deferred taxation		24
Depreciation on office machinery (for the year to 31 March 19X6)	8	
Depreciation on delivery vans (for the year to 31 March 19X6)	19	
Distribution costs	33	
Dividends received (from a UK listed company on 31 July 19X5)		14
Factory closure expenses (closed on 1 April 19X5)	12	
Interest payable on bank overdraft (repayable within five years)	6	
Interim dividend (paid on 30 September 19X5)	21	
Interest receivable		25
Purchases	401	
Retained profit at 31 March 19X5		160
Sales (net of VAT)		642
Stock at 1 April 19X5	60	

Additional information:
1 Administrative expenses include the following items:

	£000
Auditors' remuneration	20
Directors' emoluments	45
Travelling expenses	1
Research expenditure	11
Hire of plant and machinery	12

2 It is assumed that the following tax rates are applicable for the year to 31 March 19X6:
    Corporation tax   50%
    Income tax   30%
3 There was an overprovision for corporation tax of £3,000 relating to the year to 31 March 19X5.
4 Corporation tax payable for the year to 31 March 19X6 (based on the profits for that year) is estimated to be £38,000. The company, in addition, intends to transfer a further £9,000 to its deferred taxation account.
5 A final dividend of £42,000 for the year to 31 March 19X6 is expected to be paid on 2 June 19X6.
6 Stock at 31 March 19X6 was valued at £71,000.
7 As a result of a change in accounting policy, a prior period charge of £15,000 (net of tax) is to be made.
8 The company's share capital consists of 420,000 ordinary shares of £1 each. There are no preference shares, and no change had been made to the company's issued share capital for some years.

Required:
(a) In so far as the information permits, prepare the company's published profit and loss account for the year to 31 March 19X6 in the vertical format in accordance with the Companies Act and with related accounting standards.
    (NB A statement of the company's accounting policies is not required.)
(b) Prepare balance sheet extracts in order to illustrate the balances still remaining in the following accounts at 31 March 19X6:
    (i)   corporation tax;
    (ii) proposed dividend; and
    (iii) deferred taxation.
    (NB: a detailed balance sheet is not required.)

(*Association of Accounting Technicians*)

12.4A The following balance has been extracted from the books of Falconer plc as on 31 August 19X4. From them draw up (*i*) a trading and profit and loss account, for internal use, for the year ended 31 August 19X4, also (*ii*) a profit and loss account for publication for the year.

	£
Purchases	540,500
Sales	815,920
Returns inwards	15,380
Returns outwards	24,620
Carriage inwards	5,100
Wages – productive	6,370
Discounts allowed	5,890
Discounts received	7,940
Stock 31 August 19X3	128,750
Wages and salaries: Sales and distribution	19,480
Wages and salaries: Administrative	24,800
Motor expenses: Sales and distribution	8,970
Motor expenses: Administrative	16,220
General distribution expenses	4,780
General administrative expenses	5,110
Rent and rates (*see* note (*c*))	9,600
Directors' remuneration	12,400
Profit and loss account: 31 August 19X3	18,270
Advertising costs	8,380
Bad debts	1,020
Hire of plant and machinery (*see* note (*b*))	8,920
Motor vehicles at cost: Sales and distribution	28,000
Administrative	36,000
Plant and machinery: Distribution	17,500
Debenture interest payable	4,800
Income from shares in group undertakings	12,800
Income from shares in undertakings in which the company has a participating interest	10,500
Preference dividend paid	15,000
Profit on disposal of investments	6,600
Tax on profit on disposal of investments	1,920

Notes:
(*a*) Stock at 31 August 19X4 £144,510.
(*b*) The hire of plant and machinery is to be apportioned: Productive £5,200, Administrative £3,720.
(*c*) Rent and rates to be apportioned: Distribution ⅔, Administrative ⅓.
(*d*) Motors are to be depreciated at 25 per cent on cost, Plant and machinery to be depreciated at 20 per cent on cost.
(*e*) Auditors' remuneration of £1,700 to be accrued.
(*f*) Corporation tax on profit from ordinary activities for the year is estimated at £59,300, excluding tax on disposal of investments.
(*g*) Transfer £25,000 to general reserve.
(*h*) Ordinary dividend of £60,000 is proposed.

12.5A From the following balance of Danielle plc you are to draw up (*i*) a trading and profit and loss account for the year ended 31 December 19X6, for internal use, and (*ii*) a profit and loss account for publication:

	£
Plant and machinery, at cost (*see* note (*c*))	275,000
Bank interest receivable	1,850
Discounts allowed	5,040
Discounts received	3,890
Hire of motor vehicles: Sales and distribution	9,470
Hire of motor vehicles: Administrative	5,710
Licence fees receivable	5,100
General distribution expenses	11,300
General administrative expenses	15,800
Wages and salaries: Sales and distribution	134,690
Administrative	89,720
Directors' remuneration	42,000
Motor expenses (*see* note (*e*))	18,600
Stock 31 December 19X5	220,500
Sales	880,000
Purchases	405,600
Returns outwards	15,800
Returns inwards	19,550
Profit and loss account as at 31 December 19X5	29,370

Notes:
(*a*) Stock at 31 December 19X6 £210,840.
(*b*) Accrue auditor's remuneration £3,000.
(*c*) Of the Plant and machinery, £150,000 is distributive in nature, whilst £125,000 is for administration.
(*d*) Depreciate plant and machinery 20 per cent on cost.
(*e*) Of the Motor expenses $\frac{2}{3}$ is for Sales and distribution and $\frac{1}{3}$ for Administration.
(*f*) Corporation tax on ordinary profits is estimated at £28,350.
(*g*) Proposed ordinary dividend is £50,000.
(*h*) A sum of £15,000 is to be transferred to general reserve.

12.6A Bunker plc is a trading company; it does not carry out *any* manufacturing operations. The following information has been extracted from the books of account for the year to 31 March 19X0:

	£000
Auditors' remuneration	30
Corporation tax: based on the accounting profit for the year to 31 March 19X0	7,200
overprovision for the year to 31 March 19X9	200
United Kingdom corporation tax relief on	
overseas operations: closure costs	30
Delivery expenses	1,200
Dividends: final (proposed – to be paid 1 August 19X0)	200
interim (paid on 1 October 19X9)	100
Fixed assets at cost:	
Delivery vans	200
Office cars	40
Stores plant and equipment	5,000
Investment income (amount received from listed companies)	1,600
Office expenses	800
Overseas operations: closure costs of entire operations on 1 April 19X9	350
Purchases (net of value added tax)	24,000
Sales (net of value added tax)	35,000
Stocks at cost:	
at 1 April 19X9	5,000
at 31 March 19X0	6,000
Storeroom costs	1,000
Wages and salaries:	
Delivery staff	700
Directors' emoluments	300
Office staff	100
Storeroom staff	400

Additional information:
1 Depreciation policy:
   Depreciation is provided at the following annual rates on a straight line basis: delivery vans 20 per cent; office cars 7.5 per cent; stores plant and equipment 10 per cent.
2 The following taxation rates may be assumed:
   corporation tax 35 per cent; income tax 25 per cent; value added tax 15 per cent.
3 The investment income arises from investments held in fixed asset investments.
4 It has been decided to transfer an amount of £150,000 to the deferred taxation account.
5 There were 1,000,000 ordinary shares of £1 each in issue during the year to 31 March 19X0. There were no preference shares in issue.

Required:
Insofar as the information permits, prepare Bunker plc's published profit and loss account for the year to 31 March 19X0 in accordance with the minimum requirements of the Companies Act 1985 and related accounting standards.

Note: A statement of accounting policies is NOT required, but where appropriate, other formal notes SHOULD be attached to your profit and loss account. Detailed workings should also be submitted with your answer.

(Association of Accounting Technicians)

12.7A Fresno Group plc have prepared their financial statements for the year ended 31 January 19X4. However, the financial accountant of Fresno Group plc had difficulty in preparing the statements required by FRS 3: *Reporting financial performance*, and approached you for help in preparing those statements. The financial accountant furnished you with the following information:

(*i*)

Fresno Group plc

Profit and Loss Account extract for year ended 31 January 19X4

	£ million
Operating profit – continuing operations	290
Profit on sale of property in continuing operations	10
Profit on ordinary activities before taxation	300
Tax on ordinary activities	(90)
Profit after taxation	210
Dividends	(15)
Retained profit for year	195

The financial accountant did not provide for the loss on any discontinued operations in the profit and loss account. (However, you may assume that the taxation provision incorporated the effects of any provision for discontinued operations.)

(*ii*) The shareholders' funds at the beginning of the financial year were as follows:

	£ million
Share capital – £1 ordinary shares	350
Merger reserve	55
Revaluation reserve	215
Profit and loss reserve	775
	1,395

(*iii*) Fresno Group plc regularly revalues its fixed assets and at 31 January 19X4, a revaluation surplus of £375 million had been credited to revaluation reserve. During the financial year, a property had been sold on which a revaluation surplus of £54 million had been credited to reserves. Further, if the company had charged depreciation on a historical cost basis rather than the revalued amounts, the depreciation charge in the profit and loss account for fixed assets would have been £7 million. The current year's charge for depreciation was £16 million.

(*iv*) The group has a policy of writing off goodwill on the acquisition of subsidiaries directly against a merger reserve. The goodwill for the period amounted to £250 million. In order to facilitate the purchase of subsidiaries, the company had issued £1 ordinary shares of nominal value £150 million and share premium of £450 million. The premium had been taken to the merger reserve. All subsidiaries are currently 100 per cent owned by the group.

(*v*) During the financial year to 31 January 19X4, the company had made a decision to close a 100 per cent owned subsidiary, Reno plc. However, the closure did not take place until May 19X4. Fresno Group plc estimated that as at 31 January 19X4 the operating loss for the period 1 February 19X4 to 31 May 19X4 would be £30 million and that in addition redundancy costs, stock and plant write-downs would amount to £15 million. In the event, the operating loss for the period 1 February 19X4 to 31 May 19X4 was £65 million, but the redundancy costs, stock and plant write-downs only amounted to £12 million.

(*vi*) The following information relates to Reno plc for the period 1 February 19X4 to 31 May 19X4.

Reno plc

	£ million
Turnover	175
Cost of sales	(195)
Gross loss	(20)
Administrative expenses	(15)
Selling expenses	(30)
Operating loss before taxation	(65)

Required:

(a) Prepare the following statements in accordance with current statutory requirements and FRS 3: *Reporting financial performance* for Fresno Group plc for the year ending 31 January 19X4:

  (i) statement of total recognised gains and losses;

  (ii) reconciliation of movements in shareholders' funds;

  (iii) analysis of movements on reserves;

  (iv) note of historical cost profits and losses.

(b) Explain to the financial accountant:

  (i) how the decision to close the subsidiary, Reno plc, affects the financial statements of Fresno Group plc for the year ended 31 January 19X4;

  (ii) how the subsidiary, Reno plc, should be dealt with in the financial statements of Fresno Group plc for the year ended 31 January 19X5.

(Association of Chartered Certified Accountants)

13

The final accounts of limited companies: balance sheets

Objectives

After you have studied this chapter, you should:

- *be aware of the alternative presentation formats available under the Companies Acts that must be used when preparing balance sheets for external reporting purposes*

- *know how to present information under the most commonly used of the Companies Acts formats*

- *be aware of the differences between the statutory format and formats generally adopted for internal use*

- *be aware of the exemptions available to 'small' and 'medium-sized' companies in respect of filing modified accounts*

- *be aware of the option available to plcs to send members a summary financial statement*

13.1 Balance sheet formats

The Companies Acts set out two formats for the balance sheet, one vertical and one horizontal. The method chosen for this book is that of Format 1 because this most resembles previous UK practice. As it is the vertical style format it will also be looked upon with favour by examiners.

Format 1 is shown as Exhibit 13.1. Monetary figures have been included to illustrate it more clearly.

Exhibit 13.1

Balance Sheet – Format 1

			£000s		
			£	£	£
A	CALLED-UP SHARE CAPITAL NOT PAID*				10
B	FIXED ASSETS				
I	Intangible assets				
	1	Development costs	20		
	2	Concessions, patents, licences, trade marks and similar rights and assets	30		
	3	Goodwill	80		
	4	Payments on account	5	135	
II	Tangible assets				
	1	Land and buildings	300		
	2	Plant and machinery	500		
	3	Fixtures, fittings, tools and equipment	60		
	4	Payments on account and assets in course of construction	20	880	
III	Investments				
	1	Shares in group undertakings	15		
	2	Loans to group undertakings	10		
	3	Participating interests	20		
	4	Loans to undertakings in which the company has a participating interest	5		
	5	Other investments other than loans	30		
	6	Other loans	16		
	7	Own shares	4	100	1,115
C	CURRENT ASSETS				
I	Stock				
	1	Raw materials and consumables	60		
	2	Work in progress	15		
	3	Finished goods and goods for resale	120		
	4	Payments on account	5	200	
II	Debtors				
	1	Trade debtors	200		
	2	Amounts owed by group undertakings	20		
	3	Amounts owed by undertakings in which the company has a participating interest	10		
	4	Other debtors	4		
	5	Called-up share capital not paid*	–		
	6	Prepayments and accrued income**	–	234	
III	Investments				
	1	Shares in group undertakings	40		
	2	Own shares	5		
	3	Other investments	30		
				75	
IV	Cash at bank and in hand			26	
				535	
D	PREPAYMENTS AND ACCRUED INCOME**			15	
				550	

E	CREDITORS: AMOUNTS FALLING DUE WITHIN ONE YEAR			
	1 Debenture loans	5		
	2 Bank loans and overdrafts	10		
	3 Payments received on account	20		
	4 Trade creditors	50		
	5 Bills of exchange payable	2		
	6 Amounts owed to group undertakings	15		
	7 Amounts owed to undertakings in which the company has a participating interest	6		
	8 Other creditors including taxation and social security	54		
	9 Accruals and deferred income***	–	162	
F	NET CURRENT ASSETS (LIABILITIES)			388
G	TOTAL ASSETS LESS CURRENT LIABILITIES			1,513
H	CREDITORS: AMOUNTS FALLING DUE AFTER MORE THAN ONE YEAR			
	1 Debenture loans	20		
	2 Bank loans and overdrafts	15		
	3 Payments received on account	5		
	4 Trade creditors	25		
	5 Bills of exchange payable	4		
	6 Amounts owed to group undertakings	10		
	7 Amounts owed to undertakings in which the company has a participating interest	5		
	8 Other creditors including taxation and social security	32		
	9 Accruals and deferred income***	–	116	
I	PROVISIONS FOR LIABILITIES AND CHARGES			
	1 Pensions and similar obligations	20		
	2 Taxation, including deferred taxation	40		
	3 Other provisions	4	64	
J	ACCRUALS AND DEFERRED INCOME***		20	200
				1,313
K	CAPITAL AND RESERVES			
I	Called-up share capital			1,000
II	Share premium account			100
III	Revaluation reserve			20
IV	Other reserves:			
	1 Capital redemption reserve	40		
	2 Reserve for own shares	10		
	3 Reserves provided for by the articles of association	20		
	4 Other reserves	13		83
V	Profit and loss account			110
				1,313

(*) (**) (***) These items may be shown in any of the positions indicated.

It should be noted that various items can be shown in alternative places, i.e.:

- **called-up share capital not paid,** either in position A or position CII 5;
- **prepayments and accrued income,** either CII 6 or as D;
- **accruals and deferred income,** either E9 or H9, or in total as J.

Items preceded by letters or roman numerals must be disclosed on the face of the balance sheet, e.g. B Fixed assets, KII Share premium account, whereas those shown with arabic numerals (you may call them ordinary numbers, 1, 2, 3, 4, etc.) may be combined where they are not material or the combination facilitates assessment of the company's affairs. Where they are combined, the details of each item should be shown in the notes accompanying the financial statements. The actual letters, roman numerals or arabic numbers do *not* have to be shown on the face of the published balance sheets.

13.2 Further details for Format 1

The following also apply to the balance sheet in Format 1.

BI Intangible assets are assets not having a 'physical' existence compared with tangible assets which do have a physical existence. For instance, you can see and touch the tangible assets of land and buildings, plant and machinery, etc., whereas goodwill does not exist in a physical sense.

For each of the items under fixed assets, whether they are intangible assets, tangible assets or investments, full details must be given in the notes accompanying the accounts of (*a*) cost, at beginning and end of financial year, (*b*) effect on that item of acquisitions, disposals, revaluations, etc. during the year, and (*c*) full details of depreciation, i.e. accumulated depreciation at start of year, depreciation for year, effect of disposals on depreciation in the year and any other adjustments.

All fixed assets, including property and goodwill, must be depreciated over the period of the useful economic life of each asset. Prior to this many companies had not depreciated property because of rising money values of the asset. Costs of research must not be treated as an asset, and development costs may be capitalised only in special cases. Any hire purchase owing must not be deducted from the assets concerned. Only goodwill which has been purchased can be shown as an asset; internally generated goodwill must not be capitalised. (This does not refer to goodwill in consolidated accounts – *see* Chapter 20.)

Where an asset is revalued, normally this will be fixed assets being shown at market value instead of cost. Any difference on revaluation must be debited or credited to a revaluation reserve – *see* KIII in the Format.

Investments shown as CIII will be in respect of those not held for the long term.

Two items which could previously be shown as assets, (*a*) preliminary expenses (these are the legal expenses etc. in forming the company), and (*b*) expenses of and commission on any issue of shares or debentures, must not now be shown as assets. They can be written off against any share premium account balance; alternatively they should be written off to the profit and loss account.

Full details of each class of share capital, and of authorised capital, will be shown in notes accompanying the balance sheet.

13.3 Choice of formats

The Acts leave the choice of a particular format for the balance sheet and the profit and loss account to the directors. Once adopted, the choice must be adhered to in subsequent years except in the case that there are special reasons for the change. If a change is made, then full reasons for the change must be stated in the notes attached to the accounts.

13.4 Fundamental accounting principles

The Companies Acts set out the accounting principles (or 'valuation rules' as they are called in the Fourth Directive of the EC) to be followed when preparing company financial statements.

The following principles are stated in the Acts. The reader is referred to Chapter 10 of *Business Accounting 1* for a fuller discussion of some of them.

(*a*) A company is presumed to be a going concern.

(*b*) Accounting policies must be applied consistently from year to year.

(*c*) The prudence concept must be followed.

(*d*) The accruals concept must be observed.

(*e*) Each component item of assets and liabilities must be valued separately. As an instance of this, if a company has five different types of stock, each type must be valued separately at the lower of cost and net realisable value, rather than be valued on an aggregate basis.

(*f*) Amounts in respect of items representing assets or income may *not* be set off against items representing liabilities or expenditure. Thus an amount owing on a hire purchase contract cannot be deducted from the value of the asset in the balance sheet.

13.5 True and fair view

If complying with the requirements of the Companies Acts would cause the financial statements not to be 'true and fair' then the directors must set aside such requirements. This should not be done lightly, and it would not be common to find such instances.

13.6 Small and medium-sized company reporting requirements

Small and medium-sized companies do not have to file a full set of final accounts with the Registrar of Companies. They could, if they wished, send a full set of final accounts, but what they *have* to file is a minimum of 'modified accounts'. They would still have to send a full set to their own shareholders – the 'modified accounts' refer only to those filed with the Registrar.

The definition of 'small' and 'medium-sized' companies is if, for the financial year in question and the previous year, the company comes within the limits of at least two of the following three criteria:

	Small	*Medium-sized*
Turnover not more than	£2.8 million net/ £3.36 million gross	£11.2 million net/ £13.44 million gross
Balance sheet total not more than	£1.4 million net/ £1.68 million gross	£5.6 million net/ £6.72 million gross
Employees not more than	50	250

In addition, there is no longer an audit requirement for small companies with a turnover of not more than £350,000 and a balance sheet total of not more than £1.4 million, unless 10 per cent or more of shareholders sign a formal notice requesting an audit and lodge this at the registered office.

13.7 Modified accounts of small companies

(*a*) Neither a profit and loss account nor a directors' report has to be filed with the Registrar.

(*b*) A modified balance sheet showing only those items to which a letter or roman numeral are attached (*see* Format 1, Exhibit 13.1) has to be shown. For example, the total for CI Stock has to be shown but not the figures for each of the individual items comprising this total.

13.8 Modified accounts of medium-sized companies

(*a*) The profit and loss account per Format 1 does not have to show item 1 (Turnover), or item 2 (Cost of sales) or item 6 (Other operating income). It will therefore begin with the figure of gross profit or loss.
(*b*) The analyses of turnover and profit normally required as notes to the accounts need not be given.
(*c*) The balance sheet, however, must be given in full.

Notes to the accounts: review questions on published company accounts including notes required by law are shown at the end of Chapter 14.

13.9 Summary financial statements

A plc may send a summary financial statement to members in place of the full statements, but any member who requests the full statements must be sent them. The summary statement must:

(*a*) state that it is only a summary of information in the company's financial statements and the directors' report;
(*b*) contain a statement by the company's auditors of their opinion as to whether the summary financial statement is consistent with those financial statements and that report and complies with the requirements of the section in the Companies Act (CA 85, section 251) that permits the distribution of this summary financial statement and the regulations made under it;
(*c*) state whether the auditors' report on the financial statements was unqualified or qualified, and if it was qualified set out the report in full together with any further material needed to understand the qualification;
(*d*) state whether the auditors' report on the annual accounts contained a statement under either:
   - CA 85, section 237(2) – accounting records or returns inadequate or financial statements not agreeing with records or returns; or
   - CA 85, section 237(3) – failure to obtain necessary information and explanations
   and, if so, set out the statement in full.

Main points to remember

1 There are set formats for the preparation of published financial statements.

2 Accounts for internal use need not comply with these set formats.

3 Accounting standards have statutory recognition and must, therefore, be complied with when preparing financial statements intended to present a true and fair view.

4 'Small' and 'medium-sized' companies may file modified accounts with the Registrar if they wish.

5 Plcs may send a summary financial statement to members in place of the full statements, but any member who requests the full statements must be sent them.

Review questions

13.1 The following balances remained in the books of Owen Ltd on 31 December 19X1, *after* the profit and loss account and appropriation account had been drawn up. You are to draft the balance sheet as at 31 December 19X1 in accordance with the Companies Acts.

	Dr £	Cr £
Ordinary share capital: £1 shares		50,000
Preference share capital: 50p shares		25,000
Calls account (ordinary shares)	150	
Development costs	3,070	
Goodwill	21,000	
Land and buildings – at cost	48,000	
Plant and machinery – at cost	12,500	
Provision for depreciation: Buildings		16,000
Provision for depreciation: Plant and machinery		5,400
Shares in undertakings in which the company has a participating interest	35,750	
Stock: Raw materials	3,470	
Stock: Finished goods	18,590	
Debtors: Trade	17,400	
Amounts owed by undertakings in which the company has a participating interest	3,000	
Prepayments	1,250	
Debentures (*see* note 1)		10,000
Bank overdraft (repayable within 6 months)		4,370
Creditors: Trade (payable within 1 year)		12,410
Bills payable (*see* note 2)		3,600
Share premium		20,000
Capital redemption reserve		5,000
General reserve		4,000
Profit and loss account		8,400
	164,180	164,180

Notes:
1 Of the debentures £6,000 is repayable in 3 months' time, while the other £4,000 is repayable in 5 years' time.
2 Of the bills payable, £1,600 is in respect of a bill to be paid in 4 months' time and £2,000 for a bill payable in 18 months' time.
3 The depreciation charged for the year was: Building £4,000, Plant and machinery £1,800.

13.2 After the profit and loss appropriation account has been prepared for the year ended 30 September 19X4, the following balances remain in the books of Belle Works plc. You are to draw up a balance sheet in accordance with the Companies Acts.

	£	£
Ordinary share capital		70,000
Share premium		5,000
Revaluation reserve		10,500
General reserve		6,000
Foreign exchange reserve		3,500
Profit and loss		6,297
Patents, trade marks and licences	1,500	
Goodwill	17,500	
Land and buildings	90,000	
Provision for depreciation: Land and buildings		17,500
Plant and machinery	38,600	
Provision for depreciation: Plant and machinery		19,200
Stock of raw materials: 30 September 19X4	14,320	
Work in progress: 30 September 19X4	5,640	
Finished goods: 30 September 19X4	13,290	
Debtors: Trade	11,260	
Debtors: Other	1,050	
Prepayments and accrued income	505	
Debentures (redeemable in 6 months' time)		6,000
Debentures (redeemable in 4½ years' time)		12,000
Bank overdraft (repayable in 3 months)		3,893
Trade creditors (payable in next 12 months)		11,340
Trade creditors (payable after 12 months)		1,260
Bills of exchange (payable within 12 months)		4,000
Corporation tax (payable in 9 months' time)		14,370
National insurance (payable in next month)		305
Pensions contribution owing		1,860
Deferred taxation		640
	193,665	193,665

13.3 The following trial balance has been extracted from the books of Baganza plc as at 30 September 19X7:

	£000	£000
Administrative expenses	400	
Called up share capital (1,200,000 ordinary shares of £1 each)		1,200
Cash at bank and in hand	60	
Corporation tax (overpayment for the year to 30 September 19X6)		20
Deferred taxation (at 1 October 19X6)		460
Distribution costs	600	
Dividends received (on 31 March 19X7)		249
Extraordinary item (net of tax)		1,500
Freehold property:		
at cost	2,700	
accumulated depreciation (at 1 October 19X6)		260
Interim dividend (paid on June 19X7)	36	
Investments in United Kingdom companies	2,000	
Plant and machinery:		
at cost	5,200	
accumulated depreciation (at 1 October 19X6)		3,600
Profit and loss account (at 1 October 19X6)		2,022
Purchases	16,000	
Research expenditure	75	
Stock (at 1 October 19X6)	2,300	
Tax on extraordinary item		360
Trade creditors		2,900
Trade debtors	2,700	
Turnover		19,500
	£32,071	£32,071

Additional information:
1 The stock at 30 September 19X7 was valued at £3,600,000.
2 Depreciation for the year to 30 September 19X7 is to be charged on the historic cost of the fixed assets as follows:
   Freehold property: 5 per cent
   Plant and machinery: 15 per cent
3 The basic rate of income tax is assumed to be 27 per cent.
4 The directors propose a final dividend of 60p per share.
5 The company was incorporated in 19X0.
6 Corporation tax based on the profits for the year at a rate of 35 per cent is estimated to be £850,000.
7 A transfer of £40,000 is to be made to the deferred taxation account.

Required:
Insofar as the information permits, prepare Baganza plc's profit and loss account for the year to 30 September 19X7, and a balance sheet as at that date in accordance with the Companies Act 1985 and appropriate accounting standards.

However, formal notes to the accounts are not required, although detailed workings should be submitted with your answer, which should include your calculation of earnings per share.

(Association of Accounting Technicians)

13.4A The trial balance of Payne Peerbrook plc as on 31 December 19X6 is as follows:

	Dr £	Cr £
Preference share capital: £1 shares		50,000
Ordinary share capital: 50p shares		60,000
General reserve		45,000
Exchange reserve		13,600
Profit and loss account as on 31 December 19X5		19,343
Stock 31 December 19X5	107,143	
Sales		449,110
Returns inwards	11,380	
Purchases	218,940	
Carriage inwards	2,475	
Wages (putting goods into a saleable condition)	3,096	
Wages: Warehouse staff	39,722	
Wages and salaries: Sales staff	28,161	
Wages and salaries: Administrative staff	34,778	
Motor expenses (see note ii)	16,400	
General distribution expenses	8,061	
General administrative expenses	7,914	
Debenture interest	10,000	
Royalties receivable		4,179
Directors' remuneration	18,450	
Bad debts	3,050	
Discounts allowed	5,164	
Discounts received		4,092
Plant and machinery at cost (see note iii)	175,000	
Provision for depreciation: Plant and machinery		58,400
Motor vehicles at cost (see note ii)	32,000	
Provision for depreciation: Motors		14,500
Goodwill	29,500	
Development costs	16,320	
Trade debtors	78,105	
Trade creditors		37,106
Bank overdraft (repayable any time)		4,279
Bills of exchange payable (all due within 1 year)		6,050
Debentures (redeemable in 5 years' time)		80,000
	845,659	845,659

Notes:
(i)   Stock of finished goods on 31 December 19X6 £144,081.
(ii) Motor expenses and depreciation on motors to be apportioned: Distribution ¾, Administrative ¼.
(iii) Plant and machinery depreciation to be apportioned: Cost of sales ⅕, Distribution ⅗, Administrative ⅕.
(iv) Depreciate the following fixed assets on cost: Motor vehicles 25 per cent, Plant and machinery 20 per cent.
(v)   Accrue corporation tax on profits of the year £14,150. This is payable 1 October 19X7.
(vi) A preference dividend of £5,000 is to be paid and an ordinary dividend of £10,000 is to be proposed.

You are to draw up:
(a) a trading and profit and loss account for the year ended 31 December 19X6 for internal use, and
(b) a profit and loss account for publication, also a balance sheet as at 31 December 19X6.

13.5A You are presented with the following information relating to Plott plc for the year to 31 March 19X1:

	£000
Bank overdraft	500
Called-up share capital (issued and fully paid)	2,100
Corporation tax (based on the profit for the year to 31 March 19X1)	900
Creditors	300
Debtors	200
Deferred taxation (credit)	150
Fixed assets: at cost	3,800
accumulated depreciation (at 31 March 19X1)	1,400
Fixed asset investments: at cost	100
Profit and loss account (at 1 April 19X0: credit)	1,200
Proposed dividend	420
Retained profit (for the year to 31 March 19X1)	585
Share premium account	315
Stocks: at cost (at 31 March 19X1)	400
Trade creditors	2,000
Trade debtors	5,300

Additional information:

1 The above information has been obtained after the compilation of the company's profit and loss account for the year to 31 March 19X1.

2 Details of fixed assets for the year to 31 March 19X1 are as follows:

		£000
(a)	At cost	
	At 1 April 19X0	3,400
	Additions	600
	Disposals	200
(b)	Accumulated depreciation	
	At 1 April 19X0	1,200
	Additions	500
	Disposals	300

3 The market value of the fixed asset investments at 31 March 19X1 was £110,000. There were no purchases or sales of fixed asset investments during the year.

4 Stocks comprise finished goods. The replacement cost of these goods is similar to the value indicated in the balance sheet.

5 Assume that the basic rate of income tax is 25 per cent.

6 The authorised share capital of the company consists of 2,500,000 ordinary shares of £1 each.

Required:

Insofar as the information permits, prepare Plott plc's balance sheet as at 31 March 19X1 in accordance with the *minimum* requirements of the Companies Act 1985 and related accounting standards.

Notes:

1 Where appropriate, formal notes must be attached to your balance sheet; and

2 detailed working should be submitted with your answer.

(*Association of Accounting Technicians*)

13.6A The following information has been extracted from the books of Quire plc as at 30 September 19X1.

	£000	£000
Bank overdraft		2,400
Called-up share capital (ordinary shares of £1 each)		4,000
Deferred taxation		200
Delivery expenses	2,800	
Fixed assets: at cost	3,500	
accumulated depreciation (at 1 October 19X0)		1,100
Debentures held	100	
Debenture interest (net)		40
Interest payable	400	
Interim dividend paid	60	
Office expenses	3,000	
Other creditors		180
Other debtors	160	
Profit and loss account (at 1 October 19X0)		820
Purchases	12,000	
Sales		19,000
Stocks (at 1 October 19X0)	500	
Trade creditors		100
Trade debtors	5,320	
	£27,840	£27,840

The following additional information is to be taken into account:
1   Stocks at 30 September 19X1 were valued at £400,000.
2   All items in the above trial balance are shown net of value added tax.
3   At 30 September 19X1, £130,000 was outstanding for office expenses, and £50,000 had been paid in advance for delivery van licences.
4   Depreciation at a rate of 50 per cent is to be charged on the historic cost of the tangible fixed assets using the reducing balance method: it is to be apportioned as follows:

	%
Cost of sales	60
Distribution	30
Administration	10
	100

There were no purchases or sales of fixed assets during the year to 30 September 19X1.
5   The following rates of taxation are to be assumed:

	%
Corporation tax	35
Income tax	25
Value added tax	17.5

The corporation tax payable based on the profits for the year to 30 September 19X1 has been estimated at £80,000.
6   A transfer of £60,000 is to be made from the deferred taxation account.
7   The directors propose to pay a final ordinary dividend of 3p per share.

Required:

Insofar as the information permits, prepare Quire plc's profit and loss account for the year to 30 September 19X1, and a balance sheet as at that date in accordance with the MINIMUM requirements of the Companies Act 1985 and related accounting standards.

Note: Formal notes to the accounts are NOT required, but detailed workings should be submitted with your answer.

(*Association of Accounting Technicians*)

13.7A The following trial balance has been extracted from the books of Patt plc as at 31 March 19X0:

	Dr £000	Cr £000
Bank overdraft		25
Called-up share capital (ordinary shares of £1 each)		1,440
Creditors		55
Debtors	50	
Fixed assets: at cost	300	
accumulated depreciation (at 1 April 19X9)		120
Marketing expenses	100	
Office expenses	200	
Profit and loss account (at 1 April 19X9)		200
Production expenses	2,230	
Purchases (net of VAT)	3,700	
Sales (amounts invoiced, net of VAT)		7,000
Stocks (at 1 April 19X9)	130	
Trade creditors		160
Trade debtors	2,290	
	£9,000	£9,000

Additional information:

1 Following the preparation of the above trial balance, the following additional matters need to be taken into account:
   (*a*) stock at 31 March 19X0 was valued at £170,000;
   (*b*) at 31 March 19X0, £20,000 was owing for office expenses, and £15,000 had been paid in advance for marketing expenses;
   (*c*) a customer had gone into liquidation owing the company £290,000; the company does not expect to recover any of this debt;
   (*d*) the company decides to set up a provision for doubtful debts amounting to 5 per cent of the outstanding trade debtors as at the end of each financial year; and
   (*e*) depreciation is to be charged on the fixed assets at a rate of 20 per cent on cost; it is to be apportioned as follows:

	%
Marketing	20
Office	10
Production	70
	100

Note: There were no acquisitions or disposals of fixed assets during the year to 31 March 19X0.

2 Corporation tax (based on the accounting profit for the year at a rate of 35 per cent) is estimated to be £160,000. The basic rate of income tax is assumed to be 25 per cent.

3 The directors are to recommend the payment of a dividend of 10p per ordinary share.

Required:

Insofar as the information permits, prepare Patt plc's profit and loss account for the year to 31 March 19X0, and a balance sheet as at that date in accordance with the Companies Act 1985 and related accounting standards.

Notes:

(*i*) Where appropriate, formal notes should be attached to your profit and loss account and balance sheet. However, a statement of accounting policies is NOT required.

(*ii*) Detailed workings should also be submitted with your solution. They should be clearly designated as such, and they must not form part of your formal notes.

(*Association of Accounting Technicians*)

14

Published accounts of limited companies: accompanying notes

Objectives

After you have studied this chapter, you should:

- *be aware of the additional notes to published financial statements that are required by the Companies Acts*

- *be aware of the requirement to include a directors' report with the published financial statements*

14.1 Notes to accompany the balance sheet

The Companies Acts require that the following additional notes are given to accompany the published balance sheet.

1 Particulars of turnover

An analysis of turnover into:

(*a*) each class of business; and by
(*b*) geographical markets;

and, in addition, the amount of profit or loss before taxation, in the opinion of the directors, attributable to each class of business.

Such disclosure does not have to be made if it would be prejudicial to the business of the company. The fact of non-disclosure would have to be stated. An example of such a note might be as in Exhibit 14.1:

Exhibit 14.1

Analysis of Turnover

	Turnover £	Profit £
Motors	26,550,000	2,310,000
Aircraft	58,915,000	4,116,000
	85,465,000	6,426,000

The geographical division of turnover is:

	£
United Kingdom	31,150,000
The Americas	43,025,000
Rest of the World	10,290,000
	84,465,000

It should be noted that these requirements were extended by SSAP 25: *Segmental reporting*, but only for:

- plcs or parent undertakings that have one or more plcs as a subsidiary
- banking and insurance companies or groups
- private companies and other entities that exceed the criteria, multiplied in each case by ten, for defining a medium-sized company under section 247 of the Companies Act 1985. (*See* Chapter 13, section 13.6 for a table of these criteria.)

It requires that for each segment, turnover (analysed between sales to external customers and sales between segments), results and net assets should be disclosed. Geographical segmental analysis should, in the first instance, be on the basis of source (i.e. the geographical location of the supplying segment). In addition, turnover to third parties should be segmentally reported on the basis of destination (i.e. the geographical location of the receiving segment).

Where associated undertakings account for at least 20 per cent of the total results or net assets of the reporting entity, additional disclosure should be made in aggregate for all associated undertakings. This comprises segmental disclosure of the reporting entity's share of the aggregate profits or losses before tax, minority interests and extraordinary items of the associated undertakings, and the reporting entity's share of the net assets of the associated undertakings (including goodwill to the extent that it has not been written off) after attributing, where possible, fair values to the net assets at the date of acquisition of the interest in each associated undertaking.

2 Particulars of staff

(*a*) Average number employed by the company (or by group in consolidated accounts), divided between categories of workers, e.g. between manufacturing and administration.
(*b*) (*i*) Wages and salaries paid to staff.
     (*ii*) Social security costs of staff.
     (*iii*) Other pension costs for employees.
(*c*) Number of employees (excluding those working wholly or mainly overseas) earning over £30,000, analysed under successive multiples of £5,000. Exclude pension contributions.

Exhibit 14.2 is an example of a note concerning higher-paid employees.

Exhibit 14.2

The number of employees earning over £30,000 was 28, analysed as follows:

Gross salaries	*Number of employees*
£30,001–35,000	16
£35,001–40,000	8
£40,001–45,000	4
	28

3 Directors' emoluments

(a) Aggregate amounts of:
- (i)   emoluments, including pension contributions and benefits in kind. Distinction to be made between those emoluments as fees and those for executive duties;
- (ii) pensions for past directors;
- (iii) compensation for loss of office.

(b) The chairman's emoluments and those of the highest paid director, if paid more than the chairman. In both cases pension contributions are to be excluded.

(c) Number of directors whose emoluments, excluding pension contributions, fall within each bracket of £5,000.

(d) Total amounts waived by directors and numbers concerned.

The disclosures under (b) and (c) above are not needed for a company being neither a parent nor subsidiary undertaking where its directors' emoluments under (a) do not exceed £60,000. The disclosures under (b) and (c) are also not necessary for directors working wholly or mainly overseas.

An illustration is now given in Exhibit 14.3:

Exhibit 14.3

Name	Fee (as directors)	Remuneration (as executives)	Pension contributions
A (Chairman)	£5,000	£85,000	£20,000
B	£2,500	£95,000	£30,000
C	£2,500	£55,000	£15,000
D	£1,500	£54,000	£12,500
E	£1,500	£30,000	£10,000

Note to accounts:
Directors' remuneration: the amounts paid to directors were as follows:

Fees as directors	£13,000
Other emoluments, including pension contributions	£406,500

Emoluments of the Chairman – excluding pension contributions – amounted to £90,000, and those of the highest paid director to £97,500. Other directors' emoluments were in the following ranges:

£30,001 to £35,000	1
£55,001 to £60,000	2

4 Various charges to be shown as notes

(a) Auditors' remuneration, including expenses.

(b) Hire of plant and machinery.

(c) Interest payable on (i) bank loans, overdrafts and other loans repayable by instalments or otherwise within five years; (ii) loans of any other kind.

(d) Depreciation:
- (i)   amounts of provisions for both tangible and intangible assets;
- (ii) effect on depreciation of change of depreciation method;
- (iii) effect on depreciation of revaluation of assets.

5 Income from listed investments

6 Rents receivable from land, after deducting outgoings

7 Taxation (see also SSAP 8: Treatment of tax under the imputation system)

(*a*) Tax charges split between:
   (*i*) UK corporation tax, and basis of computation;
   (*ii*) UK income tax, and basis of computation;
   (*iii*) irrecoverable VAT;
   (*iv*) tax attributable to franked investment income.
(*b*) If relevant, split between tax on ordinary and tax on extraordinary activities.
(*c*) Show, as component part, charge for deferred tax.
(*d*) Any other special circumstances affecting tax liability.

8 Extraordinary and exceptional items and prior period adjustments

See FRS 3.

9 Redemption of shares and loans

Show amounts set aside for these purposes.

10 Earnings per share (listed companies only)

See FRS 14.

11 Statement showing movements on reserves

14.2 The directors' report

As well as a balance sheet and profit and loss account, the shareholders must also receive a directors' report. The contents of the report are given in the Companies Acts, but no formal layout is given. Such a report is additional to the notes, which have to be attached to the accounts; the directors' report does not replace such notes.

(*a*) A fair review of the development of the business of the company (and its subsidiaries) during the financial year and of the position at the end of the year. The dividends proposed and transfers to reserves should be given.
(*b*) Principal activities of the company and any changes therein.
(*c*) Post-balance sheet events, i.e. details of important events affecting the company (and its subsidiaries) since the end of the year.
(*d*) Likely future developments in the business.
(*e*) An indication of research and development carried on.
(*f*) Significant changes in fixed assets. In the case of land, the difference between book and market values, if significant.
(*g*) Political and charitable contributions; if, taken together, these exceed £200 there must be shown:
   (*i*) separate totals for each classification;
   (*ii*) where political contributions exceeding £200 have been made, the names of recipients and amounts.
(*h*) Details of own shares purchased.

(i) Employees:
   (i) statement concerning health, safety and welfare at work of company's employees;
   (ii) for companies with average workforce exceeding 250, details of employment of disabled people.
(j) Directors:
   (i) names of all persons who had been directors during any part of the financial year;
   (ii) their interests in contracts;
   (iii) for each director, the name; also:
   • the number of shares held at the start of the year;
   • the number of shares held at the end of the year;
   • for each director elected in the year there shall also be shown shares held when elected;
   • all the above to show nil amounts where appropriate.

Note: Under the Companies Acts the directors' report is considered during the external audit. If the external auditors' judgement is that the directors' report is inconsistent with the audited company accounts, then this must be stated in the auditors' report.

14.3 Illustrative company accounts: specimen question 1

F Clarke Ltd are specialist wholesalers. This is their trial balance at 31 December 19X4.

	Dr £	Cr £
Ordinary share capital: £1 shares		1,000,000
Share premium		120,000
General reserve		48,000
Profit and loss account as at 31.12.19X3		139,750
Stock: 31.12.19X3	336,720	
Sales		4,715,370
Purchases	2,475,910	
Returns outwards		121,220
Returns inwards	136,200	
Carriage inwards	6,340	
Carriage outwards	43,790	
Warehouse wages (average number of workers 59)	410,240	
Salesmen's salaries (average number of workers 21)	305,110	
Administrative wages and salaries	277,190	
Plant and machinery	610,000	
Motor vehicle hire	84,770	
Provisions for depreciation: plant and machinery		216,290
General distribution expenses	27,130	
General administrative expenses	47,990	
Directors' remuneration	195,140	
Rents receivable		37,150
Trade debtors	1,623,570	
Cash at bank and in hand	179,250	
Trade creditors (payable before 31.3.19X5)		304,570
Bills of exchange payable (payable 28.2.19X5)		57,000
	6,759,350	6,759,350

Notes:
(*a*) Stock at 31.12.19X4: £412,780, consists of goods for resale.
(*b*) Plant and machinery is apportioned: distributive 60 per cent; administrative 40 per cent.
(*c*) Accrue auditors' remuneration: £71,000.
(*d*) Depreciate plant and machinery: 20 per cent on cost.
(*e*) Of the motor hire, £55,000 is for distributive purposes.
(*f*) Corporation tax on profits, at a rate of 35 per cent, is estimated at £238,500, and is payable on 1.10.19X5.
(*g*) There is a proposed ordinary dividend of 37½ per cent for the year.
(*h*) All of the sales are of one type of goods. Net sales of £3,620,000 have been made in the UK with the remainder in Europe, and are shown net of VAT.
(*i*) Pension contributions for staff amounted to £42,550 and social security contributions to £80,120. These figures are included in wages and salaries in the trial balance. No employee earned over £30,000.
(*j*) Plant of £75,000 had been bought during the year.
(*k*) Directors' remuneration has been as follows:

	£
Chairman	46,640
Managing Director	51,500
Finance Director	46,000
Marketing Director	43,000
	187,140

In addition each of them drew £2,000 as directors' fees. Pensions are the personal responsibility of directors.

Required:
Subject to the limits of the information given you, draw up a profit and loss account for the year ended 31 December 19X4, and a balance sheet as at that date. They should be in published form and accompanied by the necessary notes prescribed by statute.

Specimen answer 1

F Clarke Ltd: Workings

	£		£	£
Turnover: Sales	4,715,370	Cost of sales:		
Less Returns in	136,200	Opening stock		336,720
	4,579,170	*Add* Purchases	2,475,910	
		Less Returns out	121,220	
			2,354,690	
		Add Carriage in	6,340	2,361,030
				2,697,750
		Less Closing stock		412,780
				2,284,970
Distribution costs:		Administrative expenses:		
Warehouse wages	410,240	Wages and salaries		277,190
Salesmen's salaries	305,110	Motor hire		29,770
Carriage out	43,790	General expenses		47,990
General expenses	27,130	Directors' remuneration		150,140
Motor hire	55,000	Auditors' remuneration		71,000
Depreciation: plant	73,200	Depreciation: plant		48,800
				624,890
Marketing Director's remuneration	45,000			
	959,470			

(a) F Clarke Ltd

Profit and Loss Account for the year ended 31 December 19X4

	£	£
Turnover		4,579,170
Cost of sales		2,284,970
Gross profit		2,294,200
Distribution costs	959,470	
Administrative expenses	624,890	1,584,360
		709,840
Other operating income		37,150
Profit on ordinary activities before taxation		746,990
Tax on profit on ordinary activities		238,500
Profit on ordinary activities after taxation		508,490
Proposed ordinary dividend		375,000
Retained profits for the year		133,490

(b) F Clarke Ltd

Balance Sheet as at 31 December 19X4

Fixed assets	£	£	£
Tangible assets			
Plant and machinery			271,710
Current assets			
Stock			
Finished goods and goods for resale		412,780	
Debtors			
Trade debtors		1,623,570	
Cash at bank and in hand		179,250	
		2,215,600	
Creditors: amounts falling due within one year			
Trade creditors	304,570		
Bills of exchange payable	57,000		
Other creditors including taxation and social security	684,500	1,046,070	
Net current assets			1,169,530
Total assets less current liabilities			1,441,240
Capital and reserves			£
Called-up share capital			1,000,000
Share premium account			120,000
Other reserves:			
General reserve			48,000
Profit and loss account			273,240
			1,441,240

Notes to the accounts

1 Turnover

This is the value, net of VAT, of goods of a single class of business. Turnover may be analysed as follows:

	£
United Kingdom	3,680,000
Europe	899,170
	4,579,170

2 Employees

Average number of workers was:

Warehousing	59
Sales	21
	80

Remuneration of employees was:

	£
Wages and salaries	869,870
Social security costs	80,120
Pension contributions	42,550
	992,540

3 Directors' remuneration

The amounts paid to directors were as follows:

	£
Fees as directors	8,000
Other emoluments	187,140

Emoluments of the Chairman amounted to £46,640, and those of the highest paid director £51,500. Other directors' emoluments were in the following ranges:

£40,001–45,000	1
£45,001–50,000	1

4 Operating profit is shown after charging

	£
Auditors' remuneration	71,000
Hire of motors	84,770

5 Fixed assets

Plant and machinery	£	£
Cost at 1.1.19X4	535,000	
Additions	75,000	610,000
Depreciation to 31.12.19X3	216,290	
Charge for the year	122,000	338,290
		271,710

6 Other creditors including taxation

	£	£
Proposed dividend	375,000	
Auditors' remuneration	71,000	
Corporation tax	238,500	684,500

14.4 Illustrative company accounts: specimen question 2

The trial balance of Quartz plc on 31 December 19X3 was as follows:

	Dr £000	Cr £000
Preference share capital: £1 shares		200
Ordinary share capital: £1 shares		1,000
Exchange reserve		75
General reserve		150
Profit and loss account 31.12.19X2		215
Sales		4,575
Purchases	2,196	
Carriage inwards	38	
Stock 31.12.19X2	902	
Wages (adding value to goods)	35	
Wages: warehousing	380	
Wages and salaries: administrative	120	
Wages and salaries: sales	197	
Motor expenses	164	
Bad debts	31	
Debenture interest	40	
Bank overdraft interest	19	
General distribution expenses	81	
General administrative expenses	73	
Directors' remuneration	210	
Investments in undertakings in which the company has a participating interest	340	
Income from shares in undertakings in which the company has a participating interest		36
Discounts allowed and received	55	39
Buildings: at cost	1,200	
Plant and machinery: at cost	330	
Motor vehicles: at cost	480	
Provisions for depreciation:		
Land and buildings		375
Plant and machinery		195
Motors		160
Goodwill	40	
Patents, licences and trade marks	38	
Trade debtors and creditors	864	392
Bank overdraft (repayable any time)		21
Debentures 10 per cent		400
	7,833	7,833

Notes:
(*a*) Stock at 31.12.19X3: £1,103,000 at cost.
(*b*) Motor expenses and depreciation on motors to be apportioned: Distribution 75 per cent; Administrative 25 per cent.
(*c*) Depreciation on buildings and plant and machinery to be apportioned: Distribution 50 per cent; Administrative 50 per cent.
(*d*) Depreciate on cost: Motor vehicles 25 per cent; Plant and machinery 20 per cent.
(*e*) Accrue corporation tax on profits of the year £266,000. This is payable 1 October 19X4.

(f) A preference dividend of 10 per cent is to be paid and an ordinary dividend of 50 per cent is to be proposed.

(g) During the year new vehicles were purchased at a cost of £60,000.

(h) During June 19X3 one of the buildings, which had originally cost £130,000, and which had a written-down value at the date of the sale of £80,000, was sold for £180,000. Depreciation on buildings to be charged against the year's profits £60,000. The buildings are revalued by B & Co., Chartered Surveyors, at £1,500,000 at 31.12.19X3 (and this figure is to be included in the accounts).

(i) Directors' remuneration was as follows:

	£
Marketing	42,000
Chairman	37,000
Managing	61,000
Finance	50,000
	190,000

In addition each director drew £5,000 fees.

(j) Of the goodwill, 50 per cent is to be written off during this year, and 50 per cent in the following year.

(k) The debentures are to be redeemed in five equal annual instalments, starting in the following year 19X4.

(l) The investments are in listed companies with a market value at 31 December 19X3 of £438,000.

(m) Auditors' remuneration, including expenses, was £7,000.

You are required to prepare a balance sheet as at 31 December 19X3. It should:

(a) conform to the requirements of the Companies Act 1985;
(b) conform to the relevant accounting standards;
(c) be shown in vertical form;
(d) give the notes necessary to the accounts.

Specimen answer 2

Quartz plc: workings

	£000		Dist. £000	Admin £000
Cost of sales:		Wages	577	120
Opening stock	902	Motor expenses	123	41
Add Purchases	2,196	General	81	73
Add Carriage in	38	Depreciation: plant	33	33
		motors	90	30
	3,136	buildings	30	30
Less Closing stock	1,103	Directors	47	163
		Discounts (net) 55–39		16
	2,033	Bad debts		31
Wages (added value)	35			
	2,068		981	537

(a) Quartz plc

Profit and Loss Account for the year ended 31 December 19X4

	£000	£000
Turnover		4,575
Cost of sales		2,068
Gross profit		2,507
Distribution costs	981	
Administrative expenses	537	1,518
		989
Income from shares in undertakings in which the company has a participating interest		36
		1,025
Interest payable and similar charges		59
Profit on ordinary activities before taxation		966
Tax on profit on ordinary activities		266
Profit for the year on ordinary activities after taxation		700
Goodwill written off	20	
Dividends paid and proposed	520	540
Retained profits for the year		160

(b) Quartz plc

Balance Sheet as at 31 December 19X3

Fixed assets	£000	£000	£000
Intangible assets			
Patents, licences and trade marks		38	
Goodwill		20	
		58	
Tangible assets			
Buildings	1,500		
Plant and machinery	69		
Vehicles	200	1,769	
Investments			
Shares in undertakings in which the company has a participating interest		340	2,167
Current assets			
Stock	1,103		
Trade debtors	864	1,967	
Creditors: amounts falling due within one year			
Debenture loans	80		
Bank overdraft	21		
Trade creditors	392		
Other creditors	786		
	1,279		
Creditors: amounts falling due after more than one year			
Debenture loans	320	1,599	368
			2,535
Capital and reserves			
Called-up share capital			1,200
Revaluation reserve			735
Other reserves			225
Profit and loss account			375
			2,535

Notes to the accounts

1 Share capital called up

	£
200,000 10 per cent preference shares of £1 each	200,000
1,000,000 ordinary shares of £1 each	1,000,000
	1,200,000

2 Accounting policies

Goodwill has been written off £20,000 against this year. The directors intend to write off the remaining £20,000 against next year's profits.

3 Tangible assets

	Buildings £000	Plant £000	Vehicles £000
Cost at 1.1.19X4	1,330	330	480
Disposals (at cost)	(130)	–	–
Adjustment for revaluation	735		
	1,935	330	480
Depreciation at 1.1.19X4	425	195	160
Provided in year	60	66	120
Disposals	(50)		
	435	261	280
Net book values	1,500	69	200

4 Investments

The market value of investments at 31 December 19X3 was £438,000.

5 Ten per cent debenture loans

These are redeemable in five equal annual instalments, starting next year. Interest of £40,000 is charged in this year's accounts.

6 Other creditors including taxation

	£
Preference dividend proposed	20,000
Ordinary dividend proposed 50 per cent	500,000
Corporation tax based on year's profits	266,000
	786,000

7 Other reserves

	£
Exchange reserve	75,000
General reserve	150,000
	225,000

8 Directors' remuneration

The amounts paid to directors were as follows:

	£	£
Fees as directors	20,000	
Other emoluments	190,000	210,000

Emoluments of the chairman amounted to £42,000 and those of the highest paid director £66,000. Other directors' emoluments were in the following ranges:

£45,001 to £50,000	1
£50,001 to £55,000	1

9 Operating profit is shown after charging

	£
Auditors' remuneration	7,000
Bank overdraft interest	19,000

Main points to remember

1   The Companies Acts require that additional notes be prepared and included with the published financial statements.

2   In some cases, the contents of these notes have been extended through the issuing of an accounting standard. For example, SSAP 25: *Segmental reporting* extended the disclosure required of many entities concerning segmental performance.

3   Along with the notes to the financial statements, a directors' report must be presented that summarises the activities and performance of the entity, along with specific details on a number of matters, including directors' shareholdings and information concerning significant changes in fixed assets.

Review questions

14.1 The following trial balance of X Limited, a non-listed company, has been extracted from the books after the preparation of the profit and loss and appropriation accounts for the year ended 31 March 19X7.

	£000	£000
Ordinary share capital – authorised, allotted and called-up fully paid shares of £1 each		1,000
12% debentures (repayable in 9 years)		500
Deferred taxation		128
Provisions for depreciation:		
Plant and machinery at 31 March 19X7		650
Freehold properties at 31 March 19X7		52
Vehicles at 31 March 19X7		135
Investments (listed), at cost	200	
Trade debtors and prepayments	825	
Corporation tax		270
Proposed final dividend		280
Tangible fixed assets:		
Freehold properties at 31 March 19X7	1,092	
Plant and machinery at 31 March 19X7	1,500	
Vehicles at 31 March 19X7	420	
Profit and loss account – balance at 31 March 19X7		356
Share premium account		150
Trade creditors and accruals		878
Research and development costs	35	
Stocks:		
Raw materials	200	
Work in progress	50	
Finished goods	250	
Bank balance	439	
Revaluation reserve on freehold properties		612
	5,011	5,011

You are also provided with the following information:

1 Investments
The listed investments consist of shares in W plc quoted on the Stock Exchange at £180,000 on 31 March 19X7. This is not considered to be a permanent fall in the value of this asset.

2 Trade debtors and prepayments
The company received notice, during April 19X7, that one of its major customers, Z Limited, had gone into liquidation. The amount included in trade debtors and prepayments is £225,000 and it is estimated that a dividend of 24p in the £ will be paid to unsecured creditors.

3 Taxation
(*a*) *Corporation tax*
The figure in the trial balance is made up as follows:

	£000
Based on profits for the year	174
Tax on exceptional item (*see* note 4)	96
	270

(*b*) *Deferred taxation*
    A transfer of £50,000 was made from the profit and loss account during the year ended 31 March 19X7.

4 Tangible fixed assets

(a) In arriving at the profit for the year, depreciation of £242,000 was charged, made up of freehold properties £12,000, plant and machinery £150,000 and vehicles £80,000.

(b) During the year to 31 March 19X7, new vehicles were purchased at a cost of £200,000.

(c) During March 19X7, the directors sold one of the freehold properties which had originally cost £320,000 and which had a written-down value at the date of the sale of £280,000. A profit of £320,000 on the sale, which was regarded as exceptional, has already been dealt with in arriving at the profit for the year. The estimated corporation tax liability in respect of the capital gain will be £96,000, as shown in note 3. After this sale, the directors decided to have the remaining freehold properties revalued, for the first time, by Messrs V & Co, Chartered Surveyors and to include the revalued figure of £1,040,000 in the 19X7 accounts.

5 Research and development costs

The company carries out research and development and accounts for it in accordance with the relevant accounting standard. The amount shown in the trial balance relates to development expenditure on a new product scheduled to be launched in April 19X7. Management is confident that this new product will earn substantial profits for the company in the coming years.

6 Stocks

The replacement cost of the finished goods, if valued at 31 March 19X7, would amount to £342,000.

You are required to prepare a balance sheet at 31 March 19X7 to conform to the requirements of the Companies Acts and relevant accounting standards insofar as the information given allows. The vertical format must be used.

The notes necessary to accompany this statement should also be prepared.

Workings should be shown, but comparative figures are not required.

(*Chartered Institute of Management Accountants*)

14.2 The following information has been extracted from the books of account of Billinge plc as at 30 June 19X6:

	Dr £000	Cr £000
Administration expenses	242	
Cash at bank and in hand	157	
Cash received on sale of fittings		3
Corporation tax (over-provision for the previous year)		10
Deferred taxation		60
Depreciation on fixtures, fittings, tools and equipment (1 July 19X5)		132
Distribution costs	55	
Factory closure costs	30	
Fixtures, fittings, tools and equipment at cost	340	
Profit and loss account (at 1 July 19X5)		40
Purchase of equipment	60	
Purchases of goods for resale	855	
Sales (net of VAT)		1,500
Share capital (500,000 authorised, issued and fully paid ordinary shares of £1 each)		500
Stock (at 1 July 19X5)	70	
Trade creditors		64
Trade debtors	500	
	£2,309	£2,309

Additional information:
1 The company was incorporated in 19X0.
2 The stock at 30 June 19X6 (valued at the lower of cost or net realisable value) was estimated to be worth £100,000.
3 Fixtures, fittings, tools and equipment all related to administrative expenses. Depreciation is charged on them at a rate of 20 per cent per annum on cost. A full year's depreciation is charged in the year of acquisition, but no depreciation is charged in the year of disposal.
4 During the year to 30 June 19X6, the company purchased £60,000 of equipment. It also sold some fittings (which had originally cost £20,000) for £3,000 and for which depreciation of £15,000 had been set aside.
5 The corporation tax based on the profits for the year at a rate of 35 per cent is estimated to be £100,000. A transfer of £40,000 is to be made to the deferred taxation account.
6 The company proposes to pay a dividend of 20p per ordinary share.
7 The standard rate of income tax is 30 per cent.

Required:
Insofar as the information permits, prepare Billinge plc's profit and loss account for the year to 30 June 19X6, and a balance sheet as at that date in accordance with the Companies Acts and appropriate accounting standards.

(*Association of Accounting Technicians*)

14.3A   Cosnett Ltd is a company principally involved in the manufacture of aluminium accessories for camping enthusiasts. Its trial balance at 30 September 19X5 was:

	£	£
Issued ordinary share capital (£1 shares)		600,000
Retained profit at 1 October 19X4		625,700
Debentures redeemable 19X9		150,000
Bank loan		25,000
Plant and machinery at cost	1,475,800	
Accumulated depreciation to 30 September 19X5		291,500
Investments in UK companies at cost	20,000	
Turnover		3,058,000
Dividends from investments		2,800
Loss arising on factory closure	86,100	
Cost of sales	2,083,500	
Political and charitable contributions	750	
Distribution costs	82,190	
Salaries of office staff	42,100	
Directors' emoluments	63,000	
Rent and rates of offices	82,180	
Hire of plant and machinery	6,700	
Travel and entertainment expenses	4,350	
General expenses	221,400	
Trade debtors	396,100	
Trade creditors and accruals		245,820
Stocks	421,440	
Bank	17,950	
Interim dividend paid	21,000	
Interest charged	19,360	
Provision for deferred taxation		45,100
	5,043,920	5,043,920

You are provided with the following additional information:
(a) The company's shares are owned, equally, by three brothers: John, Peter and Henry Phillips; they are also the directors.
(b) The bank loan is repayable by five annual instalments of £5,000 commencing 31 December 19X5.
(c) The investments were acquired with cash, surplus to existing operating requirements, which will be needed to pay for additional plant the directors plan to acquire early in 19X6.
(d) On 1 January 19X5 the company closed a factory which had previously contributed approximately 20 per cent of the company's total production requirements.
(e) Trade debtors include £80,000 due from a customer who went into liquidation on 1 September 19X5; the directors estimate that a dividend of 20p in the £ will eventually be received.
(f) Trade creditors and accruals include:
   (i) £50,000 due to a supplier of plant, of which £20,000 is payable on 1 January 19X6 and the remainder at the end of the year;
   (ii) accruals totalling £3,260.
(g) The mainstream corporation tax liability for the year is estimated at £120,000.
(h) The directors propose to pay a final dividend of 10.5p per share and to transfer £26,500 to the deferred tax account.

Required:
The profit and loss account of Cosnett Ltd for the year to 30 September 19X5 and balance sheet at that date together with relevant notes attached thereto. The accounts should comply with the minimum requirements of the Companies Acts and accounting standards so far as the information permits.

(*Institute of Chartered Secretaries and Administrators*)

14.4A The following trial balance has been extracted from the books of Arran plc as at 31 March 19X7:

	£000	£000
Administrative expenses	95	
Called-up share capital (all ordinary shares of £1 each)		200
Cash at bank and in hand	25	
Debtors	230	
Deferred taxation (at 1 April 19X6)		60
Distribution costs	500	
Fixed asset investments	280	
Franked investment income		12
Interim dividend paid	21	
Overprovision of last year's corporation tax		5
Land and buildings at cost	200	
Land and buildings: accumulated depreciation at 1 April 19X6		30
Plant and machinery at cost	400	
Plant and machinery: accumulated depreciation at 1 April 19X6		170
Profit and loss account (at 1 April 19X6)		229
Profit on exceptional item		50
Purchases	1,210	
Sales		2,215
Stocks at 1 April 19X6	140	
Trade creditors		130
	£3,101	£3,101

Additional information
1   Stocks at 31 March 19X7 were valued at £150,000.
2   Depreciation for the year to 31 March 19X7 is to be charged against administrative expenses as follows:

	£000
Land and buildings	5
Plant and machinery	40

3   Assume that the basic rate of income tax is 30 per cent.
4   Corporation tax of £180,000 is to be charged against profits on ordinary activities for the year to 31 March 19X7.
5   £4,000 is to be transferred to the deferred taxation account.
6   The company proposes to pay a final ordinary dividend of 30p per share.

Required:
Insofar as the information permits, prepare the company's profit and loss account for the year to 31 March 19X7 and a balance sheet as at that date in accordance with the Companies Acts and related accounting standards. (*Note*: Profit and loss account and balance sheet notes are not required, but you should show the basis and computation of earnings per share at the foot of the profit and loss account, and your workings should be submitted.)

(*Association of Accounting Technicians*)

14.5A The following trial balance has been extracted from the books of account of Greet plc as at 31 March 19X8:

	Dr £000	Cr £000
Administrative expenses	210	
Called up share capital (ordinary shares of £1 fully paid)		600
Debtors	470	
Cash at bank and in hand	40	
Corporation tax (overprovision in 19X7)		25
Deferred taxation (at 1 April 19X7)		180
Distribution costs	420	
Exceptional item		60
Fixed asset investments	560	
Investment income		72
Plant and machinery: at cost	750	
accumulated depreciation (at 31 March 19X8)		220
Profit and loss (at 1 April 19X7)		182
Purchases	960	
Stock (at 1 April 19X7)	140	
Trade creditors		261
Turnover		1,950
	£3,550	£3,550

Additional information:

1 Stock at 31 March 19X8 was valued at £150,000.
2 The following items *are already included* in the balances listed in the above trial balance:

	Distribution costs £000	Administrative expenses £000
Depreciation (for the year to 31 March 19X8)	27	5
Hire of plant and machinery	20	15
Auditors' remuneration	–	30
Directors' emoluments	–	45

3 The following rates of taxation are to be assumed:

	%
Corporation tax	35
Income tax	27

4 The corporation tax charge based on the profits for the year is estimated to be £52,000.
5 A transfer of £16,000 is to be made to the credit of the deferred taxation account.
6 The exceptional item relates to the profit made on the disposal of a factory in Belgium following the closure of the company's entire operations in that country.
7 The company's authorised share capital consists of 1,000,000 ordinary shares of £1 each.
8 A final ordinary payment of 50p per share is proposed.
9 There were no purchases or disposals of fixed assets during the year.
10 The market value of the fixed assets investments as at 31 March 19X8 was £580,000. There were no purchases or sales of such investments during the year.

Required:

Insofar as the information permits, prepare the company's published profit and loss account for the year to 31 March 19X8 and a balance sheet as at that date in accordance with the Companies Acts and with related accounting standards.

Relevant notes to the profit and loss account and balance sheet and detailed workings should be submitted with your answer, but a statement of the company's accounting policies is not required.

(*Association of Accounting Technicians*)

14.6 The accountant of Scampion plc, a retailing company listed on the London Stock Exchange, has produced the following draft financial statements for the company for the year to 31 May 19X7.

Profit and Loss Account for year to 31 May 19X7

	£000	£000
Sales		3,489
Income from investments		15
		3,504
Purchases of goods and services	1,929	
Value added tax paid on sales	257	
Wages and salaries including pension scheme	330	
Depreciation	51	
Interest on loans	18	
General administration expenses		
– Shops	595	
– Head office	25	
		3,205
Net profit for year		299
Corporation tax at 40%		120
Profit after tax for year		179

Balance Sheet at 31 May 19X7

	£000	£000
Fixed assets		
Land and buildings		1,178
Fixtures, fittings, equipment and motor vehicles		194
Investments		167
		1,539
Current assets		
Stock	230	
Debtors	67	
Cash at bank and in hand	84	
	381	
Current liabilities		
Creditors	487	
		(106)
		1,433
Ordinary share capital (£1 shares)		660
Reserves		703
Loans		70
		1,433

You discover the following further information:

(*i*)   Fixed assets details are as follows:

	Cost	Depreciation	Net
	£000	£000	£000
Freehold land and buildings	1,212	34	1,178
Fixtures, fittings and equipment	181	56	125
Motor vehicles	137	68	69

Purchases of fixed assets during the year were freehold land and buildings £50,000, fixtures, fittings and equipment £40,000, motor vehicles £20,000. The only fixed asset disposal during the year is referred to in note (x). Depreciation charged during the year was £5,000 for freehold buildings, £18,000 for fixtures, fittings and equipment and £28,000 for motor vehicles. Straight-line depreciation method is used assuming the following lives: Freehold buildings 40 years, fixtures, fittings and equipment 10 years and motor vehicles 5 years.

(ii)   A dividend of 10 pence per share is proposed.

(iii) A valuation by Bloggs & Co Surveyors shows the freehold land and buildings to have a market value of £1,350,000.

(iv)   Loans are:
£20,000 bank loan with a variable rate of interest repayable by 30 September 19X7;
£50,000 12 per cent debenture repayable 20X1;
£100,000 11 per cent debenture repaid during the year.
There were no other loans during the year.

(v)   The income from investments is derived from fixed asset investments (shares in related companies) £5,000 and current asset investment (government securities) £10,000.

(vi)   At the balance sheet date the shares in related companies (cost £64,000) are valued by the directors at £60,000. The market value of the government securities is £115,000 (cost £103,000).

(vii) After the balance sheet date but before the financial statements are finalised there is a very substantial fall in share and security prices. The market value of the government securities had fallen to £50,000 by the time the directors signed the accounts. No adjustment has been made for this item in the accounts.

(viii) Within two weeks of the balance sheet date a notice of liquidation was received by Scampion plc concerning one of the company's debtors. £45,000 is included in the balance sheet for this debtor and enquiries reveal that nothing is likely to be paid to any unsecured creditor. No adjustment has been made for this item in the accounts.

(ix)   The corporation tax charge is based on the accounts for the year and there are no other amounts of tax owing by the company.

(x)   Reserves at 31 May 19X6 were:

	£
Revaluation reserve	150,000
Share premium account	225,000
Profit and loss account	149,000

The revaluation reserve represents the after-tax surplus on a property which was valued in last year's balance sheet at £400,000 and sold during the current year at book value.

Required:
A profit and loss account for the year to 31 May 19X7 and a balance sheet at that date for Scampion plc complying with the Companies Acts insofar as the information given will allow.
   Ignore advance corporation tax.

(*Association of Chartered Certified Accountants*)

14.7A   The Companies Acts and accounting standards require a great deal of information to be disclosed in a company's annual report and accounts.

Required:
List the disclosure requirements for the following items:
(i)   employees;
(ii)   directors' emoluments; and
(iii) fixed assets.

(*Association of Accounting Technicians*)

15

FRS 1: Cash flow statements

Objectives

After you have studied this chapter, you should be able to:

- *discuss the purpose of cash flow information*
- *understand the difference between cash flow and profit*
- *prepare a cash flow statement for a company following the format given in FRS 1*

15.1 Introduction

Business Accounting 1 introduced cash flow statements and this chapter moves on to consider the accounting standard relating to these statements – FRS 1: *Cash flow statements*. The standard requires that a cash flow statement be prepared according to prescribed formats for all companies other than those exempt from doing so, either because they are 'small', as defined by the Companies Act (*see* Chapter 13), or because they are subsidiary undertakings and the group they belong to is publishing group accounts in the European Union. The standard requires that the statement be included as a primary statement within the financial statements, i.e. it has the same status as the profit and loss account and the balance sheet.

15.2 Standard headings

The objective of FRS 1 is to ensure that reporting entities report the cash generation and cash absorption for a period by highlighting the significant components of cash flow in a way that facilitates comparison of the cash performance of different businesses; and that they provide information that assists in the assessment of their liquidity, solvency, and financial adaptability. For this reason, the statement must show the flows of cash and cash equivalents for the period under the headings:

- operating activities;
- returns on investments and servicing of finance;
- taxation;
- capital expenditure and financial investment;
- acquisitions and disposals;
- equity dividends paid;
- management of liquid resources; and
- financing.

The first six headings should be in this order. The other two can be combined under a single heading provided that each of their cash flows are shown separately and separate subtotals are given. Operating cash flows can be presented by either the *direct* method (showing the relevant constituent cash flows) or the *indirect* method (calculating operating cash flows by adjustment to the operating profit reported in the profit and loss account).

The standard indicates in which section various items are to be located and these are described in sections 15.4-15.11. Further guidance concerning where items appear in the statement can be seen in the examples presented later in the chapter.

The standard requires that either adjoining the statement, or in a separate note, reconciliations are presented between operating profit and net cash flow from operating activities for the period, and between the movement in cash in the period and the movement in net debt. Neither reconciliation forms part of the statement. The reconciliation to net debt should identify the cash flows of the entity, the acquisition or disposal of subsidiary undertakings (excluding cash balances), other non-cash changes, and the recognition of changes in the market value and exchange rate movements.

15.3 Cash flow

The cash flow statement reports cash flow. Cash flow is defined in paragraph 2 of FRS 1 as 'an increase or decrease in an amount of cash'. Anything that falls outside this definition is not a cash flow and should not appear in the statement (though it could appear in the notes).

Cash is defined as 'cash in hand and deposits repayable on demand with any qualifying financial institution, less overdrafts from any qualifying financial institution repayable on demand'.

'Deposits repayable on demand' are deposits that can be withdrawn at any time without notice and without penalty or if a maturity or period of notice of not more than 24 hours or one working day has been agreed.

Cash includes cash in hand and deposits denominated in foreign currencies.

15.4 Operating activities and cash flows

Operating activities are generally the cash effects of transactions and other events relating to operating or trading activities. The net cash flow from operating activities represents the net increase or decrease in cash resulting from the operations shown in the profit and loss account in arriving at operating profit.

The reconciliation between operating profit and net cash flow from operating activities for the period should disclose separately the movements in stocks, debtors, and creditors related to operating activities, and other differences between cash flows and profits. It should also show separately the difference between dividends received and results taken into account for equity accounted entities.

In the cash flow statement, **operating cash flows** may be shown using either the **indirect** method or the **direct** method. Using the **indirect** method, it would be laid out in a manner similar to that shown in Exhibit 15.1.

Exhibit 15.1

	£
Operating profit	12,000
Depreciation charges	500
Loss on sale of tangible fixed assets	10
Increase in stocks	(200)
Increase in debtors	(100)
Increase in creditors	300
Net cash inflow from operating activities	12,510

FRS 1 requires that a reconciliation be shown between the net cash flow from operating activities and the operating profit as shown in the profit and loss account, which is precisely what is produced if the *indirect* method is adopted. Consequently, by adopting the *indirect* method, as the detailed information is to be included in a reconciliation, the main part of the statement may only include a single line 'net cash flow from operating activities'. Thus, instead of being included in the body of the cash flow statement, the details shown in Exhibit 15.1 would be included in the notes to the statement. When the *indirect* method is adopted, no details of the equivalent *direct* method analysis is required.

On the other hand, when the **direct** method is adopted for preparation of the statement, the reconciliation (i.e. the *indirect* method analysis) must also be prepared and included as a note to the statement. The **direct** method, would produce an analysis in the cash flow statement similar to that shown in Exhibit 15.2.

Exhibit 15.2

Operating activities	£
Cash received from customers	120,000
Cash payments to suppliers	(40,000)
Cash paid to and on behalf of employees	(60,000)
Other cash payments	(7,490)
Net cash inflow from operating activities	12,510

It is generally easier for an entity to adopt the *indirect* method – the figures are readily available from the profit and loss account and balance sheet data. The *direct* method, on the other hand, requires that the cash book is analysed. Despite there being much more work involved in preparing it, in Appendix III to FRS 1, the ASB encourages the use of the *direct* method when the potential benefits to users outweigh the costs of doing so – it does help provide a far clearer view of cash flow than the bookkeeping adjustments to profit that are undertaken under the *indirect* method. In an examination, if sufficient information on cash flows is provided for you to adopt the *direct* method, you should assume that is the approach to take – however, you would still require to adopt the *indirect* method when completing the reconciliation if that was also required by the question set.

15.5 Returns on investment and servicing of finance

This section concerns receipts resulting from the ownership of an investment and payments to providers of finance, non-equity shareholders, and minority interests.

Generally, the standard endeavours to classify all cash flows according to the substance of the transaction that gave rise to them. As a result, this section of the statement excludes any item that may be classified under one of the other headings. For example, payments to *non-equity* shareholders (e.g. holders of preference shares in the entity) are included in this section, but payments to *equity* shareholders appear in the 'equity dividends paid' section.

Among the cash inflows included in this section are interest and dividends received (other than dividends from equity accounted entities whose results are included as part of operating profit). Cash outflows in this section include interest paid; finance costs, as defined under FRS 4 (*Capital instruments*) – *see* Chapter 11; the interest element of finance lease rental payments, as defined under SSAP 21 (*Accounting for leases and hire purchase contracts*) – *see* Chapter 2; and dividends paid to minority interests and to non-equity shareholders of the entity.

15.6 Taxation

This section includes cash flows to and from taxation authorities in respect of the reporting entity's revenue and capital profits. Other tax cash flows should be included under the same heading as the cash flow which gave rise to them – VAT, for example, is seen as relating to 'operating activities'. Consequently, the net amount of VAT paid to or received from the tax authorities is included under that section. The exception to this arises when VAT is irrecoverable, in which case it is added to the originating transaction value and not distinguished from it within the cash flow statement.

15.7 Capital expenditure and financial investment

Included in this section are cash flows relating to the acquisition or disposal of any fixed asset other than those required to be classified under the 'acquisitions and disposals' section of the statement, and those relating to any current asset investment not included in the 'management of liquid resources' section.

The heading can be reduced to 'capital expenditure' if there are no cash flows relating to financial investment.

The cash inflows include:
- receipts from the sale or disposal of property, plant, or equipment, and,
- receipts from the repayment of the reporting entity's loans to other entities and sales of debt instruments of other entities (other than receipts forming part of an acquisition or disposal or a movement in liquid resources and classified as falling within either of those two sections of the statement).

The cash outflows include:
- payments to acquire property, plant, or equipment, and,
- loans made by the reporting entity and payments to acquire debt instruments of other entities (other than payments forming part of an acquisition or disposal or a movement in liquid resources and classified as falling within either of those two sections of the statement).

15.8 Acquisitions and disposals

Included in this section are those cash flows relating to the acquisition or disposal of any trade or business, or of an investment in an entity that is or, as a result of the transaction, becomes or ceases to be either an associate, a joint venture, or a subsidiary undertaking.

15.9 Equity dividends paid

This section includes the dividends paid on the reporting entity's or, in a group, the parent's equity shares.

15.10 Management of liquid resources

Cash flows in respect of liquid resources are included in this section. The FRS defines liquid resources as 'current asset investments held as readily disposable stores of value'. A 'readily disposable investment' is one that is disposable without curtailing or disrupting the entity's business and is either readily convertible into known amounts of cash or traded in an active market.

Each entity must explain what it includes in liquid resources and declare any change in its policy.

Cash inflows in this section include withdrawals from short-term deposits not qualifying as cash and inflows from the disposal or redemption of any other investments held as liquid resources.

Cash outflows in this section include payments into short-term deposits not qualifying as cash and outflows to acquire any other investment held as a liquid resource.

15.11 Financing

Receipts and repayments of the principal amounts (i.e. the advance, not the interest) from or to external providers of finance are entered in this section. Examples include receipts from issuing and payments towards the redemption of shares and other equity instruments, debentures, loans, notes, bonds, and from long-term and short-term borrowings (other than overdrafts); the capital element of finance lease rental payment; and payments of expenses or commission on any issue of equity shares.

The amount of any financing cash flows received from or paid to an equity accounted entity should be disclosed separately.

15.12 Material transactions not resulting in any cash flows

FRS 1 also requires that details of material transactions that do not result in any cash flows should be included in a note if it is necessary for an understanding of the underlying transactions. A possible example would be an operating lease. It would involve the acquisition of an asset, but the reporting entity is paying rent, not purchasing the asset.

15.13 Exceptional and extraordinary items

Cash flows relating to items classed as exceptional or extraordinary in the profit and loss account should be shown under the appropriate standard headings, according to their nature. They should be identified in the cash flow statement or a note to it and the relationship between the cash flows and the originating exceptional or extraordinary item should be explained.

Where the cash flows themselves are exceptional because of their size or incidence but the underlying event that gave rise to them are not, sufficient disclosure should be given to explain their cause and effect.

15.14 An example of the FRS 1 layout using the indirect method

Exhibit 15.3

X LIMITED

Cash Flow Statement for the year ended 31 December 19X7

	£000	£000
1 **Net cash inflow/(outflow) from operating activities** (*see* Note 1)		XXX
2 Returns on investments and servicing of finance		
Interest received	XXX	
Interest paid	(XXX)	
Preference dividends paid	(XXX)	
Net cash inflow/(outflow) from returns on investments and servicing of finance		XXX
3 Taxation		XXX
4 Capital expenditure and financial investment		
Payments to acquire intangible fixed assets	XXX	
Payments to acquire tangible fixed assets	XXX	
Receipts from sales of tangible fixed assets	XXX	
Net cash inflow/(outflow) from capital expenditure and financial investment		XXX
5 Acquisitions and disposals		
Purchase of subsidiary undertaking	(XXX)	
Sale of business	XXX	
Net cash inflow/(outflow) from acquisitions and disposals		XXX
6 Equity dividends paid		(XXX)
7 Management of liquid resources		
Cash withdrawn from 7 day deposit	XXX	
Purchase of government securities	(XXX)	
Sale of corporate bonds	XXX	
Net cash inflow/(outflow) from management of liquid resources		XXX
8 Financing		
Issue of ordinary share capital	XXX	
Repurchase of debenture loan	(XXX)	
Expenses paid in connection with share issues	(XXX)	
Increase/(decrease) in cash in the period		XXX

Reconciliation of net cash flow to movement in net debt/funds

Increase/(decrease) in cash in the period	XXX
Cash inflow/(outflow) from increase/decrease in debt and lease financing	XXX
Cash inflow/(outflow) from decrease/increase in liquid resources	<u>XXX</u>
Change in net debt resulting from cash flows	XXX
Loans and finance leases acquired with subsidiary	(XXX)
New finance leases	(XXX)
Exchange rate translation differences	<u>XXX</u>
Movement in net debt in the period	XXX
Net funds at 1 January 19X7	<u>XXX</u>
Net debt at 31 December 19X7	<u><u>(XXX)</u></u>

Note to the cash flow statement

1   *Reconciliation of operating profit to net cash inflow/(outflow) from operating activities*

	£000
Operating profit	XXX
Depreciation charges	XXX
(Profit)/Loss on sale of tangible fixed assets	XXX
(Increase)/Decrease in stocks	XXX
(Increase)/Decrease in debtors	XXX
Increase/(Decrease) in creditors	XXX
Net cash inflow/(outflow) from operating activities	<u><u>XXX</u></u>

Each of the eight headings of the cash flow statement can be shown as one line in the statement and the detail in a note. (The numbers have been shown in exhibit 15.3 in order to make it clear what the 8 headings are. The numbers would not normally be included.)

The reconciliation to net debt does not form part of the statement, nor does the reconciliation of operating profit to net cash flow from operationg activities. Either can be shown in a separate note (as the reconciliation of operating profit to net cash flow from operating activities is shown above) or adjoining the statement (as in the case of the reconciliation of the movement of cash to net debt above).

15.15 Two further examples

Exhibits 15.4 and 15.5 further illustrate how a cash flow statement is prepared, this time using numbers to add clarity. Some key points to remember include:

- It is amounts paid rather than charged or accrued that are included. Thus for both tax and dividends, it is the actual payments and receipts that occurred during the period that are included in the statement, not the amounts provided for that will be paid or received in a future period.

- Profit on sale of fixed assets is already included in the sale amount and should not be included a second time.

- Care should be taken to identify and eliminate non-cash adjustments to the original profit before tax figure, for example depreciation and bad debt provisions.

- If the layout presented in Exhibits 15.4 and 15.5 is followed, the entries in the 'Financing' section will have the opposite signs to the others, i.e. income will be shown with negative values, rather than positive as is the case in the other sections of the statement.

Exhibit 15.4

From the following profit and loss and balance sheet information, prepare a cash flow statement as required by FRS 1 *using the indirect method*.

Profit and Loss Account for the year ending 31 December 19X4

	£000	£000
Sales		10,000
Cost of goods sold		6,000
		4,000
Expenses		
Depreciation	600	
Interest	150	
Other expenses	2,100	
		2,850
Profit for the year before tax		1,150
Tax		200
Profit for the year after tax		950
Proposed dividend		150
Retained profit		800

Balance Sheet as at 31 December

	£000	19X4 £000	£000	19X3 £000
Fixed assets at cost		6,000		6,000
Less accumulated depreciation		3,000		2,400
Net book value		3,000		3,600
Current assets				
Stock	650		700	
Trade debtors	200		250	
Cash	1,610		150	
		2,460		1,100
Less current liabilities				
Trade creditors	310		300	
Taxation	200		150	
Proposed dividends	150		250	
		660		700
		4,800		4,000
Financed by				
Ordinary share capital		2,000		2,000
Revenue reserves		2,800		2,000
		4,800		4,000

Outline solution

Cash Flow Statement (using the indirect method) for the year ended 31 December 19X4

	£000
Net cash inflow from operating activities	2,010
Returns on investments and servicing of finance	
Interest paid	(150)
Taxation	(150)
Capital expenditure and financial investment	–
Acquisitions and disposals	–
Equity dividends paid	(250)
Management of liquid resources	–
Financing	–
Increase in cash in the period	1,460

Notes to the cash flow statement
1. Reconciliation of operating profit to net cash inflow from operating activities:

	£000
Operating profit	1,300
Depreciation charges	600
Decrease in stocks	50
Decrease in debtors	50
Increase in creditors	10
Net cash inflow from operating activities	2,010

Working:
Operating profit = Retained profit (800) + Interest (150) + Dividend (150) + Tax (200)
= 1,300

Exhibit 15.5

From the summarised cash account and the fixed asset schedule of Thistle Ltd for 19X2, prepare a cash flow statement as required by FRS 1 *using the direct method*.

Summarised Cash Account

	£000		£000
Opening balance	500	Wages	1,350
Cash from cash sales	3,500	Other expenses	600
Cash from credit sales	5,750	Cash paid to suppliers	4,320
Cash from issue of shares	1,200	Tax paid	100
Cash from sale of building	970	Cash paid on finance lease	700
		Final dividend for 19X1	100
		Interim dividend 19X2	50
		Closing balance	4,700
	11,920		11,920

Fixed Asset Schedule

	Plant £000	Buildings £000	Total £000
Cost at 1.1.19X2	10,000	15,000	25,000
Acquisitions	4,730	–	4,730
Disposals	–	(5,000)	(5,000)
Cost at 31.12.19X2	14,730	10,000	24,730
Accumulated depreciation at 1.1.19X2	3,500	6,000	9,500
Charge for year	650	1,500	2,150
Disposals	–	(4,500)	(4,500)
Accumulated depreciation at 31.12.19X2	4,150	3,000	7,150

Other information

(a) The tax charge for the year was £400,000. The opening balance on the tax liability was £100,000.

(b) The proposed final dividend for 19X2 was £120,000.

(c) Other expenses include insurance, which is paid a year in advance, on 30 June. In 19X1, insurance of £300,000 was paid. The amount paid in 19X2 was £400,000.

(d) Accrued wages were £75,000 at 1.1.19X2, and £95,000 at 31.12.19X2.

(e) Stocks were £1,500,000 at 1.1.19X2, and £1,700,000 at 31.12.19X2.

(f) All £700,000 paid on the finance lease in 19X2 represented capital. This was the first year of the lease and interest was not paid until the second payment, which was made in 19X3. Interest of £403,000 was included in the 19X3 payment and was accrued in the 19X2 financial statements.

(g) Opening and closing trade debtors and trade creditors were:

	1.1.19X2	31.12.19X2
Trade debtors	300,000	450,000
Trade creditors	500,000	475,000

(h) 600,000 £1 ordinary shares were issued at a premium on 1.3.19X2.

(i) Retained profits for the year to 31.12.19X2 were £732,000.

Outline Solution

Cash Flow Statement (using the direct method) for Thistle Ltd for the year ended 31 December 19X2

	£000	£000
Operating activities		
Cash received from customers	9,250	
Cash paid to suppliers	(4,320)	
Cash paid to employees	(1,350)	
Other cash payments	(600)	
Net cash inflow from operating activities		2,980
Returns on investment and servicing of finance		–
Taxation		(100)
Capital expenditure and financial investment		
Sale of buildings		970
Acquisitions and disposals		–
Equity dividend paid		(150)
Management of liquid resources		–
Financing		
Issue of share capital	1,200	
Capital element of finance lease rental payments	(700)	
Net cash inflow from financing		500
Increase in cash in the period		4,200

Note to the cash flow statement:

1 Reconciliation of operating profit to net cash inflow from operating activities:	£000
Operating profit	1,705
Depreciation charges	2,150
Profit on sale of building	(470)
Increase in stocks	(200)
Increase in debtors	(150)
Increase in prepayments	(50)
Decrease in creditors	(25)
Increase in accruals	20
Net cash inflow from operating activities	2,980

Workings

1 Dividends paid in 19X2 are the proposed dividends from the previous year, plus the interim dividend paid during 19X2. The dividend charge in the profit and loss account will be the interim dividend and the proposed dividend for 19X2.

2 Assume tax paid during 19X2 is the amount outstanding at the opening balance sheet date. The tax charge for 19X2 in the profit and loss account is £400,000.

3		£
	Retained profit	732,000
	Add Dividends	170,000
	Add Tax	400,000
	Add Interest	403,000
	Operating profit	1,705,000

Main points to remember

1 The objective of FRS 1 is to require entities to report their cash generation and absorption for a period on a standard basis.

2 This aids comparison between entities.

3 The statement must show the flows of cash for the period under the headings:

- operating activities;
- returns on investments and servicing of finance;
- taxation;
- capital expenditure and financial investment;
- acquisitions and disposals;
- equity dividends paid;
- management of liquid resources; and
- financing.

4 The headings should be in that order and the statement should include a total for each heading.

5 Cash flow is an increase or decrease in cash resulting from a transaction.

6 Operating activities are generally the cash effects of transactions and other events relating to operating and trading activities.

7 Operating cash flows can be shown using either the *indirect* method or the *direct* method.

8 Reconciliations are presented between operating profit and net cash flow from operating activities for the period, and between the movement in cash in the period and the movement in net debt.

9 The ASB recommends that the *direct* method be used if the benefits of doing so outweigh the costs.

Review questions

15.1 List the eight headings in the cash flow statement, as required by FRS 1.

15.2A Give an example of the information to be included under each of the headings in the cash flow statement and indicate why this information might be useful.

15.3 Prepare a cash flow statement for Lee Ltd for the year ended 31 December 19X4 as required under FRS 1 using the direct method, together with note 1 to the statement. The profit and loss account, balance sheet and cash account for Lee Ltd for the year 19X4 are given below. (Do not attempt to provide the reconciliation of net cash flow to net debt.)

Profit and Loss Account for the year ending 31 December 19X4

	£	£
Sales		6,500
Less Cost of goods sold		3,000
		3,500
Less expenses		
Wages	2,000	
Other costs	600	
Depreciation	500	
Interest	100	
		3,200
Profit for the year		300
Proposed dividend		40
Retained profit		260

Balance Sheet as at 31 December

	19X4		19X3	
	£	£	£	£
Fixed assets at cost		4,500		3,800
Less Accumulated depreciation		2,300		1,800
Net book value		2,200		2,000
Current assets				
Stock	400		500	
Trade debtors	150		200	
Cash	200		100	
		750		800
Less current liabilities				
Trade creditors	275		250	
Accrued wages	25		50	
Proposed dividends	40		50	
		(340)		(350)
		2,610		2,450
Financed by				
Debentures		900		1,000
Ordinary share capital		1,000		1,000
Retained profits		710		450
		2,610		2,450

Cash Account for 19X4

	£		£
Opening balance	100	Wages	2,025
Cash from customers	6,550	Other expenses	600
		Cash paid to suppliers	2,875
		Interest paid	100
		Cash purchase of fixed assets	700
		Cash paid to debenture holders	100
		Dividends paid	50
		Closing balance	200
	6,650		6,650

15.4A The balance sheets and additional information relating to Pennylane Ltd are given below. Prepare a cash flow statement for Pennylane Ltd for the year ended 31 December 19X3 as required under FRS 1 using the indirect method, together with note 1 to the statement. (Do not attempt to provide the reconciliation of net cash flow to net debt.)

Pennylane Ltd

Balance Sheets as at 31 December

	19X3 £000	19X2 £000
Fixed assets		
Tangible assets	400	325
Intangible assets	230	180
Investments	–	25
	630	530
Current assets		
Stocks	120	104
Debtors	400	295
Short-term investments	50	–
Cash in hand	10	4
	580	403
Creditors: amounts falling due within one year		
Trade creditors	122	108
Bank overdraft	88	105
Taxation	120	110
Dividends proposed	100	80
	430	403
Net current assets	150	–
Total assets less current liabilities	780	530
Creditors: amounts falling due after one year		
Long-term loan	(100)	–
Provisions for liabilities and charges: deferred taxation	(80)	(60)
	600	470
Capital and reserves		
Share capital (£1 ordinary shares)	200	150
Share premium account	160	150
Revaluation reserve	100	90
Profit and loss account	140	80
	600	470

Additional information:

(a) During the year interest of £75,000 was paid, and interest of £25,000 was received.

(b) The following information relates to tangible fixed assets.

At 31 December	19X3 £000	19X2 £000
Cost	740	615
Accumulated depreciation	340	290
Net book value	400	325

(c) The proceeds of the sale of fixed asset investments were £30,000.

(d) Plant, with an original cost of £90,000 and a net book value of £50,000, was sold for £37,000.

(e) Tax paid to the Inland Revenue during 19X3 amounted to £110,000.

15.5 State the purposes of a cash flow statement.

(*Association of Chartered Certified Accountants*)

15.6 The following information has been extracted from the books of Nimmo Limited for the year to 31 December 19X9:

Profit and Loss Accounts for year to 31 December

	19X8 £000	19X9 £000
Profit before taxation	9,500	20,400
Taxation	(3,200)	(5,200)
Profit after taxation	6,300	15,200
Dividends:		
Preference (paid)	(100)	(100)
Ordinary: interim (paid)	(1,000)	(2,000)
final (proposed)	(3,000)	(6,000)
Retained profit for the year	£2,200	£7,100

Balance Sheets at 31 December

	19X8 £000	19X9 £000
Fixed assets		
Plant, machinery and equipment, at cost	17,600	23,900
Less: Accumulated depreciation	9,500	10,750
	8,100	13,150
Current assets		
Stocks	5,000	15,000
Trade debtors	8,600	26,700
Prepayments	300	400
Cash at bank and in hand	600	–
	14,500	42,100
Current liabilities		
Bank overdraft	–	(16,200)
Trade creditors	(6,000)	(10,000)
Accruals	(800)	(1,000)
Taxation	(3,200)	(5,200)
Dividends	(3,000)	(6,000)
	(13,000)	(38,400)
	£9,600	£16,850
Share capital		
Ordinary shares of £1 each	5,000	5,000
10% preference shares of £1 each	1,000	1,000
Profit and loss account	3,000	10,100
	9,000	16,100
Loans		
15% debenture stock	600	750
	£9,600	£16,850

Additional information:

1 The directors are extremely concerned about the large bank overdraft as at 31 December 19X9

and they attribute this mainly to the increase in trade debtors as a result of alleged poor credit control.

2   During the year to 31 December 19X9, fixed assets originally costing £5,500,000 were sold for £1,000,000. The accumulated depreciation on these assets as at 31 December 19X8 was £3,800,000.

Required:
Prepare a cash flow statement for the year to 31 December 19X9.

Author's note: Use the indirect method but do not attempt to provide the reconciliation of net cash flow to net debt.

(*Association of Accounting Technicians*)

15.7   The following summarised balance sheets relate to Track Limited:

Balance Sheets at 30 June

	19X0 £000	19X1 £000
Fixed assets at cost	500	650
Less Accumulated depreciation	200	300
	300	350
Investments at cost	200	50
Current assets		
Stocks	400	700
Debtors	1,350	1,550
Cash and bank	100	–
	1,850	2,250
Current liabilities		
Bank overdraft	–	(60)
Creditors	(650)	(790)
Taxation	(230)	(190)
Proposed dividend	(150)	(130)
	(1,030)	(1,170)
	£1,320	£1,480
Capital and reserves		
Called-up share capital (£1 ordinary shares)	500	750
Share premium account	150	200
Profit and loss account	670	530
	£1,320	£1,480

Additional information:
1   During the year to 30 June 19X1, some fixed assets originally costing £25,000 had been sold for £20,000 in cash. The accumulated depreciation on these fixed assets at 30 June 19X0 amounted to £10,000. Similarly, some of the investments originally costing £150,000 had been sold for cash at their book value.
2   The taxation balances disclosed in the above balance sheets represent the actual amounts agreed with the Inland Revenue. All taxes were paid on their due dates. Advance corporation tax may be ignored.
3   No interim dividend was paid during the year to 30 June 19X1.
4   During the year to 30 June 19X1, the company made a 1-for-2 rights issue of 250 ordinary £1 shares at 120p per share.

Required:
Prepare Track Ltd's cash flow statement for the year to 30 June 19X1 in accordance with the requirements of FRS 1 using the indirect method. (Do not attempt to provide the reconciliation of net cash flow to net debt.)

(*Association of Accounting Technicians*)

15.8A   You are presented with the following summarised information relating to Ward plc:

Profit and Loss Account for the Year to 30 June 19X8

	£000
Net profit for the year before taxation	900
Taxation (*see* Note 1)	(636)
Profit for the year after taxation	264
Extraordinary item (after tax relief of £35,000)	(90)
Profit for the year after taxation and extraordinary item	174
Dividends paid and proposed	(119)
Retained profit for the year	£55

Balance Sheet at 30 June 19X8

	19X7 £000	19X8 £000
Fixed assets (*see* Note 2)	1,515	1,810
Investments	40	40
Current assets		
Stocks	175	200
Debtors	100	60
Cash at bank and in hand	20	–
	295	260
Creditors: amounts falling due within one year		
Bank loans and overdrafts	–	(30)
Trade creditors	(130)	(100)
Other creditors including taxation and social security (*see* Note 3)	(500)	(595)
	(630)	(725)
Creditors: amounts falling due after more than one year		
Debenture loans	(200)	(50)
Provisions for liabilities and charges		
Taxation, including deferred taxation (*see* Note 4)	(120)	(220)
	£900	£1,115
Capital and reserves		
Called-up share capital	750	910
Profit and loss account	150	205
	£900	£1,115

Notes:
1   The taxation charge in the profit and loss account includes the following items:

	£000
Corporation tax based on the profit for the year	542
Overprovision of last year's corporation tax	(15)
Transfer to deferred taxation account	109
	£636

2   During the year to 30 June 19X8, Clinic sold an asset originally costing £150,000 for £5,000 in cash. The depreciation charged on this asset was £135,000. The total depreciation charged in the profit and loss account for the year to 30 June 19X8 was £384,000.

3   Other creditors including taxation and social security includes the following items:

	19X7 £000	19X8 £000
Corporation tax	400	465
Proposed dividend	100	130
Advance corporation tax on the proposed dividend	30	39
	£500	£595

4   The deferred taxation balances include the following items:

	19X7 £000	19X8 £000
Opening balance	70	120
Transfer from the profit and loss account	50	109
	£120	£220

Required:

Insofar as the information permits, prepare Clinic plc's statement of cash flow for the year to 30 June 19X8 in accordance with FRS 1.

(*Association of Accounting Technicians*)

15.9A   The accountant of a private company has been able to get the use of a computer to produce the spreadsheets shown below but as yet the computer lacks a program to print out final accounts. The accountant nevertheless expects to use the spreadsheet data to reconstruct a summary profit and loss account and a cash flow statement for the year to 30 April 19X6.

Movements of Assets during the year 19X5/X6 (£000)

	Balance sheet value last year	Depreci- ation or amortis- ation for year	Additions during year	Sales during year	Other changes	Balance sheet value this year
Goodwill	–	–	40	–	–	40
Property	760	(36)	–	–	–	724
Plant and vehicles	540	(84)	420	(60)	–	816
Stocks	230	–	–	–	24	254
Debtors	254	–	–	–	76	330
Bank and cash	50	–	–	–	14	64
	1,834	(120)	460	(60)	114	2,228

Movement of Liabilities during the year 19X5/X6 (£000)

	Balance sheet value last year	New capital issued	Payments during year	Transfers to reserves and for provisions	Other changes	Balance sheet value this year
Ordinary shares (£1 each)	1,060	440	–	–	–	1,500
Deferred taxation	36	–	–	176	–	212
General reserve	152	–	–	32	–	184
Creditors	136	–	–	–	24	160
Provision for corporation tax	340	–	(340)	52	–	52
Provision for net dividend	110	–	(110)	120	–	120
	1,834	440	(450)	380	24	2,228

Notes:
(*i*) Proceeds of £40,000 were received from the sale of plant and vehicles.
(*ii*) During the year the company redeemed 10,000 of its £1 ordinary shares for £125,000 wholly out of distributable profits and this transaction has not been included in the spreadsheets.

Required:
(*a*) Reconstruct the profit and loss account for the year to 30 April 19X6.
(*b*) Prepare a cash flow statement for the year to 30 April 19X6.

(*Institute of Chartered Secretaries and Administrators*)

15.10 You are presented with the following forecasted information relating to Baker Limited for the nine months to 30 September 19X7.
Forecasted profit and loss accounts (abridged) for the three quarters to 30 September 19X7:

	March 19X7 £000	June 19X7 £000	Sept 19X7 £000
Sales	250	300	350
Cost of goods sold	(200)	(240)	(280)
Gross profit	50	60	70
Depreciation	(3)	(20)	(4)
Administration, selling and distribution expenses	(37)	(40)	(42)
Forecasted net profit	£10	–	£24

Forecasted balances at	31 Dec 19X6 £000	31 March 19X7 £000	30 June 19X7 £000	30 Sept 19X7 £000
Debit balances				
Tangible fixed assets at cost	360	240	480	480
90 day deposit at cost	15	5	5	10
Stocks at cost	40	30	40	55
Trade debtors	50	65	75	80
Cash at bank and in hand	80	–	–	–
Credit balances				
Debentures (10%)	–	–	–	50
Trade creditors	80	120	140	150
Taxation	8	–	–	–
Proposed dividend	15	–	–	–

Additional information:

1 Sales of tangible fixed assets in March 19X7 were expected to realise £12,000 in cash.
2 Administration, selling and distribution expenses were expected to be settled in cash during the month in which they were incurred.
3 Baker Limited includes as liquid resources term deposits of less than one year.

Required:

(*a*) Calculate Baker Limited's forecasted net cash position at 31 March, 30 June, and 30 September 19X7 respectively; and

(*b*) prepare a forecasted statement of cash flow for the nine months to 30 September 19X7.

(*Association of Accounting Technicians*)

15.11A The following information has been extracted from the draft financial information of V Ltd:

Profit and Loss Account for the year ended 31 December 19X3

	£000	£000
Sales		495
Raw materials consumed	(49)	
Staff costs	(37)	
Depreciation	(74)	
Loss on disposal	(4)	
		(164)
Operating profit		331
Interest payable		(23)
Profit before tax		308
Taxation		(87)
		221
Dividend		(52)
Profit retained for year		169
Balance brought forward		389
		558

Balance Sheets

	31 December 19X3		31 December 19X2	
	£000	£000	£000	£000
Fixed assets (*see below*)		1,145		957
Current assets:				
Stock	19		16	
Trade debtors	38		29	
Bank	21		37	
	88		82	
Current liabilities:				
Trade creditors	(12)		(17)	
Taxation	(79)		(66)	
Proposed dividend	(21)		(15)	
	(112)		(98)	
Working capital		(24)		(16)
		1,121		941
Long-term liabilities:				
Long-term loans		(70)		(320)
		1,051		621
Share capital		182		152
Share premium		141		80
Revaluation reserve		170		
Profit and loss		558		389
		1,051		621

	Land & Buildings £000	Machinery £000	Fixtures & fittings £000	Total £000
Fixed assets:				
Cost or valuation:				
At 31 December 19X2	830	470	197	1,497
Additions	–	43	55	98
Disposals	–	(18)	–	(18)
Adjustment on revaluation	70	–	–	70
At 31 December 19X3	900	495	252	1,647
Depreciation:				
At 31 December 19X2	(90)	(270)	(180)	(540)
Charge for year	(10)	(56)	(8)	(74)
Disposals	–	12	–	12
Adjustment on revaluation	100	–	–	100
At 31 December 19X3	0	(314)	(188)	(502)
Net book value:				
At 31 December 19X3	900	181	64	1,145
At 31 December 19X2	740	200	17	957

(a) **You are required to** prepare a cash flow statement for V Ltd for the year ended 31 December 19X3 in accordance with the requirements of Financial Reporting Standard 1 (FRS 1).

(b) It has been suggested that the management of long-term profitability is more important than short-term cash flow. Explain why this might be so.

(*Chartered Institute of Management Accountants*)

16

Contract accounts

Objectives

After you have studied this chapter, you should:

- *be aware of the factors that are involved in accounting for contracts*

- *be aware of how accounting records of contracts are maintained*

- *be aware of the need to apply prudence when assessing profit or loss on a contract that is still in progress*

16.1 Accounts and the business cycle

The span of production differs between businesses, and some fit into the normal pattern of annual accounts more easily than others do. A farmer's accounts are usually admirably suited to the yearly pattern, as the goods they produce are in accordance with the seasons, and therefore repeat themselves annually. With a firm whose production span is a day or two the annual accounts are also quite suitable.

On the other hand, there are businesses whose work does not conform to a financial year's calculation of profits. Assume that a firm of contractors has only one contract being handled, and that is the total construction of a very large oil refinery complex. This might take five years to complete. Not until it is completed can the actual profit or loss on the contract be correctly calculated. However, if the company was formed especially with this contract in mind, the shareholders would not want to wait for five years before the profit could be calculated and dividends paid. Therefore an attempt is made to calculate profits yearly. Obviously, most firms will have more than one contract under way at a time, and also it would be rare for a contract to take such a long time to complete.

16.2 Opening contract accounts

For each contract an account is opened. It is, in fact, a form of trading account for each contract. Therefore if the firm has a contract to build a new technical college it may be numbered Contract 71. Thus a Contract 71 Account would be opened. All expenditure traceable to the contract will be charged to the contract account. This is far easier than ascertaining direct expenses in a factory, as any expenditure on the site will be treated as direct, e.g. wages for the manual workers on the site, telephone rental for telephones on the site, hire of machinery for the contract, wages for the timekeepers, clerks, etc., on the site.

16.3 Certification of work done

The contractor is paid by agreement on the strength of architects' certificates in the case of buildings, or engineers' certificates for an engineering contract. The architect, or engineer, will visit the site at regular intervals and will issue a certificate stating his estimate of the value of the work done, in terms of the total contract price (the sale price of the whole contract). Thus he may issue a certificate for £10,000. Normally the terms governing the contract will contain a clause concerning retention money. This is the amount, usually stated as a percentage, which will be retained, i.e. held back, in case the contract is not completed by a stated date, or against claims for faulty workmanship, etc. A 10 per cent retention in the case already mentioned would lead to £9,000 being payable by the person for whom the contract was being performed.

16.4 Allocation of overheads

The administration overhead expenses not traceable directly to the sites are sometimes split on an arbitrary basis and charged to each contract. Of course, if there were only one contract then all the overhead expenses would quite rightly be chargeable against it. On the other hand if there are twenty contracts being carried on, any apportionment must be arbitrary. No one can really apportion on a 'scientific' basis the administration overhead expenses of the managing director's salary, the cost of advertising to give the firm the right 'image', or the costs of running accounting machinery for the records of the whole firm, and these are only a few of such expenses. In a fashion similar to the departmental accounts principle in Chapter 37 of *Business Accounting 1*, it sometimes gives misleading results, and it is therefore far better left for the administrative overhead expenses which are obviously not chargeable to a contract to be omitted from the contract accounts. The surplus left on each contract account is thus the 'contribution' of each contract to administrative overhead expenses and to profit.

16.5 Example

Exhibit 16.1

Contract 44 is for a school being built for the Blankshire County Council. By the end of the year the following items have been charged to the Contract Account:

Contract 44

	£
Wages – labour on site	5,000
Wages – foreman and clerks on the site	600
Materials	4,000
Subcontractors on the site	900
Other site expenses	300
Hire of special machinery	400
Plant bought for the contract	2,000

The entries concerning expenditure traceable direct to the contract are relatively simple.

These are charged to the contract account. These can be seen in the contract account shown on the next page.

Architects' certificates have been received during the year amounting to £14,000. It is assumed for this example that the certificates related to all work done up to the year end. A retention of 10 per cent is to be made, and the Blankshire County Council has paid £12,600. The £14,000 has been credited to a holding account called an Architects' Certificates Account and debited to the Blankshire County Council Account. The total of the Architects' Certificates Account now needs transferring to the Contract 44 Account. It is, after all, the 'sale' price of the work done so far, and the contract account is a type of trading account. The £12,600 received has been debited to the cash book and credited to Blankshire County Council Account, which now shows a balance of £1,400 that is equal to the retention money.

The cost of the stock of the materials on the site unused is not included in the value of the architects' certificates and is therefore carried forward to the next year at cost price. The value of the plant at the end of the year is also carried forward. In this case the value of the cost of the plant not yet used is £1,400. This means that £2,000 has been debited for the plant and £1,400 credited, thus effectively charging £600 for depreciation. Assume that the stock of unused materials cost £800.

The Contract 44 Account will now appear as follows:

Contract 44

	£		£
Wages – labour on site	5,000	Architects' certificates	14,000
Wages – foreman and clerks on the site	600	Stock of unused materials c/d	800
		Value of plant c/d	1,400
Materials	4,000		
Subcontractors on the site	900		
Other site expenses	300		
Hire of special machinery	400		
Plant bought for the contract	2,000		

16.6 Profit estimation

The difference between the two sides (Credit side £16,200, Debit side £13,200) can be seen to be £3,000. It would be a brave person indeed who would assert that the profit made to date was £3,000. The contract is only part completed, and costly snags may crop up which would dissipate any potential profit earned, or snags may have developed already, such as subsidence which has remained unnoticed as yet. The concept of prudence now takes over and the profit is reduced according to an 'appropriate' modifier. In the past, the custom developed of multiplying the profit by a fraction of two-thirds and then multiplying the result by the proportion of work certified for which cash had been received, as in the following example:

$$\text{Apparent profit} \times \frac{2}{3} \times \frac{\text{Cash received}}{\text{Work certified}} = \text{Amount available for dividends, etc.}$$

$$\text{e.g. } £3,000 \times \frac{2}{3} \times \frac{12,600}{14,000} = £1,800$$

On the basis of the £1,800 profit calculated above, the Contract 44 Account can now be completed:

Profit and Loss Account

	£
Profits from contracts:	
Contract 43	
Contract 44	1,800
Contract 45	

Contract 44

	£		£
Wages – labour on site	£5,000	Architects' certificates	14,000
Wages – foreman and clerks on the site	600	Stock of unused materials c/d	800
		Value of plant c/d	1,400
Materials	4,000		
Subcontractors on the site	900		
Other site expenses	300		
Hire of special machinery	400		
Plant bought for the contract	2,000		
Profit to the profit and loss account	1,800		
Reserve (the part of the apparent profit not yet recognised as earned) c/d	1,200		
	16,200		16,200
Stock of unused materials b/d	800	Reserve b/d	1,200
Value of plant b/d	1,400		

16.7 Anticipated losses

In the case shown there has been an apparent profit of £3,000, but the action would have been different if instead of revealing such a profit, the contract account had in fact shown a loss of £3,000. In such a case it would not be two-thirds of the loss to be taken into account but the whole of it. Thus £3,000 loss would have been transferred to the profit and loss account. This is in accordance with the concept of prudence which states that profits may be underestimated but never losses.

It is in fact not always the case that an engineer or architect will certify the work done up to the financial year end. He may call several days earlier than the year end. The cost of work done, but not certified at the year end, will therefore need carrying down as a balance to the next period when certification will take place.

16.8 The SSAP 9 rules

When a revised version of SSAP 9: *Stocks and long-term contracts* was issued in 1988, this custom-based *rule of thumb* was replaced with a far more complex calculation that focuses upon turnover and the work certified valued in relation to the overall contract amount.

According to SSAP 9, long-term contracts should be assessed on a contract by contract basis. They should be reflected in the profit and loss account by recording turnover and related costs as contract activity progresses. Turnover should be ascertained in a manner appropriate to the stage of completion of the contract, the business and the industry in which it operates. Where the outcome of the contract can be assessed with reasonable accuracy, profit should be recognised (so far as prudence permits) as the difference between recognised turnover and related costs. Any foreseeable losses identified should be immediately recognised.

The amount of long-term contracts, at costs incurred, net of amounts transferred to cost of sales, after deducting foreseeable losses and payments on account not matched with turnover should be classified as 'long term contract balances' and separately disclosed within the balance sheet heading of 'stocks'. The balance sheet note should disclose separately the balances of 'net cost less foreseeable losses' and 'applicable payments on account'.

The standard is extremely complex and it is beyond the scope of *Business Accounting*, where this topic is being introduced rather than developed in detail, to extend coverage of it to the level of complexity that would be required in order to cover the SSAP 9 rules adequately. Students who require a sound understanding of the SSAP 9 rules concerning long-term contracts should refer to the standard, where the appendix covers the topic in detail, or to a specialised text on the subject.

From the perspective of the review questions that follow at the end of this chapter, apart from question 16.5A, *unless otherwise indicated in the question*, you should apply the ⅔ rule of thumb given above. Doing so will develop an awareness of the complexity of contract accounts without the added complexity of applying the SSAP 9 rules. By adopting this approach, students will be well-placed to progress to an understanding of the SSAP 9 rules, knowing well the underlying factors involved in contract accounts. The answer to question 16.5A is based on the SSAP 9 rules, and is provided for the benefit of any student who chooses to study those rules independently of this book.

New term

Work certified (p. 264): The value of work in progress on a contract as certified by, for example, an architect or engineer.

Main points to remember

1 Separate accounts should be opened in respect of every contract.

2 Profits or losses on contracts require to be estimated at the end of each accounting period.

3 Losses should be written off immediately they are identified.

4 An appropriate amount of any profit should be included in the financial statements.

5 The profit/loss ascertainment approach adopted in this chapter is necessarily simplified in order to ensure the topic is well understood; SSAP 9 should be consulted for the definitive approach to adopt.

Review questions

16.1 The final accounts of Diggers Ltd are made up to 31 December in each year. Work on a certain contract was commenced on 1 April 19X5 and was completed on 31 October 19X6. The total contract price was £174,000, but a penalty of £700 was suffered for failure to complete by 30 September 19X6.

The following is a summary of receipts and payments relating to the contract:

	During 19X5	During 19X6
Payments:		
Materials	25,490	33,226
Wages	28,384	45,432
Direct expenses	2,126	2,902
Purchases of plant on 1 April 19X5	16,250	–
Receipts		
Contract price (*less* penalty)	52,200	121,100
Sale, on 31 October 19X6, of all plant purchased on 1 April 19X5	–	4,100

The amount received from the customer in 19X5 represented the contract price of all work certified in that year less 10 per cent retention money.

When the annual accounts for 19X5 were prepared it was estimated that the contract would be completed on 30 September 19X6, and that the market value of the plant would be £4,250 on that date. It was estimated that further expenditure on the contract during 19X6 would be £81,400.

For the purposes of the annual accounts, depreciation of plant is calculated, in the case of uncompleted contracts, by reference to the expected market value of the plant on the date when the contract is expected to be completed, and is allocated between accounting periods by the straight-line method.

Credit is taken, in the annual accounts, for such a part of the estimated total profit, on each uncompleted contract, as corresponds to the proportion between the contract price of the work certified and the total contract price.

Required:
Prepare a summary of the account for this contract, showing the amounts transferred to profit and loss account at 31 December 19X5 and 31 December 19X6.

16.2 Stannard and Sykes Ltd are contractors for the construction of a pier for the Seafront Development Corporation. The value of the contract is £300,000, and payment is by engineer's certificate subject to a retention of 10 per cent of the amount certified; this is to be held by the Seafront Development Corporation for six months after the completion of the contract.

The following information is extracted from the records of Stannard and Sykes Ltd.

	£
Wages on site	41,260
Materials delivered to site by supplier	58,966
Materials delivered to site from store	10,180
Hire of plant	21,030
Expenses charged to contract	3,065
Overheads charged to contract	8,330
Materials on site at 30 November 19X8	11,660
Work certified	150,000
Payment received	135,000
Work in progress at cost (not the subject of a certificate to date)	12,613
Wages accrued to 30 November 19X8	2,826

Required:
Prepare the Pier Contract Account to 30 November 19X8, and suggest a method by which profit could be prudently estimated.

(*Association of Chartered Certified Accountants*)

16.3A Cantilever Ltd was awarded a contract to build an office block in London and work commenced at the site on 1 May 19X5.

During the period to 28 February 19X6, the expenditure on the contract was as follows:

	£
Materials issued from stores	9,411
Materials purchased	28,070
Direct expenses	6,149
Wages	18,493
Charge made by the company for administration expenses	2,146
Plant and machinery purchased on 1 May 19X5, for use at site	12,180

On 28 February 19X6, the stock of materials at the site amounted to £2,164 and there were amounts outstanding for wages £366 and direct expenses £49.

Cantilever Ltd has received on account the sum of £64,170 which represents the amount of Certificate No. 1 issued by the architects in respect of work completed to 28 February 19X6, after deducting 10 per cent retention money.

The following relevant information is also available:

(*a*) the plant and machinery has an effective life of five years, with no residual value, and
(*b*) the company only takes credit for two-thirds of the profit on work certified.

Required:
(*a*) prepare a contract account for the period to 28 February 19X6, and
(*b*) show your calculation of the profit to be taken to the credit of the company's profit and loss account in respect of the work covered by Certificate No 1.

(*Institute of Chartered Accountants*)

16.4A You are required to prepare the contract account for the year ended 31 December 19X0, and show the calculation of the sum to be credited to the profit and loss account for that year.

On 1 April 19X0 MN Ltd commenced work on a contract which was to be completed by 30 June 19X1 at an agreed price of £520,000.

MN Ltd's financial year ended on 31 December 19X0, and on that day expenditure on the contract totalled £263,000 made up as under:

	£
Plant	30,000
Materials	124,000
Wages	95,000
Sundry expenses	5,000
Head office charges	9,000
	263,000

Cash totalling £195,000 had been received by 31 December 19X0 representing 75 per cent of the work certified as completed on that date, but in addition, work costing £30,000 had been completed but not certified.

A sum of £9,000 had been obtained on the sale of materials which had cost £8,000 but which had been found unsuitable. On 31 December 19X0 stocks of unused materials on site had cost £10,000 and the plant was valued at £20,000.

To complete the contract by 30 June 19X1 it was estimated that:

(a) the following additional expenditures would be incurred:

	£
Wages	64,000
Materials	74,400
Sundry expenses	9,000

(b) further plant costing £25,000 would be required;
(c) the residual value of all plant used on the contract at 30 June 19X1 would be £15,000;
(d) head office charges to the contract would be at the same annual rate plus 10 per cent.

It was estimated that the contract would be completed on time but that a contingency provision of £15,000 should be made. From this estimate and the expenditure already incurred, it was decided to estimate the total profit that would be made on the contract and to take to the credit of the profit and loss account for the year ended 31 December 19X0, that proportion of the total profit relating to the work actually certified to that date.

(*Chartered Institute of Management Accountants*)

16.5A *General information on the Lytax group of companies*

Lytax Ltd is a company in the building construction industry.

It has three regional offices, North Borders, Midlands and South Downs which are constituted as separate units for accounting purposes.

On 25 May 19X0 Lytax Ltd acquired 90 per cent of the ordinary share capital of Ceprem Ltd, a company which manufactures building materials.

Lytax Ltd has for 3 years held 15 per cent of the ordinary share capital of Bleco plc. This company carries out specialist research and development activities into building and construction materials, technology and techniques. It then sells the results of these activities to other companies.

Details of long-term contract work undertaken by Lytax Ltd

At 31 October 19X0, Lytax Ltd was engaged in various contracts including five long-term contracts, details of which are given below:

	1	2	3	4	5
	£000	£000	£000	£000	£000
Contract price	1,100	950	1,400	1,300	1,200
At 31 October 19X0:					
Cumulative costs incurred	664	535	810	640	1,070
Estimated further costs to completion	106	75	680	800	165
Estimated cost of post-completion					
guarantee/rectification work	30	10	45	20	5
Cumulative costs incurred					
transferred to cost of sales	580	470	646	525	900
Progress payments					
Cumulative receipts	615	680	615	385	722
Invoiced:					
Awaiting receipt	60	40	25	200	34
Retained by contractee	75	80	60	65	84

It is not expected that any contractees will default on their payments.

Up to 31 October 19X9, the following amounts had been included in the turnover and cost of sales figures.

	1	2	3	4	5
	£000	£000	£000	£000	£000
Cumulative turnover	560	340	517	400	610
Cumulative costs incurred					
transferred to cost of sales	460	245	517	400	610
Foreseeable loss transferred to cost of sales	–	–	–	70	–

It is the accounting policy of Lytax Ltd to arrive at contract turnover by adjusting contract cost of sales (including foreseeable losses) by the amount of contract profit or loss to be regarded as recognised, separately for each contract.

Required:

(*a*) Calculate the amounts to be included within the turnover and cost of sales figures of the profit and loss account of Lytax Ltd for the year ended 31 October 19X0, in respect of the long-term contracts.

(*b*) Prepare extracts from the balance sheet of Lytax Ltd at 31 October 19X0 incorporating the financial effects of the long-term contracts.

Your answer should comply with the requirements of SSAP 9 (Stocks and Long-Term Contracts) and should include any supporting notes required by that standard.

Workings for individual contracts which build up to the total for each item must be shown.

All calculations should be made to the nearest £1,000.

(Association of Chartered Certified Accountants)

17

Value added statements

Objectives

After you have studied this chapter, you should:

- *be aware of the benefits of presenting statements of value added*

17.1 The need for additional information

A great deal of discussion has taken place in recent years about the desirability of not simply interpreting results in terms of profits only. One way of doing this is in terms of the value added by the business itself to the resources acquired by it in transforming them into the final product. The production of such 'value added statements' was recommended in the *Corporate Report 1975*.

Such value added can be taken to represent in monetary terms the net output of an enterprise. This is the difference between the total value of its output and the value of the inputs of materials and services obtained from other enterprises. The value added is seen to be due to the combined efforts of capital, management and employees, and the statement shows how the value added has been distributed to each of these factors.

17.2 Example

As an example, the profit and loss account of Growth Ltd shown below is then restated in value added terms:

Growth Ltd

Profit and Loss Account for the year ended 31 December 19X1

	£	£
Turnover		765,000
Cost of sales*		439,000
Gross profit		326,000
Distribution costs*	93,000	
Administrative expenses*	108,000	201,000
		125,000
Interest payable		2,000
Profit on ordinary activities before taxation		123,000
Tax on profit on ordinary activities		44,000
Profit for the year on ordinary activities after taxation		79,000
Undistributed profits from last year		55,000
		134,000
Transfer to general reserve	15,000	
Proposed ordinary dividend	60,000	75,000
Undistributed profits carried to next year		59,000

Note: Costs* include:	£
Wages, pensions and other employee benefits	220,000
Depreciation	74,000
All other costs were bought in from outside	346,000
(£439,000 + £93,000 + £108,000)	£640,000

Growth Ltd

Statement of Value Added for the year ended 31 December 19X1

	£	£
Turnover		765,000
Bought in materials and services		346,000
Value added		419,000
Applied the following way:		
To pay employee wages, pensions and other benefits		220,000
To pay providers of capital:		
Interest on loans	2,000	
Dividends to shareholders	60,000	62,000
To pay government:		
Corporation tax payable		44,000
To provide for maintenance and expansion of assets:		
Depreciation	74,000	
Retained profits	19,000	93,000
		419,000

The reader can see that the retained profits figure of £19,000 is made up of the increase in undistributed profits (£59,000 – £55,000) £4,000 + transfer to general reserve £15,000 = £19,000.

The value added statement can be seen to be a means of reporting the income for all the groups which contribute to an organisation's performance. It is therefore relevant to the information needed by all of these groups, something which is not well served by an ordinary profit and loss account.

New term

Value added (p. 272): The difference between the total value of outputs and the total value of inputs.

Main points to remember

1   Traditional financial statements tend to focus on profit.

2   A statement of value added focuses instead on the income contributed by each group within an organisation that is included in the statement.

Review questions

17.1   Manvers Ltd includes with its financial statements each year a statement of value added. The draft value added statement for the year ended 31 May 19X6 is as follows:

	£	£
Revenue from sales		204,052
Bought in materials and services		146,928
Value added by the company		57,124
Applied to:		
The benefit of employees		
Salaries	16,468	
Deductions for income tax and national insurance	3,352	
	13,116	
Pension schemes	2,810	
Employees' profit sharing schemes	525	
Welfare and staff amenities	806	
		17,257
Central and local government		
Value added tax	30,608	
Corporation tax	985	
Local rates	325	
Tax etc. deducted from salaries and loan interest	3,832	
		35,750
The providers of capital		
Interest on loan capital	1,600	
Income tax deducted	480	
	1,120	
Interest on bank overdrafts	250	
Dividends to shareholders of the company	500	
		1,870
The replacement of assets and the expansion of the business		
Depreciation	1,835	
Retained profits	412	
		2,247
		57,124

Discussion among the board of directors on the draft figures has revealed a wide variation of opinion on the usefulness of the value added statement to the readers of the accounts.

Some board members say that the added value statement is confusing as it is only a redrafting of the results which are shown in the profit and loss account which gives all the information necessary. Another view is that the statement of changes in financial position is far more important and this should be given in place of the value added statement.

Required:

(a) A report to the directors showing the advantages of the value added statement comparing it with the profit and loss account and the cash flow statement. Your report should deal specifically with the points raised in discussion by the directors.

(b) Construct a profit and loss account from the information given.

(c) Calculate the operating profit for use in a statement of changes in financial position.

(*Association of Chartered Certified Accountants*)

17.2.A The following information relates to the Plus Factors Group plc for the years to 30 September 19X8 and 19X9.

	Notes	19X9 £000	19X8 £000
Associated company share of profit		10.9	10.7
Auditors' remuneration		12.2	11.9
Creditors for materials			
at beginning of year		1,109.1	987.2
at end of year		1,244.2	1,109.1
Debtors			
at beginning of year		1,422.0	1,305.0
at end of year		1,601.0	1,422.0
11% debentures	1	500.0	600.0
Depreciation		113.7	98.4
Employee benefits paid		109.9	68.4
Hire of plant, machinery and vehicles	2	66.5	367.3
Materials paid for in year		3,622.9	2,971.4
Minority interest in profit of the year		167.2	144.1
Other overheads incurred		1,012.4	738.3
Pensions and pension contributions paid		319.8	222.2
Profit before taxation		1,437.4	1,156.4
Provision for corporation tax		464.7	527.9
Salaries and wages		1,763.8	1,863.0
Sales	3	9,905.6	8,694.1
Shares at nominal value:			
Ordinary at 25p each fully paid	4	2,500.0	2,000.0
7% Preference at £1 each fully paid	4	500.0	200.0
Stocks of materials:			
beginning of year		804.1	689.7
end of year		837.8	804.1

Other information:
Ordinary dividends were declared as follows:
  Interim 1.12 pence per share (19X8 1.67p)
  Final 3.57 pence per share (19X8 2.61p)
Average number of employees was 196 (19X8 201)

Notes

1 £300,000 of debentures were redeemed at par on 31 March 19X9 and £200,000 new debentures at the same rate of interest were issued at 9 per cent on the same date.

The new debentures are due to be redeemed on 31 March 19X4.

2 This is the amount for inclusion in the profit and loss account in accordance with SSAP 21.

3 All the group's sales are subject to value added tax at 15 per cent and the figures given include such tax. All other figures are exclusive of value added tax.

4 All shares have been in issue throughout the year.

Required:

(*a*) Prepare a statement of value added for the year to 30 September 19X9 and give comparative figures for 19X8. Include a percentage breakdown of the distribution of value added for both years.

(*b*) Produce ratios related to employees' interests, based on the statement in part (*a*), and explain how they might be of use.

(*c*) Explain briefly what are the difficulties of measuring and reporting financial information in the form of a statement of value added.

(*Association of Chartered Certified Accountants*)

18

Investment accounts

Objectives

After you have studied this chapter, you should:

- *understand the differences between investments in government stocks and investments in limited companies*
- *know how to record investments in the financial records*

18.1 Basic investment

It is possible to envisage a situation where the only external investment made by a firm is in the form of money in an account with a **savings bank**, which had, say, an interest rate of 5 per cent per annum. Interest is calculated to 31 December each year and a cheque for the interest is sent to the account holder to arrive on 31 December. Such a type of account adhering to these dates would be very rare in practice. However, with such an account the accounting entries needed by the investing firm would be very simple indeed. If £400 was invested by a firm in such an account on 1 January 19X4 and eventually withdrawn on 31 December 19X7, then assuming that the firm's financial year was equated with the calendar year, the cash book for each year would be debited with £20 while each year's investment income account would be credited with £20. The balance of the investment income account, £20, would be transferred to the credit side of the profit and loss account for each of the years ended 31 December 19X4, 19X5, 19X6 and 19X7. On the withdrawal of the £400 the cash book would be debited with £400 and the credit entry would be made in the investment account, thereby cancelling the original debit entry made when the cash was invested.

Most investments are not of this sort, and have complicating factors. They can be divided into two main classes, **government stocks** and **investments in limited companies**, the latter may take the form of shares, stocks or debentures. In this chapter, government stocks will be dealt with first. Taxation will be ignored until it is mentioned specifically.

18.2 Government stocks

With government stock the price is always quoted for that of £100 nominal value. Prices on the Stock Exchange will vary in accordance with supply and demand. Thus, Treasury 3 per cent Stock may be shown as 45. This means that on the Stock Exchange the price for £100 nominal value of the stock was £45. The purchaser of the stock will receive interest at the rate of £3 each year as interest payable is always based on the nominal value and not the Stock Exchange value.

Interest is payable at regular intervals depending on the stock concerned. Taking a government stock which carried interest at 5 per cent per annum, interest may be payable quarterly on 31 March, 30 June, 30 September and 31 December. Imagine that a person is willing to sell stock of £1,200 nominal value at 80, i.e. for £960 on 1 Jan (£80 for £100 nominal value, therefore £80 × 12 = £960 for £1,200 nominal value). The purchaser is to receive the whole of the next interest on 31 March, this being £1,200 at 5 per cent per annum for three months = £15. The seller has received interest up to 31 December, the day before he sold the stock. Ownership of stock and ownership of interest have therefore both been on the same time scale. If market conditions do not change, consider the case of a person who is to sell the stock on 1 February, and the purchaser was still to receive all of the £15 interest on 31 March. The seller will not want to sell at the same price, for as January's interest is not to be received by him, the ownership of the stock and the right to receive interest have moved on to a different time scale. The seller is not now merely selling stock, he is also selling the right to one month's interest in addition. He would therefore now want £960 + one month's interest £5 = £965. When the purchaser pays £965 he will want to record the purchase in his own books. He will accordingly split this price as to £960 paid for the stock, a capital item, and the cost of income £5. When the full quarter's interest £15 is received, the £5 cost will be deducted in the income calculation leaving net income for the period as £10. This accords with the evidence, as two months' ownership for February and March is worth £1,200 × 5 per cent per annum × two months = £10. The seller would also apportion the selling price £965 as to £960 for the stock and £5 for the interest. The £5 interest would then be shown as investment income in his books. This is in fact, saying that where the interest is bought and sold as part of a total price, then interest received is not equal to interest accrued. The apportionment of cost and selling price is the way by which investment income can be equated with the duration of the ownership of the investment, i.e. fifteen months' ownership should show fifteen months' investment income.

18.3 Dividend rights

Where the price of the stock does not include the right to the next instalment of interest it is stated to be *ex div* or e.d.; this stands for **excluding dividend**. Where it does include the right to receive the next instalment of interest, irrespective of how long the stock has been owned it is known as *cum div*, meaning **including dividend**. All prices are *cum div* unless stated specifically to be *ex div*.

Because of the necessity to keep income separate from the capital cost of the investment, each Investment Account has a column for income and a column for capital. In addition a column is used to show the nominal value of the stock, this being used for convenience and does not form part of the double entry system. Brokerage charges and stamp duties are part of the capital cost of the investment and are included in the cheque paid to the firm's stockbrokers. Brokerage charges on sale are deducted from the cheque remitted by the stockbrokers for the sale proceeds, so that as the sale price is brought in net they have been effectively charged.

Exhibit 18.1

Brent Ltd bought £10,000 3 per cent Government Stock at 40 *ex div* on 1 January 19X6 (remember that the *ex div* means that the interest due for the quarter ending 31 December 19X5, which will not yet have been paid, belongs to the seller). The cheque for the stock £4,000 plus brokerage charges £100 was £4,100. The interest is received on 31 March, 30 June, 30 September and 31 December 19X6. During 19X7 interest is received on 31 March, and all the stock is sold for 43 *cum div* on 31 May, the cheque being £4,190, made up of £4,300 total proceeds *less* £110 brokerage charges. The financial year end of Brent Ltd is 31 December.

The following shows the entries in the investment account for the years ended 31 December 19X6 and 19X7.

Investment – 3 per cent Government Stock

			Nominal	Income	Capital				Nominal	Income	Capital
			£	£	£				£	£	£
19X6						**19X6**					
Jan	1	Cash	10,000		4,100	Mar	31	Cash		75	
Dec	31	Investment				Jun	30	,,		75	
		income to				Sep	30	,,		75	
		profit and loss		300		Dec	31	,,		75	
						Dec	31	Balance c/d	10,000		4,100
			10,000	300	4,100				10,000	300	4,100
19X7						**19X7**					
Jan	1	Balance b/d	10,000		4,100	Mar	31	Cash		75	
Dec	31	Investment				May	31	Cash sale			
		income to						proceeds (A)	10,000	50	4,140
		profit and loss		125							
Dec	31	Profit on sale to									
		profit and loss			40						
			10,000	125	4,140				10,000	125	4,140

(A) As the stock is sold *cum div*, Brent Ltd is therefore including in the selling price the value of two months' interest for April and May = $\frac{2}{12} \times 3$ per cent $\times$ £10,000 = £50. The £4,190 sale price is accordingly apportioned £50 as to income and £4,140 as to capital.

18.4 Comprehensive example

To illustrate matters further, Exhibit 18.2 shows an investment where there are both extra purchases and sales of part of the investment.

Exhibit 18.2

On 1 January 19X4 Green Ltd bought £4,000 6 per cent Government Stock at £90, the cheque of £3,680 paid being £3,600 for the stock and £80 for the brokerage charges. Interest is receivable each year on 31 March, 30 June, 30 September, and 31 December.

On 1 February 19X5 £1,000 nominal value of the stock is sold *cum div*, the net proceeds being £950.

1 June 19X5, £2,000 nominal value sold *ex div*, net proceeds after brokerage being £1,710.

1 February 19X6, £5,000 nominal value bought *cum div*, the cost including brokerage being £4,370.

1 June 19X6, £1,000 nominal value bought *ex div*, cost including brokerage being £910.

On page 288 is the Investment Account in Green's books for the financial years ended 31 December 19X4, 19X5 and 19X6. Taxation is ignored.

Investment – 6 per cent Government Stock

Debit

Date	Particulars	Ref	Nominal £	Income £	Capital £
19X4					
Jan 1	Cash		4,000		3,680
Dec 31	Investment income to profit and loss			240	
			4,000	240	3,680
19X5					
Jan 1	Balance b/d		4,000		3,680
Jun 1	Adjustment for sale at *ex div* price	(b)		10	
Dec 31	Investment income to profit and loss	(c)		115	
			4,000	125	3,680
19X6					
Jan 1	Balance b/d		1,000		920
Feb 1	Cash		5,000	25	4,345
Jun 1	Cash		1,000		910
Jun 1	Adjustment of purchase at *ex div* price	(e)			5
Dec 31	Investment income to profit and loss	(f)		370	
			7,000	395	6,180
19X7					
Jan 1	Balance b/d		7,000		6,180

Credit

Date	Particulars	Ref	Nominal £	Income £	Capital £
19X4					
Mar 31	Cash			60	
June 30	Cash			60	
Sep 30	Cash			60	
Dec 31	Cash			60	
Dec 31	Balance c/d		4,000		3,680
			4,000	240	3,680
19X5					
Feb 1	Cash sale proceeds	(a)	1,000	5	945
Mar 31	Cash ($£3,000 \times 6\% \times 3$ months)			45	
Jun 1	Cash sale proceeds	(b)	2,000		1,710
Jun 1	Adjustment for sale at *ex div* price				10
Jun 30	Cash ($£3,000 \times 6\% \times 3$ months)			45	
Sep 30	Cash ($£1,000 \times 6\% \times 3$ months)			15	
Dec 31	Cash ($£1,000 \times 6\% \times 3$ months)			15	
Dec 31	Profit and loss – on sale of investments	(d)			95
Dec 31	Balance c/d		1,000		920
			4,000	125	3,680
19X6					
Mar 31	Cash ($£6,000 \times 6\% \times 3$ months)			90	
Jun 1	Adjustment of purchase at *ex div* price	(e)		5	
Jun 30	Cash ($£6,000 \times 6\% \times 3$ months)			90	
Sep 30	Cash ($£7,000 \times 6\% \times 3$ months)			105	
Dec 31	Cash ($£7,000 \times 6\% \times 3$ months)			105	
Dec 31	Balance c/d		7,000		6,180
			7,000	395	6,180

Notes:

(*a*) The sale proceeds £950 represent the sale of the right to one month's interest, £1,000 × 6 per cent per annum for one month = £5, plus the right to the actual stock itself. This must therefore be the balance of the net sale proceeds, £950 – £5 = £945.

(*b*) The sale at an *ex div* price means that Green Ltd will receive interest for June on this £2,000 of stock even though the stock itself had passed out of Green Ltd's ownership. The actual net sale price is therefore £1,720 made up of £1,710 actually received plus £10 for the right to one month's interest retained. This is adjusted by debiting the Income column with £10 to cancel the income which was not equated with ownership, and crediting the Capital column with £10 representing the actual reduction in the sale price caused by selling at an *ex div* price. (*c*) will illustrate the validity of debiting the income column, as without this entry the amount of investment income transferred to the profit and loss account would not agree with the facts relating to the duration of the investment and the rate of interest.

(*c*) The correctness of this can be proved if the interest actually accrued during ownership is calculated:

		£
6 per cent per annum on £4,000 for one month	=	20
6 per cent per annum on £3,000 for four months	=	60
6 per cent per annum on £1,000 for seven months	=	35
		115

(*d*)

		£	£	
Cost of £1,000 nominal value of stock £3,680 × ¼	=	920		
Sold on 1 February 19X5 for		945	25	profit
Cost of £2,000 nominal value of stock £3,680 × ½	=	1,840		
Sold on 1 June 19X5 for (adjusted net sale price)		1,720	120	loss
			95	net loss

(*e*) The stock bought on 1 June 19X6 for £910 *ex div* meant that June's ownership would not bring in any interest on this stock. The price paid for the stock would have been reduced by the amount of June's interest, i.e. £1,000 at 6 per cent per annum for one month = £5. The true price paid therefore was £915. This is represented by a debit of £5 in the Capital column, while a credit of £5 in the Income column is made to show that ownership of fixed interest stock does in fact bring in a return of interest in accordance with the length of ownership.

(*f*) This can be proved to be correct.

		£
£1,000 at 6 per cent per annum for one month	=	5
£6,000 at 6 per cent per annum for four months	=	120
£7,000 at 6 per cent per annum for seven months	=	245
		370

18.5 Investment in limited companies

In the cases where stocks, shares and debentures carry a fixed rate of interest the treatment is the same as with Government Stocks. However, where the investment is not of the fixed interest type, e.g. ordinary shares, the next dividend receivable is not known on purchase or sale. On the declaration of the next dividend an adjustment can be made, so that the account will contain the same balances as it would have done if the next dividend had been known, and the necessary apportionments had taken place at sale or purchase rather than waiting until the dividend had been declared. In theory these adjustments should always be made, but in practice they are usually ignored where the purchase and sale of investments do not constitute the main business of the firm.

New terms

Ex Div (p. 278): Where the price of the stock excludes the right to the next payment of interest or dividend..

Cum Div (p. 278): Where the price of the stock includes the right to the next payment of interest or dividend.

Main point to remember

1   With government stock, the price quoted is always for £100 nominal value. For shares, the price quoted is for one share in the company irrespective of its nominal value.

Review questions

18.1   The following transactions of Trust Ltd took place during the year ended 30 June 19X7:

19X6
1 July	Purchased £12,000 4 per cent Consolidated Loan (interest payable 1 February and 1 August) at 60½ *cum div*.
12 July	Purchased 2,000 ordinary shares of £0.5 each in Abee Ltd for £4,000.
1 August	Received half-year's interest on 4 per cent Consolidated Loan.
15 August	Abee Ltd made a bonus issue of three ordinary shares for every two held. Trust Ltd sold 2,500 of the bonus shares for £1 each.
1 October	Purchased 5,000 ordinary shares of £1 each in Ceedee Ltd at £0.775 each.

19X7
2 January	Sold £3,000 4 per cent Consolidated Loan at 61 *ex div*.
1 February	Received half-year's interest on 4 per cent Consolidated Loan.
1 March	Received dividend of 18 per cent on shares in Abee Ltd.
1 April	Ceedee Ltd made a 'rights' issue of one share for every two held at £0.5 per share. 'Rights' sold on market for £0.25 per share.
1 June	Received dividend of 12½ per cent on shares in Ceedee Ltd.

Required:
Write up the relevant investment accounts as they would appear in the books of Trust Ltd for the year ended 30 June 19X7, bringing down the balances as on that date.

  Ignore brokerage and stamp duty.

(*Institute of Chartered Accountants*)

18.2 On 31 March 19X5 the investments held by Jowetts of Mayfair Ltd included 6,000 ordinary shares of £1 each fully paid in Composite Interest Ltd, such shares appearing in the books at £7,200. It is not the practice of Jowetts of Mayfair Ltd to make apportionments of dividends received or receivable.

Jowetts of Mayfair Ltd sold 1,000 shares on 31 May 19X5 for £1,965. On 20 September 19X5 Composite Interest Ltd:

(a) Issued by way of a bonus issue three fully paid shares for every five held on 31 August 19X5.
(b) It gave the right to shareholders to apply for one share for every two actually held on 31 August 19X5, the price to be £1.05 per share payable in full on application.

The shares issued under (a) and (b) were not to participate in the dividend for the year ended 31 August 19X5.

The bonus shares were received. For the rights issue 1,800 shares were taken up and paid for on 30 September 19X5. The rights on the remaining shares were sold for £0.3 per share, the money for this being received on 15 November 19X5.

On 17 December 19X5 Composite Interest Ltd declared and paid a final dividend of 20 per cent for the year ended 31 August 19X5, and on 15 March 19X6 an interim dividend of 5 per cent for the year ended 31 August 19X6.

Show the investment account for the year ended 31 March 19X6 as it would appear in the books of Jowetts of Mayfair Ltd.

Expenses of sale are to be ignored.

18.3A Stag Ltd is an investment company making up its accounts to 31 December in each year. The following transactions have been extracted from the company's records for 19X9.

1 January	Purchased 1,000 ordinary shares of £0.25 each in Bull Ltd at £1.75 per share.
12 February	Purchased £2,000 ordinary stock in Bear Ltd for £1,500.
1 March	Received dividend of 20 per cent on shares in Bull Ltd.
24 April	Bull Ltd made a bonus issue of one share for every four held.
2 May	Received dividend of 2½ per cent on ordinary stock in Bear Ltd.
10 May	Bull Ltd announced a rights issue of two ordinary shares for every five held on that date, at £1.25 per share. Rights sold on market for £0.5 per share.
1 August	Applied for £5,000 7¼ per cent loan stock in Bear Ltd issued at £98 per cent, and payable half on application and the balance in two equal instalments on 1 October and 1 December. The application was successful.
16 September	Received dividend of 30 per cent on shares in Bull Ltd.
1 October	Paid instalment on loan stock in Bear Ltd.
20 November	Received dividend of 3 per cent on ordinary stock in Bear Ltd.
1 December	Paid final instalment on loan stock in Bear Ltd.

Required:
Write up the accounts for the investments in Bull Ltd and Bear Ltd as they would appear in the books of Stag Ltd for the year ended 31 December 19X9, bringing down the balances as on that date.

Ignore stamp duty, brokerage and taxation.

(*Institute of Chartered Accountants*)

18.4A HM Ltd bought £10,000 nominal of Peatshire 6 per cent loan stock at 92 *cum div* on 30 April 19X8. Interest on the stock is paid half-yearly on 30 June and 31 December. £4,000 of the stock was sold at 94 *ex div* on 30 November 19X8. HM Ltd prepares final accounts annually to 31 March.

Prepare the investment account in the company's ledger from the date of the purchase to 1 April 19X9. You should ignore brokerage, stamp duty and taxation and make apportionments in months.

18.5A On 1 April 19X7, FRY Ltd purchased 10,000 ordinary shares of £1 each, fully paid, in TLS Ltd at a cost of £20,500.

- On 1 September 19X7, TLS Ltd declared and paid a dividend of 15 per cent on its ordinary shares for the year ended 30 June 19X7.

- On 1 November 19X7, TLS Ltd gave its eight members the right to subscribe for one ordinary share for every eight held on 1 November 19X7, at a price of £1.5 per share, payable in full on application.

- On 15 November 19X7, FRY Ltd purchased for £0.4 per share the rights of another shareholder in TLS Ltd to subscribe for 750 shares under the rights issue.

- On 30 November 19X7, FRY Ltd applied and paid for all the shares in TLS Ltd to which it was then entitled.

- On 8 September 19X8, TLS Ltd declared and paid a dividend for the year ended 30 June 19X8, of 15 per cent on all ordinary shares, including those issued in 19X7.

- On 1 October 19X8, FRY Ltd sold 4,500 ordinary shares in TLS Ltd for £9,875.

- The accounting year of FRY Ltd ends on 31 December.

- FRY Ltd does not make apportionments of dividend received or receivable. When part of a holding of shares is sold, it is the practice of this company to calculate the cost of the shares sold as an appropriate part of the average cost of all the shares held at the date of the sale.

You are required to show the investment account in the books of FRY Ltd for the two years ended 31 December 19X7, and 31 December 19X8, bringing down the balance at the end of each year.

Ignore taxation.

(*Institute of Chartered Secretaries and Administrators*)

Part 3

GROUPS

Introduction

This part is concerned with group accounts – how they are prepared, how various transactions should be dealt with, and how their presentation is regulated by the Companies Acts and accounting standards.

19

Group accounts: an introduction

Objectives

After you have studied this chapter, you should:

- *understand the difference between a parent undertaking and a subsidiary undertaking*

- *be aware of why it is important to produce consolidated financial statements*

- *know some of the alternative methods whereby control can be acquired by one company over another*

- *be aware of the relevance of 'dominant influence' to the identification of a parent–subsidiary relationship*

- *be aware of the relevance of 'significant influence' to the identification of the existence of an 'associated undertaking'*

19.1 Shareholders and their rights

The owners of a company are its shareholders. When someone buys ordinary shares in a company then they are usually given three rights. These are:

- voting rights at shareholders' meetings;
- a right to an interest in the net assets of the company;
- a right to an interest in the profits earned by the company.

Preference shareholders do not normally have such voting rights, but sometimes they can have such power. This could be when their dividends are in arrears, or their special rights are being changed by the company. Debenture holders have no rights at all to vote at general meetings.

By using their voting rights at shareholders' meetings, the shareholders are able to show their approval, or disapproval, of the election of directors. It is the directors who manage the affairs of the company. Therefore any group of shareholders, who between them own more than 50 per cent of the voting shares of the company, can control the election of directors. As a consequence they can therefore control the policies of the company through the directors. This would also be true if any one shareholder owned more than 50 per cent of the voting shares.

One company may hold shares in another company. Therefore if one company wishes to obtain control of another company it can do so by obtaining more than 50 per cent of the voting shares in that company.

19.2 Parent undertakings and subsidiary undertakings

- S Ltd has an issued share capital of 1,000 ordinary shares of £1 each.
- On 1 January 19X6, P Ltd buys 501 of these shares from Jones, a shareholder, for £600.
- P Ltd will now have control of S Ltd because it has more than 50 per cent of the voting shares.
- P Ltd is now called the 'parent undertaking'.
- S Ltd is now called the 'subsidiary undertaking' of P Ltd.

Just because the identity of S Ltd's shareholders has changed it does not mean that the balance sheet of S Ltd will be drafted in a different fashion. Looking only at the balance sheet of S Ltd no one would be able to deduce that P Ltd owned more than 50 per cent of the shares, or even that P Ltd owned any shares at all in S Ltd. After obtaining control of S Ltd both P Ltd and S Ltd will continue to maintain their own sets of accounting records and to draft their own balance sheets. If the balance sheets of P Ltd and S Ltd are looked at, both before and after the purchase of the shares, any differences can be noted.

Exhibit 19.1

(*a*) Before P Ltd acquired control of S Ltd.

P Ltd Balance Sheet as at 31 December 19X5	£	£	S Ltd Balance Sheet as at 31 December 19X5	£	£
Fixed assets		2,000	Fixed assets		400
Current assets:			*Current assets:*		
Stock-in-trade	2,900		Stock-in-trade	400	
Debtors	800		Debtors	200	
Bank	1,300		Bank	100	
		5,000			700
		7,000			1,100
Share capital		5,000	Share capital		1,000
Profit and loss account		2,000	Profit and loss account		100
		7,000			1,100

(*b*) After P Ltd acquired control of S Ltd the balance sheets would appear as follows before any further trading took place:

P Ltd Balance Sheet as at 1 January 19X6	£	£	S Ltd Balance Sheet as at 1 January 19X6	£	£
Fixed assets		2,000	Fixed assets		400
Investment in subsidiary			*Current assets:*		
undertaking		600	Stock-in-trade	400	
Current assets:			Debtors	200	
Stock-in-trade	2,900		Bank	100	
Debtors	800				700
Bank	700				1,100
		4,400	Share capital		1,000
		7,000	Profit and loss account		100
					1,100
Share capital		5,000			
Profit and loss account		2,000			
		7,000			

The only differences can be seen to be those in the balance sheets of P Ltd. The bank balance has been reduced by £600, this being the cost of shares in S Ltd, and the cost of the shares now appears as 'Investment in subsidiary undertaking £600'. The balance sheets of S Ltd are completely unchanged.

We shall see later that FRS 2: *Accounting for subsidiary undertakings* gives a much wider meaning to 'subsidiary undertaking' than we have seen so far. This has been deliberately excluded up to this point to let you see the basic structure without complicating it.

19.3 Profit and loss account

From the profit and loss account point of view, the appropriation section of S Ltd would also be completely unchanged after P Ltd takes control. P Ltd would however see a change in its profit and loss account when a dividend is received from S Ltd: in this case the dividends received would be shown as investment income in the profit and loss account. Remember that dividends payable are charged to the appropriation section of the paying company's profit and loss account, while dividends received are in the main part of the receiving company's profit and loss account.

The terms 'parent undertaking' and 'subsidiary undertaking' have been in use for only a fairly short time. Previously, a 'parent undertaking' was called a 'holding company', and a 'subsidiary undertaking' was a 'subsidiary company'. In Chapter 29 we will see exactly why the terms were changed. One of the reasons is that consolidated accounts used to be concerned only with companies. Now, as you will see, 'subsidiary undertakings' can include unincorporated businesses as well.

In the chapters which follow, 20 to 28 inclusive, we will show the consolidations only of companies, to demonstrate the principles involved. In addition we will often simply call a 'parent undertaking' by the title of 'parent' and a 'subsidiary undertaking' may also be shortened to 'subsidiary'.

In Chapter 29 we will examine Financial Reporting Standard 2 which covers the accounting needed for parent and subsidiary undertakings. This book, in the chapters which follow, fully complies with all the requirements of FRS 2.

19.4 The need for consolidated financial statements

Imagine being a shareholder of P Ltd. Each year you would receive a set of P Ltd's final accounts. After P's acquisition of the shares in S Ltd then £600 would appear as an asset in the balance sheet of P Ltd. It would be normal for it to be shown at cost £600, using the cost concept.

When you looked at the profit and loss account of P Ltd you would see the dividends received from S Ltd. This plus the cost of the investment in the balance sheet would therefore be the only things you would know about the subsidiary.

However, you have invested in P Ltd, and because of its majority shareholding in S Ltd you have in effect also invested in S Ltd as well. Just as you want to know how the assets and liabilities in P Ltd change over the years, you will now also like to know exactly the same for S Ltd.

You are not, however, a shareholder of S Ltd, and therefore you would not be sent a copy of its final accounts. If the situation were to stay like that, you could not get a proper view of your investment.

This would be even worse if in fact P Ltd was a parent undertaking with twenty subsidiaries, and held a different percentage stake in each of them. It would also be almost certain that the companies would trade with each other, and owe money to one another or be owed money by them. This would also raise complications.

Fortunately there is a remedy for this sort of problem. The Companies Acts provide for parent undertakings distributing to their shareholders a set of consolidated financial statements. These bring together all of the financial statements for the parent undertaking and its subsidiaries in such a way that the shareholders can get an overall view of their investments.

19.5 Different methods of acquiring control of one company by another

So far the acquisition of control in S Ltd was by P Ltd buying more than 50 per cent of the shares in S Ltd from Jones, i.e. buying shares on the open market. This is by no means the only way of acquiring control, so by way of illustration some of the other methods are now described.

(a) S Ltd may issue new shares to P Ltd amounting to over 50 per cent of the voting shares. P Ltd pays for the shares in cash.

(b) P Ltd could purchase over 50 per cent of the voting shares of S Ltd on the open market by exchanging for them newly issued shares of P Ltd.

Or, acting through another company:

(c) P Ltd acquires more than 50 per cent of the voting shares in S1 Ltd for cash, and then S1 Ltd proceeds to acquire all of the voting shares of S2 Ltd. S2 Ltd would then be a sub-subsidiary of P Ltd.

These are only some of the more common ways by which one company becomes a subsidiary of another company.

19.6 Control by dominant influence

The issue of FRS 2 in 1992 introduced a further way of looking at whether or not one company had control of another. If one company has 'the right to exercise a dominant influence' over another undertaking, then the company with the dominating influence is deemed to have control of the other. A dominant influence means that the holder of it has a right to give directions with regard to the operating and financial policies of another undertaking, and that the directors of that latter undertaking are obliged to comply, whether or not they are for the benefit of the undertaking.

In other words, if one undertaking can tell another undertaking what to do, both from an operating and financial point of view, and the directors of that latter undertaking have to carry out such instructions, then such an undertaking will be a subsidiary undertaking. This is a much wider definition than merely looking at the amounts of the shareholdings.

19.7 The nature of a group

Wherever two or more companies are in the relationship of parent and subsidiary undertakings then a 'group' is said to exist. When such a group exists then, besides the final accounts of the parent undertaking itself, to comply with legal requirements, there must be a set of financial statements prepared in respect of the group as a whole. These group accounts are usually known as **consolidated financial statements**, because the accounts of all the companies have had to be consolidated together to form one set of financial statements.

Sometimes parent undertakings carry on trading as well as investing in their subsidiaries. There are, however, other parent undertakings that do not trade at all, the whole of their activities being concerned with investing in other companies.

19.8 Subsidiary undertakings which are not limited companies

At one time, group accounts consolidated only those accounts which belonged to limited companies. In 1992, FRS 2 widened this so that a subsidiary undertaking can be other than a limited company. Share of ownership or the dominant influence approach will determine whether or not an entity is a 'subsidiary undertaking'. If so, its financial statements are then consolidated in a similar fashion to those of limited companies.

Other forms of entity – associates and joint ventures – are not subsidiaries and are not consolidated. They are included in the financial statements according to the rules contained in FRS 9 (and, for small entities applying the FRSSE, by SSAP 1). These rules are dealt with in Chapter 29.

19.9 FRS 2: Accounting for subsidiary undertakings

The main changes brought about by FRS 2 were as follows:

(a) The concept of 'dominant influence' widened the scope of which companies could be seen as subsidiary undertakings, rather than relying on share ownership.

(b) Unincorporated businesses (i.e. not companies) were brought into its scope and came to be classed as subsidiary undertakings which have to have their financial statements consolidated with the rest of the group.

19.10 Teaching method

The method used in this book for teaching consolidated accounts is that of showing the reader the adjustments needed on the face of the consolidated balance sheet, together with any workings necessary shown in a normal arithmetical fashion. The reasons why this method of illustrating consolidated accounts has been chosen are as follows:

(a) The authors believe that it is their job to try to help the reader understand the subject, and not just to be able to perform the necessary manipulations. They believe that, given understanding of what is happening, then the accounting entries necessary follow easily enough. Showing the adjustments on the face of the balance sheet gives a 'bird's-eye view' so that it is easier to see what is happening, rather than trace one's way laboriously through a complex set of double-entry adjustments made in ledger accounts.

(b) Secondly, this would be a much lengthier and more costly book if all of the double entry accounts were shown. It is better for a first look at consolidated accounts to be an introduction to the subject only, rather than both an introduction and a very detailed survey of the subject. If the reader can understand the consolidated accounts shown in this book, then he/she will have a firm foundation which will enable him/her to tackle the more difficult and complicated aspects of the subject.

New terms

Consolidation accounting (p. 291): This term means bringing together into a single balance sheet and profit and loss account the separate financial statements of a group of companies. Hence they are known as group financial statements.

Parent undertaking (p. 289): Although FRS 2 should be studied for a full and proper definition, the one that will suffice for the time being is 'an undertaking which controls or has a dominating influence over the affairs of another undertaking'.

Subsidiary undertaking (p. 289): An undertaking which is either controlled by another undertaking or where that other undertaking exercises a dominating influence over it.

Holding company (p. 289): The outdated term for what is now known as 'parent undertaking'.

Subsidiary company (p. 289): The outdated term for what is now known as a 'subsidiary undertaking'.

Main points to remember

1 Ordinary shareholders generally have voting rights, a right in the net assets of the company, and a right to an interest in profits earned.

2 Ordinary shareholders receive copies of the financial statements for the company whose shares they hold, but not for any company whose shares are owned by the company they hold their shares in.

3 Consolidated financial statements provide shareholders in parent undertakings with financial statements incorporating the relevant data for all companies in the group – not just the parent company's own accounts data.

4 The status of 'subsidiary undertaking' is dependent upon the existence of control over that undertaking by another entity.

5 'Control' is determined by whether 'dominant influence' can be exerted, not simply by the level of investment in the company.

Review questions

19.1 What determines whether or not one company is a subsidiary undertaking of another company?

19.2 How are incorporated businesses affected by the provisions of FRS 2?

19.3 What benefits accrue to the investor in a parent undertaking by the use of consolidated financial statements?

19.4 In what ways did FRS 2 change the ways in which consolidated financial statements should be drawn up?

20
Consolidation of balance sheets: basic mechanics I

Objectives

After you have studied this chapter, you should:

- *understand the principle of cancellation that is adopted when preparing consolidated financial statements*

- *be aware of why goodwill and capital reserves may arise on consolidation*

- *understand what is meant by the term 'minority interest'*

- *be aware of how the existence of reserves at the time of acquisition affects the preparation of consolidated financial statements*

20.1 Introduction

This chapter is concerned with the basic mechanics of consolidating balance sheets. The figures used will be quite small ones, as there is no virtue in obscuring the principles involved by bringing in large amounts. For the sake of brevity some abbreviations will be used. As the consolidation of the accounts of either two or three companies, but no more, will be attempted, then the abbreviations will be 'P' for the parent undertaking, 'S1' the first subsidiary undertaking, and 'S2' the second subsidiary undertaking. Where there is only one subsidiary undertaking it will be shown as 'S'. Unless stated to the contrary, all the shares will be ordinary shares of £1 each.

It will make the problems of the reader far easier if relatively simple balance sheets can be used to demonstrate the principles of consolidated accounts. To this end, the balance sheets which follow in the next few chapters will usually have only two sorts of assets, those of stock and cash at bank. This will save a great deal of time and effort. If every time a consolidated balance sheet were to be drawn up the reader had to deal with assets of land, buildings, patents, motor vehicles, plant and machinery, stock, debtors and bank balances, then this would be an unproductive use of time.

20.2 The principle of cancellation

The various final accounts of the parent undertaking and its subsidiary undertakings have to be brought together and consolidated into one set of accounts for the whole of the group. Some items in one of the original sets of accounts will also be found to refer to exactly the same transactions in one of the other sets of original final accounts.

Let us look at some of the more common examples:

- An item which is a debtor in one balance sheet may be shown as a creditor in another balance sheet. If P Ltd had sold goods to S Ltd, its subsidiary, but S Ltd had not yet paid for them, then the item would be shown as a debtor in the balance sheet of P Ltd and as a creditor in the balance sheet of S Ltd.
- Sales by one of the group to another company in the group will appear as sales in one company's accounts and purchases in another company's accounts.
- Shares bought in one of the subsidiary undertakings by the parent undertaking will be shown as an investment on the assets side of the parent undertaking's balance sheet. In the balance sheet of the subsidiary, exactly those same shares will be shown as issued share capital.
- Dividends paid by a subsidiary undertaking to its parent undertaking will be shown as paid dividends in the final accounts of the subsidiary, and as dividends received in the final accounts of the parent undertaking.

The group or consolidated financial statements are supposed to show how the group as a whole has dealt with the world outside. Transactions which are simply within the group do not represent dealings with the outside world. When all of the separate accounts of the companies within the group are put together such items need to be deleted, and will not appear in the consolidated financial statements of the group.

This therefore is the principle of cancellation. Like things in different final accounts within the group should be cancelled out from each to arrive at the group's final accounts. All of the items already listed will therefore not appear in the consolidated financial statements.

This can be shown in the form of the diagram in Exhibit 20.1.

Exhibit 20.1 Consolidation of accounts of a group

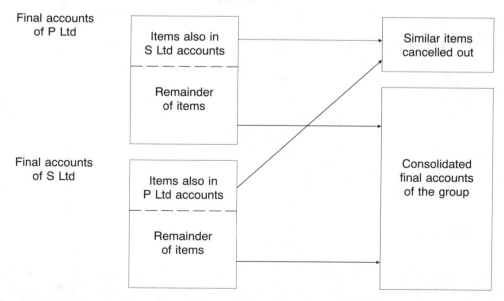

This means that a consolidated set of financial statements, where the subsidiaries are 100 per cent owned by the parent undertaking, will appear as follows:

Group Balance Sheet as at .....

	£	£
Fixed Assets (*less* Cancelled items)		xxxx
Current Assets (*less* Cancelled items)	xxxx	
Less Current liabilities (*less* Cancelled items)	xxxx	xxxx
		xxxx
Financed by		
Share capital (of the parent undertaking only, as the purchase of shares in the subsidiaries have cancelled out)		xxxx
Reserves (*less* Cancelled items)		xxxx
		xxxx

20.3 Rule 1

The first rule, therefore, is that in consolidation like things cancel out each other. In fact **cancellation accounts** are what consolidation accounts are all about. It also helps the reader to see the issue more clearly if the consolidated balance sheet is constructed immediately after P has bought the shares in S. In fact, this may not be done in practice, but it is useful to use the method from a teaching point of view.

Exhibit 20.2

100 per cent of the shares of S bought at balance sheet value.

P has just bought all the shares of S. Before consolidation the balance sheets of P and S appear as follows:

P Balance Sheet

		£
Investment in subsidiary sincerely	(A)	6
Bank		4
		10
Share capital		10
		10

S Balance Sheet

		£
Stock		5
Bank		1
		6
Share capital	(B)	6
		6

Now the consolidated balance sheet can be drawn up. The rule about like things cancelling out each other can now be applied. As can be seen, item (A) in P's balance sheet and item (B) in S's balance sheet are concerned with exactly the same thing, namely the 6 ordinary shares of S, and for the same amount, for the shares are shown in both balance sheets at £6. These are cancelled when the consolidated balance sheet is drafted.

P & S Consolidated Balance Sheet

	£
Stock	5
Bank (£4 + £1)	5
	10
Share capital	10
	10

Exhibit 20.3

100 per cent of the shares of S bought for more than balance sheet value.

P Balance Sheet

		£
Investment in subsidiary S: 6 shares	(C)	9
Bank		1
		10
Share capital		10
		10

S Balance Sheet

		£
Stock		5
Bank		1
		6
Share capital	(D)	6
		6

Now (C) and (D) refer to like things, but the amounts are unequal. What has happened is that P has given £3 more than the book value for the shares of S. In accounting, where the amount paid (or 'consideration') for something exceeds the stated value, the difference is known as 'goodwill'; and, when the consideration is less than the stated value, the difference is known as 'negative goodwill'. (In practice, the accounting standards require that 'fair values', rather than book values are used – *see* Section 25.3; however, for the sake of clarity, unless otherwise indicated, the book values will be used throughout this book.) The consolidated balance sheet is therefore:

P and S Consolidated Balance Sheet

	£
Goodwill (C) £9 – (D) £6	3
Stock	5
Bank (£1 + £1)	2
	10
Share capital	10
	10

Exhibit 20.4

100 per cent of the shares of S bought for less than balance sheet value.

P Balance Sheet

		£
Investment in subsidiary S: 6 shares	(E)	4
Stock		5
Bank		1
		10
Share capital		10
		10

S Balance Sheet

		£
Stock		5
Bank		1
		6
Share capital	(F)	6
		6

P has bought all the shares of S, but has given only £4 for £6 worth of shares at balance sheet values. The £2 difference is 'negative goodwill'. The uninitiated might look upon the £2 as being 'profit' but your knowledge of company accounts should tell you that this difference could never be distributed as cash dividends. This negative goodwill is treated as a minus entry in the Goodwill section of the balance sheet under FRS 10, or as a **capital reserve** under SSAP 22 and shown accordingly in the consolidated balance sheet.

Under SSAP 22, the consolidated balance sheet appears as:

P and S Consolidated Balance Sheet (SSAP 22)

	£
Stock (£5 + £5)	10
Bank (£1 + £1)	2
	12
Share capital	10
Capital reserve (F) £6 – (E) £4	2
	12

In contrast, under FRS 10, the consolidated balance sheet appears as:

P and S Consolidated Balance Sheet (FRS 10)

	£
Goodwill: negative goodwill (E) £4 – (F) £6	(2)
Stock (£5 + £5)	10
Bank (£1 + £1)	2
	10
Share capital	10

20.4 Cost of control

The expression 'cost of control' could be used instead of goodwill. This expression probably captures the essence of the purchase of the shares rather than calling it goodwill. It is precisely for the sake of gaining control of the assets of the company that the shares are bought. However, the expression goodwill is more widely used and is correspondingly the one that will be used through the remainder of this book. Details of how to record entries in a 'cost of control' account can be seen in section 26.4. (You can now attempt Review Questions 20.1, 20.2 and 20.3, giving answers based on both SSAP 22 and FRS 10, where appropriate.)

Important note: Remember that either FRS 10 – *Goodwill and intangible assets* – or, for some smaller entities, SSAP 22: *Accounting for goodwill* applies when goodwill is calculated. It will be up to the company exactly how it applies the relevant accounting standard. Unless otherwise indicated, you should apply the SSAP 22 rules to the examples contained in the next few chapters. However, you should be prepared to apply the FRS 10 rules if required, and should know how to apply them in case you are required to do so in your examinations.

20.5 Rule 2

This states that, although the whole of the shares of the subsidiary have not been bought, nonetheless the whole of the assets of the subsidiary (subject to certain inter-company transactions described later) will be shown in the consolidated balance sheet.

This rule comes about because of the choice made originally between two possible methods that could have been chosen. Suppose that P bought 75 per cent of the shares of S then the balance sheets could be displayed in one of two ways, e.g.

P and S Consolidated Balance Sheet

	£
Goodwill	xxxx
Assets of P: 100 per cent	xxxx
Assets of S: 75 per cent	xxxx
	xxxx
Share capital of P	xxxx
	xxxx

P and S Consolidated Balance Sheet

	£
Goodwill	xxxx
Assets of P: 100 per cent	xxxx
Assets of S: 100 per cent	xxxx
	xxxx
Share capital of P	xxxx
Claims of outsiders which equal 25 per cent of the assets of S	xxxx
	xxxx

It can be seen that both balance sheets show the amount of assets which P owns by virtue of its proportionate shareholding. On the other hand the second balance sheet gives a fuller picture, as it shows that P has control of all of the assets of S, although in fact it does not own all of them. The claims of outsiders come to 25 per cent of S and obviously they cannot control the assets of S, whereas P, with 75 per cent, can control the whole of the assets even though they are not fully owned by it. The second balance sheet method gives rather more meaningful information and is the method that is used for consolidated accounts in accordance with FRS 2.

Assume that S has 6 shares of £1 each and that it has one asset, namely stock £6. P buys 4 shares for £1 each, £4. If the whole of the assets of S £6 are to be shown on the assets side of the consolidated balance sheet, and the cancellation of only £4 is to take place on the other side, then the consolidated balance sheet would not balance. Exhibit 20.5 shows this in detail before any attempt is made to get the consolidated balance sheet to balance.

Exhibit 20.5

P Balance Sheet

	£
Investment in subsidiary: 4 shares (bought today)	4
Stock	5
Bank	1
	10
Share capital	10
	10

S Balance Sheet

	£
Stock	6
Share capital	6

Now as the two extra shares have not been bought by P then they cannot be brought into any calculation of goodwill or capital reserve. P has in fact bought four shares with a balance sheet value of £1 each, £4, for precisely £4. There is therefore no element of goodwill or capital reserve. But on the other hand the consolidated balance sheet per Rule 2 must show the whole of the assets of S. This gives a consolidated balance sheet as follows:

P and S Consolidated Balance Sheet

	£
Stock (£5 + £6)	11
Bank	1
Share capital	10

Quite obviously, if you now inserted the totals, they would differ by £2. What is this £2? On reflection it can be seen to be the £2 shares not bought by P. These shares belong to outsiders, they are not owned by the group. These outsiders also hold less than 50 per cent of the voting shares of S. In fact, if they owned more, then S would probably not be a subsidiary company. The title given to the outside shareholders is the apt one therefore of **minority interest**. As the whole of the assets of S are shown in the consolidated balance sheet then part of these assets are owned by the minority interest. This claim against the assets is therefore shown on the capital side of the consolidated balance sheet. The consolidated balance sheet becomes:

P and S Consolidated Balance Sheet

	£
Stock (£5 + £6)	11
Bank	1
	12
Share capital	10
Minority interest	2
	12

This therefore is the convention of showing the whole of the assets of the subsidiary (less certain inter-company transactions) in the consolidated balance sheet, with the claim of the minority interest shown on the other side of the balance sheet.

Exhibit 20.6

Where less than 100 per cent of the subsidiary's shares are bought at more than book value.

P Balance Sheet

		£
Investment in subsidiary: 6 shares	(G)	8
Stock		11
Bank		1
		20
Share capital		20
		20

S Balance Sheet

		£
Stock		7
Bank		3
		10
Share capital	(I)	10
		10

P has bought 6 shares only, but has paid £8 for them. As the book value of the shares is £6, the £2 excess must therefore be goodwill. The cancellation is therefore £6 from (G) and £6 from (I), leaving £2 of (G) to be shown as goodwill in the consolidated balance sheet. The remaining £4 of (I) is in respect of shares held by the minority interest.

P and S Consolidated Balance Sheet

	£
Goodwill	2
Stock (£11 + £7)	18
Bank (£1 + £3)	4
	24
Share capital	20
Minority interest	4
	24

Exhibit 20.7

Where less than 100 per cent of the shares in the subsidiary are bought at less than book value.

P Balance Sheet

		£
Investment in subsidiary: 7 shares	(J)	5
Stock		13
Bank		2
		20
Share capital		20
		20

S Balance Sheet

		£
Stock		9
Bank		1
		10
Share capital	(K)	10
		10

Seven shares of S have now been bought for £5. This means that £5 of (J) and £5 of (K) cancel out with £2 shown as capital reserve. The remaining £3 of (K) is in respect of the shares held by the minority interest and will be shown as such in the consolidated balance sheet.

P and S Consolidated Balance Sheet

	£
Stock (£13 + £9)	22
Bank (£2 + £1)	3
	25
Shares	20
Capital reserve	2
Minority interest	3
	25

You can now attempt Review Questions 20.6 and 20.7.

20.6 Taking over subsidiaries with reserves

So far, for reasons of simplification, the examples given have been of subsidiaries having share capital but no reserves. When reserves exist, as they do in the vast majority of firms, it must be remembered that they belong to the ordinary shareholders. This means that if P buys all the 10 shares of S for £15, and S at that point of time has a credit balance of £3 on its profit and loss account and a general reserve of £2, then what P acquires for its £15 is the full entitlement/rights of the 10 shares measured by/shown as:

	£
10 Shares	10
Profit and loss	3
General reserve	2
	15

This means that the £15 paid and the £15 entitlements as shown will cancel out each other and will not be shown in the consolidated balance sheet. This is shown by the balance sheets shown in Exhibit 20.8.

Exhibit 20.8

Where 100 per cent of the shares are bought at book value when the subsidiary has reserves.

P Balance Sheet

		£
Investment in subsidiary: 10 shares	(L)	15
Stock		11
Bank		2
		28
Share capital		20
Profit and loss		5
General reserve		3
		28

S Balance Sheet

		£
Stock		9
Bank		6
		15
Share capital	(M1)	10
Profit and loss	(M2)	3
General reserve	(M3)	2
		15

P and S Consolidated Balance Sheet

	£
Stock (£11 + £9)	20
Bank (£2 + £6)	8
	28
Share capital	20
Profit and loss	5
General reserve	3
	28

The cost of the shares (L) £15 is cancelled out exactly against (M1) £10 + (M2) £3 + (M3) £2 = £15. These are therefore the only items cancelled out and the remainder of the two balance sheets of P and S are then combined to be the consolidated balance sheet.

Exhibit 20.9

Where 100 per cent of the shares are bought at more than book value when the subsidiary has reserves.

P Balance Sheet

		£
Investment in subsidiary: 10 shares	(N)	23
Stock		7
Bank		5
		35
Share capital		20
Profit and loss		9
General reserve		6
		35

S Balance Sheet

		£
Stock		15
Bank		2
		17
Share capital	(O1)	10
Profit and loss	(O2)	4
General reserve	(O3)	3
		17

P paid £23 (N) for the entitlements (O1) £10 + (O2) £4 + (O3) £3 = £17, so that a figure of £6 will be shown in the consolidated balance sheet for Goodwill.

P and S Consolidated Balance Sheet

	£
Goodwill	6
Stock (£7 + £15)	22
Bank (£5 + £2)	7
	35
Share capital	20
Profit and loss	9
General reserve	6
	35

Exhibit 20.10

Where 100 per cent of the shares in the subsidiary are bought at below book value when the subsidiary has reserves.

P Balance Sheet

		£
Investment in subsidiary: 10 shares	(Z)	17
Stock		10
Bank		8
		35
Share capital		20
Profit and loss		6
General reserve		9
		35

S Balance Sheet

		£
Stock		16
Bank		5
		21
Share capital	(Q1)	10
Profit and loss	(Q2)	8
General reserve	(Q3)	3
		21

P has paid £17 (Z) for the benefits of (Q1) £10 + (Q2) £8 + (Q3) £3 = £21. This means that there will be a Capital Reserve of £21 − £17 = £4 in the consolidated balance sheet, while (Z), (Q1), (Q2) and (Q3), having been cancelled out, will not appear.

P and S Consolidated Balance Sheet

	£
Stock (£10 + £16)	26
Bank (£8 + £5)	13
	39
Share capital	20
Profit and loss	6
General reserve	9
Capital reserve	4
	39

Exhibit 20.11

Where less than 100 per cent of the shares are bought in a subsidiary which has reserves, and the shares are bought at the balance sheet value.

P Balance Sheet

		£
Investment in subsidiary: 8 shares	(R)	24
Stock		15
Bank		6
		45
Share capital		20
Profit and loss		17
General reserve		8
		45

S Balance Sheet

		£
Stock		21
Bank		9
		30
Share capital	(T1)	10
Profit and loss	(T2)	5
General reserve	(T3)	15
		30

The items (R) and the parts of (T1), (T2) and (T3) which are like things need to be cancelled out. The cancellation takes place from the share capital and reserves of S as follows:

	Total at acquisition date £	Bought by P 80 per cent £	Held by minority interest £
Share capital	10	8	2
Profit and loss	5	4	1
General reserve	15	12	3
	30	24	6

The amount paid by P was £24, and as P acquired a total of £24 value of shares and reserves the cancellation takes place without there being any figure of goodwill or capital reserve. The consolidated balance sheet therefore appears:

P and S Consolidated Balance Sheet

	£
Stock (£15 + £21)	36
Bank (£6 + £9)	15
	51
Share capital	20
Profit and loss	17
General reserve	8
Minority interest	6
	51

20.7 Partial control at a price not equal to balance sheet value

In Exhibit 20.11 the amount paid for the 80 per cent of the shares of S was equal to the balance sheet value of the shares in that it amounted to £24. Very rarely will it be so, as the price is normally different from balance sheet value. If an amount paid is greater than the balance sheet value then the excess will be shown as goodwill in the consolidated balance sheet, while if a smaller amount than balance sheet value is paid then the difference is a capital reserve and will be shown as such in the consolidated balance sheet. Using the balance sheet figure of S in Exhibit 20.11 then if P had paid £30 for 80 per cent of the shares of S then the consolidated balance sheet would show a goodwill figure of £6, while if instead £21 only had been paid then the consolidated balance sheet would show £3 for capital reserve.

When the acquisition of two subsidiaries brings out in the calculations a figure of goodwill in respect of the acquisition of one subsidiary, and a figure for capital reserve in respect of the acquisition of the other subsidiary, then the net figure only will be shown in the consolidated balance sheet. For instance if P had acquired two subsidiaries S1 and S2 where the calculations showed a figure of £10 for goodwill on the acquisition of S1 and a figure of £4 for capital reserve on the acquisition of S2, then the consolidated balance sheet would show a figure for goodwill of £6. Given figures instead of £11 goodwill for S1 and £18 capital reserve for S2 then the consolidated balance sheet would show a capital reserve of £7.

The final exhibit in this chapter is a composite one, bringing in most of the points already shown.

Exhibit 20.12

Where two subsidiaries have been acquired, both with reserves, full control being acquired of one subsidiary and a partial control of the other subsidiary.

P Balance Sheet

		£
Investment in subsidiaries:		
S1 10 shares	(U)	37
S2 7 shares	(V)	39
Stock		22
Bank		2
		100
Share capital		40
Profit and loss		50
General reserve		10
		100

S1 Balance Sheet

		£
Stock		19
Bank		11
		30
Share capital	(W1)	10
Profit and loss	(W2)	12
General reserve	(W3)	8
		30

S2 Balance Sheet

		£
Stock		42
Bank		18
		60
Share capital	(X1)	10
Profit and loss	(X2)	30
General reserve	(X3)	20
		60

With the acquisition of S1 P has paid £37 for (W1) £10 + (W2) £12 + (W3) £8 = £30, giving a figure of £7 for goodwill. With the acquisition of S2 P has given £39 for $\frac{7}{10}$ of the following: (X1) £10 + (X2) £30 + (X3) £20 = £60 × $\frac{7}{10}$ = £42, giving a figure of £3 for capital reserve. As the net figure only is to be shown in the consolidated balance sheet then it will be Goodwill £7 − Capital reserve £3 = Goodwill (net) £4.

P and S1 and S2 Consolidated Balance Sheet

		£
Goodwill		4
Stock (£22 + £19 + £42)		83
Bank (£2 + £11 + £18)		31
		118
Share capital		40
Profit and loss		50
General reserve		10
Minority interest:		
$\frac{3}{10}$ of (X1)	3	
$\frac{3}{10}$ of (X2)	9	
$\frac{3}{10}$ of (X3)	6	
		18
		118

Now work through Review Questions 20.10 and 20.11.

New terms

Minority interests (p. 301): Shareholders in subsidiary undertakings other than the holding undertaking who are not therefore part of the group.

Cost of control (p. 299): An alternative expression to goodwill.

Capital reserve (p. 298): Where less than fair value has been paid for the shares of the subsidiary.

Main points to remember

1 Some items in the accounts of one of the group companies will refer to exactly the same transactions as in the accounts of one of the other group companies and they will need to be cancelled out when the consolidated financial statements are prepared (*Rule 1*).

2 Where the consideration exceeds the balance sheet value acquired, goodwill arises.

3 Where the consideration is less than the balance sheet value acquired, the negative goodwill is treated as a negative entry in the Goodwill section of the balance sheet under FRS 10, or as a capital reserve under SSAP 22.

4 The treatment of goodwill is governed by FRS 10 or, for some small entities, by SSAP 22. (*See* Chapter 11.)

5 Minority interests exist when less than 100 per cent of the share capital of a subsidiary is owned at the balance sheet date.

6 All the assets of a subsidiary are included in the consolidated financial statements, even where less than 100 per cent of the share capital has been acquired (*Rule 2*).

7 When a subsidiary has reserves at the date of acquisition, those reserves are treated as part of the capital acquired and the calculation of goodwill includes the relevant proportion of the reserves.

8 When goodwill arises in respect of consolidation of one subsidiary and a capital reserve arises on another, the two amounts should be offset in the consolidated financial statements, leaving a net balance to be shown.

Review questions

20.1 The following balance sheets were drawn up immediately P Ltd had acquired control of S Ltd. You are to draw up a consolidated balance sheet.

P Balance Sheet

	£
Investment in S: 100 shares	110
Stock	60
Bank	30
	200
Share capital	200
	200

S Balance Sheet

	£
Stock	80
Bank	20
	100
Share capital	100
	100

20.2 You are to draw up a consolidated balance sheet from the following balance sheets of P Ltd and S Ltd which were drawn up immediately P Ltd had acquired the shares in S Ltd.

P Balance Sheet

	£
Investment in S Ltd: 3,000 shares	2,700
Fixed assets	2,000
Stock	800
Debtors	400
Bank	100
	6,000
Share capital	6,000
	6,000

S Balance Sheet

	£
Fixed assets	1,800
Stock	700
Debtors	300
Bank	200
	3,000
Share capital	3,000
	3,000

20.3 Draw up a consolidated balance sheet from the following balance sheets which were drawn up as soon as P Ltd had acquired control of S Ltd.

P Balance Sheet

	£
Investment in S Ltd: 60,000 shares	60,000
Fixed assets	28,000
Stock	6,000
Debtors	5,000
Bank	1,000
	100,000
Share capital	100,000
	100,000

S Balance Sheet

	£
Fixed assets	34,000
Stock	21,000
Debtors	3,000
Bank	2,000
	60,000
Share capital	60,000
	60,000

20.4A P Ltd acquires all the shares in S Ltd and then the following balance sheets are drawn up. You are to draw up a consolidated balance sheet.

P Balance Sheet

	£
Investment in S Ltd	29,000
Fixed assets	5,000
Stock	4,000
Debtors	3,000
Bank	1,000
	42,000
Share capital	42,000
	42,000

S Balance Sheet

	£
Fixed assets	12,000
Stock	6,000
Debtors	4,000
Bank	2,000
	24,000
Share capital	24,000
	24,000

20.5A Draw up a consolidated balance sheet from the balance sheets of P Ltd and S Ltd that were drafted immediately the shares in S Ltd were acquired by P Ltd.

P Balance Sheet

	£
Investment in S Ltd: 63,000 shares	50,000
Fixed assets	18,000
Stock	5,000
Debtors	4,000
Bank	3,000
	80,000
Share capital	80,000
	80,000

S Balance Sheet

	£
Fixed assets	48,000
Stock	6,000
Debtors	5,000
Bank	4,000
	63,000
Share capital	63,000
	63,000

20.6 P Ltd acquires 60 per cent of the shares in S Ltd. Balance sheets are then drafted immediately. You are to draw up the consolidated balance sheet.

P Balance Sheet

	£
Investment in S Ltd: 1,200 shares	1,500
Fixed assets	900
Stock	800
Debtors	600
Bank	200
	4,000
Share capital	4,000
	4,000

S Balance Sheet

	£
Fixed assets	1,100
Stock	500
Debtors	300
Bank	100
	2,000
Share capital	2,000
	2,000

20.7 P Ltd acquires 95 per cent of the shares of S Ltd. The following balance sheets are then drafted. You are to draw up the consolidated balance sheet.

P Balance Sheet

	£
Investment in S: 2,850 shares	2,475
Fixed assets	2,700
Stock	1,300
Debtors	1,400
Bank	125
	8,000
Share capital	8,000
	8,000

S Balance Sheet

	£
Fixed assets	625
Stock	1,700
Debtors	600
Bank	75
	3,000
Share capital	3,000
	3,000

20.8A P Ltd buys 66⅔ per cent of the shares in S Ltd. You are to draw up the consolidated balance sheet from the following balance sheets constructed immediately control had been achieved.

P Balance Sheet

	£
Investment in S: 600 shares	540
Fixed assets	1,160
Stock	300
Debtors	200
Bank	100
	2,300
Share capital	2,300
	2,300

S Balance Sheet

	£
Fixed assets	400
Stock	200
Debtors	240
Bank	60
	900
Share capital	900
	900

20.9A   After P Ltd acquired 75 per cent of the shares of S Ltd the following balance sheets are drawn up. You are to draw up the consolidated balance sheet.

P Balance Sheet

	£
Investments in S Ltd: 1,200 shares	1,550
Fixed assets	2,450
Stock	1,000
Debtors	800
Bank	200
	6,000
Share capital	6,000
	6,000

S Balance Sheet

	£
Fixed assets	800
Stock	400
Debtors	250
Bank	150
	1,600
Share capital	1,600
	1,600

20.10   Immediately after P Ltd had acquired control of S1 Ltd and S2 Ltd the following balance sheets were drawn up. You are to draw up a consolidated balance sheet.

P Balance Sheet

	£
Investments in subsidiaries:	
S1 Ltd (3,000 shares)	3,800
S2 Ltd (3,200 shares)	4,700
Fixed assets	5,500
Current assets	2,500
	16,500
Share capital	10,000
Profit and loss account	6,500
	16,500

S1 Balance Sheet

	£
Fixed assets	2,200
Current assets	1,300
	3,500
Share capital	3,000
Profit and loss account	400
General reserve	100
	3,500

S2 Balance Sheet

	£
Fixed assets	4,900
Current assets	2,100
	7,000
Share capital	4,000
Profit and loss account	1,000
General reserve	2,000
	7,000

20.11 Immediately after P Ltd had acquired control of S1 Ltd and S2 Ltd the following balance sheets were drawn up. You are to draw up a consolidated balance sheet.

P Balance Sheet

	£
Investment in subsidiaries:	
S1 Ltd (1,800 shares)	4,200
S2 Ltd (2,000 shares)	2,950
Fixed assets	4,150
Current assets	2,100
	13,400
Share capital	10,000
Profit and loss account	2,000
General reserve	1,400
	13,400

S1 Balance Sheet

	£
Fixed assets	3,500
Current assets	2,500
	6,000
Share capital	3,000
Profit and loss account	1,200
General reserve	1,800
	6,000

S2 Balance Sheet

	£
Fixed assets	1,800
Current assets	1,400
	3,200
Share capital	2,000
Profit and loss account	500
General reserve	700
	3,200

20.12A Immediately after P Ltd had achieved control of S1 Ltd and S2 Ltd the following balance sheets are drawn up. You are to draw up the consolidated balance sheet.

P Balance Sheet

	£
Investments in subsidiaries:	
S1 Ltd 4,000 shares	6,150
S2 Ltd 6,000 shares	8,950
Fixed assets	3,150
Current assets	2,050
	20,300
Share capital	15,000
Profit and loss account	2,000
General reserve	3,300
	20,300

S1 Balance Sheet

	£
Fixed assets	5,300
Current assets	1,200
	6,500
Share capital	4,000
Profit and loss account	1,100
General reserve	1,400
	6,500

S2 Balance Sheet

	£
Fixed assets	6,000
Current assets	3,450
	9,450
Share capital	7,000
Profit and loss account	1,400
General reserve	1,050
	9,450

20.13A The following balance sheets of P Ltd, S1 Ltd and S2 Ltd were drawn up as soon as P Ltd had acquired the shares in both subsidiaries. You are to draw up a consolidated balance sheet.

P Balance Sheet

	£
Investments in subsidiaries:	
S1 Ltd 3,500 shares	6,070
S2 Ltd 2,000 shares	5,100
Fixed assets	2,030
Current assets	1,400
	14,600
Share capital	11,000
Profit and loss account	1,000
General reserve	2,600
	14,600

S1 Balance Sheet

	£
Fixed assets	4,800
Current assets	2,400
	7,200
Share capital	5,000
Profit and loss account	900
General reserve	1,300
	7,200

S2 Balance Sheet

	£
Fixed assets	2,800
Current assets	900
	3,700
Share capital	2,000
Profit and loss account	1,400
General reserve	300
	3,700

21

Consolidation of balance sheets: basic mechanics II

Objectives

After you have studied this chapter, you should:

- *understand the implications when the date of acquisition and the group balance sheet date do not coincide*

- *know that the calculation of goodwill is performed as at the date of acquisition*

- *be aware of the difference in treatment between pre- and post-acquisition reserves of subsidiary undertakings*

21.1 Introduction

In the last chapter, the consolidation of balance sheets was looked at as if the consolidated balance sheets were drawn up immediately the shares in the subsidiary had been acquired. However, this is very rarely the case in practice yet, even though the consolidation will likely be performed at the end of the accounting period and some time after the acquisition, it must also be looked at as at the time the acquisition occurred. Correspondingly, the balance on the profit and loss account of the subsidiary, and possibly the balances on the other reserve accounts, will have altered when compared with the figures at the date of acquisition.

21.2 Goodwill in later years' accounts

In Chapter 20 the goodwill, or capital reserve, was calculated at the date of acquisition, and this calculation will stay unchanged as the years go by. It is important to understand this. Say, for instance, that the calculation was made of goodwill on 31 December 19X3 and that the figure was £5,000. Even if the calculation were made one year later, on 31 December 19X4, then the calculation must refer to the reserves etc. as on 31 December 19X3 as this is when they were acquired, and so the figure of goodwill will still be £5,000. This would be true even if five years went by before anyone performed the calculation. In practice, therefore, once the figure of goodwill has been calculated then there is absolutely no need to recalculate it every year. However, in examinations the goodwill figure will still have to be calculated by the student even though the consolidated balance sheet that he is drawing up is 5, 10 or 20 years after the company became a subsidiary. This has to be done because the previous working papers are not available to an examinee.

21.3 Capital reserves

Since 1981, companies have had the power to purchase their own shares, previous holders of the shares ceasing to be shareholders upon completion of the transaction. However, unless special permission were granted by the court, it is outside the law for any company to otherwise return its capital to the shareholders. If a parent undertaking were to pay its money in order to acquire a company as a subsidiary, and then distributed as dividends the assets that it had bought, this would really be the same as returning its capital to its shareholders. This can best be illustrated by a simple example.

P pays £15 to acquire 100 per cent of the shares of S, and the share capital of S consists of £10 of shares and £5 profit and loss account. Thus to acquire a capital asset, i.e. ownership of S, the holding company has parted with £15. If the balance of the profit and loss account of S were merely added to the profit and loss balance of P in the consolidated balance sheet, then the £5 balance of S could be regarded as being distributable as cash dividends to the shareholders of P. As this £5 of reserves has been bought as a capital asset then such a dividend would be the return of capital to the shareholders of S. To prevent this, the balance of the profit and loss account of S on acquisition is capitalised, i.e. it is brought into the balance sheet through the calculation of goodwill and is not shown in the consolidated balance sheet as a profit and loss account balance. On the other hand, the whole of any profit made by S since acquisition will clearly belong to P's shareholders as P owns 100 per cent of the shares of S.

Exhibit 21.1

Where the parent undertaking holds 100 per cent of the subsidiary undertaking's shares.

P acquires the shares on 31 December 19X4. The balance sheets one year later are as follows:

P Balance Sheet as at 31 December 19X5

		£
Investment in subsidiary: 10 shares bought 31.12.19X4	(A)	18
Stock		11
Bank		3
		32
Share capital		20
Profit and loss		12
		32

S Balance Sheet as at 31 December 19X5

			£
Stock			14
Bank			2
			16
Share capital	(B)		10
Profit and loss:		£	
As at 31.12.19X4	(C)	5	
Profit for 19X5	(D)	1	
			6
			16

The shares were acquired on 31 December 19X4, therefore the calculation of the goodwill or capital reserve is as the position of those firms were at that point in time. Thus for (A) £18 the firm of P obtained the following at 31 December 19X4: Shares (B) £10 and profit and loss (C) £5 = £15. Goodwill therefore amounted to £3. The profit of S made during 19X5 is since acquisition and does not therefore come into the goodwill calculation. The figure of (D) £1 is a reserve which belongs wholly to P, as P in fact owns all of the shares of S. This (D) £1 is added to the reserves shown in the consolidated balance sheet.

P Consolidated Balance Sheet as at 31 December 19X5

	£
Goodwill	3
Stock (£11 + £14)	25
Bank (£3 + £2)	5
	33
Share capital	20
Profit and loss (P £12 + S £1)	13
	33

Exhibit 21.2
Where the parent holds 100 per cent of the shares of the subsidiary and there is a post-acquisition loss.

P Balance Sheet as at 31 December 19X5

			£
Investment in subsidiary:			
10 shares bought 31.12.19X4	(E)		19
Stock			10
Bank			4
			33
Share capital			20
Profit and loss:		£	
As at 31.12.19X4		7	
Add Profit 19X5		6	
			13
			33

S Balance Sheet as at 31 December 19X5

			£
Stock			9
Bank			2
			11
Share capital	(F)		10
Profit and loss		£	
As at 31.12.19X4	(G)	4	
Less Loss 19X5	(I)	3	
			1
			11

In calculating goodwill, against the amount paid (E) £19 are cancelled the items (F) £10 and (G) £4, thus the goodwill is £5. The loss (I) has been incurred since acquisition. A profit since acquisition, as in Exhibit 21.1, adds to the reserves in the consolidated balance sheet, therefore a loss must be deducted.

P Consolidated Balance Sheet as at 31 December 19X5

	£
Goodwill	5
Stock (£10 + £9)	19
Bank (£4 + £2)	6
	30
Share capital	20
Profit and loss (£13 − (I)£3)	10
	30

Exhibit 21.3

Where the parent acquires less than 100 per cent of the shares of the subsidiary and there is a post-acquisition profit.

P Balance Sheet as at 31 December 19X5

			£
Investment in subsidiary: 8 shares bought 31.12.19X4	(J)		28
Stock			7
Bank			3
			38
Share capital			20
Profit and loss		£	
As at 31.12.19X4		10	
Add Profit 19X5		8	
			18
			38

S Balance Sheet as at 31 December 19X5

			£
Stock			28
Bank			2
			30
Share capital	(K)		10
Profit and loss		£	
As at 31.12.19X4	(L)	15	
Add Profit 19X5	(M)	5	
	(N)		20
			30

P has given (J) £28 to take over 80 per cent of (K) + (L), i.e. 80 per cent of (£10 + £15) = £20. Therefore goodwill is £8. The profit for 19X5 (M) £5 is also owned 80 per cent by P = £4, and as this has been earned since the shares in S were bought the whole of this belongs to the shareholders of P and is also distributable to them, therefore it can be shown with other profit and loss account balances in the consolidated balance sheet.

The minority interest is 20 per cent of (K) £10 + (N) £20 = £6. It must be pointed out that, although the holding company splits up the profit and loss account balances into pre-acquisition and post-acquisition, there is no point in the minority interest doing likewise. It would, however, amount to exactly the same answer if they did, because 20 per cent of (K) £10 + (L) £15 + (M) £5 still comes to £6, i.e. exactly the same as 20 per cent of (N) £20 + (K) £10 = £6.

P Consolidated Balance Sheet as at 31 December 19X5

	£
Goodwill	8
Stock (£7 + £28)	35
Bank (£3 + £2)	5
	48
Share capital	20
Profit and loss (P £18 + £4)	22
Minority interest (shares £2 + profit and loss £4):	6
	48

If there had been a post-acquisition loss, then this would have been deducted from P's profit and loss account balance of £18 when the consolidated balance sheet was drawn up.

Main points to remember

1 Goodwill must be calculated on the basis of the fair values at the date of acquisition of the consideration given and the net assets acquired.

2 Once calculated, there is no point in recalculating the goodwill on an acquisition at a future balance sheet date as the value determined will not alter.

3 Pre-acquisition reserves of a subsidiary are part of the capital acquired and are cancelled out on consolidation; they are not treated as reserves of the group.

4 The group's share of a subsidiary undertaking's post-acquisition profits and losses are included on consolidation with the reserves of the rest of the group.

Review questions

21.1 P Ltd buys 100 per cent of the shares of S Ltd on 31 December 19X5. The balance sheets of the two companies on 31 December 19X6 are as shown. You are to draw up a consolidated balance sheet as at 31 December 19X6.

P Balance Sheet as at 31 December 19X6

	£	£
Investment in subsidiary:		
4,000 shares bought 31.12.19X5		5,750
Fixed assets		5,850
Current assets		2,400
		14,000
Share capital		10,000
Profit and loss account:		
As at 31.12.19X5	1,500	
Add Profit for 19X6	2,500	
		4,000
		14,000

S Balance Sheet as at 31 December 19X6

	£	£
Fixed assets		5,100
Current assets		1,500
		6,600
Share capital		4,000
Profit and loss account:		
As at 31.12.19X5	800	
Add Profit for 19X6	1,800	
		2,600
		6,600

21.2 P Ltd buys 70 per cent of the shares of S Ltd on 31 December 19X8. The balance sheets of the two companies on 31 December 19X9 are as follows. You are to draw up a consolidated balance sheet as at 31 December 19X9.

P Balance Sheet as at 31 December 19X9

	£	£
Investment in S Ltd:		
7,000 shares bought 31.12.19X8		7,800
Fixed assets		39,000
Current assets		22,200
		69,000
Share capital		50,000
Profit and loss account:		
As at 31.12.19X8	4,800	
Add Profit for 19X9	9,200	
		14,000
General reserve		5,000
		69,000

S Balance Sheet as at 31 December 19X9

	£	£
Fixed assets		8,400
Current assets		4,900
		13,300
Share capital		10,000
Profit and loss account:		
As at 31.12.19X8	1,700	
Less Loss for 19X9	400	
		1,300
General reserve (unchanged since 19X5)		2,000
		13,300

21.3A P Ltd bought 55 per cent of the shares in S Ltd on 31 December 19X6. From the following balance sheets you are to draw up the consolidated balance sheet as at 31 December 19X7.

P Balance Sheet as at 31 December 19X7

	£	£
Investment in S Ltd: 2,750 shares		4,850
Fixed assets		13,150
Current assets		13,500
		31,500
Share capital		30,000
Profit and loss account:		
As at 31.12.19X6	900	
Add Profit for 19X7	600	
		1,500
		31,500

S Balance Sheet as at 31 December 19X7

	£	£
Fixed assets		4,600
Current assets		3,100
		7,700
Share capital		5,000
Profit and loss account:		
As at 31.12.19X6	700	
Add Profit for 19X7	500	
		1,200
General reserve (unchanged since 19X6)		1,500
		7,700

21.4 P buys shares in S1 and S2 on 31 December 19X4. You are to draft the consolidated balance sheet as at 31 December 19X5 from the following:

P Balance Sheet as at 31 December 19X5

	£	£
Investment:		
S1: 6,000 shares		8,150
S2: 8,000 shares		11,400
Fixed assets		21,000
Current assets		12,000
		52,550
Share capital		40,000
Profit and loss account:		
As at 31.12.19X4	2,350	
Add Profit for 19X5	5,200	
		7,550
General reserve		5,000
		52,550

S1 Balance Sheet as at 31 December 19X5

	£	£
Fixed assets		9,900
Current assets		4,900
		14,800
Share capital		10,000
Profit and loss account:		
As at 31.12.19X4	1,100	
Add Profit for 19X5	1,700	
		2,800
General reserve (same as 31.12.19X4)		2,000
		14,800

S2 Balance Sheet as at 31 December 19X5

	£	£
Fixed assets		6,000
Current assets		4,000
		10,000
Share capital		8,000
Profit and loss account:		
As at 31.12.19X4	500	
Less Loss for 19X5	300	
		200
General reserve (same as 31.12.19X4)		1,800
		10,000

21.5A P Ltd bought 40,000 shares in S1 Ltd and 27,000 shares in S2 Ltd on 31 December 19X2. The following balance sheets were drafted as at 31 December 19X3. You are to draw up a consolidated balance sheet as at 31 December 19X3.

P Balance Sheet as at 31 December 19X3

	£	£
Investments in subsidiaries		
S1 Ltd 40,000 shares		49,000
S2 Ltd 27,000 shares		30,500
Fixed assets		90,000
Current assets		80,500
		250,000
Share capital		200,000
Profit and loss account:		
As at 31.12.19X2	11,000	
Add Profit for 19X3	16,000	
		27,000
General reserve		23,000
		250,000

S1 Balance Sheet as at 31 December 19X3

	£	£
Fixed assets		38,200
Current assets		19,200
		57,400
Share capital		50,000
Profit and loss account:		
As at 31.12.19X2	3,000	
Less Loss for 19X3	1,600	
		1,400
General reserve (as at 31.12.19X2)		6,000
		57,400

S2 Balance Sheet as at 31 December 19X3

	£	£
Fixed assets		31,400
Current assets		14,600
		46,000
Share capital		36,000
Profit and loss account:		
As at 31.12.19X2	4,800	
Add Profit for 19X3	3,400	
		8,200
General reserve (as at 31.12.19X2)		1,800
		46,000

21.6A   The following information relates to Heather Limited and its subsidiary, Thistle Limited.

1   *Heather Limited*
Retained profits as at 31 March 19X8 £700,000.
80,000 ordinary shares were purchased in Thistle Limited on 1 April 19X1 for £150,000.
2   *Thistle Limited*
Retained profits as at 1 April 19X1 £50,000.
Retained profits as at 31 March 19X8 £120,000.
There were no other capital or revenue account balances at either of these dates.
Issued share capital: 100,000 ordinary shares of £1 each.
3   Goodwill arising on consolidation is written off immediately on acquisition against reserves.

Required:
Make the following calculations:
(*a*)   the goodwill arising on the acquisition of Thistle Limited;
(*b*)   the retained profits to be shown in the Heather Group balance sheet as at 31 March 19X8;
(*c*)   the minority interest in the Heather Group as at 31 March 19X8.

(*Association of Accounting Technicians*)

22

Inter-company dealings: indebtedness and unrealised profit in stocks

Objectives

After you have studied this chapter, you should:

- *know how to treat intra-group indebtedness upon consolidation*
- *know how to treat unrealised intra-group profits upon consolidation*

22.1 Inter-company debts

When a subsidiary owes money to the parent, then the amount owing will be shown as a debtor in the parent's balance sheet and as a creditor in the subsidiary's balance sheet. Such debts in fact have to be shown separately from other debts so as to comply with the Companies Acts. Such a debt between these two companies is, however, the same debt and, following the rule that like things cancel out, the consolidated balance sheet will show neither debtor nor creditor for this amount as cancellation will have taken place. The same treatment would apply to debts owed by the parent to the subsidiary, or to debts owed by one subsidiary to another subsidiary. The treatment is exactly the same whether the subsidiary is 100 per cent owned or not.

Exhibit 22.1
Where the subsidiary owes money to the parent.

P Balance Sheet

		£	£
Investment in subsidiary: 10 shares			10
Stock			13
Debtors:			
Owing from subsidiary	(A)	4	
Other debtors		7	
			11
Bank			1
			35
Share capital			20
Profit and loss			6
Creditors			9
			35

S Balance Sheet

		£	£
Stock			6
Debtors			13
Bank			3
			22
Share capital			10
Creditors:			
Owing to parent	(B)	4	
Other creditors		8	
			12
			22

P & S Consolidated Balance Sheet

	£
Stock (£13 + £6)	19
Debtors (£7 + £13)	20
Bank (£1 + £3)	4
	43
Share capital	20
Profit and loss	6
Creditors (£9 + £8)	17
	43

22.2 Unrealised profit in stock-in-trade

It is possible that companies in a group may not have traded with each other. In that case the stocks-in-trade at the balance sheet date will not include goods bought from another member of the group. Again it is also possible that the companies may have traded with each other, but at the balance sheet date all of the goods traded with each other may have been sold to firms outside the group, and the result is that none of the companies in the group will have any of such goods included in its stock-in-trade.

However, it is also possible that the companies have traded with each other, and that one or more of the companies has goods in its stock-in-trade at the balance sheet date which have been bought from another group member. If the goods have been traded between members of the group at cost price, then the consolidated balance sheet will not be altered just because of a change in the location of stocks-in-trade. This means that it will not offend accounting practice by adding together all of the stock figures and showing them in the consolidated balance sheet, as the total will be the total of the cost of the unsold goods within the group.

Conversely, goods are usually sold between members of the group at prices above the original cost price paid by the first member of the group to acquire them. If all such goods are sold by group members to firms outside by the balance sheet date then no adjustments are needed in the consolidated balance sheet, because the goods will not then be included in the stocks-in-trade. It would, however, be more usual to find that some of the goods had not been sold by one of the companies at the balance sheet date, so that company would include these goods in its stock-in-trade in its own balance sheet. Suppose that the parent owns all the shares in S, the subsidiary, and that P had sold goods which had cost it £12 to S for £20. Assume in addition that S had sold none of these goods by the balance sheet date. In the balance sheet of S the goods will be included in stock-in-trade at £20, while the profits made by P will include the £8 profit recorded in buying the goods for £12 and selling them for £20. Although this is true from each company's point of view, it most certainly is not true from the group viewpoint. The goods have not passed to anyone outside the group, and therefore the profit of £8 has not been realised by the group.

22.3 Realisation of profits

Going back to the basic accounting concepts, the realisation concept states that profit should not be recognised until the goods have been passed to the customer. As the consolidated accounts are concerned with an overall picture of the group, and the profits have not been realised by the group, then such profits should be eliminated. Accordingly the figure of £8 should be deducted from the profit and loss account of P on consolidation, and the same amount should be deducted from the stock-in-trade of S on consolidation. This cancels an unrealised intra-group profit.

If P had sold goods which had cost it £12 to S, a 100 per cent owned subsidiary, for £20, and S had sold ¾ of the goods for £22 by the balance sheet date then the picture would be different. P will have shown a profit in its profit and loss account for these sales of £8. In addition S will have shown a profit in its profit and loss account for the sales made of £7, i.e. £22 – ¾ of £20. The two profit and loss accounts show total profits of £8 + £7 = £15. So far, however, looking at the group as a whole, these goods have cost the group £12. Three-quarters of these have been sold to firms outside the group, so that the cost of goods sold outside the group is ¾ of £12 = £9, and as these were sold by S the profit realised by the group is £22 – £9 = £13. This is £2 less than that shown by adding up the separate figures for each company in the group. Thus the group figures would be overstated by £2 if the separate figures were merely added together without any adjustment. In addition the stock-in-trade would be overvalued by £2 if the two separate figures were added together because the remaining stock-in-trade of S includes one-quarter of the goods bought from P, i.e. $\frac{1}{4}$ of £20 = £5, but the original cost of the group was $\frac{1}{4}$ of £12 = £3. The adjustment needed is that in the consolidation process £2 will be deducted from the profit and loss balance of P and £2 will be deducted from the stock-in-trade of S, thus removing any unrealised intra-group profits.

This could be expressed in tabular form as:

		£
(a)	Cost of goods to P	12
(b)	Sold to S for	20
(c)	Sold by S, $\frac{3}{4}$ for	22
(d)	Stock of S at balance sheet date at cost to S $\frac{1}{4}$ of (b)	5
(e)	Stock of S at balance sheet date at cost to P $\frac{1}{4}$ of (a)	3
(f)	Excess of S balance sheet value of stock over cost to group (d) – (e)	2

(g) Profit shown in P profit and loss account (b) – (a) = £8

(h) Profit shown in S profit and loss account (c) £22 – $\frac{3}{4}$ of (b) = £7

(i) Profit shown in the profit and loss accounts of P and S = (g) + (h) = £15

(j) Actual profit made by the group dealing with outsiders (c) £22 less [$\frac{3}{4}$ of (a) £12] £9 = £13

(k) Profit recorded by individual companies exceeds profit made by the group's dealing with outsiders (i) – (j) = £2

The action needed for the consolidated balance sheet is therefore to deduct (f) £2 from the combined stock figure, and to deduct (k) £2 from the combined profit and loss account figure.

Exhibit 22.2

Where the stock-in-trade of one company includes goods bought from another company in the group.

P Balance Sheet as at 31 December 19X3

		£	£
Investment in subsidiary:			
10 shares bought 31.12.19X2			16
Stock-in-trade			24
Bank			6
			46
Share capital			20
Profit and loss account:			
As at 31.12.19X2		8	
Profit for 19X3	(C)	18	
			26
			46

S Balance Sheet as at 31 December 19X3

		£	£
Stock-in-trade	(D)		22
Bank			3
			25
Share capital			10
Profit and loss account:			
As at 31.12.19X2		6	
Profit for 19X3		9	
			15
			25

During the year P sold goods which had cost it £16 to S for £28, i.e. recording a profit for P of £12. Of these goods two-thirds had been sold by S at the balance sheet date, leaving one-third in stock-in-trade. This means that the stock-in-trade of S (D) includes £4 unrealised profit ($\frac{1}{3} \times £12$). The figure of P's profit for the year (C) £18 also includes £4 unrealised profit. When consolidating the two balance sheets £4 therefore needs to be deducted from each of those figures.

In Exhibit 22.2 the subsidiary has been wholly owned by the parent. The final figures would have been exactly the same if it had been the subsidiary which had sold the goods to the parent instead of vice versa.

P Consolidated Balance Sheet as at 31 December 19X3

	£
Stock-in-trade (S £22 − £4 + P £24)	42
Bank (P £6 + S £3)	9
	51
Share capital	20
Profit and loss accounts (S £9 + P £8 + £18 − £4)	31
	51

22.4 Partially-owned subsidiaries and unrealised profits

In Exhibit 22.2 the unrealised profit in stock-in-trade was £4, and in that case the subsidiary was 100 per cent controlled. A few years ago there were three possible methods of dealing with the adjustments needed, two of the methods taking into account the actual percentage of shares owned. However, with FRS 2 the elimination of intra-group profits or losses is to be made in full.

This means that if in Exhibit 22.2 S had been owned 75 per cent by P it would still be the full inter-group profit of £4 that would be deducted from the stock-in-trade in the consolidated balance sheet, and the full £4 would also be deducted from the profit and loss account of P when it is consolidated, there being no adjustment for minority interest.

Main points to remember

1 Intra-group indebtedness must be eliminated upon consolidation, irrespective of the proportion of the holding in the subsidiary undertaking(s) involved.

2 Unrealised intra-group profits must be eliminated upon consolidation, irrespective of the proportion of the holding in the subsidiary undertaking(s) involved.

Review questions

Note: Wherever appropriate, you should provide answers to these questions according to both SSAP 22 and FRS 10.

22.1 You are to draw up a consolidated balance sheet from the following details as at 31 December 19X9.

P Balance Sheet as at 31 December 19X9

	£	£
Investment in subsidiary: 1,000 shares bought 31.12.19X8		2,800
Fixed assets		1,100
Stock		1,200
Debtors		2,100
Bank		200
		7,400
Share capital		2,000
Profit and loss account:		
As at 31.12.19X8	1,500	
Profit for 19X9	2,200	
		3,700
General reserve		800
Creditors		900
		7,400

S Balance Sheet as at 31 December 19X9

	£	£
Fixed assets		1,200
Stock		900
Debtors		1,400
Bank		300
		3,800
Share capital		1,000
Profit and loss account:		
As at 31.12.19X8	950	
Profit for 19X9	1,150	
		2,100
Creditors		700
		3,800

During the year P had sold goods which had cost £150 to S for £240. None of these goods had been sold by the balance sheet date.

At the balance sheet date P owes S £220.

22.2 Draw up a consolidated balance sheet as at 31 December 19X4 from the following:

P Balance Sheet as at 31 December 19X4

	£	£
Investment in subsidiary: 6,000 shares bought 31.12.19X3		9,700
Fixed assets		9,000
Stock		3,100
Debtors		4,900
Bank		1,100
		27,800
Share capital		20,000
Profit and loss account:		
As at 31.12.19X3	6,500	
Loss for 19X4	2,500	
		4,000
Creditors		3,800
		27,800

S Balance Sheet as at 31 December 19X4

	£	£
Fixed assets		5,200
Stock		7,200
Debtors		3,800
Bank		1,400
		17,600
Share capital		10,000
Profit and loss account:		
As at 31.12.19X3	3,500	
Profit for 19X4	2,000	
		5,500
Creditors		2,100
		17,600

At the balance sheet date S owes P £600.

During the year P sold goods which had cost £300 to S for £500. Three-quarters of these goods had been sold by S by the balance sheet date.

22.3 Draw up a consolidated balance sheet from the following details as at 31 December 19X8.

P Balance Sheet as at 31 December 19X8

	£	£
Investment in subsidiaries:		
S1 30,000 shares bought 31.12.19X7		39,000
S2 25,000 shares bought 31.12.19X7		29,000
Fixed assets		22,000
Stock		26,000
Debtors		13,000
Bank		5,000
		134,000
Share capital		100,000
Profit and loss account		
As at 31.12.19X7	14,000	
Add Profit for 19X8	9,000	
		23,000
General reserve		2,000
Creditors		9,000
		134,000

S1 Balance Sheet as at 31 December 19X8

	£	£
Fixed assets		22,000
Stock		11,000
Debtors		8,000
Bank		3,000
		44,000
Share capital		30,000
Profit and loss account:		
As at 31.12.19X7	8,000	
Less Loss for 19X8	5,000	
		3,000
General reserve (as at 31.12.19X7)		4,000
Creditors		7,000
		44,000

S2 Balance Sheet as at 31 December 19X8

	£	£
Fixed assets		21,000
Stock		9,000
Debtors		7,000
Bank		1,000
		38,000
Share capital		30,000
Profit and loss account:		
As at 31.12.19X7	1,200	
Add Profit for 19X8	1,800	
		3,000
Creditors		5,000
		38,000

At the balance sheet date S2 owed S1 £500 and P owed S2 £900.

During the year P had sold goods costing £2,000 to S1 for £2,800. Of these goods one-half had been sold by the year end. P had also sold goods costing £500 to S2 for £740, of which none had been sold by the year end.

22.4A You are presented with the following information from the Seneley group of companies for the year to 30 September 19X6:

	Seneley plc £000	Lowe Ltd £000	Wright Ltd £000
Tangible fixed assets	225	300	220
Investments			
Shares in group companies:			
Lowe Ltd	450	–	–
Wright Ltd	130	–	–
	580	–	–
Current assets			
Stocks	225	150	45
Trade debtors	240	180	50
Cash at bank and in hand	50	10	5
	515	340	100
Creditors: amounts falling due within one year			
Trade creditors	(320)	(90)	(70)
Net current assets	195	250	30
	1,000	550	250
Capital and reserves			
Called-up share capital	800	400	200
Profit and loss account	200	150	50
	1,000	550	250

Additional information:
(a) The authorised, issued and fully paid share capital of all three companies consists of £1 ordinary shares.
(b) Seneley purchased 320,000 shares in Lowe Ltd on 1 October 19X3, when Lowe's profit and loss account balance stood at £90,000.
(c) Seneley purchased 140,000 shares in Wright Ltd on 1 October 19X5, when Wright's profit and loss account balance stood at £60,000.
(d) During the year to 30 September 19X6, Lowe had sold goods to Wright for £15,000. These goods had cost Lowe £7,000, and Wright still had half of these goods in stock as at 30 September 19X6. Minority interests are not charged with their share of any unrealised stock profits.
(e) Included in the respective trade creditor and trade debtor balances as at 30 September 19X6 were the following inter-company debts:
   • Seneley owed Wright £5,000;
   • Lowe owed Seneley £20,000; and
   • Wright owed Lowe £25,000.
(f) Seneley writes off any goodwill arising on consolidation to reserves.

Required:
Prepare the Seneley group's consolidated balance sheet as at 30 September 19X6. Your workings should be submitted.

(Association of Accounting Technicians)

22.5A You are to draw up a consolidated balance sheet as at 31 December 19X3 from the following:

P Balance Sheet as at 31 December 19X3

	£	£
Investment in subsidiaries:		
S1 75,000 shares bought 31.12.19X2		116,000
S2 45,000 shares bought 31.12.19X2		69,000
Fixed assets		110,000
Stock		13,000
Debtors		31,000
Bank		6,000
		345,000
Share capital		300,000
Profit and loss account:		
As at 31.12.19X2	22,000	
Less Loss for 19X3	7,000	
		15,000
General reserve (as at 31.12.19X2)		7,000
Creditors		23,000
		345,000

S1 Balance Sheet as at 31 December 19X3

	£	£
Fixed assets		63,000
Stock		31,000
Debtors		17,000
Bank		3,000
		114,000
Share capital		75,000
Profit and loss account:		
As at 31.12.19X2	11,000	
Add Profit for 19X3	12,000	
		23,000
Creditors		16,000
		114,000

S2 Balance Sheet as at 31 December 19X3

	£	£
Fixed assets		66,800
Stock		22,000
Debtors		15,000
Bank		4,000
		107,800
Share capital		80,000
Profit and loss account:		
As at 31.12.19X2	12,800	
Less Loss for 19X3	2,400	
		10,400
General reserve (as at 31.12.19X2)		6,400
Creditors		11,000
		107,800

At the balance sheet date S1 owed P £2,000 and S2 £500, and P owed S2 £1,800.

P had sold goods which had cost £2,000 to S2 for £3,200, and of these goods one-half had been sold by S2 by the year end.

22.6 The following summarised information relates to the Pagg group of companies.

Balance Sheet at 31 March 19X0

	Pagg plc £000	Ragg Ltd £000	Tagg Ltd £000
Tangible fixed assets at net book value	2,000	900	600
Investments			
800,000 ordinary shares in Ragg Ltd	3,000	–	–
300,000 ordinary shares in Tagg Ltd	1,000	–	–
	4,000	–	–
Current assets			
Stocks	1,300	350	100
Debtors	3,000	200	300
Cash	200	20	50
	4,500	570	450
Current liabilities			
Creditors	(4,000)	(270)	(400)
	6,500	1,200	650
Capital and reserves			
Called-up share capital (all ordinary shares of £1 each)	5,500	1,000	500
Profit and loss account	1,000	200	150
	6,500	1,200	650

Additional information:

1 Pagg acquired its shareholding in Ragg Ltd on 1 April 19X5. Ragg's profit and loss account balance at that time was £600,000.
2 The shares in Tagg Ltd were acquired on 1 April 19X9 when Tagg's profit and loss account balance was £100,000.
3 All goodwill arising on consolidation is amortised in equal amounts over a period of 20 years commencing from the date of acquisition of each subsidiary company.
4 At 31 March 19X0, Ragg had in stock goods purchased from Tagg at a cost to Ragg of £60,000. These goods had been invoiced by Tagg at cost plus 20 per cent. Minority interests are not charged with any inter-company profit.
5 Inter-company debts at 31 March 19X0 were as follows:
Pagg owed Ragg £200,000 and Ragg owed Tagg £35,000.

Required:

Insofar as the information permits, prepare the Pagg group of companies' consolidated balance sheet as at 31 March 19X0 in accordance with the Companies Acts and standard accounting practice.

Note: Formal notes to the accounts are NOT required, although detailed working must be submitted with your answer.

(Association of Chartered Certified Accountants)

22.7A You are presented with the following summarised information relating to Block plc for the year to 30 September 19X8:

	Block plc £000	Chip Ltd £000	Knot Ltd £000
Fixed assets	8,900	3,240	2,280
Investments			
Shares in group companies:			
Chip Ltd	2,500	–	–
Knot Ltd	1,600	–	–
	4,100	–	–
Current assets			
Stocks	300	160	80
Trade debtors	1,600	130	50
Cash at bank and in hand	400	110	120
	2,300	400	250
Creditors: amounts falling due within one year			
Trade creditors	(200)	(90)	(110)
Proposed dividend	(100)	(50)	(20)
	(300)	(140)	(130)
	15,000	3,500	2,400
Capital and reserves			
Called-up share capital (ordinary shares of £1 each)	10,000	3,000	2,000
Profit and loss account	5,000	500	400
	15,000	3,500	2,400

Additional information:

1 Block purchased 80 per cent of the share capital of Chip on 1 October 19X3 when Chip's profit and loss account balance was £200,000 credit.

2 On 1 October 19X7 Block purchased 60 per cent of the share capital of Knot. Knot's profit and loss account balance at that date was £500,000 credit.

3 Goodwill is written off against reserves immediately on acquisition.

4 During the year to 30 September 19X8, Block sold goods costing £200,000 to Chip for £300,000. Half of these goods remained in stock at the year end.

5 Inter-company debts at the year end were as follows:

	£000
Chip owed Block	20
Knot owed Chip	30

Required:

Prepare the Block plc group of companies' consolidated balance sheet as at 30 September 19X8. Formal notes to the accounts are NOT required, although detailed working should be submitted with your answer.

(Association of Chartered Certified Accountants)

23

Consolidated financial statements: acquisition of shares in subsidiaries at different dates

Objectives

After you have studied this chapter, you should:

- *know how to calculate goodwill when an interest in a subsidiary undertaking was acquired in blocks over a period of time*

- *know how to calculate goodwill when a subsidiary undertaking was acquired part way through its accounting period*

23.1 Shares bought at different dates

Up to this point the shares in subsidiaries have all been bought at one point in time for each company. However, it is a simple fact that shares are often bought in blocks at different times, and that the first purchase may not give the buyer a controlling interest.

There used to be two possible methods of calculating pre-acquisition profits, and therefore goodwill or capital reserve. However, FRS 2 states that only one method should be used, and this is the method used in this book. FRS 2 requires that the consolidation be based on the fair values at the date the undertaking actually becomes a subsidiary, even though the acquisition has been made in stages.

For instance, a company, S, has an issued share capital of 100 ordinary shares of £1 each. The only reserve of S is the balance on the profit and loss account which was £50 on 31 December 19X4, and two years later on at 31 December 19X6 it was £80. P buys 20 shares on 31 December 19X4 for £36, and a further 40 shares on 31 December 19X6 for £79. The date that S became a subsidiary was therefore 31 December 19X6. The calculation of goodwill becomes:

	£	£
Shares bought (20 + 40)	60	
Profit and loss account of subsidiary, 60 per cent × £80 (date control achieved)	48	108
Paid 31.12.19X4	36	
Paid 31.12.19X6	79	115

Goodwill therefore £115 − £108 = £7

23.2 Shares bought during an accounting period

In addition it has been conveniently assumed so far that all shares have been bought exactly on the last day of an accounting period. This will just not be so, most shares being bought part way through an accounting period. Unless specially audited accounts are drawn up as at the date of acquisition there is no up-to-date figure of profit and loss account as at the date of acquisition. As this is needed for the calculation of goodwill or capital reserve the figure has to be obtained somehow. Naturally enough, specially audited accounts would be the ideal for the purpose of the calculation, but if they are not available a second-best solution is necessary. In this instance the profit and loss balance according to the last balance sheet before the acquisition of the shares is taken, and an addition made (or deduction – if a loss) corresponding to the proportion of the year's profits that had been earned before acquisition took place. This is then taken as the figure of pre-acquisition profits for goodwill and capital reserve calculations.

Exhibit 23.1

Calculation of pre-acquisition profits, and goodwill, where the shares are bought part way through an accounting period.

P bought 20 of the 30 issued ordinary shares of S for £49 on 30 September 19X5. The accounts for S are drawn up annually to 31 December. The balance sheet of S as at 31 December 19X4 showed a balance on the profit and loss account of £24. The profit and loss account of S for the year ended 31 December 19X5 disclosed a profit of £12.

	£	£
Shares bought		20
Profit and loss account:		
Balance at 31.12.19X4	24	
Add Proportion of 19X5 profits before acquisition $\frac{9}{12} \times £12$	9	
	33	
Proportion of pre-acquisition profits		
20 shares owned out of 30, $\frac{2}{3} \times £33$		22
		42

Paid for shares £49
Therefore goodwill is £49 – £42 = £7

Main points to remember

1   When an interest in a subsidiary undertaking is acquired in blocks over a period of time, goodwill is calculated as if all the blocks had been purchased at the date when control was achieved.

2   When a subsidiary undertaking is acquired part way through its accounting period, in the absence of specially audited financial statements, the proportion of profit (or loss) applicable to that part of the financial period that preceded the acquisition date should be treated as being part of the pre-acquisition reserves for the calculation of goodwill upon consolidation.

Review questions

Note: Wherever appropriate, you should provide answers to these questions according to both SSAP 22 and FRS 10.

23.1 On 31 December 19X4 S Ltd had share capital of £40,000 ordinary £1 shares and reserves of £24,000. Two years later the share capital has not altered but the reserves have risen to £30,000. The following shares were bought by P Ltd: 10,000 on 31 December 19X4 for £23,500, and on 31 December 19X6 14,000 for £31,000. You are to calculate the figure of goodwill for the consolidated balance sheet as at 31 December 19X6.

23.2A On 31 December 19X6, S Ltd had share capital of £400,000 ordinary £1 shares and reserves of £260,000. Three years later the share capital is unchanged but the reserves have risen to £320,000. The following shares were bought by P Ltd: 100,000 on 31 December 19X6 for £210,000, and 200,000 on 31 December 19X9 for £550,000. Calculate the figure of goodwill for the consolidated balance sheet as at 31 December 19X9.

23.3 P Ltd bought 50,000 of the 80,000 issued ordinary £1 shares of S Ltd for £158,000 on 31 August 19X8. S Ltd accounts are drawn up annually to 31 December. The balance sheet of S Ltd on 31 December 19X7 showed a balance on the profit and loss account of £36,000. The profit and loss account of S Ltd for the year ended 31 December 19X8 showed a profit of £42,000. Calculate the figure for the goodwill to be shown in the consolidated balance sheet as at 31 December 19X8.

23.4A On 1 January 19X1 S Ltd had a share capital of £300,000, a profit and loss account balance of £28,000 and a general reserve of £20,000. During the year ended 31 December 19X1 S Ltd made a profit of £36,000, none of which was distributed. P Ltd bought 225,000 shares on 1 June 19X1 for £333,000. Calculate the figure of goodwill to be shown in the consolidated balance sheet as at 31 December 19X1.

24

Intra-group dividends

Objectives

After you have studied this chapter, you should:

- *know how to treat intra-group dividends*

- *know how to treat dividends from a newly acquired subsidiary undertaking that were proposed prior to the acquisition date*

- *know how to treat dividends proposed by subsidiary undertakings at the balance sheet date*

24.1 Not from pre-acquisition profits

Intra-group dividends are dividends paid by one member of a group to another, i.e. from one company in the group to another. They will, therefore, be shown in the receiving company's own profit and loss account as investment income, with a subsequent increase in the bank balance. From the point of view of the paying company's own accounts, it will show the dividend as a charge against its own profit and loss account, thus reducing the final balance on that account; when paid, there will be a reduction of the bank balance. If the dividend has been proposed, but not paid at the accounting year end, then it will be normal for the proposed dividend to be shown as a current liability in the subsidiary's balance sheet, and as a current asset on the parent undertaking's balance sheet as a dividend owing from the subsidiary.

From the point of view of the consolidated balance sheet (making an assumption about pre-acquisition profit shown in detail later) no action is needed. It is a past event that is automatically cancelled when drafting the consolidated balance sheet, as they are like things.

24.2 If paid from pre-acquisition profits

In Chapter 21, the company law principle that dividends should not be paid out of capital was reiterated. To prevent this happening, the pre-acquisition profits were capitalised and brought into the goodwill or capital reserve calculation. A company cannot circumvent the principle by buying the shares of a company, part of the purchase price being for the reserves of the subsidiary, and then utilising those reserves by paying itself dividends, and consequently adding those dividends to its own profits and then declaring an increased dividend itself. The next two exhibits are drawn up to illustrate this.

Exhibit 24.1

Dividends paid from post-acquisition profits.

P buys 100 per cent of the shares of S on 31 December 19X4. In 19X5, S pays a dividend of 50 per cent = £5 which P receives. To simplify matters the dividend is declared for 19X5 and paid in 19X5.

P Balance Sheet as at 31 December 19X5

	£	£
Investment in subsidiary:		
10 shares bought 31.12.19X4		23
Stock		11
Bank		1
		35
Share capital		20
Profit and loss account:		
As at 31.12.19X4	7	
Add Profit for 19X5 (including dividend of £5 from S)	8	
		15
		35

S Balance Sheet as at 31 December 19X5

	£	£	£
Stock			19
Bank			7
			26
Share capital			10
Profit and loss account:			
As at 31.12.19X4		12	
Profit for 19X5	9		
Less Dividend paid to P	5	4	16
			26

The dividend is £5 out of profits made since the acquisition of £9. The dividend can be treated as being from post-acquisition profits, and can therefore be shown in the profit and loss account of P as investment income and so swell the profits of P available for dividend purposes.

P Consolidated Balance Sheet as at 31 December 19X5

	£
Goodwill (£23 − £10 − £12)	1
Stock (P £11 + S £19)	30
Bank (P £1 + S £7)	8
	39
Share capital	20
Profit and loss account:	
(P £7 + £8 + S £4)	19
	39

Exhibit 24.2
Dividends paid from pre-acquisition profits.

P Balance Sheet as at 31 December 19X4

	£
Investment in subsidiary:	
10 shares bought 31.12.19X4	23
Stock	7
Bank	1
	31
Share capital	20
Profit and loss account	11
	31

S Balance Sheet as at 31 December 19X4

	£
Stock	14
Bank	3
	17
Share capital	10
Profit and loss account	7
	17

P Consolidated Balance Sheet as at 31 December 19X4
(immediately after acquisition)

	£
Goodwill (P £23 – S £10 – S £7)	6
Stock	21
Bank (P £1 + S £3)	4
	31
Share capital	20
Profit and loss account	11
	31

The consolidated balance sheet already shown was drafted immediately after acquisition. The following balance sheets show the position one year later. It is helpful to remember that the calculation of goodwill does not alter.

P Balance Sheet as at 31 December 19X5

	£	£
Investment in subsidiary:		
($23 originally calculated less dividend from pre-acquisition profits £7)		16
Stock		18
Bank		5
		39
Share capital		20
Profit and loss account:		
As at 31.12.19X4	11	
Add Profit for 19X5 (does not include the dividend from S)	8	
		19
		39

S Balance Sheet as at 31 December 19X5

	£	£
Stock		8
Bank		2
		10
Share capital		10
Profit and loss account:		
As at 31.12.19X4	7	
Add Profit for 19X5*	0	
Less Dividend paid	7	
		–
		10

*For simplicity the profit of S for 19X5 is taken as being exactly nil.

P Consolidated Balance Sheet as at 31 December 19X5

	£
Goodwill	6
Stock	26
Bank	7
	39
Share capital	20
Profit and loss	19
	39

It will be noticed that when a dividend is paid out of pre-acquisition profits it is in fact a return of capital to the parent company. Accordingly, the dividend is deducted from the original cost of the investment – it is a return of the purchase money – rather than treated as investment income of the holding company. A common practice of many examiners, or 'trick' if you prefer to call it that, would have been to treat the receipt as investment income instead of as a refund of capital. Thus the balance sheet of P as at 31 December 19X5 in this exhibit would have read 'Profit and loss account £26' instead of 'Profit and loss account £19', and the investment would be shown at £23 instead of £16. This means that the examiner really wants the examinee to adjust what is in fact an incorrect balance sheet, so that the only way is to adjust the parent's balance sheet before proceeding with the consolidation of the balance sheets of P and S.

24.3 Proposed dividend at date of acquisition of shares

Quite frequently there will be a proposed dividend as at the date of the acquisition of the shares, and the holding company will receive the dividend even though the dividend was proposed to be paid from profits earned before acquisition took place. The action taken is similar to that in Exhibit 24.2, in that it will be deducted from the price paid for the shares in order that the net effective price is calculated.

Exhibit 24.3

Shares acquired in a subsidiary at a date when a proposed dividend is outstanding.

P Balance Sheet as at 31 December 19X3

	£	£
Investment in subsidiary:		
10 shares bought 31.12.19X2	22	
Less Dividend from pre-acquisition profits	6	
		16
Stock		11
Bank		2
		29
Share capital		20
Profit and loss account:		
As at 31.12.19X2	4	
Profit for 19X3	5	
		9
		29

S Balance Sheet as at 31 December 19X3

	£	£
Stock		19
Bank		4
		23
Share capital		10
Profit and loss account:		
As at 31.12.19X2 (after deducting the proposed dividend £6)	5	
Add Profit for 19X3	8	
		13
		23

P Consolidated Balance Sheet as at 31 December 19X3

	£	£
Goodwill (see workings below)		1
Stock		30
Bank		6
		37
Share capital		20
Profit and loss account:		
(P £9 + S £8)		17
		37

Calculation of goodwill

	£	£
Paid		22
Less Shares taken over	10	
Less Profit and loss balance at 31.12.19X2	5	
Less Dividend paid from pre-acquisition profits	6	
		21
Goodwill		1

24.4 Proposed dividends

When a dividend is proposed by a company it will be shown as a current liability in its balance sheet. This is just as true for a subsidiary company as it would be for a company which is not controlled by another company. It is common practice for the parent to show a proposed dividend from a subsidiary for an accounting period as being receivable in the same accounting period. Thus the subsidiary will show the proposed dividend as a current liability and the parent will show it as a current asset. However, as this is merely another form of intra-group indebtedness, the amounts owing must be cancelled out when drawing up the consolidated balance sheet. Where the subsidiary is owned 100 per cent by the parent then the two items will cancel out fully.

When the subsidiary is only part-owned, there is the question of the minority interest. The cancellation of the part of the proposed dividend payable to the parent is effected, and the remainder of the proposed dividend of the subsidiary will be that part owing to the minority interest. This can be dealt with in two ways, both acceptable in accounting:

(a) The part of the proposed dividend due to the minority interest is added back to the minority interest figure in the consolidated balance sheet.
(b) The part of the proposed dividend due to the minority interest is shown as a current liability in the consolidated balance sheet.

It must be borne in mind that nothing that has been said refers in any way to the proposed dividends of the parent. These will simply be shown as a current liability in the consolidated balance sheet.

Method (b) would seem to be the better method. For instance, when considering the working capital or liquidity of the group it is essential that all current liabilities due to external parties should be brought into calculation. If the proposed dividend soon to be paid to persons outside the group was excluded, this could render the calculations completely invalid.

Exhibit 24.4

Where a subsidiary has proposed a dividend, and there is a minority interest share in the subsidiary.

This will be shown using method (*b*) just described.

P Balance Sheet as at 31 December 19X3

	£
Investment in subsidiary:	
6 shares bought 31.12.19X1	17
Stock	19
Proposed dividend receivable from S	3
Bank	1
	40
Share capital	20
Profit and loss account	11
Proposed dividend (of the holding company)	9
	40

S Balance Sheet as at 31 December 19X3

	£
Stock	23
Bank	7
	30
Share capital	10
Profit and loss account	15
Proposed dividend	5
	30

Note: At the date of acquisition of the shares on 31 December 19X1 the profit and loss account balance of S was £10, and there were no proposed dividends at that date.

P Consolidated Balance Sheet as at 31 December 19X3

	£	£
Goodwill (*see workings*)		5
Stock		42
Bank		8
		55
Share capital		20
Profit and loss account (*see workings*)		14
Minority interest:		
Shares	4	
Profit and loss ⅖	6	
		10
Current liabilities:		
Proposed dividends of parent	9	
Owing to minority interest	2	
		11
		55

	£	£	£
Workings:			
Profit and loss account:			
P's profit and loss balance			11
S's profit and loss balance		15	
Less Owned by minority interest: ⅖ of £15	6		
Less Pre-acquisition profits at 31.12.19X1 bought by parent: ⅗ of £10	6		
		12	
			3
			14
Goodwill:			
Paid			17
Less Shares bought		6	
Less Pre-acquisition profits ⅗ of £10		6	
			12
			5

If method (*a*) had been used then the consolidated balance sheet would be as shown except for Minority interest and Current liabilities. These would have appeared:

	£	£
Minority interest:		
Shares	4	
Profit and loss	8	12
Current liabilities:		
Proposed dividend		9

Main points to remember

1 Intra-group dividends paid out of post-acquisition reserves will not appear in the consolidated financial statements, the entries in the individual company financial statements cancelling out upon consolidation.

2 Dividends from a newly acquired subsidiary that were declared prior to the date of acquisition are treated as repayment of capital and the investment in the subsidiary in the parent company balance sheet is reduced by the amount received.

3 Where a subsidiary undertaking is 100 per cent owned, dividends proposed by the subsidiary undertaking that are unpaid at the balance sheet date will be cancelled out upon consolidation.

4 Where a subsidiary undertaking is not 100 per cent owned, dividends proposed by the subsidiary undertaking that are unpaid at the balance sheet date will be cancelled out upon consolidation to the extent that ownership is held; the remainder of the dividend (that relates to the minority interest in the subsidiary undertaking) is shown as either an addition to the minority interest figure in the consolidated balance sheet, or as a current liability in the consolidated balance sheet.

Review questions

24.1 The following balance sheets were drawn up as at 31 December 19X7. The person drafting the balance sheet of P Ltd was not too sure of an item and has shown it as a suspense amount.

P Balance Sheet as at 31 December 19X7

	£	£
Investment in subsidiary:		
20,000 shares bought 31.12.19X6		29,000
Fixed assets		40,000
Current assets		5,000
		74,000
Share capital		50,000
Profit and loss account:		
As at 31.12.19X6	8,000	
Add Profit for 19X7	11,000	
		19,000
Suspense*		5,000
		74,000

*The suspense item consists of the dividend received from S in January 19X7.

S Balance Sheet as at 31 December 19X7

	£	£
Fixed assets		17,000
Current assets		10,000
		27,000
Share capital		20,000
Profit and loss account:		
As at 31.12.19X6*	3,000	
Add Profit for 19X7	4,000	
		7,000
		27,000

*The balance of £3,000 is after deducting the proposed dividend for 19X6 of £5,000.

Draw up the consolidated balance sheet as at 31 December 19X7.

24.2A The following balance sheets of P Ltd and S Ltd were drawn up as at 31 December 19X4. Draw up the consolidated balance sheet as at that date.

P Balance Sheet as at 31 December 19X4

	£	£
Investment in subsidiary:		
100,000 shares bought 31.12.19X3		194,000
Fixed assets		250,000
Current assets		59,000
		503,000
Share capital		400,000
Profit and loss account:		
As at 31.12.19X3	39,000	
Add Profit for 19X4*	64,000	
		103,000
		503,000

*The profit figure for 19X4 includes the dividend of £20,000 received from S Ltd for the year 19X3.

S Balance Sheet as at 31 December 19X4

	£	£
Fixed assets		84,000
Current assets		49,000
		133,000
Share capital		100,000
Profit and loss account:		
As at 31.12.19X3*	11,000	
Add Profit for 19X4	22,000	
		33,000
		133,000

*The balance of £11,000 is after deducting the proposed dividend for 19X3 £20,000.

24.3 Draw up a consolidated balance sheet as at 31 December 19X9 from the following information.

P Balance Sheet as at 31 December 19X9

	£	£
Investment in subsidiary:		
30,000 shares bought 31.12.19X8		47,000
Fixed assets		44,000
Current assets		12,000
		103,000
Share capital		80,000
Profit and loss account:		
As at 31.12.19X8	14,000	
Add Profit for 19X9	9,000	
		23,000
		103,000

S Balance Sheet as at 31 December 19X9

	£	£
Fixed assets		36,000
Current assets		21,000
		57,000
Share capital		40,000
Profit and loss account:		
As at 31.12.19X8	4,000	
Add Profit for 19X9	7,000	
		11,000
Proposed dividend for 19X9		6,000
		57,000

The proposed dividend of S has not yet been brought into the accounts of P Ltd.

24.4A The balance sheets of P Ltd and S Ltd are as follows:

P Balance Sheet as at 31 December 19X4

	£	£
Investment in subsidiary:		
120,000 shares bought 31.12.19X3		230,000
Fixed assets		300,000
Current assets		75,000
		605,000
Share capital		500,000
Profit and loss account:		
As at 31.12.19X3	64,000	
Add Profit for 19X4	41,000	
		105,000
		605,000

S Balance Sheet as at 31 December 19X4

	£	£
Fixed assets		203,000
Current assets		101,000
		304,000
Share capital		200,000
Profit and loss account:		
As at 31.12.19X3	51,000	
Add Profit for 19X4	13,000	
		64,000
Proposed dividend for 19X4		40,000
		304,000

The proposed dividend of S has not yet been brought into the accounts of P Ltd. Draw up the consolidated balance sheet as at 31 December 19X4.

24.5 The following are the summarised balance sheets of P Ltd and S Ltd at 31 December 19X6.

	P Limited £	P Limited £	S Limited £	S Limited £
Tangible fixed assets (see note (a))		320,000		360,000
Loan to S Ltd		50,000		
Investment in S Ltd		250,000		
Current assets:				
Stocks	110,000		50,000	
Debtors	100,000		40,000	
Bank	30,000		10,000	
		240,000		100,000
Creditors: amounts falling due within one year:				
Trade creditors	190,000		22,000	
Proposed preference dividend	–		8,000	
		(190,000)		(30,000)
Total assets less current liabilities		£670,000		£430,000
Capital and reserves:				
Ordinary shares of £1 each, fully paid		500,000		200,000
8% preference shares of £1 each, fully paid		–		100,000
Reserves		170,000		80,000
Loan from P Ltd		–		50,000
		£670,000		£430,000

Notes:
(A) Tangible fixed assets:
  P Limited

	Cost £	Cumulative Depreciation £	WDV £
Buildings	120,000	10,000	110,000
Plant and machinery	200,000	40,000	160,000
Motor vehicles	80,000	30,000	50,000
	400,000	80,000	320,000

Tangible fixed assets:
  S Limited

	Cost £	Cumulative Depreciation £	WDV £
Buildings	300,000	100,000	200,000
Plant and machinery	120,000	30,000	90,000
Motor vehicles	130,000	60,000	70,000
	550,000	190,000	360,000

There were no additions or disposals of fixed assets by the group during the year.
(b) P Limited acquired its holding on 1 January 19X6, when the balance on S Limited's reserves stood at £50,000. The investment consists of 150,000 ordinary shares of £1 each, fully paid, purchased for £250,000.
(c) P Limited credited to its profit and loss account a dividend of £7,500 from S Limited in March 19X6, in respect of the shares acquired on 1 January 19X6. S Limited does not intend to pay an ordinary dividend for the year ended 31 December 19X6.

Required:
Prepare a consolidated balance sheet for P Limited and its subsidiary S Limited at 31 December 19X6.

Note: Ignore taxation.

(Chartered Institute of Management Accountants)

24.6 X plc acquired 80 per cent of the ordinary share capital of Y plc on 1 January 19X6 for £300,000.

The lists of balances of the two companies at 31 December 19X6 were as follows:

	X plc £000	Y plc £000
Called-up share capital:		
400,000 ordinary shares of £1 each, fully paid	400	
300,000 ordinary shares of £0.50 each, fully paid		150
Reserves as at 1 January 19X6	220	90
Retained profits for 19X6	20	18
Trade creditors	130	80
Taxation	30	14
Proposed final dividend	20	10
Depreciation provisions:		
Freehold property	12	6
Plant and machinery	40	12
Current account		14
	872	394
Tangible fixed assets:		
Freehold property, at cost	120	160
Plant and machinery, at cost	183	62
Investment in Y plc	300	
Stocks	80	70
Debtors	160	90
Bank	10	12
Current account	19	
	872	394

Notes:

(a) A remittance of £2,000 from Y plc to X plc in December 19X6 was not received by X plc until January 19X7.

(b) Goods, with an invoice value of £3,000, were despatched by X plc in December 19X6 but not received by Y plc until January 19X7. The profit element included in this amount was £400.

(c) Included in the stock of Y plc at 31 December 19X6 were goods purchased from X plc for £10,000. The profit element included in this amount was £2,000.

(d) It is group policy to exclude all profit on any intra-company transactions.

(e) No interim dividend was paid in 19X6 by either company.

(f) Goodwill is to be written off against reserves.

Required:

Prepare a consolidated balance sheet for X plc and its subsidiary Y plc as at 31 December 19X6.

(*Chartered Institute of Management Accountants*)

24.7A P plc acquired 80 per cent of the ordinary share capital of S plc for £150,000 and 50 per cent of the issued 10 per cent cumulative preference shares for £10,000, both purchases being effected on 1 May 19X7. There have been no changes in the issued share capital of S plc since that date. The following balances are taken from the books of the two companies at 30 April 19X8:

	P plc	S plc
	£000	£000
Ordinary share capital (£1 shares)	300	100
10% cumulative preference shares (50p shares)	–	20
Share premium account	20	10
General reserve	68	15
Profit and loss account	50	35
Trade creditors	35	22
Taxation	50	30
Proposed dividends	15	10
Depreciation		
Freehold property	40	15
Plant and machinery	100	48
	678	305
Freehold property at cost	86	55
Plant and machinery at cost	272	168
Investment in S plc	160	–
Stocks	111	65
Debtors	30	15
Cash	19	2
	678	305

The following additional information is available:
(a) Stocks of P plc include goods purchased from S plc for £20,000. S plc charged out these stocks at cost plus 25 per cent.
(b) Proposed dividend of S plc includes a full year's preference dividend. No interim dividends were paid during the year by either company.
(c) Creditors of P plc include £6,000 payable to S plc in respect of stock purchases. Debtors of S plc include £10,000 due from P plc. The holding company sent a cheque for £4,000 to its subsidiary on 29 April 19X8 which was not received by S plc until May 19X8.
(d) At 1 May 19X7 the balances on the reserves of S plc were as follows:

	£000
Share premium	10
General reserve	20
Profit and loss account	30

(e) Goodwill is to be written off against reserves.

Required:
(a) Prepare a consolidated balance sheet for P plc and its subsidiary S plc at 30 April 19X8. Notes to the accounts are not required. Workings must be shown.
(b) Explain what is meant by the term 'cost of control' and justify your treatment of this item in the above accounts.

(*Chartered Institute of Management Accountants*)

25

Consolidated balance sheets: sundry matters

Objectives

After you have studied this chapter, you should:

- *know how to calculate goodwill on the purchase of preference shares*

- *know how to treat unrealised profits and losses on intra-group asset sales*

- *be aware of the effect of 'fair value' on the calculation of goodwill and on the preparation of the consolidated financial statements*

25.1 Preference shares

It should be remembered that preference shares do not carry voting powers under normal conditions, nor do they possess a right to the reserves of the company. Contrast this with ordinary shares which, when bought, will give the parent company voting rights and also a proportionate part of the reserves of the company.

This means that the calculation of goodwill or capital reserve on the purchase of preference shares is very simple indeed. If 9 preference shares of £1 each are bought for £12 then goodwill will be £3, while if 20 preference shares of £1 each are bought for £16 then the capital reserve will be £4. The amount of goodwill or capital reserve on the purchase of preference shares is not shown separately from that calculated on the purchase of ordinary shares. Instead the figures will be amalgamated to throw up one figure only on the consolidated balance sheet.

Preference shares owned by the minority interest are simply shown as part of the minority interest figure in the consolidated balance sheet, each share being shown at nominal value.

25.2 Sale of fixed assets between members of the group

There is obviously nothing illegal in one company in the group selling items in the nature of fixed assets to another company in the group. If the sale is at the cost price originally paid for it by the first company, then no adjustment will be needed in the consolidated balance sheet. Rather more often, the sale will be at a price different from the original cost price. The intra-group unrealised profit must be eliminated in a similar fashion to that taken for the unrealised profit in trading stock as described in Chapter 22.

If the fixed asset is shown at its cost to the group in the consolidated balance sheet rather than at the cost to the particular company, then obviously the depreciation figure on that fixed asset should be adjusted to that based on the group cost rather than on the cost of the particular company.

Exhibit 25.1

P Balance Sheet as at 31 December 19X6

	£	£
Investment in S:		
50 shares bought 31.12.19X5		95
Fixed assets	78	
Less Depreciation	23	
		55
Current assets		20
		170
Share capital		100
Profit and loss account:		
As at 31.12.19X5	30	
For the year 19X6	40	
		70
		170

S Balance Sheet as at 31 December 19X6

	£	£
Fixed assets	80	
Less Depreciation	20	
		60
Current assets		35
		95
Share capital		50
Profit and loss account:		
As at 31.12.19X5	20	
For the year 19X6	25	
		45
		95

During the year P Ltd had sold a fixed asset which had cost it £20 to S Ltd for £28. Of the figure of £20 depreciation in the balance sheet of S, £7 refers to this asset and £13 to the other assets. The rate of depreciation is 25 per cent. The £8 profit is included in the figure of £40 profit for 19X6 in the balance sheet of P.

This means that the figure of £8 needs cancelling from the asset costs in the consolidated balance sheet and from the profit and loss account balance. In addition the figure of depreciation needs adjusting downward, from the £7 as shown on the balance sheet of S, to the figure of £5, i.e. 25 per cent depreciation based on the cost of the asset to the group. This in turn means that the figure of profit for S, £25, needs increasing by £2, as, instead of the expense of £7 depreciation, there will now be a reduced expense of £5. The consolidated balance sheet becomes:

P and S Consolidated Balance Sheet as at 31 December 19X6

	£	£
Goodwill		25
Fixed assets	150	
Less Depreciation	41	
		109
Current assets		55
		189
Share capital		100
Profit and loss account: (P £70 − £8 + S £25 + £2)		89
		189

25.3 Fair values in acquisition accounting

The consolidated balance sheet should give a picture that is not clouded by the method of drafting consolidated accounts. The consolidation process is looked at from the point of view that the parent undertaking acquires shares in a company, and thereby achieves control of that company. In addition, it is recognised that the reserves are also taken over. It has been said previously that the economic view is that of taking over the assets of another company – after all one does not buy such shares just to possess the share certificates. Rather, the exercise is for the assets which are taken over and used. The consolidated balance sheet should therefore give the same picture as that which would have been recorded if, instead of buying shares, the assets themselves had been bought directly.

Prior to the issue of FRS 6: *Acquisitions and mergers* and FRS 7: *Fair values in acquisition accounting* in September 1994, the way in which acquisitions were accounted for varied from case to case. One of the areas of greatest diversity was in the revaluation of assets and liabilities to 'fair values'. 'Fair value' is defined as the amount for which an asset or liability could be exchanged in an arm's length transaction (i.e. as in an exchange between strangers). Generally, acquiring companies set their own 'fair values' on the assets and liabilities acquired, and then follow the FRS 10 (*goodwill and intangible assets*) [or, for smaller companies applying the FRSSE, the SSAP 22 (*accounting for goodwill*)] rules that the amount to be attributed to purchased goodwill should be the difference between the 'fair value' of the consideration given and the aggregate of the 'fair values' of the separable net assets acquired. Where assets are revalued, this should apply to all the assets, i.e. including those attributable to minority interests.

Under acquisition accounting, the investment is shown at cost (= the 'fair value' given) in the parent company's own financial statements. On consolidation, if the fair value of the net assets (excluding goodwill) acquired is less than the fair value of the purchase consideration, FRS 10 requires that the difference should be treated as goodwill and capitalised and, normally, amortised (SSAP 22, on the other hand, permits immediate write-off); if the fair value of the net assets (excluding goodwill) acquired exceeds the fair value of the purchase consideration, the difference should be treated as negative goodwill. (*See* Chapter 20 for a description of the SSAP 22 treatment.) This is similar to the treatment that has been adopted throughout the previous few chapters, the only difference being that 'fair values' should be used rather than the values as shown in the balance sheet of the acquired company.

FRS 7 seeks to ensure that upon acquisition, all assets and liabilities that existed in the acquired entity at that date are recorded at *fair values* reflecting their condition at that date. In addition it seeks to ensure that all changes to the acquired assets and liabilities, and the resulting gains and losses that arise after control of the acquired entity has passed to the acquirer, are reported as part of the post-acquisition financial performance of the reporting group.

There are a number of rules given in FRS 7 governing the determination of the appropriate fair value.

- The fair value of **tangible fixed assets** should be based upon either *market value* (if assets similar in type and condition are bought and sold on an open market) or *depreciated replacement cost* (reflecting the acquired business's normal buying process and the sources of supply and prices available to it). However, the fair value should not exceed the recoverable amount (i.e. the greater of the net realisable value and the value in use) of the asset.
- The fair value of **intangible assets** should be based on their *replacement cost*, which is normally their estimated market value.
- **Stocks**, including commodity stocks, that **the acquired entity trades on a market in which it participates as both a buyer and seller** should be valued at *current market prices*.
- **Other stocks and work in progress** should be valued at the lower of *replacement cost* and *net realisable value*. As with the use of *depreciated replacement cost* for *tangible fixed assets*, *replacement cost* for stock should be the cost at which it would have been replaced by the acquired entity, reflecting the acquired business's normal buying process and the sources of supply and prices available to it. The standard suggests that this is synonymous with 'the current cost of bringing the stocks to their present location and condition'.
- **Quoted investments** should be valued at *market price*.
- **Monetary assets and liabilities**, including accruals and provisions, should take into account their timing and the amounts expected to be received and paid. The *fair value* should be determined by reference to *market prices*, or by discounting to present value.
- **Contingencies** should be measured at *fair values* where these can be determined, using reasonable estimates of the expected outcome if necessary.

The cost of acquisition is defined in FRS 7 as the amount of cash paid and the fair value of other purchase consideration given by the acquirer, together with the expenses of the acquisition.

The effect of the use of 'fair values' can be seen from what would occur if 'fair values' were used by the acquiring company in arriving at the price it wished to pay, but then were never incorporated into the financial statements. For instance, if P buys all the 10 shares of S for £18 when the reserves are £5, then the goodwill calculation if 'fair values' are not used is:

	£	£
Cost		18
Less Shares	10	
Less Reserves	5	
		15
Goodwill		£3

However, P might have bought the shares of S because it thought that the 'fair value' of the net assets of S was £17.

In P's eyes, it is giving £18 for physical assets worth £17 and the goodwill figure is correspondingly £18 − £17 = £1. Assuming that the difference is in the recorded value of fixed assets, then the consolidated balance sheet will not be showing a true and fair view if it shows goodwill £3 and assets £15. The revaluation upwards of the fixed assets by £2, and the consequent reduction of the goodwill figure by £2 will correct the view. Where there are depreciation charges on the revalued assets, this will also require to be adjusted.

Exhibit 25.2

P Balance Sheet as at 31 December 19X6

	£	£
Investment in subsidiary:		
30 shares bought 31.12.19X5		56
Fixed assets	80	
Less Depreciation for the year	16	
		64
Current assets		26
		146
Share capital		100
Profit and loss account:		
As at 31.12.19X5	20	
Add Profit 19X6	26	
		46
		146

S Balance Sheet as at 31 December 19X6

	£	£
Fixed assets	50	
Less Depreciation for the year	10	
		40
Current assets		14
		54
Share capital		30
Profit and loss account:		
As at 31.12.19X5	3	
Add Profit 19X6	21	
		24
		54

At the time when P bought the shares in S, the assets in S were shown at a value of £33 in the balance sheet of S. In fact, however, P valued the fixed assets as being worth £20 higher than that shown. The consolidated balance sheet will therefore show them at this higher figure. In turn the depreciation, which is at the rate of 20 per cent, will be £4 higher. The consolidated balance sheet therefore appears:

P and S Consolidated Balance Sheet as at 31 December 19X6

	£	£
Goodwill		3
Fixed assets		
(£80 + £70)	150	
Less Depreciation (£16 + £14)	30	
		120
Current assets		40
		163
Share capital		100
Profit and loss account:		
(P £46 + S £21 − increased depreciation £4)		63
		163

Main points to remember

1 Goodwill on the purchase of preference shares is the difference between their nominal value and the amount paid.

2 Unrealised profit on the sale of fixed assets between companies in a group must be eliminated upon consolidation.

3 'Fair values' at the time of acquisition should be used in the calculation of goodwill, rather than the value shown in the balance sheet of the subsidiary, and the consolidation of the subsidiary undertaking should also be based on those 'fair values'.

4 'Fair value' is dependent upon the nature of the item being valued. However, the general rule is that it represents the amount for which an asset or liability could be exchanged in an arm's length transaction, i.e. as in an exchange between strangers.

Review questions

25.1 From the following balance sheets and further information you are to draw up a consolidated balance sheet as at 31 December 19X8.

P Balance Sheet as at 31 December 19X8

	£	£
Investment in S:		
200,000 shares bought 31.12.19X7		340,000
Fixed assets	300,000	
Less Depreciation	100,000	
		200,000
Current assets		103,000
		643,000
Share capital		500,000
Profit and loss account:		
As at 31.12.19X7	77,000	
Add Profit for 19X8	66,000	
		143,000
		643,000

S Balance Sheet as at 31 December 19X8

	£	£
Fixed assets	210,000	
Less Depreciation	40,000	
		170,000
Current assets		102,000
		272,000
Share capital		200,000
Profit and loss account:		
As at 31.12.19X7	40,000	
Add Profit for 19X8	32,000	
		72,000
		272,000

During the year P Ltd had sold a fixed asset, which had cost it £40,000 to S for £50,000. S has written off 20 per cent, i.e. £10,000 as depreciation for 19X8.

25.2A From the following balance sheets and supplementary information you are to draw up a consolidated balance sheet as at 31 December 19X5.

P Consolidated Balance Sheet as at 31 December 19X5

	£	£
Investment in S: 10,000 shares bought 31.12.19X4		23,000
Fixed assets	84,000	
Less Depreciation	14,000	
		70,000
Current assets		20,000
		113,000
Share capital		75,000
Profit and loss account:		
As at 31.12.19X4	15,000	
Add Profit for 19X5	23,000	
		38,000
		113,000

S Balance Sheet as at 31 December 19X5

	£	£
Fixed assets	26,000	
Less Depreciation	10,000	
		16,000
Current assets		12,000
		28,000
Share capital		10,000
Profit and loss account:		
As at 31.12.19X4	6,000	
Add Profit for 19X5	7,000	
		13,000
General reserve (as at 31.12.19X4)		5,000
		28,000

During the year P sold a fixed asset to S. It had cost P £3,000 and it was sold to S for £5,000. S had written off £500 as depreciation during 19X5.

25.3

P Balance Sheet as at 31 December 19X7

	£	£
Investment in S: 60,000 shares bought on 31.12.19X6		121,000
Fixed assets	90,000	
Less Depreciation for year	24,000	
		66,000
Current assets		40,000
		227,000
Share capital		150,000
Profit and loss account:		
As at 31.12.19X6	44,000	
Add Profit for 19X7	33,000	
		77,000
		227,000

S Balance Sheet as at 31 December 19X7

	£	£
Fixed assets	70,000	
Less Depreciation for year	7,000	
		63,000
Current assets		28,000
		91,000
Share capital		60,000
Profit and loss account:		
As at 31.12.19X6	17,000	
Add Profit for 19X7	14,000	
		31,000
		91,000

When P Ltd bought the shares of S Ltd it valued the fixed assets at £95,000 instead of the figure of £70,000 as shown in the balance sheet of S.

Draw up a consolidated balance sheet as at 31 December 19X7.

25.4A

P Balance Sheet as at 31 December 19X5

	£	£
Investment in S: 30,000 shares bought 31.12.19X4		53,400
Fixed assets	60,000	
Less Depreciation for year	6,000	
		54,000
Current assets		10,600
		118,000
Share capital		80,000
Profit and loss account:		
As at 31.12.19X4	27,000	
Add Profit for 19X5	11,000	
		38,000
		118,000

S Balance Sheet as at 31 December 19X5

	£	£
Fixed assets	40,000	
Less Depreciation for year	4,000	
		36,000
Current assets		11,000
		47,000
Share capital		30,000
Profit and loss account:		
As at 31.12.19X4	8,000	
Add Profit for 19X5	9,000	
		17,000
		47,000

When P Ltd took control of S Ltd it valued the fixed assets at 31.12.19X4 at £50,000 instead of £40,000 as shown.

Draw up the consolidated balance sheet as at 31 December 19X5.

26

Consolidation of the accounts of a vertical group of companies

Objectives

After you have studied this chapter, you should:

- *understand how a company that is the subsidiary of another is also a subsidiary of its parent's own parent undertaking*

- *know how to consolidate groups that include subsidiaries of subsidiaries*

26.1 Subsidiaries that control other companies

So far we have considered the case of parent undertakings having a direct interest in their subsidiary undertakings. In each case the parent itself has bought the shares in its subsidiaries. In each case over 50 per cent of the voting shares have been bought. In a straightforward case, where the parent company, P1, has bought shares in subsidiaries S1 and S2, it could be represented by a diagram (Exhibit 26.1).

Exhibit 26.1

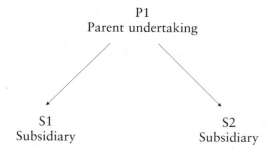

P1
Parent undertaking

S1
Subsidiary

S2
Subsidiary

Suppose instead that P2 bought 100 per cent of the shares in S3, and that S3 then itself bought 100 per cent of the shares in S4. Because P2 controls S3 completely, and S3 controls S4 completely, therefore P2 controls both S3 and S4. This is shown as Exhibit 26.2.

If P3 owned S5 100 per cent, but S5 only owned 80 per cent of S6, then we can say that P3 owns 100 per cent of 80 per cent of S6 = 80 per cent (*see* Exhibit 26.3). Similarly if in another case P4 owned 75 per cent of S7, and S7 owns 80 per cent of S8, then P4 owns 75 per cent × 80 per cent = 60 per cent of S8 (*see* Exhibit 26.4).

Exhibit 26.2

P2
Parent

↓ 100% owned

S3
Subsidiary
100% owned | 100% owned

↓

S4
Subsidiary
P2 owns S4
100% × 100% = 100%

Exhibit 26.3

P3
Parent

↓ 100% owned

S5
Subsidiary
80% owned | 80% owned

↓

S6
Subsidiary
P3 owns S6
100% × 80% = 80%

Exhibit 26.4

P4
Parent

↓ 75% owned

S7
Subsidiary
60% owned | 80% owned

↓

S8
Subsidiary
P4 owns S8
75% × 80% = 60%

In Exhibits 26.2, 26.3 and 26.4 the eventual ownership by P of each subsidiary's subsidiary exceeds 50 per cent.

There will be cases where the ownership of the subsidiary of a subsidiary by the parent is less than 50 per cent. Exhibit 26.5 shows where P5 owns 80 per cent of S9, and S9 owns 60 per cent of S10. This means that P5 owns 80% × 60% = 48% of S10. Exhibit 26.6 similarly shows where P6 owns 60 per cent of S11 and S11 owns 55 per cent of S12. Therefore P6 owns 60% × 55% = 33% of S12.

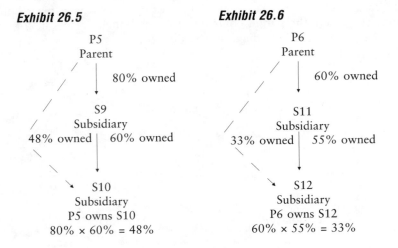

Exhibit 26.5

P5
Parent

↓ 80% owned

S9
Subsidiary
48% owned | 60% owned

↓

S10
Subsidiary
P5 owns S10
80% × 60% = 48%

Exhibit 26.6

P6
Parent

↓ 60% owned

S11
Subsidiary
33% owned | 55% owned

↓

S12
Subsidiary
P6 owns S12
60% × 55% = 33%

It might look as though S10 is not a subsidiary of P5, because P5 owns less than 50 per cent of S10. However, P5 controls S9 as its ownership is over 50 per cent, and in turn S9 controls S10 as it owns more than 50 per cent. Effectively, therefore, P5 controls S10, and as such S10 is its subsidiary.

26.2 Legal exemptions from preparing consolidated accounts

Section 228 of the Companies Act 1985 exempts a wholly owned subsidiary from preparing consolidated accounts. For instance, in Exhibit 26.2 the subsidiary S3 would not have to prepare consolidated accounts; neither would S5 in Exhibit 26.3.

In each of cases S7, S9 and S11 in Exhibits 26.4, 26.5 and 26.6, there are minority shareholders. In practice, therefore, those subsidiary companies may have to prepare consolidated accounts, e.g. in Exhibit 26.4 consolidating S7 and S8 if sufficient of the minority interests demand it. See also Chapter 29 for FRS 2 re exemptions.

26.3 Methods of consolidating accounts

There are two methods of consolidating the accounts.

(a) The 'indirect' or 'single-stage' method follows the reasoning already given in this chapter, i.e. computing the parent's interest in the subsidiaries and their subsidiaries and taking that percentage of the capital and reserves of these companies into the consolidation process. For instance, in Exhibit 26.5 the capital and reserves would give 100% of P5 + 80% of S9 + 48% of S10.
(b) The 'multi-stage' method first consolidates the balance sheets of the subsidiary and its subsidiary, and when that is done it is then consolidated with the balance sheet of the holding company. This recognises the fact that subsidiaries with minority interests have to produce consolidated accounts and is more generally used in practice than the indirect method.

For an examination method (a) is to be preferred. It is a quicker method, and usually you will be short of time in an examination. Also an examination question will almost certainly ask for consolidation for all the companies and therefore there will be no need to do the intermediate consolidation. This book will therefore use method (a) only.

26.4 Consolidation technique

We are concerned here with the **indirect** method. It follows mainly the same techniques as described in earlier chapters, but two points need stressing:

(a) **Cost of control account,** and the entry for the cost of investment:
   (i) For subsidiaries, debit total cost of investment to cost of control account.
   (ii) For subsidiaries of subsidiaries, debit cost of control account only with the proportion concerned with the parent's share in the subsidiary which controls the subsidiary. Debit minority interest account with the balance.

Given P investing £20,000 to buy 80 per cent of shares of S1, then S1 investing £10,000 to buy 60 per cent of shares of S2, the entries in the cost of control account (or its workings) would be:

Cost of Control

	£	
Cost of shares in S1	20,000	
Cost of shares in S2 (80%)	8,000	

The remaining proportion of investment by S1 is then debited to a minority interest account (or its workings).

Minority Interest

	£
Cost of shares in S2 (20%)	2,000

(b) **Apportionment of share capital and reserves** to cost of control account and to minority interest account:

    (i) *Cost of control*: take only the group's ultimate share of subsidiary of subsidiary's share capital and reserves.

    (ii) *Minority interest*: include the balance of subsidiary of subsidiary's share capital and reserves.

In the illustration given in (a)(ii) where P bought 80 per cent of S1, and S1 bought 60 per cent of S2, the ultimate share of the group is 80% × 60% = 48%. Therefore, in the consolidated financial statements 48 per cent should come into group calculations and 52 per cent shown in minority interest workings. Double entry: Cr Cost of control account: Dr (appropriate) Reserve account.

26.5 A worked example (without proposed dividends)

Exhibit 26.7

P Ltd owns 80 per cent of the ordinary share capital of S1 Ltd. In turn S1 Ltd owns 75 per cent of the ordinary share capital of S2 Ltd. Both investments had been acquired on 31 December 19X4, one year previous to the following balance sheets:

Balance Sheets December 19X5

	P Ltd £000	P Ltd £000	S1 Ltd £000	S1 Ltd £000	S2 Ltd £000	S2 Ltd £000
Fixed assets		40		4		27
Investments:						
Shares in S1		41				
Shares in S2				25		
Net current assets		19		6		28
		100		35		55
Share capital		40		10		20
Profit and loss						
As at 31.12.19X4	24		5		15	
Add Profit 19X5	36	60	10	15	20	35
General reserve at 31.12.19X4				10		
		100		35		55

Ownership of P can be seen to be 80 per cent of S1 and 80% × 75% = 60 per cent of S2. Any goodwill on acquisition to be written off to profit and loss.

We now will prepare a consolidated balance sheet on 31 December 19X5, one year after both acquisitions. In previous chapters the illustrations have been given on the face of the balance sheets. In this more complicated example we will use double entry accounts for the main items.

P Ltd and its subsidiaries

Consolidated Balance Sheet as at 31 December 19X5

	£000
Fixed assets	71
Net current assets	53
	124
Share capital	40
Profit and loss (*see* account below)	60
	100
Minority interest (*see* account below)	24
	124

In the accounts which follow (*a*)(*i*), (*a*)(*ii*), (*b*)(*i*) and (*b*)(*ii*) refer to consolidation techniques already described.

Cost of Control

	£000		£000
Cost of shares in S1 (*a*)(*i*)	41	Share capital S1 80% × 10	8
Cost of shares in S2 80% (*a*)(*ii*)	20	Share capital S2 60% × 20 (*b*)(*i*)	12
		Pre-acquisition reserves:	
		Profit and loss S1 80% × 5	4
		Profit and loss S2 60% × 15	9
		General reserve S1 80% × 10	8
		Profit and loss: goodwill written off	20
	61		61

Minority Interest

	£000		£000
Cost of shares in S2 20% (*a*)(*ii*)	5	Share capital S1 20%	2
Balance to consolidated balance sheet	24	Share capital S2 40% (*b*)(*ii*)	8
		Profit and loss S1 20%	3
		Profit and loss S2 40% (*b*)(*ii*)	14
		General reserve S1 20% × 10	2
	29		29

Profit and Loss

	£000		£000
Minority interest S1	3	P	60
Minority interest S2	14	S1	15
Cost of control S1: pre-acquisition	4	S2	35
Cost of control S2: pre-acquisition	9		
Cost of control: goodwill written off	20		
Balance to consolidated balance sheet	60		
	110		110

General Reserve

	£000		£000
Cost of control 80% × 10	8	S1 balance b/d	10
Minority interest 20% × 10	2		
	10		10

26.6 A worked example (with proposed dividends)

Take the same companies as in Exhibit 26.7 but in this case the companies have proposed dividends at 31 December 19X5 of P Ltd £16,000; S1 Ltd £5,000; S2 Ltd £20,000. The balance sheets would have appeared:

Balance Sheets as at 31 December 19X5

		P Ltd		*S1 Ltd*		*S2 Ltd*
		£000		£000		£000
Fixed assets		40		4		27
Investments						
Shares in S1		41				
Shares in S2				25		
Net current assets (as before)		19		6		28
Dividends to be received	(80% of S1)	4	(75% of S2)	15		
		104		50		55
Share capital	£000	40	£000	10	£000	20
Profit and loss as at 31.12.19X4	24		5		15	
Retained profits for 19X5						
(*see* below)	24	48	20	25	–	15
General reserve				10		
Proposed dividends		16		5		20
		104		50		55

Note:

	P	*S1*	*S2*
Retained profit			
Net profits 19X5	36	10	20
Less Proposed dividends	16	5	20
	20	5	–
Add Dividends receivable			
P 80% of S1 × 5	4		
S1 75% of S2 × 20		15	
	24	20	–

Now a consolidated balance sheet can be drawn up.

P Ltd and its subsidiaries

Consolidated Balance Sheet as at 31 December 19X5

	£000
Fixed assets	71
Net current assets	53
	124
Share capital	40
Profit and loss (*see* account below)	44
	84
Minority interest (*see* account below)	24
Proposed dividend	16
	124

The cost of control figures and goodwill in this exhibit are the same as for Exhibit 26.7 as circumstances at dates of acquisition had not changed.

Profit and Loss

	£000			£000
Minority interest:		Balances P		48
S1 20% × 25	5	S1		25
S2 40% × 15	6	S2		15
Cost of control (as before) S1	4			
Cost of control (as before) S2	9			
Cost of control: goodwill written off	20			
Balance to consolidated balance sheet	44			
	88			88

Minority Interest

	£000		£000
Cost of shares in S2 (20%)	5	Profit and loss S1	5
Balance to consolidated balance sheet	24	Profit and loss S2	6
		General reserve 20%	2
		Share capital S1 20%	2
		Share capital S2 40%	8
		Proposed dividends S1	1
		Proposed dividends S2 (*see* note (*a*))	5
	29		29

Proposed Dividends

	£000		£000
Minority interest S1	1	P	16
Minority interest S2 (25%)	5	S1	5
Consolidated balance sheet (P)	16	S2	20
Cancel against dividends receivable	19		
	41		41

Dividends Receivable

	£000		£000
P	4	Cancel against proposed dividends	
S1	15	(note (b))	19
	19		19

Notes:

(a) Credit is given to minority for 25 per cent of S2 dividend, not 40 per cent. This is because 25 per cent is the amount actually received by them, while 75 per cent is received by S1, and the minority interest in this dividend is automatically calculated when we calculate the S1 minority interest in profit and loss balance £25,000 at 20 per cent. As the £25,000 figure already includes the dividend from S2 it should not be double-counted.

(b) The balances on dividends proposed and receivable cancel out, so nothing appears in the consolidated balance sheet.

(c) It would have been possible to show the proposed dividends applicable to minority shareholders, S1 £1,000 and S2 £5,000, as a current liability in the consolidated balance sheet, rather than show it as part of minority interest. This would seem to be the better method. For instance, when considering the working capital or liquidity of the group it is essential that all current liabilities due to external parties should be brought into the calculation. If the proposed dividend soon to be paid to persons outside the group was excluded, this could render the calculations completely invalid.

Main points to remember

1   A company that is the subsidiary of another is also a subsidiary of its parent's own parent undertaking, even where the ultimate parent's shareholding is below 50 per cent.

2   There are two recognised methods of consolidating the financial statements of groups that contain subsidiaries of subsidiaries:
   (a) the multi-stage method is generally more common in practice, but
   (b) the indirect single-stage method is recommended for examinations.

3   The indirect method involves computing the parent undertaking's interest in the subsidiaries and their subsidiaries and taking that percentage of the capital and reserves of these companies into the consolidation process.

Review questions

26.1 From the following balance sheets you are to draft a consolidated balance sheet for the group of P, S1 and S2.

P Balance Sheet as at 31 December 19X7

	£	£
Investment in S1:		
9,000 shares bought 31.12.19X6		23,000
Fixed assets		99,000
Current assets		25,000
		147,000
Share capital		100,000
Profit and loss account:		
As at 31.12.19X6	15,000	
Add Profit for 19X7	22,000	
		37,000
General reserve		10,000
		147,000

S1 Balance Sheet as at 31 December 19X7

	£	£
Investment in S2:		
3,500 shares bought 31.12.19X6		6,000
Fixed assets		22,000
Current assets		5,000
		33,000
Share capital		10,000
Profit and loss account:		
As at 31.12.19X6	7,000	
Add Profit for 19X7	16,000	
		23,000
		33,000

S2 Balance Sheet as at 31 December 19X7

	£	£
Fixed assets		6,000
Current assets		3,000
		9,000
Share capital		5,000
Profit and loss account:		
As at 31.12.19X6	1,000	
Add Profit for 19X7	3,000	
		4,000
		9,000

26.2A From the following balance sheets prepare a consolidated balance sheet for the group of P, S1 and S2.

P Balance Sheet as at 31 December 19X9

	£	£
Investment in S1:		
16,000 shares bought 31.12.19X8		39,000
Fixed assets		200,000
Current assets		40,000
		279,000
Share capital		200,000
Profit and loss account:		
As at 31.12.19X8	43,000	
Add Profit for 19X9	36,000	
		79,000
		279,000

S1 Balance Sheet as at 31 December 19X9

	£	£
Investment in S2:		
7,000 shares bought 31.12.19X8		13,000
Fixed assets		16,000
Current assets		4,000
		33,000
Share capital		20,000
Profit and loss account:		
As at 31.12.19X8	6,000	
Add Profit for 19X9	4,000	
		10,000
General reserve (as at 31.12.19X8)		3,000
		33,000

S2 Balance Sheet as at 31 December 19X9

	£	£
Fixed assets		10,500
Current assets		5,500
		16,000
Share capital		10,000
Profit and loss account:		
As at 31.12.19X8	1,000	
Add Profit for 19X9	5,000	
		6,000
		16,000

26.3 On 1 April 19X1 Machinery Limited bought 80 per cent of the ordinary share capital of Components Limited and on 1 April 19X3 Machinery Limited was itself taken over by Sales Limited who purchased 75 per cent of the ordinary shares in Machinery Limited.

The balance sheets of the three companies at 31 October 19X5 prepared for internal use showed the following position:

	Sales Ltd £	£	Machinery Ltd £	£	Components Ltd £	£
Fixed assets						
Freehold land at cost		89,000		30,000		65,000
Buildings at cost	100,000		120,000		40,000	
Less:						
Accumulated depreciation	36,000		40,000		16,400	
		64,000		80,000		23,600
Plant and equipment at cost	102,900		170,000		92,000	
Less:						
Accumulated depreciation	69,900		86,000		48,200	
		33,000		84,000		43,800
		186,000		194,000		132,400
Investments						
Shares in Machinery at cost		135,000				
Shares in Components at cost				96,000		
Current assets						
Stocks	108,500		75,500		68,400	
Debtors	196,700		124,800		83,500	
Cash at bank	25,200		–		25,400	
		330,400		200,300		177,300
		651,400		490,300		309,700
Current liabilities						
Creditors	160,000		152,700		59,200	
Bank overdraft	–		37,400		–	
Corporation tax	57,400		47,200		24,500	
Proposed dividends	80,000		48,000		12,000	
		297,400		285,300		95,700
		354,000		205,000		214,000
Ordinary shares		200,000		120,000		100,000
10% preference shares		–		–		40,000
Revenue reserves		154,000		85,000		74,000
		354,000		205,000		214,000

Additional information
(a) All ordinary shares are £1 each, fully paid.
(b) Preference shares in Components Ltd are 50p each fully paid.
(c) Proposed dividends in Components Ltd are:
   on ordinary shares £10,000;
   on preference shares £2,000.
(d) Proposed dividends receivable by Sales Ltd and Machinery Ltd are included in debtors.
(e) All creditors are payable within one year.
(f) Items purchased by Machinery Ltd from Components Ltd and remaining in stock at 31 October 19X5 amounted to £25,000. The profit element is 20 per cent of selling price for Components Ltd.
(g) Depreciation policy of the group is to provide for:
   (i) buildings – at the rate of 2 per cent on cost each year;

(*ii*) plant and equipment – at the rate of 10 per cent on cost each year including full provision in the year of acquisition.

These policies are applied by all members of the group.

Included in the plant and equipment of Components Ltd is a machine purchased from the manufacturers, Machinery Ltd, on 1 January 19X4 for £10,000. Machinery Ltd recorded a profit of £2,000 on the sale of the machine.

(*h*) Intra-group balances are included in debtors and creditors respectively and are as follows:

			£
Sales Ltd	Creditors	– Machinery Ltd	45,600
		– Components Ltd	28,900
Machinery Ltd	Debtors	– Sales Ltd	56,900
Components Ltd	Debtors	– Sales Ltd	28,900

(*i*) A cheque drawn by Sales Ltd for £11,300 on 28 October 19X5 was received by Machinery Ltd on 3 November 19X5.

(*j*) At 1 April 19X1, reserves in Machinery Ltd were £28,000 and in Components Ltd £20,000. At 1 April 19X3 the figures were £40,000 and £60,000 respectively.

Required:
Prepare a group balance sheet at 31 October 19X5 for Sales Ltd and its subsidiaries complying, so far as the information will allow, with the accounting requirements of the Companies Acts.

(*Association of Chartered Certified Accountants*)

26.4A Bryon Ltd has held 1,500,000 shares in Carlyle Ltd for many years. At the date of acquisition, the reserves of Carlyle Ltd amounted to £800,000. On 31 March 19X6 Carlyle Ltd bought 400,000 shares in Doyle Ltd for £600,000 and a further 400,000 shares were purchased on 30 June 19X6 for £650,000.

At 30 September 19X6 the balance sheets of the three companies were:

	Bryon Ltd £	Bryon Ltd £	Carlyle Ltd £	Carlyle Ltd £	Doyle Ltd £	Doyle Ltd £
Freehold land and buildings						
– cost		950,000		1,375,000		300,000
Plant and equipment						
Cost	500,000		10,000,000		750,000	
Depreciation	280,000		7,500,000		500,000	
		220,000		2,500,000		250,000
		1,170,000		3,875,000		550,000
Investments						
1,500,000 shares in						
Carlyle Ltd		1,600,000				
800,000 shares in						
Doyle Ltd				1,250,000		
Stocks	50,000		2,050,000		850,500	
Debtors	325,000		2,675,000		1,700,000	
Cash at bank	25,500		–		16,500	
		400,500		4,725,000		2,567,000
		3,170,500		9,850,000		3,117,000
Creditors under 1 year	91,500		2,385,750		1,395,800	
Proposed dividend	200,000					
Bank overdraft	–		1,450,850		–	
		291,500		3,836,600		1,395,800
		2,879,000		6,013,400		1,721,200
10% debenture		–		2,000,000		–
		2,879,000		4,013,400		1,721,200

	£	£	£
Ordinary shares of			
£1 each	2,000,000		1,200,000
50p each		1,000,000	
8% redeemable preference			
shares of £1 each		2,000,000	
Reserves	879,000	1,013,400	521,200
	2,879,000	4,013,400	1,721,200

Proposed dividends have not yet been provided for on the shares in Carlyle Ltd and Doyle Ltd although Bryon Ltd has included dividends of 5p per share as receivable from Carlyle Ltd in debtors. Dividends on the preference shares were paid for one-half year on 1 April 19X6; the next payment date was 1 October 19X6. Dividends on the ordinary shares in Doyle Ltd are proposed at the rate of 10p per share and on Carlyle's shares as anticipated by Bryon.

Profits for the year in Doyle Ltd were £310,000, before making any adjustments for consolidation, accruing evenly through the year.

The directors of Bryon Ltd consider that the assets and liabilities of Carlyle Ltd are shown at fair values, but fair values for Doyle Ltd for the purposes of consolidation are:

	£	£
Freehold land and building		500,000
Plant and equipment – Valuation	968,400	
– Depreciation	639,600	
		328,800

Other assets and liabilities are considered to be at fair values in the balance sheet.

Additional depreciation due to the revaluation of the plant and equipment in Doyle Ltd amounts to £40,000 for the year to 30 September 19X6.

Included in stocks in Carlyle Ltd are items purchased from Doyle Ltd during the last three months of the year, on which Doyle Ltd recorded a profit of £80,000.

On 30 September 19X6 Carlyle Ltd drew a cheque for £100,000 and sent it to Doyle Ltd to clear the current account. As this cheque was not received by Doyle Ltd until 3 October, no account was taken of it in the Doyle Ltd balance sheet.

Required:
Prepare a balance sheet as at 30 September 19X6 for Bryon Ltd and its subsidiaries, conforming with the Companies Acts so far as the information given will permit.

Ignore taxation.

(*Association of Chartered Certified Accountants*)

27

Consolidated profit and loss accounts

Objectives

After you have studied this chapter, you should:

● *know how to prepare consolidated profit and loss accounts for groups with wholly owned subsidiaries*

● *know how to prepare consolidated profit and loss accounts for groups with partly owned subsidiaries*

27.1 Wholly-owned subsidiaries

The consolidated profit and loss account is drawn up to show the overall profit (or loss) of the companies in the group, treating the group as a single entity. If all of the subsidiaries are owned 100 per cent, and there are no inter-company dividends or unrealised profits in stock, then it is simply a case of adding together all of the separate profit and loss accounts to form the consolidated profit and loss account. However, such a situation would very rarely be found.

Exhibit 27.1 shows the framework for a consolidated profit and loss account giving details of adjustments needed. Notes (*a*) to (*g*) follow the account.

Exhibit 27.1

Specimen Profit and Loss Account for the Year ended ...

		£000	£000	
Turnover	(*a*)		200	Parent plus
Cost of sales	(*b*)		120	subsidiaries
Gross profit			80	less cancellation
Distribution costs		10		of inter-company
Administrative expenses		20	30	items
Profit on ordinary activities before taxation			50	
Tax on profit on ordinary activities	(*c*)		14	
Profit on ordinary activities after taxation			36	
Minority interest	(*d*)		4	
Profit for the financial year			32	
Retained profits from last year	(*e*)		7	
			39	
Proposed dividend	(*f*)	15		Parent only
Transfer to reserves	(*g*)	8	23	
Retained profits carried to next year			16	

Notes:
(*a*) Turnover. Sales within the group to be deducted.
(*b*) Cost of sales: (*i*) Deduct purchases within the group. This is the same figure as for (*a*), as the price at which sales are made by one group company is the same figure at which the other group company has bought them. (*ii*) Adjust for unrealised profit in stock, by reducing closing stock. As cost of sales = opening stock + purchases – closing stock, any reduction in closing stock will increase 'cost of sales'. The balance sheet stock figure will be reduced by unrealised profits.
(*c*) Tax on profit on ordinary activities. This is the sum of tax for all companies within the group.
(*d*) Minority interest:
  (*i*) If ordinary shares only issued by subsidiary: take requisite percentage of subsidiary's profits after taxation.
  (*ii*) If preference shares also issued by subsidiary found by:
    Minority interest percentage of preference share capital × total preference dividend for the year
    plus
    Minority interest percentage of ordinary share capital × balance of profits (i.e. after preference dividend) for the year
    e.g.
    Total preference shares £1,000: Minority interest £400.
    Total ordinary shares £2,000: Minority interest £500.
    Total preference dividend for year £150.
    Profit of subsidiary after tax but before dividend: £950.
    Minority interest is:

Share of preference dividend: 40% × £150	=	£60
Share of balance of profits: 25% × (£950 – £150)	=	£200
		£260

(*e*) This is parent's retained profits plus group's share of post-acquisition profit of subsidiaries.
(*f*) In respect of parent only.
(*g*) Those of the parent plus the group's share of the subsidiary's transfers to reserves.

We can now look at two examples:

(*a*) Exhibit 27.2: consolidation of accounts where subsidiary owned 100 per cent;
(*b*) Exhibit 27.3: consolidation where there is a minority interest in subsidiary company.

Exhibit 27.2

P Ltd owns 100 per cent of shares in S Ltd. Profit and loss accounts of these companies for the year to 31 December 19X4 are as follows:

Profit and loss accounts		P Ltd		S Ltd
	£000	£000	£000	£000
Turnover		400		280
Cost of sales		270		190
Gross profit		130		90
Distribution costs	20		10	
Administrative expenses	30	50	15	25
Profit on operating activities		80		65
Dividend receivable		30		–
Profit on ordinary activities before taxation		110		65
Tax on profit on ordinary activities		17		11
Profit on ordinary activities after taxation		93		54
Retained profits from last year		11		7
		104		61
Proposed dividend	40		30	
Transfer to reserves	5	45	2	32
Retained profits carried to next year		59		29

Notes:

(a) P Ltd had sold goods costing £10,000 to S Ltd for £15,000.

(b) At the balance sheet date 40 per cent of the goods in (a) had not been sold by S Ltd.

(c) Of the £7,000 retained profits from last year for S Ltd, £3,000 is in respect of post-acquisition profits.

The consolidated profit and loss of the group can now be drawn up.

P Ltd and subsidiary S Ltd

Consolidated Profit and Loss Account for the year ended 31 December 19X4

	£000	£000
Turnover (W1)		665
Cost of sales (W2)		447
Gross profit		218
Distribution costs	30	
Administrative expenses	45	75
Profit on ordinary activities before taxation		143
Tax on profit on ordinary activities		28
Profit on ordinary activities after taxation		115
Retained profits from last year (W3)		14
		129
Proposed dividend (W4)	40	
Transfer to reserves (W5)	7	47
Retained profits carried to next year		82

Workings: Letters (a) to (g) refer to the descriptions given above and in Exhibit 27.1.

(W1) P 400 + S 280 − 15 inter-company sales = 665 (a).

(W2) P 270 + S 190 − 15 inter-company purchases + unrealised profit in stock (40% × 5 = 2) = 447 (b) (i) and (ii).

(W3) P 11 + S 3 = 14. Only post-acquisition profits of S included. (*See* (e) in Exhibit 27.1.)

(W4) Only dividend of P included as S dividend will be received by P and will cancel out. (*See* item (f) in Exhibit 27.1.)

(W5) P 5 + S (100%)2 = 7. (*See* item (g) in Exhibit 27.1.)

27.2 Partly-owned subsidiaries

Exhibit 27.3

P Ltd owns 80 per cent of shares in S Ltd. Profit and loss accounts of the companies for the year to 31 December 19X2 are as follows:

Profit and loss accounts	P Ltd		S Ltd	
	£000	£000	£000	£000
Turnover		640		330
Cost of sales		410		200
Gross profit		230		130
Distribution costs	35		20	
Administrative expenses	70	105	55	75
Profit on operating activities		125		55
Dividend receivable		28		–
Profit on ordinary activities before taxation		153		55
Tax on profit on ordinary activities		26		10
Profit on ordinary activities after taxation		127		45
Retained profits from last year		29		35
		156		80
Proposed dividend	60		35	
Transfers to reserves	22	82	10	45
Retained profits carried to next year		74		35

Notes:

(*a*) S Ltd had sold goods costing £20,000 to P Ltd for £30,000.
(*b*) At the balance sheet date 30 per cent of the goods in (*a*) had not been sold by P Ltd.
(*c*) Of the £35,000 retained profits of S Ltd, £15,000 is post-acquisition profits.

P Ltd and subsidiary S Ltd

Consolidated Profit and Loss Account for the year ending 31 December 19X2

	£000	£000
Turnover (W1)		940
Cost of sales (W2)		583
Gross profit		357
Distribution costs	55	
Administrative expenses	125	180
Profit on ordinary activities before taxation		177
Tax on profit on ordinary activities		36
Profit on ordinary activities after taxation		141
Minority interest (W3)		9
Profit for the financial year		132
Retained profits from last year (W4)		41
		173
Proposed dividend (W5)	60	
Transfer to reserves (W6)	30	90
Retained profits carried to next year		£83

Workings:

Letters (*a*) to (*g*) refer to the descriptions given above and in Exhibit 27.1.

(W1) P 640 + S 330 – inter-company sales 30 = 940 (*a*).

(W2) P 410 + S 200 – inter-company purchases 30 + unrealised profit in stock (30% × 10 = 3) =

583 (*b*) (*i*) and (*ii*).
(W3) 20 per cent × 45: profit after taxation of S Ltd = 9 (*d*) (*i*).
(W4) P 29 + S (80% × 15 = 12) = 41 (*e*).
(W5) Only the dividend of P shown. *See* (*f*).
(W6) P 22 + S (80% × 10 = 8) = 30 (*g*).

Main points to remember

1 When consolidating profit and loss accounts for groups with wholly-owned subsidiaries with no intra-group transactions or indebtedness, it is simply a case of adding together all the separate profit and loss accounts to form the consolidated profit and loss account.

2 When consolidating profit and loss accounts, adjustments for unrealised profits on intra-group transactions and for intra-group indebtedness must be made where they exist (as per Chapters 22, 24, and 25).

3 When consolidating profit and loss accounts for groups with partly owned subsidiaries, the approaches detailed in Chapters 20 and 26 should be followed.

Review questions

27.1 The following information relates to the Brodick group of companies for the year to 30 April 19X7:

	Brodick plc £000	Lamlash Ltd £000	Corrie Ltd £000
Turnover	1,100	500	130
Cost of sales	(630)	(300)	(70)
Gross profit	470	200	60
Administrative expenses	(105)	(150)	(20)
Dividend from Lamlash Ltd	24	–	–
Dividend from Corrie Ltd	6	–	–
Profit before tax	395	50	40
Taxation	(65)	(10)	(20)
Profit after tax	330	40	20
Interim dividend	(50)	(10)	–
Proposed dividend	(150)	(20)	(10)
Retained profit for the year	130	10	10
Retained profits brought forward	460	106	30
Retained profits carried forward	£590	£116	£40

Additional information:
(*a*) The issued share capital of the group was as follows:
Brodick plc: 5,000,000 ordinary shares of £1 each;
Lamlash Ltd: 1,000,000 ordinary shares of £1 each; and
Corrie Ltd: 400,000 ordinary shares of £1 each.
(*b*) Brodick plc purchased 80 per cent of the issued share capital of Lamlash Ltd in 19X0. At that time, the retained profits of Lamlash amounted to £56,000.
(*c*) Brodick plc purchased 60 per cent of the issued share capital of Corrie Ltd in 19X4. At that time, the retained profits of Corrie amounted to £20,000.
(*d*) Brodick plc recognises dividends proposed by other group companies in its profit and loss account.

Required:

Insofar as the information permits, prepare the Brodick group of companies' consolidated profit and loss account for the year to 30 April 19X7 in accordance with the Companies Acts and related accounting statements. (*Note*: Notes to the profit and loss account are not required, but you should append a statement showing the make-up of the 'retained profits carried forward', and your workings should be submitted.)

(*Association of Accounting Technicians*)

27.2 You are presented with the following summarised information for Norbreck plc and its subsidiary, Bispham Ltd:

Profit and Loss Accounts for the year to 30 September 19X7

	Norbreck plc £000	Bispham Ltd £000
Turnover	1,700	450
Cost of sales	(920)	(75)
Gross profit	780	375
Administration expenses	(300)	(175)
Income from shares in group company	120	–
Profit on ordinary activities before taxation	600	200
Tax on profit on ordinary activities	(30)	(20)
Profit on ordinary activities after taxation	570	180
Dividends paid	(90)	(50)
proposed	(270)	(100)
Retained profit for the year	210	30
Retained profit brought forward	220	70
Retained profit carried forward	£430	£100

Balance Sheets at 30 September 19X7

	Norbreck plc £000	Bispham Ltd £000
Fixed tangible assets	1,280	440
Investments: Shares in group company	400	–
Current assets:		
Stocks	300	250
Debtors (including, for Norbreck plc, the dividend proposed by the subsidiary)	280	150
Cash at bank and in hand	40	10
	620	410
Creditors (amounts falling due within one year):		
Trade creditors	(80)	(160)
Other creditors, taxation and social security	(160)	(70)
Proposed dividend	(270)	(100)
	(510)	(330)
Net current assets	110	80
Total assets *less* current liabilities	1,790	520
Provisions for liabilities and charges		
Taxation, including deferred taxation	(460)	(20)
	£1,330	£500

	Norbreck plc £000	Bispham Ltd £000
Capital and reserves:		
Called-up share capital (ordinary shares of £1 each)	900	400
Profit and loss account	430	100
	£1,330	£500

Additional information:
(a) Norbreck plc acquired 80 per cent of the shares in Bispham Ltd on 1 October 19X4. Bispham's profit and loss account balance as at that date was £40,000.
(b) Goodwill arising on acquisition is to be written off against the group's retained profits.
(c) Norbreck takes credit within its own books of account for any dividends receivable from Bispham.

Required:
Prepare Bispham plc's consolidated profit and loss account for the year to 30 September 19X7 and a consolidated balance sheet as at that date.

Note: Formal notes to the account are not required, although detailed workings should be submitted with your answer. You should also append to the consolidated profit and loss account your calculation of earnings per share and a statement showing the make-up of 'retained profits carried forward'.

(*Association of Accounting Technicians*)

27.3A The following figures for the year to 30 April 19X6 have been extracted from the books and records of three companies which form a group:

	Old plc £	Field Ltd £	Lodge Ltd £
Revenue reserves at 1 May 19X5	30,000	40,000	50,000
Stocks at 1 May 19X5	90,000	150,000	80,000
Sales	1,250,000	875,000	650,000
Purchases	780,000	555,000	475,000
Distribution expenses	125,000	85,000	60,000
Administration expenses	28,000	40,000	72,000
Interim dividends:			
Paid 31 July 19X5, ordinary	45,000	35,000	15,000
Paid 31 October 19X5, preference		4,000	
Share capital – fully paid ordinary shares of £1 each	450,000	350,000	200,000
8% preference shares of £1 each		100,000	
Stocks at 30 April 19X6	110,000	135,000	85,000

Profits are deemed to accrue evenly throughout the year.

Other information:
(a) Corporation tax of the following amounts is to be provided on the profits of the year:

Old plc	£125,000
Field Ltd	£75,000
Lodge Ltd	£20,000

(b) Final dividends proposed are:

Old plc	15p per share
Field Ltd	12.5p per share on the ordinary shares and a half-year's dividend on the preference shares
Lodge Ltd	7.5p per share

(c) Field Ltd sells goods for resale to both Old plc and Lodge Ltd. At 30 April 19X6, stocks of goods purchased from Field Ltd are:

in Old plc	£40,000
in Lodge Ltd	£28,000

The net profit percentage for Field Ltd on sales of these goods is 25 per cent.
Old plc has £36,000 of these goods in stock at 1 May 19X5.
Total sales in the year by Field Ltd to Old plc were £150,000 and to Lodge Ltd £120,000.

(d) Old plc acquired the whole of the ordinary shares in Field Ltd many years ago. 50,000 of the preference shares were acquired on 1 August 19X5. Old plc acquired 120,000 shares in Lodge Ltd on 1 August 19X5.

Required:

A consolidated profit and loss account for Old plc and its subsidiaries for the year ended 30 April 19X6, together with any relevant notes.

(*Association of Chartered Certified Accountants*)

27.4A The following are the trial balances of ATH Ltd, GLE Ltd, and FRN Ltd as on 31 December 19X8.

	ATH Ltd £	GLE Ltd £	FRN Ltd £
Ordinary share capital (shares of £1 each, fully paid)	100,000	30,000	20,000
7 per cent cumulative preference share capital (shares of £1 each, fully paid)	–	–	5,000
Profit and loss account – balance at 31.12.19X7	15,600	6,000	1,900
Current liabilities	20,750	15,900	18,350
Sales	194,000	116,000	84,000
Dividend received from GLE Ltd	1,200		
	331,550	167,900	129,250
Fixed assets	45,000	29,000	25,000
Current assets	46,000	27,500	22,500
24,000 ordinary shares in GLE Ltd at cost	33,700	–	–
20,000 ordinary shares in FRN Ltd at cost	21,250	–	–
Cost of goods sold	153,000	87,000	63,000
General expenses	32,600	22,900	18,750
Dividend for 19X8, paid on 31.12.19X8	–	1,500	–
	331,550	167,900	129,250

ATH Ltd acquired the shares in FRN Ltd on 31 December 19X6, when the credit balance on the profit and loss account of FRN Ltd was £700, and acquired the shares in GLE Ltd on 31 December 19X7. No dividend was paid by either ATH Ltd or GLE Ltd for the year 19X7.

No dividend has been paid by FRN Ltd for the years 19X6, 19X7 and 19X8 and none is proposed. The directors of ATH Ltd propose to pay a dividend of £7,000 for 19X8.

The sales of GLE Ltd for 19X8 (£116,000) include £1,000 for goods sold to FRN Ltd and this amount has been debited to purchases account in the books of FRN Ltd.

All these goods were sold by FRN Ltd during 19X8.

Required:

A consolidated trading and profit and loss account for the year 19X8 and a consolidated balance sheet as on 31 December 19X8 (not necessarily in a form for publication).

Ignore depreciation of fixed assets and taxation.

(*Institute of Chartered Secretaries and Administrators*)

28

Consolidated financial statements – FRS 6: Acquisitions and mergers

Objectives

After you have studied this chapter, you should:

- *know when merger accounting should be used*

- *know the difference between the acquisition and the merger methods of preparing consolidated financial statements*

28.1 Methods of combination of companies

When two limited companies are going to combine together in some way, then it is obvious that the shares must come under common ownership. There are two main methods of achieving this, with different possible methods of accounting for the combination: **acquisition accounting**, which would normally be applied (and which has been assumed throughout Chapters 19–27); and **merger accounting**, which is restricted to specific circumstances. Acquisition accounting is dealt with in FRS 2: **Accounting for subsidiary undertakings**; FRS 6: **Acquisitions and mergers**; and FRS 7: **Fair values in acquisition accounting**. FRS 6 presents the merger accounting approach.

Examples of combinations where it would be appropriate to adopt acquisition accounting

A common approach to the formation of new business combinations is for one company, A, to purchase the shares of another company, B. Often, this is achieved by A making a cash payment to shareholders in B. In accepting the cash, the shareholders sever their links with the company. Company A shareholders now control both companies.

Another common approach is where company A issues debentures (loan stock) to company B's shareholders in exchange for their shareholdings in B: the new debenture holders would have no voting power in the new group, which would be controlled by the shareholders of A.

In both of these cases, **acquisition accounting** should be used.

Exhibit 28.1 Requirements to be met if merger accounting is to be used

Examples of combinations where it would be appropriate to adopt merger accounting

When company A does not pay cash or issue debentures to the old shareholders of company B, but instead issues new equity (ordinary voting) shares to the old shareholders of B, this means that the shareholders of A and B have 'merged' into one, and between them have a joint interest in the new group. It is often called a pooling of interest.

A variation on this is the 'new entity' method of combination. Here a new company, C, is formed to take over A and B, giving the old shareholders of A and B new shares in C. Once again the shareholders have 'merged' into one.

In both these cases, **merger accounting** may be used, but only if a number of conditions contained in FRS 6 are met; otherwise, **acquisition accounting** must be used.

Exhibit 28.1 shows the conditions to be considered if merger accounting is to be used.

28.2 Acquisition accounting method

As mentioned above, this is the method that has been assumed in Chapters 19–27. In the books of the parent undertaking:

(a) shares purchased in a subsidiary should be shown at cost less dividends received out of pre-acquisition profits;

(b) dividends out of pre-acquisition profits cannot be regarded as available for distribution as dividends by the parent.

In the consolidated financial statements:

(c) assets and liabilities of the subsidiary at the date of acquisition should be shown in the balance sheet at their fair value at that date;

(d) the difference at the date of acquisition between the fair value of the purchase consideration and the fair value of the net assets is treated as goodwill, positive or negative;

(e) only post-acquisition profits of the subsidiary should be included in the consolidated reserves of the group.

The idea underlying these rules is to stop capital receipts, i.e. dividends from pre-acquisition profits, being paid out as dividends.

The consolidation of balance sheets using the **acquisition method** is now shown in Exhibit 28.2.

Exhibit 28.2

A Ltd has just made an offer of £270,000 for the whole of the share capital of B Ltd and this has been accepted. Payment to be by cash. The 'fair value' placed on the tangible fixed assets of B Ltd for the purposes of the merger is £148,000. Following are the two companies' balance sheets, immediately before the merger on 31 December 19X3.

	A Ltd		B Ltd	
	£000	£000	£000	£000
Tangible fixed assets		400		120
Current assets	450		200	
Less Current liabilities	130	320	90	110
		720		230
Ordinary shares £1		500		150
Revenue reserves		220		80
		720		230

The balance sheets of A Ltd, and of the group, immediately following the merger, are as follows:

Balance Sheet at 31 December 19X3

		A Ltd £000	A Ltd £000		Group £000	Group £000
Fixed assets						
Intangible (goodwill)		–		(W2)	12	
Tangible		400		(W3)	548	
Investments		270	670		–	560
Current assets	(W1)	180		(W4)	380	
Less Current liabilities		130	50		220	160
			720			720
Share capital			500			500
Reserves			220			220
			720			720

Workings (£000):
(W1) Original current assets 450 – cash paid 270 = 180
(W2) Paid for shares 270
      Less Net assets at takeover date 230
      Add Increase in value of fixed assets to a
      'fair value' 148 – 120 = ... 28 258
      Goodwill (intangible fixed asset) 12
(W3) Fixed assets A Ltd 400 + B Ltd 148 = 548
(W4) A Ltd (after payment) 180 + B Ltd 200 = 380

28.3 Merger accounting method

(a) Shares issued by the parent are merely the means of achieving the merger in a technical sense. Consequently, no share premium arises. They are shown in the parent's balance sheet (A Ltd) at nominal value, as addition to share capital.

(b) As share premium is not recognised in (a) the cost of the investment in the parent's balance sheet (A Ltd) is the nominal value of shares issued. If the nominal value of the shares is not the same as the Stock Exchange or similar market valuation then, obviously, the 'true' value of the subsidiary is not shown in the 'cost' of the investment.

(c) Any dividends received by the parent (A Ltd) from the subsidiary (B Ltd) can be distributed in full by the parent. This means that the whole of the subsidiary's reserves can be included in the consolidated balance sheet reserves.

(d) The assets of the subsidiary are not revalued at 'fair value' at the date of merger. It would not make sense to revalue B Ltd's assets while leaving A Ltd's assets valued at the old amounts. Sometimes, however, under the 'new entity' method of merger described on p. 388, both companies revalue their assets.

(e) Where the total nominal value of the shares issued by the parent, A Ltd, is more than the total nominal value of the shares of B Ltd, the difference is deducted from group reserves. If the total is less, then the shortfall becomes a non-distributable group reserve.

Exhibit 28.3

Taking the same firms, A Ltd and B Ltd, as in Exhibit 28.2, but instead of a cash offer of £270,000 the offer is 200,000 ordinary shares of £1 each at a stock exchange value of £270,000.

The balance sheets of A Ltd and the group immediately after the merger are now:

	A Ltd £000	A Ltd £000	Group £000	Group £000
Fixed assets				
Tangible	400			520
Investments	200	600		–
Current assets	450		650	
Less Current liabilities	130	320	220	430
		920		950
Share capital		700		700
Reserves		220		250
		920		950

Workings:

(W1)	Reserve	A Ltd	220	
		B Ltd	80	300

Less Excess of nominal value shares issued by A Ltd over those exchanged of B Ltd, i.e. 200 – 150

	50
	250

28.4 The advantages of merger accounting to a group

Merger accounting has a number of advantages from the perspective of the investing group:

(a) The subsidiary's results are included in the group for the whole accounting period, not just for the post-acquisition period. Consequently, the group can appear to the casual reviewer as more profitable than it was. However, as the amounts relating to pre- and post-merger must be disclosed, this is not as great an advantage as it may appear.

(b) The parent company can appear misleadingly successful if it is in receipt of pre-acquisition dividends which it treats as revenue income. (The investment is normally recorded at the nominal value of the holding company shares issued, plus any other consideration given, and is unlikely to need to be reduced to account for the pre-acquisition distribution.)

(c) Assets may be understated (compared to equivalent situations where **acquisition accounting** has been applied), providing an opportunity for instant earnings by selling assets, and resulting in higher returns on capital.

(d) Lower depreciation charges and an absence of goodwill will result in a correspondingly higher return on capital employed than would be the case were the **acquisition accounting** approach adopted.

(e) Most importantly, all the pre-acquisition distributable reserves of the companies involved are available for distribution to the group's shareholders (though this may be subject to a reduction resulting from the nominal value of the new shares exceeding the nominal value of the shares received).

However, despite these advantages, the merger method has only been used infrequently in the UK. Furthermore, with the release in September 1994 of FRS 6, which significantly tightened the restriction on its use, future adoption of merger accounting in the UK is likely to be very rare indeed.

28.5 Final points concerning FRS 6

Under **merger accounting** per FRS 6, it is not necessary to adjust values of the subsidiaries' assets and liabilities to fair values. However, adjustments should be made to achieve uniformity of accounting policies within the group.

Remember that, in a merger, there is no such thing as **pre-acquisition profits**. The distribution of pre-acquisition profits is not restricted in the way it is under **acquisition accounting**.

Finally, while **acquisition accounting** will generally give rise to goodwill (positive or negative), **merger accounting** never does – not because a difference cannot arise between the consideration given and the value received, but because such differences arising under the merger accounting approach do not conform to the fair-value-based definition of goodwill given in FRS 10 and SSAP 22.

Main points to remember

1 Merger accounting should be used only when certain conditions are met, and must be used when they are.

2 Otherwise, acquisition accounting should be used.

3 Under merger accounting, assets and liabilities do not require to be stated at their fair values on acquisition.

4 Goodwill can only arise under acquisition accounting.

5 No distinction is made between pre- and post-acquisition reserves under merger accounting.

Review questions

Note: Wherever appropriate, you should provide answers to these questions according to both SSAP 22 and FRS 10.

28.1 Large plc, a manufacturer and wholesaler, purchased 600,000 of the 800,000 issued ordinary shares of a smaller company, Small Ltd, on 1 January 19X5 when the retained earnings account of Small Ltd had a credit balance of £72,000.

The latest accounts of the two companies are:

Summary Profit and Loss Accounts for the year to 30 September 19X6 (£000s)

		Large plc		Small Ltd
Credit sales		10,830		2,000
Cost of sales and production services		3,570		1,100
Gross profit		7,260		900
Administrative and marketing expenses		2,592		180
(including depreciation, audit fee and directors' remuneration)				
Operating profit		4,668		720
Dividend received from Small Ltd		180		–
Net profit before tax		4,848		720
Taxation	2,304		200	
Net dividend	2,400		240	
		4,704		440
Profit retained		144		280
Brought forward from last year		1,200		192
Carried forward to next year		1,344		472

Summary Balance Sheets at 30 September 19X6 (£000s)

	Large plc	Small Ltd
Intangible assets:		
Research and development:		
– pure research	20	–
– applied research	30	–
– development	180	–
Goodwill – purchased (at cost less amounts written off)	48	–
– unpurchased	50	–
Fixed assets at cost less depreciation	3,920	728
Investment in Small Ltd	525	–
Current account with Large plc	–	75
Stock	594	231
Debtors	2,250	370
Bank	99	24
	7,716	1,428
Less Current account with Small Ltd	75	–
Creditors for goods and services	297	156
	7,344	1,272
Share capital	6,000	800
Retained earnings	1,344	472
	7,344	1,272

Notes:

The intangible asset section of the balance sheet of Large plc has not yet been amended prior to consolidation to take account of the provisions of the Companies Acts or the recommendations contained in accounting standards regarding intangible assets.

The stock of Large plc contained goods valued at £108,000 purchased from Small Ltd at production cost plus 50 per cent.

Required:

(a) Prepare the consolidated profit and loss account of Large plc and its subsidiary Small Ltd for the year to 30 September 19X6 using the acquisition (purchase) method of consolidation.

(b) Prepare the consolidated balance sheet of Large plc and its subsidiary Small Ltd at 30 September 19X6 using the acquisition method of consolidation.

(c) What would the reserves of the group be if the merger method of consolidation were used instead of the acquisition method? Briefly explain why there is a difference between the values of the reserves arising from the two methods of consolidation.

(*Institute of Chartered Secretaries and Administrators*)

28.2A Huge plc acquired a holding of 600,000 of the 800,000 ordinary £1 shares of Large plc on 1 October 19X5 when the revenue reserves of Large stood at £320,000.

On 1 October 19X6, the directors of Medium plc agreed to appoint the commercial manager of Huge as one of its directors to enable Huge to participate in its commercial, financial and dividend policy decisions. In exchange, Huge agreed to provide finance to Medium for working capital. On the same day, Huge acquired its holding of 100,000 of the 400,000 ordinary £1 shares of Medium when the revenue reserves of Medium were £150,000. Three months later, the directors of Small plc, who supplied materials to Large, heard of the arrangement between Huge and Medium and suggested that they would be pleased to enter into a similar relationship. The board of Huge were interested in the proposal and showed their good faith by acquiring a 10 per cent holding in Small which at that time had a debit balance of £2,000 on its profit and loss account.

Balance Sheets of the four companies on 30 September 19X7

	Huge	Large	Medium	Small
	£000	£000	£000	£000
Property, plant and machinery	2,004	780	553	85
Investment in Large	650			
Investment in Medium	180			
Investment in Small	12			
Current a/c Medium	40			
Current a/c Small		10		
Stocks	489	303	72	28
Debtors	488	235	96	22
Bank/cash	45	62	19	5
	3,908	1,390	740	140
Less Liabilities due in one year: Creditors	318	170	90	10
	3,590	1,220	650	130
Ordinary share capital	2,400	800	400	80
Revenue reserves	1,190	420	210	40
Current a/c Huge			40	
Current a/c Large				10
	3,590	1,220	650	130

Required:

(a) Identify which of the four companies should be included in a group consolidation, explaining how and why the treatment of one company in the consolidation may be different from another. Mention any appropriate accounting standards or legislation applicable.

(b) Prepare the consolidated balance sheet of the group at 30 September 19X7 using the acquisition method of accounting.

(*Institute of Chartered Secretaries and Administrators*)

29

Standards covering subsidiary and associated undertakings

Objectives

After you have studied this chapter, you should:

- *understand the importance of the control concept*

- *know the circumstances under which a parent:subsidiary relationship is recognised*

- *know of the conditions whereby companies are exempt from preparing consolidated financial statements*

- *know of the conditions under which a subsidiary company should not be included in the consolidated financial statements*

- *know what to do when a company has investments in associated undertakings but does not prepare consolidated financial statements because it has no investments in subsidiary undertakings*

29.1 Introduction

The whole field of accounting relating to consolidated financial statements and groups in general has recently undergone considerable changes. In the last few years, FRS 2 has been introduced to clarify and extend business operations for which consolidated financial statements are needed, and to define those situations where exemptions from their preparation should apply; FRS 9 has been introduced, updating the requirements of SSAP 1 concerning associates, and introducing regulations relating to joint ventures; and FRS10 has replaced SSAP 22 as the accounting standard relating to goodwill.

29.2 FRS 2: Accounting for subsidiary undertakings

Financial Reporting Standard 2 superseded SSAP 14: *Group accounts*. While it must comply with the Companies Acts, it redefines the legal requirements by reducing the number of alternatives and making the requirements and definitions more precise, thereby, improving the standardisation and hence comparability of accounts.

Main changes recently have concerned consolidated financial statements. Specifically:

(*a*) the definitions of parents and subsidiaries are now based upon control, rather than on ownership;

(*b*) instead of 'company' the term 'undertaking' is used. This means that unincorporated bodies are now covered;

(*c*) there are now more exemptions available from the need to prepare consolidated financial statements.

In the remainder of this chapter the more important provisions are discussed. As chapters 19 to 28 have already incorporated the actual mechanics of implementing FRS 2, those points will not be looked at again. While this chapter is concerned with the other most important aspects of FRS 2 and of FRS 9 and SSAP 1, it does not cover every detail. This would be needed only in your studies at a later stage.

29.3 Parent and subsidiary relationship

In general terms, the main test as to the existence of a parent:subsidiary relationship is one of control. A group consists of all the various enterprises, including unincorporated businesses as well as companies, under the control of the parent. If you can understand that, the detail contained in FRS 2 and the Companies Acts will become much clearer. In fact, control and ownership usually go together, but it is the exceptions to this that have brought about the need for the changes that have been made to the Companies Acts and that have led to the issue of replacement accounting standards.

FRS 2 states that an undertaking is a parent undertaking of another undertaking (this being the subsidiary undertaking) if any of the following can apply to it:

1 it holds a majority of the voting rights (i.e. shares carrying a right to vote) in the undertaking;

2 it is a member of the undertaking and has the right to appoint or remove directors holding a majority of the voting rights at meetings of the board on substantially all matters;

3 it has the right to exercise a 'dominant influence' over the undertaking. This could be by virtue of provisions in the undertaking's memorandum or articles, or by a control contract which must be in writing and be legally valid. By 'dominant influence' is meant influence that can be exercised to achieve the operating and financial policies desired by the holder of the influence, not withstanding the rights or influence of any other party – in other words, it has the right to give directions as to the functioning of the operating and financial policies of the undertaking, whether or not they are to the benefit of that undertaking;

4 it is a member of the undertaking and controls alone a majority of the voting rights by agreement with other members;

5 it has a 'participating interest' (i.e. an interest in the shares of the undertaking which is held for the long term for the purpose of securing a contribution to its activities by the exercise of control or influence arising from that interest – this would normally be a holding of more than 20 per cent of the shares of the undertaking) and either (a) it exercises a dominant influence over the undertaking, or (b) it and the undertaking are managed on a unified basis (i.e. where the whole of the operations of the undertakings are integrated and they are managed as a single unit);

6 a parent undertaking is also treated as the parent undertaking of the subsidiary undertakings of its subsidiary undertakings.

Points 1 and 6 above are the more traditional and more usual ways of establishing the existence of a parent:subsidiary relationship in the UK.

29.4 Exemption from preparing consolidated financial statements

The Companies Act 1989 contains provisions which exempt some groups from having to prepare consolidated accounts. Exactly the same provisions are contained in FRS 2. The main points contained therein are:

1 Small and medium-sized groups can claim exemption on the grounds of size. They must comply with at least two of the following criteria:

	Small	Medium-sized
Aggregate turnover not more than	£2.8 million net/ £3.36 million gross	£11.2 million net/ £13.44 million gross
Aggregate gross assets not more than	£1.4 million net/ £1.68 million gross	£5.6 million net/ £6.72 million gross
Aggregate employees not more than	50	250

(This exemption does not apply to groups whose members include a plc, a bank, an insurance company, or an authorised person under the Financial Services Act (1986).)

In the past small and medium-sized companies could file modified group accounts. This is no longer possible. Small and medium-sized companies now have to choose between filing *full* consolidated accounts or *individual* company accounts.

2 Except for companies who have any of their securities listed on any stock exchange in the European Union, any parent undertaking that is itself a wholly owned subsidiary whose immediate parent is established in the European Union does not have to prepare consolidated financial statements. Individual company accounts must still be prepared for the parent and they must include the name of its own parent undertaking; the country where its own parent is incorporated, if it is not the United Kingdom; and the fact that it is exempt from preparing group financial statements. As well as this, a copy of the audited consolidated financial statements of its own parent must be filed with its own individual company accounts. (This exemption can be overturned by minority shareholders who can require that consolidated accounts are prepared.)

3 If all of the subsidiary undertakings are permitted or required to be excluded from consolidation under the Companies Acts, consolidated financial statements are not required.

29.5 Exemption from the inclusion of a subsidiary in consolidated financial statements

There are three grounds for exclusion of a subsidiary given in FRS 2:

1 where severe long-term restrictions substantially hinder the rights of the parent undertaking over the assets or management of the subsidiary undertaking;
2 where the interest in the subsidiary undertaking is held exclusively for subsequent resale; and
3 where activities are so different from those of other undertakings to be included in the consolidation that their inclusion would be incompatible with the obligation to give a true and fair view.

A subsidiary that is excluded on the grounds of long-term restriction should be treated as a fixed asset investment. However, if the parent still exercises significant influence it should be treated as an associated undertaking.

Subsidiaries excluded on the grounds that they are being held exclusively for resale should be included as current assets at the lower of cost and net realisable value.

Where exclusion is due to the activities of the subsidiary being so different from those of other undertakings to be included in the consolidation that their inclusion would be incompatible with the obligation to give a true and fair view, they should be accounted for using the equity method.

29.6 SSAP 1: Accounting for associated companies

For most entities, this accounting standard was replaced by FRS 9 – *Associates and joint ventures* – in November 1997. However, it remains in force for small enterprises who apply the FRSSE.

SSAP 1 says that B Ltd will be considered as an associated company of A Ltd if A Ltd can *significantly* influence the financial and operating decisions of B Ltd. As a normal rule the amount of B Ltd's equity shares that A Ltd would have to hold would be 20 per cent. This, however, is only a guideline. What is important is the presence or absence of significant influence.

The idea behind the SSAP was to ensure that if one company has invested in another company, and can significantly influence the affairs of that company, then ordinary investment accounting is not suitable. Rather than simply show dividends received as a measure of income, it would be much more realistic for the investing company's *full* share of the profit of that company to be incorporated in the investing company's accounts. The method of doing this is known as 'equity accounting'.

29.7 FRS 9: Associates and joint ventures

This standard updated and expanded the content of SSAP 1 to encompass joint ventures, which it defines as entities in which the reporting entity holds an interest on a long-term basis and which are jointly controlled by the reporting entity and one or more other venturers under a contractual arrangement.

The definition of an associate was altered to include entities only where the investing entity *exercises* a significant influence, rather than one that is *in a position to exercise* significant influence. Hence, less entities should be defined as associates under FRS 9 than was the case under SSAP 1. At the same time, the amount of disclosure required in the financial statements was increased.

No change was made to the treatment of associates in the balance sheet, 'investments in associates' appearing as a line under fixed asset investments. In the profit and loss account, the share of the associate's results are shown as a separate line under group operating profit. Under SSAP 1, they were shown as part of the group profit before tax.

The standard introduced the 'gross equity' method of accounting, which is a form of equity accounting applicable to joint ventures under which the investor's share of the aggregate gross assets and liabilities of the joint venture is shown on the face of the balance sheet and the investor's share of the joint venture's turnover is noted in the profit and loss account.

29.8 Equity accounting

Equity accounting is a modified form of consolidation that requires similar adjustments to be made as apply under FRS 2: *Accounting for subsidiary undertakings* for full, acquisition-accounting-based consolidations. In the consolidated profit and loss account, the investing company should take into account the whole of its share of the earnings of the associate, whether or not the associate has distributed the earnings as dividends. In the consolidated balance sheet the investment is shown at cost, adjusted each year by the share of retained profits belonging to the investor, subject to an adjustment for any goodwill arising on acquisition written off.

We will shortly see how this is carried out. You will note that there are considerable differences between equity accounting and consolidation accounting of a subsidiary's results. With subsidiary accounting, the group would take credit for the whole of the turnover, cost of sales, etc. and then make a one-line adjustment to remove any minority share. With equity accounting, the associated company's turnover, cost of sales, etc. are not amalgamated with those of the group. Instead, only the items concerned with the group's share of the associated company's results are brought into account.

As it would be quite rare for the investing company not to have subsidiaries, we will use an example that brings the necessary equity accounting into a consolidated set of financial statements.

Effect upon consolidated profit and loss account

Take out:
(a) dividends received or receivable from the associate.

Include instead the group's share of the associate's:

(b) pre-tax profit;
(c) taxation charge;
(d) post-acquisition retained profits brought forward.

Effect upon consolidated balance sheet

Rather than   the cost of the investment
Show instead   the cost of the investment
        plus
        the group's share of associate's post-acquisition retained profit.

Exhibit 29.1 shows how the associated company's results are incorporated into a set of consolidated financial statements.

Exhibit 29.1

A Ltd is a holding company with subsidiaries. It also has 25 per cent of the equity share capital of B Ltd. This was bought for £100,000 three years ago when B Ltd had reserves (retained profits) of £20,000.

Profit and Loss Accounts for the year ending 31 December 19X3

	A Ltd & Subsidiaries (consolidated)		B Ltd (associated co.)	
	£000	£000	£000	£000
Turnover		540		200
Cost of sales		370		130
Gross profit		170		70
Distribution costs	20		3	
Administrative expenses	40	60	7	10
		110		60
Dividends receivable from B Ltd	(A)	10		–
Profit on ordinary activities before taxation		120	(B)	60
Tax on profit on ordinary activities		28	(C)	16
Profit on ordinary activities after taxation		92		44
Retained profits from last year		43		40
		135		84
Proposed dividends		60		40
Retained profits carried to next year		75		44

Balance Sheet as at 31 December 19X3 (abbreviated)

	£000	£000
Fixed assets	145	130
Investment in B Ltd at cost	100	–
Net current assets	180	114
	425	244
Share capital (ordinary shares)	350	200
Reserves	75	44
	425	244

Now we can move to the consolidation of B Ltd with A Ltd. As you have already been told the items needing adjusting are:

Take out: (A) Dividends receivable
Include: (B) Group share of pre-tax profit
            (C) Group share of taxation
            (D) Group's share post-acquisition retained profit brought forward.

The answer is:

A Ltd Group
Consolidated Profit and Loss Account for the year ending 31 December 19X3

		£000	£000
Turnover			540
Cost of sales			370
			170
Distribution costs		20	
Administrative expenses		40	60
			110
Share of profit of associated company (*see* W1)	(B)		15
Profit on ordinary activities before taxation			125
Tax on profit on ordinary activities (*see* W2)	(C)		32
Profit on ordinary activities after taxation			93
Retained profits from last year (*see* W3)	(D)		48
			141
Proposed dividend			60
Retained profits carried to next year			81

Consolidated Balance Sheet as at 31 December 19X3

	£000
Fixed assets	145
Investment in B Ltd (*see* W4)	106
Net current assets	180
	431
Share capital	350
Reserves (*see* W5)	81
	431

Workings:

(W1) 25% of profit before taxation of B Ltd × £60 = £15

(W2) A £28 + 25% of B £16 = £32

(W3) A £43 + 25% of B's post-acquisition profits (£40 − £20) £20 = £48

(W4) Cost of 25% share in B =   100
       Add Retained profits B c/d   44
       Less Pre-acquisition profits   20
       Post-acquisition profits   24
       25% share   6
                                      106

(W5) Reserves A   75
       Add 25% of post-acquisition
       profit of B (*see* W4)   6   81

29.9 Investing companies without subsidiaries

If no consolidated financial statements are produced by the investing company and it is not exempt from preparing consolidated statements, or would not be if it had subsidiaries, a separate profit and loss account (or a supplement to the investing company's own profit and loss account) should be prepared showing the information that would have been included in respect of the associated undertaking had consolidated financial statements been prepared. Similar requirements apply to the balance sheet. An example of a supplementary statement incorporating the results of associated companies is shown in Exhibit 29.2.

Exhibit 29.2

Example of a profit and loss account of a company without subsidiaries:

Profit and Loss Account of an Investing Company

	£000	£000
Turnover		2,000
Cost of sales		1,400
Gross profit		600
Distribution costs	175	
Administrative expenses	125	300
Profit on ordinary activities before taxation		300
Tax on profit on ordinary activities		85
Profit on ordinary activities after taxation		215
Dividends – proposed		80
Amount set aside to reserves		135

Supplementary statement incorporating results of associated companies:

	£000
Share of profits less losses of associated companies	50
Less Tax	15
Share of profits after tax of associated companies	35
Profit on ordinary share activites after taxation (as above)	215
Profit attributable to members of the investing company	250
Dividends – proposed	80
Net profit retained (£35,000 by associated companies)	170

Note: The earnings per share figure would be based on £250,000.

29.10 The control concept

The control concept underlies the presentation of consolidated financial statements for a group as a single economic entity. While the list given in section 29.3 can be used to identify a parent:subsidiary relationship, it may result in more than one undertaking being classified as the parent. However, FRS 2 states that control can only be held by one parent, and that the control that identifies undertakings as parent and subsidiary undertakings should be distinguished from shared control, for example as in a joint venture. If more than one undertaking is identified as the parent, their interests in the subsidiary are in effect interests in a joint venture, and no parent:subsidiary relationship exists.

On the other hand, one or more of these parents may exercise a non-controlling but significant influence over the company in which it has invested. In that case it would be appropriate to account for it as an associate undertaking.

New terms

Associated undertaking (p. 397): A company which is not a subsidiary of the investing group or company but in which the investing group or company has a long-term interest and over which it exercises significant influence.

Joint venture (p. 397): An entity in which the reporting entity holds an interest on a long-term basis and which is jointly controlled by the reporting entity and one or more other venturers under a contractual arrangement

Equity accounting (p. 397): A method of accounting for associated undertakings that brings into the consolidated profit and loss account the investor's share of the associated undertaking's results and that records the investment in the consolidated balance sheet at the investor's share of the associated undertaking's net assets including any goodwill arising to the extent that it has not previously been written off.

Gross equity accounting (p. 397): A form of equity accounting applicable to joint ventures under which the investor's share of the aggregate gross assets and liabilities of the joint venture is shown on the face of the balance sheet and the investor's share of the joint venture's turnover is noted in the profit and loss account.

Main points to remember

1   The existence of a parent:subsidiary relationship depends upon whether the 'parent' undertaking can exercise *dominant* influence over the 'subsidiary' undertaking.

2   The existence of a parent:associate relationship depends upon whether the 'parent' undertaking actually exercises *significant* influence over the 'associate' undertaking.

3 There are some circumstances where groups are exempted from the preparation of consolidated financial statements.

4 Equity accounting is used when including associate undertakings in consolidated financial statements.

5 When a company has investments in associated undertakings but does not prepare consolidated financial statements because it has no investments in subsidiary undertakings, it should prepare a supplement to its financial statements detailing the information that would have been included in respect of the associated undertaking had consolidated financial statements been prepared.

6 Subsidiary undertakings can only have one parent; however, more than one parent may have a significant influence over an associated undertaking.

Review questions

29.1 Q plc has three subsidiaries: L Ltd, M Ltd, and N Ltd. All three were acquired on 1 January at the start of the financial year which has just ended. Q has a 55 per cent, 70 per cent, and 95 per cent holding respectively and holds a majority of the voting equity in L and M. It has changed the composition of both these companies' boards since they were acquired. However, despite its 95 per cent holding in N Ltd, it only has a 45 per cent holding of the voting equity and has so far failed in all its attempts to have a director appointed to the board. How should these three investee companies be treated in the Q group consolidated financial statements?

29.2 At the end of 19X5, a parent company, P plc, with one subsidiary had a holding representing 10 per cent of the equity of R Ltd, a clothing company. It had cost £80,000 when purchased at the start of 19X4. At the time of that investment, R Ltd had net assets of £560,000 which increased to £840,000 by the end of that year. At the start of the current year, the investment was increased by a further 11 per cent of the equity at a cost of £110,000.

(a) How would the investment be shown in the financial statements if it were treated as a *trade investment*?

(b) How would the investment be shown in the financial statements if it were treated as an *associated undertaking*?

29.3A Relevant balance sheets as at 31 March 19X4 are set out below:

	Jasmin (Holdings) plc £000	Kasbah plc £000	Fortran plc £000
Tangible fixed assets	289,400	91,800	7,600
Investments			
Shares in Kasbah (at cost)	97,600		
Shares in Fortran (at cost)	8,000		
	395,000		
Current assets			
Stock	285,600	151,400	2,600
Cash	319,000	500	6,800
	604,600	151,900	9,400
Creditors: amounts falling			
due within one year	289,600	238,500	2,200
Net current assets	315,000	(86,600)	7,200
Total assets less current liabilities	710,000	5,200	14,800

Capital and reserves:			
Called up share capital			
Ordinary £1 shares	60,000	20,000	10,000
10% £1 Preference shares		4,000	
Revaluation reserve	40,000		1,200
Profit and loss reserve	610,000	(18,800)	3,600
	710,000	5,200	14,800

You have recently been appointed chief accountant of Jasmin (Holdings) plc and are about to prepare the group balance sheet at 31 March 19X4. The following points are relevant to the preparation of those accounts.

(a) Jasmin (Holdings) plc owns 90 per cent of the ordinary £1 shares and 20 per cent of the 10 per cent £1 preference shares of Kasbah plc. On 1 April 19X3 Jasmin (Holdings) plc paid £96 million for the ordinary £1 shares and £1.6 million for the 10 per cent £1 preference shares when Kasbah's reserves were a credit balance of £45 million.

(b) Jasmin (Holdings) plc sells part of its output to Kasbah plc. The stock of Kasbah plc on 31 March 19X4 includes £1.2 million of stock purchased from Jasmin (Holdings) plc at cost plus one-third.

(c) The policy of the group is to revalue its tangible fixed assets on a yearly basis. However, the directors of Kasbah plc have always resisted this policy, preferring to show tangible fixed assets at historical cost. The market value of the tangible fixed assets of Kasbah plc at 31 March 19X4 is £90 million. The directors of Jasmin (Holdings) plc wish to follow the requirements of FRS 2 'Accounting for Subsidiary Undertakings' in respect of the value of tangible fixed assets to be included in the group accounts.

(d) The ordinary £1 shares of Fortran plc are split into 6 million 'A' ordinary £1 shares and 4 million 'B' ordinary £1 shares. Holders of 'A' shares are assigned 1 vote and holders of 'B' ordinary shares are assigned 2 votes per share. On 1 April 19X3 Jasmin (Holdings) plc acquired 80 per cent of the 'A' ordinary shares and 10 per cent of the 'B' ordinary shares when the profit and loss reserve of Fortran plc was £1.6 million and the revaluation reserve was £2 million. The 'A' ordinary shares and 'B' ordinary shares carry equal rights to share in the company's profit and losses.

(e) The fair values of Kasbah plc and Fortran plc were not materially different from their book values at the time of acquisition of their shares by Jasmin (Holdings) plc.

(f) Goodwill arising on acquisition is amortised over five years.

(g) Kasbah plc has paid its preference dividend for the current year but no other dividends are proposed by the group companies. The preference dividend was paid shortly after the interim results of Kasbah plc were announced and was deemed to be a legal dividend by the auditors.

(h) Because of its substantial losses during the period, the directors of Jasmin (Holdings) plc wish to exclude the financial statements of Kasbah plc from the group accounts on the grounds that Kasbah plc's output is not similar to that of Jasmin (Holdings) plc and that the resultant accounts therefore would be misleading. Jasmin (Holdings) plc produces synthetic yarn and Kasbah plc produces garments.

Required:

(a) List the conditions for exclusion of subsidiaries from consolidation for the directors of Jasmin (Holdings) plc and state whether Kasbah plc may be excluded on these grounds.

(b) Prepare a consolidated balance sheet for Jasmin (Holdings) Group plc for the year ending 31 March 19X4. (All calculations should be made to the nearest thousand pounds.)

(c) Comment briefly on the possible implications of the size of Kasbah plc's losses for the year for the group accounts and the individual accounts of Jasmin (Holdings) plc.

(*Association of Chartered Certified Accountants*)

Part 4

FINANCIAL ANALYSIS

Introduction

This part considers how accounting information is analysed and used.

30

Accounting ratios

Objectives

After you have studied this chapter, you should:

- *know of the existence of various groups of accounting ratios, where they would be used, why they would be of interest, and to whom*

- *know how to calculate a number of commonly used accounting ratios*

- *be aware of some of the difficulties that may arise in the calculation and interpretation of accounting ratios*

- *be aware of the dangers in overtrading and of how ratio analysis can be used to identify it*

30.1 Introduction

Accounting ratios and the interpretation of final accounts were introduced in Volume 1. This chapter takes that material forward, re-examining the material for reinforcement, and developing greater depth of knowledge and understanding.

Information is data organised for a purpose. Information contained in financial statements is organised so as to enable users of the financial statements to draw conclusions concerning the financial well-being and performance of the reporting entity. In the case of the financial statements of companies, independent auditors review the manner in which the data has been presented and provide a filter mechanism attesting to the reliability of the information presented. For partnerships and sole traders, there is generally no such independent review. However, as the financial statements are generally subject to review by the tax authorities, there is some justification in assuming that they are a reasonable reflection of reality.

Yet, being 'reasonably assured' of their reliability is not generally sufficient for tax authorities and they will review the financial statements of partnerships and sole traders to determine whether there may be cause to doubt their reliability. One of the key instruments at their disposal is ratios, and they use ratio analysis to compare those found in the entity under review with those typically existing in that sector of the economy. Hence, through ratio analysis, factors can be identified that would not otherwise be apparent.

Ratio analysis can also be used to review trends and compare entities with each other. A number of commercial organisations specialise in this service, providing detailed ratio analysis of the financial statements of plcs to subscribers and enabling analysts to see, at a glance, how one entity is performing, or how its financial structure compares to others of a similar nature.

Without ratios, financial statements would be largely uninformative to all but the very skilled. With ratios, financial statements can be interpreted and usefully applied to satisfy the needs of the reader.

There are, however, a vast number of parties interested in analysing financial statements – shareholders, lenders, customers, suppliers, employees, government agencies and competitors are just some of the groups who may all be interested in the financial statements of an entity. Yet, in many respects they will be interested in different things, and so there is no definitive, all-encompassing list of points for analysis that would be useful to all the groups. Nevertheless, it is possible to construct a series of ratios that together will provide all these groups with something that they will find relevant, and from which they can choose to investigate further, if necessary. Ratio analysis is a first step in assessing an entity which removes some of the mystique surrounding the financial statements and makes it easier to pinpoint items which it would be interesting to investigate further.

Exhibit 30.1 shows some of categories of ratios and indicates some of the groups that would be interested in them.

Exhibit 30.1

Ratio category	Examples of interested groups
Solvency	Shareholders, suppliers, creditors, competitors
Profitability	Shareholders, management, employees, creditors, competitors, potential investors
Efficiency	Shareholders, potential purchasers, competitors
Capital structure	Shareholders, lenders, creditors, potential investors
Shareholder	Shareholders, potential investors

30.2 Solvency

It is essential that a business is aware if a customer or borrower is at risk of not repaying the amount due. New customers are usually vetted prior to being allowed to trade on credit rather than by cash. For private individuals there are credit rating agencies with extensive records of the credit histories of many individuals. For a small fee a company can receive a report indicating whether a new customer might be a credit risk. Similarly, information can be purchased concerning companies that indicates their solvency, i.e. whether they are liable to be bad credit risks. The difference between these two sources of information is that, while the information on private individuals is based on their previous credit record, that of the companies is generally based on a ratio analysis of their financial statements. The ratio analysis will focus upon the solvency (or liquidity) ratios. Of these the best known are the current ratio and the acid test ratio.

Current ratio

This compares total current assets to total current liabilities and is intended to indicate whether there are sufficient short-term assets to meet the short-term liabilities. Traditionally, in order to provide some general guide, a value is given that may generally be taken to be the 'norm'. This has become increasingly less meaningful and is really more misleading (as it instils undue confidence) than helpful – the ratio is so sector-dependent as to be incapable of being defined as 'generally best if around x'. Consequently, no such guidance will be given here. Rather, a set of factors will be suggested that ought to be considered:

- What is the norm in this industrial sector?
- Is this company significantly above or below that norm?
- If so, can this be justified after an analysis of the nature of these assets and liabilities, and of the reasons for the amounts of each held?

The ratio when calculated may be expressed as either a ratio to 1, with current liabilities being set to 1, or as a 'number of times', representing the relative size of the amount of total current assets compared with total current liabilities.

Example

If total current assets are £40,000 and total current liabilities are £20,000, the current ratio could be expressed as either:

$$£40,000:£20,000 \quad = 2:1$$

or as:

$$\frac{£40,000}{£20,000} \quad = 2 \text{ times}$$

Acid test ratio

As with the current ratio, there is little benefit in suggesting a norm for the value to expect. The only difference in the items involved between the two ratios is that the acid test (or 'quick') ratio does not include stock. Otherwise, it is identical to the current ratio, comparing current assets, excluding stock, to current liabilities. Stock is omitted as it is considered to be relatively illiquid, because it depends upon prevailing and future market forces and may be impossible to convert to cash in a relatively short time.

Many companies operate with acid test ratios below 1:1. That is, they have insufficient liquid assets to meet their short-term liabilities. The great majority of companies in this situation have no problem paying their creditors when due. Consideration of a simple example should explain how this is possible.

Example

If total current assets, including stock of £22,000, are worth £40,000 and total current liabilities stand at £20,000, the acid test ratio will be £18,000:£20,000 = 0.9:1 (or 0.9 times). This means that at the balance sheet date, had all current liabilities been due for payment, it would not have been possible to do so without converting some assets (e.g. stock, or fixed assets) into cash that were likely to only be convertible into cash at a discount on their true value – that is, the company would have had to pay a premium in order to meet its obligations, and would not be able to continue to do so indefinitely.

However, the reality is generally that the current liabilities are due for payment at varying times over the coming financial period and some, for example a bank overdraft, may not, in reality, ever be likely to be subject to a demand for repayment.

The current assets, on the other hand, are within the control of the company and can be adjusted in their timing to match the due dates for payment to creditors. They can be renewed many times before one or other of the current liabilities is due for payment. For example, debtors may be on a ten-day cycle while trade creditors are paid after 90 days' credit has expired. Clearly, in this case, receipts from nine times the balance sheet debtors' figure could be received and available to meet the trade creditor figure shown in the balance sheet.

As with the current ratio, when calculated, the acid test ratio should be compared to the norms for the industrial sector, and then the underlying assets and liabilities should be considered to determine whether there is any cause for concern in the result obtained.

30.3 Profitability

These measures indicate whether the company is performing satisfactorily. They are used, among other things, to measure the performance of management, to identify whether a company may be a worthwhile investment opportunity, and to determine a company's performance relative to its competitors.

There are a large number of these ratios. Some of the most commonly used are:

Gross profit:Sales

If gross profit is £120,000 and sales are £480,000, the ratio would be 25 per cent. (This should not be confused with the gross margin:cost of sales ratio which compares the gross profit to the cost of sales which, in this case, would have a value of 33.33 per cent.)

Net profit after tax:Sales

If net profit is £38,400 and sales are £480,000, the ratio would be 8 per cent. It indicates how much safety there is in the price, i.e. current prices could be reduced by up to 8 per cent without causing the company to make a loss. Of course, it is much more complex than this. As any student of economics knows only too well, if a commodity's price falls, generally demand for it rises. This could result in costs increasing (if unexpected demand has to be met in a hurry) or falling (as bulk discounts become available that were not previously obtainable due to the lower level of demand). Nevertheless, as a general guide, it is a sensible indicator of safety, as well as an indicator of success.

While a high value for this ratio may suggest successful performance, it is not always the case. It is possible for selling prices to be so high that demand is reduced causing overall profitability to be significantly lower than it could be were a lower price being used. In this circumstance, the ratio would produce a high percentage, but performance would certainly not be as good as it ought to have been.

Return on capital employed

This is one of the more awkward ratios to deal with. Unlike the current ratio, for example, there is no widely agreed definition of return on capital employed (ROCE). Hence, care must be taken when comparing this ratio as calculated for one company and as reported for another. Use of financial analysis bureaux that use the same formula to calculate the ratios of all the companies they consider is one way around this difficulty. Another is to ensure that the formula used by the companies being compared against is known and, where necessary, the result is revised to bring it into line with the internally calculated ratio.

The ratio compares the profit earned (usually before interest and tax) to the funds used to generate that return (often the total of shareholders' funds at the beginning of the accounting period plus long-term creditors – most simply defined as total assets minus current liabilities). Were the profit before interest and tax £40,000 and the opening capital employed shown in the balance sheet £800,000, the return on capital employed would be 5 per cent. In theory, the higher the ratio, the more profitably the resources of the company have been used.

Return on share capital

As with ROCE, there are a number of different ways in which this may be calculated.

One is the comparison of profit on ordinary activities before tax with share capital and reserves. For example, if profit on ordinary activities before tax were £40,000 and the share capital and reserves at the start of the accounting period £720,000, the return on share capital (ROSC) would be 5.56 per cent. In theory, the higher the ratio, the more profitably the shareholders' investment in the company has been used, and it is often used to compare performance between accounting periods, rather than to draw comparison with the ROSC of other companies.

Net profit after tax:Total assets

Net profit after tax is compared to the total of all assets other than current assets, plus working capital (i.e. current assets less current liabilities). If working capital is £20,000 and all non-current assets total £820,000, total assets are £840,000. If net profit after tax is £30,000, the ratio is £30,000/£840,000, i.e. 3.57 per cent.

There are problems with the integrity of this ratio – some items of expenditure that are relevant, e.g. interest on debentures, will have been charged against the profit in arriving at the figure for profit after tax. Strictly speaking, these other payments to investors and creditors ought to be reviewed and included in the profit figure used in the ratio, otherwise the profit may be significantly understated, giving a less healthy view than would be appropriate to present.

Intangible assets, e.g. goodwill, are included in the value of total assets used in the ratio. However, many would argue that this is inappropriate as there is not an agreed view on how such assets should be valued, thus inter-company comparisons may be difficult.

Net operating profit:Operating assets

This is an alternative to *Net profit after tax:Total assets*. It takes the net profit before interest, taxes and dividends, and before inclusion of any investment income. This is then compared with the assets other than intangibles and investments outside the company. Working capital would be included, but bank overdrafts would be excluded from the current liabilities on the basis that they are not generally short-term in nature. If net operating profit before interest, tax and dividends is £36,000, tangible fixed assets excluding investments made outside the company are £600,000, working capital is £20,000, and there is a bank overdraft of £5,000, the ratio is:

$$\frac{£36,000}{£625,000} = 5.76\%$$

30.4 Efficiency ratios

Profitability is affected by the way that the assets of a business are used. If plant and machinery are only used for a few hours a day, the business is failing to utilise these assets efficiently. This may be because there is limited demand for the product produced. It could be due to the business restricting supply in order to maximise profitability per unit produced. On the other hand, it could be that there is a shortage of skilled labour and that there is no one to operate the plant and machinery the rest of the time. Alternatively, it could be that the plant and machinery is unreliable, breaking down a lot, and that the limited level of use is a precautionary measure designed to ensure that production targets are met.

In common with all accounting ratios, it is important that the results of efficiency ratio computations are not treated as definitively good or bad. They must be investigated further through consideration both of the underlying variables in the ratios, and of the broader context of the business and its relation to the industrial sector in which it operates.

These ratios include the following.

Asset turnover

This is a measure of how effectively the assets are being used to generate sales. It is one of the ratios that would be considered when interpreting the results of profitability ratio analyses like ROCE, but is of sufficient importance to be calculated and analysed irrespective of that fact. The calculation involves dividing sales by total assets less current liabilities.

As a general guide, where a company's asset turnover is significantly lower than those of its competitors, it suggests there may be over-investment in assets which could, in turn, make it vulnerable to takeover from a company interested in selling off any surplus assets while otherwise retaining the business in its current form. However, considerable care must be taken when interpreting this ratio: the assets may be much newer than those of other companies; the company may use a lower rate of depreciation than its competitors; or the company may purchase its plant and machinery, whereas the industry norm is to lease them. On the other side of the ratio, the result may be high because selling prices are being suppressed in order to maximise volume.

Stock turnover

Included in virtually every case where accounting ratios are being calculated, this measures the number of times (approximately) that stock is replenished in an accounting period. If stock is £100,000 and cost of sales are £800,000, the stock turnover ratio would be 8 times. The ratio can also be expressed as a number of days – the number of days stock held. In this example, 365 would be divided by 8 producing a result of 45.6 days.

There are two major difficulties in computing this ratio: if cost of sales is not available, it is tempting to use sales instead. This should not be done. Sales are expressed at selling prices; stock is expressed at cost price. Use of sales instead of cost of sales in the equation will not be comparing like with like.

In addition, there are at least three possible stock values that could be used – opening, closing and the average of these figures. The average figure would be the more commonly used, but use of any of the three can be justified.

Whichever approach is taken, the result will, at best, be a crude estimate. Due to seasonality of the business, stock, as shown in the balance sheet for example, may not be representative of the 'normal' level of stock. However, it is still useful for comparing trends over time and should be used mainly for that purpose. The result it produces needs careful consideration. A rising stock turnover may indicate greater efficiency, or it may be an indicator that stocks are being run down and that there may be problems in meeting demand in future. A falling stock turnover may indicate lower efficiency, perhaps with a build-up of obsolete stocks, or it could indicate higher stock volumes are being held because stock purchasing has become more efficient and the higher stock levels are financially beneficial for the company. In addition, it is important not to overlook that any change in the ratio may have nothing to do with the stock, but be due to changes in factors relating to the sales for the period.

Debtor days

This indicates how efficient the company is at controlling its debtors. If debtors are £50,000 and sales £800,000, debtors are taking, on average, 22.8 days credit, i.e.

$$\frac{£50,000}{£800,000} \times 365 = 22.8$$

Strictly speaking, the two figures are not comparable. Debtors include the VAT on sales; the figure for sales excludes VAT. However, the adjustment is not difficult to make if required for clarity.

As with stock, the amount shown in the balance sheet for debtors may not be representative of the 'normal' level. Nevertheless, this is generally a very useful ratio to calculate and comparison with those of other companies in the same industrial sector may be very interesting. However, as with stock turnover, its strength lies in trend analysis between periods.

Creditor days

This ratio indicates how the company uses short-term financing to fund its activities and further investigation will reveal whether or not the result is due to efficiency. It is calculated by dividing creditors by purchases, and multiplying the result by 365. The purchases figure is not usually available in published financial statements, and the cost of sales amount would be used in its place. As with stock turnover and debtor days, its strength lies in trend analysis between periods.

30.5 Capital structure ratios

There are a number of ratios that can be used to assess the way in which a company finances its activities. One, creditor days, was referred to in the last section. The ratios discussed in this section differ in that they are longer-term in nature, being more concerned with the strategic rather than the operational level of corporate decision making. Some of the more commonly analysed ratios of this type are described below.

Net worth:Total assets

This ratio indicates the proportion of fixed and current assets that are financed by net worth (the total of shareholders' funds, i.e. share capital plus reserves). If fixed assets are shown at a value of £500,000, current assets £100,000 and net worth is £300,000, 50 per cent of total assets are financed by shareholders' funds. As with many accounting ratios, it is the trend in this ratio between periods that is important.

Fixed assets:Net worth

This ratio focuses on the longer-term aspects of the net worth:total assets ratio. By matching long-term investment with long-term finance it is possible to determine whether borrowing has been used to finance some long-term investment in assets. Where this has occurred, there may be a problem when the borrowing is to be repaid (as the fixed assets it was used to acquire cannot be readily converted into cash). Again, this ratio is of most use when the trend over time is analysed.

Fixed assets:Net worth + Long-term liabilities

This ratio focuses on whether sufficient long-term finance has been obtained to meet the investment in fixed assets.

Debt ratio

This ratio compares the total debts to total assets and is concerned with whether the company has sufficient assets to meet all its liabilities when due. For example, if total liabilities are £150,000 and total assets are £600,000, the debts represent 25 per cent of total assets. Whether this is good or bad will, as with all accounting ratios, depend upon the norm for the industrial sector in which the company operates and on the underlying items within the figures included in the ratio.

Capital gearing ratio

This ratio provides the proportion of a company's total capital that has a prior claim to profits over those of ordinary shareholders. Prior claim (or prior charge) capital includes debentures and preference share capital and is any capital carrying a right to a fixed return. Total capital includes ordinary share capital and reserves, prior charge capital, and long-term liabilities.

Debt:Equity ratio

This is the ratio of prior charge capital to ordinary share capital and reserves.

Borrowing:Net worth

This ratio indicates the proportion that borrowing represents of a company's net worth. If long-term liabilities are £100,000 and current liabilities are £50,000, total borrowing is £150,000. If net worth is £300,000, the ratio is 1:2, or 50 per cent.

This and the *debt:equity ratio* indicate the degree of risk to investors in ordinary shares in a company. The higher these ratios are, the greater the possibility of risk to ordinary shareholders – both in respect of expectations of future dividends (especially in times of depressed performance where much of the profits may be paid to the holders of prior charge capital), and from the threat of liquidation should there be a slump in performance that leads to a failure to meet payments to holders of prior charge capital. Whether these risks may be relevant can be investigated by reference to the next ratio.

Interest cover

This ratio shows whether enough profits are being earned to meet interest payments when due. It is calculated by dividing profit before interest and tax by the interest charges. Thus, the interest cover is 20 times if profit before interest and tax is £400,000 and the total interest charges are £20,000. In this case, there would be little cause for immediate concern that there was any risk of the company failing to meet its interest charges when due. However, just because a company is making profits does not guarantee that there will be sufficient cash available to make the interest charge payments when due.

30.6 Shareholder ratios

These ratios are those most commonly used by anyone interested in an investment in a company. They indicate how well a company is performing in relation to the price of its shares and other related items including dividends and number of shares in issue. The ratios usually calculated are described below.

Dividend yield

This measures the real rate of return by comparing the dividend paid to the market price of a share. It is calculated as:

$$\frac{\text{Gross dividend per share}}{\text{Market price per share}}$$

Earnings per share (EPS)

This is the most frequently used of all the accounting ratios and is generally felt to give the best view of performance. It indicates how much of a company's profit can be attributed to each ordinary share in the company. In an amendment to the origoinal accounting standard on this topic (SSAP 3) FRS 3 (*Reporting financial performance*) defined earnings per share as:

$$\frac{\text{Earnings after tax, minority interests and extraordinary items available for equity shareholders}}{\text{Number of equity shares in issue and ranking for dividend in the period}}$$

FRS 14 (*Earnings per share*) simplified the formula, but not the figures to be used, to:

$$\frac{\text{Net profit or loss attributable to ordinary shareholders}}{\text{The weighted average number of ordinary shares outstanding during the period}}$$

Dividend cover

This compares the amount of profit earned per ordinary share with the amount of dividend paid, thereby showing the proportion of profits that could have been distributed and were. It differs from EPS only in having a different denominator. The formula is:

$$\frac{\text{Net profit or loss attributable to ordinary shareholders}}{\text{Net dividend on ordinary shares}}$$

Price earnings (P/E) ratio

This relates the earnings per share to the market price of the shares. It is calculated by:

$$\frac{\text{Market price}}{\text{Earnings per share}}$$

and is a useful indicator of how the stock market assesses the company. It is also very useful when a company proposes an issue of new shares, in that it enables potential investors to better assess whether the expected future earnings make the share a worthwhile investment.

30.7 Overtrading

A very high proportion of new businesses fail within the first two years of trading. This can occur because there was insufficient demand for the goods or service provided, because of poor management, or a number of other reasons of which possibly the most common to arise would be **overtrading**. However, unlike the other common causes of business failure, overtrading often arises when a business is performing profitably. Furthermore, despite the introduction to this paragraph referring to 'new' businesses, overtrading can just as easily affect established businesses.

Overtrading occurs when there is insufficient control over working capital resulting in there being insufficient liquid funds to meet the demands of creditors. As the cash dries up, so do the sources of supply of raw materials and other essential inputs – they will not continue to supply a business that fails to settle its bills when due. Overtrading is generally the result of sales growth being at too fast a rate in relation to the level of trade debtors, trade creditors and stock.

Take an example where, over a twelve-month period, profits increased by 20 per cent, sales doubled from £1 million to £2 million, trade debtors doubled from £80,000 to £160,000, trade creditors quadrupled from £60,000 to £240,000, stock quadrupled from £50,000 to £200,000, and the bank balance moved from positive £20,000 to an overdraft of £80,000. No changes occurred during the period in long-term financing of the business, though £100,000 was spent on some new equipment needed as a result of the expansion.

Working capital was 2.5:1; now it is 1.125:1 and the acid test ratio is now 0.5:1 from 1.67:1. Liquidity appears to have deteriorated significantly (but may have been high previously compared to other businesses in the same sector). Debtor days are unchanged (as the ratio of sales to debtors is unaltered). However, creditor days have probably doubled (subject to a slight reduction due to some cheaper purchasing costs as a result of the higher volumes involved). If the bank overdraft is currently at its limit, the business would be unable to meet any requests from creditors for immediate payment, never mind pay wages and other regular expenses.

This situation can be addressed by raising long-term finance, or by cutting-back on the expansion – clearly, the first option is likely to be the more attractive one to the business.

Signals suggesting overtrading include:

- significant increases in the volume of sales;
- lower profit margins;
- deteriorating debtor, creditor and stock turnover ratios;
- increasing reliance on short-term finance.

30.8 Summary of ratios

Ratio category   *Formula*

Solvency

Current ratio

$$\frac{\text{Current assets}}{\text{Current liabilities}}$$

Acid test ratio

$$\frac{\text{Current assets} - \text{Stock}}{\text{Current liabilities}}$$

Profitability

Gross profit:Sales

$$\frac{\text{Gross profit}}{\text{Sales}}$$

Net profit after tax:Sales

$$\frac{\text{Net profit after tax}}{\text{Sales}}$$

Return on capital employed

$$\frac{\text{Profit before interest and tax}}{\text{Total assets} - \text{Current liabilities}}$$

Return on share capital

$$\frac{\text{Profit before tax}}{\text{Share capital + Reserves}}$$

Net profit after tax:Total assets

$$\frac{\text{Net profit after tax}}{\text{Fixed and other non-current assets + Working capital}}$$

Net operating profit:Operating assets

$$\frac{\text{Net profit before interest, tax, dividends, and investment income}}{\text{Tangible fixed assets – Outside investments + Working capital + Bank overdraft}}$$

Efficiency

Asset turnover

$$\frac{\text{Sales}}{\text{Total assets – Current liabilities}}$$

Stock turnover

$$\frac{\text{Cost of goods sold}}{\text{Average stock}}$$

Debtor days

$$\frac{\text{Debtors}}{\text{Sales}} \times 365$$

Creditor days

$$\frac{\text{Creditors}}{\text{Purchases}} \times 365$$

Capital structure

Net worth:Total assets

$$\frac{\text{Shareholders' funds}}{\text{Total assets}}$$

Fixed assets:Net worth

$$\frac{\text{Fixed assets}}{\text{Shareholders' funds}}$$

Fixed assets:Net worth + Long-term liabilities

$$\frac{\text{Fixed assets}}{\text{Shareholders' funds + Long-term liabilities}}$$

Debt ratio

$$\frac{\text{Total liabilities}}{\text{Total assets}}$$

Capital gearing ratio

$$\frac{\text{Prior charge capital}}{\text{Total capital}}$$

Debt:Equity ratio

$$\frac{\text{Prior charge capital}}{\text{Ordinary share capital and reserves}}$$

Borrowing:Net worth

$$\frac{\text{Total borrowing}}{\text{Shareholders' funds}}$$

Interest cover

$$\frac{\text{Profit before interest and tax}}{\text{Interest charges}}$$

Shareholder ratios

Dividend yield

$$\frac{\text{Gross dividend per share}}{\text{Market price per share}}$$

Earnings per share

$$\frac{\text{Net profit or loss attributable to ordinary shareholders}}{\text{Weighted average number of ordinary shares outstanding during the period}}$$

Dividend cover

$$\frac{\text{Net profit or loss attributable to ordinary shareholders}}{\text{Net dividend on ordinary shares}}$$

Price earnings ratio

$$\frac{\text{Market price}}{\text{Earnings per share}}$$

Main points to remember

1 There are many different categories of accounting ratios and many different ratios within each category.

2 Ratios that are of interest to one group of readers of financial statements may not be of interest to another.

3 Ratios may be used in order to review reliability of financial statements.

4 Ratios may be used to review trends between periods for the same company.

5 Ratios may be used to compare a company to others in the same industrial sector.

6 Some ratios are in wide use for which there is no agreed 'correct' formula to calculate them. This makes comparison between analysis reported elsewhere of limited value unless the formula used can be identified.

7 The ratios derived can be misleading if taken at face value. It is essential that they are placed in context and that interpretation goes beyond a superficial comparison to general norms.

8 Used casually, accounting ratios can mislead and result in poor quality decision making.

9 Used carefully, accounting ratios can provide pointers towards areas of interest in an entity, and provide a far more complete picture of an entity than that given by the financial statements.

10 Overtrading can be financially disastrous for a business and ratios can be used to help detect it.

Review questions

30.1 Five categories of accounting ratios are described in this chapter. What are they?

30.2A Why should different groups of people be interested in different categories of accounting ratios?

30.3 Describe two ratios from each of the five groups of ratios, including how to calculate them.

30.4A What is the purpose in using each of the following ratios:

(a) current ratio;
(b) net profit after tax:sales;
(c) asset turnover;
(d) interest cover;
(e) dividend cover?

30.5 If you wished to assess the efficiency of a company, which of these ratios would you use:

(a) stock turnover;
(b) interest cover;
(c) return on capital employed;
(d) acid test ratio;
(e) dividend yield?

30.6A A company has capital of 1 million ordinary shares of £1 each. It pays a dividend of 6 per cent out of its profits after tax of £480,000 on sales of £4 million. The market price of the shares is £2.40. What is the:

(a) net profit after tax:sales;
(b) dividend yield;
(c) earnings per share;
(d) price earnings ratio?

30.7 In respect of each of the following events, select all the effects resulting from that event that are shown in the list of effects:

(i)   a bad debt written-off;
(ii) an increase in the bank overdraft;
(iii) a purchase of six months' stock;
(iv) payment of all amounts due to trade creditors that had been outstanding for longer than 90 days;
(v)   an offer of 5 per cent discount to all customers who settle their accounts within two weeks.

List of effects
(a) increased current ratio
(b) reduced current ratio
(c) increased acid test ratio
(d) reduced acid test ratio

30.8A Using the following balance sheet and profit and loss accounts, calculate and comment on ten accounting ratios (ignore taxation):

Balance Sheet as at 31 December 19X1 (£000s)

Fixed Assets			
Equipment at cost			6,000
Less Depreciation to date			2,000
			4,000
Current assets			
Stock		600	
Debtors		60	
Bank		–	
		660	
Less Current liabilities			
Creditors	90		
Dividends payable	80		
Bank overdraft	450		
		620	
			40
			4,040
Long-term liabilities			
10% debentures			500
			3,540
Financed by			
Share capital – £1 ordinary shares			2,000
Reserves			
General reserve			800
Profit and loss account			740
			3,540

Profit and Loss Account for period ending 31 December 19X1 (£000s)

Sales		8,000
Less Cost of sales		
Opening stock	500	
Add Purchases	1,300	
	1,800	
Less Closing stock	600	
		1,200
		6,800
Gross profit		
Less Depreciation	800	
Other expenses	5,500	
		6,300
Net operating profit		500
Less Debenture interest		50
Net profit		450
Add Balance b/f		490
		940
Less Appropriations		
General reserve	120	
Dividend	80	
		200
		740

30.9 You are to study the following financial statements for two similar types of retail store and then answer the questions which follow.

Summary of Financial Statements

Trading and Profit and Loss Account	A £	A £	B £	B £
Sales		80,000		120,000
Less Cost of goods sold				
Opening stock	25,000		22,500	
Add Purchases	50,000		91,000	
	75,000		113,500	
Less Closing stock	15,000	60,000	17,500	96,000
Gross profit		20,000		24,000
Less Depreciation	1,000		3,000	
Other expenses	9,000	10,000	6,000	9,000
Net profit		10,000		15,000

Balance sheets	A	A	B	B
Fixed assets				
Equipment at cost	10,000		20,000	
Less Depreciation to date	8,000	2,000	6,000	14,000
Current assets				
Stock	15,000		17,500	
Debtors	25,000		20,000	
Bank	5,000		2,500	
	45,000		40,000	
Less Current liabilities				
Creditors	5,000	40,000	10,000	30,000
		42,000		44,000

Financed by:
Capitals

Balance at start of year	38,000	36,000
Add Net profit	10,000	15,000
	48,000	51,000
Less Drawings	6,000	7,000
	42,000	44,000

Required:

(*a*) Calculate the following ratios:

    (*i*) gross profit as percentage of sales;   (*vi*) current ratio;
    (*ii*) net profit as percentage of sales;   (*vii*) acid test ratio;
    (*iii*) expenses as percentage of sales;   (*viii*) debtor:sales ratio;
    (*iv*) stockturn;   (*ix*) creditor:purchases ratio.
    (*v*) rate of return of net profit on capital
        employed (use the average of the
        capital account for this purpose);

(*b*) Drawing upon all your knowledge of accounting, comment upon the differences and similarities of the accounting ratios for *A* and *B*. Which business seems to be the most efficient? Give possible reasons.

30.10A Study the following accounts of two companies and then answer the questions which follow. Both companies are stores selling textile goods.

Trading and Profit and Loss Accounts

	R Ltd		T Ltd	
	£	£	£	£
Sales		250,000		160,000
Less Cost of goods sold				
Opening stock	90,000		30,000	
Add Purchases	210,000		120,000	
	300,000		150,000	
Less Closing stock	110,000	190,000	50,000	100,000
Gross profit		60,000		60,000
Less Expenses				
Wages and salaries	14,000		10,000	
Directors' remuneration	10,000		10,000	
Other expenses	11,000	35,000	8,000	28,000
Net profit		25,000		32,000
Add Balance from last year		15,000		8,000
		40,000		40,000
Less Appropriations				
General reserve	2,000		2,000	
Dividend	25,000	27,000	20,000	22,000
Balance carried to next year		13,000		18,000

Balance Sheets

	R Ltd		T Ltd	
Fixed assets				
Equipment at cost	20,000		5,000	
Less Depreciation to date	8,000	12,000	2,000	3,000
Motor lorries	30,000		20,000	
Less Depreciation to date	12,000	18,000	7,000	13,000
		30,000		16,000

Current assets				
Stock	110,000		50,000	
Debtors	62,500		20,000	
Bank	7,500		10,000	
	180,000		80,000	
Less Current liabilities				
Creditors	90,000		16,000	
		90,000		64,000
		120,000		80,000
Financed by				
Issued share capital		100,000		50,000
Reserves				
General reserve	7,000		12,000	
Profit and loss	13,000	20,000	18,000	30,000
		120,000		80,000

Required:

(a) Calculate the following ratios for each of R Ltd and T Ltd:

(*i*)   gross profit as percentage of sales;
(*ii*) net profit as percentage of sales;
(*iii*) expenses as percentage of sales;
(*iv*) stockturn;
(*v*)   rate of return of net profit on capital employed (for the purpose of this question only, take capital as being total of share capitals + reserves at the balance sheet date);

(*vi*)   current ratio;
(*vii*) acid test ratio;
(*viii*) debtor:sales ratio;
(*ix*)   creditor:purchases ratio.

(b) Comment briefly on the comparison of each ratio as between the two companies. State which company appears to be the most efficient, giving what you consider to be possible reasons.

30.11 The directors of L Ltd appointed a new sales manager towards the end of 19X2. This manager devised a plan to increase sales and profit by means of a reduction in selling price and extended credit terms to customers. This involved considerable investment in new machinery early in 19X3 in order to meet the demand which the change in sales policy had created.

The financial statements for the years ended 31 December 19X2 and 19X3 are shown below. The sales manager has argued that the new policy has been a resounding success because sales and, more importantly, profits have increased dramatically.

Profit and loss accounts	19X2	19X3
	£000	£000
Sales	900	2,800
Cost of sales	(360)	(1,680)
Gross profit	540	1,120
Selling expenses	(150)	(270)
Bad debts	(18)	(140)
Depreciation	(58)	(208)
Interest	(12)	(192)
Net profit	302	310
Balance b/fwd	327	629
	629	939

Balance sheets		*19X2*		*19X3*	
	£000	£000	£000	£000	
Fixed assets:					
Factory		450		441	
Machinery		490		1,791	
		940		2,232	
Current assets:					
Stock	30		238		
Debtors	83		583		
Bank	12				
	125		821		
Current liabilities:					
Creditors	(36)		(175)		
Bank			(11)		
	(36)		(186)		
Current assets *less* Current liabilities		89		635	
		1,029		2,867	
Borrowings		(100)		(1,600)	
		929		1,267	
Share capital		300		328	
Profit and loss		629		939	
		929		1,267	

(a) **You are required to** explain whether you believe that the performance for the year ended 31 December 19X3 and the financial position at that date have improved as a result of the new policies adopted by the company. You should support your answer with appropriate ratios.

(b) All of L Ltd's sales are on credit. The finance director has asked you to calculate the immediate financial impact of reducing the credit period offered to customers. Calculate the amount of cash which would be released if the company could impose a collection period of 45 days.

(*Chartered Institute of Management Accountants*)

31

Interpretation of financial statements

Objectives

After you have studied this chapter, you should:

- *be aware of the importance of trend analysis when analysing financial statements*

- *appreciate that there is no such thing as a generally 'good' or 'bad' value for any ratio*

- *be aware of the need to compare 'like with like' if attempting to assess the quality of the result found from ratio analysis*

- *appreciate the existence of a pyramid of ratios that can be used in order to enhance the view obtained from ratio analysis*

- *be aware that different groups of users of financial statements have access to different sources of information that may help in developing an understanding of and explanation for the results of ratio analysis*

31.1 Introduction

When shareholders receive the annual financial statements of a business, many simply look to see whether it has made a profit, and then put the document away. They are aware of only one thing – that the company made a profit of £x. They do not know if it was a 'good' profit. Nor do they know whether it was any different from the profit earned in previous years. (Even if they had noticed the previous period's profit figure in the comparative column, they would be unaware of the equivalent figures for the periods that preceded it.) In addition, they would have no perception of how the performance compared to those of other companies operating in the same sector.

In order that performance within a period can be assessed, ratio analysis may be undertaken, as explained in Chapter 30. However, such analysis is relatively useless unless a similar task is undertaken on the financial figures for previous periods. Trend analysis is very important in the interpretation of financial statements, for it is only then that the relative position can be identified, i.e. whether things are improving, etc.

Of similar importance if financial statements are to be usefully interpreted is comparison of the position shown with that of other companies operating in the same sector.

31.2 Sector relevance

The importance of ensuring that any comparison of analysis between companies is between companies in the same sector can best be illustrated through an extreme example – that of the contrast between service companies and manufacturing companies.

Stating the obvious, a firm of consultants that advise their clients on marketing strategies will have far fewer tangible assets than a company with the same turnover which manufactures forklift trucks. The service industry will need premises, but these could easily be rented, and in addition would need very little in the way of machinery. Some computer equipment and office equipment as well as motor cars would be all that would be needed.

Compared with the service industry firm, a manufacturing company, such as that making forklift trucks, would need a great deal of machinery as well as motor lorries and various types of buildings and so on. The manufacturing firm would also have stocks of materials and unsold trucks. The service firm would have very little in the way of stocks of tangible assets.

Especially with the service industries it is also likely that the number of people working for the firm, but who do most, sometimes all, of their work in their homes will grow apace. The need for people to turn up at offices at given times every day is falling dramatically with the wider use of computers and various communication and link-up devices.

All of this has an effect on the ratios of performance calculated from the accounts of manufacturers and service industry firms. The figure of return on capital employed for a service firm, simply because of the few tangible assets needed, may appear to be quite high. For a manufacturing firm the opposite may well be the case.

If this distinction between these completely different types of organisation is understood, then the interpreter of the accounts will judge them accordingly. Failure to understand the distinction will bring forth some very strange conclusions.

31.3 Trend analysis

What is important for a business is not just what the accounting ratios are for one year, but what the trend has been. In *Business Accounting 1*, the example was introduced of two companies G and H. The example is now reintroduced and further developed: Exhibit 31.1 presents four ratios derived from the financial statements of G over the past five periods.

Exhibit 31.1

Period:	X1	X2	X3	X4	X5 (*now*)
Gross profit as % of sales	40	38	36	35	34
Net profit as % of sales	15	13	12	12	11
Net profit as % of capital employed	13	12	11	11	10
Current ratio	3.0	2.8	2.6	2.3	2.0

If the trends in these four ratios are considered, it is clear that they are all deteriorating, but there is no indication whether there should be cause for concern as a result. For example, the industry may be becoming more competitive, causing margins to shrink, and the falling current ratio may be due to an increase in efficiency over the control of working capital.

A company with this trend of figures could state that these were the reasons for the decline in margins and for the reduction in liquidity. A reader of the financial statements could then accept the explanation and put the calculations away. However, there is no guarantee that an explanation of this kind actually indicates a beneficial situation, whether or not it is accurate. In order to gain a fuller view of the company, comparison with other comparable companies in the same sector is needed. Exhibit 31.2 presents the information from Exhibit 31.1 for company G plus information on another company of similar size operating in the same sector, company H.

Exhibit 31.2

Period:		X1	X2	X3	X4	X5 (now)
Gross profit as % of sales	G	40	38	36	35	34
	H	30	32	33	33	34
Net profit as % of sales	G	15	13	12	12	11
	H	10	10	10	11	11
Net profit as % of capital employed	G	13	12	11	11	10
	H	8	8	9	9	10
Current ratio	G	3.0	2.8	2.6	2.3	2.0
	H	1.5	1.7	1.9	1.9	2.0

Another way in which these results may be compared is through graphs, as shown by the example in Exhibit 31.3 which compares the trend in gross profit as a percentage of sales of the two companies. (Note that the vertical axis does not show the percentage below 30 as there is no percentage below that amount. Omitting the lower figures on the graph allows for a more informative display of the information.)

Exhibit 31.3

The trend of gross profit as a percentage of sales

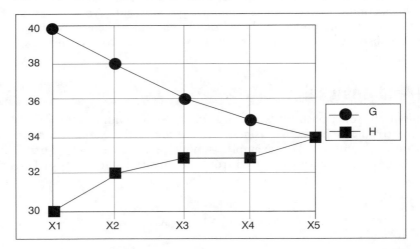

The companies have identical ratios for the current period – does that make them equally desirable as investments? Given one year's accounts it appears so, but the five-year trend analysis reveals a different picture.

From these figures, G appears to be the worse investment for the future, as the trend for it appears to be downwards, while that of H is upwards. It suggests that the explanation made earlier for the falling margins may not be valid. If the trend for G is continued it could be in a very dangerous financial situation in a year or two. H, on the other hand, is strengthening its position all the time.

While it would be ridiculous to assert that H will continue on an upward trend, or that

G will continue downwards, a consistent trend of this type does suggest that the situation may well continue into the foreseeable future. It is certainly cause for further investigation.

31.4 Comparisons over time

As shown in the previous section, one of the best ways of using ratios is to compare them with the ratios for the same organisation in respect of previous years. Take another example, the net profit percentage of a company for the past six years, including the current year 19X8:

	19X3	*19X4*	*19X5*	*19X6*	*19X7*	*19X8* *(now)*
Net profit %	5.4	5.2	4.7	4.8	4.8	4.5

This could be graphed as in Exhibit 31.4.

Exhibit 31.4

It is obvious that there is a long-term decline in net profit percentage. This prompts us to examine why this should be so. Without measuring against past years our understanding of the direction in which the business seems to be heading would be much diminished.

We would not look only at the long-term changes in net profit percentages, but would also compare similar long-term figures in relation to other aspects of the business.

In considering trends, problems may arise from the use of the historical cost accounting concept during a period of significant price increases because of inflation.

31.5 Comparisons with other businesses

No one can say in isolation that a firm is 'very profitable'. It could be the case that it has made £6 million a year, which to most people may seem profitable. On the other hand, if firms of a similar size in the same type of industry are making £20 million a year, then the firm making £6 million cannot be said to be 'very profitable'.

Ideally we would like to be able to compare the results of one firm with those of other similar firms in the same sort of industry. Then, and only then, would we really be able to judge how well, or how badly, it was doing.

The size of firm can have an important effect upon ratios. Just as we would not try to compare a chemist's shop with a building firm, it would also be wrong to judge a small supermarket against Sainsbury's, which owns hundreds of supermarkets.

Interfirm comparisons are also sometimes misleading because of the different accounting treatment of various items, and the location and ages of assets. Some industries have, however, set up interfirm comparisons with guidelines to the companies to ensure that the figures have been constructed using the same bases so that the information is properly comparable. The information does not disclose data which can be traced to any one firm, ensuring that full confidentiality is observed.

The information available may take the form shown in Exhibit 31.5.

Exhibit 31.5

Published ratios for the widget industry (extract)

	Solvency		Efficiency			
	Current	*Acid test*	*Asset T/O*	*Stock T/O*	*Debtor days*	*Creditor days*
19X6	2.4	0.7	5.4	8.2	56.4	80.4
19X7	2.2	0.8	5.7	9.3	52.6	66.8

The equivalent figures for the company being assessed can then be tabulated alongside the industry figures to enable comparisons to be made, as in Exhibit 31.6.

Exhibit 31.6

	Company ratios		Industry ratios	
	19X6	*19X7*	*19X6*	*19X7*
Current ratio	2.9	2.8	2.4	2.2
Acid test ratio	0.5	0.6	0.7	0.8
Asset turnover	5.2	5.3	5.4	5.7
Stock turnover	4.4	4.7	8.2	9.3
Debtor days	65.9	65.2	56.4	52.6
Creditor days	58.3	56.8	80.4	66.8

The financial status of the company is now much clearer. What appeared to be a situation of improving liquidity and efficiency is now clearly shown to be an increasingly poorer liquidity and efficiency position compared to the industry as a whole.

However, it should be borne in mind that the industry figures probably include many companies that are either much larger or much smaller than the company being assessed. To obtain a more complete picture, information is needed concerning companies of a similar size, such as in the comparison between G and H earlier in this chapter (section 31.3). This information may be available from the source of the interfirm comparison. If not, other sources would need to be used, for example the published financial statements of appropriate companies.

The other information missing from the above comparison is data from previous periods. While not so relevant to the current position, it can be useful in explaining why a situation has developed, and in determining whether the current position is likely to persist into the future.

31.6 Pyramid of ratios

Once ratios have been analysed and compared, explanations must be sought for the results obtained. Sometimes, it will be obvious why a certain result was obtained – for example, if a company has moved from traditional stock-keeping to a 'just-in-time' system during the period, its stock turnover will bear no resemblance to that which it had in the previous period.

For those inside the company – its directors and management – the management accounting records are available to assist in finding explanations, as are the company's staff. Outsiders – shareholders, analysts, lenders, suppliers, customers, etc. – do not have access to all this internal information (though some of these user groups will have access to more internal information than others – banks, for example, can usually obtain copies of a company's management accounts upon request). They must fall back upon other sources of information – newspaper reports and industry publications, for example. One source of additional information available to everyone is the **pyramid of ratios**. Most ratios can be further subdivided into secondary ratios, which themselves can also be subdivided. By following through the pyramid of a given ratio, the source of the original ratio can often be isolated, enabling a far more focused investigation than would otherwise be possible.

For example, one of the most important ratios is the return on the capital employed (ROCE). This ratio has not happened by itself. If the ratio of net profit to sales had not been a particular figure and the ratio of sales to capital employed had not been a particular figure, then the ROCE would not have turned out to be the figure that it is.

Thus, the ROCE comes about as a result of all the other ratios which have underpinned it. It is the final summation of all that has happened in the various aspects of the business. The ROCE pyramid of ratios is shown in Exhibit 31.7.

By itself the pyramid of ratios may not tell you much. It comes into full effect when compared with similar figures of the ratios for previous years, or with pyramids in respect of other firms. If the ROCE has been falling over the past year then a study of the pyramids for the two years may enable you to pinpoint exactly where the changes have been made to bring about the worsening position. Investigation of these matters may then give you some answers for action to be taken.

31.7 Return on capital employed: company policy

The pyramid of ratios in Exhibit 31.7 illustrates the interdependence of each ratio. This can be examined in greater detail by investigating the policies of two companies to achieve their desired return on capital employed.

The first part of the pyramid tells us that the ROCE is dependent on both net profit as a percentage of sales and also sales as a percentage of capital employed. This means that:

$$ROCE = \frac{Net\ profit}{Capital\ employed}$$

which by splitting the equation between profitability ratios and resource utilisation ratios means also that:

$$ROCE = \frac{Net\ profit}{Sales} \times \frac{Sales}{Capital\ employed}$$

This interrelationship of the subsidiary ratios can be illustrated through an example. At the same time, it can be seen that the result of computing a primary ratio is dependent upon the items comprising it; and that there is no guarantee that a value of x will be 'good', and y 'bad'. Whether the result obtained is 'good' or 'bad' depends on the underlying factors that give rise to the result obtained (what, for example, is the company's policy on depreciation and replacement of assets? This can significantly affect the ROCE), the sector in which the business operates and its relative size. Without knowledge of these items, comparison of the ratio analysis of two companies is likely to be misleading at best.

Exhibit 31.7

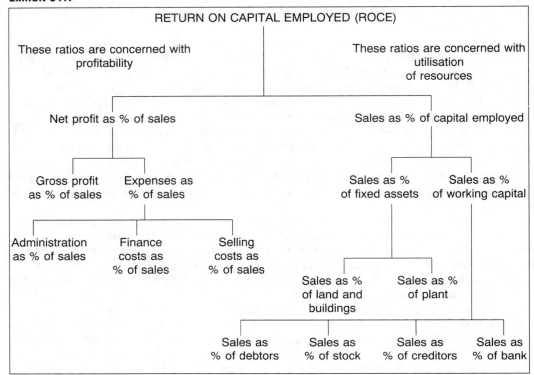

Two companies, both in the grocery business, may decide to aim for the same ROCE of 10 per cent. This can be achieved in completely different ways by the two companies.

A Ltd is a large company operating a supermarket. It seeks to attract customers by offering low prices and only makes a net profit of 1.25 per cent on sales. Its sales for the year are £8,000,000 on which its net profit is £100,000. Its capital employed is £1,000,000. The ROCE is, therefore, 10 per cent (i.e. £100,000 net profit on capital employed of £1,000,000). This can also be expressed as:

$$\text{ROCE} = \frac{\text{Net profit}}{\text{Sales}} \times \frac{\text{Sales}}{\text{Capital employed}}$$

$$= \frac{£100,000}{£8,000,000} \times \frac{£8,000,000}{£1,000,000} = 10\%$$

B Ltd by comparison, is a small local retailer. It seeks a higher margin per £100 sales, but because of higher prices it will achieve a lower volume of business. It makes a net profit of 5 per cent on sales. Its sales for the year amount to £200,000 on which it makes a net profit of £10,000. The capital employed is £100,000. The ROCE is therefore 10 per cent (i.e. £10,000 on capital employed of £100,000). This can also be expressed as:

$$\text{ROCE} = \frac{\text{Net profit}}{\text{Sales}} \times \frac{\text{Sales}}{\text{Capital employed}}$$

$$= \frac{£10,000}{£200,000} \times \frac{£200,000}{£100,000} = 10\%$$

It can be seen that two firms, despite different sizes of business and operating different pricing policies, can have the same ROCE.

Main points to remember

1   Ratios on their own are frequently misleading – they should not be considered in isolation from similar computations:
    (a) in previous periods; and/or
    (b) on similar sized firms in the same sector.

2   The items in the financial statements are affected by company policy – for example, the rate of depreciation to use, and the policy of asset replacement – and the policies adopted, therefore, directly affect the ratio analysis.

3   Companies of very different size and in very different sectors can have the same ratio results despite their being different in every respect.

4   The importance and impact of size, sector and company policies upon ratios mean that there is no such thing as a 'good' or 'bad' value that can be treated as a yardstick for any ratio.

5   All ratios are part of one or more pyramids of ratios.

6   When the results of ratio analysis are being investigated further, the relevant pyramid of ratios can be analysed in order to pinpoint the element giving rise to the situation being investigated.

Advice

This is a topic that causes more marks to be thrown away in exams than probably every other topic combined. No other topic is as concerned with understanding rather than knowledge, and examiners tend to expect students to be able to demonstrate their understanding rather than simply their ability to prepare the accounts or calculate the ratios.

There is no one set pattern to the questions, which depend upon the examiner's ingenuity and background experience. The usual shortcomings in the answers handed in by examinees, particularly on questions relating to this topic but also on questions in other areas, can be listed as follows:

1   Not following the instructions as laid down. If the question says 'list the' then the examiner expects a list as an answer, 'Discuss the' means exactly that, 'Write a report' needs a report as the answer, and so on. You will lose a lot of marks for not giving the examiner exactly what has been asked for.

2   Very often all the ratios etc. are calculated, but then the candidate does not offer any comments even though they have been asked for. *Make certain you cover this part of the question in an appropriate amount of detail.*

3   Even where students have written something about the ratios, they often repeat what the calculations are and offer nothing else, e.g. 'you can see that the gross profit ratio has increased from 18 to 20 per cent' and the answer has finished there. The examiner can already see from your calculations that the gross profit percentage has increased, and wants you to write about why it might have increased, what conclusions, if any, can be arrived at, or what further information may be needed to discover why it has changed.

4   Remember that when the examiner asks you 'what other information you would like to have' about a firm when trying to interpret the accounts so as to give advice to

someone then, ideally, you would like to know more about the plans for the future of the business, how it compares with others in the same industry, whether or not there are going to be changes in the management and so on. We should not limit ourselves to information about the past, we really need to know as much about the future as we possibly can.

5 Do not restrict your examination answers to what you have read in a textbook. Keep your eyes and ears open as you go shopping, visit factories, work, buy petrol at the filling station, go to the theatre, and so on. Reading a 'quality' newspaper helps, as there are quite a lot of items about business. Bring all of this sort of knowledge and experience into your answers. You will impress the examiners. They are bored to death reading regurgitations of textbook learning with nothing else added.

6 Quite a few questions will concern the type of business of which you will have first-hand experience and can introduce your own personal knowledge into your answer. A typical instance would be comparing two grocery businesses. One would be a large supermarket and the other would be a small corner shop. The policies of the two firms would be quite different. The supermarket would have decided on a policy of attracting new customers by lowering sales margins and yet boosting ROCE. The corner shop might have a policy of high margins, but remain open on Sundays and late at nights, and thus be a 'convenience shop', i.e. customers might well go there when other shops are closed or are too far away to be worth the extra cost in petrol, etc. when compared with the extra cost of shopping at the corner shop.

7 Last, but not least, *show your workings*. If you make a mistake in your calculations and do not show your workings you cannot be awarded any credit for a partially incorrect calculation. Consider how much longer it takes to show the detail contained in section 31.7 above, rather than simply the result of the calculation – maybe 30 seconds. *Now consider whether you would rather spend five minutes in an exam showing the workings of ten ratio calculations, or six months studying to retake the exam you failed because you made a mistake in two of your calculations and lost five marks because the examiner could not tell why you got the answer wrong.*

Review questions

31.1 Adrian Frampton was considering the purchase of one of two businesses. However, Frampton had only been provided with limited information about the businesses, as follows:

Summarised financial information for the year ended 31 December 19X9

Information	Business X	Business Y
Cost of goods sold	£400,000	£600,000
Administrative expenses	£50,000	£60,000
Average stock at cost	£40,000	£50,000
Working capital as at 31 December 19X9	£90,000	£250,000
Selling and distribution expenses	£15,000	£35,000
Proprietor's capital at 1 January 19X9	£200,000	£350,000
Gross profit percentage mark-up on cost	20	25

Additional information

1 Average stock had been calculated by using the year's opening and closing stocks. Subsequently it was discovered that Business Y had overvalued its stock on 31 December 19X9 by £10,000.

2 Business X's administrative expenses included a payment for rent of £15,000 which covered a three-year period to 31 December 19X1.

3   A sum of £2,500 was included in the administrative expenses of Business Y in respect of a holiday taken by the owner and his family.

4   Cash drawings for the year ended 31 December 19X9 were:

	£
Business X	20,000
Business Y	25,000

5   The owners of the businesses had stipulated the following prices for their businesses:

	£
Business X	190,000
Business Y	400,000

Required:

(a) Based on the information available prepare comparative trading and profit and loss accounts for the year ended 31 December 19X9.

(b) Using the information provided and the accounting statements prepared in (a), calculate relevant accounting ratios in order to give Frampton a basis for assessing the performances of the two businesses. Comment on the results.

(c) What additional information is needed in order to assess more accurately
    (i) the liquidity of the businesses;
    (ii) the future prospects of the businesses?

(*Associated Examining Board: GCE A–level*)

31.2   Three companies have the capital structures shown below.

Company	A	B	C
	£000	£000	£000
Ordinary shares	600	400	50
12% debentures	–	200	550
	600	600	600

The return on capital employed was 20 per cent for each firm in 19X4, and in 19X5 was 10 per cent. Corporation tax in both years was assumed to be 55 per cent, and debenture interest is an allowable expense against corporation tax.

(a) Calculate the percentage return on the shareholders' capital for each company for 19X4 and 19X5. Assume that all profits are distributed.

(b) Use your answer to explain the merits and the dangers of high gearing.

(*Edexcel Foundation, London Examinations: University of London GCE A–level*)

31.3A   Martha is the accountant of a trading business. During the past year she produced interim accounts for the six months ended 30 November 19X5, and draft final accounts for the year ended 31 May 19X6, as follows:

	Interim accounts	Draft final accounts
	£	£
Sales (all on credit terms)	140,000	336,000
Cost of sales (note 1)	42,000	112,000
Gross profit	98,000	224,000
Less Expenses	56,000	168,000
Net profit	42,000	56,000
Fixed assets	70,000	63,000
Current assets (note 2)	42,000	71,000
Current liabilities (note 3)	(22,000)	(30,000)
	90,000	104,000

Share capital	30,000	30,000
Retained earnings	60,000	74,000
	90,000	104,000

Notes:

1 Average stock was £14,000 during the first six months.
2 Current assets were:

	30 Nov 19X5	31 May 19X6
	£	£
Stock	16,000	25,000
Debtors	24,000	28,000
Bank	2,000	18,000
	42,000	71,000

3 Current liabilities consisted entirely of trade creditors.

Martha informs you that the business leased additional premises from 1 December 19X5, and that sales arising therefrom totalled £70,000 for the six months to 31 May 19X6, with an average mark-up on cost prices of 150 per cent being made on those goods.

Expenses relating to these additional premises totalled £21,000 for the period. Two-fifths of the closing stock of the business was located at these premises.

Prepare a report, using appropriate accounting ratios, to explain the changes in the financial situation of the business during the year ended 31 May 19X6.

(Edexcel Foundation, London Examinations: University of London GCE A–level)

31.4 John Jones is considering purchasing shares in one of two companies and has extracted the following information from the balance sheet of each company.

	Company A Plc £000	Company B Plc £000
Authorised share capital		
£1 ordinary shares	600	1,000
8% £1 preference shares	400	
Issued share capital		
£1 ordinary shares	300	800
8% £1 preference shares	200	
Reserves		
Share premium	300	400
Retained earnings	400	200
Loan capital		
10% debentures (19X0)		200
12% debentures (19X6)	400	

Required:
(a) Define the term 'gearing' stating clearly what is meant by a low gearing ratio.
(b) Calculate the gearing factor for each company.
(c) Explain to John Jones the significance of gearing to an ordinary shareholder in each of the companies above.
(d) Assuming for each company a trading profit of £200,000 before interest and an ordinary dividend of 15 per cent complete the profit and loss appropriation account for a year for each company. You should ignore taxation.

(Associated Examining Board GCE A–level)

31.5A The following are extracts from the balance sheets as at 31 March 19X4 and 31 March 19X5 of Glebe Ltd:

	31 March 19X4		31 March 19X5	
	£	£	£	£
Current assets				
Stocks	20,000		25,000	
Trade debtors	10,000		17,000	
Cash	5,000		3,000	
		35,000		45,000
Less				
Current liabilities				
Trade creditors	12,000		16,000	
Proposed dividends	6,000		5,000	
Bank overdraft	7,000		29,000	
		25,000		50,000
		10,000		(5,000)

Required:

(a) Calculate for each of the two years two ratios that indicate the liquidity position of the company.

(b) (i) From the information given, give reasons for the changes which have occurred in the working capital.

(ii) What other information regarding the current assets and current liabilities would you consider necessary to assess the ability of the business to continue in operation?

(c) Discuss any other information available from a balance sheet that may affect an assessment of the liquidity of a business.

(*Associated Examining Board GCE A–level*)

31.6 Colin Black is considering investing a substantial sum in the ordinary shares of Jacks Ltd. Having some accounting knowledge he has extracted the following information from the accounts for the last two financial years.

	As at 31 March 19X4	As at 31 March 19X5
	£	£
Issued share capital		
£1 ordinary shares, fully paid	100,000	150,000
Reserves		
Share premium	10,000	60,000
Retained earnings	140,000	160,000
Loan capital		
10% debentures 19X7–X9	40,000	40,000

	For year ended 31 March 19X4	For year ended 31 March 19X5
	£	£
Net profit after tax	60,000	70,000

Because he was disappointed with the result he obtained when he calculated the return on the equity capital employed, Colin Black has asked for your advice.

Required:

(a) Calculate the figures which prompted Colin Black's reaction.

(b) Prepare a memorandum to Colin Black pointing out other information to be considered when comparing the return on equity capital employed over two years as a basis for his investment decision.

(c) Explain why a company builds up and maintains reserves.

(*Associated Examining Board GCE A–level*)

31.7A The following information has been extracted from the accounts of Witton Way Ltd:

Profit and Loss Account for the year to 30 April

	19X5	19X6
	£000	£000
Turnover (all credit sales)	7,650	11,500
Less Cost of sales	(5,800)	(9,430)
Gross profit	1,850	2,070
Other expenses	(150)	(170)
Loan interest	(50)	(350)
Profit before taxation	1,650	1,550
Taxation	(600)	(550)
Profit after taxation	1,050	1,000
Dividends (all ordinary shares)	(300)	(300)
Retained profits	£750	£700

Balance Sheet at 30 April

	19X5	19X6
	£000	£000
Fixed assets		
Tangible assets	10,050	11,350
Current assets		
Stocks	1,500	2,450
Trade debtors	1,200	3,800
Cash	900	50
	3,600	6,300
Creditors: Amounts falling due within one year	2,400	2,700
Net current assets	1,200	3,600
Total assets less current liabilities	11,250	14,950
Creditors:		
Amounts falling due after more than one year		
Loans and other borrowings	350	3,350
	£10,900	£11,600
Capital and reserves		
Called-up share capital	5,900	5,900
Profit and loss account	5,000	5,700
	£10,900	£11,600

Additional information:
During the year to 30 April 19X6, the company tried to stimulate sales by reducing the selling price of its products and by offering more generous credit terms to its customers.

Required:
(a) Calculate six accounting ratios specifying the basis of your calculations for each of the two years to 30 April 19X5 and 19X6 respectively which will enable you to examine the company's progress during 19X6.
(b) From the information available to you, including the ratios calculated in part (a) of the question, comment upon the company's results for the year to 30 April 19X6 under the heads of 'profitability', 'liquidity', 'efficiency' and 'shareholders' interests'.
(c) State what additional information you would require in order to assess the company's attempts to stimulate sales during the year to 30 April 19X6.

(*Association of Accounting Technicians*)

31.8 You are presented with the following information for three quite separate and independent companies:

Summarised Balance Sheets at 31 March 19X7

	Chan plc £000	Ling plc £000	Wong plc £000
Total assets *less* current liabilities	600	600	700
Creditors: amounts falling due after more than one year			
10% debenture stock	–	–	(100)
	£600	£600	£600
Capital and reserves:			
Called-up share capital			
Ordinary shares of £1 each	500	300	200
10% cumulative preference shares of £1 each	–	200	300
Profit and loss account	100	100	100
	£600	£600	£600

Additional information:

1 The operating profit before interest and tax for the year to 31 March 19X8 earned by each of the three companies was £300,000.
2 The effective rate of corporation tax for all three companies for the year to 31 March 19X8 is 30 per cent. This rate is to be used in calculating each company's tax payable on ordinary profit.
3 An ordinary dividend of 20p for the year to 31 March 19X8 is proposed by all three companies, and any preference dividends are to be provided for.
4 The market prices per ordinary share at 31 March 19X8 were as follows: £
   Chan plc 8.40
   Ling plc 9.50
   Wong plc 10.38
5 There were no changes in the share capital structure or in long-term loans of any of the companies during the year to 31 March 19X8.

Required:

(*a*) Insofar as the information permits, prepare the profit and loss account for each of the three companies (in columnar format) for the year to 31 March 19X8 (formal notes to the accounts are not required);

(*b*) calculate the following accounting ratios for each company:
   (*i*) earnings per share;
   (*ii*) price earnings;
   (*iii*) gearing (taken as total borrowings (preference share capital and long-term loans) to ordinary shareholders' funds); and

(*c*) using the gearing ratios calculated in answering part (*b*) of the question, briefly examine the importance of gearing if you were thinking of investing in some ordinary shares in one of the three companies assuming that the profits of the three companies were fluctuating.

(*Association of Accounting Technicians*)

31.9A The chairman of a family business has been examining the following summary of the accounts of the company since it began three years ago.

Balance Sheet (at 30 June) £000s

	19X4 Actual		19X5 Actual		19X6 Actual	
Freehold land and buildings		150		150		150
Plant	150		150		450	
Less: Depreciation	15	135	30	120	75	375
		285		270		525

Stock and work in progress	20		45		85		
Debtors	33		101		124		
Bank and cash	10		15		–		
	63		161		209		
Less: Creditors	20		80		35		
Taxation	4		17		6		
Overdraft	–	39	–	64	25	143	
		324		334		468	
Less: Loan		–		–		200	
		324		334		468	
Ordinary share capital (£1 shares)		300		300		400	
General reserve		17		25		45	
Deferred tax account		7		9		23	
		324		334		468	

Profit and Loss Account (for year to 30 June) £000s

	19X4 Actual		19X5 Actual		19X6 Actual	
Sales		260		265		510
Trading profit		53		50		137
Depreciation	15		15		45	
Loan interest	–	15	–	15	43	88
Net profit		38		35		49
Taxation (including transfer to or from deferred tax account)		11		15		15
Net profit after tax		27		20		34
Dividend (proposed*)		10		12		14*
Retained		17		8		20

The company's products are popular in the locality and in the first two years sales could have been higher if there had been extra machine capacity available.

On 1 January 19X6, additional share and loan capital was obtained which enabled extra machinery to be purchased. This gave an immediate increase in sales and profits.

Although 19X5/X6 showed the best yet results, the chairman is not very happy; the accountant has suggested that a dividend should not be paid this year because of the overdraft. The accountant has, however, shown a proposed dividend of £14,000 (£2,000 up on last year) for purposes of comparison pending a decision by the directors.

Naturally, the chairman is displeased and wants some explanations from the accountant regarding the figures in the accounts. He specifically asks:

(i) Why, if profits are the best ever and considering the company has obtained extra capital during the year, has the company gone into overdraft? Can there really be a profit if there is no cash left in the bank to pay a dividend?

(ii) Why is the freehold still valued at the same price as in 19X4? The real value seems to be about £225,000. Why is this real value not in the balance sheet?

Required:
Write a report to the chairman:

(a) commenting on the state and progress of the business as disclosed by the accounts and the above information, supporting your analysis by appropriate key accounting ratios, and

(b) giving reasoned answers, in the context of recognised accounting law, rules and practices, to each of the questions raised by the chairman.

(Institute of Chartered Secretaries and Administrators)

31.10 The following information is provided for Bessemer Ltd which operates in an industry subject to marked variations in consumer demand.

(*i*) Shareholders' equity at 30 September 19X5:

	£000
Issued ordinary shares of £1 each fully paid	5,000
Retained profits	1,650
	6,650

There were no loans outstanding at the balance sheet date.

(*ii*) Profit and loss account extracts: year to 30 September 19X5:

	£000
Net profit before tax	900
Less Corporation tax	270
	630
Less Dividends	600
Retained profit for the year	30
Retained profit at 1 October 19X4	1,620
Retained profit at 30 September 19X5	1,650

(*iii*) The directors are planning to expand output. This will require an additional investment of £2,000,000 which may be financed either by issuing 1,000,000 ordinary shares each with a nominal value of £1, or by raising a 12 per cent debenture.

(*iv*) Forecast profits before interest charges, if any, for the year to 30 September:

	£000
19X6	1,800
19X7	500
19X8	2,200

A corporation tax rate of 30 per cent on reported profit before tax may be assumed; the directors plan to pay out the entire post-tax profit as dividends.

Required:

(*a*) The forecast profit and loss appropriation accounts for each of the next three years and year-end balance sheet extracts, so far as the information permits, assuming that the expansion is financed by:
  (i) issuing additional shares, or
  (ii) raising a debenture.
(*b*) Calculate the forecast return on shareholders' equity, for each of the next three years, under the alternative methods for financing the planned expansion.
(*c*) An assessment of the merits and demerits of the alternative methods of finance based on the calculations made under (*a*) and (*b*) and any other relevant methods of comparison.

(*Institute of Chartered Secretaries and Administrators*)

31.11A An investor is considering the purchase of shares in either AA plc or BB plc whose latest accounts are summarised below. Both companies carry on similar manufacturing activities with similar selling prices and costs of materials, labour and services.

Balance Sheets at 30 September 19X7 (£000s)

	AA plc		BB plc	
Freehold property at revaluation 19X5		2,400		–
Plant, machinery and equipment:				
at cost	1,800		1,800	
depreciation	1,200		400	
		600		1,400
Goodwill		–		800
Stocks: finished goods		400		200
work in progress		300		100
Debtors		800		500
Bank deposit		–		400
		4,500		3,400
Less Liabilities due within one year				
Creditors	600		900	
Overdraft	200		–	
	800		900	
Liabilities due after one year	1,400		1,000	
		2,200		1,900
		2,300		1,500
Ordinary £1 shares		1,000		500
Reserves		1,300		1,000
		2,300		1,500

Profit and Loss Accounts – Year to 30 September 19X7 (£000s)

	AA plc		BB plc	
Sales		2,500		2,500
Operating profit		400		600
Depreciation – plant, machinery and equipment	180		180	
Loan interest	150		160	
		330		340
		70		260
Bank interest		–		100
		70		360
Taxation		20		90
Available to ordinary shareholders		50		270
Dividend		40		130
Retained		£10		£140
Price/earnings ratio		30		5
Market value of share		£1.50		£2.70

Required:

(a) Write a report to the investor, giving an appraisal of the results and state of each business, and

(b) advise the investor whether, in your opinion, the price earnings ratios and market price of the shares can be justified in the light of the figures in the accounts, giving your reasons.

(*Institute of Chartered Secretaries and Administrators*)

31.12 The following are the summarised accounts for B Limited, a company with an accounting year ending on 30 September.

Summarised Balance Sheets for	19X5/6		19X6/7	
	£000	£000	£000	£000
Tangible fixed assets – at cost				
Less Depreciation		4,995		12,700
Current assets:				
Stocks	40,145		50,455	
Debtors	40,210		43,370	
Cash at bank	12,092		5,790	
	92,447		99,615	
Creditors: amounts falling due within one year:				
Trade creditors	32,604		37,230	
Taxation	2,473		3,260	
Proposed dividend	1,785		1,985	
	36,862		42,475	
Net current assets		55,585		57,140
Total assets less current liabilities		60,580		69,840
Creditors: amounts falling due after more than one year:				
10% debentures 20X6/20X9		19,840		19,840
		40,740		50,000
Capital and reserves:				
Called-up share capital of £0.25 per share		9,920		9,920
Profit and loss account		30,820		40,080
Shareholders' funds		40,740		50,000

Summarised Profit and Loss Accounts for	19X5/6	19X6/7
	£000	£000
Turnover	486,300	583,900
Operating profit	17,238	20,670
Interest payable	1,984	1,984
Profit on ordinary activities before taxation	15,254	18,686
Tax on profit on ordinary activities	5,734	7,026
Profit for the financial year	9,520	11,660
Dividends	2,240	2,400
	7,280	9,260
Retained profit brought forward	23,540	30,820
Retained profit carried forward	30,820	40,080

You are required to:

(a) calculate, for each year, two ratios for each of the following user groups, which are of particular significance to them:
  (i)   shareholders;
  (ii) trade creditors;
  (iii) internal management;

(b) make brief comments upon the changes, between the two years, in the ratios calculated in (a) above.

(*Chartered Institute of Management Accountants*)

31.13A The following are the financial statements of D Limited, a wholesaling company, for the year ended 31 December:

Profit and Loss Accounts	19X4 £000	19X4 £000	19X5 £000	19X5 £000
Turnover – credit sales	2,200		2,640	
cash sales	200		160	
		2,400		2,800
Cost of sales		(1,872)		(2,212)
Gross profit		528		588
Distribution costs		(278)		(300)
Administration expenses		(112)		(114)
Operating profit		138		174
Interest payable		–		(32)
Profit on ordinary activities before tax		138		142

Balance Sheets as at 31 December	19X4 £000	19X4 £000	19X5 £000	19X5 £000
Tangible fixed assets		220		286
Current assets: Stocks	544		660	
Debtors	384		644	
Cash at bank	8		110	
	936		1,414	
Creditors: amounts falling due within one year:				
Trade creditors	(256)		(338)	
Net current assets		680		1,076
Total assets less current liabilities		900		1,362
Creditors: amounts falling due after more than one year:				
Debenture loans				(320)
Shareholders' funds		900		1,042

The following information should be taken into consideration.

1 You may assume that:
   (i) The range of products sold by D Limited remained unchanged over the two years;
   (ii) the company managed to acquire its products in 19X5 at the same prices as it acquired them for in 19X4;
   (iii) the effects of any inflationary aspects have been taken into account in the figures.
2 Ignore taxation.
3 All calculations must be shown to one decimal place.

You are required, using the information above, to assess and comment briefly on the company, from the point of view of:
(a) profitability;
(b) liquidity.

(*Chartered Institute of Management Accountants*)

31.14 G plc is a holding company with subsidiaries that have diversified interests. G plc's board of directors is interested in the group acquiring a subsidiary in the machine tool manufacturing sector. Two companies have been identified as potential acquisitions, A Ltd and B Ltd. Summaries of both these companies' accounts are shown below:

Profit and Loss Accounts for the year ended 30 April 19X8

	A Ltd £000	B Ltd £000
Turnover	985	560
Cost of goods sold		
Opening stock	150	145
Materials	255	136
Labour	160	125
Factory overheads	205	111
Depreciation	35	20
Closing stock	(155)	(140)
	650	397
Gross profit	335	163
Selling and administration expenses	(124)	(75)
Interest	(35)	(10)
Profit before taxation	176	78
Taxation	65	25
Profit after taxation	111	53

Balance Sheets at 30 April 19X8

	A Ltd £000	A Ltd £000	B Ltd £000	B Ltd £000
Fixed assets		765		410
Current assets				
Stock	155		140	
Debtors	170		395	
Bank	50		45	
	375		580	
Current liabilities				
Trade creditors	235		300	
Other	130		125	
	365		425	
Net current assets		10		155
Debentures		(220)		(70)
		555		495
Share capital		450		440
Profit and loss account		105		55
		555		495

You are required to prepare a report for the board of G plc assessing the financial performance and position of A Ltd and B Ltd. Your report should be prepared in the context of G plc's interests in these two companies and should be illustrated with financial ratios where appropriate. You should state any assumptions you make as well as any limitations of your analysis.

(*Chartered Institute of Management Accountants*)

31.15A J plc supplies and fits car tyres, exhaust pipes and other components. The company has branches throughout the country. Roughly 60 per cent of sales are for cash (retail sales). The remainder are credit sales made to car hire companies and large organisations with fleets of company cars (business sales). Business sales tend to be more profitable than retail and the company is keen to expand in this area. There is, however, considerable competition. Branch managers are responsible for obtaining business customers and have some discretion over terms of trade and discounts.

The company's computerised accounting system has recently produced the following report for the manager of the Eastown branch for the six months ended 30 September 19X4:

	Eastown Branch	Average for all branches
Return on capital employed	22%	16%
Gross profit	38%	45%
Selling and promotion costs/sales	9%	6%
Wages/sales	19%	14%
Debtors turnover (based on credit sales only)	63 days	52 days
Stock turnover	37 days	49 days

The Eastown branch manager has only recently been appointed and is unsure whether his branch appears well managed. He has asked for your advice.

You are required to compare the performance of the Eastown branch with the average for all branches. Suggest reasons for the differences you identify.

(*Chartered Institute of Management Accountants*)

31.16A Company managers are aware that the readers of financial statements often use accounting ratios to evaluate their performance. **Explain** how this could lead to decisions which are against the company's best interests.

(*Chartered Institute of Management Accountants*)

Part 5

ISSUES IN FINANCIAL REPORTING

Introduction

This part looks at the theories upon which accounting practice is based, considers issues affecting accounting and financial reporting, and reviews the place of accounting information in the context of the environment in which business entities operate.

32

Accounting theory

Objectives

After you have studied this chapter, you should:

- *appreciate that there is no one overall accepted general theory of accounting*

- *realise that there are possible valuation alternatives other than that of historical cost*

- *understand the difference between current purchasing power and current cost accounting*

- *know the characteristics of useful information*

PART I: GENERAL THEORY

32.1 An introduction

To many students it will seem strange that a discussion of accounting theory has been left until this late stage of the book. Logically you could argue that it should have preceded all the practical work.

The reason for not dealing with theory at the beginning is simple. From a teaching point of view, it could easily have confused you then, and made it more difficult to assimilate the basic rules of accounting. The terms used in theory, such as what is meant in accounting by capital, liabilities, assets, net profit and so on, would not then have been understood. Leaving it until now, if theory points out what is wrong with accounting methods, at least you know those methods. Theory taught in a vacuum is counter-productive for most students.

In the discussion which follows, we want you to remember that this is your first proper look at accounting theory. We do not intend it to be an exhaustive examination, but simply an introduction to give you an overall appreciation. If you carry your studies to a higher level you will have to study accounting theory in much greater depth. At this level all you will need is an appreciation aspect only.

32.2 An overall accepted theory?

It would not be surprising if you were expecting to read now exactly what the overall accepted theory of accounting is, and then proceed to examine the details later. We are afraid there is no such 'accepted' theory. This is much regretted by those accountants who have chosen an academic life. Many 'practical' accountants, and you will meet quite a few of them, are quite pleased that no such theory exists. To them, accounting is what accountants do, and they feel theory has little place in that. Such a narrow view is to be deprecated. Accounting theory provides a general frame of reference by which accounting practices can be judged, and it also guides the way to the development of new practices and procedures.

The lack of an accepted theory of accounting does not mean that it has not been attempted; there have been numerous attempts. At first they consisted of an **inductive** approach. This involved observing and analysing the practices of accountants to see if any consistent behaviour could be detected. Should a general principle be observed, anyone deviating from it could be criticised accordingly. Such attempts failed. First, it was impossible to find consistent patterns of behaviour amongst the mass of practices which had developed over the years. Second, such an approach would not have brought about any important improvements in accounting practices, as it looked at 'what accountants do' rather than 'what accountants *should* be doing'.

A different approach emerged, as recently as the 1950s. It was a **normative** approach, in that it was aimed at the improvement of accounting practice. It also included elements of the inductive approach in attempting to derive rules based on logical reasoning when given a set of objectives. The combination of these approaches has been a valuable and productive one, albeit still in its infancy. For instance, it had an important effect upon current value accounting which we will examine later. The main problem has been that of a general agreement as to the objectives of accounting.

As you might expect, general attention has more recently tended to switch away to a less ambitious approach. This is based, first, on identifying the users of accounts, and then finding out what kind of information they require. Such an approach was used in *The Corporate Report*, produced under the auspices of the Accounting Standards Committee (ASC), and published in 1975. We will look later at the user groups which were identified. The other important report using this approach was that of the Sandilands Committee in 1975. This will also be considered more fully later.

There is still a major problem here. Should accountants give the user groups the information they are asking for, or the information for which they should be asking? With management accounts this is not such a great problem, as management and accountants get together to agree on what should be produced. The financial accounts present greater problems. First, there is not such a close relationship between the accountant and the user groups. Second, there are the legal and other regulations governing financial accounts which the accountant must observe. Another point which will be considered later is whether only one report should be issued for all user groups, or whether each group should have its own report.

Having had an overall look at how theory construction is proceeding, we can now turn to look at theory in more detail.

32.3 Measurement of income

The syllabus uses the word 'income', but the words 'net profit' mean exactly the same. In this book the calculation of net profit is done within fairly strict guidelines. Chapter 10 in *Frank Wood's Business Accounting 1* provided guidance on the overall concepts ruling such calculations. However, just because the business world and the accounting profession use this basic approach does not mean it is the only one available. We will now consider possible alternatives to the basic method.

Let us start by looking at the simplest possible example of the calculation of profit, where everyone would agree with the way it is calculated. John is starting in business, his only asset being cash £1,000. He rents a stall in the market for the day, costing him £40. He then buys fruit for cash £90, and sells it all during the day for cash £160. At the end of the day John's only asset is still cash: £1,000 – £40 – £90 + 160 = £1,030. Everyone would agree that his profit for that day was £30, i.e. £160 sales – £90 purchases – £40 expenses = £30. In this case his profit equals the increase in his cash.

Suppose that John now changes his style of trading. He buys the market stall, and he also starts selling nuts and dried fruit, of which he can keep a stock from one day to another. If we now want to calculate profit we cannot do it simply in terms of cash, we will also have to place a value both on the stock of fruit and nuts and on his stall, both at the beginning and end of each day.

The argument just put forward assumes that we can all agree that profit represents an increase in wealth or 'well-offness'. It assumes that John will make a profit for a period if either:

(a) he is better off at the end of it than he was at the beginning; or
(b) he would have been better off at the end than the beginning had he not consumed some of the profits by taking drawings.

Sir John Hicks, the economist, expressed this view by saying that the profit was the maximum value which a person could consume during a period and still be as well off at the end of the period as at the beginning.

In terms of a limited company, the Sandilands Committee, which will be mentioned in greater detail later, said that a company's profit for the year is the maximum value which the company can distribute as dividends during the year, and still be as well off at the end of the year as it was at the beginning. There are some important questions here which need answering. They are:

(a) how can we measure wealth at the beginning and end of a period?
(b) how do we measure the change in wealth over a period?
(c) having measured wealth over a period, how much can be available for consumption and how much should not be consumed?

There are basically two approaches to the measurement of wealth of a business:

(a) Measuring the wealth by finding the values of the individual assets of a business.
(b) Measuring the expectation of future benefits.

In Chapter 46, you will learn the technique of discounting. We will use it here to calculate the present value of the expected future net flow of cash into the firm.

We will first look at the different methods of valuation on an individual asset basis.

32.4 Asset valuation alternatives

1 Historical cost

This method is the one you have used so far in the financial accounting in this book. Even in that case there is not always one single figure to represent it. Let us look at a few examples.

(a) **Depreciation.** How do we 'precisely' charge the cost of using an asset to a particular period? As you have already seen, there is no one 'true' answer; the choice of method, expected length of use of the asset, etc., is quite arbitrary.
(b) Stocks to be used during the period can be charged out at FIFO, LIFO, AVCO, and so on. There is no one 'true' figure.

(c) Suppose we buy a block of assets, e.g. we take over the net assets of another organisation. How do we allocate the cost exactly? There is no precise way, we simply use a 'fair value' for each asset. Any excess of cost over the total of fair values we call goodwill.

2 Adjusted historical cost

Because of the changes in the value or purchasing power of money, the normal historical cost approach can be very unsatisfactory. Take the case of a buildings account; in it we find that two items have been debited. One was a warehouse bought in 1950 for £100,000 and the other an almost identical warehouse bought in 1985 for £400,000. These two figures are added together to show cost of warehouses £500,000, quite clearly a value which has little significance.

To remedy this defect, the original historical cost of an asset is adjusted for the changes in the value or purchasing power of money over the period from acquisition to the present balance sheet date. The calculations are effected by using a price index.

This method does not mean that the asset itself is revalued. What is revalued is the money for which the asset was originally bought. This method forms the basis of what is known as **current purchasing power** accounting, abbreviated as CPP.

It does not remove the original problems of historical accounting which we have already described (see above). All this does is to take the original historical cost as accurate and then adjust it.

To illustrate this method, let us take an instance which works out precisely, just as the proponents of CPP would wish.

A machine which will last for five years, depreciated using the straight line method, was bought on 1 January 19X4 for £5,000. On 1 January 19X6 exactly the same kind of machine (there have been no technological improvements) is bought for £6,000. The price index was 100 at 1 January 19X4, 120 at 1 January 19X6 and 130 at 31 December 19X6. The machines would appear in the balance sheet at 31 December 19X6 as follows, the workings being shown in the box alongside.

	Historical cost £	Conversion factor £		Balance sheet CPP at 31 Dec 19X6 £
Machine 1	5,000	130/100	6,500	
Machine 2	6,000	130/120	6,500	13,000
Less Depreciation				
Machine 1	3,000	130/100	3,900	
Machine 2	1,200	130/120	1,300	5,200
				7,800

You can see that the CPP balance sheet shows two exactly similar machines at the same cost, and each has been depreciated £1,300 for each year of use. In this particular case CPP has achieved exactly what it sets out to do, namely put similar things on a similar basis.

Underlying this method are the problems inherent in the price index used to adjust the historical cost figures. Any drawbacks in the index will result in a distortion of the adjusted historical cost figures.

3 Replacement cost

Replacement cost, abbreviated as RC, is the estimated amount that would have to be paid to replace the asset at the date of valuation. You will often see it referred to as an 'entry value' as it is the cost of an asset entering the business.

How do we 'estimate' the replacement cost? As we are not in fact replacing the asset we will have to look at the state of the market at the date of valuation. If the asset is exactly the same as those currently being traded, perhaps we can look at suppliers' price lists.

Even with exactly the same item, there are still problems. Until you have actually negotiated a purchase it is impossible to say how much discount you could get – you might guess but you could not be certain. Also, if the asset consists of, say, ten drilling machines, how much discount could you get for buying ten machines instead of one only?

If we have those difficulties looking at identical assets, what happens when we are trying to find out these figures for assets which cannot still be matched on the market? Technological change has greatly speeded up in recent years. If there is a second-hand market, it may be quite possible to get a valuation. However, in second-hand markets the price is often even more subject to negotiation. It becomes even more complicated when the original asset was specially made and there is no exactly comparable item, new or second-hand.

The difficulties outlined above mean that solutions to valuation can be sought under three headings:

(a) **Market prices.** As already mentioned, there will often be a market, new or second-hand, for the assets. For instance, this is particularly true for motor vehicles. If our asset differs in some way an adjustment may be necessary, thus cutting into the desirable degree of objectivity.

(b) **Units of service.** Where a market price is unobtainable, this being especially so with obsolete assets, a value is placed on the units of service which the asset can provide, rather than trying to value the asset itself.

For instance, assume that a machine has an estimated future production capacity of 1,000 units. A new machine producing the same type of product might have a total future capacity of 5,000 units. If the running costs of the machines are the same, the value of the old machine can be said to be one-fifth of the cost of the new one, as that is the proportion its future capacity bears to the new one. If the running costs were different an adjustment would be made.

(c) **Cost of inputs.** If the asset was made or constructed by the owner, it may be possible to calculate the cost of replacing it at the balance sheet date. Present rates of labour and materials costs could be worked out to give the replacement cost.

4 Net realisable value

Net realisable value means the estimated amount that would be received from the sale of the asset less the estimated costs on its disposal. The term '**exit value**' is often used as it is the amount receivable when an asset leaves the business.

A very important factor affecting such a valuation is the conditions under which the assets are to be sold. To realise in a hurry would often mean accepting a very low price. Look at the sale prices received from stock from bankruptcies – usually very low figures. The standard way of approaching this problem is to value as though the realisation were 'in the normal course of business'. This is not capable of an absolutely precise meaning, as economic conditions change and the firm might never sell such an asset 'in the normal course of business'.

The difficulties of establishing an asset's net realisable value are similar to those of the replacement value method when similar assets are not being bought and sold in the market-place. However, the problems are more severe as the units of service approach cannot be used, since that takes the seller's rather than buyer's viewpoint.

5 Economic value (present value)

As any economist would be delighted to tell you, they would value an asset as the sum of the future expected net cash flows associated with the asset, discounted to its present value. The technicalities of discounting are discussed in Chapter 46.

Certainly, if you really did know (not guess) the future net cash flows associated with the asset and you had the correct discount rate, your valuation would be absolutely correct. The trouble is that it is impossible to forecast future net cash flows with certainty, neither will we necessarily have chosen the correct discount rate. It is also very difficult to relate cash flows to a particular asset, since a business's assets combine together to generate revenue.

6 Deprival value

The final concept of value is based on ideas propounded in the USA by Professor Bonbright in the 1930s, and later developed in the UK for profit measurement by Professor W T Baxter.

Deprival value is based on the concept of the value of an asset being the amount of money the owner would have to receive to compensate them exactly for being deprived of it. We had better point out immediately that the owner does not have to be deprived of the asset to ascertain this value, it is a hypothetical exercise. This leads to a number of consequences.

(a) Deprival value cannot exceed replacement cost, since if the owner were deprived of the asset they could replace it for a lesser amount. Here we will ignore any costs concerned with a delay in replacement.

(b) If the owner feels that the asset is not worth replacing, its replacement cost would be more than its deprival value. They simply would not pay the replacement cost, so the value to the owner is less than that figure.

(c) If the asset's deprival value is to be taken as its net realisable value, that value must be less than its replacement cost. It would otherwise make sense for someone to sell the asset at net realisable value and buy a replacement at a lower cost. Again, delays in replacement are ignored.

(d) Take the case where an owner would not replace the asset, but neither would they sell it. It is possible to envisage a fixed asset which has become obsolete but might possibly be used, for example, when other machines break down. It is not worth buying a new machine, as the replacement cost is more than the value of the machine to the business. Such a machine may well have a very low net realisable value.

The benefit to the business of keeping such a machine can be said to be its 'value in use'. This value must be less than its replacement cost, as pointed out above, but more than its net realisable value for otherwise the owner would sell it.

It is probably easier to summarise how to find 'deprival value' by means of the diagram in Exhibit 32.1.

Exhibit 32.1 Deprival value

This can be illustrated by a few examples, using assets A, B and C.

	Asset A	Asset B	Asset C
	£	£	£
Replacement cost (RC)	1,000	800	600
Net realisable value (NRV)	900	500	400
Economic value (EV)	2,000	700	300

The deprival values can be explained as follows. Check them against Exhibit 32.1.

(a) Asset A. If the firm were deprived of asset A, what would it do? As economic value is greater than replacement cost it would buy another asset A. The deprival value to the business is therefore £1,000, i.e. replacement cost.

(b) Asset B. If deprived of asset B, what would the firm do? It would not replace it, as RC £800 is greater than its value to the business – its economic value £700. If deprived, the firm would therefore lose the present value of future cash flows, i.e. economic value £700. This then is the deprival value for asset B.

(c) Asset C. With this asset there would be no point in keeping it, as its economic value to the firm is less than the firm could sell it for. Selling it is the logical way, so the deprival value is net realisable value £400.

32.5 Capital maintenance

Let us go back to Sir John Hicks's definition of income (profit): 'A man's income is the maximum value which he can consume during a week, and still expect to be as well off at the end of the week as he was at the beginning.'

We have looked at the different ways we could value assets as a preliminary to totalling them to find the wealth or 'well-offness' at a particular date. Before going any further we must examine the problems of measuring the maintenance of wealth (or 'well-offness') over a period. We could call this **capital maintenance**.

The basic method used in accounting, and described earlier throughout this book, is that of **money capital maintenance**. Using this approach, if a firm has £1,000 in capital or net assets on 1 January 19X1 it must have £1,000 in capital or net assets at 31 December 19X1 to be as well off at the end of the period. This means that, provided no new share capital has been issued and no dividends have been paid or share capital withdrawn, a company starting with capital of £1,000 on 1 January 19X2 and finishing with capital of £1,600 on 31 December 19X2 must have made a profit of £600, using this approach to capital maintenance.

Such a method would be acceptable to everyone in a period when there is no change in prices. However, most people would agree that the approach is not satisfactory when either prices in general, or specific prices affecting the firm, are changing. In these two cases, to state that £600 profit has been made for 19X2 completely ignores the fact that the £1,000 at 1 January 19X2 and the £1,000 at 31 December 19X2 do not have the same value. From this we can see the possibilities of three different concepts.

1   **Money capital maintenance.** The traditional system of accounting as already described.
2   **Real capital maintenance.** This concept is concerned with maintaining the general purchasing power of the equity shareholders. This takes into account changes in the purchasing power of money as measured by the retail price index.
3   **Maintenance of specific purchasing power of the capital of the equity.** This uses a price index which is related to the specific price changes of the goods in which the firm deals.

From these we can look at the following example, which illustrates three different figures of profit being thrown up for a firm.

32.6 A worked example

A company has only equity share capital. Its net assets on 1 January 19X5 are £1,000, and on 31 December 19X5 £1,400. There have been no issues or withdrawal of share capital during the year. The general rate of inflation, as measured by the retail price index, is 10 per cent, whereas the specific rate of price increase for the type of goods in which the company deals is 15 per cent. The profits for the three measures are as follows:

	(a) Money maintenance of capital	(b) Real capital maintenance	(c) Maintenance of specific purchasing power
	£	£	£
Net assets 31 Dec 19X5	1,400	1,400	1,400
Less What net assets would have to be at 31 Dec 19X5 to be as well off on 1 Jan 19X5			
(a) Money maintenance	1,000		
(b) Real capital £1,000 + 10%		1,100	
(c) Specific purchasing power maintenance £1,000 + 15%			1,150
Profit	400	300	250

Note that under the three methods:

(a) here the normal accounting method gives £400 profit;
(b) this case recognises that there has been a fall in the purchasing power of money;
(c) this takes into account that it would cost £1,150 for goods whose value at the start of the year was £1,000.

32.7 Combinations of different values and capital maintenance concepts

We have just looked at three ways of calculating profits based on historical cost allied with three capital maintenance concepts. This can be extended by using replacement cost or net realisable value instead. Each of these, when adjusted by each capital maintenance concept, will give three separate figures for profit. Together the three different means of valuation, multiplied by three different concepts of capital maintenance, will give us nine different profit figures.

At this stage in your studies it will be difficult to understand how such different profit measures could be useful for different purposes. We can leave this until your studies progress to more advanced examinations. However, we can use one simple example to illustrate how using only the traditional way of calculating profits can have dire consequences. The next example shows how this can happen.

32.8 A worked example

A company has net assets on 1 January 19X7 of £100,000 financed purely by equity share capital. During 19X7 there has been no injection or withdrawal of capital. At 31 December 19X7 net assets have risen to £115,000. Both the retail price index and the specific price index for the goods dealt in have risen by 25 per cent. Taxation, based on traditional historical cost calculations (maintenance of money capital), is at the rate of 40 per cent. The profit may be calculated as follows.

	Maintenance of money capital	Maintenance of real capital and of specific purchasing power
	£	£
Net assets on 31 Dec 19X7	115,000	115,000
Less Net assets needed to be as well off at 31 Dec 19X7 as with £100,000 on 1 Jan 19X7		
(a) Money capital	100,000	
(b) Both real capital and specific purchasing power £100,000 + 25%		125,000
Profit/loss	15,000	(10,000)

Tax payable is £15,000 × 40% = £6,000. Yet the real capital or that of specific purchasing power has fallen by £10,000. When tax is paid that would leave us with net assets of £115,000 − £6,000 = £109,000. Because of price changes £109,000 could not finance the amount of activity financed by £100,000 one year before. The operating capacity of the company would therefore be reduced.

Obviously it is not equitable for a company to have to pay tax on what is in fact a loss. It is only the traditional way of measuring profits that has thrown up a profit figure.

32.9 Operating capital maintenance concept

This approach looks at the output which could be generated by the initial holding of assets. A profit will only be made if the assets held at the end of the period are able to maintain the same level of output.

A very simple example of this is that of a trader who sells only one product, a particular kind of watch. The only costs the trader incurs are those of buying the watches. They have no assets apart from watches. In this case the operating capital consists solely of watches.

Using the historical cost concept the trader will recognise a profit if the revenue from the sale of a watch exceeded the historic cost of it. However, using the operating capital maintenance concept they will recognise a profit only if the revenue from the sale is greater than the cost of buying another watch to replace the watch sold.

PART II: ACCOUNTING FOR CHANGING PRICE LEVELS

32.10 Introduction

As you have seen already in this chapter, changes in price levels can lead to both profit and asset valuation figures being far from reality if simple historical cost figures are used. This is not a recently observed phenomenon. As far back as 1938, Sir Ronald Edwards wrote several classic articles which were published in *The Accountant*. You can find these in the book, *Studies in Accounting Theory*, edited by W T Baxter and S Davidson and published by the Institute of Chartered Accountants, London, 1977.

The greater the rate of change in price levels, the greater the distortion. The clamour for changes to simple historical cost accounting is noticeably greater when the inflation rate is high – at such times the deficiencies of historical cost accounts are most obvious. If there were a period of deflation, however, the historical cost accounts would be still misleading.

In certain countries in the world the annual rate of inflation in recent years has been several hundred per cent. Historical cost accounts in those countries would certainly be at odds with accounts adjusted for inflation. In the UK the highest rate in recent years, based on the RPI, was 17.8 per cent for 1979, falling to less than 5 per cent in some years.

We can now look, in outline only, at suggestions made in the UK since 1968 as to methods which could be used to adjust accounts for changing price levels.

32.11 Current purchasing power (CPP)

This proposal is something you have already read about. It is the adjustment of historical cost accounting figures by a price index figure to give figures showing what we called real capital maintenance. It will convey more of the problems and uncertainties facing the accounting profession in this regard, if we look at the history of the various proposals.

First came *Accounting for stewardship in a period of inflation*, published in 1968 by the Research Foundation of the Institute of Chartered Accountants in England and Wales (ICAEW). Stemming from this came Exposure Draft No 8 (ED 8), published in 1973. ED 8 contained the proposal that companies should be required to publish, in addition to their conventional accounts, supplementary statements which would be, in effect, their final accounts amended to conform to CPP principles. In May 1974 a Provisional Statement of Standard Accounting Practice No 7 (PSSAP 7) was published. Notice the sign of uncertainty; it was a **provisional** standard – the only one yet published. Compared with ED 8, which said that a company should be *required* to publish CPP accounts, PSSAP 7 simply *requested* them to publish such accounts. Many companies would not accede to such a request.

PSSAP 7 stipulated that the price index to be used in the conversion of accounts from historical cost should be the retail price index (RPI). As the actual price index relating to the goods dealt in by the firm might be quite different from RPI, the CPP accounts could well be distant from the current values of the firm itself.

The exact nature of the calculations needed for CPP accounts is not part of your syllabus, and we will not repeat them here.

Many people, including the government, were completely dissatisfied with the CPP approach. After ED 8 was issued the government set up its own committee of inquiry into inflation accounting. The chairman of the committee was Sir Francis Sandilands. The report, often known as the Sandilands Report, was published in September 1975.

32.12 Current cost accounting (CCA)

The Sandilands Committee's approach was quite different from ED 8 and PSSAP 7. The committee recommended a system called **current cost accounting** (CCA). This basically approved the concept of capital maintenance as the maintenance of operating capacity.

After the Sandilands Report appeared, the accounting bodies, as represented by their own Accounting Standards Committee (ASC), abandoned their proposals in PSSAP 7. A working party, the Inflation Accounting Steering Group (IASG), was set up to prepare a Statement of Standard Accounting Practice based on the Sandilands Report.

This group published ED 18, 'Current cost accounting', in November 1976. It was attacked by many members of the ICAEW, whose members passed, in July 1977, a resolution rejecting compulsory use of CCA. However, the government continued its support, and in November 1977 the accounting profession issued a set of interim recommendations called the Hyde guidelines (named after the chairman of the committee). The second exposure draft, ED 24, was issued in April 1979, followed by SSAP 16 in March 1980. SSAP 16 was to last three years to permit the evaluation of the introduction of CCA. After this, ED 35 was published in July 1984.

In November 1986 the CCAB Accounting Standards Committee published its handbook, *Accounting for the effects of changing prices*. At the same time presidents of five of the leading accountancy bodies issued the following statement:

'The presidents of five of the leading accountancy bodies welcome the publication by the CCAB Accounting Standards Committee of its Handbook on *Accounting for the effects of changing prices*.

The presidents endorse the CCAB Accounting Standards Committee's view that, where a company's results and financial position are materially affected by changing prices, historical cost accounts alone are insufficient and that information on the effects of changing prices is important for an appreciation of the company's results and financial position. The presidents join the Accounting Standards Committee in encouraging companies to appraise and, where material, report the effects of changing prices.

The five bodies have proposed that SSAP 16, "Current cost accounting", which was made non-mandatory by all the CCAB bodies in June 1985, should now be formally withdrawn. They take the view, however, that the subject of accounting for the effects of changing prices is one of great importance. Accordingly, they support the Accounting Standards Committee in its continuing work on the subject and agree that an acceptable accounting standard should be developed.'

The Institute of Chartered Accountants in England and Wales; The Institute of Chartered Accountants of Scotland; The Institute of Chartered Accountants in

Ireland; The Chartered Institute of Management Accountants; The Chartered Institute of Public Finance and Accountancy.

So once again the idea of forcing companies to produce accounts adjusted for changing prices was rejected. The emphasis is now on encouragement, rather than trying to force companies to do it.

The reason why, at this early stage in your studies, we have given you some of the history behind the efforts to compel companies to produce CCA accounts is to illustrate the conflicts that have taken place inside and outside the accountancy profession. Opinions on the merits of CCA accounts are widely divided. You will study this in greater detail in the later stages of more advanced examinations, but we feel we should make clear at the outset that it is a controversial topic.

32.13 Handbook on *Accounting for the effects of changing price levels*

We can now look at the main outline of this handbook. The ASC encouraged companies to co-operate in an attempt to produce accounts suitable for the effects of changing price levels. In doing this it did not try to recommend any one method, or even recommend one way only of publishing the results. The handbook says that the information may be presented:

(a) as the main accounts; or
(b) in the notes to the accounts; or
(c) as information supplemental to the financial statements.

The handbook first examines the problems.

32.14 Problems during a period of changing price levels

Obviously, the greater the rate of change, the greater will be the problems. We can now list some of them.

1   **Fixing selling prices.** If you can change your prices very quickly, an extreme case being a market trader, this problem hardly exists. For a company setting prices which it is expected to maintain for a reasonably long period, the problems are severe. It dare not price too highly, as early demand may be reduced by an excessive price; on the other hand, the company has to guess how prices are going to change over a period so that sufficient profit is made.

2   **Financial planning.** As it is so difficult to guess how prices are going to change over a period, planning the firm's finances becomes particularly trying. Obviously, it would be better if the plans were revised frequently as conditions changed.

3   **Paying taxation and replacing assets.** We have seen earlier how, during a period of inflation, traditional historic accounting will tend to overstate profits. Such artificial 'profits' are then taxed. Unless various supplementary tax allowances are given, the taxation paid is both excessive and more than true profits, adjusted for inflation, can bear easily. This tends to lead to companies being short of cash, too much having been taken in tax. Therefore, when assets which have risen in price have to be replaced, adequate finance may not be available.

4   **Monetary assets.** If stocks of goods are held, they will tend to rise in money terms during a period of inflation. On the other hand, holding monetary assets, e.g. cash,

bank and debtors, will be counter-productive. A bank balance of £1,000 held for six months, during which the purchasing power of money has fallen 10 per cent, will in real terms be worth only 90 per cent of its value six months before. Similarly, in real terms debt of £5,000 owed continually over that same period will have seen its real value fall by 10 per cent.

5 **Dividend distribution.** Just as it is difficult to calculate profits, so is it equally difficult to decide how much to pay as dividends without impairing the efficiency and operating capability of the company. At the same time the shareholders will be looking to payment of adequate dividends.

32.15 Solutions to the problems

The handbook recommends the use of one of two concepts. These will now be examined fairly briefly, in as much detail as is needed at this stage of your examinations.

1 Profit under the operating capital maintenance concept

This has been mentioned previously, with a simple example given of a trader buying and selling watches. Under this concept several adjustments are needed to the profit calculated on the historical cost basis. Each adjustment is now considered.

Adjustment 1: holding gains and operating gains

Nearly all companies hold fixed assets and stocks. For each of these assets the opportunity cost will bear little relationship to its historic cost. Instead it is the asset's value to the business at date of consumption, and this is usually the replacement cost of the asset.

Accordingly the historic cost profit, which was based on money capital maintenance, can be divided into two parts.

(a) Current cost profit, or operating gains. This is the difference between sales revenue and the replacement cost of the assets.
(b) Holding gains. This is the replacement cost of the assets less historical cost of those assets.

For example, a company buys an asset for £1,000 on 1 January 19X4. It holds it for one year and sells it for £1,600 when the replacement cost is £1,200. There has been a historical cost profit of £600. This can be analysed as in Exhibit 32.2.

Exhibit 32.2

Profit for 19X4	£
Historical cost profit (£1,600–£1,000)	600
Less Holding gain (£1,200–£1,000)	200
Current cost profit (or operating gain)	400

To put it another way, the company makes £200 historical profit by simply holding the asset from when its replacement cost (i.e. original cost) was £1,000, until the date of sale when its replacement cost was £1,200. The actual current cost profit at point of sale must reflect conditions at date of sale, i.e. the company has sold for £1,600 something which would currently cost £1,200 to replace. The current cost profit is therefore £400.

The holding gains are often described as a cost of sales adjustment (COSA).

Adjustment 2: depreciation

Depreciation is to be adjusted to current replacement cost values. Without going into complicated examples, this means that if the historical cost of depreciation is £4,000 and the current cost of depreciation, based on current replacement cost values, is £7,000, the adjustment should be £3,000 as follows:

	£
Depreciation based on historical cost	4,000
Adjustment needed to bring depreciation charge to CCA basis	3,000
CCA depreciation	7,000

Adjustment 3: monetary working capital adjustment

The monetary working capital needed to support the operating capability of the business will be affected by inflation. An adjustment will be needed to the historic profits in respect of this.

Adjustment 4: gearing adjustment

If we borrow £1,000 now, and have to pay back exactly £1,000 in five years, we will gain during a period of inflation. We will be able to put the £1,000 to use at current purchasing power. In five years' time, if £1 now is worth only 60p then, we will have gained because we will only be giving up £600 of current purchasing power now. The gearing adjustment is an attempt to adjust current cost operating profits for this factor.

2 Profit and loss account based on the operating capital maintenance concept

A general idea how such a profit and loss account could appear can now be given.

RST Ltd

Profit and Loss Account incorporating Operating Capital Maintenance Concept adjustments

	£	£
Profit on the historical cost basis, before interest and taxation		100,000
Less Current cost operating adjustments:		
(1) Holding gains (COSA)	15,000	
(2) Depreciation	10,000	
(3) Monetary working capital	5,000	30,000
Current cost operating profit		70,000
(4) Gearing adjustment	(2,000)	
Interest payable less receivable	6,000	4,000
Current cost profit before taxation		66,000
Taxation		25,000
Current cost profit attributable to shareholders		41,000
Dividends		30,000
Retained current cost profit for the year		11,000

3 Profit under the financial capital maintenance concept

According to the handbook this method is sometimes known as the 'real terms' system of accounting. The steps by which the profit is calculated can be summarised as:

(a) calculate shareholders' funds at the beginning of the period, based on current cost asset values; then

(b) restate that opening amount in terms of pounds at the end of the period, by adjusting (a) by the relevant change in a general price index (e.g. RPI); then

(c) calculate shareholders' funds at the end of the period, based on current cost values.

Assuming that there have been no introductions or withdrawals of capital, including dividends, if (c) is greater than (b) a 'real terms' profit will have been made. Otherwise a loss will have been incurred.

Allowance will have to be made in steps (a) to (c) above where there have been introductions or withdrawals of capital, or where there have been dividends.

The calculation of 'real terms' profit, as described, has been by way of comparing opening and closing balance sheets. Suppose that the 'real terms' profit figure had been £10,000, it could in fact have been calculated in the following manner:

	£	£
Historical cost profit		7,800
Add Holding gains: the amount by which the current costs of the assets have increased over the period	3,400	
Less Inflation adjustment: the amount by which general inflation has eroded shareholders' funds	1,200	
Real holding gains		2,200
Total real gains		10,000

The balance sheet approach was described first, as it is probably the easier to understand in the first instance. Obviously the link between opening and closing balance sheets can be traced to total real gains, which can also be explained using the profit and loss account concept.

4 Current cost balance sheet

The two main differences between a current cost balance sheet and a historical cost balance sheet are as follows:

(a) assets are shown at value to the business on the balance sheet date, rather than at any figure based on historical cost or at any previous revaluation;

(b) obviously the balance sheet would not balance if asset values were altered without an amendment somewhere else. A current cost reserve account is opened, additions to historical cost account values are debited to each asset account, whilst a credit will be made in the current cost reserve account. Entries are also made here to complete the double entry in respect of the four adjustments in the current cost profit and loss account. As a result, all double entry adjustments are made in this account and so the balance sheet will now balance.

32.16 More on current cost accounting

Chapter 33 further explores this topic.

PART III: OBJECTIVES OF FINANCIAL STATEMENTS

32.17 Introduction

Earlier in this chapter we pointed out that a recent development in accounting theory had been towards identifying the users of accounts, and then finding out the type of information they require. Both *The Corporate Report 1975* and the 1975 *Sandilands Report* were directed in this fashion.

32.18 Users of accounts

The main users of published accounts of large companies are now identified with the main reasons they require the accounts.

1 **Shareholders of the company,** both existing and potential, will want to know how effectively the directors are performing their stewardship function. They will use the accounts as a base for decisions to dispose of some or all of their shares, or to buy some.

2 **The loan-creditor group.** This consists of existing and potential debenture and loan stock holders, and providers of short-term secured funds. They will want to ensure that interest payments will be made promptly and capital repayments will be made as agreed. Debenture and loan stock holders, whether redeemable or irredeemable, will also want to be able to assess how easily they may dispose of their debentures or loan stocks, should they so wish.

3 **Employee groups,** including existing, potential and past employees. These can include trade unions whose members are employees. Past employees will be mainly concerned with ensuring that any pensions, etc., paid by the company are maintained. Present employees will be interested in ensuring that the company is able to keep on operating, so maintaining their jobs and paying them acceptable wages, and that any pension contributions are maintained. In addition, they may want to ensure that the company is being fair to them, so that they get a reasonable share of the profits accruing to the firm from their efforts. Trade unions will be upholding the interests of their members, and will possibly use the accounts in wage and pension negotiations. Potential employees will be interested in assessing whether or not it would be worth seeking employment with the company.

4 **Bankers.** Where the bank has not given a loan or granted an overdraft, there will be no great need to see the accounts. Where money is owed to the banks, they will want to ensure that payments of interest will be made when due, and that the firm will be able to repay the loan or overdraft at the correct time.

5 **The business contact group.** This includes trade creditors and suppliers, who will want to know whether or not they will continue to be paid, and the prospects for a profitable future association. Customers are included, since they will want to know whether or not the company is a secure source of supply. Business rivals in this group will be trying to assess their own position compared with the firm. Potential takeover bidders, or those interested in a merger will want to assess the desirability of any such move.

6 **The analyst/adviser group.** These will need information for their clients or their

readers. Financial journalists need information for their readers. Stockbrokers need it to advise investors. Credit agencies want it to be able to advise present and possible suppliers of goods and services to the company as to its creditworthiness.

7 **The Inland Revenue** will need the accounts to assess the tax payable by the company.

8 **Other official agencies.** Various organisations concerned with the supervision of industry and commerce may want the accounts for their purposes.

9 **Management.** In addition to the internally produced management accounts the management is also vitally concerned with any published accounts. It has to consider the effect of such published accounts on the world at large.

10 **The public.** This consists of groups such as ratepayers, taxpayers, political parties, pressure groups and consumers. The needs of these parties will vary accordingly.

32.19 Characteristics of useful information

From the various reports which have appeared since 1975 the following characteristics have been noted.

1 **Relevance.** This is regarded as one of the two main qualities. The information supplied should be that which will satisfy the needs of its users.

2 **Reliability.** This is regarded as the other main quality. Obviously, if such information is also subject to an independent check, such as that of the auditor, this will considerably enhance the reliance people can place on the information.

3 **Objectivity.** Information which is free from bias will increase the reliance people place on it. It is, therefore, essential that the information is prepared as objectively as possible. Management may often tend to give a better picture of its own performance that is warranted, and is therefore subjective. It is the auditor's task to counter this view, and to ensure objectivity in the accounts.

4 **Ability to be understood.** Information is not much use to a recipient if it is presented in such a manner that no one can understand it. This is not necessarily the same as simplicity.

5 **Comparability.** Recipients of accounts will want to compare them both with previous accounts of that company and with the results of other companies; without comparability the accounts would be of little use.

6 **Realism.** This can be largely covered by the fact that accounts should show a 'true and fair' view. It has also been contended that accounts should not give a sense of absolute precision when such precision cannot exist.

7 **Consistency.** This is one of the basic concepts, but it is not to be followed slavishly if new and improved accounting techniques indicate a change in methods.

8 **Timeliness.** Up-to-date information is of more use to recipients than outdated news.

9 **Economy of presentation.** Too much detail can obscure the important factors in accounts and cause difficulties in understanding them.

10 **Completeness.** A rounded picture of the company's activities is needed.

32.20 Problems of information production in accounting

You have seen that a company's profit and loss account and balance sheet produced for general publication is a multi-purpose document. The present state of the art of accounting is such that we have not yet arrived at producing specific financial reports for each group of users, tailored to their special needs.

At times, companies do produce special reports for certain groups of users. A bank, for instance, will almost certainly want to see a forecast of future cash flows before granting a loan or overdraft. The Inland Revenue will often require various analyses in order to agree the tax position. Some companies produce special reports for the use of their employees. In total, such extra reports are a very small part of the reports which could be issued.

Of course, producing reports is not costless. To produce special reports, exactly tailored to every possible group of users, would be extremely costly and time-consuming. It is hardly likely that any existing company would wish to do so. There is, however, no doubt that this is the way things are moving and will continue to move.

For the present, however, most companies produce one set of accounts for all the possible users, with the exception that management will have produced its own management accounts for its own internal purposes. Obviously such a multi-purpose document cannot satisfy all the users. In fact, it will almost certainly not fully satisfy the needs of any one user group – save that it must satisfy the legal requirements of the Companies Act.

Published accounts are, therefore, a compromise between the requirements of users and the maintenance of accounting concepts, subject to the overriding scrutiny of the auditor. Judgement has a major impact on the information presented. It can be said that if two large companies operating in the same industry and in the same location had identical share capitals, liabilities, numbers of employees, assets, turnover, costs, transactions, and so on, the published accounts of the two companies would not be identical. Differences would arise for a number of reasons. For example, depreciation methods and policies may vary, as may stock valuation assessments, bad debt provisions, figures for revaluation of properties, etc. There will also probably be rather more subtle distinctions, many of which you will come across in the later stages of your studies.

33

Alternatives to historic cost accounting

Objectives

After you have studied this chapter, you should:

- *know why historic cost accounts are deficient in times of rising prices*

- *understand different valuation methods*

- *know the purposes of specific price indices for assets and liabilities*

- *have an understanding of the adjustments necessary in order to convert historic costs to current costs*

- *be able to prepare a current cost balance sheet and current cost profit and loss account*

33.1 Introduction

Accounts have traditionally been prepared for two main purposes, stewardship and decision making. The Accounting Standards Board's Exposure Draft: Statement of Principles, published in 1991, outlined several user groups with varying needs, all of whom are interested in financial information. Shareholders are interested in different information than trade creditors. This information has traditionally been provided by financial statements prepared under the historic cost convention. However, there are circumstances when financial statements prepared under this traditional approach can present financial information in a misleading way.

Consider the following example. On 1 January 19X4, a company invests in 500 widgets for £1,000, that is £2 per unit. Shortly before the year end, when the replacement cost of a widget is £2.20 per unit, the stock is sold for £1,200. On a historic cost basis, the profit is recorded as follows:

	£
Sales	1,200
Cost of Sales	1,000
Profit	200

However, in order to maintain the same operating capacity, the company will need to invest in more widgets at a cost of £1,100 (500 × £2.20). If the company distributes the £200 as a dividend, it will only be left with £1,000 and cannot make this investment. From this simple example, one of the major criticisms of historic cost accounting is evident – its inability to reflect the effects of changing prices. Obviously, this criticism is dependent upon the level of inflation at the time.

An acceptable alternative to historic cost accounting has been sought by the accountancy profession in the United Kingdom for several years. The attempts of the Accounting Standards Committee (ASC) to introduce a system of inflation accounting, which are outlined in Chapter 32, failed. The culmination of great effort and numerous exposure drafts and standards was the ASC Handbook, *Accounting for the Effects of Changing Prices*, published in 1986. The remainder of this chapter considers several of the issues dealt with in the Handbook in the context of the preparation of a set of current cost accounts. It is worth noting that the ASB recognises that the present system of historic cost accounting, modified by voluntary revaluations of certain assets, is unsatisfactory. The ASB aims to tackle the issue, and current values are once again on the agenda. It is unlikely, however, that a system of current cost accounting will be introduced without difficulty.

33.2 Valuation

Under historic cost accounting, assets and liabilities are recorded at their actual cost at the date of transaction. For example, when a new machine is purchased, the price per the invoice can be recorded in the books of the business. Whilst this is a familiar and reasonably cheap method of recording the assets and liabilities of an entity, its main advantage is its objectivity. The historic cost of an item is an objective verifiable fact that can easily be ascertained from the records of the business. It is worth noting that there is some degree of subjectivity in the preparation of historic cost accounts. Consider, for example, the choice of suitable depreciation method for a fixed asset which is left to the discretion of the directors of the company. The size of the bad debts provision is also dependent upon the exercise of judgement. Notwithstanding this, it is fair to say that historic values have a high degree of reliability. The main disadvantage, particularly in times of changing prices, is their relevance, as demonstrated in the widget example in the previous section.

Current value accounting considers the following valuation methods which are covered in Chapter 32: **economic value, value to the business, replacement cost, net realisable value** and **recoverable amount**.

The **economic value** of an asset is the sum of the future expected net cash flows associated with the asset, discounted to its present value. **Value to the business**, or **deprival value**, can be considered an appropriate valuation basis for accounting purposes. If a business were deprived of an asset, it could either replace it, or choose not to. If the asset were replaced, then its current value to the business is its net current **replacement cost**. This is normally the current cost of a fixed asset, except where it has suffered a permanent diminution in value, in which case it will be written down to its **recoverable amount**. This may happen, for example, because there is no longer a market for the product. Alternatively, if the business would choose not to replace the asset, then it would sell it and its current cost is its **net realisable value**, i.e. the price at which it can be sold in the market.

How are these values determined by a business? The replacement cost of an asset can be approximated using a relevant index. Indices, published for example by the UK Government Statistical Service, are usually specific to a class of asset. A company may prepare its own index based on experience or, where it is not appropriate to use an index, a valuer may be relied upon. This is usual in the case of revaluing property. The index will indicate the change in value of the asset or class of asset.

Consider the following example. A machine was purchased on 1 January 19X2 for £75,000 when the relevant specific price index was 90. Its current value at 31 December 19X4, when the relevant specific price index is 120, is:

$$\frac{\text{Index at accounting date}}{\text{Index at date of purchase}} \times £75,000 = \frac{120}{90} \times £75,000 = £100,000$$

Replacement does not necessarily mean replacement of the asset with a similar asset. Rather, it focuses on replacement of the service potential of the asset and its contribution to the business.

Net realisable value is the price at which the asset could be sold in an arm's length transaction. A problem may arise where no market exists for the asset. The main problem with current values is the level of subjectivity involved in ascertaining valuations. A business may need to spend considerable time and effort ascertaining current values for its assets and liabilities.

33.3 Current cost accounts

The directors of Hillcrest Ltd are interested in preparing current cost accounts to reflect changing prices. They have prepared a historic cost balance sheet and profit and loss account (Exhibit 33.1). The relevant price indices for plant and machinery, stock, debtors and creditors, are given in Exhibit 33.2.

Exhibit 33.1

Hillcrest Ltd

Balance Sheet as at 30 June (£000s)

	19X5		19X4	
Fixed assets				
Plant and machinery				
Cost		800		800
Depreciation		320		240
Net book value		480		560
Current assets				
Stock	250		200	
Trade debtors	180		110	
Cash	105		75	
	535		385	
Current liabilities				
Trade creditors	(90)		(100)	
Net current assets		445		285
10% loan stock		(310)		(310)
		615		535
Financed by				
Ordinary shares		200		200
Reserves		415		335
		615		535

Hillcrest Ltd

Profit and Loss Account for year ending 30 June 19X5 (£000s)

Sales		1,700
Cost of sales		
Opening stock	200	
Purchases	1,375	
	1,575	
Less Closing stock	250	
		1,325
Gross profit		375
Interest	31	
Depreciation	80	
Other expenses	184	
		295
Net profit		80

Exhibit 33.2

Price index for stock at the end of each month:

March	19X4	109
April	19X4	112
June	19X4	114
December	19X4	116
March	19X5	122
April	19X5	126
June	19X5	130

Average for the year ending 30 June 19X5   126

Plant and machinery index			*Debtors and creditors index*		
June	19X1	80	June	19X4	110
June	19X2	90	June	19X5	200
June	19X3	100			
June	19X4	105			
June	19X5	110	Average for	19X5	155

In order to prepare current cost accounts, the first step is to calculate current values for the assets. Hillcrest Ltd's plant and machinery was purchased for £800,000 on 1 July 19X1. The current value of the plant and machinery at 30 June 19X5 is:

$$\text{Plant and machinery at cost} \times \frac{\text{Index at balance sheet date}}{\text{Index at date of purchase}} = £800,000 \times \frac{110}{80} = £1,100,000$$

The accumulated depreciation of £320,000 charged in the historic cost accounts, representing 40 per cent of the asset which has been consumed, is also restated. The current value of the depreciation is:

$$£320,000 \times \frac{110}{80} = £440,000$$

On average, Hillcrest Ltd's stock was acquired three months before the year end. Hence, its current value, rounded to the nearest £000, at 30 June 19X5 is:

$$£250,000 \times \frac{130}{122} = £266,393$$

Monetary assets, for example trade debtors and cash, and monetary liabilities, including trade creditors, are not restated. These items have a fixed monetary value which does not change. For example, if you borrow £1,000 today under an agreement to repay in 12 months, the monetary value of the amount borrowed will not change, that is you will repay £1,000. However, in times of rising prices, the market value of the amount will decrease. This gain will be dealt with later in the chapter.

33.4 Current cost reserve

Having revalued both plant and machinery and stock to their current values, the following revaluation gains are recorded:

	Plant and machinery £	Stock £
Current book value	660,000[1]	266,393
Historic book value	480,000	250,000
Surplus on revaluation	180,000	16,393

[1] Plant at current cost less accumulated depreciation, i.e. £1,100,000 – £440,000

The total gain of £196,393 (£180,000 + £16,393) is not a gain which has been realised through a transaction, for example sale of goods at a profit. In addition, Hillcrest Ltd cannot distribute this revaluation gain as a dividend if it wishes to maintain its operating capacity. In this example the gain of £196,393 will be credited to a non-distributable reserve called the Current Cost Reserve. The balance sheet incorporating these revaluations is shown in Exhibit 33.3.

Exhibit 33.3, however, does not incorporate the effect of changing prices on the profit for the year. The reserves figure of £415,000 includes historic cost profit of £80,000 for the year ended 30 June 19X5. We will now consider adjustments necessary in order to calculate the current cost profit for Hillcrest Ltd for the year.

Exhibit 33.3

Hillcrest Ltd
Balance Sheet as at 30 June 19X5 (£000s)

Plant and machinery		
Current value		1,100
Depreciation		440
Net book value		660
Current assets		
Stock	266	
Debtors	180	
Cash	105	
	551	
Current liabilities		
Trade creditors	(90)	
Net current assets		461
10% loan stock		(310)
		811
Financed by		
Ordinary shares		200
Reserves		415
Current cost reserve		196
		811

33.5 Cost of sales adjustment

In calculating the profit for an accounting period, the cost of the goods sold (or cost of sales) is charged against sales. In Exhibit 33.1, sales of £1,700,000 are recorded at their invoiced prices during the year to 30 June 19X5. Likewise, purchases of £1,375,000 are recorded at their actual cost prices during the year. If we assume that activity occurs evenly throughout the year, a reasonable assumption unless trade is seasonal, then these figures will reflect the average prices for the period. The opening and closing stock valuations, in times of rising prices, will not reflect average prices under the historic cost convention. It is therefore necessary to adjust these figures in order to calculate the current cost of sales. This is carried out using an averaging method.

Using the price index for stock, the current cost of sales for Hillcrest Ltd is:

		£
Opening stock at average prices: £200,000 × $\frac{130}{109}$	=	238,532
Purchases (assume occur evenly through year)	=	1,375,000
		1,613,532
Closing stock at average prices: £250,000 × $\frac{130}{122}$	=	266,393
Current cost of sales	=	1,347,139

The cost of sales adjustment is the difference between the current cost of sales of £1,347,139 and the historic cost of sales of £1,325,000, i.e. £22,139. This is charged to the historic cost profit and loss account as an adjustment in order to arrive at the current cost profit. A corresponding amount will be credited to the current cost reserve.

33.6 Depreciation adjustment

Depreciation charged in the profit and loss account should be based on the value of the asset as stated in the balance sheet. Hence, an adjustment is necessary where depreciation has been based on the historic cost of a fixed asset. Consider the following example in which the depreciation charge is based on the value of the asset at the year end. A fixed asset is purchased on 1 January 19X3 for £10,000 when the relevant price index is 100. It is planned to depreciate this asset on a straight line basis at 20 per cent per annum. At the end of 19X3, when the index has moved to 110, the current value of the asset is:

$$£10,000 × \frac{110}{100} = £11,000$$

and depreciation based on current cost of the asset is:

$$£10,000 × \frac{110}{100} × 20\% = £2,200$$

The net book value of the asset as stated in the current cost balance sheet is:

	£
Asset at current value	11,000
Accumulated depreciation	2,200
	8,800

At the end of 19X4 the relevant index is 120, and the current value of the asset is:

$$£10,000 × \frac{120}{100} = £12,000$$

and the depreciation charge based on current cost is:

$$£10,000 × \frac{120}{100} × 20\% = £2,400$$

Hence, at the end of 19X4, the net book value of the asset in the current cost balance sheet is:

	£
Asset at current value	12,000
Accumulated depreciation	4,600
	7,400

Whilst 40 per cent of the value of the asset has been consumed at 31 December 19X4, it is noted that £4,600 is not 40 per cent of £12,000. This is due to an undercharge of £200 depreciation in 19X3 in current value terms. Hence, as the original cost of the asset is altered to reflect current values, so too must the aggregate depreciation. The term given to depreciation relating to earlier years is **backlog depreciation**. Backlog depreciation is not charged against this period's profit. As we saw in the Hillcrest example, only an adjustment for this year's depreciation is charged against profit. Backlog depreciation is charged to the current cost reserve.

For Hillcrest Ltd, depreciation charged at 10 per cent on the current value of the plant and machinery of £1,100,000 is £110,000. Comparing this with the historic cost depreciation charge in the historic cost profit and loss account of £80,000 gives an additional depreciation adjustment of £30,000. This is a charge in arriving at current cost profit for the year, the corresponding credit going to the current cost reserve.

33.7 Monetary working capital adjustment

The effect of changing prices on stock values has already been considered. In addition, during inflationary periods, the market value of monetary assets, e.g. trade debtors, trade creditors and cash, will change. In order for a business to maintain its operating capacity, this change needs to be reflected in the accounts. The **monetary working capital adjustment** represents the increase (or decrease) in finance necessary to provide an appropriate level of monetary working capital due to price changes, rather than a change in the volume of working capital. Cash is usually excluded from the calculation as the amount of cash held by a business may not relate to its operating activities. For example, cash may be held in order to make a capital investment. However, in the case of a bank, cash balances which are required to support daily operations are included in the **monetary working capital adjustment**.

Calculation of the monetary working capital adjustment is similar to the calculation of the cost of sales adjustment. The index for debtors should reflect changes in the cost of goods or services sold which are included in debtors. Likewise, the index for creditors should reflect changes in the cost of goods or services purchased which are included in creditors. A single index may be appropriate, and in some businesses, a fair approximation may be the index used for stock. Consider the following example:

	31 December 19X4 £	31 December 19X5 £
Trade debtors	9,000	12,000
Trade creditors	7,500	11,000
Monetary working capital	1,500	1,000

Relevant indices applicable to the business are:

31 December 19X4	100
31 December 19X5	200
Average for the year	150

The monetary working capital at 31 December 19X4 in the historic cost accounts is £1,500 (£9,000 – £7,500). Stating this at average values for the year gives:

$$£1,500 \times \frac{150}{100} = £2,250$$

The monetary working capital at 31 December 19X5 in the historic cost accounts is £1,000 (£12,000 – £11,000). Stating this at average values for the year gives:

$$£1,000 \times \frac{150}{200} = £750$$

The historic cost accounts show a decrease in monetary working capital over the year of £500. However, at average values for the year the monetary working capital is reduced by £1,500 (£2,250 – £750). The difference between the change under the historic cost convention and under the current cost convention of £1,000 (£1,500 – £500) – the monetary working capital adjustment – represents the change in working capital due to price changes during the year.

For Hillcrest Ltd the monetary working capital adjustment is calculated as follows:

	19X5 £	19X4 £
Trade debtors	180,000	110,000
Trade creditors	90,000	100,000
Net monetary working capital	90,000	10,000

Hence, the increase in monetary working capital in historic cost terms is £80,000 (£90,000 – £10,000).

Restating opening monetary working capital at average prices gives (to the nearest £000):

$$£10,000 \times \frac{155}{110} = £14,000$$

The value of closing monetary working capital at average prices is (to the nearest £000):

$$£90,000 \times \frac{155}{200} = £70,000$$

The increase in monetary working capital which is due to change in volume is £56,000 (£70,000 – £14,000). The increase due to price changes – the monetary working capital adjustment – is £24,000 (£80,000 – £56,000).

33.8 Current cost operating profit

Hillcrest Ltd's current cost operating profit, having applied the above adjustments, is given in Exhibit 33.4.

Exhibit 33.4

Hillcrest Ltd

Current Cost Operating Profit for year ending 30 June 19X5 (£000s)

Sales		1,700
Trading profit (add back interest)		111
Adjustments		
Cost of sales adjustment	22	
Monetary working capital adjustment	24	
Additional depreciation adjustment	30	76
Current cost operating profit		35

From the point of view of a business and maintenance of its operating capacity, the current cost operating profit is relevant. However, maintenance of financial capital is also relevant where a business is not financed solely by equity. In this case, account should be taken of the capital structure of the business.

33.9 Gearing adjustment

If a company is financed by debt, and prices increase, whilst the monetary value of the loan has not changed, the market value has reduced. This gain for shareholders is recorded by making a gearing adjustment. The gearing adjustment is calculated in the following way.

Firstly, a gearing proportion is calculated. This is:

Average net borrowings for the year (L) : Shareholders' interest (S) + L

For Hillcrest Ltd, its net borrowings for the two years to 30 June 19X5 are:

	19X5 £	19X4 £
Loan stock	310,000	310,000
Cash	105,000	75,000
Net borrowing	205,000	235,000

Hence, average net borrowings for the year to 30 June 19X5 are:

$$\frac{£205,000 + £235,000}{2} = £220,000$$

Shareholders' interest for both years are:

	19X5 £	19X4 £
Ordinary shares	200,000	200,000
Reserves	415,000	335,000
	615,000	535,000

Average shareholders' interest (S) for the year to 30 June 19X5 is:

$$\frac{£615,000 + £535,000}{2} = £575,000$$

The gearing proportion is:

$$\frac{L}{L + S} = \frac{£220,000}{£220,000 + £575,000} = 27.67\%$$

To calculate the gearing adjustment, this proportion is applied to the sum of the current cost adjustments for the year, that is:

	£
Cost of sales adjustment	23,000
Depreciation adjustment	30,000
Monetary working capital adjustment	24,000
	77,000

The gearing adjustment for Hillcrest Ltd (to the nearest £000) is:

27.67% × £77,000 = £21,000

Exhibit 33.5 shows the current cost reserve having made the above adjustments.

Exhibit 33.5

Current cost reserve	£000
Surplus on revaluation of plant and machinery	180
Additional depreciation adjustment	30
Surplus on revaluation of stock	16
Cost of sales adjustment	22
Monetary working capital adjustment	24
Gearing adjustment	(21)
Balance at 30 June 19X5	251

The current cost profit for the year to 30 June 19X5 is given in Exhibit 33.6.

Exhibit 33.6

Hillcrest Ltd

Current Cost Profit and Loss Account for year ending 30 June 19X5

			£000
Sales			1,700
Trading profit (add back interest)			111
Adjustments			
Cost of sales adjustment	22		
Monetary working capital adjustment	24		
Additional depreciation adjustment	30		
			76
Current cost operating profit			35
Gearing adjustment		21	
Less Interest payable		31	
			(10)
Current cost profit			25

The balance sheet for Hillcrest Ltd for 30 June 19X5, based on current costs, is given in Exhibit 33.7.

Exhibit 33.7

Hillcrest Ltd

Current Cost Balance Sheet as at 30 June 19X5

		£000
Plant and machinery		
Cost		1,100
Depreciation		440
Net book value		660
Current assets		
Stock	266	
Debtors	180	
Cash	105	
	551	
Current liabilities		
Trade creditors	(90)	
Net current assets		461
10% loan stock		(310)
		811
Financed by		
Ordinary shares		200
Reserves (335+25)		360
Current cost reserve		251
		811

Main points to remember

1 During inflationary periods, one of the main criticisms of historic cost accounting is its inability to reflect changing prices.

2 Deprival value is a suitable valuation basis for accounting purposes.

3 One of the major difficulties with current cost accounting is the level of subjectivity which can be involved in converting historic costs to current costs.

4 Relevant price indices, specific to an asset or class of assets, can approximate replacement cost.

5 The purpose of the cost of sales adjustment is to restate historic cost of sales in current cost terms by including opening and closing stock at average prices.

6 The depreciation adjustment ensures that the depreciation charge in the current cost profit and loss account is based on the current value of the asset as stated in the current cost balance sheet.

7 The monetary working capital adjustment reflects the change in the market value of monetary assets and liabilities, usually trade debtors and trade creditors, in the current cost accounts.

8 Gains or losses for shareholders, which arise due to debt financing in times of changing prices, are accounted for in the gearing adjustment.

9 Surpluses and deficits on revaluations are credited or charged to the current cost reserve, which is a non-distributable reserve.

Review questions

33.1 State whether you consider the following statements to be true or false:

(a) During inflationary periods, historic cost accounts do not reflect a true and fair view.
(b) The preparation of historic cost accounts does not involve subjectivity.
(c) Current cost accounting involves estimating future events.
(d) An index number must relate to a specific asset in order to be useful in converting historic cost accounts to current cost accounts.
(e) Where no market exists for an asset, conversion from historic cost to current cost can be difficult.

33.2A State whether you consider the following statements to be true or false:

(a) The current cost of plant and machinery is likely to be its net realisable value.
(b) A company should distribute dividends from the current cost reserve.
(c) The market value of a monetary asset, for example trade debtors, will decrease during inflationary periods.
(d) A gearing adjustment is necessary where a company is financed solely by equity capital.
(e) Backlog depreciation is charged to the current cost reserve.

33.3A What are the practical difficulties a company may encounter in ascertaining the current values of its assets?

33.4 Plant and machinery was purchased on 1 January 19X3 for £30,000, when the relevant specific price index was 90. What is the current cost value of the asset at 31 December 19X4 if the index at that date is 120?

33.5A The plant and machinery, details of which are given in question 33.4, is depreciated on a straight line basis at 10 per cent per annum. The depreciation charge is based on year-end values. What is the current cost depreciation charge for the year ended 31 December 19X5, if the index at that date is 160?

33.6 Calculate backlog depreciation at 31 December 19X5 for the plant and machinery whose details are given in question 33.5A.

33.7A A firm purchased machinery on 1 January 19X4 for £40,000, at which date the relevant price index for machinery was 100. Depreciation is charged on a straight line basis at 25 per cent per annum. The index at 31 December 19X4 had moved to 150, and at 31 December 19X5 it was 200. Show the current cost balance sheet entries for machinery at 31 December 19X4 and 31 December 19X5. Calculate the adjustments to the current cost reserve in respect of machinery.

33.8 The historic cost of sales figure for Apple Ltd for the year ended 31 December 19X3 is calculated as follows:

	£
Opening stock	50,000
Purchases	450,000
	500,000
Closing stock	70,000
Cost of sales	430,000

Price indices for stock are as follows:

Index at date of purchase of opening stock	80
Index at date of purchase of closing stock	120
Average index for 19X3	100
Index at 31 December 19X3	130

Assuming that purchases occur evenly throughout the year, calculate the cost of sales adjustment for Apple Ltd for 19X3.

33.9A The balance sheet of Seafield Ltd at 31 December 19X4 shows the following balances:

	31 December 19X4	31 December 19X3
	£	£
Trade debtors	35,000	30,000
Trade creditors	25,000	23,000

The relevant price indices for trade debtors and trade creditors are:

31 December 19X3	120
31 December 19X4	180
Average for the year ending 31 December 19X4	150

Using the above information, calculate the monetary working capital adjustment at 31 December 19X4 for Seafield Ltd.

33.10 If the relevant price indices for trade debtors and trade creditors are as follows, calculate the monetary working capital adjustment for Seafield Ltd, using the details given in question 33.9A.

31 December 19X3	200
31 December 19X4	280
Average for the year ending 31 December 19X4	240

33.11A The information given below has been extracted from the accounting records of Cedarwood Ltd for the year ended 30 June 19X4. Prepare a statement showing the current cost operating profit to 30 June 19X4.

	£
Sales	2,500,000
Historic cost operating profit	1,400,000
Current cost adjustments	
Additional depreciation adjustment	500,000
Cost of sales adjustment	750,000
Monetary working capital adjustment	25,000

33.12 The balance sheet for Cremore Ltd at 31 December 19X3 is given below (£000s):

	19X3		19X2	
Plant and machinery				
Cost		800		800
Depreciation		320		160
		480		640
Current assets				
Stock	210		130	
Debtors	100		60	
Cash	145		50	
	455		240	
Current liabilities				
Trade creditors	(80)		(60)	
Net current assets		375		180
10% loan stock		(200)		(200)
		655		620
Financed by				
Ordinary shares		250		250
Reserves		370		340
Current cost reserve		35		30
		655		620

Using the above information, calculate the gearing adjustment percentage:

$$\frac{L}{L + S}$$

33.13A The following information has been extracted from the accounting records of Sycamore Ltd for the year ended 30 June 19X3.

	£
Sales	9,000,000
Historic cost trading profit	4,000,000
Interest payable	500,000
Corporation tax charge for the year	1,500,000
Ordinary dividend	600,000
Additional depreciation adjustment	200,000
Cost of sales adjustment	800,000
Monetary working capital adjustment	370,000
Gearing adjustment: $\dfrac{L}{L + S}$	20%

Prepare a current cost profit and loss account for Sycamore Ltd for the year ended 30 June 19X3.

33.14 During a period of inflation, many accountants believe that financial reports prepared under the historical cost convention are subject to the following major limitations:

1 stocks are undervalued;
2 depreciation is understated;
3 gains and losses on net monetary assets are undisclosed;
4 balance sheet values are unrealistic; and
5 meaningful periodic comparisons are difficult to make.

Required:

Explain briefly the limitations of historical cost accounting in periods of inflation with reference to each of the items listed above.

(*Association of Accounting Technicians*)

33.15A You are presented with the following information relating to Messiter plc:

Year to 31 December	19X4	19X5
	£m	£m
Profit and loss accounts:		
Turnover, all on credit terms	1,300	1,400
Cost of sales	650	770
Gross profit	650	630
Profit before taxation	115	130
Balance sheets at 31 December:		
Fixed assets at cost	850	850
Less Accumulated depreciation	510	595
Net book value	340	255
Stock at cost	105	135
Trade debtors	142	190

Required:

(a) Using the historic cost accounts and stating the formulae you use, calculate the following accounting ratios for both 19X4 and 19X5:
   (i)   Gross profit percentage;
   (ii) Net profit percentage;
   (iii) Stock turnover, stated in days;
   (iv) Trade debtor collection period, stated in days; and
   (v)   Fixed asset turnover.

(b) Using the following additional information:
   (i)   Restate the turnover for 19X4 and 19X5 incorporating the following average retail price indices:
      Year to 31.12.19X4   85
      Year to 31.12.19X5   111

   (ii) Calculate the additional depreciation charge required to finance the replacement of fixed assets at their replacement cost. The company's depreciation policy is to provide 10 per cent per annum on original cost, assuming no residual value.
      The replacement cost of fixed assets at 31 December was as follows:

	£ millions
19X4	1,140
19X5	1,200

   (iii) Based upon these two inflation adjustments, why may it be misleading to compare a company's results for one year with that of another without adjusting for changes in general (RPI) or specific inflation?

(*Association of Accounting Technicians*)

34

Social accounting

Objectives

After you have studied this chapter, you should:

- *have an understanding of the term 'social accounting'*
- *be aware of the implications of 'social accounting' for the accounting function*
- *appreciate some of the difficulties in the measurement of qualitative factors*
- *be aware of the conflict between shareholders' interests and social considerations*

34.1 Introduction

Over time, the objective of financial statements has changed. In addition to reporting to shareholders of the company, directors are aware of a wide range of other user groups who are interested in accounting information. These user groups include employees of the company and, more controversially, the public at large. The controversy arises when considering whether or not organisations are responsible for 'social actions', that is actions which do not have purely financial implications.

34.2 Costs and measurement

One of the problems associated with actions of this type is the difficulty of identifying costs and measuring the effects of (often intangible) factors that contribute to the 'value' of an organisation. It is obvious that employee loyalty and commitment to quality performance increase this value, but how are such intangibles to be measured using objective and verifiable techniques?

Some of the input costs of 'social' activities can be evaluated reasonably accurately. Providing 'social' information required under the 1985 Companies Act is not particularly difficult – it requires information regarding employees to be presented in the accounts, including numbers of employees, wages and salaries data, and details regarding the company's policy on disabled persons. Also, even where 'social' actions are required by legislation, they can often be costed reasonably accurately. For example, there are a large number of European Union directives which have been implemented in the UK relating to social and environmental policies, including the monitoring and control of air and water pollution. The costs of complying with these disclosure requirements and operational control measures can be high and, as the numbers of regulations increase, these costs will become a basic and essential part of financial statements. It will become increasingly important that not only the costs are reported, but also the benefits, and this is where the difficulties arise – how can the benefits of controlling pollution from a factory be evaluated? Indeed, should an attempt be made to evaluate them at all? Would they be better reported in qualitative or non-financial quantitative terms?

As soon as a company seeks to incorporate social criteria alongside other more traditional performance measures, problems of objectivity, comparability, and usefulness arise. For example, social criteria for a paper manufacturer may include environmental issues concerning reforestation; and an oil extraction company would include the environmentally safe disposal of oil rigs at the end of their useful economic lives among its social criteria.

However, issues of this type become problematic when viewed using conventional capital appraisal techniques. Not only may the measurable financial payback be so long as to be immaterial – as in the case of an environmental project such as reforestation – it may be virtually non-existent, as in the case of the disposal of obsolete oil rigs. Assessment of issues of this type require different techniques from those traditionally used, and organisations' accounting information systems will need to take this into account, not just in terms of using more qualitative value criteria, but also in selecting the information which is sought in order to assist in the decision-making process.

34.3 The pressure for social actions and social accounting

Despite the existence of many environmental laws, much of the pressure for social actions comes from pressure groups like Greenpeace. These groups can have an enormous impact upon an organisation's profitability, in ways that governments have singularly failed to do. For example, an air pollution law may concentrate on monitoring the quality of air around a factory, rather than on measuring emissions from the factory, making it far more difficult to enforce action against the factory, as it can always argue that another factory is the cause of any pollution found. Also, powerful cartels can influence legislation to create enormous delays in introducing socially responsible legislative controls. On the other hand, a pressure group can stop demand for a company's products, make it difficult for it to send its products to its customers, and may give it so much negative publicity that it can find its public image materially and irreversibly altered in a very short time.

While pressure groups are not a new phenomenon, their power is now far greater than it has ever been. Organisations need to be aware of the social, particularly environmental issues inherent in and/or related to their activities, and must be in a position to assess how best to approach these issues. They can only do so if they identify all the variables, both quantitative and qualitative, and both the inputs (costs) and the outputs (effects) of these variables, and determine methods with which to determine what actions to take. Social accounting is concerned with how to report upon the application of the social policies adopted by an organisation, and upon how they have impacted upon the organisation and its environment. An organisation that does so effectively will not only be providing user groups with rich information from which to form a view concerning its social ethos, it will also be enhancing its ability to take decisions appropriate for its own longer-term survival and prosperity.

34.4 Corporate social reporting

The reporting of the social effects of a company's activities became an issue in the UK in the 1970s. The reporting of non-financial information usually takes the form of narrative disclosure, sometimes supported by a statistical summary. As much social reporting is non-mandatory, comparison with other companies is difficult, if not virtually pointless and misleading. This is partially due to a positive bias in what is reported – most companies tend to report only 'good news' in their social reports. It is also due to the lack of standards governing what to include and how to present social reports.

Environmental issues have been firmly on the political agenda since the early 1980s and large corporations have responded to public demands for more information about 'green issues'. Oil companies, in particular, produce a notable amount of additional information in their annual reports. This environmental information usually includes details about the company's waste disposal practices, attitudes towards pollution and natural resource depletion, as well as the overall corporate environmental policy. However, many continue to avoid any non-mandatory social reporting, and many instances have been reported of organisations claiming to be socially responsible, when they were, in fact, anything but.

34.5 Types of social accounting

Social accounting can be divided into five general areas:

- national social income accounting;
- social auditing;
- financial social accounting in profit-oriented organisations;
- managerial social accounting in profit-oriented organisations;
- financial and/or managerial social accounting for non-profit organisations.

34.6 National social income accounting

Such accounts have now been in existence for many years. The measure of the nation's productivity recorded in the accounts – basically in sales terms – gives an income called the Gross National Product, usually referred to as GNP.

To an outsider an increase in GNP would seem to indicate a betterment or progress in the state of affairs existing in the country. This is not necessarily true. The following example illustrates this point.

A new chemical factory is built in a town. Fumes are emitted during production which cause houses in the surrounding areas to suffer destruction of paintwork and rotting woodwork, and it also causes extensive corrosion of bodywork on motor vehicles in the neighbourhood. In addition it also affects the health of the people living nearby. An increase in GNP results because the profit elements in the above add to GNP. These profit elements include:

- to construction companies and suppliers of building materials: profit made on construction of plant;
- to house paint dealers and paint manufacturers, painters and decorators, joiners and carpenters: profit made on all work effected in extra painting, woodwork, etc.;
- to garages and car paint manufacturers: profit made on all extra work needed on motor vehicles;
- to chemists and medical requirement manufacturers: profit made on dealing with effects on residents' health, because of extra medical purchases, etc.

However, in real terms one can hardly say that there has been 'progress'. Obviously the quality of life has been seriously undermined for many people.

As national income accounts do not record the 'social' well-being of a country, other national measures have been proposed. The one most often mentioned is a system of 'social indicators'. These measure social progress in such ways as:

- national life expectancies;
- living conditions;
- levels of disease;
- nutritional levels;
- amount of crime;
- road deaths.

Thus if national life expectancies rose, or road deaths per 100,000 people decreased, etc. there could be said to be social progress, while the converse would apply were the opposite signals found to be occurring.

The main difficulty with this approach is that (given present knowledge and techniques) it cannot be measured in monetary terms. Because of this, the national social income accounts cannot be adjusted to take account of social indicators. On the level of an individual organisation, however, social indicators similar to the above are used in planning, programming, budgeting systems (PPBS). This will be discussed later.

34.7 Social auditing

Whilst national social accounting would measure national social progress, many individuals and organisations are interested in their own social progress. This form of social progress is usually called 'social responsibility'.

To identify activities to be measured, a 'social audit' is required, investigating:

(*a*) which of their activities contribute to, or detract from, being socially responsible;
(*b*) measurement of those activities;
(*c*) a report on the results disclosed by the investigation.

An example of this might be to discover how the organisation had performed in respect of such matters as:

- employment of women;
- employment of disabled people;
- occupational safety;
- occupational health;
- benefits at pensionable age;
- air pollution;
- water pollution;
- charitable activities;
- help to third world countries.

Social audits may be carried out by an organisation's own staff or by external auditors. The reports may be for internal use only or for general publication.

34.8 Financial social accounting in profit-oriented organisations

This is an extension to normal financial accounting. The objective may either be to show how the social actions have affected financial performance, or otherwise to put a social value on the financial statements of the organisations. The two main types of financial social accounting envisaged to date are those of human resource accounting and how the organisation has responded to governmental or professional bodies' regulations concerning environmental matters.

Human resource accounting

One of the main limitations of normal financial accounting is the lack of any inclusion of the 'value' of the workforce to an organisation. The value may be determined by either:

- capitalising recruitment and training costs of employees and apportioning value over employees' period of employment; or
- calculating the 'replacement cost' of the workforce and taking this as the value of human resources; or
- extending either of the above to include the organisation's suppliers and customers.

It is contended that such measurements have the benefits that (a) financial statements are more complete, and (b) managerial decisions can be made with a fuller understanding of their implications.

For instance, suppose that a short-term drop in demand for a firm's goods led to a manufacturer laying off part of the workforce. This might mean higher profits in the short term, because of wages and salaries saved. In the long term, it could do irreparable damage, as recruitment could then be made difficult, or because of the effect on the morale of the rest of the workforce, or changes in attitudes of suppliers and customers.

Compliance costs of statutory/professional requirements

As the effects of organisations upon societies are more widely recognised there will be more and more regulations with which to comply. The costs of compliance will obviously then become a basic and essential part of financial statements.

34.9 Managerial social accounting in profit-oriented organisations

All that has been described has an effect upon the accounting information systems of an organisation. They will have to be established on an ongoing basis, rather than be based purely on adjustments to the financial accounts at the year end.

The information will be used to affect the day-to-day decisions needed to run the organisation.

34.10 Financial and/or managerial social accounting for non-profit organisations

As profit is not a measure in these organisations it can be difficult to measure how well they are performing. Two approaches to measurement have been used, **planning, programming, budgeting systems (PPBS)**, and **social programme measurement**.

Both of these approaches can be said to be part of what politicians in recent years have called 'value for money'. The general attitude is that whilst there may be a need for all sorts of social programmes, including health, there is a great need for ensuring that money is not wasted in doing this. The demand is that we should ensure that we get 'value for money' in that the outputs from such schemes should be worth the amount of money expended in carrying them out.

Planning, programming, budgeting systems (PPBS)

It has been said that in the past there was a great deal of confusion between planning and budgeting. Annual budgeting takes a short-term financial view. Planning on the other hand should be long-term and also be concerned with strategic thinking.

PPBS enables management of non-profit organisations to make decisions on a better-informed basis about the allocation of resources to achieve their overall objectives. PPBS works in four stages:

1 Review organisational objectives.
2 Identify programmes to achieve objectives.
3 Identify and evaluate alternative ways of achieving each specific programme.
4 On the basis of cost-benefit principles, select appropriate programme.

PPBS necessitates the drawing up of a long-term corporate plan. This shows the objectives which the organisation is aiming to achieve. Such objectives may not be in accord with the existing organisational structure.

For instance, suppose that the objective of a local government authority, such as a city, is the care of the elderly. This could include providing:

- services to help them keep fit;
- medical services when they are ill;
- old people's housing;
- 'sheltered' accommodation;
- recreational facilities;
- educational facilities.

These services will usually be provided by separate departments, e.g. housing, welfare, education. PPBS relates the total costs to the care of the elderly, rather than to individual departmental budgets.

Management is therefore forced by PPBS to identify exactly which services or activities should be provided, otherwise the worthiness of the programme could not be evaluated. PPBS also provides information which enables management to assess the effectiveness of their plans, such as giving them a base to decide whether for every thousand pounds they are giving as good a service as possible.

As the structure of the programme will not match up with the structure of the organisation, e.g. the services provided will cut across departmental borders, a specific individual must be made responsible for controlling and supervising the programme.

Social programme measurement

The idea that governmental social programmes should be measured effectively is, as yet, in its infancy.

A government auditor would determine whether the agency had complied with the relevant laws, and had exercised adequate cost controls. The auditor would determine whether or not the results expected were being achieved and whether there were alternatives to the programmes at a lower cost.

There should be cost-benefit analyses to show that the benefits are worth the costs they incur. However, the benefit side of the analysis is often very difficult to measure. How, for instance, do you measure the benefits of not dumping a particular substance or an obsolete oil rig into the sea?

As a consequence, most social programmes do not yet measure results (benefits). Instead they measure 'outputs', e.g. how many prosecutions for dumping waste: a high number of prosecutions is 'good', a low number 'bad'. This is hardly a rational way of assessing results, and quite a lot of research is going into better methods of audit.

34.11 Conflict between shareholders' interests and social considerations

Obviously, an organisation has to come to a compromise about how far it should look after the interests of its shareholders and how far it should bother about social considerations. For instance, a company could treat its employees so well in terms of pay, pensions and welfare that the extra costs would mean very low profits or even losses.

On the other hand there must be instances that, no matter what the effects on profits, the expenses just have to be incurred. If the company has a chemical plant which could easily explode, causing widespread destruction and danger to people, then there cannot be any justification for not spending the money either to keep the plant safe or to demolish it. The full severity of the law must bear down on transgressors of the law in such cases of wilful neglect.

All the facts of the particular case must be brought into account. Let us look at a typical case where the answer may seem obvious, but perhaps there may be other factors which may make the answer not so obvious. Workers in underdeveloped countries are usually paid far lower wages than those in the developed countries. What happens if a large multinational company pays its workers in a given country three or four times as much as home-based companies? Immediately everyone wants to work for the multinational company, which can afford high wages, and leave the home-based companies which cannot. Is that sensible? What chance is there for the development of the country's own home-based industries if the outside companies constantly take all the best brains and more able people?

In such a case it would probably make more sense for the multinational company to pay wages more in keeping with the particular economy, and to help that country in other ways such as by improving the health care generally for all, better education for all, and so on. Obviously a topic such as this will engender discussions and arguments for some considerable time.

34.12 Reports from companies

Companies, mainly those in the USA at first, have begun to declare their philosophy towards such matters as the environment. These are usually included in the annual reports which accompany the accounts.

One company, for instance, has stated that it has ten principles of environmental policy:

1 To comply with both governmental and community standards of environmental excellence.
2 To use only materials and packaging selected to be good for the health of consumers, and for the safety and quality of the environment.
3 To keep energy use per unit of output down to a low level.
4 To minimise waste.
5 To get to as low a level as possible the discharge of pollutants.
6 To use other firms which have shown commitment to environmental excellence.
7 To research fully the ecological effect of the company's products and packaging.
8 To carry on business operations in an open, honest and co-operative manner.
9 To make certain that on the board of directors there would be scientifically knowledgeable directors, and ensure that they were regularly provided with environmental reports.
10 To ensure that all the above principles are fully observed and that challenges posed by the environment are vigorously and effectively pursued.

Main points to remember

1 To whom organisations are responsible is a controversial area, and there is no exact definition of 'social accounting'.

2 Social indicators measure social progress, but as yet, given their inability to measure progress in monetary terms, they cannot be incorporated into social income accounts.

3 A social audit will test the social responsibility of an organisation, including compliance with regulations, for example legislation relating to employees.

4 If an organisation wishes to take account of social and environmental factors, these items need to be incorporated into its accounting information system.

5 There is a conflict between shareholders' interests, for example profit maximisation, and social considerations.

6 Corporate social reporting is the reporting of a company's activities and how they are related to social, including environmental, issues.

7 There are five areas into which social accounting can be divided:
   (*a*) national social income accounting;
   (*b*) social auditing;
   (*c*) financial social accounting in profit-oriented organisations;
   (*d*) managerial social accounting in profit-oriented organisations;
   (*e*) financial and/or managerial social accounting for non-profit organisations.

8 Social accounting is as yet in its infancy. There is obviously a great difficulty in trying to put money values on the various aspects of being 'better off' or 'worse off'. There are also problems connected with exactly what 'better off' and 'worse off' mean. One person's 'worsening' in some way may be someone else's 'betterment'.

Review questions

34.1 Describe how an increase in Gross National Product may not have a positive effect on the well-being of the country.

34.2 What types of measures could be used to measure social well-being? What difficulties would be discovered in trying to use accounting in measuring these?

34.3 What aspects of an organisation's activities could be measured in a 'social audit'?

34.4 Describe how there could be conflicts between short-term and long-term benefits.

34.5 Describe how PPBS may conflict with departmental budgets.

34.6A Review a set of company accounts for social disclosures. Consider the usefulness of such disclosures to different user groups.

34.7 Why has the traditional model of income measurement failed to account for the impact of business activities on the environment?

(*Association of Chartered Certified Accountants*)

35

Accounting as an information system

Objectives

After you have studied this chapter, you should:

- *be aware of some of the deficiencies of financial accounting if it were used for management control purposes*

- *be aware of the need to avoid potential conflicts between alternative or competing objectives that may be adopted within an organisation*

- *know that decision making should involve more than just the financial figures involved*

- *be aware that the information needs of organisations are, in part at least, a function of their size*

- *understand the difference between the three areas in which management operates, and their different information needs*

- *be aware that accounting information is only one part of the overall system in which organisations operate*

- *understand that the accounting system is affected by the surrounding environment both inside and outside the organisation in which it operates*

35.1 The part played by financial accounting

So far your studies have been concerned primarily with the recording function of accounting, often called bookkeeping, and the drafting of the final accounts of different types of organisations, such as partnerships or limited companies. The term generally used for your studies up to this point is that of **financial accounting**. Much of it is concerned with legal requirements, such as complying with the provisions of the Companies Acts when drafting final accounts, or keeping an accounting record of a customer's legal indebtedness, i.e. a debtor's account.

With companies the final accounts represent the account given to the shareholders by the directors of their running of the company during a particular year, in other words it is a statement of the directors' 'stewardship'. These accounts are also given to other interested parties such as the bankers to the firm, creditors, Inspectors of Taxes, etc.

Whilst financial accounting is necessary from a legal point of view, it cannot be said to be ideal from the point of view of controlling the activities of a firm. Your studies would therefore be incomplete if you had seen only the 'stewardship' function of accounting. The use of accounting for controlling the activities of a firm is probably more important. In this chapter, we shall briefly consider accounting for 'management control' purposes.

The word 'management' does not necessarily mean that the firm is a limited company, although most of the large organisations in the private sector of industry would in fact be limited companies. It means instead the people who are managing the affairs of the firm, whether they are directors, partners, sole traders or 'managers' classified as those employees who are in charge of other employees.

35.2 Deficiencies of financial accounting

Before starting to examine accounting for management control let us look first at the deficiencies of financial accounting when we want to control the activities of an organisation.

Its first deficiency is that it deals with operations that have already occurred: it deals with the past, not the future. It is possible to control something whilst it is happening, and control can be arranged for something that is going to happen, but when it has already happened without being controlled then the activity has ended and we are too late to do anything about control. In this way if a company incurs a loss and we do not realise it until long after the event then the loss cannot be prevented.

What we really want to do is to control affairs so that a loss is not incurred if at all possible, and we should be able to call on accounting techniques to help in the control of activities. However, it certainly does not mean that we are not interested in the past. We can learn lessons from the past which can be very useful in understanding what is going on now, and what is likely to be happening in the future.

The second deficiency of financial accounting is that it is concerned with the whole of the firm. Thus the trading account of a firm may show a gross profit of £60,000, and whilst it is better to know that than to have no idea at all of what the gross profit is, it does not tell management much about past transactions. Suppose that in fact the firm manufactures three products – watches, pens and cigarette lighters. Some possibilities of how much profit (or loss) was attributable to each of the products might be as in Exhibit 35.1.

Exhibit 35.1

Various possibilities of profits and loss for each product

	1	2	3	4
Watches	20,000	5,000	30,000	(30,000)*
Pens	20,000	70,000	28,000	65,000
Lighters	20,000	(15,000)*	2,000	25,000
Total gross profit	£60,000	£60,000	£60,000	£60,000

*Losses are shown in brackets

These are only some of the possible figures of profit and loss for each product which could result in an overall gross profit of £60,000. Just the figure of total gross profit would give you very few clues as to what lessons can be learned from studying the past to help you control the firm in the future. If possibility number 2 was in fact the correct solution then it would stimulate further discussion and investigation as to why these results had occurred.

It could result in the closing down of the section of the firm which makes cigarette lighters if, after investigation, it was found to be in the interests of the firm to cease manufacturing them. Many more lessons can therefore be learned from events if the firms' activities can be examined for each part of its activities instead of just the whole of its activities.

This means that financial accounting is of little use by itself for management control purposes. It does not mean that it is of no use at all for control purposes, as for instance the financial accounting system may reveal that the debtors at a point in time are £50,000. Management need to know this if they are to control their finances properly, but although this is true of some accounting figures in financial accounting, many of the other accounting figures may not be much use in controlling the business. For example, if a building was bought in 1930 for £20,000 it may well be worth £200,000 today, whilst if we rented a similar building now it might cost us £30,000 a year. We would surely not use the original cost of £20,000 as the deciding factor as to what we will do now with the building. The original cost is now completely irrelevant for the control of the business now or in the future.

35.3 Objectives of the firm

If we want to discuss management control we must first of all ask ourselves what is its purpose. We can only have control if it is for a particular purpose, otherwise how can we possibly draw up any plans?

It might seem obvious to you that the objectives of an organisation should be spelled out clearly and unambiguously. In fact the writing down of objectives is not done by quite a few organisations. This means that all the employees of the firm could well be pulling in different directions, as they all have different ideas as to the firm's objectives.

Let us look at some of the possible objectives:

- To ensure that the maximum profit is made. This still is not clear; do we mean profits in the long term or the short term?
- To obtain a given percentage share of the market for our sort of goods or services.
- To achieve a high quality in the goods being manufactured or services offered.
- To ensure that our customers are fully satisfied with our goods and services.
- To ensure full employment for our employees.
- To ensure that our employees' welfare is maintained at a high level, in terms of back-up facilities and other things such as adequate pension schemes.
- To ensure that our employees receive the best training and are kept fully up to date with the latest technology for our sort of business.
- To cause as little damage as possible ecologically.

35.4 Conflicts between objectives

Each objective of the firm is not 'mutually exclusive'. By that we mean that one objective may affect another objective, and that it cannot be considered completely on its own.

Let us take the case of the objective of maximum profit with that of causing as little damage as possible ecologically. We could have to spend a lot of money ensuring that dangerous chemical substances are not released into the atmosphere. This could mean less profits. There would be a conflict here if the improvements were being made voluntarily by the firm instead of being forced on it by the authorities.

Similarly, to maintain a very high quality of goods could mean lower profits if a large number of items manufactured are scrapped because they are not up to this standard. Lowering the quality could possibly increase profits.

This could again be interpreted in more than one way. Lowering the quality could possibly increase the profits in the short term, but it could mean less profits in the long term if our customers deserted us because our goods were second-rate. This could apply similarly to services.

It is thus essential to ensure that the objectives are very clearly spelled out. Otherwise people will easily misunderstand them and because of this the firm may not proceed in the direction that is desired.

35.5 People and management control

It is also important to point out that the most important resource of any firm is the people who work in it. A danger exists that a great deal of care and attention may be given to designing a management control system and operating it, but this is absolutely of no use to management if it does not result in action by the human beings in the firm. Systems and figures do not themselves do anything; instead it is the people in the firm who take (or do not take) the necessary action.

You must bear in mind that figures thrown up by systems are only part of the evidence available when a decision has to be made as to the necessary action. A particular department may be incurring losses now, but the sales manager may give as his considered opinion that sales will increase soon and that the department will become profitable. If people accepted accounting figures as the only criteria on which action should be based then there would be some very bad actions by management. Many of the now very successful products have started off by incurring losses in the early stages, and have been eventually successful because the firm has persevered with the product because it had the faith that it would eventually make the grade.

If it was possible to have exactly the same system of management control in three different firms, it might be found in firm A that the control system was useless because no one acted on the data produced. In firm B the control system might result in damage being done to the firm because management used the data as though it were the only criterion in gauging the actions it should take. In firm C it might be an extremely good system because the management saw the data as a useful guide in the planning and control of the firm, and had also made certain that the rest of the organisation took the same view.

How human beings react to a management control system is therefore right at the heart of the problem of ensuring that an effective management control system is in use.

35.6 Different sizes of organisations

Part of this book is about information which is intended to be used by the management of an organisation. For a small and simple organisation the information needs of management may be limited and can be obtained by direct observation – using eyes to look and the voice to ask questions. For example, a person managing a greengrocery stall on a market can often operate effectively without formal records to help him. What he buys is determined by the goods available in the local wholesale market and his personal knowledge of what his customers are prepared to buy at a given price. His records will probably centre around the recording of cash – the details of his sales and expenditures in order to prepare financial accounts. However, apart from the essential requirement of maintaining proper cash levels these records do not help him in the day-to-day management of his business operations.

If in contrast we look at the manager responsible for buying greengrocery for a large supermarket chain certain differences emerge. The basic decision about what to buy at a given price remains the same. However, in the large organisation there is a much wider choice of where and how to buy than in the small organisation. The large buyer may, for example, be able to enter into contracts directly with growers and to enter forward contracts for the supply of produce (for example, a farmer agrees to sell all his potatoes at the end of the summer to the firm at a fixed price).

In the large organisation the buyer will not be in direct contact with the many different sales outlets and therefore needs written information to keep him in touch with demand. He does not have to listen to complaining customers! Similarly because the sources of supply are likely to be much wider for the big firm, he needs more formal information to keep him in touch with market prices.

One of the other features about the large organisation which distinguishes it from the small is that responsibility for running the business is shared between many different people. In order to ensure that the operations of the firm are carried out efficiently and effectively there needs to be some criterion to measure the performance of the managers. In a small firm the inadequate proprietor will either make a very poor living or become a bankrupt. Thus his success or failure is clearly his own responsibility. In a large firm the same things can happen overall, but the situation may be obscured by a swings and roundabouts effect of some good sections making up for some bad. A management information system should help identify these problems in an organisation.

35.7 The management process

The way that management operates in an organisation may be conveniently described by a division into three areas:

- forecasting and planning;
- controlling operations;
- evaluating performance.

Forecasting and planning

Forecasting and planning is the process by which senior management decide on major overall issues concerning what the business is going to do, and how it is going to do it. It involves an assessment of information about the future which is called forecasting. When the forecast has been prepared, then the company can plan how to achieve the objectives set by management based on the forecast. Planning is the process of co-ordinating the resources available to attain an objective.

Controlling operations

Controlling operations involves management in a number of processes and requires several different kinds of information. It involves converting top management plans into an operating pattern which matches the parts into which a company is divided. This changes the overall plan into detailed operating plans which relate to the management structure of the company. This process is called budgeting.

When actual events occur, then the information recording the events needs to be measured in such a way that it can be compared with the plan. This important process of management gives a feedback on the success of the plan to those who set it up in the first instance.

Controlling operations effectively also requires information designed to help managers take the decisions which their jobs require. For example, information about the profit produced by one product as compared to another will enable a decision about how many of each product to make.

Evaluating performance

Evaluating performance involves the analysis and assessment of actual results. This is partly a process of comparison with plans but not exclusively. The information on which plans were based may have been wrong. Thus the analysis of performance, whilst involving comparison of actual with planned results, needs considerable judgement as to what the plans should have been had all the facts been known in advance.

The three elements we have described are by no means completely independent. One way of looking at them is as a cycle in which information is circulating continually from one area to another as in Exhibit 35.2.

Exhibit 35.2

In this diagram information is shown to flow around from one part into the other. Thus, for example, forecasts in one period may be improved by taking account of the analysis of what happened last period.

It is also useful, as in Exhibit 35.3, to include a time dimension in the diagram. Forecasting and planning must relate to the future. Controlling operations relates to concurrent events – the here and now. Evaluating performance can only be concerned with the past.

The diagram we have just considered only looks at internal information. Exhibit 35.3 takes into account that information is being fed into the process from outside. Top management will have to take into account all the information it can about the outside environment such as competition, economic cutbacks, etc. The control of operations also receives information about actual events.

Exhibit 35.3

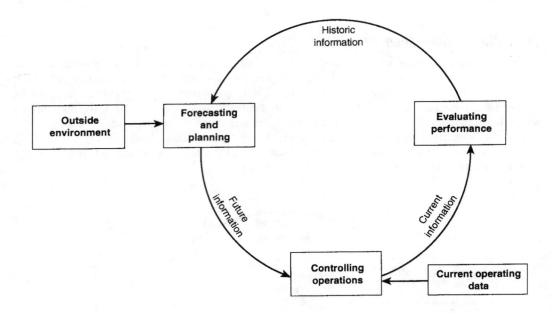

35.8 Types of management information

So far in this chapter no attempt has been made to describe the nature of the information which management requires. Information may come in many shapes and forms. In this book we are only concerned with information which is capable of being expressed in numerical terms, which in other words may be 'quantified'. Information of a more general nature about people's 'feelings' or 'views' may be very useful to management but cannot be quantified, and therefore is usually part of the informal rather than the formal information systems.

Within the body of quantified information it is normal to identify that part which can be measured in money terms. This is the part of the information system which is called accounting information. Accounting information is a very important element in the whole system since the organisation is basically an economic unit which must survive in conditions of economic scarcity and competition. In other words an organisation which does not meet its economic objectives will eventually fail or be taken over, hence the central importance of accounting information.

However, other quantified information may be very important for management. For example, if you are a farmer you will measure the yield of milk from your cows in the first instance as litres. A production manager will be very concerned to monitor the tonnages produced on his machines.

35.9 Quantitative methods in the information system

A modern management information system collects all the data together (into what is called a data bank) and issues that part which is important to each manager. Thus the distinction between accounting and other types of management information has tended to become less meaningful in modern data processing systems. The techniques of quantitative analysis (or statistics) apply to all the data in this system whether it be accounting data or not.

Main points to remember

1 Financial accounting fulfils a stewardship function by reporting past performance and financial position.

2 Financial accounting information is only of limited use for management control purposes, for which other forms of data and information are required.

3 It is important that organisational objectives are clearly defined and that the financial accounting information system is designed to meet and support those objectives in the most efficient and effective way.

4 Management is concerned with three areas of activity:
(a) forecasting and planning;
(b) control;
(c) evaluating performance.

5 The financial accounting information system does not exist in a vacuum, it interacts with and is affected by the environment in which it is operating and must be designed accordingly.

Review questions

35.1 'Financial accounting looks behind, whilst management accounting looks ahead.' To what extent does this quotation accurately reflect the role of the two branches of accountancy?

(*Edexcel Foundation, London Examinations: GCE A–Level*)

35.2 'Financial accounting is non-dynamic, backward looking, conservative, as objective as possible, and subject to statutory and other regulation. Management accounting is future oriented, is dynamic, produces forward looking figures, should not be too concerned with objectivity, and is not generally subject to external regulation.' (Prof. Michael Bromwich)
   Justify this statement, giving examples to illustrate your answer.

(*Edexcel Foundation, London Examinations: GCE A–Level*)

35.3 What are some of the deficiencies of financial accounting?

35.4 Why is it important that the employees of an organisation should clearly understand what the objectives of the organisation are?

35.5 How can there be a conflict between the various objectives of an organisation?

35.6 Describe how the management process is carried out.

Part 6

COSTING

Introduction

This part looks at what constitutes cost and at four techniques used to derive cost.

36

Elements of costing

Objectives

After you have studied this chapter, you should:

- *know why knowing the purpose for which data about costs is required is important*

- *know the advantages of having an effective costing system*

- *appreciate that the benefits to be derived from a costing system should always outweigh the costs of operating the costing system*

36.1 Costs for different purposes

Cost accounting is needed so that there can be an effective management accounting system. Without a study of costs such a system could not exist. Before entering into any detailed description of costs it is better if we ask ourselves first of all what use we are going to make of information about costs in the business.

This can best be done by referring to something which is not accounting, and then relating it to accounting. Suppose that your employer asked you to measure the distance between Manchester and London, but walked away from you without giving any further information. As you thought about his request the following thoughts might go through your head:

1   *HOW* does he want the distance measured? Some possibilities are:
   - from the southern outskirts of Manchester to the northern outskirts of London.
   - from the accepted geographical centre of London to the accepted geographical centre of Manchester.
   - to the centres of the two cities calculated as mathematically precise points.
   - by road – this could be just major roads, just minor roads, or could be a mixture of both – the main requirement being the quickest route by road.
   - by canal.
   - by train.
   - by air; allowance may or may not be made for the distance covered by the aircraft which would include climbing to an altitude of 5,000 feet or perhaps 40,000 feet, or might ignore the distance travelling in achieving an altitude.

2   The *COST* of obtaining the information. Measuring distances (or measuring costs) is not costless itself. Using very sophisticated instruments to get accurate measurement can be very expensive indeed. On the other hand it might just be a matter of measuring the distance on a map with a rule and converting it into miles – this would cost hardly anything at all.

3   What is the *PURPOSE* for which the measurement will be used? This has been deliberately left as the last point, but in fact it should have been the first question that came into your mind. Illustrations of the use could have been as follows:

- he is going to drive from Manchester to London by car and wants a rough idea of the mileage so that he can gauge what time to set off if he is to arrive before it goes dark in London.
- he might conceivably want to walk it.
- he might be submitting a tender for the building of a motorway by the shortest possible route, cutting tunnels through ranges of hills.
- perhaps he wants to send goods by canal.
- maybe he wants to arrive as close as possible to an underground station.
- he might be an amateur pilot who wants to fly from Manchester Airport to London Airport.

The lesson to be learned from this is that measurement depends entirely on the use that is to be made of the data. Far too often firms make measurements of financial and other data without looking first at the use that is going to be made of it. In fact it could be said that 'information' is useful data that is provided for someone.

Data given to someone which is not relevant to the purpose required is just not information. Data which is provided for a particular purpose, and which is completely wrong for the purpose, is worse than having no data at all. At least when there is no data the manager knows that he is making a guess. When useless data is collected it first of all has cost money to collect, in itself a waste of money; secondly it often gets taken to be useful data and misleads a manager into taking steps which are completely wrong and would not have happened if he had relied instead on his own hunches. Third it clogs up the communication system within a firm, so that other data is not acted on properly because of the general confusion that has been caused.

How is all this reflected in a study of costs?

1   What is the data on costs wanted for? It might be needed for the financial accounts, for management control or for decision making. Different data on costs are wanted for different purposes.

2   How are the costs to be measured? Only when the purpose for which the costs are to be used has been decided can the measurement process be decided. Financial accounting for instance needs a certain precision in calculating costs which is often not needed in management accounting, where sometimes the nearest thousand pounds will be good enough for the purpose.

3   The cost of obtaining costing data should not exceed the benefits to be gained from having it. This does not refer to some cost data which is needed to comply with various provisions of the law. We can, however, look at several cases to illustrate the cost/benefit factor:

- Spending £100 to obtain costs which will be used as a basis for pricing many of the products of the firm. If the costs had been 'guessed' an error could have meant large losses for the firm.
- Spending £10,000 to find data on sales which the sales manager will toss into the wastebasket, because it is not the sort of data he wants, is obviously money wasted.
- Spending a lot of time and money to find out that the stock values on a particular day were £2,532,198, when such precision was not needed. Perhaps the chairman was having a general chat with the bank manager, and all he needed to know was an approximate figure for stock of £2,500,000. The approximate figure could have been found easily and at little cost, so here costs have exceeded benefits.

When it is known what the costs are for, and how much is to be spent on studying them, the appropriate method for measuring them can be decided.

36.2 Past costs in trading companies

Past costs – often aptly called historic costs – are part of the ordinary financial accounting done in firms. Here the 'original cost' concept is used. A diagram – Exhibit 36.1 – shows costs flowing through financial accounts.

Exhibit 36.1

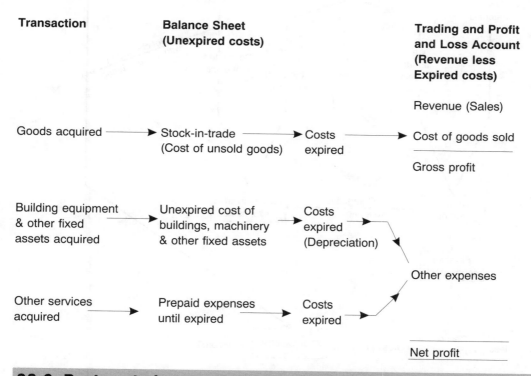

36.3 Past costs in manufacturing companies

You have probably already covered the topic of manufacturing accounts earlier in your studies. In this chapter we will examine some of the detailed aspects of them a little further, as this is essential for a study of costing.

Exhibit 36.2 shows costs flowing through a manufacturing company.

Exhibit 36.2

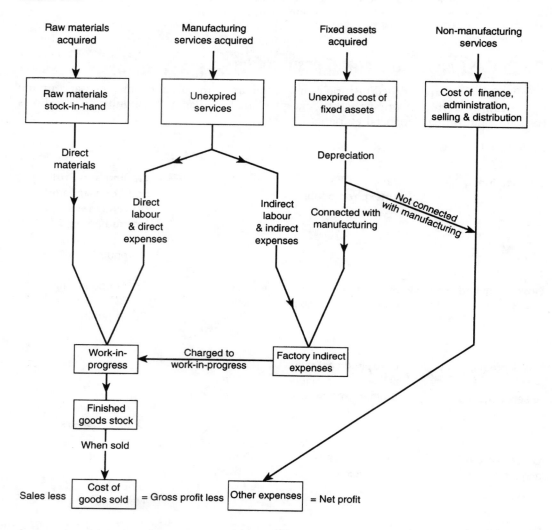

The following is a more detailed description of costs than you will have encountered previously.

- *Direct materials* are those materials which become part of the finished goods, subject to the proviso that the expense involved in tracing the cost is worth while. Some items, usually of insignificant amounts, are treated as indirect materials even though they are part of the finished product because the cost cannot be ascertained easily.
- *Direct labour* are those labour costs which are applied to convert the direct materials into the finished goods, also subject to the proviso that the expense involved in tracing this cost is worth while.
- *Direct expenses* are those expenses which can be traced directly to the product being manufactured. These are fairly rare, but an instance would be a royalty where the production of each item resulted in say £1 being due to the owner of a patent.

- Prime cost: The total of Direct materials + Direct labour + Direct expenses is called prime cost.

  Naturally there will be disagreement between accountants as to whether certain costs are worth tracing as being of a direct type, as it will often be a matter of judgement which defies any easy proof whether or not the expense of tracing the cost exceeds the benefit from so doing. You should get used to the idea in accounting that disagreement will often occur, which will only be settled by a compromise or appeal to someone in higher authority to settle the argument. This obviously relates to many things in accounting beside the decision as to whether an item is of a direct type or not.

- *Factory indirect expenses or manufacturing overheads* are all those other expenses concerned with the manufacturing process which have not been treated as of the direct type. Because there is no easily traceable direct connection with the goods being manufactured these costs must be apportioned between the goods being manufactured in a logical fashion.

- *Production cost:* The total of Prime cost + Factory indirect expenses is called production cost.

- *Administration, selling and distribution and finance expenses* are common to both trading and manufacturing firms.

- *Total cost:* If we add together production cost and administration, selling and distribution, and finance expenses, the resultant figure is known as total cost. To summarise:

	Direct materials
ADD	Direct labour
ADD	Direct expenses
Gives:	PRIME COST
ADD	Factory indirect expenses
Gives:	PRODUCTION COST
ADD	Administration expenses
ADD	Selling and distribution expenses
ADD	Finance expenses
Gives:	TOTAL COST

Exhibit 36.3 is a list of typical types of expenses found in a manufacturing firm. These can be analysed as to whether they are direct materials, direct labour, direct expenses, factory indirect expenses, administration expenses, selling and distribution expenses, or finance expenses. See how well you can do yourself by covering up the right-hand column with a piece of paper, then sliding your paper down to reveal one answer at a time after you have mentally analysed it yourself.

Exhibit 36.3

	Cost	Cost Analysis
1	Raw materials for goods – identifiable with product made.	Direct materials
2	Rent of factory buildings.	Factory indirect expenses
3	Sales staff salaries.	Selling and distribution
4	Wages of machine operators in factory.	Direct labour
5	Wages of accounting machine operators in office.	Administration expenses
6	Depreciation of lathes in factory.	Factory indirect expenses
7	Depreciation of typewriters in office.	Administration expenses
8	Depreciation of fixtures in sales showrooms.	Selling and distribution expenses
9	Supervisors' wages in factory.	Factory indirect expenses
10	Royalty paid for each item manufactured.	Direct expenses
11	Works manager's salary: he reckons that he spends ¾ of his time in the factory and ¼ in general administration of the firm.	¾ Factory indirect expenses ¼ Administration expenses
12	Raw materials incorporated in goods sold, but too difficult to trace to the goods being made.	Indirect expenses
13	Depreciation of motor vehicles used for delivery of finished goods to customers.	Selling and distribution expenses
14	Interest on bank overdraft.	Finance expenses
15	Wages of crane drivers in factory.	Factory indirect expenses
16	Discounts allowed.	Finance expenses
17	Company secretary's salary.	Administration expenses
18	Advertising.	Selling and distribution expenses
19	Wages of staff of canteen used by factory staff only.	Factory indirect expenses
20	Cost of hiring special machinery for use in manufacturing one special item.	Direct expenses

36.4 Product costs and period costs

Product costs are those costs which are allocated to the units of goods manufactured. In fact product costs make up production cost. Such costs are charged up to the cost of goods manufactured in the trading account, and would normally be part of the valuation of unsold goods if the goods to which they refer had not been sold by the end of the period. Product costs are therefore matched up against revenue as and when the goods are sold and not before.

Period costs are those of a non-manufacturing nature and represent the selling and distribution, administration and the financial expenses. They are treated as expenses of the period in which they were incurred irrespective of the volume of goods sold.

36.5 Advantages of a costing system

You have now looked at the various elements of cost as far as the whole of the firm is concerned. Such a classification of costs is necessary so that the overall production cost can be ascertained in the case of a manufacturing company with its effect on the valuation of the closing stock of finished goods and of work in progress. What most businesses want to know is how much each item has cost to make. This means that the total costs for the whole firm are not sufficient, and so these costs must be analysed further.

Any costing system must bring about the better control of the firm in guiding it towards its objectives, and the benefits to be derived from the costing system must be greater than the expense of operating the costing system. We must, therefore, look at the possible advantages to be gained in carrying on further analyses of cost:

(a) Because expenditure is traced down to each item produced, or each batch of items, it becomes possible to ascertain the contribution of each item to the profitability of the business. The desirability of stopping unprofitable activities can then be assessed.

(b) Once the profitability of each item is known, the reasons for increases or decreases in profits can be seen more clearly.

(c) It becomes easier to forecast future results if we know more about the operations of all the various parts of the business. When forecasted results are not achieved it becomes possible to highlight the reasons for the failure to achieve the forecasted results.

(d) Estimates and tenders can be prepared in future with far greater confidence – previously such calculations as were done must have been largely guesswork. Fewer errors should be made because of the greater knowledge gained via the costing system.

(e) Improvements in various activities of the firm may come about because of the more relevant information that can be supplied. Thus a machine which had always been thought to be quite cheap to use may turn out to be very expensive to use. This may bring about an investigation which would not otherwise have happened, and it may consequently be found that a simple attachment to the machine costing £10 brings about a saving of £100 a year.

(f) As we will see, a very important advantage is the control of expenditure, and it can be achieved because an individual can be made responsible for the expenditure under his/her control.

The possible advantages which can be gained from having a costing system can be seen to be quite considerable. It is, however, now a convenient point to remind you that accounting techniques themselves do not solve problems. Instead it is people within the firm who, when armed with the information that accounting techniques can provide, are far more able to make sensible decisions about what should be done to aid the progress of the firm towards its objectives.

Imagine trying to decide which item to stop producing out of twelve items made by a firm if you have little information as to the contribution of each item towards the profitability of the firm. Very often the solution will be that a new layout in the factory is needed; special training given to certain employees; changes made in the system of remunerating employees, and so on. The information provided by accounting is, therefore, only one part of the whole story for any problem. It is important to remember that often it will be the least important information available to the decision-taker.

36.6   The control of costs

One of the most important features of cost accounting is its use for control purposes meaning, in this context, the control of expenditure. But control of expenditure is possible only if you can trace the costs down to employees who are responsible for such costs. A convenient and frequently adopted approach to collecting costs is through '**cost centres**' – production or service locations, functions, activities, or items of equipment. Costs are collected from cost centres for individual '**cost units**' – units of product or service. For example, in a manufacturing firm all direct materials, direct labour and direct expenses are traced to cost centres. (In this case, they may be known as 'product centres'.)

A cost centre may be such as a single machine used for jobbing work, i.e. quite a lot of separate jobs performed specially to conform with the customer's specifications. It could, however, be a group of similar machines or a production department. Thus, if a firm makes metal boxes on one machine, all the costs incurred directly relating to that machine (cost centre) would be gathered and then shared (allocated) among all the metal boxes (cost units) made by that machine.

By comparison, factory indirect expenses are 'indirect' expenses and so cannot be traced (or it is not worth while tracing them) to product centres. Instead, these are traced to cost centres which give service rather than being concerned with work directly on the products, and such cost centres are, therefore, known as 'service centres'. Examples of service centres would be the factory canteen or the maintenance department. The costs from these service centres will then need allocating to the product centres in a logical fashion – for example, canteen costs may be allocated to product cost centres according to the number of employees working at each of them.

In practice there are a number of possible ways of allocating costs to cost centres. What must not be lost sight of is the endeavour to trace costs to a person responsible for the expenditure so that the costs can be controlled.

36.7   Costing: manufacturing firms compared with retailing or wholesale firms

It is quite wrong to think that costing is concerned only with manufacturing firms. Both textbooks and examination papers often give the impression that only in manufacturing is costing needed or found. This is quite incorrect, as costing is just as relevant to retailing and wholesaling firms and service industries as it is to those in manufacturing. It is simply that manufacturing, which usually has more complex sorts of activities because of the manufacturing element, has attracted greater attention than other types of firms. There are, in addition, many other forms of organisations such as farming, shipping, banking and even charitable organisations where costing can aid management control. It would indeed be difficult to find any organisation which could not use some form of costing system profitably.

New terms

Cost centre (p. 506): A production or service location, function, activity, or item of equipment whose costs may be attributed to cost units.

Cost unit (p. 506): A unit of product or service in relation to which costs are ascertained.

Main points to remember

1 Cost accounting is needed for there to be an effective management accounting system.

2 The benefits of operating a costing system should always outweigh the costs of operating it.

3 Information is data prepared for a purpose. To qualify as 'information', the 'information' must be useful.

4 Accounting techniques themselves do not solve problems. It is people within the organisation who, when armed with the information that accounting techniques can provide, are far more able to make sensible decisions about what should be done to aid the progress of the organisation towards its objectives.

Review questions

36.1   Analyse the following costs between:
(*i*)   Direct materials
(*ii*) Direct labour
(*iii*) Factory indirect expenses
(*iv*) Administration expenses
(*v*)   Selling and distribution expenses
(*vi*) Finance expenses

(*a*) Wages for staff maintaining machines in factory
(*b*) Wages for staff maintaining accounting machinery
(*c*) Expenses of canteen run exclusively for factory workers
(*d*) Expenses of canteen run exclusively for administrative workers
(*e*) Grease used for factory machinery
(*f*) Cost of raw materials
(*g*) Carriage inwards on fuel used in factory boiler-house
(*h*) Carriage inwards on raw material
(*i*) Wages of managing director's chauffeur
(*j*) Wages of cleaners in factory
(*k*) Discounts allowed
(*l*) Rent of salesrooms
(*m*) Wages of lathe operators in factory
(*n*) Wages of security guards; the area of the factory buildings is four times as great as the other buildings
(*o*) Debenture interest
(*p*) Rent of annexe used by accounting staff
(*q*) Managing director's remuneration
(*r*) Sales staff salaries
(*s*) Running costs of sales staff cars
(*t*) Repairs to factory buildings
(*u*) Audit fees
(*v*) Power for machines in factory
(*w*) Rates: $\frac{3}{4}$ for factory buildings and $\frac{1}{4}$ for other buildings
(*x*) Rent of internal telephone system in factory
(*y*) Bank charges
(*z*) Costs of advertising products on television.

36.2A   Analyse the following costs between

(*i*)   Direct materials
(*ii*)   Direct labour
(*iii*) Factory indirect expenses
(*iv*)   Administration expenses
(*v*)   Selling and distribution expenses
(*vi*)   Finance expenses

    (*a*)   Interest on bank overdraft
    (*b*)   Factory storekeepers' wages
    (*c*)   Hire of Rolls-Royce for managing director's use
    (*d*)   Repairs to factory roof
    (*e*)   Hotel bills incurred by sales staff
    (*f*)   Motor tax for vans used for delivering goods to customers
    (*g*)   Chief accountant's salary
    (*h*)   Lubricants for factory machinery
    (*i*)   Cost of disks for firm's computer
    (*j*)   Helicopter hire charges re special demonstration of company's products
    (*k*)   Debt collection costs
    (*l*)   Costs of painting advertising signs on London buses
    (*m*)   Cost of airplane tickets for sales staff
    (*n*)   Wages of painters engaged in production
    (*o*)   Wages of timekeepers in factory
    (*p*)   Postal charges for letters
    (*q*)   Wages of office boy in general office
    (*r*)   Postal charges – parcels sent to customers
    (*s*)   Repairs to vans used for taking goods to customers
    (*t*)   Cost of raw materials included in product
    (*u*)   Wages for cleaners engaged in administration block
    (*v*)   Carriage inwards on raw materials
    (*w*)   Repairs to neon sign in Piccadilly Circus
    (*x*)   Advertising agency fees
    (*y*)   Wages of crane drivers in factory
    (*z*)   Power costs of accounting machinery.

36.3   From the following information work out:

(a) Prime cost
(b) Production cost
(c) Total cost

Wages and salaries of employees:

	£	£
In factory (70 per cent is directly concerned with units being manufactured)		220,000
Salaries: Sales staff		8,000
Commission on sales paid to sales staff		1,400
Salaries of administrative staff		72,000
Travelling expenses:		
Sales staff	2,900	
Factory workers not directly concerned with production	100	
Administrative staff	200	
		3,200
Haulage costs on raw material bought		4,000
Carriage costs on goods sold		7,800
Depreciation:		
Factory machinery	38,000	
Accounting and office machinery	2,000	
Motor vehicles:		
Sales staff cars	3,800	
Administrative staff	1,600	
Sales display equipment	300	
		45,700
Royalties payable per unit of production		1,600
Canteen costs used by all the workers, ⅔ work in the factory, ⅓ in other parts of the firm		6,000
Raw materials:		
Stock at start of period		120,000
Stock at close of period		160,000
Bought in the period		400,000
Interest on loans and overdrafts		3,800
Other factory indirect expenses		58,000
Other administrative expenses		42,000
Other selling expenses		65,000

36.4A From the following information work out:

(a) Prime cost

(b) Production cost

(c) Total cost

	£	£
Wages and salaries of employees:		
In factory (60 per cent is directly concerned with units being manufactured)		150,000
In sales force		15,000
In administration		26,000
Carriage costs:		
On raw materials brought into the firm		1,800
On finished goods delivered to customers		1,100
Rent and rates:		
Of factory block	4,900	
Of sales department and showrooms	1,000	
Of administrative block	1,100	
		7,000
Travelling expenses:		
Sales staff	3,400	
Administrative staff	300	
Factory workers not connected directly with production	200	
		3,900
Raw materials:		
Stock at start of period		11,400
Bought in the period		209,000
Stock at close of the period		15,600
Royalties: payable per unit of production		400
Depreciation:		
Sales staff cars	500	
Vehicles used for deliveries to customers	300	
Cars of administrative staff	400	
Machinery in factory	1,800	
Office machinery	200	
		3,200
Interest costs on borrowed money		800
Other factory indirect expenses		6,000
Other administrative expenses		4,000
Other selling expenses		1,000

36.5A

(a) The terms *cost behaviour* and *analysis of total cost* are regularly used in cost accounting to classify costs. Distinguish between the two terms.

(b) Explain how the following costs will:

(i) behave;

(ii) be analysed.

- Factory Power and Lighting
- Production Line Workers' Wages
- Sales Manager's Salary
- Office rent

(Edexcel Foundation, London Examinations: GCE A–Level)

37

Absorption and marginal costing

Objectives

After you have studied this chapter, you should:

- *know the difference between absorption costing and marginal costing*

- *know why marginal costing, not absorption costing, should be used when deciding how to utilise spare capacity through additional production*

- *know what is meant by the term 'contribution'*

- *know how contribution is used in decision making*

37.1 Allocation of factory indirect expenses

The most commonly accepted cost accounting theory used for purposes of the determination of profit is where all the factory indirect expenses are allocated to the products manufactured. The factory indirect expenses are seen as adding to the value of work in progress and thence to finished goods stock. The production cost of any article is thus comprised of direct materials, direct labour, any direct expenses and a share of factory indirect expense.

After the financial year it is possible to look back and calculate exactly what the factory indirect expenses were. This means that this figure is used when calculating the valuation of the closing stock. For a firm which had produced 1,000 units, of which 200 units have not yet been sold, with a total production cost of £100,000, the closing stock valuation becomes:

$$\frac{\text{Unsold units}}{\text{Total units produced}} \times \text{Production cost of goods completed} = \frac{200}{1,000} \times £100,000$$

$$= £20,000 \text{ closing stock valuation}$$

Cost data is, however, used for purposes other than that of valuing stock. The question is, therefore, whether or not this method is suitable for all costing purposes. The method we have just used above, of allocating all factory indirect expenses to products is known as **absorption costing**, sometimes called full costing.

37.2 Absorption costing: effect upon future action

We can now look at a decision we might have to come to about a future action. Exhibit 37.1 shows a firm which has to make a decision about whether or not to take on an extra order.

Exhibit 37.1

Donald Ltd's factory has been making 1,000 units annually of a particular product for the past few years. Last year costs were:

	£
Direct labour	2,000
Direct materials	3,000
Factory indirect expenses	4,000
Production cost	9,000
Administration and other expenses	1,000
	10,000

The units, 1,000 had been sold for £12 each = £12,000

The production cost per unit can be seen to be $\frac{£9,000}{1,000}$ = £9.

The current year is following exactly the same pattern of production and costs. Suddenly, part-way through the year, a foreign buyer says he will take 200 units if the price for him can be cut from £12 each to £8 each. A meeting is held and the managing director says, 'What a pity. This could have been our first export order, something we have been waiting to happen for several years. The selling price overseas has no bearing on our selling price at home. But it costs us £9 a unit in production costs alone. We just cannot afford to lose money so as to export. Our shareholders would not tolerate the profits of the company falling to less than £2,000.'

'I think that you are wrong,' says John the accountant. 'Let's look at this year's results (a) if we do not accept the order and (b) if the order is accepted.' He then drafts the following:

	(a) Order not taken		(b) Order taken	
	£	£	£	£
Sales 1,000 × £12		12,000		
1,000 × £12 + 200 × £8				13,600
Less Expenses:				
Direct labour	2,000		2,400	
Direct materials	3,000		3,600	
Factory indirect expenses	4,000		4,200	
Other expenses	1,000	10,000	1,000	11,200
Net profit		2,000		2,400

'More profit. This means that we take the order,' says the sales director enthusiastically.

'Surely you've got your figures wrong, John,' says the managing director. 'Check your arithmetic.'

'There's nothing wrong with my arithmetic,' says John, 'but perhaps it will be a little more enlightening if I draft (b), Order taken, more fully.'

	£	£
(b) Order taken		
Sales		13,600
Less Costs which vary with production: Direct labour. The men are on piece work of a type that means 20 per cent more production brings 20 per cent more wages (i.e. £2,000 for 1,000 units, £2,400 for 1,200 units).	2,400	
Direct materials. 20 per cent greater production gives 20 per cent more materials (£3,000 + £600).	3,600	
Factory indirect expenses: Some would not change at all, e.g. factory rent, factory rates. Some would alter, e.g. cost of electric power because machines are used more. Of the factory indirect expenses one-quarter is variable. For this part £1,000 costs for 1,000 units means £1,200 costs for 1,200 units.	1,200	7,200
Sales *less* Variable costs		6,400
Costs: i.e. costs which will not alter at all if 200 more units are produced.		
Factory indirect expenses; fixed part	3,000	
Administration and other expenses	1,000	4,000
Net profit		2,400

'We can do all this without borrowing any money,' says the managing director, 'so I'll phone now to tell them we will start production immediately. By the way, John, come to my office this afternoon and tell me more about variable and fixed costs.'

37.3 The lesson to be learned

We must not get lost in the technicalities of accounting. It is easy to think that calculations which look complicated must give the right answer. Logic must be brought to bear on such problems. This last case shows that different costs will often be needed when making decisions about the future than the costs which were used for calculating profit earned in the past. £9 per unit had been taken for stock valuation, but this case proves that a firm could still manufacture units and sell at less than £9 each and still increase profits. The reason for this state of affairs is the very essence of the differences between fixed and variable costs which we will now consider.

37.4 Fixed and variable costs

The division of costs into those that are fixed and those that are variable is not an easy matter. Even factory rent is not always a fixed cost, for if production had to be increased to a certain figure the firm might have to rent further premises. Such a change would not usually happen in the short term, it would take a while to rent and set up a new factory or extra premises before production could start. When fixed costs are mentioned it is normally assumed that this means costs which are fixed in the short term.

In the firm Donald Ltd, Exhibit 37.1 assumed that variable costs were 100 per cent variable, by this meaning that if production rose 20 per cent then the cost would rise 20 per cent, if the production rose 47 per cent then the cost would also rise 47 per cent. This is not necessarily true. The cost of power may rise 20 per cent if production rose 20 per cent, but the cost of repairing and maintaining the machines may rise by only 10 per cent if production rose 20 per cent. In this case the machine maintenance would be a semi-variable cost, this being the term for a cost which varies with production but not at a proportionate rate.

37.5 Cost behaviour

Intelligent cost planning and control is dependent on the knowledge of how costs behave under certain conditions. What is important is how costs behave in a particular firm; there is no substitute for experience in this respect.

Raw materials are examples of variable costs which normally vary in strict proportion to the units manufactured. Labour costs, on the other hand, usually move in steps, thus the name 'step-variable' costs. For instance, a job may be done by two men, and then a slight increase in activity means that the two men, cannot manage it so that a third man is added. In fact it may represent only $2\frac{1}{3}$ men's work, but the acquisition of workers come in indivisible chunks. There can still be a further increase in activity without any more workers, but then the time will come when a fourth man is needed. This is shown on the two graphs in Exhibit 37.2

Exhibit 37.2

Variable cost behaviour

£   Volume
Costs which are strictly
variable e.g. materials

£   Volume
Costs which increase
in steps

37.6 Marginal costing and absorption costing contrasted

Where costing is used which takes account of the variable cost of products rather than the full production cost, then this is said to be **marginal costing**. We have seen that a marginal costing approach to the decision as to whether or not to accept the foreign order by Donald Ltd gave us the answer which increased the firm's profitability, whereas to use absorption costing of £9 a unit in a blind fashion would have meant our rejecting the order and therefore passing up the chance to increase profits and break into the foreign market. Let us look now at what would happen if we used either marginal costing or absorption costing in the calculation of profits for a whole firm, i.e. income determination.

Exhibit 37.3

The final accounts of a firm, Burke Ltd, are now shown drafted as if (A) marginal costing had been used, (B) absorption costing had been used. The following information is available:

1 All fixed factory overheads amounted to £4,000 per annum.
2 Variable overheads amounted to £2 per unit.
3 Direct labour and direct materials total £3 per unit.
4 Sales remain constant at 1,000 units per annum at £12 per unit.
5 Production in year 1 is 1,200 units, year 2 is 1,500 units and year 3 is 900 units.

Year 1	(A) Marginal costing		(B) Absorption costing	
	£	£	£	£
Sales		12,000		12,000
Less Variable costs:				
Direct labour and material, 1,200 × £3	3,600		3,600	
Variable overheads, 1,200 × £2	2,400		2,400	
Total variable cost	6,000			
Less in (A) Valuation closing stock*				
$\frac{200}{1,200} \times £6,000$	1,000			
	5,000			
Fixed factory overhead	4,000	9,000	4,000	
Total production costs			10,000	
Less in (B) Valuation closing stock*				
$\frac{200}{1,200} \times £10,000$			1,666	8,334
Gross profit		3,000		3,666

Year 2				
Sales		12,000		12,000
Less Variable costs:				
Direct labour and material 1,500 × £3	4,500		4,500	
Variable overheads, 1,500 × £2	3,000		3,000	
Total variable cost	7,500			
Add in (A) Opening stock b/d	1,000			
	8,500			
Less in (A) Closing stock*				
$\frac{700}{1,500} \times £7,500$	3,500			
	5,000			
Fixed factory overhead	4,000	9,000	4,000	
Total production costs			11,500	
Add Opening stock in (B) b/d			1,666	
			13,166	
Less Closing stock in (B)*				
$\frac{700}{1,500} \times £11,500$			5,366	7,800
Gross profit		3,000		4,200

Year 3		(A) Marginal costing		(B) Absorption costing	
	£	£		£	£
Sales		12,000			12,000
Less Variable costs:					
Direct labour and material, 900 × £3	2,700			2,700	
Variable overheads, 900 × £2	1,800			1,800	
Total variable cost	4,500				
Add in (A) Opening stock b/d	3,500				
	8,000				
Less in (A) Closing stock $\frac{600}{900}$ × £4,500	3,000				
	5,000				
Fixed factory overheads	4,000	9,000		4,000	
				8,500	
Add in (B) Opening stock b/d				5,366	
				13,866	
Less in (B) Closing stock $\frac{600}{900}$ × £8,500				5,666	8,200
Gross profit		3,000			3,800

Notes: The closing stock each year for (A) is made up of:

$$\frac{\text{Unsold units}}{\text{Number of units produced in year}} \times \text{total variable cost of that year}$$

Units produced year 1   1,200 – sold 1,000 = Stock 200 units

Units produced year 2   1,500 + 200 opening stock – sales 1,000 = Closing stock 700 units

Units produced year 3   900 units + 700 opening stock – sales 1,000 = Closing stock 600 units

So in year 1 unsold units are 200 units; units produced 1,200; total variable cost is £6,000, therefore stock valuation is:

$$\frac{200}{1,200} \times £6,000 = £1,000$$

The closing stock each year for (B) is made up of:

$$\frac{\text{Unsold units}}{\text{Number of units produced in year}} \times \text{total production cost of that year}$$

So in year 1 stock valuation becomes $\frac{200}{1,200} \times £10,000 = £1,666.$

Exhibit 37.4 shows in diagrammatic form the reported profits shown in Exhibit 37.3.

Exhibit 37.4

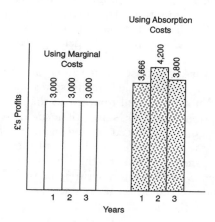

37.7 Comparison of reported profits – constant sales and uneven production

Exhibits 37.3 and 37.4 have illustrated that Burke Ltd, a firm which has had the same amount of sales each year at the same prices, and the same variable costs per unit have not changed at all, shows quite different profit figures using a marginal costing approach compared with absorption costing. As these were the gross profits that were calculated let us assume that the selling, distribution, administration and finance expenses were £1,000 for each of these years. The net profits would therefore be as follows:

	(A) *Marginal costing*	(B) *Absorption costing*
	£	£
Year 1	2,000	2,666
Year 2	2,000	3,200
Year 3	2,000	2,800

Because of the absorption costing approach, year 2 shows the biggest profit. As sales etc. are the same, only production being different, this means that the year which has the greatest closing stock has shown the greatest profit. Because of greater production, the amount of fixed factory overhead per unit is less. For instance in year 1 with 1,200 units produced and £4,000 fixed factory overhead this means:

$$\frac{£4,000}{1,200} = £3.3 \text{ per unit, year 2 } \frac{£4,000}{1,500} = £2.7 \text{ per unit, year 3 } \frac{£4,000}{900} = £4.4 \text{ per unit}$$

(only taken to one decimal place).

By calculating the value of closing stock to include the fixed factory overhead means that less gets charged per unit for fixed factory overhead when production is greatest, and thus there is a tendency for a greater profit to be shown.

Of course the situation gets more complicated because the closing stock of one year is the opening stock of the next year, and under absorption costing the values of units of stock will vary. Look at year 3: the opening stock of 700 units is shown as £5,366 = £7.7 approximately; the closing stock of 600 units is shown as £5,666 = £9.4 approximately. Yet these are exactly the same kind of things, and because we have made costs the same each year we have been ignoring inflation. To show a higher profit in a year when the closing stock is higher than usual is often dangerous. In fact the stock may be rising because we cannot sell the goods, we are really getting into trouble, yet the accounts sublimely show a higher profit!

Many experts have argued for or against the marginal and the absorption approach in income determination. The marginal approach really states that fixed factory overhead is a function of time and should not be carried forward to the next period by including it in stock valuations. The absorption approach states that such overhead is concerned with production and therefore the goods produced in that year, but not yet sold, should have such overhead brought into the calculation of their value carried forward to the next period. Put bluntly – do such costs 'attach' to the product or to time? Accountants are divided on this issue, perhaps what has been written in this chapter may have brought you down in favour of one side or the other. It does seem that the marginal approach will become used much more frequently than in the past.

Of course, during the complete life of a business the recorded profits of a firm will be the same in total whichever method is in use. If A Ltd exists for 20 years before it closes down, the profits as calculated for each year using the different methods will result in different recorded profits year by year (except by coincidence). The total profit during the complete life of the business of (say) £20 million will, however, be the same. However, the intermediate reporting of profits may induce decisions which may change the pattern of activities.

37.8 Contribution

Which approach, absorption or marginal costing, is relevant in deciding whether to continue the manufacture of a certain product or to cease production? The marginal cost approach. If the marginal cost is less than the selling price, then the difference will make a **contribution** towards fixed overheads, thus reducing the burden of the fixed overhead on the other products. This can be seen in the following example concerning which of two additional products to make when there is some spare production capacity:

	Product A	Product B
	£	£
Selling price	45	45
Marginal cost	26	22
Contribution towards fixed overhead and profit	19	23

Either product could be usefully considered, both making a positive contribution towards fixed costs. However, all other things being equal, Product B would appear the better option. Thus, if there is spare capacity, and an opportunity arises to use some of it, marginal costing would be used in order to determine whether the projected income exceeds the marginal cost. If it does, it would be appropriate to consider taking-on the work. As absorption costing includes an element of fixed cost, it is not appropriate to use it when considering decisions of this type.

37.9 Using marginal costs

Let us test this out in Exhibit 37.5 using a firm that produces five products and has the following cost and selling information. The firm would sell 100 of each product it manufactured. Total fixed overhead is £4,800 – allocated A £5 (100), B £7 (100), C £11 (100), D £15 (100), E £10 (100), i.e. £4,800 total.

Exhibit 37.5

Violet Ltd	Products				
	A	B	C	D	E
Cost: (per unit)	£	£	£	£	£
Direct labour and materials	8	9	16	25	11
Variable overhead	7	8	10	13	14
Marginal cost	15	17	26	38	25
Fixed overhead	5	7	11	15	10
Full cost	20	24	37	53	35
Selling price per unit	30	21	31	80	20

On the full-cost basis only A and D would seem to be profitable. Should production of B, C and E be discontinued? According to what has been said production should cease only when the selling price is less than marginal cost. In Exhibit 37.6 we will see if following our own advice brings about the greatest profit. We will also see at the same time what would have happened if production was not cut at all.

Exhibit 37.6

	(1) Following full-cost pricing, cease producing B, C and E	(2) Using marginal costing, cease producing E only	(3) Ignore costing altogether and produce all items
	£	£	£
Sales: A 100 × £30	3,000	3,000	3,000
B 100 × £21		2,100	2,100
C 100 × £31		3,100	3,100
D 100 × £80	8,000	8,000	8,000
E 100 × £20			2,000
Total revenue	11,000	16,200	18,200
Less Costs:			
Direct labour and materials:			
100 × cost per product	(£33) 3,300	(£58) 5,800	(£69) 6,900
Variable cost: 100 × cost per product	(£20) 2,000	(£38) 3,800	(£52) 5,200
Fixed overhead (does not change)	4,800	4,800	4,800
Total costs	10,100	14,400	16,900
Net profit	£900	£1,800	£1,300

The £s figures in brackets show the cost of each product, e.g. in (1) the Direct labour and Materials are A £8 + D £25 = £33.

As you can see, in Exhibit 37.6 it would be just as well if we followed our own advice. This would give a profit of £1,800 compared with £900 using the full-cost method or £1,300 if we disregarded costing altogether. Sometimes the full-cost method will give far better results than ignoring costing altogether, but this case shows that in fact the wrong kind of costing can be even worse than having no costing at all! The marginal costing approach will, however, give the better answer in this sort of situation.

There is, however, a danger in thinking that if the marginal cost of each product is less than the selling price then activities will be profitable. This is certainly not so, and full consideration must be given to the fact that the total contributions from all the products should exceed the fixed costs, otherwise the firm will incur an overall loss. Different volumes of activity will affect this. Let us look in Exhibit 37.7 with a two-product firm making products A and B given different volumes of activity. Product A has a marginal cost of £10 and a selling price of £14. Product B has a marginal cost of £6 and a selling price of £8. Fixed costs are £1,400.

Exhibit 37.7

	Profit, or loss, at different volumes of activity							
	A	B	A	B	A	B	A	B
Units sold	100	100	200	200	300	300	400	400
	£	£	£	£	£	£	£	£
Contribution (Selling price *less* Marginal cost) A £4 per unit, B £2 per unit	400	200	800	400	1,200	600	1,600	800
Total contributions	600		1,200		1,800		2,400	
Fixed overhead	1,400		1,400		1,400		1,400	
Net loss	£800		£200					
Net profit					£400		£1,000	

Here the selling price always exceeds marginal cost, but if activity is low the firm will incur a loss. This is shown where activity is only 100 or 200 units of each product.

The main lessons to be learned about selling prices are that:

(*a*) Selling prices should exceed marginal costs.

(*b*) In the long term, the total contributions at given volumes must exceed the fixed costs of the firm.

37.10 Maximisation of total contribution

It should be stressed that it is the maximisation of the total contribution from a product that is important. In this, the volumes of activity cannot be disregarded. Suppose, for instance, that a firm could only manufacture two products in future, whereas to date it had manufactured three. It may be that per unit the contribution may well have been (A) £10, (B) £8 and (C) £6. If a decision was made on this basis only then (C) would be discontinued. However, if the volumes were (A) 20, (B) 15 and (C) 30, then the total contributions would be (A) 20 × £10 = £200: (B) 15 × £8 = £120: (C) 30 × £6 = £180. As (B) has the lowest *total* contribution it should be (B) that is discontinued, not (C).

Where there is a limit of one of the items used in production of the product, the contribution per product per unit of that **limiting factor** (or key factor) should be used as the basis for the decision taken.

Take, for example, a situation where there are only 200 spare hours of machine capacity available and a choice has to be made between increasing current production levels of a range of products. The contribution per machine hour of each product is: A £2; B £3; C £5; D £1. Product C should be produced. It will generate the greatest amount of contribution. If there is any spare capacity remaining after all product C has been produced (for example, if there is only enough material available to make a few of product C) then product B should be produced, etc.

New terms

Absorption costing (p. 511): The method of allocating all factory indirect expenses to products. (All fixed costs are allocated to cost units.)

Marginal costing (p. 514): An approach to costing that takes account of the variable cost of products rather than the full production cost. It is particularly useful when considering utilisation of spare capacity.

Contribution (p. 518): The difference between sales income and marginal cost. (It can also be defined as sales income minus variable cost, which would virtually always produce the same answer.)

Limiting factor (p. 521): Anything that limits activity. Typically, this would be the shortage of supply of something required in production, for example, machine hours, labour hours, raw materials, etc. However, it could also be something that prevents production occuring, for example, a lack of storage for finished goods, or a lack of a market for the products.

Main points to remember

1 Different costs will often be needed when making decisions about the future than were used when calculating profit in the past.

2 Marginal cost, not full (or absorption cost) is the relevant cost when considering a change in what and/or how much is produced.

3 Selling prices should exceed marginal costs. (Almost the only exception to this would be where a product was being promoted as a 'loss leader'.)

4 In the long term, the total contributions at given volumes must exceed the fixed costs of the firm.

Review questions

37.1 Drake Ltd's cost and revenues for the current year are expected to be:

		£
Direct labour		6,000
Direct materials		7,000
Factory indirect expenses:		
Variable	4,500	
Fixed	500	
		5,000
Administration expenses		1,200
Selling and distribution expenses		600
Finance expenses		200
		£20,000

It was expected that 2,000 units would be manufactured and sold, the selling price being £11 each.

Suddenly during the year two enquiries were made at the same time which would result in extra production being necessary. They were:

(A) An existing customer said that he would take an extra 100 units, but the price would have to be reduced to £9 per unit on this extra 100 units. The only extra costs that would be involved would be in respect of variable costs.

(B) A new customer would take 150 units annually. This would mean extra variable costs and also an extra machine would have to be bought costing £1,500 which would last for 5 years before being scrapped. It would have no scrap value. Extra running costs of this machine would be £600 per annum. The units are needed for an underdeveloped country and owing to currency difficulties the highest price that could be paid for the units was £10 per unit.

On this information, and assuming that there are no alternatives open to Drake Ltd, should the company accept or reject these orders? **Draft the memo** that you would give to the managing director of Drake Ltd.

37.2A Hawkins Ltd expects its cost per unit, assuming a production level of 100,000 per annum, to be:

	£
Direct materials	2.8
Direct labour	2.4
Factory indirect expenses: Variable	0.8
Fixed	0.4
Selling and distribution expenses	0.2
Administration expenses	0.3
Finance	0.1
	£7.0

Selling price is £7.5 per unit.

The following propositions are put to the managing director. Each proposition is to be considered on its own without reference to the other propositions.

(a) If the selling price is reduced to £7.4 per unit, sales could be raised to 120,000 units per annum instead of the current 100,000 units. Apart from direct materials, direct labour and factory variable expenses there would be no change in costs.

(b) If the selling price is put up to £7.7 per unit, sales would be 80,000 per annum instead of 100,000. Apart from variable costs there would also be a saving of £2,000 per annum in finance costs.

(c) To satisfy a special order, which would not be repeated, 5,000 extra units could be sold at £6.3 each. This would have no effect on fixed expenses.

(d) To satisfy a special order, which would not be repeated, 3,000 extra units could be sold for £5.9 each. This would have no effect on fixed expenses.

Draft a memo stating what you would advise the managing director to do giving your reasons and workings.

37.3 Assume that by coincidence two firms have exactly the same costs and revenue, but that Magellan Ltd uses a marginal costing approach to the valuation of stock-in-trade in its final accounts, whilst Frobisher Ltd has an absorption cost approach. **Calculate** the gross profits for each company for each of their first three years of operating from the following:

(a) All fixed factory overhead is £9,000 per annum.
(b) Direct labour costs over each of the three years – £3 per unit.
(c) Direct material costs over each of the three years – £5 per unit.
(d) Variable overheads which vary in direct ratio to production were £2 per unit.
(e) Sales are: Year 1 900 units: Year 2 1,200 units: Year 3 1,100 units.
    The selling price remained constant at £29 per unit.
(f) Production is at the rate of: Year 1 1,200 units: Year 2 1,300 units: Year 3 1,250 units.

37.4A Your firm has been trading for three years. It has used a marginal costing approach to the valuation of stock-in-trade in its final accounts. Your directors are interested to know what the recorded profits would have been if the absorption cost approach had been used instead. **Draw up the three year's accounts using both methods.**

(a) Fixed factory overhead is £16,000 per annum.
(b) Direct labour costs per unit over each of the three years £4 per unit.
(c) Direct material costs over each of the three years £3 per unit.
(d) Variable overheads which vary in direct ratio to production were £5 per unit.
(e) Sales are: Year 1 9,000 units; Year 2 10,000 units; Year 3 15,000 units. All at £16 per unit.
(f) Production is at the rate of: Year 1 10,000 units; Year 2 12,000 units; Year 3 16,000 units.

37.5 Greatsound Ltd manufactures and sells compact disc players, the cost of which is made up as follows:

	£
Direct material	74.80
Direct labour	18.70
Variable overhead	7.50
Fixed overhead	30.00
Total cost	131.00

The current selling price is £187.

Greatsound Ltd works a day shift only, at present producing 120,000 compact disc players per annum, and has no spare capacity.

Market research has shown that there is a demand for an additional 60,000 compact disc players in the forthcoming year. However, these additional sales would have a selling price of £150 each. One way of achieving the extra production required is to work a night shift. However, this would increase fixed costs by £2,500,000 and the labour force would have to be paid an extra 20 per cent over the day shift rate.

The company supplying the materials to Greatsound Ltd has indicated that it will offer a special discount of 10 per cent on total purchases if the annual purchases of materials increase by 50 per cent.

The selling price and all other costs will remain the same.

Assuming that the additional purchases will only be made if the night shift runs, **you are required to:**

(*a*) advise Greatsound Ltd whether it should proceed with the proposal to commence the night shift, based on financial considerations.

(*b*) calculate the minimum increase in sales and production required to justify the night shift.

(*c*) give **four** other matters which should be taken into consideration when making a decision of this nature.

(*Northern Examinations and Assessment Board: GCE A–Level*)

37.6A

(*a*) What is meant by the terms *contribution* and *marginal cost*?

(*b*) Barton & Co Ltd make and sell 2,000 units per month of a product 'Barco'. The selling price is £65 per unit, and unit costs are: direct labour £8; direct materials £17; variable overheads £11. Fixed costs per month are £29,400.

The company receives two export orders for completion in September 19X2. Order A requests 600 items at a special total price of £20,000; order B requires 750 items at a total price of £34,000. Order A will require no special treatment, but order B will demand extra processing at a cost of £6 per item. The company has sufficient capacity to undertake *either* A *or* B in addition to its current production, but only by paying its direct labour force an overtime premium of 25 per cent.

Calculate the company's contribution and the profits for the month if:

(*i*) normal production only takes place;

(*ii*) order A is accepted in addition to normal production;

(*iii*) order B is accepted in addition to normal production.

(*c*) Use your answer to (*b*) to demonstrate that a company will normally accept an order which produces a *contribution* towards overheads.

(*Edexcel Foundation, London Examinations: GCE A–Level*)

37.7

Arncliffe Limited manufactures two types of product marketed under the brand names of 'Crowns' and 'Kings'. All the company's production is sold to a large firm of wholesalers.

Arncliffe is in something of a crisis because the chief accountant has been taken ill just as the company was about to begin negotiating the terms of future contracts with its customer. You have been called in to help and are given the following information relating to each product for the last year. This information has been prepared by a junior assistant.

Report on revenues/costs for the year just ended:

	Crowns £	Kings £
Sales	60,000	25,000
Floor space costs (rent and rates)	10,000	5,000
Raw materials	8,000	2,000
Direct labour	20,000	10,000
Insurances	400	200
Machine running costs	12,000	3,000
Net profit	9,600	4,800

The junior assistant says in his report. 'As you can see, Crowns make twice as much profit as Kings and we should therefore stop manufacturing Kings if we wish to maximise our profits. I have allocated floor space costs and insurances on the basis of the labour costs for each product. All other costs/revenues can be directly related to the individual product.'

Further investigation reveals the following information:

(*i*) The wholesaler bought all the 20,000 Crowns and 10,000 Kings produced last year, selling them to their customers at £4 and £3 each respectively. The wholesaler is experiencing an increasing demand for Crowns and intends to raise his price next year to £4.50 each.
(*ii*) Crowns took 8,000 hours to process on the one machine the company owns, whereas Kings took 2,000 hours. The machine has a maximum capacity of 10,000 hours per year.
(*iii*) Because all production is immediately sold to the wholesaler no stocks are kept.

Required:

(*a*) Prepare the revenue/cost statement for the year just ended on a marginal cost basis, and calculate the rate of contribution to sales for each product.
(*b*) You are told that in the coming year the maximum market demand for the two products will be 40,000 Crowns and 36,000 Kings and that the wholesaler wishes to sell a minimum of 6,000 units of each product. Calculate the best product mix and resulting profit for Arncliffe Limited.
(*c*) Calculate the best product mix and resulting profit for Arncliffe Limited if another machine with identical running costs and capacity can be hired for £20,000 per annum. Floor space and insurance costs would not change and the maximum and minimum conditions set out in (*b*) above continue to apply.
(*d*) What points does Arncliffe Limited need to bear in mind when negotiating next year's contract with the wholesaler?

(*Reproduced by permission of the University of Cambridge Local Examinations Syndicate*)

37.8A Reed Ltd manufactures three products A, B and C. Budgeted costs and selling prices for the three months ending 30 September 19X2 are as follows:

	A	B	C
Sales (units per month)	6,000	8,000	5,000
	£	£	£
Selling price per unit	45	44	37
Unit costs			
Direct labour	6	9	6
Direct materials*	20	24	16
Variable overhead	4	3	2
Fixed overhead	5	5	6

Labour costs are £3 per hour, and material costs are £4 per kilo for all products. The total fixed costs are of a general factory nature, and are unavoidable.

The company has been advised by its supplier that due to a material shortage, its material requirement for the month of September will be reduced by 15 per cent. No other changes are anticipated.

Required:

A A statement to show the maximum net profit for the three months ending 30 September 19X2, taking into account the material shortage for the month of September.
B Explain how the fixed cost element is dealt with in marginal costing and in absorption costing. Briefly explain how this affects any closing stock valuation.

(*University of Oxford Delegacy of Local Examinations: GCE A–Level*)

Authors' note : assume that the materials used in each product are of the same kind.

37.9 Paul Wagtail started a small manufacturing business on 1 May 19X8. He has kept his records on the double entry system, and has drawn up a trial balance at 30 April 19X9 before attempting to prepare his first final accounts.

Extract from the trial balance of Paul Wagtail at 30 April 19X9

	£	£
Purchases of raw materials	125,000	
Sales		464,360
Selling expenses	23,800	
Insurance	4,800	
Factory repairs and maintenance	19,360	
Carriage on raw materials	1,500	
Heating and lighting	3,600	
Direct factory power	12,430	
Distribution expenses	25,400	
Production wages	105,270	
Factory supervisor's wages	29,600	
Administration expenses	46,700	
Plant and machinery at cost	88,000	
Delivery vehicles at cost	88,000	
Raw materials returned to supplier	2,100	

At 30 April 19X9, he has closing stocks of raw materials costing £8,900. He has manufactured 9,500 completed units of his product, and sold 8,900. He has a further 625 units that are 80 per cent complete for raw materials and production labour, and also 80 per cent complete for factory indirect costs.

He has decided to divide his insurance costs and his heating and lighting costs 40 per cent for the factory and 60 per cent for the office/showroom.

He wishes to depreciate his plant and machinery at 20 per cent p.a. on cost, and his delivery vehicles using the reducing balance method at 40 per cent p.a.

He has not yet made up his mind how to value his stocks of work in progress and finished goods. He has heard that he could use either marginal or absorption costing to do this, and has received different advice from a friend running a similar business and from an accountant.

Required:

(*a*) Prepare Paul Wagtail's manufacturing, trading and profit and loss accounts for the year ended 30 April 19X9 using *both* marginal and absorption costing methods, preferably in columnar format.

(*b*) Advise Paul Wagtail of the advantages and disadvantages of using each method.

(*University of Oxford Local Delegacy Examinations: GCE A–Level*)

37.10A The figures given below are all that could be salvaged from the records after a recent fire in the offices of Firelighters Limited. The company manufactures a single product, has no raw materials or work in progress and values its stocks at marginal cost (i.e. at variable manufacturing cost) using the FIFO basis. It is known that the unit closing stock valuation in 19X0 was the same as in 19X9.

	19X0	19X1
Selling price per unit	£10.00	£10.00
Variable manufacturing cost (per unit produced)	£4.00	£4.00
Variable selling cost (per unit sold)	£1.25	?
Quantity sold (units)	100,000	?
Quantity manufactured (units)	105,000	130,000
Contribution	?	£585,000
Fixed manufacturing costs	£105,000	£117,000
Other fixed costs	£155,000	?
Operating profit before interest charges	?	£292,000
Interest charges	£70,000	?
Opening finished stock (units)	?	?
Closing finished stock (units)	20,000	20,000
Net profit for the year	?	£210,000

Required:

Prepare a revenue statement for management showing contribution, operating profit and net profit for each year in as much detail as the information given above permits.

(*Reproduced by permission of the University of Cambridge Local Examinations Syndicate*)

37.11A Gainford Ltd is a manufacturing company which produces three specialist products — **A**, **B** and **C**. For costing purposes the company's financial year is divided into thirteen periods of four weeks. There is always sufficient raw material in stock to meet any planned level of production but there is a maximum number of labour hours available to the company. The production of each product requires a different physical layout of the factory equipment although the labour tasks are broadly similar. For this reason the company only produces one type of product at any time, and the decision as to which product to manufacture is taken before each four week period commences.

A forty hour working week is in operation and the following factory staff are employed:

> Grade 1   28 staff paid at a rate of £8 per hour
> Grade 2   12 staff paid at a rate of £6 per hour

In addition, a limited number of qualified part-time staff can be employed when required. Both full-time and part-time staff are paid at the same rate. The next four week period is number 7 and the following maximum part-time hours are available for that period:

> Grade 1   2,240 hours
> Grade 2   1,104 hours

The production costs and selling costs per unit for each product are:

		A £	B £	C £
Direct raw material		147	87	185
Direct labour:	Grade 1	64	56	60
	Grade 2	24	27	21
Variable overheads		15	10	15
Fixed Overheads		12	12	12
Selling price of each product		400	350	450

There is a strong demand for all three products and every unit produced is sold.

Required:
(a) Explain the terms:
   (i) 'contribution'
   (ii) 'key factor'
(b) Calculate the contribution and profit obtained when **each** product is sold.
(c) Prepare a statement from the available information, for each period number 7 which will assist management to decide which product to produce in order to maximise contribution. This statement should include details of the:
   (i) total production labour hours available
   (ii) number of hours required to produce one unit of **each** type of product
   (iii) maximum production (in units) possible of **each** type of product
   (iv) product which will give the greatest contribution in period number 7
(d) Outline the main steps in the manufacturing decision-making process which ought to be adopted by a business.

(Associated Examining Board: GCE A–Level)

37.12A Vale Manufacturing started in business on 1 April 19X3, and incurred the following costs during its first three years.

Year ending 31 March	19X4 £	19X5 £	19X6 £
Direct materials	60,000	49,900	52,200
Direct labour	48,000	44,000	45,000
Variable overheads	24,000	30,000	40,000
Fixed costs	40,000	40,600	41,300

Sales during the first three years were all at £20 per unit.

	19X4	19X5	19X6
Production each year (units)	16,000	14,000	14,000
Sales each year (units)	14,000	14,000	15,000

Required:
(a) Prepare a statement showing the gross profit for each of the three years if the company used:
   (i) the marginal costing approach to valuing stock;
   (ii) the absorption costing approach to valuing stock.
(b) Advise the company of the advantages and disadvantages of using each method.

(University of Oxford Delegacy of Local Examinations: GCE A–Level)

37.13 Glasses Ltd make four different products, Q, R, S and T. They have ascertained the cost of direct materials and direct labour and the variable overhead for each unit of product. An attempt is made to allocate the other costs in a logical manner. When this is done 10 per cent is added for profit. The cost of direct labour and materials per unit is Q £14; R £28; S £60; T £32. Variable overheads per unit are Q £4; R £8; S £13; T £12. Fixed overhead of £1,900 is allocated per unit as Q £2; R £4; S £7; T £6.

You are required to:

(a) Calculate the prices at which the units would be sold by Glasses Ltd if the full-cost system of pricing was adhered to.

(b) What would you advise the company to do if, because of market competition, prices had to be fixed at Q £33; R £39; S £70; T £49?

(c) Assuming production of 100 units of each item per accounting period, what would be the net profit (i) if your advice given in your answer to (b) was followed, (ii) if the firm continued to produce all of the items?

(d) What would you advise the company to do if, because of market competition, prices had to be fixed at Q £17; R £48; S £140; T £39?

(e) Assuming production of 100 units of each item per accounting period, what would be the net profit (i) if your advice given in your answer to (d) was followed, (ii) if the firm continued to produce all of the items?

37.14A Bottles Ltd makes six different products, F, G, H, I, J and K. An analysis of costs ascertains the following:

Per unit	F	G	H	I	J	K
	£	£	£	£	£	£
Direct labour and direct materials	15	17	38	49	62	114
Variable cost	6	11	10	21	22	23

Fixed costs of £11,400 are allocated per unit as F £4; G £7; H £7; I £10; J £16 and K £13. Using full-cost pricing 20 per cent is to be added per unit for profit.

You are required to:

(a) Calculate the prices that would be charged by Bottles Ltd if the full-cost pricing system was adhered to.

(b) What advice would you give the company if a survey of the market showed that the prices charged could be F £26; G £26; H £66; I £75; J £80; K £220?

(c) Assuming production of 200 units per period of each unit manufactured what would be the profit of the firm, (i) if your advice in (b) was followed, (ii) if the firm continued to produce all of the items?

(d) Suppose that in fact the market survey had revealed instead that the prices charged could be F £30; G £33; H £75; I £66; J £145 and K £130, then what would your advice have been to the company?

(e) Assuming that production of each item manufactured was 200 units per month, then what would have been the profit (i) if your advice in (d) had been followed, (ii) if the company chose to continue manufacturing all items?

38

Job and process costing

Objectives

After you have studied this chapter, you should:

- *know how indirect costs are apportioned among cost centres*

- *understand the system of job costing*

- *understand the system of process costing*

- *be aware of the appropriate treatment for under- and over-absorbed overheads*

- *know the difference between scrap, by-products, and joint products*

38.1 Introduction

The earlier chapters on costing have been concerned mainly with the firm as a whole. You have seen the effects of marginal and absorption costing if applied to the firm, and you have seen the flow of costs through manufacturing and retail businesses. Now we have to consider the use of these concepts in the application of costing in firms. So far there has been a certain amount of simplification just so that the concepts could be seen without too much detail obscuring your view. For instance, it has been usually assumed in most of the *exhibits* that the firms have been making only one kind of product, and that there has really been only one cost centre. Without stretching your imagination greatly you will realise that firms manufacture many different types of goods, and that there are many cost centres in most firms.

When looking at the costing systems in use it can be seen that they can usually be divided into two main types, (*a*) job costing, (*b*) process costing. These two main types have either an absorption or marginal costing approach, they use FIFO or LIFO or AVCO methods of pricing issues etc. It is important to realise that marginal costing is not a costing system, it is instead an approach to costing which is used when job or processing costing systems are used. The same applies to absorption costing.

38.2 The choice of job costing or process costing

Process costing is relevant where production is regarded as a continuous flow, and would be applicable to industries where production is repetitive and continuous. One example would be an oil refinery where crude oil is processed continually, emerging as different grades of petrol, paraffin, motor oil, etc. Another instance would be a salt works where brine (salt water) is pumped into the works, and the product is slabs or packets of salt.

Salt works and oil refineries will have a repetitive and continuous flow of production and would, therefore, use process costing.

Contrasted with this would be production which consisted of separate jobs for special orders which could be just one item or of a batch of items. For instance, where bodies of Rolls-Royce cars are made to each customer's specifications, each car can be regarded as a separate job. Compared with this would be a printer's business where books are printed, so that the printing of say 5,000 copies of a book can also be regarded as a job. The 'job' can thus be one item or a batch of similar items.

We can compare the two approaches by using diagrams of the different types of costing. These are shown as Exhibit 38.1.

Exhibit 38.1

Process costing

Costs *not* allocated to individual units. Instead direct costs and overheads allocated to Process A, or Process B, or Process C

All units same as each other. Valued at average unit cost of production

Job costing

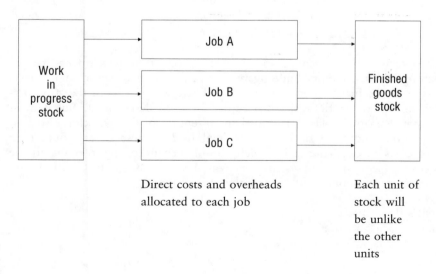

Direct costs and overheads allocated to each job

Each unit of stock will be unlike the other units

38.3 Job costing

Each job will be given a separate job number, and direct materials and direct labour used on the job will be charged to the job. The accumulation of the costs will be done on a 'job cost sheet'. The materials will have been charged to the job on FIFO, or LIFO, or AVCO, etc., basis. The direct labour costs will be found by recording the number of direct labour hours of each type of direct worker, and multiplying by the labour cost per hour for each type.

The job is thus the cost centre, and direct labour and direct materials can be charged direct to the cost centre. The indirect expenses cannot be charged direct to the job, such costs are charged instead to a service cost centre and the cost of the service centre is then apportioned between the various jobs to give the cost of each job including indirect expenses. Now it is only after the accounting period is over that the exact costs of each service centre are known, but you will want to know how much each job costs as it is finished. You will not want to wait months to find out the cost of each job. This is solved by estimating the indirect expenses, and then fixing the method of apportioning these estimated expenses as will be seen in Exhibit 38.2.

Suppose there are three jobs being performed and these are in separate production departments, Departments A, B and C. There are also two service centres, Departments G and H. Some of the indirect labour expenses and other indirect expenses can be allocated direct to the production departments – for instance the wages of the foremen of each of Departments A, B and C, or items such as lubricating materials if each department used quite different lubricants. Other indirect labour can be traced to the two centres G and H as well as expenses. The problem then is that of apportioning the costs of G and H between Departments A, B and C. We can now look at Exhibit 38.2, and see what answer this firm came up with.

Exhibit 38.2

Indirect labour costs and other indirect expenses have been allocated to Production Departments A, B and C and Service Departments G and H as follows:

	Production Departments			Service Departments	
	A	B	C	G	H
Indirect labour	2,000	3,000	4,000	500	1,000
Other expenses	1,000	2,000	3,000	1,500	2,000
	£3,000	£5,000	£7,000	£2,000	£3,000

The problem is to apportion the costs of G and H to the production departments. G was a department which maintained factory buildings whilst H maintained factory machinery. A study of the costs of G produced a very easy answer. There was no doubt that the costs were in direct relationship to the floor space occupied by each department. But it must not be overlooked that department H also needed the attention of G's workforce so that part of the costs of G would have to be apportioned to H. These costs would then increase the total of costs of department H which would then need apportioning to the production departments. Floor space in square feet was A 2,000, B 4,000, C 3,000, and H 1,000. The £2,000 costs of department G were therefore apportioned:

$$\frac{\text{Each department's floor space}}{\text{Total floor space}} \times £2,000$$

Therefore:

A $\dfrac{2,000}{10,000} \times £2,000 = £400$:   B $\dfrac{4,000}{10,000} \times £2,000 = £800$

C $\dfrac{3,000}{10,000} \times £2,000 = £600$:   H $\dfrac{1,000}{10,000} \times £2,000 = £200$

(Department H's costs have now increased by £200 and become £3,200.)

Department H's costs presented a far more difficult problem. Consideration was given to apportionment based on numbers of machines, volumes of production, and types of machinery. It was, however, felt that there was a high relationship in this case (although this would certainly not always be true in other firms) between the values of machinery in use and the costs of maintaining them. The more costly equipment was very complicated and needed a lot of attention. Consequently it was decided to apportion H's costs between A, B and C on the basis of the value of machinery in each department. This was found to be A £3,000; B £6,000; C £7,000. The costs were therefore apportioned:

$$\dfrac{\text{Value of machinery in department}}{\text{Total value of machinery in all 3 departments}} \times £3,200$$

Therefore:

A $\dfrac{3,000}{16,000} \times £3,200 = £600$:   B $\dfrac{6,000}{16,000} \times £3,200 = £1,200$

C $\dfrac{7,000}{16,000} \times £3,200 = £1,400$

The costs and their apportionment can, therefore, be shown:

	Production Departments			Service Departments	
	A	B	C	G	H
Indirect labour	2,000	3,000	4,000	500	1,000
Other expenses	1,000	2,000	3,000	1,500	2,000
	3,000	5,000	7,000	2,000	3,000
Department G's costs apportioned	400	800	600	(2,000)	200
					3,200
Department H's costs apportioned	600	1,200	1,400		(3,200)
	£4,000	£7,000	£9,000	–	–

This continuous method of apportioning service department overheads is sometimes called the repeated distribution method. See Question 38.7 for a discussion of this and another method, the elimination method.

We now have the estimated overhead for each department for the ensuing accounting period. However, another problem faces us concerning how the overhead is going to be taken into the calculation of the cost of each job in these departments. After investigation the conclusion is that in departments A and B there is a direct relationship between direct labour hours and overhead, but in department C the guiding fact is machine hours. If the total overheads of departments A and B are therefore divided by the estimated number of direct labour hours this will give the overhead rate per direct labour hour. In department

C, the total overhead will be divided by the estimated machine hours. The calculation of the overhead rates is therefore:

	Production Departments		
	A	B	C
Direct labour hours	5,000	4,000	
Machine hours			6,000
Overhead rate per direct labour hour	$\dfrac{£4,000}{5,000}$	$\dfrac{£7,000}{4,000}$	
	= £0.8	= £1.75	
Overhead rate per machine hour			$\dfrac{£9,000}{6,000}$
			= £1.5

We can now calculate the costs of four jobs performed in this factory:

Job A/70/144
> *Department A*
> Started 1.7.19X2. Completed 13.7.19X2
> Cost of direct materials £130
> Number of direct labour hours 100
> Cost rate of direct labour per hour £0.9

Job B/96/121
> *Department B*
> Started 4.7.19X2. Completed 9.7.19X2
> Cost of direct materials £89
> Number of direct labour hours 40
> Cost rate of direct labour per hour £1.1

Job C/67/198
> *Department C*
> Started 8.7.19X2. Completed 16.7.19X2
> Cost of direct materials £58
> Number of direct labour hours 50
> Cost rate of direct labour per hour £1.0
> Number of machine hours 40

Job AC/45/34
> *Departments A and C*
> Started in A 3.7.19X2. Passed on to C 11.7.19X2. Completed in C 16.7.19X2
> Cost of materials £115
> Number of direct labour hours (in Dept. A) 80
> Number of direct labour hours (in Dept. C) 90
> Cost rate per direct labour hour Dept. A £0.9
>   Dept. C £1.0
> Number of machine hours, Dept. C 70

The job cost sheets for these four jobs are shown below. At no point during this Exhibit has it been stated whether a marginal costing or an absorption costing approach has been adopted. If an absorption costing approach had been used, overhead would include both fixed and variable overhead. If a marginal costing approach had been used, the overhead brought into the calculations of job costs would exclude fixed overhead, so that the overhead rate would be a variable overhead rate.

Job Cost Sheet. Job No. A/70/144

Started 1.7.19X2   Completed 13.7.19X2
                                                                £
Materials   130

	Hours	Rates £	
Direct labour	100	0.9	90
Factory overhead	100	0.8	80
Total job cost			£300

Job Cost Sheet. Job No. B/96/121

Started 4.7.19X2   Completed 9.7.19X2
                                                                £
Materials   89

	Hours	Rates £	
Direct labour	40	1.1	44
Factory overhead	40	1.75	70
Total job cost			£203

Job Cost Sheet. Job No. C/67/198

Started 8.7.19X2   Completed 16.7.19X2
                                                                £
Materials   58

	Hours	Rates £	
Direct labour	50	1.0	50
Factory overhead	40	1.5	60
Total job cost			£168

Job Cost Sheet. Job No. AC/45/34

Started 3.7.19X2   Completed 16.7.19X2
                                                                £
Materials   115

	Hours	Rates £	
Direct labour (Dept. A)	80	0.9	72
Direct labour (Dept. C)	90	1.0	90
Factory overhead (Dept. A)	80	0.8	64
Factory overhead (Dept. C)	70	1.5	105
Total job cost			£446

38.4 Cost centres – job costing and responsibility

It must be pointed out that a cost centre for job costing is not necessarily the same as tracing the costs down to the individual who is responsible for controlling them. There are two questions here: (*a*) Finding the cost of a job to check on its profitability and (*b*) Controlling the costs by making someone responsible for them so that he/she will have to answer for any variations from planned results. Many firms therefore keep separate records of costs to fulfil each of these functions.

38.5 Process costing

Job costing treats production as a number of separate jobs being performed, whereas process costing sees production as a continuous flow. In process costing there is correspondingly no attempt to allocate costs to specific units being produced.

There is, however, usually more than one process in the manufacture of goods. We can take as an example a bakery producing cakes. There are three processes: (*a*) the mixing of the cake ingredients, (*b*) the baking of the cakes, and (*c*) the packaging of the cakes. Each process is treated as a cost centre, and therefore costs for (*a*), (*b*) and (*c*) are collected separately. Overhead rates are then calculated for each cost centre in a similar fashion to that in job costing.

In the case of the bakery, each accounting period would probably start and finish without any half-mixed or half-baked cakes, but some types of firms which use process costing have processes which take rather longer to complete than baking cakes. A typical case would be the brewing of beer. At the beginning and end of each period there would be partly processed units. It is a matter of arithmetic to convert production into 'equivalent production'. For instance, production during a particular period may be as in Exhibit 38.3.

Exhibit 38.3

Started in previous year ¾ completed then, and ¼ completed in current period, 400 units, 400 × ¼	100
Started and completed in current period	680
Started in current period and ⅛ completed by end of period, 160 units, 160 × ⅛	20
Equivalent production	800 units

If the total costs of the cost centre amounted to £4,000 then the unit cost would be:

$$\frac{£4,000}{800} = £5.$$

In fact, process costing can become very complicated because some of the part-produced items are complete in terms of say, materials, but incomplete in terms of labour, or else say ⅔ complete for materials and ¼ complete for labour. Although the situation becomes complicated, the principles are no different from those described for calculating equivalent production.

We can now look at an example of process costing in Exhibit 38.4. So that we do not get involved in too many arithmetical complications, we will assume that there are no partly completed goods in each process at the start and end of the period considered.

Exhibit 38.4

A bakery making cakes has three processes, process (A) the mixing of the cake ingredients, (B) the baking of the cakes, and (C) the packaging of the cakes.

January activity was as follows:

Materials used:	£
Process (A)	4,000
Process (B)	–
Process (C)	1,000
Direct labour:	
Process (A)	1,500
Process (B)	500
Process (C)	800
Factory overhead:	
Variable:	
Process (A)	400
Process (B)	1,300
Process (C)	700
Fixed: (allocated to processes)	
Process (A)	600
Process (B)	500
Process (C)	400

During January 100,000 cakes were made.
The process cost accounts will appear as:

Process (A)

	£		£
Materials	4,000	Transferred to Process (B)	
Direct labour	1,500	100,000 units at £0.065	6,500
Variable overhead	400		
Fixed overhead	600		
	£6,500		£6,500

Process (B)

	£		£
Transferred from Process (A)		Transferred to Process (C)	
100,000 units at £0.065	6,500	100,000 units at £0.088	8,800
Direct labour	500		
Variable overhead	1,300		
Fixed overhead	500		
	£8,800		£8,800

Process (C)

	£		£
Transferred from Process (B)		Transferred to finished goods stock	
100,000 units at £0.088	8,800	100,000 units at £0.117	11,700
Materials	1,000		
Direct labour	800		
Variable overhead	700		
Fixed overhead	400		
	£11,700		£11,700

38.6 Normal and abnormal losses

There are some losses that are basically part of the production process and cannot be eliminated. For instance, when printing books, losses occur in the cutting of paper, when brewing beer there will be losses due to evaporation, when cutting steel there will be losses. These losses are inevitable, even in the most efficient firms, and as such they are called normal or uncontrollable losses.

On the other hand, there are losses which should be avoided if there are efficient operating conditions. Such things as the incorrect cutting of cloth so that it is wasted unnecessarily, not mixing ingredients properly so that some of the product is unusable, and the use of inferior materials so that much of the product cannot pass production tests and is wasted. These are abnormal or controllable losses.

The accounting treatment varies between these two sorts of losses:

Normal losses: These are not transferred from the process account but are treated as part of the process costs.

Abnormal losses: These are transferred from out of the process account to an abnormal loss account. The double entry is:

Dr Abnormal loss account
Cr   Process account

The **abnormal loss** is then treated as a period cost. Accordingly it is written off to the debit of the profit and loss account at the end of the period.

38.7 Under/over absorption of overheads

When an overhead rate is based on estimated annual overhead expenditure and estimated activity, it would be very rare for it to be exactly the same as the actual overhead incurred. Either the costs themselves will have changed, or the activity, or both.

If therefore £300,000 has been allocated to the year's production, but actual costs were £298,000 then too much has been allocated; in other words, it is a case of over-absorption of overheads amounting to £2,000. If on the other hand £305,000 had been allocated but the actual costs were £311,000 then too little has been allocated, and this is an under-absorption of overheads amounting to £6,000.

At the closing balance sheet date the stock-in-trade has been valued and this will include something for overheads. In the case of an under-absorption the question arises as to whether the closing stock valuation should be amended to include something for the under-absorbed overheads. The accounting answer is that no adjustment should be made to the stock valuation. Similarly the stock valuation should not be reduced to take account of over-absorption of overheads.

Exhibit 38.5 shows how the costs should be treated.

Exhibit 38.5

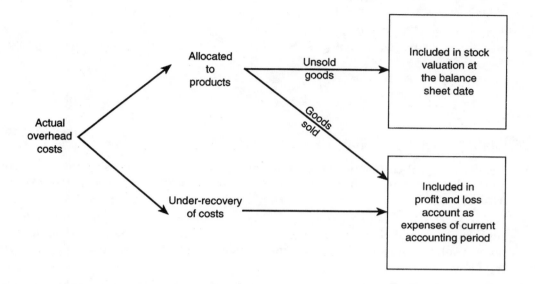

38.8 Other kinds of firms

Process costing is found most often in industries such as oil, canning, paint manufacture, steel, textiles, and food processing.

38.9 The problem of joint costs

Usually a manufacturing operation results in one simple product. Any excess is regarded as scrap, and the small cost that could be traced to it is ignored, e.g. the manufacture of a suit where the cost is traced to the suit, the small unusable bits of cloth being ignored.

This is not always the case. Sometimes a second product of some minor value is produced – a 'by-product'. An example would be the sawdust produced when wood is being prepared for furniture manufacture.

Something else that may occur arises where a group of separate products is produced simultaneously, each of the products having relatively substantial sales values – 'joint products'. Thus crude oil taken into an oil refinery is processed and the output is in terms of different grades of petrol, paraffin, motor oil, etc. This means that in costing terms the costs of the materials and processes, etc. have to be split between the joint products.

Many problems exist in this area. Perhaps you will see why when the problem of allocating costs between joint products is concerned with the cutting up of a cow for beef. From a cow there is rump steak, the fillet steaks, the T-bone steaks, sirloin, silverside, brisket, etc. If the cow costs the butcher £300, then how would you allocate the cost between all of these various joint products? This gives you some idea of the problem which exists; in many industries this becomes involved with complex technological problems.

New terms

Job costing (p. 530): A costing system that is applied when goods or services are produced in discrete jobs, either one item at a time, or in batches.

Process costing (p. 530): A costing system that is applied when goods or services are produced in a continuous flow.

Abnormal loss (p. 538): A loss arising in the production process that should have been avoided.

By-product (p. 539): Products of minor sales value that result from the production of a main product.

Joint product (p. 539): Two or more products, each of which have significant sales value, created in the same production process.

Main points to remember

1   Neither marginal costing nor absorption costing are costing 'systems'; rather, they are approaches to costing which are used when job or processing costing systems are used.

2   Direct costs can be allocated directly to the relevant cost centre. However, indirect costs have to be apportioned among cost centres on an appropriate basis, as there is no way of knowing precisely how much indirect cost was incurred on each item produced.

Review questions

Advice:

Questions on job and process costing are usually fairly easy to answer and it is also relatively simple to gain quite high marks by tackling them.

38.1   In a firm there are four types of jobs performed in separate production departments A, B, C and D. In addition there are three service departments, K, L and M. Costs have been allocated to the departments as follows:

	Production Departments				Service Departments		
	A	B	C	D	K	L	M
	£	£	£	£	£	£	£
Indirect labour	4,000	6,000	8,000	2,000	1,500	3,000	4,100
Other expenses	2,700	3,100	3,600	1,500	4,500	2,000	2,000

The expenses of the service departments are to be allocated between other departments as follows:

Dept K to Depts A 25 per cent: B 30 per cent: C 20 per cent: D 10 per cent: M 15 per cent.
Dept L to Depts A 60 per cent: C 30 per cent: D 10 per cent.
Dept M to Depts B 30 per cent: C 50 per cent: D 20 per cent.

In departments A and C the job costing is to use an overhead rate per direct labour hour, whilst in B and D a machine hour rate will be used. The number of direct hours and machine hours per department is expected to be:

	A	B	C	D
Direct labour hours	2,000	4,000	4,450	2,700
Machine hours	1,900	2,600	2,900	2,400

You are required to calculate:

(*a*) The overhead rates for departments A and C.
(*b*) The overhead rates for departments B and D.

(Keep your answer – it will be used as a basis for the next question.)

38.2 In the firm mentioned in Question 38.1 what would be the costs of the following jobs given that the direct labour costs per hour are: Dept A £2.1; B £1.7; C £2.4; D £2.3?

Job 351: Dept A	Direct materials cost	£190
	Number of direct labour hours	56
	Number of machine hours	40
Job 352: Dept B	Direct materials cost	£1,199
	Number of direct labour hours	178
	Number of machine hours	176
Job 353: Dept C	Direct materials cost	£500
	Number of direct labour hours	130
	Number of machine hours	100
Job 354: Dept D	Direct materials cost	£666
	Number of direct labour hours	90
	Number of machine hours	64
Job 355: Dept C	Direct materials cost	£560
	Number of direct labour hours	160
	Number of machine hours	150
	Job passed on to Dept B where additional direct materials cost	£68
	Number of direct labour hours	30
	Number of machine hours	20

38.3A In a firm there are five types of jobs performed in separate production departments P, Q, R, S and T. In addition there are two service departments F and G. Costs have been allocated to the departments as follows:

	Production Departments				Service Departments		
	P	Q	R	S	T	F	G
	£	£	£	£	£	£	£
Indirect labour	5,000	7,000	3,000	6,000	8,000	10,000	9,000
Other expenses	500	1,800	1,000	1,200	1,300	6,000	7,000

The expenses of the service departments are to be allocated between other departments as follows:

Dept F to Depts P 10 per cent: Q 20 per cent: S 30 per cent: T 15 per cent: G 25 per cent.

Dept G to Depts P 12.5 per cent: Q 20 per cent: R 25 per cent: S 30 per cent: T 12.5 per cent.

In departments R and T the job costing is to use an overhead rate per direct labour hour, whilst in the other production departments a machine hour rate will be used. The number of direct labour hours and machine hours per department are expected to be:

	P	Q	R	S	T
Direct labour hours	4,000	5,000	3,600	10,000	3,550
Machine hours	3,000	4,000	3,000	8,000	2,800

You are required to calculate:
(*a*) The overhead rates for departments R and T.
(*b*) The overhead rates for departments P, Q and S.

(Keep your answer – it will be used for Question 38.4A.)

38.4A   In the firm mentioned in Question 38.3X what would be the costs of the following jobs, given that the direct labour rate per hour is Dept P £1.9; Q £2.5; R £2.0; S £2.7; T £2.4?

Job 701: Dept R	Direct materials cost	£115
	Number of direct labour hours	35
	Number of machine hours	29
Job 702: Dept T	Direct materials cost	£1,656
	Number of direct labour hours	180
	Number of machine hours	160
Job 703: Dept P	Direct materials cost	£546
	Number of direct labour hours	100
	Number of machine hours	90
Job 704: Dept S	Direct materials cost	£65
	Number of direct labour hours	250
	Number of machine hours	60
Job 705: Dept Q	Direct materials cost	£4,778
	Number of direct labour hours	305
	Number of machine hours	280
Job 706: Dept P	Direct materials cost	£555
	Number of direct labour hours	200
	Number of machine hours	180
	Then passed to Dept T for completion where direct materials cost	£11
	Number of direct labour hours	18
	Number of machine hours	2

38.5

(*a*)   Define the term *equivalent production* and state when the principle is used.

(*b*)   During May 1991, M Wurzel & Co. Limited's output was 4,000 finished items plus 600 partly finished items. There was no work in progress on 1 May 19X1.

	Materials	Labour	Overheads	Total
Total cost (£)	8,172	7,120	5,196	20,488
WIP degree of completion %	90	75	55	–

Calculate for the month of May 19X1:

(*i*)   the total equivalent production for each cost element;

(*ii*)   the cost per complete unit;

(*iii*)   the value of the work in progress.

(*Edexcel Foundation, London Examinations: GCE A–Level*)

38.6A

(*a*)   What is meant by the term *equivalent production*?

(*b*)   At Earith Industries at the beginning of April there were no partially finished goods on hand. During the month, 6,000 completed units were produced, together with 800 units partially completed. Details of the partially finished items were:

	Total cost (£)	Percentage completed
Materials	12,540	75
Labour	8,476	65
Overheads	7,084	55

Calculate:

(*i*)   the total equivalent production,

(*ii*)   the cost per complete unit,

(*iii*)   the total value of work in progress

(*Edexcel Foundation, London Examinations: GCE A–Level*)

38.7

(a) Explain the difference between the terms *overhead allotment, overhead apportionment,* and *overhead absorption.*

(b) Why are *estimated* figures used in calculating overhead absorption rates?

(c) The following information relates to the Flyby Knight Plc for the six months ended 31 December 19X1:

	Production Departments			Service Departments	
	A	B	C	X	Y
Overheads (£)	14,000	12,000	8,000	4,000	3,000
Overheads to be apportioned:					
Dept X (%)	35	30	20	–	15
Dept Y (%)	30	40	25	5	–

(i) Use the continuous apportionment (repeated distribution) method to apportion the service departments' overheads between each other.
(ii) Apportion the service departments' overheads calculated in (i) to the production departments.
(iii) Show how the overheads apportioned to the production departments would have differed if the elimination method had been used for the service departments.
(iv) State how far it is true to say that the elimination method produces an inaccurate answer, and is therefore not to be recommended.

(Edexcel Foundation, London Examinations: GCE A–Level)

38.8A Kalmo Ltd offers a subcontracting service in assembly, painting and packing. Components are supplied by customers to the company, the required operations are then carried out, and the completed work returned to the customer. The company is labour intensive, with only a relatively small amount of materials purchased.

Currently, one factory overhead recovery rate is used which is a percentage of total direct labour costs. This is calculated from the following budgeted costs.

Department	Direct labour costs £	Direct labour hours	Machine hours	Factory overheads £
Assembly	450,000	150,000	6,000	180,000
Painting	500,000	140,625	–	225,000
Packing	250,000	100,000	8,000	75,000

The cost sheet for Job 131190 shows the following information:

Department	Direct labour costs £	Direct labour hours	Machine hours	Direct material costs £
Assembly	2,500	1,000	120	100
Painting	2,200	900	–	400
Packing	4,800	960	80	500

General administration expenses of 20 per cent are added to the total factory costs, and then a further 25 per cent of the total cost is added as profit, to arrive at the selling price.

Although the company has been using the blanket factory overhead recovery rate for a number of years, one of the directors has questioned this method, and asks if it would be possible to apply overhead recovery rates for each department.

Required:

A   Calculate the current factory overhead recovery rate, and apply this to arrive at the selling price for Job 131190.

B   In line with the director's comments, calculate overhead recovery rates for each department, using two alternative methods, and apply both to arrive at new selling prices for Job 131190.

C   Briefly evaluate the methods you have used for the recovery of factory overheads, justifying which one you consider to be most appropriate.

D   Outline how an unsatisfactory method of overhead absorption can affect the profits of a business.

(*University of Oxford Delegacy of Local Examinations: GCE A–Level*)

38.9

(*a*) What is meant by the term, 'specific order costing'?

(*b*) In what ways does specific order costing differ from process costing?

(*c*) The Acme Shelving Co. Ltd manufactures shelving brackets in batches of 300. During May, Batch No. 23 was machined at a rate of 15 per hour. Sixty of the brackets failed to pass inspection, but of these, 40 were thought to be rectifiable. The remaining 20 were scrapped, and the scrap value was credited to the batch cost account. Rectification work took nine hours.

Batch No. 23

	£
Raw materials per bracket	1.60
Scrap value per bracket	0.86
Machinists' hourly rate	4.20
Machine hour overhead rate	3.60
(running time only)	
Setting up of machine: normal machining	21.00
rectification	18.00

Calculate:

(*i*) the cost of Batch No. 23 in total and per unit, if all units pass inspection;

(*ii*) the *actual* cost of Batch No. 23, in total and per unit, after crediting the recovery value of the scrapped components, and including the rectification costs;

(*iii*) the loss incurred because of defective work.

(*Edexcel Foundation, London Examinations: GCE A–Level*)

38.10A Horden Products Ltd manufactures goods which could involve any or all of three production departments. These departments are simply entitled **A**, **B** and **C**. A direct wages cost percentage absorption rate for the recovery of production overheads is applied to individual job costs.

Details from the company's budgets for the year ended 31 March 19X5 are as follows:

	Dept A	Dept B	Dept C
Indirect materials	£23,000	£35,000	£57,000
Indirect wages	£21,000	£34,000	£55,000
Direct wages	£140,000	£200,000	£125,000
Direct labour hours	25,000	50,000	60,000
Machine hours	100,000	40,000	10,000

The following information is also available for the production departments:

	Dept A	Dept B	Dept C
Area (square metres)	30,000	20,000	10,000
Cost of machinery	£220,000	£160,000	£20,000
Horse power of machinery	55	30	15

Other budgeted figures are:

	£
Power	120,000
Rent, rates, light, heat	90,000
Insurance (machinery)	20,000
Depreciation	80,000

Machinery is depreciated on the basis of 20% on cost.
Job No 347 passed through all three departments and incurred the following actual direct costs and times:

	Direct material £	Direct wages £	Direct Labour hours £	Machine hours £
Dept A	152	88	35	60
Dept B	85	192	90	30
Dept C	52	105	45	10

A sum amounting to 30% of the production cost is added to every job to enable a selling price to be quoted.

Required:

(a) A statement to show the total production overheads per department and calculate the absorption rate which the company has adopted.
(b) Calculate the selling price to be quoted for Job No 347.
(c) Using the available data, calculate absorption rates when based on:
  (i) direct labour hour rate;
  (ii) machine hour rate.
(d) Explain clearly the meaning of the following terms relating to overheads:
  (i) allotment;
  (ii) allocation;
  (iii) apportionment.

(*Associated Examining Board: GCE A–Level*)

38.11A

(*a*) Explain the following terms as used in process costing:

    (*i*)   normal losses

    (*ii*) abnormal losses

    (*iii*) equivalent production

    (*iv*) joint cost

    (*v*) split-off point

(*b*) In process costing, it is neither the technology nor the costs incurred, but the market price of the item, which determines whether an item is classed as:

    (*i*)   scrap or waste; and

    (*ii*) a joint product or a by-product.

    How far do you agree?

(*Edexcel Foundation, London Examinations: GCE A–Level*)

Part 7

BUDGETS

Introduction

This part looks at how management can institute a system to support planning, evaluation, and control through the use of budgets.

39

Budgeting and budgetary control

Objectives

After you have studied this chapter, you should:

- *have an awareness of the budgetary process*
- *be aware of the importance of budgets for planning and control*
- *know how to apply the economic order quantity approach to stock control*

39.1 Introduction

It can be stated that management control is needed to try to ensure that the organisation achieves its objectives. Once the objectives have been agreed, plans should be drawn up so that the progress of the firm can be directed towards the ends specified in the objectives. Now it must not be thought that plans can be expressed only in accounting terms. For example, quality of the product might be best shown in engineering terms, or social objectives shown in a plan concerned with employee welfare. But some of the objectives, such as the attainment of a desired profit, or the attainment of a desired growth in assets, can be expressed in accounting terms. When a plan is expressed quantitatively it is known as a **budget** and the process of converting plans into budgets is known as **budgeting**. In this book we are concerned primarily with budgets shown in monetary terms, i.e. financial budgets.

The budgeting process may be quite formal in a large organisation with committees set up to perform the task. On the other hand in a very small firm the owner may jot down his budget on a piece of scrap paper or even on the back of a used envelope. Some even manage without writing anything down at all – they have done the budgets in their heads and can easily remember them. This book is concerned with budgeting in a formal manner.

39.2 Budgets and people

Probably in no other part of accounting is there a greater need for understanding other people than in the processes of budgeting. Budgets are prepared in order to try to guide the firm towards its objectives. There is no doubt that some budgets that are drawn up are even more harmful to a firm than if none were drawn up at all.

Budgets are drawn up for control purposes, that is, as an attempt to control the direction that the firm is taking. Many people, however, look upon them, not as a guide, but as a straitjacket. We can look at a few undesirable actions that can result from people regarding budgets as a straitjacket rather than as a guide.

(a) The sales manager refuses to let a salesman go to Sweden in response to an urgent and unexpected request from a Swedish firm. The reason – the overseas sales expenses budget has already been spent. The result – the most profitable order that the firm would have received for many years is taken up instead by another firm.

(b) The works manager turns down requests for overtime work, because the budgeted overtime has already been exceeded. The result – the job is not completed on time, and the firm has to pay a large sum under a penalty clause in the contract for the job which stated that if the job was not finished by a certain date then a penalty of £20,000 would become payable.

(c) Towards the end of the accounting year a manager realises that he has not spent all of his budget for a particular item. He then launches on a spending spree, completely unnecessary items being bought, on the basis that 'If I don't spend this amount this year they will cut down next year when I will really need the money.' The result: a lot of unusable and unnecessary equipment.

(d) The education budget has been spent, therefore the education manager will not let anyone go on courses for the rest of the year. The result: the firm starts to fall behind in an industry which is highly technical, the staff concerned become fed up, and the better ones start to look for jobs in other firms which are more responsive to the need to allow personnel to keep in touch with changing technology.

Studies have shown that the more that managers are brought into the budgeting process, then the more successful budgetary control is likely to be. A manager on whom a budget is imposed, rather than a manager who had an active part in the drafting of his budget, is more likely to pay less attention to the budget and use it unwisely in the control process.

Having sounded the warning that needs to be borne in mind constantly when budgeting, we can now look at the positive end of budgeting – to see the advantages of a good budgetary control system.

39.3 Budgets, planning, and control

The methodology of budgetary control is probably accountancy's major contribution to management. Before we get down to the mechanics of constructing budgets we should first of all look at the main outlines of drafting budgets.

When the budgets are being drawn up the two main objectives must be uppermost in the mind of top management, that is that the budgets are for:

(a) **Planning.** This means a properly co-ordinated and comprehensive plan for the whole business. Each part must interlock with the other parts.

(b) **Control.** Just because a plan is set down on paper does not mean that the plan will carry itself out. Control is exercised via the budgets, thus the name budgetary control. To do this means that the responsibility of managers and budgets must be so linked that the responsible manager is given a guide to help him to produce certain desired results, and the actual achieved results can be compared against the expected, i.e. actual compared with budget.

39.4 Preparation of estimates

The first thing to establish is what the limiting factors are in a firm. It may well be the fact that sales cannot be pushed above a certain amount, or it might be the fact that the firm could sell as much as it can produce, but the productive capacity of the firm sets a limit. Whatever the limiting factor is, there is no doubt that this aspect of the firm will need more attention than probably any other. There would not, for instance, be much point in budgeting for the sale of 1,000 units a year if production could not manufacture more that 700, or to manufacture 2,000 a year if only 1,300 of them could be sold.

There is no doubt that usually the most difficult estimate to make is that of sales revenue. This can be done by using one of two methods:

(a) Make a statistical forecast on the basis of the economic conditions applying with reference to the goods sold by the company, and what is known about the actions of competitors.

(b) The opposite is to make an internal forecast. This is usually done by asking each salesperson, or group of salespeople, to estimate the sales in their own areas, and then total the estimates. Sometimes, however, they are not asked at all.

Now we should remember that much of the subject matter that you have read about, or are currently reading, in Economics is very relevant here. A knowledge of elasticity of demand, whether the product is a complementary product, e.g. the price of egg-cups is linked to the demand for eggs, or whether it is a substitute, e.g. that a rise in the price of butter may induce housewives to turn to other commodities instead, is very relevant in this area. Factors such as whether the firm has a monopoly, whether the firm has many small customers, a few large customers, or even one large customer, are of crucial importance. Estimating sales revenue is very much a matter of taking all the economic factors into account allied to other factors.

The sales budget is, however, more than just a sales forecast. Budgets should show the actions that management is taking to influence future events. If an increase in sales is desired the sales budget may show extra sales, which may well be an indication of the action that management is going to take by means of extra television advertising, making a better product, or giving retailers better profit margins and pushing up sales in that way.

39.5 The production budget

The production budget stems from the sales budget, but the first question that has to be settled is that of the level of the stock of finished goods which will be held by the firm.

If sales are even over the year, then production can also be in keeping with the sales figure, and the stock figure can remain constant. Suppose that the firm sells 50 units every month, then the firm can produce 50 units per month. In almost every firm, a stock level will have to be maintained, the amount of stock being dependent on factors such as amount of storage space, the estimated amount needed to cater for breakdowns in production or for delays in receiving raw materials, etc. Nonetheless, if the stock level was to be a minimum of 70 units it would still mean that production was at the rate of 50 units per month.

On the other hand sales may not be constant. Sales may average 50 units per month, but the figures may well be as follows:

January	20 units	February	30 units	March	60 units
April	80 units	May	70 units	June	40 units

This would mean that if production levels were kept at 50 units per month the stock levels would usually have to be more than 100 units, whilst if the stock levels were to be kept at 100 units minimum the production figures each month would equal the sales figures. We can now compare the two levels of production.

39.6 Even production flow

The problem here is to find the stock level that the firm would need on 1 January if (*a*) sales are as shown, (*b*) the stock must not fall below 100 units, (*c*) production is to be 50 units per month. It can be found by trial and error. For instance, if you decided to see what would happen if the firm started off with 100 units in stock at 1 January, you would find that, after adding production and deducting sales each month, the stock level would fall to 90 units in May. As 100 units of stock is the minimum needed you would need to start off on 1 January with 110 units. The method is that if you start off your calculation with an estimated figure of stock, which must at least be the minimum figure required, then if you find that the lowest figure of stock shown during the period is 10 units less than the minimum stock required, go back and add 10 units to the stock to be held on 1 January. If the lowest figure is 30 units less than required add 30 units to the 1 January stock, and so on. We can now look at the figures in Exhibit 39.1.

Exhibit 39.1

Units	January	February	March	April	May	June
Opening stock	110	140	160	150	120	100
Add Units produced	50	50	50	50	50	50
	160	190	210	200	170	150
Less Sales	20	30	60	80	70	40
Closing stock	140	160	150	120	100	110

Before we look at the implications of maintaining an even production flow we can look at another example. Try to work it out for yourself before looking at the answer in Exhibit 39.2. The sales are expected to be January 70, February 40, March 50, April 120, May 140 and June 70. The stock level must not fall below 120 units and an even production flow of 80 units is required. What stock level would there have to be on 1 January?

Exhibit 39.2

Units	January	February	March	April	May	June
Opening stock	140	150	190	220	180	120
Add Units produced	80	80	80	80	80	80
	220	230	270	300	260	200
Less Sales	70	40	50	120	140	70
Closing stock	150	190	220	180	120	130

It is more important in many firms to ensure a smooth production flow than to bother unduly about stock levels, assuming that the minimum stock level is always attained. If the work is skilled then that type of labour force may take several years to become trained, and skilled labour in many industries does not take kindly to being sacked and re-employed as the demand for the goods fluctuates. This is not always true with skilled labour. For instance, in the building industry such craftsmen as bricklayers may go to a builder until he has completed a contract such as building a college, a hospital or a housing estate, and then leave and go to another employer on the completion of the job.

On the other hand, a skilled engineer concerned with the manufacture of, say, diesel engines would not expect to be fired and re-employed continuously. The bricklayer has a skill that is easily transferable to many other building employers in an area, whereas the diesel engineer may have only one firm within fifty miles of his home where he can perform his skills properly. A man employed as a labourer might work on a building site in one part of the year and then transfer to an engineering factory as a labourer in another part of the year. Whether a firm could carry on production with widely uneven production levels depends so much on the type of firm and the type of labour involved. A firm would only sack skilled labour which it needed again shortly if it could persuade the men or women to come back when required. If the people who had been sacked were likely to find other employment, and not return to the firm when required, then this would mean that the firm would probably keep them on its payroll and production would continue and stocks of finished goods would begin to pile up. Many firms do in fact realise their social obligations by only laying off workers when no other alternative is at all reasonable. In many organisations there are probably more workers from time to time than the firm actually needs – this is known as 'organisational slack', so that there is a leeway between the increasing of production and having to take on extra workers.

39.7 Uneven production levels

Some firms by their very nature will have uneven production levels, and this will be accepted by their labour force. An ice-cream firm would find sales at the highest levels in summer, tailing off in winter. It is not really possible to build up stocks of ice-cream very much in the winter for summer sales! Even if it could be done technically, the costs of refrigerating large quantities of ice-cream for several months could hardly be economic. The large labour force used in the summer months will probably include quite a few students occupying their vacation periods profitably, and not able anyway to work at the job all the year round even if they wanted to. Such a kind of firm will normally have a far greater relationship between current stock levels and current sales than a firm which has even production levels. The calculation of the quantity to be produced is then:

Opening stock + Units produced – Sales = Closing stock

This means that if the opening stock will be 80 units, the sales are expected to be 100 units and the desired closing is 50 units the quantity to be produced becomes:

	Units
Opening stock	80
Add Production	?
	?
Less Sales	100
Closing stock	50

Production will, therefore, be the missing figure, i.e. 70 units (80 + Production 70 = 150 for sale less actually sold 100 = closing stock 50).

Exhibit 39.3 shows the units to be produced if the following information is known – Stock required 1 January 40, at end of each month, January 60, February 110, March 170, April 100, May 60, June 20. Sales are expected to be January 100, February 150, March 110, April 190, May 70, June 50.

Exhibit 39.3

Units	January	February	March	April	May	June
Opening stock	40	60	110	170	100	60
Production required (?)	120	200	170	120	30	10
	160	260	280	290	130	70
Less Sales	100	150	110	190	70	50
Closing stock	60	110	170	100	60	20

Linked with the production budget will be a materials purchase budget. It may well be that an order will have to be placed in January, received in March and issued to production in April. The purchase of materials will have to be planned as scientifically as possible.

39.8 Stock control

In your first-year studies you will have examined the different methods by which stocks are valued — *see Frank Wood's Business Accounting 1*, eighth edition, Chapter 28). Although this is important, it is also important for an accountant to ensure that the stocks being carried are not greater than they need be.

Let us look at how excessive stocks can have a detrimental effect upon the financial results of a firm:

1   Money tied up in unnecessarily large stocks is not earning anything. If, therefore, an extra £1 million is tied up in stocks which do not have to be so large, then the money which we could have earned from utilising that extra £1 million somewhere else has been lost. If we could have earned 10 per cent return on that money, then the unnecessary stocks have cost us £100,000 a year without any alternative benefit.
2   Too much stock needs extra storage space. Therefore the rent for the extra space, heating, lighting, insurance, wages of extra storekeepers, etc. is all money being spent for no benefit.

One thing that anyone should look for when examining the affairs of a business is to see if stocks are larger than they need be. For someone controlling the business there are three methods of cutting down on unnecessarily high stocks which have become much more popular in recent times. These are:

(*a*) Economic Order Quantity (EOQ). This is a mathematical method of deciding what is the lowest amount of stock that should be ordered at a time so that the costs of financing and keeping stock are kept down to the minimum.
  The formula for this is:

$$\text{EOQ} = \sqrt{\frac{2CO}{S}}$$

where:
C = consumption (usage) per annum in units
O = cost of placing one order
S = cost of storage and holding of one unit per year

S will include the costs of operating the stores, transport and insurance, and also the costs concerned with interest on capital which has been invested in stock. We then take the square root of the above as the answer.
  Exhibit 39.4 shows the calculation of the minimum order to be made.

Exhibit 39.4

Annual consumption = 800 units
Cost of reordering = £4
Storage and holding costs per unit = £1

$$EOQ = \sqrt{\frac{2 \times 800 \times £4}{£1}} = \sqrt{\frac{6,400}{1}} = 80 \text{ units (10 orders per year)}$$

(b) **Just-in-time** approach (JIT). This has been seen as one of the major factors which have resulted in the past success of Japanese manufacturers. It is not just an approach which is concerned with stock levels, but that is part of it.

The JIT approach requires that delivery of materials should occur immediately before their use. If arrangements are made with suppliers for more frequent deliveries then stocks can be cut to a minimum. Getting suppliers to inspect the materials before they deliver them, and getting them to guarantee their quality, also cuts down on costs, including the need to keep larger stocks in case there are deficiencies.

This sort of service is obtained by giving more business to fewer suppliers, and also placing longer-term orders. This enables the supplier to plan ahead more effectively to give you a better service.

(c) The last few years have also seen a new approach to the management of production called **optimised production technology** (OPT). The object is to distinguish between 'bottleneck' and 'non-bottleneck' resources. To give an example, the 'bottleneck' resource might be a machine which has a limited capacity. As a result, everything else can only be operated at that same level. Rather than other parts of the business produce more than the 'bottleneck' machine can absorb, a lower overall level of activity takes place. This needs less stocks.

Of course if a 'bottleneck' can be eliminated it will be. The above applies when a bottleneck, for whatever reason, cannot be eliminated.

It is better to have a smooth-running business, operating within its 'bottleneck' capacities, than to have one which operates very irregularly. One run irregularly would have to have parts of the business shut down at times. One running smoothly, besides all the other economies, needs fewer stocks.

Of these three methods, the existence of a formula makes EOQ particularly easy to examine. It is a useful aid to management in ensuring that they are making best use of their stock-related resources. Also, because of the precise nature of the calculation, it lends itself to incorporation within a computerised managerial decision support system.

New terms

Budget (p. 549): A plan quantified in monetary terms in advance of a defined time period – usually showing planned income and expenditure and the capital employed to achieve a given objective.

Economic Order Quantity [EOQ] (p. 554): A mathematical method of identifying the amount of stock that should be ordered at a time and how frequently to order it, so that the overall total of the costs of holding the stock and the costs of ordering the stock can be minimised.

Main points to remember

1 Budgets are prepared in order to guide the firm towards its objectives.
2 They should be drawn up within the context of *planning* and *control*.

3 While budgets are drawn up for control purposes, a budget should not be seen as a straitjacket.

4 There are a number of methods or techniques available to management wishing to ensure that excessive stocks are not carried by their organisations. These include economic order quantity (EOQ), just-in-time (JIT), and optimised production technology (OPT).

Review questions

39.1 What would the production levels have to be for each month if the following data was available:

Units 19X5	Jan	Feb	Mar	Apr	May	Jun
(a) Stocks levels wanted at the end of each month	690	780	1,100	1,400	1,160	940
(b) Expected sales each month	800	920	1,090	1,320	1,480	1,020

(c) The stock level at 1 January, 19X5 will be 740 units.

39.2 For the year ended 31 December 19X9 the sales of units are expected to be:

January	110	July	70
February	180	August	30
March	170	September	170
April	150	October	110
May	120	November	150
June	100	December	190

The opening stock at 1 January 19X9 will be 140 units. The closing stock desired at 31 December 19X9 is 150 units.

Required:

(a) What will production be per month if an even production flow is required and stock levels during the year could be allowed to fall to zero?

(b) Given the same information plus the constraint that stock levels must never fall below 80 units, and that extra production will be undertaken in January 19X9 to ensure this, what will be the January production figure?

39.3A

(a) For each of the following, state three reasons why a firm may wish to keep:
  (i) a minimum stock level of finished goods, and
  (ii) an even level of production in the face of fluctuating demand.

(b) The sales forecast for Douglas & Co for July–December 19X7 is:

	J	A	S	O	N	D
Units	280	200	260	360	400	420

Produce a production budget showing monthly opening and closing stock figures if the firm wishes to maintain an even level of producing 300 units each month, and a minimum stock level of 150 units.

  What must the opening stock be at 1 July to achieve this?

(c) Under what circumstances, in budgetary control, may a firm's productive capacity prove to be its limiting or key factor?

(Associated Examining Board: GCE A–Level)

40

Cash budgets

Objectives

After you have studied this chapter, you should:

- *know what is meant by the term 'cash budget'*

- *know how to prepare a cash budget*

- *know why a cash budget may be prepared*

40.1 The need for cash budgets

It is no use budgeting for production and for sales if during the budget period the firm runs out of cash funds. When talking about cash in budgets we are also usually including bank funds, and therefore in this book we will not be differentiating between cash and cheque payments or between cash and cheques received. Cash is, therefore, also budgeted for, so that any shortage of cash can be known in advance and action taken to obtain permission for a loan or a bank overdraft to be available then, rather than wait until the shortage or deficiency occurs. Bank managers, or anyone concerned with the lending of money, certainly resent most strongly one of their customers needing a bank overdraft without prior warning, when in fact the customer could have known if he had drawn up a cash budget in advance which revealed the need for cash funds on a particular date.

The finance needed may not just be by way of borrowing from a bank or finance house; it may well be a long-term need that can only be satisfied by an issue of shares or debentures. Such issues need planning well in advance, and a cash budget can reveal (a) that they will be needed, (b) how much is needed and (c) when it will be needed.

We can now look at a very simple case. Without being concerned in this first exhibit with exactly what the receipts and payments are for, just to keep matters simple at this stage, we can see the dangers that are inherent in not budgeting for cash.

Exhibit 40.1

Mr Muddlem had a meeting with his accountant on 1 July 19X3. He was feeling very pleased with himself. He had managed to get some very good orders from customers, mainly because he was now allowing them extra time in which to pay their accounts. Sprite, the accountant, said, 'Can you afford to do all that you are hoping to do?'

Muddlem laughed, 'Why, I'll be making so much money I won't know how to spend it.'

'But have you got the cash to finance everything?' asked Sprite.

'If I'm making a good profit then of course I'll have the cash,' said Muddlem. 'I know the bank manager says that any bank overdraft could not be more than £1,000, but I doubt if I need it.'

'Don't let's rely on guesses,' says Sprite. 'Let's work it out.'

After an hour's work the following facts emerge.

(*a*) Present cash balance (including bank balance) £800.

(*b*) Receipts from debtors will be: July £2,000, August £2,600, September £5,000, October £7,000, November £8,000, December £15,000.

(*c*) Payments will be July £2,500, August £2,700, September £6,900, October £7,800, November £9,900, December £10,300.

This is then summarised:	*Jul* £	*Aug* £	*Sep* £	*Oct* £	*Nov* £	*Dec* £
Balance at start of the month:	+800	+300	+200			
Deficit at the start of the month:				−1,700	−2,500	−4,400
Receipts	2,000	2,600	5,000	7,000	8,000	15,000
	2,800	2,900	5,200	5,300	5,500	10,600
Payments	2,500	2,700	6,900	7,800	9,900	10,300
Balance at end of the month:	+300	+200				+300
Deficit at the end of the month:			−1,700	−2,500	−4,400	

'I'm in an awkward position now,' says Muddlem. 'I just cannot borrow £4,400 nor can I cut down on my sales, and anyway I don't really want to as these new sales are very profitable indeed. If only I'd known this, I could have borrowed the money from my brother only last week but he's invested it elsewhere now.'

'Come and see me tomorrow,' says Sprite. 'There may well be something we can do.'

Fortunately for Muddlem his luck was in. He arrived to see his accountant the following morning waving a cheque. 'My wife won £5,000 on a jackpot bingo last night,' he said.

'Thank goodness for that. At least in future you'll learn to budget ahead for cash requirements. You can't be lucky all the time,' says Sprite.

40.2 Timing of cash receipts and payments

In drawing up a cash budget it must be borne in mind that all the payments for units produced would very rarely be at the same time as production itself. For instance, the raw materials might be bought in March, incorporated in the goods being produced in April, and paid for in May. On the other hand the raw materials may have been in hand for some time, so that the goods are bought in January, paid for in February, and used in production the following August. Contrary to this, the direct labour part of the product is usually paid for almost at the same time as the unit being produced. Even here a unit may be produced in one week and the wages paid one week later, so that a unit might be produced on, say, 27 June and the wages for the direct labour involved paid for on 3 July.

Similarly the date of sales and the date of receipt of cash will not usually be the same, except in many retail stores. The goods might be sold in May and the money received in August, or even paid for in advance so that the goods might be paid for in February but the goods not shipped to the buyer until May. This is especially true, at least for part of the goods, when a cash deposit is left for specially made goods which will take some time to manufacture. A simple example of this would be a made-to-measure suit on which a deposit would be paid at the time of order, the final payment being made when the completed suit is collected by the buyer.

Exhibit 40.2

A cash budget for the six months ended 30 June 19X3 is to be drafted from the following information.

(*a*) Opening cash balance at 1 January 19X3 £3,200.
(*b*) Sales, at £12 per unit, cash received three months after sale: in units.

19X2			19X3								
Oct	Nov	Dec	Jan	Feb	Mar	Apr	May	Jun	Jul	Aug	Sep
80	90	70	100	60	120	150	140	130	110	100	160

(*c*) Production: in units.

19X2			19X3								
Oct	Nov	Dec	Jan	Feb	Mar	Apr	May	Jun	Jul	Aug	Sep
70	80	90	100	110	130	140	150	120	160	170	180

(*d*) Raw materials used in production cost £4 per unit of production. They are paid for two months before being used in production.
(*e*) Direct labour, £3 per unit paid for in the same month as the unit produced.
(*f*) Other variable expenses, £2 per unit, ¾ of the cost being paid for in the same month as production, the other ¼ paid in the month after production.
(*g*) Fixed expenses of £100 per month are paid monthly.
(*h*) A motor van is to be bought and paid for in April for £800. Schedules of payments and receipts are as follows:

Payments (the month shown in brackets is the month in which the units are produced):

January	£
Raw materials: 130 (March) × £4	520
Direct labour: 100 (January) × £3	300
Variable: 100 (January) × ¾ × £2	150
90 (December) × ¼ × £2	45
Fixed	100
	£1,115

February	£
140 (April) × £4	560
110 (February) × £3	330
110 (February) × ¾ × £2	165
100 (January) × ¼ × £2	50
Fixed	100
	£1,205

March	£
Raw materials: 150 (May) × £4	600
Direct labour: 130 (March) × £3	390
Variable: 130 (March) × ¾ × £2	195
110 (February) × ¼ × £2	55
Fixed	100
	£1,340

April	£
120 (June) × £4	480
140 (April) × £3	420
140 (April) × ¾ × £2	210
130 (March) × ¼ × £2	65
Fixed	100
Motor van	800
	£2,075

May	£
Raw materials: 160 (July) × £4	640
Direct labour: 150 (May) × £3	450
Variable: 150 (May) × ¾ × £2	225
140 (April) × ¼ × £2	70
Fixed	100
	£1,485

June	£
170 (August) × £4	680
120 (June) × £3	360
120 (June) × ¾ × £2	180
150 (May) × ¼ × £2	75
Fixed	100
	£1,395

Receipts: (the month shown in brackets is the month in which the sale was made):

				£
January	80	(October)	× £12	960
February	90	(November)	× £12	1,080
March	70	(December)	× £12	840
April	100	(January)	× £12	1,200
May	60	(February)	× £12	720
June	120	(March)	× £12	1,440

	Cash budget					
	Jan	*Feb*	*Mar*	*Apr*	*May*	*Jun*
	£	£	£	£	£	£
Balance from previous month	3,200	3,045	2,920	2,420	1,545	780
Add Receipts (per schedule)	960	1,080	840	1,200	720	1,440
	4,160	4,125	3,760	3,620	2,265	2,220
Less Payments (per schedule)	1,115	1,205	1,340	2,075	1,485	1,395
Balance carried next month	3,045	2,920	2,420	1,545	780	825

40.3 Advantages of cash budgets

These can be said to be:

1   Having to think ahead and plan for the future and express the plans in figures, focuses one's mind in a way that thinking in a general fashion about the future will not do. A general optimistic feeling that 'all will be well' will often not stand up to scrutiny when the views of the future are expressed in a cash budget.

2   Seeing that money will have to be borrowed at a particular date will mean that you can negotiate for a loan in advance, rather than at the time when you have actually run out of cash. Bankers and other lenders do not like someone attempting to borrow money in a panic, and which has to be instantly available.

   In borrowing money you have to give the lender the confidence that the loan will be repaid at the proper time, plus any interest and charges that may accrue. Attempted last-minute borrowing, probably not substantiated by any calmly thought-out plan will not inspire such confidence, and will often lead to the loan being refused as the lender may think that the risk is too great.

   It is not only that you risk the loan being refused. Lenders will often realise that they have you at their mercy, and will charge much higher rates of interest and impose other conditions that otherwise they would not have done.

3   Knowing about the need to borrow in advance also widens the possible pool of lenders. Such people as friends, relations, and businessmen or investors other than bankers rarely have large sums of cash quickly available. They need time to turn their own investments into cash before they can lend to you.

4   Alternatively you may find that you will have cash funds surplus to requirements. Knowing this in advance will enable you to investigate properly how you can invest this surplus cash until required, thus earning interest or other investment income. Surplus cash lying in bank current accounts very often earns absolutely no interest at all, no matter how large the amount. Banks often have deposit accounts into which surplus current account cash can be invested to earn interest, then transferring the

necessary sums back into the current account when required by the business. There are also other sorts of short-term investments which your bank or accountant can advise you to put your surplus cash into at appropriate times.

40.4 Profits and shortages of cash funds

Just because a firm is making good profits it does not mean that it will not be short of cash funds. Let us look at how some firms may have good profits and yet still be short of cash funds, possibly having bank overdrafts or loans which are getting steadily bigger.

1   Firm A has increased its sales by 50 per cent, is making the same percentage gross profit and its expenses have hardly increased, yet its overdraft has got bigger. The reason is that it increased its sales by giving all of its customers four months to pay instead of the usual one month. This has attracted a lot of new customers.

   This means that the debtors are increasing by very large amounts, as they can wait another three months in which to pay their bills. Thus the equivalent of three months' cash receipts have not come into the bank. Meanwhile the firm is making extra purchases for goods for the new customers, with a consequent outflow of more cash than usual, especially if it has not got longer credit terms from its suppliers. So hardly any cash is coming in in the short term, whilst more cash than usual is going out.

   The answer to this is: large increase in profits and fewer cash funds probably resulting in higher bank overdrafts or loans.

2   Firm B has the same sales, purchases and expenses as usual. However, the proprietor, for whatever reason, is now taking much higher drawings than before. In fact his drawings are exceeding the profits he is making.

   Such a situation cannot go on for ever. He will start to find his cash funds in the business are decreasing, possibly meaning higher loans or overdrafts being needed.

3   Firm C has just spent a lot of money on fixed assets. It will be several years before the firm recoups the money it has paid out. In the meantime only the depreciation provisions are charged against profits. However, the cash funds have seen the disappearance of the whole amount paid for fixed assets. The net result is that profits may be recorded but the firm is hard-up for cash funds.

4   Firm D is going through a bad patch in that sales are very difficult to make, but it does not want to get rid of any of its workforce. Production is kept going at normal rates, and the products not sold are simply kept in stock. Thus the stock is increasing at an alarming rate.

   If stock is not being sold then cash obviously is not being received in respect of such production. Meanwhile all the expenses and wages are still being paid for. This can result in a severe shortage of funds if carried on for long if no further finance is received.

5   A long-term loan has been paid off but no extra finance from anywhere else has been received. This could equally apply to a partner retiring and the balance due to him being paid out of the firm's funds, without a new partner being introduced. Similarly a company buying back its shares without a new issue of shares could face the same situation.

In the long term there is a connection between profits and cash funds available, even though it may not be that marked. In the short term you can see that there may be no relationship at all. This simple fact is one that surprises most people. It is because the calculation of profits follows one set of concepts, whereas the calculation of cash funds follows a completely different set of rules.

Main point to remember

1   When undertaking a cash budget, 'cash' includes both money held in the form of cash and amounts held in the bank.

Review questions

Advice:
Cash budgeting is an extremely important part of accounting. Questions on this topic are relatively easy to do, and high marks can be gained quite easily.

40.1   Ukridge comes to see you in April 19X3. He is full of enthusiasm for a new product that he is about to launch on to the market. Unfortunately his financial recklessness in the past has led him into being bankrupted twice, and he has only just got discharged by the court from his second bankruptcy.

'Look here laddie,' he says, 'with my new idea I'll be a wealthy man before Christmas.'

'Calm down,' you say, 'and tell me all about it.'

Ukridge's plans as far as cash is concerned for the next six months are:

(*a*)   Present cash balance (including bank) £5.

(*b*)   Timely legacy under a will – being received on 1 May, 19X3, £5,000. This will be paid into the business bank account by Ukridge.

(*c*)   Receipts from debtors will be: May £400, June £4,000, July £8,000, August £12,000, September £9,000, October £5,000.

(*d*)   Payments will be: May £100, June £5,000, July £11,000, August £20,000, September £12,000, October £7,000.

You are required:

(*a*)   To draw up a cash budget, showing the balances each month, for the six months to 31 October 19X3.

(*b*)   The only person Ukridge could borrow money from would charge interest at the rate of 100 per cent per annum. This is not excessive considering Ukridge's past record. Advise Ukridge.

40.2   Draw up a cash budget for N. Morris showing the balance at the end of each month, from the following information for the six months ended 31 December 19X2:

(a) Opening cash (including bank) balance £1,200

(b) Production in units:

19X2								19X3		
Apr	May	Jun	Jul	Aug	Sep	Oct	Nov	Dec	Jan	Feb
240	270	300	320	350	370	380	340	310	260	250

(c) Raw materials used in production cost £5 per unit. Of this 80 per cent is paid in the month of production and 20 per cent in the month after production.

(d) Direct labour costs of £8 per unit are payable in the month of production.

(e) Variable expenses are £2 per unit, payable one-half in the same month as production and one-half in the month following production.

(f) Sales at £20 per unit:

19X2									
Mar	Apr	May	Jun	Jul	Aug	Sep	Oct	Nov	Dec
260	200	320	290	400	300	350	400	390	400

Debtors to pay their accounts three months after that in which sales are made.

(g) Fixed expenses of £400 per month payable each month.

(h) Machinery costing £2,000 to be paid for in October 19X2.

(i) Will receive a legacy £2,500 in December 19X2.

(j) Drawings to be £300 per month.

40.3   Herbert Limited make a single product, whose unit budget details are as follows:

	£	£
Selling price		30
Less Costs		
Direct material	9	
Direct labour	4	
Direct production expenses	6	
Variable selling expenses	4	23
Contribution		7

Additional information

1   Unit sales are expected to be:

June	July	August	September	October
1,000	800	400	600	900

2   Credit sales will account for 60 per cent of total sales. Debtors are expected to pay in the month following sale for which there will be a cash discount of 2 per cent.

3   Stock levels will be arranged so that the production in one month will meet the next month's sales demand.

4   The purchases of direct materials in one month will just meet the next month's production requirements.

5   Suppliers of direct materials will be paid in the month following purchase.

6   Labour costs will be paid in the month in which they are incurred. All other expenses will be paid in the month following that in which they are incurred.

7   Fixed expenses are £2,000 per month and include £180 for depreciation.
8   The bank balance at 1 July 19X9 is £3,900 favourable to the business.

Required:

(a) A cash budget for Herbert Limited for the three month period ending on 30 September 19X9 showing the balance of cash at the end of each month.

(b) List and explain **three** ways in which the preparation of a cash flow budget could be of advantage to the management of Herbert Limited.

(*Associated Examining Board: GCE A–Level*)

40.4A   Mtoto Ltd operate as wholesale 'cash and carry' stores and in addition to its main store have two other depots. The company's summarised balance sheet as at 31 August 19X1 was as follows.

	£	£		£	£
Fixed assets			*Authorised and issued capital*		
(at net book value)		549,600	450,000 £1 *Ordinary shares*		
Current assets			Fully paid		450,000
Stock	399,900		Retained earnings at		
Trade debtors	21,000	420,900	1 Sept 19X0	300,000	
			Less Current year ended		
			31 Aug 19X1 loss.	130,000	170,000
			Current liabilities		
			Trade (and other)		
			creditors	110,500	
			Bank overdraft	240,000	350,500
		970,500			970,500

- Over the past year the company has experienced increased competition and as a consequence reported a net trading loss for the year ended 31 August 19X1.
- The company has decided that in the new financial year tighter control must be exercised over cash resources.
- The following information is available:

1   All goods are purchased by the main store.

Purchases 19X1

Actual			*Forecast*		
Jul	*Aug*	*Sep*	*Oct*	*Nov*	*Dec*
£	£	£	£	£	£
55,800	61,200	64,300	41,000	46,000	41,800

- Mtoto Ltd pays suppliers two months after the month of purchase.
- Forecast purchases are being reduced since the managing director regarded current stock levels as too high.
- In addition, shop-soiled stock which cost £20,000 is to be sold for cash in October. It is anticipated that this stock will be sold for £17,000. This sale is not included in the sales of note 2 below.

2 All sales are on a cash basis only except for several important customers who trade only with Mtoto's main store.

Sales 19X1

		Actual		Forecast		
		Jul £	Aug £	Sep £	Oct £	Nov £	Dec £
Mainstore							
Cash sales		21,500	21,600	18,000	26,300	19,200	24,700
Credit sales		24,000	21,000	32,500	26,000	25,400	27,800
Depot	1	15,500	17,400	19,700	18,000	17,600	17,900
Depot	2	21,000	24,000	26,300	19,700	21,000	19,100

3 Mtoto Ltd pays £9,500 fixed overhead costs per month.

4 Wages and salaries are paid each month through a centralised payroll system.

Wages and salaries 19X1

Actual	Forecast			
Aug £	Sep £	Oct £	Nov £	Dec £
16,000	17,000	19,000	13,000	12,000

In October, 10 staff were made redundant and are to receive their redundancy compensation of £12,000 in December. This amount is not included in the above figures.

5 Other variable overhead charges are paid by Mtoto Ltd in the month following the month they are incurred.

Variable overhead charges 19X1

Aug £	Sep £	Oct £	Nov £	Dec £
5,600	6,800	6,100	7,400	6,900

6 Plant surplus to requirement is to be sold in September for £26,500 cash. The plant cost £55,000 and depreciation to date is £20,000.

Required:

(a) A detailed cash budget, on a month by month basis, for the first four months of the financial year ending 31 August 19X2 for Mtoto Ltd.
(b) A report commenting on:
  (i) the current and forecast liquidity position.
  (ii) the action that Mtoto Ltd could take to attempt a return to a profit situation.

(*Associated Examining Board: GCE A–Level*)

40.5 David Llewelyn has been advised by his bank manager that he ought to provide a forecast of his cash position at the end of each month. This is to ensure that his cash inputs will be sufficient to allow a bank loan to be repaid when due and to check that his outgoings are properly controlled. It is estimated that at 30 June 19X0 his current account will be £5,000 in credit, whereas the amount owing in respect of the bank loan taken out on 1 July 19X5 will be £15,000. Monthly deductions from the current account balance amount to £242 including interest charges on account of this loan. In addition to these outgoings, David has to allow for the following:

(i)   The payment of wages of £2,000 per month.

(ii) Personal drawings of £500 per month.

(iii) On average David earns a margin of 15 per cent (of sales) and expects to sell stocks purchased in the previous month. Of the sales in any one month, 20 per cent are paid for within that month, 70 per cent the following month and the remainder two months after sale.

     Other receipts from debtors are expected to be £40,000 in July 19X0, £32,000 in August 19X0 and £4,000 in September 19X0.

(iv) Purchases of supplies will amount to £38,250 per month from July 19X0 payable one month in arrears. In addition, purchases of £7,500 to increase stocks will be delivered in September 19X0 and must be paid for in October 19X0. Creditors of £34,000 for purchases made in June 19X0 are to be paid in July 19X0.

(v)   Monthly payments to the Inland Revenue for the taxation of his employees' earnings will amount to £500 per month.

(vi) Rent which has to be paid quarterly in advance amounts to £5,000 per annum. These payments commenced in January 19X0.

(vii) Business rates are to be paid in two instalments as due in October 19X0 and in March 19X1. This estimated expenditure will amount to £4,500 per annum.

(viii) Payment of Value Added Tax to H.M. Customs and Excise of £5,000 in July 19X0 and every third month thereafter (but see also (ix)).

(ix) David intends to purchase a van for £8,150 in August 19X0. He will then be entitled to deduct £1,050 from the VAT payment due to H.M. Customs and Excise in October 19X0.

Required:
A forecast cash flow statement in columnar form showing the estimated current account balance at the close of each of the four months ending 31 October 19X0.

(*Welsh Joint Examining Board: GCE A–Level*)

40.6 The managing director of Pumpkin Ltd was reviewing the results of the company for the financial year ended 31 March 19X0. The following summarised information was available:

	£
Balances as at 1 April 19X9	
Issued ordinary share capital:	
£1 fully paid shares	150,000
Share premium account	100,000
Balance of retained earnings	40,000
Balances as at 31 March 19X0	
Net profit for year 19X9/X0	70,000
Fixed assets	300,000
Bank overdraft	150,000
Other net current assets	210,000

Note: There were no other accounts with balances. The balances as at 1 April 19X9 had remained unchanged throughout the year.

The managing director was pleased that the company had made a good profit, but he was rather concerned that a healthy bank balance at the beginning of the year had now become a large bank overdraft.

Consequently he asked the company accountant to prepare forecast information for 19X0/X1 in order that the cash situation could be improved.

The following information was prepared by the accountant:

1 Company sales – March 19X0

		£
	Cash sales	30,000
	Credit sales	65,000

In each month April to September (inclusive) the sales per month would be:

		£
	Cash sales	40,000
	Credit sales	70,000

All credit sales are settled the month after the sale.

2 All goods purchased are from a single supplier. The goods are purchased on credit and each month's purchases are paid for three months after the month of purchase.

The following purchase schedule had been prepared for the first 9 months of 19X0:

	January	*February*	*March*
Purchases	£60,000	£58,000	£61,000

Purchases in April, May and June
    £55,000 in each month
Purchases in July, August and September
    £45,000 in each month

Note: The company had successfully negotiated lower prices from its supplier commencing 1 July 19X0.

3 Dividends would be paid as follows:
  (*i*) Final ordinary dividend of 5p per share payable on 31 May 19X0 in respect of financial year 19X9/X0.
  (*ii*) Interim ordinary dividend of 2p per share payable on 31 July 19X0 in respect of financial year 19X0/X1.

4 Selling and distribution expenses are expected to be 6 per cent of a given month's total sales. They are paid one month in arrears.

5 Administration charges would be incurred as follows:

19X0 February, March, April	£10,000 per month
19X0 May to September (inclusive)	£13,500 per month

Administration charges are settled two months after the month in which they were incurred.

6 The company had decided to make a bonus issue of shares of one share for every three held. The issue would be made on 30 April 19X0. The bonus shares would not qualify for the final dividend of 19X9/X0, but would qualify for the interim dividend to be paid on 31 July 19X0.

Required:

(*a*) Comment on the liquidity of the company as at 31 March 19X0 and explain to the managing director why a company can apparently make a good profit but have no cash in the bank.

(*b*) Prepare a cash budget for each of the four months ending 31 July 19X0.

(*c*) Comment on the forecast bank balance as shown by your cash budget. Identify ways in which the bank overdraft could be reduced over the last five months of 19X0.

(*Associated Examining Board: GCE A–Level*)

40.7A Belinda Raglan owns a clothing factory. Trading over the last two years has been very successful and she feels that having achieved good results it is now time to request an increase in the overdraft facility.

- In the past the bank has been willing to offer business overdraft facilities and at present there is an agreed limit of £15,000.
- On 1 May 19X4 the overdraft stands at £5,000.
- In order to support her request for the increased facility, she has produced a forecast profit statement for the four months ended 31 August 19X4 as follows:

	May	May	June	June	July	July	August	August
	£000	£000	£000	£000	£000	£000	£000	£000
Sales		74		28		116		168
Cost of sales		51		12		78		101
Gross Profit		23		16		38		67
Less: Rent	4		4		4		4	
Other expenses	8		3		10		14	
Depreciation	5	17	5	12	5	19	5	23
Net profit		6		4		19		44

Although Belinda thought these figures would be sufficient to satisfy the requirements of the bank, the manager has asked for a cash budget for the period concerned to be submitted.

The following additional information concerning the business is available.
(1) Rent is paid quarterly in advance on the first day of May, August, November and February.
(2) All other expenses are payable in the month in which they are incurred.
(3) Purchases for the period are expected to be — May £60,000; June £120,000; July £40,000 and August £43,000. These will be paid for in the month of purchase. Purchases will be unusually high in May and June because they will be subject to a special reduction of 3% of the amounts quoted.
(4) 80% of the sales are on a credit basis payable two months later. Sales in march and April were £88,000 and £84,000 respectively.
(5) A compensation payment of £10,000 to a former employee for an industrial injury, not covered by insurance, is due to be paid in May.

Required:
(a) Prepare a forecast cash budget on a month by month basis for the period May to August 19X4.
(b) Discuss the advantages and disadvantages of cash budgeting.
(c) Draft notes, to be used by the bank manager for a letter to Ms Raglan, indicating why the request for an increased overdraft facility may be refused.

(*Associated Examining Board: GCE A–Level*)

40.8A Ian Spiro, formerly a taxi-driver, decided to establish a car-hire business after inheriting £50,000.

His business year would be divided into budget periods each being four weeks.

He commenced business on a Monday the first day of period 1, by paying into a business bank account £34,000 as his initial capital.

All receipts and payments would be passed through his bank account.

The following additional forecast information is available on the first four budget periods of his proposed business venture.

1   At the beginning of period 1 he would purchase 6 saloon cars of a standard type; list price £6,000 each, on which he had negotiated a trade discount of 11 per cent.

2 He estimates that four of the cars will be on the road each Monday to Friday inclusive, and at weekends all six cars will be on the road. Hire charges as follows:

Weekday rate £10 per day per car
Weekend rate £18 per day per car

He estimates that this business trading pattern will commence on the Monday of the second week of period 1, and then continue thereafter.
All hire transactions are to be settled for cash.
Note: a weekend consists of Saturday and Sunday. All remaining days are weekdays.

3 An account was established with a local garage for fuel, and it was agreed to settle the account two periods in arrear. The forecast gallon usage is as follows:

Period 1	*Period 2*	*Period 3*	*Period 4*
200	200	400	500

The fuel costs £1.80 per gallon.

4 Servicing costs for the vehicles would amount to £300 per period, paid during the period following the service. Servicing would commence in period 1.

5 Each of his vehicles would be depreciated at 25 per cent per annum on a reducing balance basis.

6 Fixed costs of £200 per period would be paid each period.

7 He had agreed with a local firm to provide two cars on a regular basis, Monday to Friday inclusive, as chauffeur driven cars. The agreed rate was £60 a day (per car), payment being made in the following period.
This contract would not commence until the first day of period 2, a Monday.

8 Drawings: Periods 1 and 2: £400 a period.
Periods 3 and 4: £800 a period.

9 Wages and salaries:
(*a*) Initially he would employ 3 staff, each on £320 a budget period. Employment would commence at the beginning of period 1.
(*b*) On commencement of the contract the two additional staff employed as chauffeurs would each receive £360 a budget period. Payments are to be made at the end of the relevant period.

10 In anticipation of more business being developed he planned to buy a further three cars for cash in period 4. The cars would cost £6,500 each and it was agreed he would be allowed a trade discount of 10 per cent.

Required:
(*a*) A detailed cash budget for the first four budget periods.
(*b*) An explanation as to why it is important that a business should prepare a cash budget.
(*c*) Identify how a sole proprietor may finance a forecast cash deficit distinguishing between internal and external financial sources.

(*Associated Examining Board: GCE A–Level*)

41

Co-ordination of budgets

Objectives

After you have studied this chapter, you should:

- *be aware of the importance of effective co-ordination of budgets for the organisation*

- *be aware of the benefits of operating a system of flexible budgeting*

41.1 Master budgets

The various budgets have to be linked together and a **master budget**, which is really a budgeted set of final accounts, drawn up. We have looked at the sales, production and cash budgets. There are, however, many more budgets for parts of the organisation; for instance, there may be:

1 a selling budget,
2 an administration expense budget,
3 a manufacturing overhead budget,
4 a direct labour budget,
5 a purchases budget,

and so on. In this book we do not wish to get entangled in too many details, but in a real firm with a proper set of budgeting techniques there will be a great deal of detailed backing for the figures that are incorporated in the more important budgets.

Now it may be that when all the budgets have been co-ordinated, or slotted together, the master budget shows a smaller profit than the directors are prepared to accept. This will mean recasting budgets to see whether a greater profit can be earned, and if at all possible the budgets will be altered. Eventually there will be a master budget that the directors can agree to. This then gives the target for the results that the firm hopes to achieve in financial terms. Remember that there are other targets such as employee welfare, product quality, etc. that cannot be so expressed.

The rest of this chapter is concerned with the drawing up of budgets for an imaginary firm, Walsh Ltd, culminating in the drawing up of the master budget.

To start with we can look at the last balance sheet of Walsh Ltd as at 31 December 19X4. This will give us our opening figures of stocks of raw materials, stock of finished goods, cash (including bank) balance, creditors, debtors, etc.

Walsh Ltd
Balance Sheet as at 31 December 19X4

Fixed assets	Cost £	Depreciation to date £	Net £
Machinery	4,000	1,600	2,400
Motor vehicles	2,000	800	1,200
	6,000	2,400	3,600

Current assets			
Stocks: Finished goods (75 units)		900	
Raw materials		500	
Debtors (19X4 October £540 + November £360 + December £450)		1,350	
Cash and bank balances		650	
		3,400	

Less Current liabilities			
Creditors for raw materials (November £120 + December £180)	300		
Creditors for fixed expenses (December)	100	400	
Working capital			3,000
			6,600

Financed by		
Share capital: 4,000 shares £1 each		4,000
Profit and loss account		2,600
		6,600

The plans for the six months ended 30 June 19X5 are as follows:

(a) Production will be 60 units per month for the first four months, followed by 70 units per month for May and June.

(b) Production costs will be (per unit):

	£
Direct materials	5
Direct labour	4
Variable overhead	3
	£12

(c) Fixed overhead is £100 per month, payable always one month in arrears.

(d) Sales, at a price of £18 per unit, are expected to be:

	January	February	March	April	May	June
No. of units	40	50	60	90	90	70

(e) Purchases of direct materials (raw materials) will be:

	January £	February £	March £	April £	May £	June £
	150	200	250	300	400	320

(*f*) The creditors for raw materials bought are paid two months after purchase.
(*g*) Debtors are expected to pay their accounts three months after they have bought the goods.
(*h*) Direct labour and variable overheads are paid in the same month as the units are produced.
(*i*) A machine costing £2,000 will be bought and paid for in March.
(*j*) 3,000 shares of £1 each are to be issued at par in May.
(*k*) Depreciation for the six months: Machinery £450, Motor vehicles £200.

We must first of all draw up the various budgets and then incorporate them into the master budget. Some of the more detailed budgets which can be dispensed with in this illustration will be omitted.

Materials Budget

	January	February	March	April	May	June
Opening stock £	500	350	250	200	200	250
Add Purchases £	150	200	250	300	400	320
	650	550	500	500	600	570
Less Used in production:						
Jan–April 60 × £5	300	300	300	300		
May and June 70 × £5					350	350
Closing stock £	350	250	200	200	250	220

Production Budget (in units)

	January	February	March	April	May	June
Opening stock (units)	75	95	105	105	75	55
Add Produced	60	60	60	60	70	70
	135	155	165	165	145	125
Less Sales	40	50	60	90	90	70
Closing stock	95	105	105	75	55	55

Production Cost Budget (in £s)

	January	February	March	April	May	June	Total
Materials cost £	300	300	300	300	350	350	1,900
Labour cost £	240	240	240	240	280	280	1,520
Variable overhead £	180	180	180	180	210	210	1,140
	720	720	720	720	840	840	4,560

Creditors Budget

	January	February	March	April	May	June
Opening balance £	300	330	350	450	550	700
Add Purchases £	150	200	250	300	400	320
	450	530	600	750	950	1,020
Less Payments £	120	180	150	200	250	300
Closing balance £	330	350	450	550	700	720

Debtors Budget

	January	February	March	April	May	June
Opening balances £	1,350	1,530	2,070	2,700	3,600	4,320
Add Sales £	720	900	1,080	1,620	1,620	1,260
	2,070	2,430	3,150	4,320	5,220	5,580
Less Received £	540	360	450	720	900	1,080
Closing balances £	1,530	2,070	2,700	3,600	4,320	4,500

Cash Budget

	January	February	March	April	May	June
Opening balance £	+650	+550	+210			+1,050
Opening overdraft £				−2,010	−2,010	
Received (see schedule) £	540	360	450	720	3,900	1,080
	1,190	910	660	−1,290	1,890	2,130
Payments (see schedule) £	640	700	2,670	720	840	890
Closing balance £	+550	+210			+1,050	+1,240
Closing overdraft £			−2,010	−2,010		

Cash Payments Schedule

	January	February	March	April	May	June
Creditors for goods bought two months previously £	120	180	150	200	250	300
Fixed overhead £	100	100	100	100	100	100
Direct labour £	240	240	240	240	280	280
Variable overhead £	180	180	180	180	210	210
Machinery £			2,000			
	640	700	2,670	720	840	890

Cash Receipts Schedule

	January	February	March	April	May	June
Debtors for goods sold three months previously £	540	360	450	720	900	1,080
Shares issued £					3,000	
					3,900	

Master Budget

Forecast Operating Statement for the Six Months ended 30 June 19X5

		£
Sales		7,200
Less Cost of goods sold:		
Opening stock of finished goods	900	
Add Cost of goods completed	4,560	
	5,460	
Less Closing stock of finished goods	660	4,800
Gross profit		2,400
Less		
Fixed overhead		600

	Depreciation: Machinery	450	

			£
Depreciation: Machinery	450		
Motors	200	650	1,250
Net profit			1,150

Forecast Balance Sheet as at 30 June 19X5

Fixed assets	Cost £	Depreciation to date £	Net £
Machinery	6,000	2,050	3,950
Motor vehicles	2,000	1,000	1,000
	8,000	3,050	4,950
Current assets			
Stocks: Finished goods		660	
Raw materials		220	
Debtors		4,500	
Cash and bank balances		1,240	
		6,620	
Creditors: amounts falling due within 1 year			
Creditors for goods	720		
Creditors for overheads	100	820	
Net current assets			5,800
Total assets less current liabilities			10,750
Capital and reserves			
Called-up share capital			7,000
Profit and loss account (2,600 + 1,150)			3,750
			10,750

41.2 Capital budgeting

The plan for the acquisition of fixed assets such as machinery, buildings, etc. is usually known as a **capital budget**. Management will evaluate the various possibilities open to it, and will compare the alternatives. This is a very important part of budgeting. So far in this book it has been assumed that the capital budgeting has already been done.

41.3 The advantages of budgeting

The process of budgeting with the necessary participation throughout management, finally producing a profit plan, is now a regular feature in all but the smallest firms. Very often budgeting is the one time when the various parts of management can really get together and work as a team rather than just as separate parts of an organisation. When budgeting is conducted under favourable conditions, there is no doubt that a firm which budgets will tend to perform rather better than a similar firm that does not budget. Budgeting means that managers can no longer give general answers affecting the running of the firm; they have to put figures to their ideas, and they know that in the end their estimated figures are going to be compared with what the actual figures turn out to be.

It has often been said that the act of budgeting is possibly of more benefit than the budgets which are produced. However, the following benefits can be claimed for good budgeting:

1   The strategic planning carried out by the board of directors or owners can be more easily linked to the decisions by managers as to how the resources of the business will be used to try to achieve the objectives of the business. The strategic planning has to be converted into action, and budgeting provides the ideal place where such planning can be changed into financial terms.

2   Standards of performance can be agreed for the various parts of the business. If sales and production targets are set as part of a co-ordinated plan, then the sales department cannot really complain that production is insufficient if they had agreed previously to a production level and this is being achieved, nor can production complain if its production exceeds the amount budgeted for and it remains unsold.

3   The expression of plans in comparable financial terms. Some managers think mainly in terms of, say, units of production, or of tons of inputs or outputs, or of lorry mileage, etc. The effect that each of them has upon financial results must be brought home to them. For instance, a transport manager might be unconcerned about the number of miles that his haulage fleet of lorries covers until the cost of doing such a large mileage is brought home to him, often during budgeting, and it may be then and only then that he starts to search for possible economies. It is possible in many cases to use mathematics to find the best ways of loading vehicles, or to plan routes taken by vehicles so that fewer miles are covered and yet the same delivery service is maintained. This is just one instance of many when the expression of the plans of a section of a business in financial terms sparks off a search for economies, when otherwise such a search may never be started at all.

4   Managers can see how their work slots into the activities of the firm. It can help to get rid of the feeling of 'I'm only a number not a person', because managers can identify their positions within the firm and can see that their jobs really are essential to the proper functioning of the firm.

5   The budgets for a firm cannot be set in isolation. This means that the situation of the business, the nature of its products and its workforce, etc., must be seen against the economic background of the country. For instance it is no use budgeting for extra labour when labour is in extremely short supply, without realising the implications, possibly that of paying higher than normal wage rates. Increasing the sales target during a 'credit squeeze' needs a full investigation of the effect of the shortage of money upon the demand for the firm's goods and so on.

The charges made against budgeting are mainly that budgets bring about inflexibility, and that managers will not depart from budget even though the departure would bring about a more desirable result. Too many budgets are set at one level of sales or production when in fact flexible budgets (discussed below) ought to be used. It is very often the case that budgeting is forced upon managers against their will. Instead the firm should really set out first of all to do a 'selling job' to convince managers that budgets are not the monsters so often thought. A trial run for part of a business is far superior to starting off by having a fully detailed budget set up right away for the whole of the business. Learning to use budgets is rather like learning to swim. Let a child get used to the water first and remove its fear of the water, then it will learn to swim fairly easily. For most children (but not all), if the first visit to the baths meant being pushed into the deep end immediately, then reaction against swimming would probably set in. Let a manager become used to the idea of budgeting during a trial period, without the fear of being dealt with severely. Most managers will then accept it and participate properly.

41.4 The use of computers in budgeting

Years ago, budgeting was a task which most accountants hated doing. It was not the concept of budgeting that accountants disliked; far from it, as it suited their needs perfectly. Instead it was the multitude of numerical manipulations that had to be performed that made the task a formidable one.

Those of you who have done some of the exercises in this book manually know the feeling when after a lot of work your master budget simply will not balance. Searching through to find the error(s) can be a daunting prospect. Imagine how much more complicated it is in a real firm dealing with real figures rather than with the simple sets of data which form your exercises. Also imagine the feeling when the managing director used to say to the accountant 'What if we increased our prices by 5 per cent and took an extra month to pay creditors?' The accountant would then have to plough his way through a large number of extra calculations.

Most of that is now a thing of the past. Computers are used instead. They either have a computer program specially written for the task, or else commercial spreadsheets can be used. By keying in the necessary basic figures or 'what if' amendments the computer will automatically produce the budgets or the amended budgets within a very short space of time.

This enables management to see the results that would be expected to be obtained from many separate propositions, thus enhancing the chance of choosing the best solution. Also as the accounting year unfolds the changes that have occurred since the year started can be incorporated very easily so as to adjust the budgets as the year progresses.

42.5 Flexible budgets

So far in this book budgets have been drawn up on the basis of one set of expectations, based on just one level of sales and production. Later, when the actual results are compared with the budgeted results expected in a fixed budget, they will have deviated for two reasons:

1   While the actual and budgeted volumes of production and sales may be the same there may be a difference on actual and budgeted costs.
2   The volumes of actual and budgeted units of sales and production may vary, so that the costs will be different because of different volumes.

The variations, or variances as they are more commonly known, are usually under the control of different managers in the organisation. Variances coming under (1) will probably be under the control of the individual department. On the other hand variances under (2) are caused because of variations in plans brought about by top management because of changing sales, or at least the expectation of changing sales.

Budgets are used for control purposes. A manager does not take kindly to being held responsible for a variance in his spending if the variance is caused by a type (2) occurrence if he is working on a fixed budget. The answer to this is to construct budgets at several levels of volume, and to show what costs etc. they should incur at different levels. For instance, if a budget had been fixed at a volume of 500 units and the actual volume is 550, then the manager would undoubtedly feel aggrieved if his costs for producing 550 units were compared with the costs he should have incurred for 500 units. Budgets which do allow for changing levels are called **flexible budgets**.

To draft a full set of flexible budgets is outside the scope of this book, but an instance of one department's flexible budget for manufacturing overhead is shown in Exhibit 41.1.

Exhibit 41.1

Data Ltd
Budget for Manufacturing Overhead, Department S
(In real life, this would be in greater detail)

Units	400	450	500	550	600
	£	£	£	£	£
Variable overhead	510	550	600	680	770
Fixed overhead	400	400	400	400	400
Total overhead (A)	£910	£950	£1,000	£1,080	£1,170
Direct labour hours (B)	200	225	250	275	300
Overhead rates (A) divided by (B)	£4.55	£4.22	£4.0	£3.92	£3.9

Notice that the variable costs in this case do not vary in direct proportion to production. In this case once 500 units production have been exceeded they start to climb rapidly. The flexible budget makes far greater sense than a fixed budget. For instance, if a fixed budget had been agreed at 400 units, with variable overhead £510, then if production rose to 600 units the manager would think the whole system unfair if he were expected to incur only £510 variable overhead (the figure for 400 units). On the contrary, if the comparison was on a flexible budget then costs at 600 units production would instead be compared with £770 (the figure at 600 units).

New terms

Flexible budget (p. 577): A budget which, by recognising the difference in behaviour between fixed and variable costs in relation to fluctuations in output, turnover or other factors, is designed to change appropriately with such fluctuations.

Master budget (p. 570): The overall summary budget encompassing all the individual budgets.

Main points to remember

1 There are a number of budgets that together comprise the 'master budget' and they must all reconcile to each other and to the master budget.

2 Budget preparation is often an iterative process as the master budget is focused more and more tightly to the objectives of the organisation.

3 Flexible budgeting permits managers to adjust their budgets in the light of variations in plan, often involving items over which they have no control.

Review questions

Advice:

In many ways drawing up a budgeted set of final accounts is very much like drawing up accounts from single-entry records. Accounts from single-entry records concern the past; budgeted accounts from estimates concern the future.

41.1 Richard Toms has agreed to purchase the business of Norman Soul with effect from 1 August 19X7. Soul's budgeted working capital at 1 August 19X7 is as follows:

	£	£	£
Current assets			
Stock at cost	13,000		
Debtors	25,000		
		38,000	
Current liabilities			
Creditors	10,000		
Bank overdraft	20,000		
		30,000	
			8,000

In addition to paying Soul for the acquisition of the business, Toms intends to improve the liquidity position of the business by introducing £10,000 capital on 1 August 19X7. He has also negotiated a bank overdraft limit of £15,000. It is probable that 10 per cent of Soul's debtors will in fact be bad debts and that the remaining debtors will settle their accounts during August subject to a cash discount of 10 per cent. The opening creditors are to be paid during August. The sales for the first four months of Toms' ownership of the business are expected to be as follows: August £24,000, September £30,000, October £30,000 and November £36,000. All sales will be on credit and debtors will receive a two-month credit period. Gross profit will be at a standard rate of 25 per cent of selling price. In addition, in order to further improve the bank position and to reduce his opening stock, Toms intends to sell on 1 August 19X7 at cost price £8,000 of stock for cash. In order to operate within the overdraft limit Toms intends to control stock levels and to organise his purchases to achieve a monthly rate of stock turnover of 3. He will receive one month's credit from his suppliers.

General cash expenses are expected to be £700 per month.

Required:
(a) A stock budget for the four months ending 30 November 19X7 showing clearly the stock held at the end of each month.
(b) A cash budget for the four months ending 30 November 19X7 showing clearly the bank balance at the end of each month.

(*Associated Examining Board: GCE A–Level*)

41.2A A company's estimated pattern of costs and revenues for the first four months of 19X7 is as follows:

Cost and Revenues: January–April 19X7 (£000)

Month	Sales	Materials	Wages	Overheads
January	410.4	81.6	16.2	273.6
February	423.6	84.8	16.8	282.4
March	460.8	93.6	18.3	306.7
April	456.3	91.2	18.6	304.5

1   One-quarter of the materials are paid for in the month of production and the remainder two months later: deliveries received in November 19X6 were £78,400, and in December 19X6 £74,800.
2   Customers are expected to pay one-third of their debts a month after the sale and the remainder after two months: sales expected for November 19X6 are £398,400, and for December 19X6, £402,600.
3   Old factory equipment is to be sold in February 19X7 for £9,600. Receipt of the money is expected in April 19X7. New equipment will be installed at a cost of £38,000. One-half of the amount is payable in March 19X7 and the remainder in August 19X7.
4   Two-thirds of the wages are payable in the month they fall due, and one-third a month later: wages for December 19X6 are estimated at £15,900.
5   £50,000 of total monthly overheads are payable in the month they occur, and the remainder one month later: total overheads for December 19X6 are expected to be £265,200.
6   The opening bank balance at 1 January 19X7 is expected to be an overdraft of £10,600.

Required:

(a) Using the information above, prepare the firm's cash budget for the period January–April 19X7.
(b) Provide a statement to show those items in part (a) which would appear in a budgeted balance sheet as at 30 April 19X7.

(*Edexcel Foundation, London Examinations: GCE A–Level*)

41.3 D Smith is to open a retail shop on 1 January 19X4. He will put in £25,000 cash as capital. His plans are as follows:

(i)   On 1 January 19X4 to buy and pay for Premises £20,000, Shop fixtures £3,000, Motor van £1,000.
(ii)   To employ two assistants, each to get a salary of £130 per month, to be paid at the end of each month. (PAYE tax, National Insurance contributions, etc., are to be ignored.)
(iii) To buy the following goods (shown in units):

	Jan	Feb	Mar	Apr	May	Jun
Units	200	220	280	350	400	330

(iv)   To sell the following number of units:

	Jan	Feb	Mar	Apr	May	Jun
Units	120	180	240	300	390	420

(v)   Units will be sold for £10 each. One-third of the sales are for cash, the other two-thirds being on credit. These latter customers are expected to pay their accounts in the second month following that in which they received the goods.
(vi)   The units will cost £6 each for January to April inclusive, and £7 each thereafter. Creditors will be paid in the month following purchase. (Value stock-in-trade on FIFO basis.)
(vii) The other expenses of the shop will be £150 per month payable in the month following that in which they were incurred.

(*viii*) Part of the premises will be sub-let as an office at a rent of £600 per annum. This is paid in equal instalments in March, June, September and December.

(*ix*) Smith's cash drawings will amount to £250 per month.

(*x*) Depreciation is to be provided on Shop fixtures at 10 per cent per annum and on the Motor van at 20 per cent per annum.

You are required to:

(*a*) Draw up a cash budget for the six months ended 30 June 19X4, showing the balance of cash at the end of each month.

(*b*) Draw up a forecast trading and profit and loss account for the six months ended 30 June 19X4 and a balance sheet as at that date.

41.4A B. Cooper is going to set up a new business on 1 January 19X8. He estimates that his first six months in business will be as follows:

(*i*) He will put £10,000 into a bank account for the firm on 1 January 19X8.

(*ii*) On 1 January 19X8 he will buy machinery £2,000, motor vehicles £1,600 and premises £5,000, paying for them immediately out of the business bank account.

(*iii*) All purchases will be effected on credit. He will buy £2,000 goods on 1 January and he will pay for these in February. He will purchase another £3,200 of goods in January and £4,000 of goods each month during February, March, April, May and June. Other than the £2,000 worth bought in January all other purchases will be paid for two months after purchase.

(*iv*) Sales (all on credit) will be £4,000 for January and £5,000 for each month after that. Debtors will pay for the goods in the third month after purchase by them.

(*v*) Stock-in-trade on 30 June 19X8 will be £2,000.

(*vi*) Wages and salaries will be £150 per month and will be paid on the last day of each month.

(*vii*) General expenses will be £50 per month, payable in the month following that in which they were incurred.

(*viii*) He will receive a legacy of £5,500 on 21 April 19X8. This will be paid into the business bank account immediately.

(*ix*) Insurance covering the 12 months of 19X8 will be paid for by cheque on 30 June 19X8, £140.

(*x*) Rates will be paid as follows: for the three months to 31 March 19X8 by cheque on 28 February 19X8: for the 12 months ended 31 March 19X9 by cheque on 31 July 19X8. Rates are £360 per annum.

(*xi*) He will make drawings of £80 per month by cheque.

(*xii*) He has substantial investments in public companies. His bank manager will give him any overdraft that he may require.

(*xiii*) Depreciate motors 20 per cent per annum, machinery 10 per cent per annum.

You are required to:

(*a*) Draft a cash budget (includes bank) month by month showing clearly the amount of bank balance or overdraft at the end of each month.

(*b*) Draft the projected trading and profit and loss account for the first six months' trading, and a balance sheet as at 30 June 19X8.

41.5A

(*a*) What is meant by the terms:

    (*i*) Budget

    (*ii*) Operating budget

    (*iii*) Master budget?

(*b*) The information below relates to the business of Madingley Ltd:

Balance Sheet as at 30 May 19X0

		(£000)	
	Cost	Aggregate depreciation	Book value
Fixed assets:			
Land and buildings	134.00	–	134.00
Plant and machinery	9.40	3.76	5.64
Fixtures and fittings	2.30	1.05	1.25
	145.70	4.81	140.89
Current assets:			
Stocks: Raw materials	91.70		
Finished goods	142.40		
Debtors	594.40		
Bank	12.40		
		840.90	
Less: Current liabilities			
Creditors: Raw materials	82.20		
Overheads	127.40		
		209.60	
Working capital			631.30
			772.19
Financed by			
Share capital		500.00	
Profit and loss account		272.19	
			772.19

The following is a schedule of the budgeted income and expenditure for the six months ended 30 November 19X0 (£000):

	Sales	Materials	Wages	Overheads
June	193.20	41.20	7.60	123.00
July	201.40	42.40	7.90	119.20
August	216.10	49.60	8.80	131.40
September	200.50	31.40	6.10	91.50
October	190.30	21.20	3.70	59.30
November	183.70	19.80	2.60	42.60

Notes:

(*i*) Generally, materials are paid for two months after receipt, and customers pay on average after three months.

(*ii*) Payments outstanding for materials at 1 June 19X0 were: April £38,500; May £43,700.

(*iii*) Debtors were: March £194,300; April £203,600; May £196,500.

(*iv*) Wages are to be paid in the month in which they fall due.

(*v*) Overheads are to be paid one month after they are incurred: the figure for May was £127,400.

(*vi*) Stocks of raw materials are to be kept at £91,700.

(*vii*) The stocks of finished goods at 30 November 19X0 are to be £136,200.

(*viii*) There are no stocks of semi-finished items on 31 May 19X0, and none are expected in stock on 30 November.

(*ix*) Forty per cent of the overheads are to be considered as fixed.

(*x*) Depreciation on plant and machinery is to be allowed at 10 per cent *per annum* on cost; the fixtures and fittings are thought to have a value at 30 November of £980.

(*xi*) There are no sales of finished goods or purchases of raw materials for cash planned during the period.

Prepare:

(a) A forecast operating statement for the period June to November 19X0; and

(b) A forecast balance sheet as at 30 November 19X0.

(*Edexcel Foundation, London Examinations: GCE A–Level*)

41.6 The following information has been extracted from the books of Issa Ltd for the financial year ended 31 December 19X0.

*Trading and Profit and Loss Account
for the year ended 31 December 19X0*

	£000s		£000s
Opening stock	90	Sales	750
Purchases	490		
	580		
Less Closing stock	80		
Cost of goods sold	500		
Gross profit	250		
	750		750
Administration expenses	60	Gross profit	250
Selling and distribution expenses	50		
Financial charges	20		
Depreciation of fixed assets	20		
Net profit	100		
	250		250

Balance Sheet as at 31 December 19X0

	£000s	£000s		£000s	£000s
Fixed assets			£1 Ordinary shares		
at cost		750	Fully paid		200
Less Aggregate depreciation		144	9% £1 Preference shares, fully paid		100
		606			
Current assets			Share premium		150
Stock	80		Retained earnings		350
Trade debtors	75				
Less Provision for			*Current liabilities*		
Doubtful debtors	5	70	Trade creditors	50	
Balance at bank	100	250	Accrued expenses	6	56
		856			856

The company had commenced the preparation of its budget for the year ending 31 December 19X1 and the following information is the basis of its forecast.

1 An intensive advertising campaign will be carried out in the first six months of 19X1 at a cost of £15,000. It is anticipated that as a result of this, sales will increase to £900,000 in 19X1.

2 The gross profit/sales ratio will be increased to 35 per cent.

3 A new stock control system is to be installed in 19X1 and it is expected that the stock level will be reduced by £15,000 as compared to the 19X0 closing stock.

4 Land and buildings which cost £50,000 (nil depreciation to date) will be sold in 19X1 for £200,000 cash. Half of the proceeds will be used to buy ordinary shares in another company, Yates Ltd, at an agreed price of £4 per share. (Ignore share commission etc.)

5 The company planned to capitalise some of its reserves on 1 April 19X1. New ordinary shares

are to be issued on a 1 for 2 basis. Half the funds required will be drawn from the share premium account and the remainder will be taken from retained earnings.

6 Preference share dividends will be paid on 1 May 19X1 and 1 November 19X1. The company planned to pay an interim ordinary share dividend on the increased share capital of 2.5p per share on 1 July 19X1. No final dividend is proposed.

7 Owing to inflation revenue expenses are expected to rise as follows:
Administration expenses will increase by 6 per cent.
Selling and distribution expenses will increase by 8 per cent.
The advertising campaign expenses are in addition to the increase above.
Financial charges will increase by 4 per cent.
These percentage increases are based on the figures for the year ended 31 December 19X0.

8 With the projected sales increases trade debtors are expected to rise to £100,000 by 31 December 19X1. The provision for doubtful debts is to be adjusted to $7\frac{1}{2}$ per cent of forecast trade debtors.

9 Other forecast figures as at 31 December 19X1.

	£000s
Balance at bank	350.1
Trade creditors	56.0
Expense creditors	15.0

10 Depreciation of 10 per cent per annum on cost is to be provided on £600,000 of the company's fixed assets.

Required:

(a) A budgeted trading, profit and loss and appropriation account for the year ending 31 December 19X1.
Show the full details of the trading account.

(b) A budgeted balance sheet as at 31 December 19X1.

(c) What advantages accrue to a business by preparing a budget with respect to
(i) forecast profitability;
(ii) forecast liquidity?

(*Associated Examining Board: GCE A–Level*)

41.7 The balance sheet of Gregg Ltd at 30 June 19X6 was expected to be as follows:

Balance Sheet 30 June 19X6 (£)

Fixed assets	Cost	Depreciation to date	Net
Land and buildings	40,000	–	40,000
Plant and machinery	10,000	6,000	4,000
Motor vehicles	6,000	2,800	3,200
Office fixtures	500	220	280
	56,500	9,020	47,480
Current assets			
Stock-in-trade: Finished goods		1,800	
Raw materials		300	
Debtors (19X6 May £990 + June £900)		1,890	
Cash and bank balances		7,100	11,090
			£58,570

Financed by

Share capital	50,000
Profit and loss account	7,820
	57,820

Current Liabilities

Creditors for raw materials		
(April £240 + May £140 + June £160)	540	
Creditors for variable overhead	210	750
		£58,570

The plans for the six months to 31 December 19X6 can be summarised as:

(*i*) Production costs per unit will be:

	£
Direct materials	2
Direct labour	5
Variable overhead	3
	10

(*ii*) Sales will be at a price of £18 per unit for the three months to 30 September and at £18.5 subsequently. The number of units sold would be:

	Jul	Aug	Sep	Oct	Nov	Dec
Units	60	80	100	100	90	70

All sales will be on credit, and debtors will pay their accounts two months after they have bought the goods.

(*iii*) Production will be even at 90 units per month.

(*iv*) Purchases of direct materials – all on credit – will be:

	Jul	Aug	Sep	Oct	Nov	Dec
	£	£	£	£	£	£
	220	200	160	140	140	180

Creditors for direct materials will be paid three months after purchase.

(*v*) Direct labour is paid in the same month as production occurs.

(*vi*) Variable overhead is paid in the month following that in which the units are produced.

(*vii*) Fixed overhead of £90 per month is paid each month and is never in arrears.

(*viii*) A machine costing £500 will be bought and paid for in July. A motor vehicle costing £2,000 will be bought and paid for in September.

(*ix*) A debenture of £5,000 will be issued and the cash received in November. Interest will not start to run until 19X7.

(*x*) Provide for depreciation for the six months: Motor vehicles £600, Office fixtures £30, Machinery £700.

You are required to draw up as a minimum:

(*a*) Cash budget, showing figures each month.

(*b*) Debtors' budget, showing figures each month.

(*c*) Creditors' budget, showing figures each month.

(*d*) Raw materials budget, showing figures each month.

(*e*) Forecast operating statement for the six months.

(*f*) Forecast balance sheet as at 31 December 19X6.

In addition you may draw up any further budgets you may wish to show the workings behind the above budgets.

41.8 The following information relates to the actual sales of Griffton Ltd during the last four months of its financial year.

	March	April	May	June
Quantity (units)	900	900	900	1,000
Price each	£55	£55	£55	£55

The budgeted information below relates to the next financial year commencing 1 July 19X2:

(i) The company forecasts that sales quantity will decrease in July by 10 per cent of the level in June. The reduced quantity will remain for August and September, but will then increase by 10 per cent in October, and remain fixed for the next three months.

The sales price will remain at £55 each until 1 September when it will be increased to £60 per unit, this price will be effective for a minimum of six months.

50 per cent of sales are on a cash basis and attract a 2 per cent cash discount, the remaining 50 per cent of sales are paid two months in arrears.

The company arranges its purchases of raw materials such that the closing stock at the end of each month exactly meets the requirement for the following month's sales. Each unit sold requires 2 kg of material at £15 per kg; this price is fixed until December 19X3.

(ii) As a separate exercise, the managing director asks for stock levels to be reviewed, and asks you about the use of Economic Order Quantities at some time in 19X3. The following budgeted data would apply to this exercise:

Material	2,000 kg per month
Price	£15 per kg
Stockholding costs	20% p.a. on average stock value
Ordering costs	£10 per order

Required:

A Draw up monthly budgets for the four-month period commencing 1 July 19X2 for:
   (a) Debtors in £s;
   (b) Raw material purchases in kg.

B From the budgeted information given in note (ii) calculate the Economic Order Quantity for the company. Briefly outline the limitations of this ordering method.

(*University of Oxford Delegacy of Local Examinations: GCE A–Level*)

41.9 Bedford Ltd is a manufacturing business with several production departments. Benjamin Kent, the manager of the machining department, submitted the following figures for the firm's annual budget for his department:

Units produced (normal production level)	64,000

	£
Raw materials	294,400
Direct labour	236,800
Power	38,400
Repairs and maintenance (25% variable at this level of budgeted cost)	51,200
Insurance	1,300
Heating and lighting	1,250
Indirect wages (15% variable at this level of budgeted cost)	64,000
Total cost	687,350

Total capacity for machining department	80,000 units

Actual production for the period is 68,000 units, and costs are:

Materials	310,750
Labour	249,100
Power	39,800
Repairs and maintenance	53,050
Insurance	1,350
Heating and lighting	1,200
Indirect wages	65,250
Total cost	720,500

Benjamin is being criticised for overspending £33,150 compared with his normal budget. It is appreciated that he has made a saving on heating and lighting, but concern is being expressed over the spending on materials and labour. Benjamin feels that he has been able to control the department's costs efficiently.

Required:

A   Construct a flexible budget for 60 per cent, 70 per cent, 75 per cent, 85 per cent and 90 per cent of production capacity, calculate any savings or overspending by Benjamin's department and comment on its efficiency.

B   Describe the operation of an efficient system of budgetary control.

(*University of Oxford Delegacy of Local Examinations: GCE A–Level*)

41.10A The summarised balance sheet of Newland Traders at 30 May 19X7 was as follows:

	£000	£000
Fixed assets at cost		610
Less depreciation		264
		346
Current assets		
Stocks	210	
Debtors	315	
Cash at bank and in hand	48	
	573	
Less Current liabilities		
Creditors	128	445
		791
Capital and reserves		
Issued capital		600
General reserve		150
Profit and loss account		41
		791

Selling and materials prices at 30 May 19X7 provide for a gross profit at the rate of 25 per cent of sales.

The creditors at 30 May 19X7 represent the purchases for May 19X7, and the debtors the sales for April of £150,000 and May of £165,000.

Estimates of sales and expenditure for the six months to 30 November 19X7 are as follows:

(*i*)   Sales for the period at current prices will be £800,000. Sales for the months of September and October will each be twice those of the sales in each of the other months.

(*ii*)   Stock at the end of each month will be the same as at 30 May 19X7 except that at 30 November 19X7 it will be increased to 20 per cent above that level.

(*iii*) Creditors will be paid one month after the goods are supplied and debtors will pay two months after the goods are supplied.

(*iv*)   Wages and expenses will be £20,000 a month and will be paid in the month in which they are incurred.

(*v*)   Depreciation will be at the rate of £5,000 a month.

(*vi*)   There will be capital expenditure of £80,000 on 1 September 19X7. Depreciation, in addition to that given in (*v*) above, will be at the rate of 10 per cent per annum on cost.

(*vii*) There will be no changes in issued capital, general reserve or prices of sales or purchases.

Required:

(*a*)   Sales and purchases budgets and budgeted trading and profit and loss accounts for the six months ended 30 November 19X7.

(*b*)   A budgeted balance sheet as at 30 November 19X7.

(*c*)   A cash flow budget for the six months ended 30 November 19X7 indicating whether or not it will be necessary to make arrangements for extra finance and, if so, your recommendation as to what form it should take.

Show all your calculations.

(*Welsh Joint Education Committee: GCE A–Level*)

41.11A Len Auck and Brian Land trade as partners in Auckland Manufacturing Company making components for minicomputers. To cope with increasing demand the partners intend to extend their manufacturing capacity but are concerned about the effect of the expansion on their cash resources during the build-up period from January to April 19X6.

The following information is available.

(*a*)   The balance sheet of Auckland Manufacturing Company at 31 December 19X5 is expected to be:

	£	£
Fixed assets		
Plant and machinery at cost		65,000
Less depreciation		28,000
		37,000
Current assets		
Stocks – raw materials	10,500	
– finished goods	18,500	
Debtors	36,000	
Cash at bank	4,550	
	69,550	
Current liabilities		
Creditors	27,550	
		42,000
		£79,000
Partners' capital accounts		
Len Auck		40,000
Brian Land		39,000
		£79,000

(b) Creditors at 31 December 19X5 are made up of:

Creditors for materials supplied in November and December at £13,000 per month	26,000
Creditors for overheads	1,550
	£27,550

(c) New plant costing £25,000 will be delivered and paid for in January 19X6.

(d) Raw material stocks are to be increased to £12,000 by the end of January 19X6, thereafter raw material stocks will be maintained at that level. Payment for raw materials is made two months after the month of delivery. Finished goods stocks will be maintained at £18,500 throughout the period. There is no work in progress.

(e) Sales for the four months are expected to be:

	£
January	18,000
February	22,000
March	22,000
April	24,000

Sales for several months prior to 31 December had been running at the rate of £18,000 per month. It is anticipated that all sales will continue to be paid for two months following the month of delivery.

(f) The cost structure of the product is expected to be:

	%
Raw materials	50
Direct wages	20
Overheads, including depreciation	$17\frac{1}{2}$
Profit	$12\frac{1}{2}$
Selling price	100

(g) Indirect wages and salaries included in overheads amount to £900 for the month of January and £1,000 per month thereafter.

(h) Depreciation of plant and machinery (including the new plant) is to be provided at £700 per month and is included in the total overheads.

(i) Wages and salaries are to be paid in the month to which they relate; all other expenses are to be paid for in the month following the month to which they relate.

(j) The partners share profits equally and drawings are £400 per month each.

(k) During the period to April an overdraft facility is being requested.

Required:

(a) A forecast profit and loss account for the four months January to April 19X6 and a balance sheet as at 30 April 19X6.

(b) A month by month cash forecast for the four months showing the maximum amount of finance required during the period.

(c) A calculation of the month in which the overdraft facility would be repaid on the assumption that the level of activity in April is maintained.

For the purposes of this question, taxation and bank interest may be ignored.

(*Association of Chartered Certified Accountants*)

Part 8

STANDARD COSTING AND VARIANCE ANALYSIS

Introduction

This part looks at how budgetary control can be exercised in a timely manner through the establishment of estimates for cost and income and the subsequent monitoring of those estimates against the actual costs and income as they arise.

42

Standard costing

Objectives

After you have studied this chapter, you should:

- *understand the difference between a standard costing system and an actual cost system*

- *be able to explain the advantages of adopting a standard costing system*

- *understand the importance of selecting appropriate standards*

42.1 Comparison with actual costs

A cost accounting system can be said to be either an *actual* cost system or a *standard* cost system. The difference lies, not in the systems themselves, but in the kind of costs that are used. In the costing systems already shown, we have seen that they have consisted of the *actual costs* for direct materials and direct labour, and overhead has been charged by reference to a predetermined overhead rate. Standard costing uses instead the *costs that should have been incurred.*

In an actual cost accounting system, costs are traced through the records as product costs. On the other hand, **standard costing** uses standards of performance and of prices derived from studying operations and of estimating future prices. Each unit being produced can have a standard material cost, a standard direct labour cost and a standard overhead cost. As with any form of management accounting, this does not in fact have to be carried out fully, for instance some companies will use standard labour and standard overhead costs but may use actual material costs. In the rest of this chapter we will consider firms that use standard costing system for all items.

As with all management accounting, the benefits flowing from using standard costing should exceed the costs of operating it, so that there should be advantages accruing from having a standard costing system, and these are:

1   Usually it is simpler and needs less work than an actual cost system. This is because once the standards have been set they are adhered to, and the standard costs will remain unchanged for fairly long periods. Other systems need constant recalculations of cost. For instance the average cost method of pricing issues of materials needs a recalculation of the price each time there are further receipts, whereas standard cost of materials will remain at a constant figure. This can bring about a reduction in the costs of clerical work.

2 The unit costs for each identical product will be the same, whereas this may not be the same with actual costing systems. For instance, in an actual cost system two men making identical units may be paid at different wage rates, the materials issued to one man may have come from a slightly later lot of raw materials received which cost more than the previous lot and therefore the issue price may be higher, and so on. In a standard costing system the same amount would be charged for each of these men, until such time as the standards were altered.

3 A standard cost system provides a better means of checking on the efficiency with which production is carried on, in that the differences between the standard costs and the actual costs, i.e. the **variances**, throw up the changes in efficiency.

4 One important advantage may be that standard costing might make faster reporting available. This is certainly most important, as generally the later information is received the less useful it will be. Standard costing has a great deal of predetermined data when compared with an actual costing system; therefore entering up job order sheets, job sheets and many other tasks can be speeded up if the actual costs do not have to be waited for.

The costs that will have been flowing through the standard costing system is that of standard costs and as actual costs will normally be different, then the difference or variance if adverse (i.e. actual costs have exceeded standard costs) will be debited to the profit and loss account. If the variance is a favourable one (i.e. actual costs have been less than standard costs) then this would be credited to the profit and loss account. This must be done, as all the costs used for the calculation of gross profit, etc. have been standard costs, and if the variances were not put in the profit and loss account then the net profit would not be the net profit actually made.

42.2 Setting standards

Standard cost accounting is a classic case of the use of the principle of 'management by exception'. Put roughly this means that when things are going according to plan leave them alone, and concentrate instead on the things that are deviating from planned results. With standard costing the actual results that conform to the standards require little attention. Instead management's interest is centred on the exceptions to standards.

Getting the 'right' standards is, therefore, of prime importance. If the 'wrong' standards are used, not only will a lot of time and money have been wasted, but it may bring worse results than if no standard had been set at all. Standards may be unsuitable because they were not set properly, or because conditions have changed greatly since they were set.

Standards of one of two types can be used; ideal standards and maintainable standards. These are as follows:

1 **Ideal standards.** These are set at a maximum level of efficiency, and thus represent conditions that really can very rarely be attained. This approach can be seriously objected to, in that if standards are too high, employees who might otherwise be motivated by standards which are possible to achieve may become discouraged.

2 **Attainable standards.** It is simple for someone to say that individuals will be motivated to attain standards that they are capable of, that they will not exert very much effort to exceed standards, and that standards outside their capabilities will not motivate them. From this follows the also easy conclusion that standards should be neither 'too easy' nor 'too difficult' but should be 'just right'. The difficult part of this

is in saying what the 'just right' figures are to ask as standards. There is no doubt that the work of behavioural scientists in this area has brought about a far greater insight into such problems. In a very large firm such specialists may be members of the team setting the standards.

The standards for materials and for labour can be divided between those which are concerned with (i) prices and (ii) quantities. Standard overhead costs are divided between standard variable overhead costs, and standard fixed overhead costs. The standard fixed overhead costs will be used in absorption costing only, as marginal costing does not bring the fixed costs into its figures.

New terms

Standard cost (p. 591): An estimate of what costs should be.

Standard costing (p. 591): A control technique that compares standard costs and standard revenues to actual costs and actual revenues in order to determine differences (variances) that may then be investigated.

Variance (p. 592): The difference between budget and actual.

Ideal standard (p. 592): A standard that is based upon the premise that everything operates at the maximum level of efficiency. It takes no account of normal losses, or of normal levels of downtime and waste.

Attainable standard (p. 592): A standard that can be achieved in normal conditions. It takes into account normal losses, and normal levels of downtime and waste.

Main points to remember

1   Standard costing is based upon costs that should have been incurred, whilst other costing systems are based upon actual costs, i.e. costs that have been incurred.

2   Under a standard costing system, management focuses upon the exceptions to the standards.

3   It is essential that the standards adopted are appropriate.

Review questions

Advice:

This is a chapter giving background information only. You will not find many computational questions limited to the contents of the chapter.

42.1 Rimham plc prepares its budgets annually and as the accountant you are responsible for this task. The following standard data is available:

Material content	Product X kg	Product Y kg	Product Z kg
Material 1	–	18	24
Material 2	4	14	–
Material 3	12	10	6
Material 4	8	–	18

Material prices	Price per kg £
Material 1	0.1
Material 2	0.15
Material 3	0.25
Material 4	0.05

Labour content	Product X hours	Product Y hours	Product Z hours
Department A	2.5	1.5	3
Department B	2.5	1.5	3

Labour rates	Rate per hour £
Department A	1.6
Department B	1.2

Additional budgeted information

Direct labour hours	635,000
Production overheads	£1,143,000

- Production overheads are absorbed on the direct labour hour rate method.
- Administration and selling overheads are absorbed as a percentage of production cost at the rates of 50 per cent and 25 per cent, respectively.
- Profit is estimated at 12½ per cent on budgeted selling price.
- Sales, at standard selling price, for the following year are budgeted as follows:

Product	£
X	800,000
Y	1,280,000
Z	2,400,000

● In order to meet the needs of an expansion programme the company considers it necessary to increase stocks as follows:

Material 1	90,000 kg
Material 2	36,000 kg
Material 3	42,000 kg
Material 4	54,000 kg

Finished goods	
Product X	5,000 units
Product Y	10,000 units
Product Z	10,000 units

You are required to prepare the following:

(a) A schedule giving a detailed standard cost and standard selling price per unit for **each** product,
(b) The sales budget in units,
(c) The production budget in units,
(d) The direct material purchases budget in both units and value.

(*Northern Examinations and Assessment Board: GCE A–Level*)

42.2A Define the terms:

(*i*)   standard costing
(*ii*) standard cost
(*iii*) standard hours
(*iv*) variance

(*Edexcel Foundation, London Examinations: GCE A–Level*)

43

Material and labour variances

Objectives

After you have studied this chapter, you should:

- *understand the difference between a favourable and an adverse variance*
- *know how to calculate materials usage and price variances*
- *know how to calculate wage rate and efficiency variances*
- *understand the similarity between the calculation of the materials usage variance and the labour efficiency variance*
- *understand the similarity between the calculation of the materials price variance and the wage rate variance*

43.1 Introduction

Variance analysis is a means of assessing the difference between a predetermined cost and the actual cost. It can improve the operating efficiency of a business by, first of all, setting up the predetermined standard cost structures and, then, measuring actual costs against them in order to measure production efficiency.

It also makes use of the principle of management by exception. When things are going according to plan they can be left alone. Management can then concentrate on the things that deviate from the planned results.

43.2 Adverse and favourable variances

The difference between standard cost and actual cost has already been stated to be a variance. Remember these are classified:

> Adverse: actual cost greater than standard cost.
> Favourable: actual cost less than standard cost.

The use of the words favourable and adverse should not be confused with their meaning in ordinary language usage, they are technical terms. Whether a variance is 'good' or 'bad' can only be determined after the cause(s) of the variance have been fully investigated and ascertained.

43.3 Computation of variances

There is a great deal of difference between the *computation* of the variances and their *analysis*. The computation is simply the mathematical calculation of the variance. The analysis of the variance is a matter requiring a fair amount of judgement, it just cannot be performed in a mechanical fashion.

We can now look at some computations of variances. In fact there are many variances which can be computed, but we will concentrate on a few of the more important ones. In order that sense can be made of the computations and a reasonable job of analysis done, it will be assumed that the standards set were calculated on a rational basis.

Note: In the computations of variances which follows this, there are diagrams to illustrate the variances which have been calculated. The lines drawn on the diagrams will be as follows:

Representing standard costs — — — — — —
Representing actual costs - - - - - - - - -
Where actual costs and standard costs are the same —·—·—·—·—·—·.

(a) Material price variances

(*i*) Favourable variance:

Material J

Standard price per metre	£4
Standard usage per unit	5 metres
Actual price per metre	£3
Actual usage per unit	5 metres

Usage is the same as standard, therefore the only variance is that of price calculated:

	£
Actual cost per unit 5 × £3	15
Standard cost per unit 5 × £4	20
Variance (favourable)	£5

The diagram illustrates this in that the variance is represented by the shaded area. This is £1 by a quantity of 5, therefore the variance is £5. The variance extends to the price line and not the quantity line, therefore it is a price variance.

(*ii*) Adverse variance:

Material K

Standard price per metre	£9
Standard usage per unit	8 metre
Actual price per metre	£11
Actual usage per unit	8 metre
Variance computed:	£
Actual cost per unit 8 × £11	88
Standard cost per unit 8 × £9	72
Variance (adverse)	£16

The shaded part of the diagram is the variance. This extends £2 times a quantity of 8. Therefore, the variance is £16. Notice that the shaded area is outside the lines marked ─ ─ ─ ─ ─ ─ ─ ─ ─ ─ ─ ─ ─ representing standard costs. In the diagrams, when the variance is outside the standard cost area as marked by the standard cost lines, it will be an adverse variance. When it is inside the standard cost area as marked by the standard cost lines, it will be a favourable variance.

(*b*) Materials usage variances

(*i*) Favourable variance:

Material L

Standard price per tonne	£5
Standard usage per unit	100 tonnes
Actual price per tonne	£5
Actual usage per unit	95 tonnes

Cost is the same as standard, therefore the only variance is that of usage calculated:

	£
Actual cost per unit 95 × £5	475
Standard cost per unit 100 × £5	500
Variance (favourable)	25

(*ii*) Adverse variance:

Material M

Standard price per centimetre	£8
Standard usage per unit	11 cm
Actual price per centimetre	£8
Actual usage per unit	13 cm
Variance computed:	£
Actual cost per unit 13 × £8	104
Standard cost per unit 11 × £8	88
Variance (adverse)	16

Here again the variances for Materials L and M are shown in diagrams by means of shaded areas. The variances extend to the quantity lines and are, therefore, usage variances. With material L the variance is shown inside the standard cost area, and is, therefore, a favourable variance, whereas Material M shows an adverse variance as it is outside the standard cost area.

(*c*) Combinations of material price and usage variances

Most variances are combinations of both material price and usage variances. Sometimes one variance will be favourable whilst the other is adverse, sometimes both will be adverse variances, and at other times both will be favourable variances.

(*i*) Favourable and adverse variances combined:

Material N

Standard price per metre	£6
Standard usage per unit	25 metres
Actual price per metre	£7
Actual usage per metre	24 metres

The net variance is calculated as:

		£
Actual cost per unit 24 × £7		168
Standard cost per unit 25 × £6		150
Variance (adverse)		£18

As the diagram shows, this is in fact made up of two variances. The first variance, shown as the shaded portion A, is an adverse price variance (i.e. it is outside the standard cost lines, therefore actual cost has exceeded standard cost). The second variance, shown as the shaded portion B, is a favourable usage variance (i.e. it is inside the standard cost lines, therefore actual usage has been less than standard usage).

The adverse price variance can therefore be seen to be £1 by a quantity of 24 = £24. The favourable usage variance can be seen to be a length of 1 metre by a price of £6 = £6. The net (adverse) variance is therefore made up:

Adverse material price variance	24
Favourable material usage variance	6
Net (adverse) variance	£18

(*ii*) Both adverse variances combined:

Material O

Standard price per kilo.	£9
Standard usage per unit	13 kilos
Actual price per kilo.	£11
Actual usage per unit	15 kilos

The net variance is computed:

	£
Actual cost per unit 15 × £11	165
Standard cost per unit 13 × £9	117
Variance (adverse)	£48

The diagram shows the shaded area A which is definitely a price variance of £2 × 13 = £26 adverse. Shaded area B is definitely a usage variance of 2 × £9 = £18 adverse. This makes up £44 of the variance, but there is the double shaded area, C, of 2 × £2 = £4. This is really an area which is common to both usage and price. Sometimes, although not very often, this would be treated as a separate variance, but as detail is necessarily limited, in this book we will just add it to the price variance, making it £26 + £4 = £30, the usage variance being left at £18.

(*iii*) Both favourable variances combined:

Material P

Standard price per tonne	£20
Standard usage per unit	15 tonnes
Actual price per tonne	£19
Actual usage per unit	13 tonnes

The net variance is computed:

	£
Actual cost per unit 13 × £19	247
Standard cost per unit 15× £20	300
Variance (favourable)	£53

The diagram shows the shaded area A which is definitely a price variance of £1 × 13 = £13 favourable. Shaded area B is a usage variance of 2 × £19 = £38 favourable. The double shaded area C of £1 × 2 = £2, making up the total variance of 53 would normally be added to the usage variance to make it £38 + £2 = £40.

43.4 Materials variances – analysis

(*a*) Price variances

The price variance is a simple one in that it is obvious that the purchasing department has not been able to buy at the anticipated price. How far this is completely outside the powers of the purchasing department depends entirely on the facts. It may simply be that the rate of inflation is far greater than it had been possible to foresee, or that special forms of extra taxes have been introduced by the government. No one can surely blame the purchasing department for not knowing the secrets of the government's budget each year!

On the other hand, it may have been that poor purchasing control has meant that orders for materials have been placed too late for the firm to manage to get the right price in the market, or that materials which ought to have been bought in bulk have been in fact bought in small lots at uneconomic prices. If there are regular suppliers, a short-term gain by buying a cheaper lot from somewhere else could militate against the firm's benefit in the long run if the firm's regular suppliers took umbrage.

Buying the cheapest materials does not always bring about the achievement of the greatest profit. It may result in more wastages, a greater amount of labour time because the men take longer to do the job with inferior materials, and a unit made up of poor materials may well damage the image of the firm because its products do not last as long as they used to do.

All the same, there must be someone to whom the responsibility for the price variance can be traced and who is then accountable for it.

(*b*) Usage variances

There are many reasons for excessive use of material. Inferior materials can bring about a lot of waste, so can workers who are not as skilled as they ought to be. Perhaps the machinery is not suitable for the job, or there might even be deliberate wastage of material, e.g. wood wasted so that it can be taken home by workers as fuel etc. The theft of material obviously aggravates a usage variance. Here again responsibility must be traced.

43.5 Key questions of variances

Before we look at the computation or analysis of any further variances this is a convenient point to raise some fundamental questions about variances. They are:

1   Why do we wish to calculate this particular variance?
2   When it has been calculated what action are we going to take about it?
3   If we are not going to make an effective use of the variance, then why bother at all to calculate it?

43.6 Formulas for material variances

We have deliberately waited until now to give you the formula for calculating each variance. We wanted you to understand what the variances were, rather than simply give you the formula to calculate them. They are as follows:

Materials price variance = (Standard price − Actual price per unit) × Quantity purchased
= (SP − AP) × QP

Materials usage variance = (Standard quantity required − Actual quantity) × Standard price
= (SQ − AQ) × SP

43.7 Inventory records under standard costing

It is worth noting at this point that when a firm adopts a standard costing system it avoids the difficulties involving FIFO, LIFO or average stock methods. In a standard costing system all materials received and issued are valued at the standard cost in the inventory account. There is no recording problem associated with changing prices during the period since they are separately recorded as variances.

Provided that standards are reviewed sufficiently often this system should ensure that the values of inventories are maintained close to their current value.

43.8 Disposition of variances

The question arises as to how the variances are to be brought into the final accounts of the business. There are, in fact, several methods of dealing with them.

They can be treated entirely as costs (if adverse variances) which are period costs and are, therefore, not included in the valuation of closing stocks of finished goods or work in progress. Alternatively they may be brought in as product costs and therefore used in the valuation of closing stocks. Another variation is to treat those variances which are controllable as period costs, but the uncontrollable variances be treated as product costs. All of these methods are acceptable for the final accounts which are used for external reporting.

Before you read further, now attempt Questions 43.1 to 43.2A.

43.9 Labour variances

The computation of labour variances is similar to that of material variances. With labour variances the analysis can be broken down into:

(a) Wage rate variances.
(b) Labour efficiency variances.

As you read and work through this section, you will notice great similarity between the labour variance formulas and the materials variance formulas. In actual fact, the only diffence is a terminological one. The wage rate formula is identical in method to the materials price formula; and the labour efficiency formula is similarly identical to the materials usage formula. This is something that students frequently fail to grasp. In effect, it means that you need only learn one of the pairs of formulas, along with the terminology for the other pair. You can then complete any variance computation on both pairs of formulas.

Because the computation of labour variances is so similar to those of material variances only a few examples will be given.

(*a*) Wage rate variance

Product A

Standard hours to produce	100
Actual hours to produce	100
Standard wage rate per hour	£0.9
Actual wage rate per hour	£1.0

As the actual and standard hours are the same, then the only variance will be a wage rate variance, computed as follows:

	£
Actual cost per unit 100 × £1.0	100
Standard cost per unit 100 × £0.9	90
Variance (adverse)	£10

The diagram illustrates this in that the variance is represented by the shaded area. This is £0.1 by a quantity of 100, therefore the variance is £10. The variance extends to the wage rate line and it is thus a wage rate variance, and as the shaded area is outside the standard cost lines, indicated by lines marked – – – – – – –, then it is an adverse variance.

(*b*) Labour efficiency variance

Product B

Standard hours to produce	400
Actual hours to produce	370
Standard wage rate per hour	£1.0
Actual wage rate per hour	£1.0

As the actual and standard wage rates are the same, then the only variance will be a labour efficiency variance, computed as follows:

	£
Actual cost per unit 370 × £1.0	370
Standard cost per unit 400 × £1.0	400
Variance (favourable)	£30

The diagram illustrates this in that the variance is represented by the shaded area. This is a quantity of 30 by a rate of £1.0, therefore the variance is £30. The variance extends to the time line, therefore this is an efficiency variance, as the job has been completed in a different number of hours than standard. As the shaded area is inside the standard cost lines indicated by lines marked – – – – – – then it is a favourable variance.

(c) Combined wage rate and efficiency variance

Product C

Standard hours to produce	500
Actual hours to produce	460
Standard wage rate per hour	£0.9
Actual wage rate per hour	£1.1

The net variance can be computed as:

	£
Actual cost per unit 460 × £1.1	506
Standard cost per unit 500 × £0.9	450
Variance (adverse)	£56

The diagram shows that this is made up of two variances. The first variance, shown as the shaded portion A, is an adverse wage rate variance (it is outside the standard cost lines, therefore it is an adverse variance because actual cost for this has exceeded standard cost). The second variance, shown as the shaded portion B, is a favourable labour efficiency variance (it is inside the standard cost lines, therefore actual hours have been less than standard hours).

The adverse wage rate variance can, therefore, be seen to be £0.2 by a quantity of 460 = £92. The favourable efficiency variance is a quantity of 40 by a price of £0.9 = £36. The net adverse variance is, therefore, made up of:

	£
Adverse wage rate variance	92
Favourable labour efficiency variance	36
	£56

43.10 Labour variances – analysis

Labour wage rates will probably be set in conjunction with the trade unions involved, so that this variance may not really be subject to control at any other level other than at the bargaining table with the unions involved. Nevertheless such a variance could arise because a higher grade of labour was being used than was necessary, even taking into account trade union needs. It might reflect a job running behind schedule that had to be finished off quickly even though higher grade labour was used. It might have been a rush job that also meant bringing in a higher grade of labour as well. The staffing policy of the firm may have come adrift because the firm had not recruited sufficient numbers of the various grades of labour.

Labour efficiency variances can be caused by a great number of things. Using unsuitable labour, unsuitable machinery, workers trying to slow work up so that more overtime rates of pay are earned, the day after a bank holiday, or the day before it, can affect performance. The morale of workers, the physical state of workers, using poor materials which slows up production, hold-ups because of bottlenecks in production and so on. The possibilities are almost endless. At the same time, if the variance was worth calculating then some form of action should follow, as otherwise there is no point at all in doing the accounting work of calculating such variances.

43.11 Formulas for labour variances

Wage rate variance = (Standard wage rate per hour − Actual wage rate) × Actual hours worked
= (SR − AR) × AH

Labour efficiency variance = (Standard labour hours for actual production − Actual labour hours worked) × Standard wage rate per hour
= (SH − AH) × SR

New terms

Variance analysis (p. 596): A means of assessing the difference between a predetermined cost/income and the actual cost/income.

Adverse variance (p. 596): A difference arising that is *apparently* 'bad' from the perspective of the organisation. For example, when the total actual material cost exceeds the total standard cost due to more material having been used than anticipated. Whether it is indeed 'bad' will only be revealed when the cause of the variance is identified. It may, for example, have arisen as a result of an unexpected rise in demand for the product being produced.

Favourable variance (p. 596): A difference arising that is *apparently* 'good' from the perspective of the organisation. For example, when the total actual labour cost is less than the total standard cost because less hours were worked than expected. Whether it is indeed 'good' will only be revealed when the cause of the variance is identified – it may be that less hours were worked because demand for the product fell unexpectedly.

Main points to remember

1   Variance analysis can improve the operating efficiency of a business by pinpointing items in need of investigation.

2   Adverse variances are not necessarily 'bad'. They result from more having been used or spent than was anticipated. Similarly, favourable variances, are not necessarily 'good'. It is the reason for the variance, not the effect, that determines whether it is 'good' or 'bad'.

3   The materials usage variance formula is identical to the labour efficiency variance formula. Only the terminology differs.

4   The materials price variance formula is identical to the wage rate variance formula. Only the terminology differs.

Review questions

Advice:

Work carefully through Questions 43.1 and 43.3. If you have any difficulty, repeat them after 24 hours. Once you get into the swing of doing this type of question, it is quite easy to tackle them and get high marks.

43.1 Calculate the materials variances from the following data.

(i)	Material Q:	Standard price per tonne	£20	
		Standard usage per unit	34	tonnes
		Actual price per tonne	£18	
		Actual usage per unit	37	tonnes
(ii)	Material R:	Standard price per metre	£17	
		Standard usage per unit	50	metres
		Actual price per metre	£19	
		Actual usage per unit	46	metres
(iii)	Material S:	Standard price per metre	£12	
		Standard usage per unit	15	metres
		Actual price per metre	£14	
		Actual usage per unit	18	metres
(iv)	Material T:	Standard price per roll	£40	
		Standard usage per unit	29	rolls
		Actual price per roll	£37	
		Actual usage per unit	27	rolls
(v)	Material U:	Standard price per kilo	£7	
		Standard usage per unit	145	kilos
		Actual price per kilo	£8	
		Actual usage per unit	154	kilos
(vi)	Material V:	Standard price per litre	£25	
		Standard usage per unit	10,000	litres
		Actual price per litre	£22	
		Actual usage per unit	9,850	litres

43.2A Calculate the materials variances from the following data.

(i)	Material E:	Standard price per metre	£6	
		Standard usage per unit	88	metres
		Actual price per metre	£6	
		Actual usage per unit	85	metres
(ii)	Material F:	Standard price per tonne	£117	
		Standard usage per unit	30	tonnes
		Actual price per tonne	£123	
		Actual usage per unit	30	tonnes
(iii)	Material G:	Standard price per litre	£16	
		Standard usage per unit	158	litres
		Actual price per litre	£16	
		Actual usage per unit	165	litres
(iv)	Material H:	Standard price per foot	£16	
		Standard usage per unit	92	feet
		Actual price per foot	£19	
		Actual usage per unit	92	feet
(v)	Material I:	Standard price per tonne	£294	
		Standard usage per unit	50	tonnes
		Actual price per tonne	£300	
		Actual usage per unit	50	tonnes
(vi)	Material J:	Standard price per kilo	£27.5	
		Standard usage per unit	168	kilos
		Actual price per kilo	£27.5	
		Actual usage per unit	156	kilos

43.3 Calculate the labour variances from the following data:

		Standard hours	Actual hours	Standard wage rate	Actual wage rate
(i)	Job A	220	218	£2.1	£2.1
(ii)	Job B	115	115	£1.7	£1.9
(iii)	Job C	200	240	£1.8	£1.8
(iv)	Job D	120	104	£2.0	£2.0
(v)	Job E	68	68	£1.8	£1.5
(vi)	Job F	30	34	£1.7	£1.7
(vii)	Job G	70	77	£1.6	£1.6
(viii)	Job H	100	100	£1.9	£2.0

43.4A Calculate the labour variances from the following data:

		Standard hours	Actual hours	Standard wage rate	Actual wage rate
(i)	Job I	150	142	£2.0	£2.2
(ii)	Job J	220	234	£1.9	£1.7
(iii)	Job K	50	48	£2.0	£1.9
(iv)	Job L	170	176	£2.0	£2.2
(v)	Job M	140	149	£2.1	£1.8
(vi)	Job N	270	263	£1.6	£2.0

43.5 The company for which you are the accountant manufactures three related, but different, products. These are dishwashers, washing machines and refrigerators. Each product has a standard time per unit of production. These are:

dishwashers	10 hours
washing machines	12 hours
refrigerators	14 hours

In the month of March the actual production was:

dishwashers	150
washing machines	100
refrigerators	90

and the labour details were:

actual hours worked	4,100
standard hourly rate of pay	£4
actual wages incurred	£18,450

You are required to:

(a) Explain the term 'standard hour'
(b) Calculate the standard hours produced in the month of March
(c) Calculate the following variances, using the above data:
    (i)   total direct labour variance
    (ii) direct labour rate variance
    (iii) direct labour efficiency variance
(d) Give **two** possible causes for **each** of the labour rate and efficiency variances in (c).

(Northern Examinations and Assessment Board: GCE A–Level)

43.6A Central Grid plc manufactures tungsten parts which pass through two processes, machining and polishing, before being transferred to finished goods. The management of the company have in operation a system of standard costing and budgetary control. The standard cost and budget information for April 19X8 has been established by the management accountant as follows:

Standard cost and budget details for April 19X8

	Machining	Polishing
Standard cost per unit		
Direct material	£5	–
Direct labour	£12	£4.50
Budgeted output – units	16,000	16,000
(*See* Note below)		
Budgeted direct labour hours	48,000	24,000

Note: Output passes through both processes and there is no opening or closing work in progress.

Additional information

1   The actual production costs and details for April 19X8 are as follows:
  (*i*)   The output that passed through the two processes was 12,000 units and there was no opening or closing work in progress.
  (*ii*) Direct material used at standard prices was £64,150.
  (*iii*) Direct material used at actual prices was £60,390.
  (*iv*) The direct wages bill and the direct labour hours clocked for the machining department were:

	£	Hours
Machining department	153,000	34,000

2   Variances for the polishing department have been calculated and reveal the following:

Labour efficiency variance	£3,000 Adverse
Labour rate variance	Nil

Required:

(*a*) Calculate the total direct material variance and its analysis into:
  (*i*)   direct material usage variance
  (*ii*) direct material price variance.
(*b*) Calculate the overall direct labour variance for the machining department and analyse this variance into:
  (*i*)   direct labour efficiency variance
  (*ii*) direct labour rate variance.
(*c*) Identify the possible reasons for each of the variances calculated for the machining department in (*a*) and (*b*) above and also for the variances given for the polishing department.
(*d*) Discuss possible interrelationships between these variances.

(*Associated Examining Board: GCE A–Level*)

43.7 Borrico Ltd manufacture a single product and they had recently introduced a system of budgeting and variance analysis. The following information is available for the month of July 19X1:

1

	Budget £	Actual £
Direct materials	200,000	201,285
Direct labour	313,625	337,500
Variable manufacturing overhead	141,400	143,000
Fixed manufacturing overhead	64,400	69,500
Variable sales overhead	75,000	71,000
Administration costs	150,000	148,650

2 Standard costs were:
Direct labour 48,250 hours at £6.50 per hour.
Direct materials 20,000 kilograms at £10 a kilogram.

3 Actual manufacturing costs were:
Direct labour 50,000 hours at £6.75 per hour.
Direct materials 18,900 kilograms at £10.65 a kilogram.

4 Budgeted sales were 20,000 units at £50 a unit.
Actual sales were
    15,000 units at £52 a unit
    5,200 units at £56 a unit

5 There was no work in progress or stock of finished goods.

Required:

(a) An accounting statement showing the budgeted and actual gross and net profits or losses for July 19X1.
(b) The following variances for July 19X1.
    (i) Direct material cost variance, direct material price variance and direct material usage variance.
    (ii) Direct labour cost variance, direct labour rate variance and direct labour efficiency variance.
(c) What use can the management of Borrico Ltd make of the variances calculated in (b) above?

(*Associated Examining Board: GCE A–Level*)

43.8A

(a) How does a system of standard costing enable a business to operate on the principle of management by exception?

(b) Some of the following materials and labour variances have been wrongly calculated, although the figures used are correct. Recalculate the variances, showing clearly the formulae you have used, and state whether the variances are adverse or favourable.

(i) *Total Materials Variance*

(Standard price – Actual price)   (Standard quantity – Actual quantity)

= (£8.42 – £8.24)   (1,940 litres – 2,270 litres)

= (£0.18)   (– 330 litres)

= £59.40 *adverse*

(ii) *Materials Price Variance*

(Standard price – Actual price)   Standard quantity

= (£8.42 – £8.24)   1,940

= £349.20 *favourable*

(iii) *Materials Usage Variance*

(Standard quantity – Actual quantity)   Standard price

= (1,940 – 2,270)   £8.42

= £2,778.6 *adverse*

(iv) *Total Labour Variance*

(Actual hours – Standard hours)   (Actual rate – Standard rate)

= (860 – 800)   (£6.14 – £6.53)

= (60 hours)   (– £0.39)

= £23.4 *adverse*

(v) *Wage Rate Variance*

(Standard rate – Actual rate)   Actual hours

= (£6.53 – £6.14)   860

= £335.4 *favourable*

(vi) *Labour Efficiency Variance*

(Actual hours – Standard hours)   Standard rate

= (860 – 800)   £6.53

= £391.80 *favourable*

(*Edexcel Foundation, London Examinations: GCE A–Level*)

43.9A Makers Ltd assembles computer games machines. Standard costs have been prepared as follows:

	Gamesmaster £	Gotchya £
Standard cost:		
Direct material: boards	5	10
components	20	30
Direct labour: assembly	5	5
testing	5	10
Overheads charged at 200%	20	30
	55	85
Profit margin	11	15
Standard selling price	66	100

The standard direct labour rate is £5 per hour.

During May 19X5, 5,000 Gamesmasters were sold at £60 each and 2,000 Gotchyas at £110 each. Actual costs were incurred as follows:

	£
5,050 Gamesmaster boards	26,000
5,060 sets Gamesmaster components	75,000
2,010 Gotchya boards	28,390
2,025 sets Gotchya components	56,409
10,000 assembly labour hours @ £4.90	49,000
7,000 testing labour hours at £5.10	35,700
Overheads	160,000
	430,499

There are no opening or closing stocks.

Required:

A schedule of direct material and direct labour variances for the month.

(*Welsh Joint Education Committee: GCE A–Level*)

44

Overhead and sales variances

Objectives

After you have studied this chapter, you should:

* *know how to calculate overhead budget, volume, and efficiency variances*
* *know how to calculate selling price, sales volume, and sales mix variances*

44.1 Management overheads

In Chapter 38 the problem of allocating manufacturing overheads to jobs or processes, was introduced. In the first instance the costs were collected in cost centres – normally recognisable departments of the organisation. The total costs of these centres is then applied to products or jobs as they pass through the operations of the cost centre.

Suppose that a firm collects costs into three manufacturing departments with the results as in Exhibit 44.1.

Exhibit 44.1

Department	A	B	C
	£	£	£
Fixed overhead cost	50,000	40,000	20,000
Variable overhead cost	30,000	35,000	40,000
Total overhead	80,000	75,000	60,000
Direct labour hours	10,000	30,000	15,000
Direct labour cost	£22,000	£59,000	£35,000

A decision has to be taken as to which activity, either labour of machine time, is the dominant factor in the department and will provide the most sensible basis for allocating the overhead.

In the case of Department A, machine hours appear to be the major factor and therefore overheads will be charged on the basis $\dfrac{£80,000}{20,000}$ hours = £4 per machine hour.

The firm will record for each job or process the number of machine hours taken and the overheads allocated on this total of hours at £4 per hour.

In Department B, labour appears to be the dominant feature and therefore overheads will be charged on a labour hour rate calculated at $\dfrac{£75,000}{30,000}$ hours = £2.50 per hour.

Department C does not exhibit any dominant activity and could either be expressed in a machine hour rate or a labour hour rate. Some firms where rates of pay in a department are stable and the mix of labour at different rates of pay stays the same prefer to express the overheads as a percentage of labour cost. In Department C it could be $\dfrac{£60,000}{£35,000} = 171$ per cent. Thus the labour cost for all work going through department C would be collected and overheads allocated at 171 per cent of this labour cost figure.

44.2 Predetermined rates

The usual procedure whether using standard costing or not is to predetermine the overhead absorption rates using budgeted figures both for the overhead costs and for the activity measure, whether machine or labour hours or cost. This process has a number of advantages – since not only does it allow proper current estimates to be made for things such as price quotations – but also it avoids the problem of fluctuating overhead rates at different times of the year due to seasonal variations. For example an ice-cream manufacturer is likely to be much more active in the summer months than in the winter. Because activity is low in winter the rate of absorption is likely to rise steeply since costs will not reduce proportionately. It makes more sense to view the overheads in this type of business on an annual cycle and recover the same amount of overhead in both summer and winter.

44.3 Variances in overhead recovery

As in all situations where budgeted figures are used there are almost certainly going to be variances at the end of a period. Take figures from Exhibit 44.1 for Department A as the budget, and compare them with actual performance (*see* Exhibit 44.2).

Exhibit 44.2

	Department A	
	Budget figures	Actual figures
	£	£
Fixed overhead	50,000	52,000
Variable overhead	30,000	37,000
Total overhead	80,000	89,000
Machine hours	20,000	25,000

The actual machine hours worked of 25,000 will have been used to allocate overheads to production at the rate of £4 per hour and therefore £100,000 will have been allocated. Compared to actual overheads of £89,000 this represents an over-absorption of £11,000.

Only if 22,250 machine hours had been worked would the recovery have been exactly equal to actual overhead costs.

In a cost accounting system not using standard costing the over- or under-absorption of overheads would be either:

1 transferred wholly to cost of goods sold in the profit and loss account for the period.
2 allocated between closing inventories and cost of goods sold.
3 carried forward to the net period.

The first choice would be used if the difference was felt to represent a shortfall in achievement; for example, if the number of hours worked had dropped due to bad management planning. The second would be applied if the differences were felt to be due to poor estimates of the original budgets. The third would only apply to interim accounts – not those at a year end.

Analysing the variances

The variance between the amount recovered of £100,000 and the actual overhead cost of £89,000 can be analysed into a number of constituent variances in the normal manner of standard costing. In the example we have used the variance can be due to

1   the prices paid for goods and services being different from original estimates or standards.

2   the volume of activity during the period being different from the original estimate.

These are known as the budget or spending variance for the first and a volume variance for the second reason.

Budget or spending variance

This represents the difference between the actual cost of overhead and the budgeted overhead cost adjusted to the actual level of operational activity. From Exhibit 44.2 the budget figures need to be increased to take account of the fact that activity measured in machine hours has increased from 20,000 to 25,000 hours. This will not, of course, increase the fixed overhead – only the variable overheads which we will assume increase by 25 per cent in line with the hours. This is shown as Exhibit 44.3.

	a Original budget	b Adjusted budget	c Actual	b – c Variance
Fixed overhead	50,000	50,000	52,000	(2,000)
Variable overhead	30,000	37,500	37,000	500
	80,000	87,500	89,000	(1,500)

Exhibit 44.3

The actual expenditure exceeds the adjusted budget by £1,500 which represents an adverse budget or spending variance.

Volume variance

The other factor apart from the cost of the overheads which was budgeted in developing the predetermined standard was the number of machine hours. In the example we estimated that 20,000 machine hours would be worked whereas 25,000 were actually worked. This difference would not matter if all the overheads were variable since the rate per hour would be constant at different activities. Where fixed costs are concerned, however, increasing the activity will increase the amount recovered above the level required, and if activity is below budget insufficient overhead will be recovered.

In the example the rate is split:

$$\text{Fixed} \qquad \frac{50,000}{20,000} = \qquad £2.50$$

$$\text{Variable} \qquad \frac{30,000}{20,000} = \qquad £1.50$$

$$\overline{£4.00}$$

When the machine hours increase from 20,000 to 25,000 we recover $5,000 \times £2.50 = £12,500$ more than required.

An alternative way of viewing this is to compare the amount of overheads recovered at 25,000 hours with the flexible budget for this level of activity:

Recovered 25,000 × £4 =		100,000
Budget variable cost £25,000 × 1.50	37,500	
Fixed cost	50,000	87,500
Volume variance		12,500

This variance shows that by increasing the utilisation of the fixed resources in a business considerable savings are made. The £12,500 is a favourable variance in terms of the original standard.

Summary of variances

The analysis so far shows:

	£
Standard overhead recovered at actual level of activity (25,000 × £4)	100,000
Budget or spending variance – adverse	1,500
	101,500
Volume variance – favourable	12,500
Actual level of manufacturing overheads	89,000

44.4 Assessing variances

In standard costing in an organisation where products are being manufactured it is common for the cost of the overheads to be related to the product. If in the example a Superwidget is manufactured in Department A which it is estimated requires 2 machine hours per widgit, then the standard cost of overhead per Superwidget will be $2 \times £4 = £8$.

If in the actual period a Superwidget takes less than two hours to make there will be a favourable variance which will be costed at £4 per hour. Similarly if more than two hours are taken there will be an unfavourable variance.

Using the example and assuming Department A exclusively manufactures Superwidgets, the original budget is to make 10,000 Superwidgets and the actual production of Superwidgets is 12,000.

	Department A	
	Original budget	*Actual*
	£	£
Total overhead	80,000	89,000
Machine hours	20,000	25,000
Hours per Superwidget	2	
Number of units	10,000	12,000

To produce 12,000 widgets should take 24,000 hours at the standard rate. Since the actual hours are 25,000 there is an adverse variance of 1,000 hours which costs £4 per hour (note this is both fixed and variable overhead in effect as it is money wasted through operating at below expected efficiency). Relating this adverse £4,000 variance to the other overhead variances we get:

	£
Standard cost of overheads for 12,000 actual Superwidgets produced × £8 =	96,000
Efficiency variance – adverse	4,000
Standard overhead recovered at actual level of activity	100,000
Budget variance – adverse	1,500
	101,500
Volume variance – favourable	12,500
Actual level of manufacturing overhead	89,000

44.5 Formulas for variances

The formula for each overhead variance is as follows:

Budget or spending variance = Budgeted fixed overheads – Actual fixed overheads

= BFO – AFO

Volume variance = (Actual production – Budgeted production) × Standard fixed overhead rate

= (AP – BP) × SR

Efficiency variance = (Standard hours of output – Actual hours) × Standard variable overhead rate

= (SH – AH) × SR

44.6 A comprehensive example

The data set out below refers to a cost centre for a particular period:

Budget

Variable overheads (extract)

| Output | | Cost |
In units	In standard hours	£
9,800	49,000	98,000
9,900	49,500	99,000
10,000	50,000	100,000
10,100	50,500	101,000
10,200	51,000	102,000
Fixed overheads		150,000

Budgeted volume of production 10,000 units

Standard Labour Hours/Unit = 5

Actual

Variable overhead	£104,000	
Fixed overhead	£160,000	
Direct labour hours worked	49,000	hours
Units of production	9,900	units

9,900 units of production is the equivalent of 9,900 × 5 = 49,500 standard direct labour hours.

Before making the variance calculations, it will be helpful to make some observations on the data given. The flexible budget shows that each unit of production has a standard variable overhead cost of £10. Alternatively, this can be expressed as £10 ÷ 5 = £2 per standard hour of labour. It should not be assumed that this rate of £2 would also apply to levels of production outside the range shown. These may well be step costs, such as additional supervision, which would alter the standard variable overhead rate at higher levels of output.

The fixed costs are thought likely to remain fixed provided the range of output does not extend too far above or below the budgeted volume of production. The fixed standard rate is £150,000 ÷ 50,000 = £3 per standard hour of labour, or £150,000 ÷ 10,000 = £15 per unit.

The standard unit cost for overhead is thus £10 + £15 = £25 per unit and £2 + £3 = £5 per labour hour.

This budgeted volume of production is likely to be the level of output thought of as being normal and acceptable in the long run. It is frequently referred to as the normal volume of production.

Calculation of variances

Firstly it is helpful to calculate the net variance which is to be analysed. This is developed from the standard cost of the actual units produced:

Standard cost of actual production 9,900 × £25 =	£247,500	
Actual overhead costs total	£264,000	
Total variance – Adverse	16,500	

This is broken down into efficiency, budget and volume variances as follows.

Efficiency variance

Actual units produced 9,900 × 5 hours =	49,500	(standard labour hours)	
Actual labour hours	49,000		
Labour hours saved	500		
Efficiency variance at the overhead rate per labour hour £5		Favourable	2,500

Budget variance

Budgeted overheads at actual labour hours worked of 49,000 – Variable	98,000		
Fixed	150,000		248,000
Actual overheads			264,000
Budget variance –		Adverse	16,000

Volume variance

Budgeted recovery of fixed overheads at standard activity 50,000 hrs × £3		150,000
Actual recovery of fixed overheads at actual activity 49,000 hrs × £3		147,000
Volume variance –	Adverse	3,000

Summary of variances

Efficiency	Favourable	2,500
Budget	Adverse	16,000
Volume	Adverse	3,000
	Net Adverse	16,500

Reconciliation of standard and actual cost

Standard cost of actual production 9,900 units × £25	247,500
Efficiency variance – favourable	2,500
Budgeted level of overhead cost on actual labour hours at standard 49,000 × £5	245,000
Budget variance – adverse	16,000
	261,000
Volume variance – adverse	3,000
Actual cost of overheads	264,000

44.7 Variances and management action

The calculation of variances and their explanation to managers is of no value unless the information so revealed is put to use in making decisions which change subsequent activities. The question then arises as to whether every variance needs some form of action. It is not possible to be dogmatic here, it really does depend on circumstances. In some cases, a fairly large variance may be fairly insignificant, whereas in others even a small amount may call for urgent action.

There is no doubt that variance calculations of the right type, transmitted to the right people at the right time, and which have an effect upon subsequent operations, can be of immense use. On the other hand, much of the effort put into variance calculation in many firms just goes to waste, as managers do not act on the information. This is very often because a poor 'selling' job has been done by the accounting staff to the managers concerned, in that they have not either been able to convince the managers that variance analysis is worth while, or possibly that the information provided is not really what the managers require to enable them to tackle their jobs properly.

44.8 Sales variances

The analysis of the difference between budgeted sales levels and actual levels can have an important bearing on the understanding of results. The main factors which are important in analysing sales are

(a) selling price variances
(b) volume variances
(c) mix variances.

The selling price variance measures the overall profit difference caused by budgeted unit selling price and actual unit selling price being different. If the budget was to sell 100 widgets at £5 each and the actual sales were 100 widgets of £4.50 each, there will be a profit reduction of £50 due to the adverse selling price variance of 50p per unit on the 100 units sold.

The volume variances in sales will be measured in terms of the difference in the total quantity being sold between budget and actual. The impact of changes in volume of sales on profit can only be measured if we know the profitability of the sales. This will be dealt with at gross profit level. Thus if the budget is to sell 100 widgets with a unit gross margin of £2 and the actual sales achieved are only 90 widgets then there is an adverse variance of 10 units at the margin of £2 which represents a loss of profit of £20. If several products are being sold the variance will be worked on total units actually sold in the proportion originally budgeted.

Exhibit 44.4

Product	Budget sales units	%	Budget gross margin £	Total budget margin £	Actual sales units	Actual sales in budget %
X	200	33.3	1	200	250	240
Y	200	33.3	1.50	300	190	240
Z	200	33.3	3.50	700	280	240
	600	100.0		1,200	720	720

The volume variance is calculated by company actual sales in budget percentage mix with the original budget at budget margins:

Product	Budget sales units	Actual sales in budget % units	Variance units	Budget margin £	Volume variances £
X	200	240	40	1.00	40.00
Y	200	240	40	1.50	60.00
Z	200	240	40	3.50	140.00
	600	720	120		240.00

The mix variance arises where more than one product is being sold and the different products have differing profit margins. If the proportions in which the actual sales of the products varies from budget then the overall profit will vary as a consequence.

In the example on volume variance the original budget was compared with actual sales split in the budget mix. For the mix variance these figures of actual sales in budget mix are compared with the actual sales and the differences evaluated at the budgeted gross profit margin.

Product	Actual sales in budget % units	Actual sales units	Variance units	Budget gross margin £	Mix variance £
X	240	250	+10	1.00	+ £10
Y	240	190	−50	1.50	− £75
Z	240	280	+40	3.50	+£140
	720	720	−		+ £75

The difference in mix between budget and actual has increased profit by £75 due to the influence of more sales of product Z, i.e. there is a favourable mix variance of £75.

Exhibit 44.5

			Budget				Actual		
Product	%	Units	Unit selling price £	Unit gross profit £	Total profit £	Units	Unit selling price £	Unit gross profit £	Total profit £
A	16.7	100	20	5	500	90	21	6	540
B	33.3	200	25	10	2,000	220	24	9	1,980
C	50.0	300	10	2	600	350	10	2	700
	100.0	600			3,100	660			3,220

Total variance =

Actual profit	3,220
Budget profit	3,100
Favourable variance	120

Firstly eliminate the price variance using the actual units sold as the basis:

	Actual units sold 1	Budget price 2 £	Actual price 3 £	Unit variance 3 − 2 = 4 £	Total price variance 1 × 4 = 5 £
A	90	20	21	+1	+90
B	220	25	24	−1	−220
C	350	10	10	–	–
			Adverse price variance		−130

Secondly eliminate the volume variance using the unit budgeted gross profit to evaluate the variance.

	Actual units sold 1	Actual units in budget % 2	Budget units sold 3	Variance in units 2 − 3 = 4	Budget unit gross profit 5 £	Total value variance 4 × 5 = 6 £
A	90	110	100	+10	5	+50
B	220	220	200	+20	10	+200
C	350	330	300	+30	2	+60
	660	660	600	+60		
			Favourable volume variance			+310

Finally eliminate the mix variance. This is done by comparing the actual total units sold in the mix as originally budgeted with the actual sales:

	Budget %	Actual total sales split in budget %	Actual sales units	Difference units	Budget unit gross profit	Mix variance
	1	2	3	3 − 2 = 4	5	4 × 5 = 6
A	16.7	110	90	−20	5	−100
B	33.3	220	220	–	10	–
C	50.0	330	350	+20	2	+40
		660	660			
				Adverse mix variance		−60

Summary of variance:

Adverse price variance	−130
Favourable volume variance	+310
Adverse mix variance	−60
Favourable total sales variance	+120

The gross profit margin may change for reasons other than changes in sales – for example, if the cost of materials varies from budgets or wage rates change. This type of variance has, however, already been dealt with under material and labour variances.

Main point to remember

1   The calculation of variances and their explanation to managers is of no value unless the information so revealed is put to use in making decisions which change subsequent activities.

Review questions

Advice:

Remember that the overhead variances consist of the difference between the standard costs at the actual level of activity and the actual costs. Remember also that sales variances consist of those for price, volume and mix.

It is important that you answer the parts of the questions that ask you to comment on exactly what might be behind the variances and what action is needed.

44.1 You are required to calculate the overhead variances from the following data.

(a) Budgeted for £6,000 variable overhead and 1,000 machine hours.

Actual overhead	£5,840
Actual machine hours	1,000

(b) Budgeted for £20,000 variable overhead and 5,000 machine hours.

Actual overhead	£21,230
Actual machine hours	5,000

(c) Budgeted for £12,000 fixed overhead and the actual overhead is found to be £11,770.
(d) Budgeted for £40,000 fixed overhead and the actual overhead is found to be £41,390.
(e) Budgeted production of 2,000 units in 8,000 hours. Standard variable overhead rate is £3 per hour. In fact 2,000 units are produced in 7,940 hours.
(f) Budgeted production of 5,000 units in 15,000 hours. Standard variable overhead rate is £4 per hour. In fact 4,860 units are produced in 15,000 hours.

44.2A You are required to calculate the overhead variances in the following cases:

(a) Budgeted for £37,000 fixed overhead. The actual fixed overhead turns out to be £36,420.
(b) Budgeted for production of 500 units in 250 hours. The variable overhead rate is £6 per hour. In fact 500 units are produced in 242 hours.
(c) Budgeted for £18,000 variable overhead and 9,000 machine hours. Actual overhead is £18,000 and actual machine hours 8,820.
(d) Budgeted for £9,000 variable overhead and 3,000 machine hours. Actual overhead is £8,790 and actual machine hours 3,000.
(e) Budgeted for £120,000 fixed overhead. The actual fixed overhead turns out to be £129,470.
(f) Budgeted for production of 10,000 units in 30,000 hours. Standard variable overhead rate is £8 an hour. In fact 9,880 units are produced in 30,000 hours.

44.3 You are required to calculate the overhead variances of Joseph Ltd. The budget is prepared as:

(a) Total budgeted variable overhead £400,000.
(b) Total budgeted fixed overhead £160,000.
(c) Budgeted volume of production 80,000 direct labour hours for 40,000 units.

The actual results turn out to be:

(d) Actual variable overhead £403,600.
(e) Actual fixed overhead £157,200.
(f) Actual volume 78,500 direct labour hours which resulted in 42,000 units of production.

44.4A You are required to calculate the overhead variances of Raymond Ltd. The budget is prepared as:

(a) Total budgeted variable overhead £100,000.
(b) Total budgeted fixed overhead £125,000.
(c) Budgeted volume of production 50,000 direct labour hours of 250,000 units.

The actual results turn out to be:

(d) Actual variable overhead £96,500.
(e) Actual fixed overhead £129,400.
(f) Actual volume 52,000 direct labour hours which resulted in 244,000 units.

44.5 The Grange Company had the following results for the year to 31 March 19X1. A single product – a toggle – was made by the company.

	Budget	Actual
Sales in units	125,000	150,000
Sales in £	312,500	356,250

The standard cost of manufacturing each unit was £1.50.

What are the price and volume variances on sales in 19X1?

44.6A Corporec PLC manufactures a detergent in one of its plants. The information for the year to 30 September 19X2 was as follows:

	Budget	Actual
Sales in litres	180,000	170,000
Sales in £	540,000	527,000

The standard cost of manufacturing a litre was £2.

Calculate the price and volume variances for 19X2.

44.7 The following data was collected for Molton Ltd for the year ended 31 March 19X3.

Product	Budget Selling price	Budget sales units	% Budget gross profit per unit	Budget gross profit total	Actual selling price	Actual sales unit	% Actual gross profit per unit	Actual gross profit total
	£			£	£	£		£	£
M	5	800	25	1.00	800	5.10	840	30	0.90	756
N	8	1,600	50	1.50	2,400	7.90	1,680	60	1.40	2,352
P	7	800	25	1.20	960	7.30	280	10	1.20	336
		3,200	100		4,160		2,800	100		3,444

Calculate price, volume and mix variances for 19X3.

44.8A The following information relates to Burton Company for the year to 30 June 19X6:

Product	Budget units	Sales %	Budget selling price per unit £	Budget gross profit per unit £	Actual units	Sales %	Actual unit selling price £	Actual unit gross profit £
A	400	14.3	30	5	500	20.8	29	4
B	600	21.4	25	4	400	16.7	27	5
C	1,800	64.3	40	10	1,500	62.5	39	9
	2,800	100.0			2,400	100.0		

Calculate price, volume and mix variances for 19X6.

44.9 Singleton has been operating for some years as a manufacturer of a single product, and after several years' growth has decided to form a company Singleton Ltd.

His accountant advised him that in an increasingly competitive world he really should achieve greater financial control of his business, and to assist Singleton in this objective the accountant prepared a simple manufacturing budget for the financial year ending 31 August 19X9.

The following schedule provides the detail of the budget and the actual results for the year ended 31 August 19X9. The actual results have been extracted from the ledger as at that date without any adjustments made.

	Budget £	Actual £
Raw materials consumed	80,000	90,000
Factory rent	10,000	12,500
Factory maintenance expenses	6,700	6,100
Heating and lighting	2,900	3,000
Direct labour wages	120,000	110,500
Direct expenses	5,800	6,000
Depreciation of plant and machinery	8,900	10,500
Wages, maintenance labour	18,000	24,000
Other factory overheads	12,700	9,600

Additional information

1 At 31 August 19X9 the following amounts were still owing:

	£
Direct labour wages	5,100
Heating and lighting	900
Other factory overhead	400

2 The factory rent paid covered the period from 1 September 19X8 to 30 November 19X9.
3 During the year the firm sold 90,000 units of its product at £4.50 a unit.
4 There was no work-in-progress. The stocks of finished goods were:

	£
1 September 19X8	28,900
31 August 19X9	35,000

Required:

(*a*) What is variance analysis and how can it contribute to the operating efficiency of Singleton's business?

(*b*) For the year ended 31 August 19X9 prepare:
   (*i*) A manufacturing account and a schedule of the relevant variances;
   (*ii*) A trading account.

(*c*) Write a report to advise Singleton whether the principles of budgeting can be applied to:
   (*i*) Non-manufacturing costs;
   (*ii*) The control of cash resources.

Your report should indicate in each case the potential benefits that the firm could achieve through extending its use of budgeting.

(*Associated Examining Board: GCE A–Level*)

44.10A Flint Palatignium Ltd calculates the prices of its output by adding a mark-up of 15 per cent to standard costs. These standard costs are arrived at by reference to budgeted outputs and estimated direct costs as follows:

	£ each	Standard price/rate
Materials	5.00	£1 per unit
Direct labour	2.50	£1.25 per hour
Overheads	7.50	£3.75 per direct labour hour
	15.00	
Mark-up	2.25	
Selling price	17.25	

Management accounts for April, 19X8 provide an analysis of operations as follows:

	£
Sales – at standard price	534,750
Standard margin on sales	69,750
Favourable sales price variance	8,691
	78,441
Other favourable variances	
Material price	4,662
Labour rate	600
Overhead expenditure	147
	83,850
Adverse variances	
Material usage	1,743
Labour efficiency	292
Overhead capacity	9
Actual operating profit	81,806

Materials in stock are valued at standard cost. At 1 April, 1,000 units of material were held, whereas at 30 April the stock of this material increased to 1.750 units.

Required:

(*i*) A trading account for the month of April 19X8 comparing the budgeted income and expenditure appropriate to actual output, to actual income and expenditure.

(*ii*) An explanation of the value of standard costing and variance analysis to a service business whose custom is to negotiate fixed price contracts.

(*Welsh Joint Education Committee: GCE A–Level*)

44.11A (Note: *this question covers material from both Chapters 43 and 44.*) HGW Limited produces a product called a Lexton. The standard selling price and the manufacturing costs of this product are as follows:

		£
Standard selling price per unit		<u>86</u>

Standard production costs:

Direct material	1.5 kilos at £12 per kilo	18
Direct labour	4.4 hours at £7.50 per hour	33
Variable overheads	4.4 hours at £5 per hour	<u>22</u>
		<u><u>73</u></u>

The projected production and sales for March 19X4 were 520 units.

On 1 April 19X4 the following actual figures were determined.

Sales	550 units at £85 each
Production	550 units
Direct material	785 kilos at £12.40 per kilo
Direct labour	2,400 hours at £7.80 per hour
Overheads	£12,500 (overall variance £400 adverse)

There was no opening stock of the product Lexton.

Required:
(a) Prepare an actual profit and loss statement for HGW Ltd for March 19X4
(b) Calculate the following variances and their respective sub-variances:
   (i)   sales – price and volume
   (ii) direct material – price and usage
   (iii) direct labour – rate and efficiency
(c) Prepare a statement reconciling the actual profit calculated in part (a) with the budgeted profit on actual sales. (Use the variances calculated in part (b) and the given overhead variance.)
(d) Write a report to the management outlining the factors that need to be considered when standards are being established.

(*Associated Examining Board: GCE A–Level*)

44.12A   The following diagram reflects costs under a standard costing system. Assume that all the variances are *unfavourable*. State, with reasons, which rectangle(s) represent:

(*i*)   the standard cost
(*ii*)   the actual cost
(*iii*) the total labour cost variance
(*iv*) the efficiency variance
(*v*)   the wage rate variance

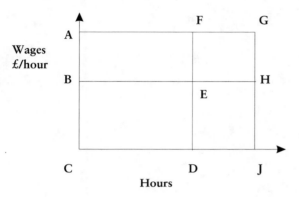

(*Edexcel Foundation, London Examinations: GCE A–Level*)

Part 9

PLANNING, CONTROL AND DECISION MAKING

45 Break-even analysis

46 Discounting techniques

Introduction

This part looks at how accounting information may be used to guide decision making within an entity.

45

Break-even analysis

Objectives

After you have studied this chapter, you should:

- *know what is meant by 'break-even'*

- *know how to use a formula in order to calculate the break-even point*

- *know how to use graphs to identify break-even point, the margin of safety, and the contribution for any level of activity*

45.1 Introduction

The level of activity achieved by a firm is of paramount importance in determining whether the firm is making a profit or loss, and the size of such profits or losses. Let us take an example to which the answer is obvious. If a firm has fixed costs of £10,000 and its total revenue is £8,000, then, no matter how much the variable costs are, the firm is bound to make a loss. A firm has to cover both its fixed costs plus its variable costs before it can make a profit. With very low revenue, as in the case already stated, a loss would be bound to be incurred.

There is, therefore, a great deal of interest in exactly how much revenue (i.e. sales) has to be earned before a profit can be made. If revenue is below fixed costs then a loss will be incurred: if revenue is below fixed costs + variable costs then a loss will still be incurred. Where revenue is greater than fixed costs plus variable costs then a profit will have been made. The question then arises – at what point does the firm stop incurring a loss and with the next unit of revenue make a profit, i.e. at what point does the firm break even or make neither a profit nor a loss?

Fixed costs stay unchanged over stated ranges in the volume of production, but variable costs are those that change with volumes in production. As revenue increases so do variable costs, so that the only item that remains unchanged is that of fixed costs. Let us look at an example of a firm showing the changing costs and revenue over differing volumes of production.

Apollo Ltd has fixed costs of £5,000. The variable costs are £2 per unit. The revenue (selling price) is £3 per unit. Looking at production in stages of 1,000 units, we can see that the figures emerge as in Exhibit 45.1.

Exhibit 45.1

No. of units	Fixed cost	Variable cost	Total cost: Variable + Fixed	Revenue (Sales)	Profit	Loss
	£	£	£	£	£	£
0	5,000	Nil	5,000	Nil		5,000
1,000	5,000	2,000	7,000	3,000		4,000
2,000	5,000	4,000	9,000	6,000		3,000
3,000	5,000	6,000	11,000	9,000		2,000
4,000	5,000	8,000	13,000	12,000		1,000
5,000	5,000	10,000	15,000	15,000	Nil	Nil
6,000	5,000	12,000	17,000	18,000	1,000	
7,000	5,000	14,000	19,000	21,000	2,000	
8,000	5,000	16,000	21,000	24,000	3,000	
9,000	5,000	18,000	23,000	27,000	4,000	

With activity of 5,000 units the firm will break even, it will make neither a profit nor a loss. Above that the firm moves into profit, below that the firm would never make a profit.

We could have calculated the **break-even point** without drawing up a schedule of costs, etc. as in Exhibit 45.1. Instead we could have said that for one unit the revenue is £3 and the variable cost is £2, so that the remaining £1 is the amount out of which the fixed costs have to come, and anything left over would be profit. The £1 is thus the 'contribution' towards fixed costs and profit. Now if the contribution was only just enough to cover fixed costs then there would be no profit, but neither would there be any loss. There are £5,000 fixed costs, so that with a contribution of £1 per unit there would have to be 5,000 units to provide a contribution of £5,000 to cover fixed costs. It could be stated as:

$$\text{Break-even point} = \frac{\text{Fixed costs}}{\text{Selling price per unit} - \text{Variable costs per unit}}$$

i.e. in the case of Apollo Ltd $\dfrac{£5,000}{£3 - £2} = \dfrac{5,000}{1} = 5,000 \text{ units}$

45.2 The break-even chart

The information given in Exhibit 45.1 can also be shown in the form of a chart. Many people seem to grasp the idea of break-even analysis rather more easily when they see it in chart form. This is particularly true of people who are not used to dealing with accounting information. We will, therefore, plot the figures from Exhibit 45.1 on a chart which is shown as Exhibit 45.2.

The use of the chart can now be looked at. It would be extremely useful if you could draw the chart as shown in Exhibit 45.2 on a piece of graph paper. The larger the scale that you use the easier it will be to take accurate readings. Plot the lines from the figures as shown in Exhibit 45.1.

Exhibit 45.2

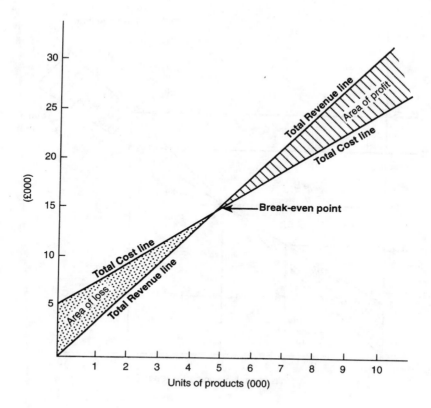

To find the break-even point in terms of units of product, draw a line straight down from the break-even point so that it meets the base line at right angles. This is shown in Exhibit 45.3 as line A, which when read off on the base line gives units of products and sales as 5,000 units.

Another item of interest that can be seen from a break-even graph is the **margin of safety,** i.e. the difference in level of activity between the break-even point and forecast activity level.

Exhibit 45.3

Now draw a line direct to the vertical £s line so that it meets that at a right angle. This is line B and shows £15,000. This means that according to the chart the break-even point is shown at 5,000 units where both costs and revenue are equal at £15,000. This is naturally the same answer as given by ordinary means in Exhibit 45.1.

As production and sales go above 5,000 units, the firm makes profits. When production and sales are above 5,000 units, the difference represents the 'safety margin', as this is the number of units in excess of the break-even point, below which the firm would incur losses.

Look at the chart again and, without consulting the book, attempt to answer the following by taking readings off your chart:

(i) What would the total costs of the firm be at (a) 2,000 units, (b) 7,000 units, (c) 8,500 units?

(Remember: take a line up from the product line for the figure needed, then from where the cost line is bisected draw a line to the £s line to meet it at right angles.)

(ii) What is the revenue for (a) 3,000 units, (b) 6,000 units, (c) 7,500 units?

Before proceeding further, look at the answers which are shown at the end of the chapter in section 45.6.

Now we will try to find the amount of profit or loss at various levels by looking at the chart in Exhibit 45.3. First let us calculate the profit made if 8,000 units are going to be made and sold. Draw a line up from the product line at right angles (shown as line C) until it bisects both the Total Cost line and the Total Revenue line, the points of intersection being shown as C1 for the Total Cost line and C2 for the Total Revenue line. Read off the amounts in £s by taking lines across to the £s vertical line until they meet it at right angles. These are shown as lines C1 and C2. The line from C1 will give a reading of £21,000 and from C2 of £24,000. As the Total Revenue exceeds the Total Costs there is a profit, and in this case the profit is £3,000.

If we now try for 3,000 units, the line drawn up from the product line will meet the Total Revenue line at point D1 and the Total Cost line at D2. Reading off to the £s line D1 shows as £9,000 whilst D2 shows as £11,000. In this case the Total Cost exceeds the Total Revenue by £2,000 and there is, therefore, a loss of £2,000.

Before you proceed further, attempt to find from your own chart the profit or loss recorded at (1) 1,000 units; (2) 4,000 units; (3) 6,500 units and (4) 8,500 units. Check your answers in section 45.6.

45.3 Changes and break-even charts

The effect of changes on profits can easily be shown by drawing fresh lines on the chart to show the changes, or intended changes, in the circumstances of the firm. Let us first of all consider what factors can bring about a change in the profits of a firm. These are:

(a) The selling price per unit could be increased (or decreased).
(b) A possible decrease (or increase) in fixed costs.
(c) A possible decrease (or increase) in variable costs per unit.
(d) Increase the volume of production and sales.

We will investigate these by starting with the same basic information for a firm and then seeing what would happen if each of the charges (a) to (d) were to happen.

The basic information, before suggested changes, is shown in Exhibit 45.4.

Exhibit 45.4

No. of units	Fixed cost	Variable cost	Total costs: Variable + Fixed	Revenue (Sales)	Profit	Loss
	£	£	£	£	£	£
100	2,000	400	2,400	900		1,500
200	2,000	800	2,800	1,800		1,000
300	2,000	1,200	3,200	2,700		500
400	2,000	1,600	3,600	3,600	Nil	Nil
500	2,000	2,000	4,000	4,500	500	
600	2,000	2,400	4,400	5,400	1,000	
700	2,000	2,800	4,800	6,300	1,500	
800	2,000	3,200	5,200	7,200	2,000	
900	2,000	3,600	5,600	8,100	2,500	

The above table shows that variable costs are £4 per unit and selling price £9 per unit.

(These figures are found by dividing the variable cost and revenue values at any number of units by that number of units. For example, dividing £400 variable cost by 100 gives £4 variable cost per unit.) We can draw a chart to incorporate this information before considering the changes being contemplated. This is shown in Exhibit 45.5.

Exhibit 45.5

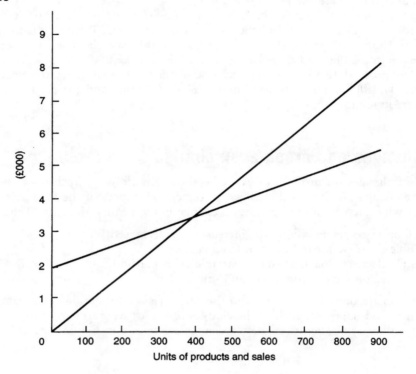

(a) Increase selling price

We can now draw an extra line onto the chart shown in Exhibit 45.5, to represent an increase in selling price. Let us suppose that the selling price could be increased by £2 per unit. This can now be shown on a break-even chart, see Exhibit 45.6. The line shown as 'New Total Revenue' could then be added. As the increased revenue would mean that costs were covered sooner, the break-even point would change. The dotted area shows the reduction in the loss area that would be incurred at the same volume of sales, whilst the shaded area shows the increase in profit at the various volumes of sales.

Exhibit 45.6

(*b*) **Reduce fixed costs**

Reverting to the original selling price of £9 (as shown in Exhibit 45.5), let us consider how things would change if fixed costs fell by £800. Exhibit 45.7 shows a new line representing New Total Costs. The reduction in loss if sales were at a low volume is represented by the dotted area whilst the shaded area shows the additional profit at various volumes of activity. The change in profit or loss will be constant at £800 over these volumes.

Exhibit 45.7

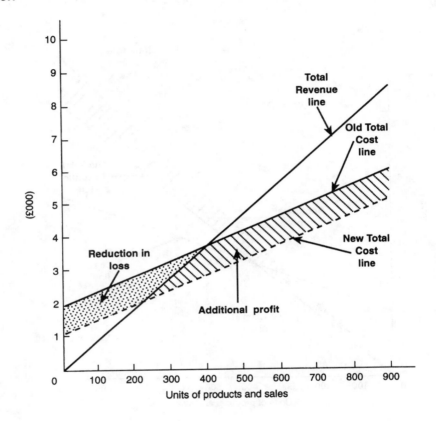

(*c*) Reduce variable costs

Reverting to the original fixed costs of £2,000, as shown in Exhibit 47.5, let us consider how things would change if variable costs per unit are reduced by £2 per unit. Exhibit 45.8 shows a new line representing New Total Costs. The dotted area shows the reduction in loss compared with the position if the costs had not changed, whilst the shaded area shows the additional profit at different levels of activity.

You will recall that a reduction in fixed costs in Exhibit 45.7 showed a constant difference of £800 compared with previously over the whole range of activity. In contrast, a reduction in variable costs (as in Exhibit 45.8) brings about different increases of profit, or reduction of loss, over the whole range of activity. The greater the activity the greater the gain with variable cost savings, whereas the gain remains constant with fixed cost savings.

Exhibit 45.8

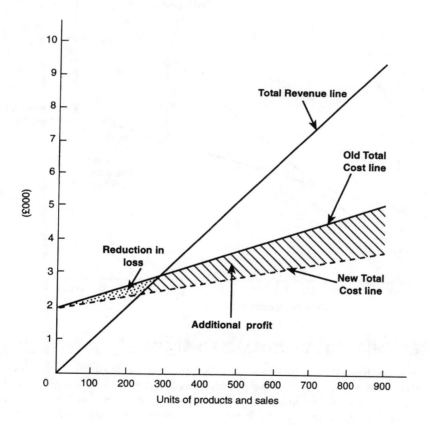

(*d*) Increased production and sales

Reverting once more to the original position as shown in Exhibit 45.5, when sales and/or production increase, all that is required is that the lines for Total Revenue and Total Costs are extended. Exhibit 45.9 shows this for an increase of 300 units. The new profit indicated will be greater than the old profit because all extra units are being sold at a profit.

Exhibit 45.9

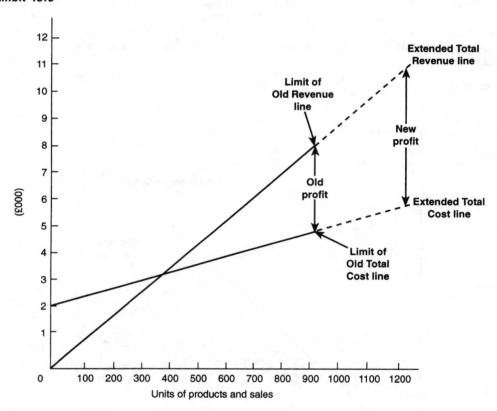

45.4 The limitations of break-even charts

In each of the cases looked at it has been assumed that only one of the factors of variable cost, fixed cost, selling price, or volume of sales has altered. This is not usually the case. An increase in price may well reduce the number sold. There may well be an increase in fixed cost which has an effect which brings down variable costs. The changes in the various factors should, therefore, be studied simultaneously rather than separately.

In addition, where there is more than one product, the proportions in which the products are sold, i.e. the product mix, can have a very important bearing on costs. Suppose that there are two products, one has a large amount of fixed costs but hardly any variable costs, and the other has a large amount of variable costs but little fixed costs. Therefore, if the proportions in which each are sold change very much this could mean that the costs and profit could vary tremendously, even though the total figures of sales stayed constant. An illustration of this can be seen in Exhibit 45.10.

Exhibit 45.10

In considering the break-even analysis we may expect that the following will occur.

Fixed costs £1,000, Variable costs: Product A £5 per unit, B £20 per unit.
Selling prices: A £10 per unit, B £30 per unit.
Expected sales: A 150, B 50. Actual sales: A 30, B90.

The expected sales are A 150 × £10 + B 50 × £30 = £3,000.
The actual sales are A 30 × £10 + B 90 × £30 = £3,000.

The total actual sales and total expected sales are the same, but sales mix is different, as are the costs and profit:

Expected:			£
Sales			3,000
Less Variable costs:	A 150 × £5 =	750	
	B 50 × £20 =	1,000	1,750
Contribution			1,250
Less Fixed costs			1,000
Net profit			£250

Actual:			
Sales			3,000
Less Variable costs:	A 30 × £5 =	150	
	B 90 × £20 =	1,800	1,950
Contribution			1,050
Less Fixed costs			1,000
Net profit			£50

Variable costs are usually taken to be in direct proportion to volume, so that 1,000 units means (say) £5,000 variable costs and therefore 2,000 units would mean £10,000 variable cost, 3,000 units equal £15,000 variable cost and so on. This is often a reasonable estimation of the situation, but may well hold true only within fairly tight limits. For instance 3,100 units could mean £16,000 costs instead of the £15,500 that it would be if a linear relationship existed. This is also true of sales, because to increase sales beyond certain points some units may be sold cheaply. Thus 1,000 units might be sold for £9,000; 2,000 units sold for £18,000; but to sell 2,200 units the revenue might be only £19,100 instead of the £19,800 (2,200 × £9) that might be expected if a linear relationship existed over all ranges.

It is assumed that everything produced is sold, and that stocks-in-trade remain constant. It would be difficult to do otherwise as both sales revenue and costs relate to one and the same measure of volume.

Another limitation, is more of a complication than a hinderance. Organisations considering a change in the level of activity outside the current range may well be faced with changed fixed costs as a result. For example, a new warehouse may need to be leased in order to cope with the extra production. In that case, the break-even graphs produced need to incorporate stepped fixed costs that increase to a new fixed level once the threshhold in activity for the higher cost has been reached. This can result in multiple break-even points.

45.5 Contribution graph

Exhibit 45.11 is a redrafting of Exhibit 45.5 that includes the addition of a line representing variable cost. It runs parallel to and below the total cost line. This is an alternative method of presentation. It highlights the total contribution. The vertical gap between the Total cost line and the Variable cost line at any particular number of units represents the contribution at that number of units.

Exhibit 45.11

45.6 Answers to questions in section 45.2

(*i*) (*a*) £9,000; (*b*) £19,000; (*c*) £22,000.

(*ii*) (*a*) £9,000; (*b*) £18,000; (*c*) £22,500.

(*1*) Loss £4,000; (*2*) Loss £1,000; (*3*) Profit £1,500; (*4*) Profit £3,500.

New terms

Break-even point (p. 636): The level of activity at which total revenues equal total costs.

Margin of safety (p. 637): The gap between the level of activity at the break-even point and the actual level of activity.

Main points to remember

1 Break-even analysis can be performed using either a formula or a graph.

2 Fixed costs are assumed to be fixed for the range of activity being considered, and variable costs per unit and sales revenue per unit are assumed to be constant within that range of activity. It is important to check whether these assumptions are correct when carrying out a break-even analysis. If they are not, the format of the analysis should be adjusted appropriately.

Review questions

Advice:

The very important concept of 'break-even' attracts quite a large number of questions. Be careful when drawing any charts, as a faulty chart will give you wrong answers for every part of your answer and you are unlikely to get marks for those wrong answers. You cannot expect examiners to assume that your faulty drawing of a graph was a simple error of draughtsmanship instead of being conceptual.

45.1 Hedges Ltd has fixed costs of £8,000. The variable costs are £4 per unit. The revenue (selling price) is £6 per unit. **You are required** (*i*) to draft a schedule as follows filling in the columns (*a*) to (*f*) for each stage of 1,000 units up to 10,000 units.

No. of units	(a) Fixed cost £	(b) Variable cost £	(c) Total cost £	(d) Revenue £	(e) Profit £	(f) Loss £
0						
1,000						
2,000						
3,000						
4,000						
5,000						
6,000						
7,000						
8,000						
9,000						
10,000						

(*ii*) **You are also required to** draw a break-even chart from the data in this schedule. Draw it carefully to scale on a piece of graph paper. Retain your answer, you will need it for some questions which follow later.

45.2 Cover up the schedule you constructed as your answer to 45.1(*i*) and look instead at the break-even chart constructed as the answer to 45.1(*ii*). **Answer the following:**

(*a*) What are the total costs at production levels of (*i*) 4,000 units; (*ii*) 7,000 units; (*iii*) 9,000 units; (*iv*) 5,500 units?

(*b*) What is the total revenue at (*i*) 3,000 units; (*ii*) 8,000 units; (*iii*) 5,500 units?

45.3A Look at your schedule in answer to 45.1 (*i*) and **answer the following:**

(*a*) What are the total costs at production levels of (*i*) 4,000 units; (*ii*) 7,000 units; (*iii*) 9,000 units; (*iv*) 5,500 units? You will have to deduce this amount as it is not shown as a figure on the schedule.

(*b*) What is the total revenue at (*i*) 3,000 units; (*ii*) 8,000 units; (*iii*) 5,500 units?

45.4 From your break-even chart for 45.1 (*ii*) **calculate** the profit or loss that will be made at levels of (*i*) 3,000 units; (*ii*) 10,000 units; (*iii*) 4,000 units; (*iv*) 7,000 units; (*v*) 8,500 units.

45.5A From the schedule in 45.1 (*i*) **calculate** the profit or loss that would be made at levels of (*i*) 3,000 units; (*ii*) 10,000 units; (*iii*) 4,000 units; (*iv*) 7,000 units; (*v*) 8,500 units (this last figure will have to be deduced as it is not a figure on the schedule).

45.6 Polemic Ltd manufacture and sell a single product. The following information is available for three financial years ending 30 September.

	Price per unit £	Unit volume 000s
Sales		
Actual 19X1	130	50
Forecast 19X2	129	52
Forecast 19X3	128.5	53

Costs per unit Produced	Actual 19X1 £	Forecast 19X2 £	19X3 £
Direct materials	50	55	55
Direct labour	30	31.5	33
Variable production overhead	10	11	12
Direct expenses	5	5	6
Variable sales overhead	15	16	16

Other costs for the year	£ 000s	£ 000s	£ 000s
Fixed production overhead	50	55	55
Other fixed overhead	200	220	220

Additional information
1 When the management of Polemic prepared its direct labour forecast unit cost for 19X2 and 19X3, direct wages were increased only by the forecast rate of inflation.

2 The trade union representatives of the production workers wished to press for a greater wage increase. They suggested that:

(*i*) Direct wages be increased at twice the rate of inflation. The effect of this would be to increase direct labour costs per unit as follows:

	19X2	19X3
	£	£
Direct labour	33.0	35.0

(*ii*) Unit selling prices be increased in order to cover the increased labour costs.

3   It is to be assumed that all expense and revenue relationships will be unchanged except where indicated.

Required:

(*a*) A schedule for 19X1, 19X2 and 19X3 for Polemic Ltd showing:

  (*i*)   the break-even points;
  (*ii*) the net profit for each year.
  Base your calculations on the original labour costs.

(*b*) A graph showing a break-even point for 19X2.

(*c*) Advise Polemic Ltd's management as to their response to the trade union's claim for higher wages. Include relevant financial analysis.

(*d*) Explain the limitation of break-even analysis.

(*Associated Examining Board: GCE A–Level*)

45.7A   The relationship between income/cost/volume suggests that there are four ways by which profit can be increased. These are:

1   Increase unit selling price.
2   Decrease unit variable cost.
3   Decrease fixed costs.
4   Increase volume.

Assume that the current situation for a product is as follows:

Sales volume	1,000 units
Selling price	£2 each
Variable cost	£1 per unit
Fixed costs	£500

You are required to:

(*a*) draw **four** separate break-even charts showing the effect of the following changes on the current situation:

  (*i*)   a 10 per cent increase in volume,
  (*ii*)   a 10 per cent increase in unit selling price,
  (*iii*) a 10 per cent decrease in unit variable cost,
  (*iv*)   a 10 per cent reduction in fixed costs.

(*b*) Use your charts to state the additional profit resulting from **each** change.

(*Northern Examinations and Assessment Board: GCE A–Level*)

45.8 At the monthly senior management meeting of Hampshire plc on 1 May 19X0, various suggestions were made to improve the profit to be made by selling the firm's single product in the last quarter of the year ending 30 September 19X0. The product is not subject to seasonal demand fluctuations, but there are several competitors producing similar items. In the first quarter of the year a suggestion was made that profit could be improved if the selling price were reduced by 5 per cent, and this was put into effect at the beginning of the second quarter. As the new price undercut that of the rival firms, demand increased, and the firm's break-even point was reduced.

The following suggestions have now been raised:

(*i*) Differentiate the product from its rivals by giving it a more distinctive shape, colour and packaging. This would increase material costs per unit by £0.30, but selling price would not be raised. Demand is then predicted to rise by 10 per cent;

(*ii*) Improve the quality of the product by strengthening it and giving it a one-year guarantee – material costs would then increase by £0.15 per unit and labour costs by £0.30 per unit. Selling price would rise by £0.40 per unit, and demand increase by 7 per cent;

(*iii*) Further reduce the selling price by 10 per cent – demand to rise by 20 per cent;

(*iv*) Pay commission plus salaries instead of fixed salaries only to all sales staff. Variable selling costs would then rise by £0.20 per unit, but fixed costs would fall by £4,100 per quarter;

(*v*) Subcontract the making of some components, and close the department responsible, making six staff redundant at an estimated cost to the firm of £12,000. 30,000 components are currently made per quarter. Each component's variable cost is £0.55. They can be bought from a recently established firm for £0.60 per unit. The department's share of the firm's fixed costs is 20 per cent and £2,500 fixed costs per quarter would cease to arise if the department were to be closed.

Data for:	First quarter	Second quarter
Number of units produced and sold	9,000	10,800
	£	£
Selling price per unit	14	13.30
Materials per unit	3.65	3.65
Labour per unit	2.10	2.10
Variable factory overhead per unit	1.40	1.40
Variable selling costs per unit	0.85	0.85
Fixed factory overhead	21,375	21,375
Fixed selling and administration costs	16,125	16,125

Required:

A Calculate the profit made in each of the first and second quarters, showing clearly the contribution per unit in each case.

B Draw one break-even chart showing the total costs and total revenues for the first and second quarters. You should label clearly the two break-even points and margins of safety.

C Taking each suggestion independently, calculate the profit that might be made in the last quarter if each of them were to be implemented.

D Discuss the implications for the firm of undertaking suggestions (*i–iv*), and for the firm and the local community of undertaking suggestion (*v*).

E Explain to the senior managers how, while break-even analysis is useful, it has limitations.

(*University of Oxford Delegacy of Local Examinations: GCE A–Level*)

45.9A You are employed by Monarch Ltd which manufactures specialist hydraulic seals for the aircraft industry. The company has developed a new seal with the following budgeted data.

	£
Variable cost per unit	
Direct materials	8
Direct labour	4
Variable overheads	4
	16

The draft budget for the following year is as follows.

Production and sales	60,000 units

		£
Fixed cost:	Production	260,000
	Administration	90,000
	Selling, marketing and distribution	100,000
Contribution		840,000

Certain departmental managers within the company believe there is room for improvement on the budgeted figures, and the following options have been suggested.

(*i*) The sales manager has suggested that if the selling price was reduced by 10 per cent, then an extra 30 per cent units could be sold. The purchasing manager has indicated that if material requirements were increased in line, then a material price reduction of 6.25 per cent could be negotiated. With this additional output, fixed production costs would increase by £30,000, administration by £5,000 and selling, marketing and distribution by £10,000. Other costs would remain unchanged.

(*ii*) The export manager has suggested that if the company increased overseas marketing by £15,000 then exports would increase from 15,000 units to 17,000 units. With this suggestion, distribution costs would increase by £12,000, and all other costs would remain unchanged.

(*iii*) The marketing manager has suggested that if an extra £40,000 were spent on advertising, then sales quantity would increase by 25 per cent. The purchasing manager has indicated that in such circumstances, material costs would reduce by £0.30 per unit. With this suggestion fixed production costs would increase by £25,000, administration by £4,000 and other selling, marketing and distribution costs by £7,000. All other costs would remain unchanged.

(*iv*) The managing director believes the company should be aiming for a profit of £486,000. He asks what the selling price would be per unit if marketing were increased by £50,000, this leading to an estimated increase in sales quantity of 30 per cent? Other fixed costs would increase by £67,000, whilst material prices would decrease by 6.25 per cent per unit. All other costs would remain unchanged.

Required:

A Taking each suggestion independently, compile a profit statement for options (*i*) to (*iii*), showing clearly the contribution per unit in each case. For suggestion (*iv*), calculate the selling price per unit as requested by the managing director.

B Calculate the break-even quantity in units if the Managing Director's suggestion were implemented. Draw a contribution/sales graph to illustrate your calculations.
   Read from the graph the profit if 60,000 units were sold.

C Whilst marginal costing has a number of applications, it also has disadvantages. In a report to the managing director, outline the main applications of marginal costing and explain its disadvantages.

(*University of Oxford Delegacy of Local Examinations: GCE A–Level*)

45.10 Magwitch Limited's finance director produced the following forecast break-even chart for the year ending 31 May 19X1:

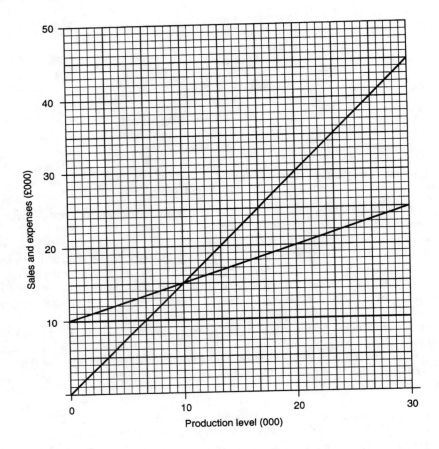

During the year the company produced and sold 20,000 units, and both revenue and expenses were 10 per cent higher than forecast.

Compeyson plc has made an agreed takeover bid for the company at a value of twelve times the net profit for the year ending 31 May 19X1.

Magwitch's assets and liabilities are to be taken over at their balance sheet values, with the exception of fixed assets, which are to be revalued at £40,000.

The summarised balance sheets of Magwitch Limited and Compeyson plc at the takeover date of 31 May 19X1 are as follows:

	Magwitch £000	Compeyson £000
Fixed assets	32	160
Current assets	65	340
Short-term liabilities	(26)	(110)
	71	390
Share capital (£1 shares)	40	200
Reserves	31	190
	71	390

The terms of the takeover are that Compeyson plc will give three of its shares (value £1.80 each) for every two shares in Magwitch Limited, plus a cash payment to make up the total agreed takeover price.

Magwitch Limited will cease to trade on 31 May 19X1, and its assets and liabilities will be assumed by Compeyson plc. Any goodwill arising is to be written off immediately against reserves.

(a) Draw up a summarised profit and loss account for Magwitch Limited for the year ended 31 May 19X1.

(b) Draw up a balance sheet for Compeyson plc after the takeover of Magwitch Limited has taken place.

(c) Calculate how many shares and how much cash would be received by a holder of 6,000 shares in Magwitch Limited as a result of the takeover.

(*Edexcel Foundation, London Examinations: GCE A–Level*)

45.11A

(a) How far is it true to state that a company's break-even point occurs where the contribution just equals the fixed costs?

(b) A company's detailed information of costs and sales has been destroyed because of a computer malfunction. The following data has, however, been gleaned from various sources:

Sales volume (units)	10,000	12,000
Costs (£):		
direct materials	30,000	36,000
direct labour	28,000	33,000
overheads	20,500	24,100

Selling price per unit at all volumes of output is £12.30.

Calculate:

(i) the cost of an additional 2,000 units of output;
(ii) the variable costs of 10,000 units of output;
(iii) the fixed element – if any – of each component cost;
(iv) the break-even point.

(*Edexcel Foundation, London Examinations: GCE A–Level*)

46

Discounting techniques

Objectives

After you have studied this chapter, you should:

- *know why interest rates are important in financial decision making*

- *understand the difference between simple and compound interest*

- *know what is meant by and be able to calculate the annual percentage rate (APR)*

- *be able to calculate the present value of a series of cash flows*

- *be able to calculate and compare the net present value (NPV), internal rate of return (IRR), and payback of a series of cash flows*

- *be able to choose between alternative projects on the basis of NPV, IRR and payback*

- *understand and compute the effects of taxation upon capital project appraisal*

- *know what an annuity is and be able to calculate the value of ordinary annuities*

- *be able to calculate the annualised amount of a series of cash flows and select between alternative projects on that basis*

- *know the difference between operating and finance leases and be able to calculate the relevant figures for use in financial statements*

46.1 Different values

Would you rather be given £10 today or in 12 months' time? As time passes, money loses value due to the effects of inflation. When a transaction involves a delay in payment for the item purchased (e.g. a new car), the loss in value of the amount to be paid will be recovered by the seller charging the buyer interest. The delay also represents a period during which the seller could have invested the money and earned interest. This 'opportunity cost' of interest lost will also be charged to the buyer. The seller may have had to borrow money in order to provide the item purchased, and the interest cost incurred will be charged to the buyer. The seller will also add interest to the amount due in order to compensate for risk – the risk that the buyer will not pay the debt when due. Thus, the amount the buyer will be required to pay depends upon both the market rate of interest and the degree of risk in the debt, as perceived by the seller.

46.2 Interest rates

If a seller adds 10 per cent interest to a debt of £100, the required payment if made 1 year later is £100 + (10 per cent × £100 = £10) = £110. The interest in this case is known as 'simple interest' – 'simple' because the rate (10 per cent) is for one year, which matches the length of the debt. Interest rates generally indicate the percentage of the amount due that will be charged as interest if the debt is unpaid for a year.

If a 10 per cent interest rate is used, but the buyer is given two years to pay the debt, the second year's interest must be based on the amount due at the end of the first year – £110 (i.e. the original debt of £100 plus the £10 interest charged for the first year). The interest for the second year is therefore 10 per cent × £110 = £11, and the amount due at the end of the second year is the original debt (£100) + the first year's interest (£10) + the second year's interest (£11) = £121. This is known as 'compound interest' – 'compound' because the amount of interest due for years beyond the first year is calculated on the basis of how much is owed at the start of each year, i.e. the original amount plus all the interest to that date.

If the buyer offers to pay £121 in two years' time, instead of paying £100 today, providing the seller charges debtors 10 per cent interest, the value to the seller of the £121 in two years' time is £100 today. However, if the seller uses a 20 per cent interest rate, the £121 will only be worth £84.03. On the other hand, if the seller uses a 5 per cent interest rate, the £121 will be worth £109.75. These different values can be checked by applying the same approach as with the 10 per cent interest rate.

At 20 per cent, the interest for the first year on a debt of £84.03 will be £16.80, and the amount due at the end of one year will be £100.84. The second year's interest will be 20 per cent of £100.84, i.e. £20.17, and the total due at the end of the second year will be £121.

At 5 per cent, the interest for the first year on a debt of £109.75 will be £5.49, and the amount due at the end of one year will be £115.24. The second year's interest will be 5 per cent of £115.24, i.e. £5.76, and the total due at the end of the second year will be £121.

46.3 Simple interest

Simple interest on a debt of one year is, therefore, calculated using the formula:

$$\text{Amount of interest (Y)} = \text{Amount due (A)} \times \text{Interest rate (r)}$$

However, simple interest also applies to periods of less than a year. In order to calculate the interest on a shorter period, the period in question is expressed as a proportion of a year, and the formula is adjusted to:

$$\text{Amount of interest (Y)} = \text{Amount due (A)} \times \text{interest rate (r)} \times \text{fraction of a year (t)}$$

Example

Interest on a debt of £100 is to be charged at 10 per cent per annum. The debt will be repaid after 60 days. The interest due can be calculated using the formula:

$$Y = £100 \times 10\% \times (60/365) = £10 \times (60/365) = £1.64$$

46.4 Annual percentage rate (APR)

Sometimes, an interest rate that appears to be a 'simple interest' rate does not actually represent the 'real' rate charged. This can arise where, for example, a 10 per cent rate is charged on a debt for a year, but part of the debt must be repaid after six months, and the interest charge ignores the fact that there is early payment of part of the debt. This 'real' rate is known as the Annual Percentage Rate (APR). Hire purchase agreements are examples of debts where APR must be calculated in order to determine the 'real' cost incurred by the debtor.

Example

Interest on a debt of £100 is to be charged at 10 per cent per annum. However, £40 must be paid after six months, and the balance plus the interest at the end of the year.

			£
• The interest to be paid is	10% of £100	= Y	= 10
• The amount due is	£100 for ½ year	=	50
	£60 for ½ year	=	30
• The equivalent amount due for a year is		= q	= 80
• The 'real' rate of interest		= r	= Y/q
			= 10/80
			= 12.5% = the APR

Another typical example of APR arises when a business is owed money by its customers and it decides to sell the debt to a factor in order to obtain cash now. In these cases, the factor will pay the business an amount equal to the amount of the debt less a discount.

Example

A business is due £10,000 from a customer and the customer has agreed to make the payment in 90 days' time. The business approaches a debt factor who agrees to pay the amount due now, less a discount rate of 10 per cent. Applying the formula for debts of less than one year

Amount of interest (Y) = Amount due (A) × Interest rate (r) × Fraction of a year (t)

the discount charged is:

$$Y = £10,000 \times 10\% \times (90/365) = £1,000 \times (90/365) = £246.58$$

The debt factor will pay the business £10,000 less £246.58, i.e. £9,753.42. However, £246.58 does not represent a charge based on the amount of the advance (£9,753.42). Rather, it is based on the higher original amount of the customer's debt of £10,000. As a proportion of the £9,753.42 advanced by the debt factor, £246.58 represents an interest rate of 10.25 per cent. This can be seen by rewriting the formula for debts of less than one year to:

$$r = \frac{Y}{(A \times t)}$$

which, substituting the example values, gives:

$$r = \frac{246.58}{9,753.42 \times (90/365)}$$

$$= 10.25\%$$

A similar approach must be adopted with *bills of exchange* and *trade bill* interest rate calculations.

46.5 Compound interest

When more than a year is involved, the interest due is compounded, i.e. each year's interest charge is based on the amount outstanding, including all previous years' interest, at the beginning of the year. The graph shown in Exhibit 46.1 illustrates the difference between two investments of £1,000 at 10 per cent per annum for 20 years. In the first case, the interest is reinvested at the same 10 per cent rate and the final value of the investment is £6,727.50. In the other case, the interest is withdrawn as soon as it is paid, leaving only the original £1,000 invested, which is also the final value of the investment. However, 20 times £100, i.e. £2,000, has been received in interest over the 20 years, resulting in the overall value (ignoring inflation) being £3,000.

Exhibit 46.1

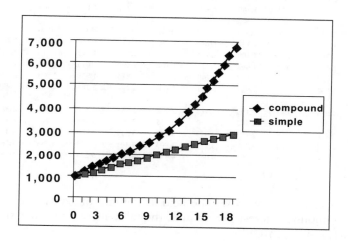

The final value of an investment that is subject to compound interest can be calculated laboriously by calculating the value at the end of the first year, calculating the interest on that amount for the next year, adding that interest to the amount at the start of the year to get the amount at the end of the year, and repeating the process for each year. However, there is a formula which enables the amount to be calculated swiftly:

Final value (V) = Amount invested (I) × $(1 + r)^n$, where n = the number of years

Example

£1,000 invested today for five years at 10 per cent would have a final value (V) of:

$$
\begin{aligned}
V &= £1,000 \times (1+0.10)^5 \\
&= £1,000 \times (1.1)^5 \\
&= £1,000 \times 1.61051 \\
&= £1,610.51
\end{aligned}
$$

Calculations of this type are easily performed on most calculators, or by the use of tables. Where such calculations are performed regularly, it is quite common for a spreadsheet to be used to perform the calculation, often using the structure of a compound interest table within the spreadsheet to make it clear how the numbers used were derived. A compound interest table is included in Appendix II, but a shorter example is reproduced in Exhibit 46.2.

Exhibit 46.2 An example of a compound interest table

Compound Interest Table
Period
Length £1 compounded at the end of each period at the interest rate shown

n	1%	2%	3%	4%	5%	6%	7%	8%	9%	10%	n
1	1.010	1.020	1.030	1.040	1.050	1.060	1.070	1.080	1.090	1.100	1
2	1.202	1.040	1.061	1.082	1.103	1.124	1.145	1.166	1.188	1.210	2
3	1.030	1.061	1.093	1.125	1.158	1.191	1.225	1.260	1.295	1.331	3
4	1.041	1.082	1.126	1.170	1.216	1.262	1.311	1.360	1.412	1.464	4
5	1.051	1.104	1.159	1.217	1.276	1.338	1.403	1.469	1.539	1.611	5
6	1.062	1.126	1.194	1.265	1.340	1.419	1.501	1.587	1.677	1.772	6
7	1.072	1.149	1.230	1.316	1.407	1.504	1.606	1.714	1.828	1.949	7
8	1.083	1.172	1.267	1.369	1.477	1.594	1.718	1.851	1.993	2.144	8
9	1.094	1.195	1.305	1.423	1.551	1.689	1.838	1.999	2.172	2.358	9
10	1.105	1.219	1.344	1.480	1.629	1.791	1.967	2.159	2.367	2.594	10

n	11%	12%	13%	14%	15%	16%	17%	18%	19%	20%	n
1	1.110	1.120	1.130	1.140	1.150	1.160	1.170	1.180	1.190	1.200	1
2	1.232	1.254	1.277	1.300	1.323	1.346	1.369	1.392	1.416	1.440	2
3	1.368	1.405	1.443	1.482	1.521	1.561	1.602	1.643	1.685	1.728	3
4	1.518	1.574	1.630	1.689	1.749	1.811	1.874	1.939	2.005	2.074	4
5	1.685	1.762	1.842	1.925	2.011	2.100	2.192	2.288	2.386	2.488	5
6	1.870	1.974	2.082	2.195	2.313	2.436	2.565	2.700	2.840	2.986	6
7	2.076	2.211	2.353	2.502	2.660	2.826	3.001	3.185	3.379	3.583	7
8	2.305	2.476	2.658	2.853	3.059	3.278	3.511	3.759	4.021	4.300	8
9	2.558	2.773	3.004	3.252	3.518	3.803	4.108	4.435	4.785	5.160	9
10	2.839	3.106	3.395	3.707	4.046	4.411	4.807	5.234	5.695	6.192	10

Example

If you want to know how much will be held at the end of seven years if you invest £100 at 6 per cent compound interest per annum, the table in Exhibit 46.2 shows that it would be £100 times 1.504 = £150.40.

Sometimes, interest accumulates more frequently than once a year. It will often be paid every three months. If so, the rate of interest used in the formula must be changed to reflect this. To do this, the number of periods is multiplied by the number of payments being made each year, and the interest rate used is divided by the same amount. The formula can then be used with these adjusted values.

Example

If £100 is invested for two years at 12 per cent compound interest paid quarterly, the interest rate used in the calculation is 3 per cent (i.e. 12 per cent divided by four). The number of periods to use is eight (i.e. two multiplied by four). Looking up the table, the amount accumulated at the end of the two years will be £126.70. Compare that to the compounded amount if interest was paid annually, £125.40. The difference is very small. However, the investment was for a short period of time. Had it been for a longer period, the difference would have become progressively greater. When large amounts of money are being invested over a long period, an increased frequency of interest payments will have a significant effect upon the amount of interest received.

Over time, most investments change their value. Investments in the stock market or in houses, for example, are made without knowing what the rate of return (interest) will be. When the investment is ended and the final amount received is known, it is often useful to know what the rate of return over the period of the investment was. This can be done using the table. If an investment was made for five years, it is the five year row in the table that would be consulted. In that row, you would search for the number that represented the proportion that the final amount represented of the initial investment. The interest rate column in which that proportion lay would represent the average rate of return on the investment.

Example

If a house were bought for £100,000 on 1 January 19X1 and sold for £140,300 on 31 December 19X5, a five-year investment was made. The proportion that £140,300 represents of the £100,000 invested is 1.403:1. Looking up the table in the row where $n = 5$, a value of 1.403 can be seen in the 7 per cent interest rate column. The rate of return is equivalent to 7 per cent compound per annum. Where the proportion calculated is not shown in the table, the table can be used to identify an approximate rate which can then be adjusted in order to arrive at the accurate rate.

Example

If a house were bought for £100,000 on 1 January 19X1 and sold for £160,000 on 31 December 19X4, a four-year investment was made. The proportion that £160,000 represents of the £100,000 invested is 1.6:1. Looking up the table in the row where $n = 4$, a value of 1.574 can be seen in the 12 per cent column and 1.630 can be seen in the 13 per cent column. The difference between these two values is 0.056 (i.e. 1.630 − 1.574). The difference between 1.574 and the amount being searched for of 1.6 is 0.026, which represents 46 per cent of the total difference of 0.056 between the 12 per cent and 13 per cent amounts. Adding 0.46 to 12 produces a percentage return of 12.46 per cent.

Rather than using the tables to identify the rate of return, a formula can be used which is the final value formula [Final value (V) = Amount invested (I) $\times (1 + r)^n$, where n = the number of years] rewritten to identify r:

$$r = \sqrt[n]{(V/I)} - 1$$

Substituting the values from the last example:

$$r = \sqrt[4]{(160,000/100,000)} - 1$$

$$= 12.46\%$$

46.6 Present value

Present value is the amount that a future cash flow is worth in terms of today's money. The £1,000 invested in the previous section for five years at 10 per cent compound resulted a final amount of £1,610.51, but what would be the value of that £1,610.51 at the date of the initial investment (i.e. today)? If it were known, it would be possible to tell whether the investment might be worthwhile.

To calculate present value, the formula to use has the same variables as that used to calculate compound interest, but it is rewritten to reflect that it is really the reciprocal of the compound interest formula:

$$\text{Amount invested (I)} = \frac{\text{Final value (V)}}{(1 + r)^n}$$

However, it would be more appropriate to describe the amount calculated as 'present value' rather than 'amount invested' and the formula becomes:

$$\text{Present value (PV)} = \frac{\text{Final value (V)}}{(1 + r)^n}$$

Example

A bank is offering a guaranteed return at the end of five years of £1,500 for every £1,000 invested. If you could usually expect to obtain a rate of interest of 8 per cent on your investments, what would be the present value of investing £1,000 in the bank?

$$PV = \frac{£1,500}{(1.08)^5} = £1,020.87$$

The 8 per cent interest rate used in this example is generally referred to as the 'discount rate', i.e. the rate at which the future flow of cash is discounted to arrive at its present value. As with compound interest, present value tables are generally used, and will often be created and used on spreadsheets. A present value table is included in Appendix II, but an extract is reproduced in Exhibit 46.3.

Exhibit 46.3 *An example of a present value table*

Present Value Table

Period
Length PV of £1 discounted over the period at the rate shown

n	1%	2%	3%	4%	5%	6%	7%	8%	9%	10%	n
1	0.990	0.980	0.971	0.961	0.952	0.943	0.935	0.926	0.917	0.909	1
2	0.980	0.961	0.943	0.925	0.907	0.890	0.873	0.857	0.842	0.826	2
3	0.971	0.942	0.915	0.889	0.864	0.840	0.816	0.794	0.772	0.751	3
4	0.961	0.924	0.889	0.855	0.823	0.792	0.763	0.735	0.708	0.683	4
5	0.951	0.906	0.863	0.822	0.784	0.747	0.713	0.681	0.650	0.621	5
6	0.942	0.888	0.838	0.790	0.746	0.705	0.666	0.630	0.596	0.564	6
7	0.933	0.871	0.813	0.760	0.711	0.665	0.623	0.583	0.547	0.513	7
8	0.923	0.853	0.789	0.731	0.677	0.627	0.582	0.540	0.502	0.467	8
9	0.914	0.837	0.766	0.703	0.645	0.592	0.544	0.500	0.460	0.424	9
10	0.905	0.820	0.744	0.676	0.614	0.558	0.508	0.463	0.422	0.386	10

n	11%	12%	13%	14%	15%	16%	17%	18%	19%	20%	n
1	0.901	0.893	0.885	0.877	0.870	0.862	0.855	0.847	0.840	0.833	1
2	0.812	0.797	0.783	0.769	0.756	0.743	0.731	0.718	0.706	0.694	2
3	0.731	0.712	0.693	0.675	0.658	0.641	0.624	0.609	0.593	0.579	3
4	0.659	0.636	0.613	0.592	0.572	0.552	0.534	0.516	0.499	0.482	4
5	0.593	0.567	0.543	0.519	0.497	0.476	0.456	0.437	0.419	0.402	5
6	0.535	0.507	0.480	0.456	0.432	0.410	0.390	0.370	0.352	0.335	6
7	0.482	0.452	0.425	0.400	0.376	0.354	0.333	0.314	0.296	0.279	7
8	0.434	0.404	0.376	0.351	0.327	0.305	0.285	0.266	0.249	0.233	8
9	0.391	0.361	0.333	0.308	0.284	0.263	0.243	0.226	0.209	0.194	9
10	0.352	0.322	0.295	0.270	0.247	0.227	0.208	0.191	0.176	0.162	10

Frequently, the cash flows arising from an investment arise throughout the period of the investment, not simply at the end. To calculate the overall present value of all the cash flows, each is calculated separately, and all the resulting present values are added together.

Example

An investment of £10,000 is made for five years. The net cash flows at the end of each of the five years are:

Period	Amount £
1	2,000
2	3,000
3	4,000
4	3,000
5	1,000

If the discount rate used is 10 per cent, the overall present value of the net cash flows is calculated as:

Period	Amount £	Discount factor 10%	Present value £
1	2,000	0.909	1,818
2	3,000	0.826	2,478
3	4,000	0.751	3,004
4	3,000	0.683	2,049
5	1,000	0.621	621
		Overall present value of cash flows	9,970

When compared to the initial investment of £10,000, it can be seen that this investment would lose £30 (i.e. £10,000 − £9,970). To make it easier to see this figure, these calculations usually incorporate the initial investment (which is not discounted as it is already at today's value) and produce a figure known as the **net present value**, or **NPV**. Incorporating the initial investment into this example produces the following table:

Period	Amount £	Discount factor 10%	Present value £
0	(10,000)	1.000	(10,000)
1	2,000	0.909	1,818
2	3,000	0.826	2,478
3	4,000	0.751	3,004
4	3,000	0.683	2,049
5	1,000	0.621	621
		Net present value	(30)

Many businesses have a rate of return that they require to achieve on investments. If a potential investment is not expected to achieve that rate of return, the investment will not be made. It is always possible to adopt the NPV approach in order to determine whether the return exceeds the required rate (which is shown by a positive NPV). However, it is often useful to know what the actual rate of return is – the proposed investment may, for example, require that some additional financing be obtained that would be at a higher rate than the business's normal rate of return.

The actual rate of return is known as the **internal rate of return**, or **IRR**. It is the discount rate that results in an NPV of zero. It can be calculated very easily using a spreadsheet – a table similar to the one above would be written in the spreadsheet, but the discount factor would be left blank. Then, by instigating an appropriate command, the spreadsheet would identify and insert the IRR into the table so as to arrive at an NPV of zero.

However, spreadsheets are not always available and IRR may need to be calculated manually. The method to adopt is similar to that adopted in the final example in section 46.5 – a guess is made as to an appropriate IRR and the NPV calculation is made using that rate. If the NPV is positive, a higher rate is selected (a lower rate is selected if the NPV is negative) and the NPV is again calculated. This continues until one positive NPV and one negative NPV are identified. The absolute difference between the two NPVs is calculated and the proportion of that difference that represents the difference between the NPV of the lower of the rates involved and zero is added to the lower rate to produce the IRR.

Example

You have been asked if you would be willing to lend £10,000 to a taxi company in order that it may expand its fleet of taxis. The money would be repaid at the rate of £3,000 per annum for four years. What is the IRR?

Step one is to select a rate that may be approximately correct. There is no simple way to select such a rate, and what would often be done is that the same rate would be used as the first step with most IRR calculations, and then the choice of the second rate to use would depend on how close to zero the first attempt came, and on whether the NPV it gave was positive or negative. If an 8 per cent rate is used, the following results:

Period	Amount £	Discount factor 8%	Present value £
0	(10,000)	1.000	(10,000)
1	3,000	0.926	2,778
2	3,000	0.857	2,571
3	3,000	0.794	2,382
4	3,000	0.735	2,205
		Net present value	(64)

Using the 8 per cent rate resulted in an NPV that was less than zero. The next rate chosen must, therefore, be less than 8 per cent. A 7 per cent rate produces the following:

Period	Amount £	Discount factor 7%	Present value £
0	(10,000)	1.000	(10,000)
1	3,000	0.935	2,805
2	3,000	0.873	2,619
3	3,000	0.816	2,448
4	3,000	0.763	2,289
		Net present value	161

Therefore, the IRR lies between 7 per cent and 8 per cent. The difference between the two NPVs is 225 (i.e. 64 + 161). A zero NPV will result if the rate is set to 7 per cent plus 161/225 (as 7 per cent is 161 away from zero). Expressed as a decimal, 161/225 = 0.72 and the IRR is, therefore, 7.72 per cent.

46.7 Annuities

Annuities are an income generating investment whereby, in return for the payment of a single lump sum, the 'annuitant' receives regular amounts of income over a predefined term (i.e. number of years). The frequency of the payments to the annuitant will depend upon the agreement reached, but would generally be either monthly, quarterly, six-monthly or annually. The timing of the payments to the annuitant vary from annuity to annuity – for example, some involve the regular payments to the annuitant being made at the start of each period, others have the payments at the end of each period. In some cases, the original investment will be repaid at the end of the agreed term, in others it is not. It is also possible for the agreement to include the annuitant making a number of payments, rather than paying everything in a single lump sum.

There is a large range of possible arrangements that can be incorporated into an annuity, and it is not possible to describe how to deal with each of them. However, by concentrating upon one specific form of annuity – one in which equal payments are made to the annuitant at the end of each period – the basic principles to be applied can be identified. These principles can then be applied to more complex situations and, as a result, there should be very few circumstances when, with a little thought, it should not be possible to perform the appropriate calculation.

Many forms of business transaction are annuity-like, and a knowledge of the calculation of annuities can be useful, for example when considering rental agreements, hire purchase agreements, and leases.

46.8 Calculation of the value of ordinary annuities

When calculating the value of an annuity, it can be helpful to think of it as being similar to the calculation of compound interest, but one period in arrears. Thus, when considering compound interest, it would be assumed that an investment of £1,000 in year two was made at the start of the year. For an annuity, all the payments are assumed to arise at the end of a year, and interest on a payment made in year two would only start to accumulate during year three – there would be no interest in year two on that part of the annuity.

The following formula may be used to calculate the value of an annuity:

$$\text{Value} = \text{Annuity per period} \times \frac{(1 + r)^n - 1}{r}$$

It can be applied to calculate the final value of a series of regular payments where a set rate of interest is being earned. For example, if £1,000 is being saved at the end of each year for five years and the interest rate is 10 per cent, the amount accumulated at the end of the fifth year will be:

$$
\begin{aligned}
\text{Value} &= £1,000 \times \frac{(1 + 0.10)^n - 1}{0.10} \\
&= £1,000 \times 6.1051 \\
&= £6,105.10
\end{aligned}
$$

This can be confirmed by treating each of the five payments as individual compound interest calculations:

Year	Invested £	Formula	Value £
1	1,000	$£1,000 \times (1 + 0.10)^4$	1,464.10
2	1,000	$£1,000 \times (1 + 0.10)^3$	1,331.00
3	1,000	$£1,000 \times (1 + 0.10)^2$	1,210.00
4	1,000	$£1,000 \times (1 + 0.10)^1$	1,100.00
5	1,000	$£1,000 \times (1 + 0.10)$	1,000.00
			6,105.10

Tables can also be used. The one provided in Appendix II also confirms that the value of an annuity of £1 for five years at 10 per cent would be £6.105, i.e. £1 times the multiplier of 6.105 given in the table.

Example

As an alternative to calculating the value of an annuity when the amounts paid are known, it can often be useful to know how much should be set aside regularly in order to accumulate a certain amount at the end of a given period. For example, if it was intended to purchase equipment estimated to cost £10,000 in five years' time, and a 10 per cent interest rate was being offered for regular investments over a five-year period, the annuity formula can be rewritten so as to provide the amount to set aside:

$$
\begin{aligned}
\text{Annuity per period} &= \frac{\text{Value} \times (r)}{(1 + r)^n - 1} \\
&= \frac{£10,000 \times 0.10}{(1.10)^5 - 1} \\
&= £1,637.97
\end{aligned}
$$

As mentioned previously, the multiplier given in the annuity table for a five-year annuity at 10 per cent is 6.105. If £1,637.97 is multiplied by 6.105, it confirms the annuity has a final value (to the nearest £1) of £10,000. It is also possible to confirm the annuity per period does result in the correct final value of £10,000 by creating a payment plus interest table:

Annuity paid	Payment £	Interest £	Increase in fund £	Balance of fund £
end of year 1	1,637.97	–	1,637.97	1,637.97
end of year 2	1,637.97	163.80	1,801.77	3,439.74
end of year 3	1,637.97	343.97	1,981.94	5,421.68
end of year 4	1,637.97	542.17	2,180.14	7,601.82
end of year 5	1,637.97	760.18	2,398.15	9,999.97

46.9 Calculation of the present value of ordinary annuities

If faced with a choice of paying for something now, or paying for it in instalments over the next year, it is useful to know which is the cheaper of the two alternatives. For example, a business may purchase a new computer costing £1,000 and have a choice of paying £1,000 now, or £200 per month for six months. It seems that the second option will be more expensive because £1,200 (i.e. six times £200) would be paid instead of £1,000.

In order to be able to compare the two alternatives, the payments must all be discounted to arrive at their cost expressed in terms of today's money, i.e. to arrive at their present values. Whether it really is more expensive to pay by instalments will depend on the discount rate used in the calculation.

As with the calculation of the value of an ordinary annuity, tables are available for the calculation of the present value of an ordinary annuity. A full table is provided in Appendix II and it shows the value now of £1 per period for n periods when an organisation uses a discount rate of r. When payments are made more frequently than once per annum, the discount rate used should be reduced accordingly – that is, if payments are half-yearly, the rate is halved; if they are made every month, the rate is divided by 12.

The formula for calculating the present value of an ordinary annuity is:

$$\text{Present value} \quad = \quad \text{payment} \times \left[\frac{1 - \dfrac{1}{(1 + r)^n}}{r} \right]$$

If a 12 per cent rate were used with the above example, the rate of 12 per cent would be divided by 12 for the calculation and the present value would be:

$$\text{Present value} \quad = \quad £100 \times \left[\frac{1 - \dfrac{1}{(1 + 0.01)^6}}{0.01} \right]$$

$$= \quad £579.55$$

The multiplier in the table in Appendix II for 1 per cent over 6 periods is 5.795 which, when multiplied by the payment of £100, confirms a present value of £579.50.

It can be shown that this is the amount required if a table of interest and withdrawals is constructed (interest is at the same rate as above – 1 per cent per month):

Period	Balance b/d £	Interest £	Payment £	Balance c/d £
1	579.55	5.80	(100)	485.35
2	485.35	4.85	(100)	390.20
3	390.20	3.90	(100)	294.10
4	294.10	2.94	(100)	197.04
5	197.04	1.97	(100)	99.01
6	99.01	0.99	(100)	–

46.10 Capital project appraisal

If you had £5,000 to spend today and had the choice of investing it in a five-year bond with a bank, or lending it to a friend who had just opened a restaurant and who offered you 10 per cent of the profits for five years, plus the return of your £5,000 at the end of the five years, which alternative would you choose?

Organisations make vast numbers of short-term decisions. They make comparatively few long-term decisions. These long-term decisions involve investing resources in something and then receiving the benefits. Examples include:

- building a new production facility;
- buying a new delivery truck;
- sponsoring a local football team for three years;
- building a bridge;
- buying an airline;
- making a new product;
- starting a new business.

Generally, only the incremental cash payments and receipts arising from the decision to invest are relevant. The relevant costs include interest, but not items that normally appear in the calculation of profit but which do not involve cash – depreciation, for example. There are two aspects of the incremental cash flows that should be distinguished: the cash outflows resulting from the decision to invest, and the cash inflows arising as a result of investing. The difference between these two groups of incremental cash flows determines whether or not an investment is made.

The techniques used to aid the selection of the appropriate long-term decision are referred to collectively as **capital project appraisal**. There are three generally acceptable capital project appraisal techniques in common use. Two have already been introduced in section 46.6 – **net present value** and **internal rate of return**. Collectively, these two are known as **discounted cash flow (DCF) techniques**, as they involve the discounting of future net cash flows of a capital project to find their present value. Both techniques assume that all cash flows occur at the end of a period.

The third technique, **payback**, involves selecting the alternative that repays the initial investment in the shortest time, providing that it does not exceed the business's maximum acceptable payback period – its payback hurdle period. It is useful when cash resources are limited and swift repayment of the investment is vital for the maintenance of working capital. Also, because risks of problems arising increase with the length of an investment, payback reduces the risk by minimising the relevant length of investment. In contrast to the DCF techniques, payback assumes all cash flows occur evenly over a period.

A fourth technique, accounting rate of return (ARR), having once been very popular, is now falling into disuse as technology becomes more sophisticated, and those performing these calculations become more aware of the benefits of using the other three techniques in preference to ARR. The technique uses profits rather than cash flows and it involves dividing the average return by the average investment over the period, i.e. if £10,000 is invested and the return is £30,000 over a ten-year period, there would be a return of £3,000 per year (£30,000 ÷ 10). If the £10,000 is repaid at the end of the ten years, the average investment is £10,000 (i.e. [£10,000 + £10,000] ÷ 2). Therefore, the (annual) accounting rate of return is £3,000 divided by £10,000, i.e. 30 per cent. Although it is generally easy to calculate, ARR produces a percentage figure that is of little practical use. It cannot, for example, be compared to an organisation's cost of capital in order to assess whether a project would achieve a greater return than the cost of the capital that financed it. It also ignores the timing of cash flows – a project whose profits all arose at the start would be rejected in favour of one with a higher ARR whose profits all came at the end, even if inflation meant that those later period profits were worth significantly less in present value terms than the earlier profits of the rejected project.

Example

When considering a capital project proposal, the first step is to identify all the incremental cash flows that would arise were the decision taken to proceed with the investment. As most decisions of this type involve cash flows over a number of years, once identified, the cash flows are then mapped against the year in which they arise.

A new machine would cost £10,000 and installation would cost a further £1,000. It would replace an existing machine that would be sold for £2,000. The machine would generate cash income of £2,500 per annum for four years, at the end of which it would be sold for £3,000.

The cash flows are:

Period		Amount £
0	purchase + installation – sale proceeds	(9,000)
1	income	2,500
2	income	2,500
3	income	2,500
4	income (including sale proceeds)	5,500
		4,000

If the business's cost of capital is 10 per cent, that would be the discount rate used and the net present value (as previously illustrated in section 46.6) would be:

Period	Amount £	Discount factor 10%	Present value £
0	(9,000)	1.000	(9,000.00)
1	2,500	0.909	2,272.50
2	2,500	0.826	2,065.00
3	2,500	0.751	1,877.50
4	5,500	0.683	3,756.50
		Overall net present value of cash flows	971.50

As the NPV is positive, the internal rate of return is higher than 10 per cent. A 15 per cent discount factor produces a negative NPV of £144:

Period	Amount £	Discount factor 15%	Present value £
0	(9,000)	1.000	(9,000)
1	2,500	0.870	2,175
2	2,500	0.756	1,890
3	2,500	0.658	1,645
4	5,500	0.572	3,146
		Overall net present value of cash flows	(144)

Interpolating between these two values, as in section 46.6, the IRR is found to be 14.35 per cent. [The absolute difference is £1,115.50 (i.e. £971.50 + £144), of which approximately 87 per cent (£971.50) is represented by the proportion relating to the 10 per cent NPV. Multiplying the difference between the two discount rates (15% − 10% = 5%) by 87 per cent gives an answer to two decimal places of 4.35 per cent. This is then added to 10 per cent to produce the IRR of 14.35 per cent.] On the basis that the business's cost of capital is 10 per cent, this project will be financially beneficial. Substituting the discount rate of 14.35 per cent into the table produces a net present value of minus 10, the failure to reach a value of zero being due to rounding.

Period	Amount £	Discount factor 14.35%	Present value £
0	(9,000)	1.000	(9,000.00)
1	2,500	0.875	2,187.50
2	2,500	0.765	1,912.50
3	2,500	0.669	1,672.50
4	5,500	0.585	3,217.50
	Overall net present value of cash flows		(10.00)

These two DCF techniques generally arrive at the selection of the same alternative when faced with a choice between two or more alternative projects. However, they can produce different choices and when they do, it is the NPV choice that should be selected.

As the following schedule shows, payback on the machine occurs after 3.27 years:

Period	Amount £	Balance £
0	(9,000)	(9,000)
1	2,500	(6,500)
2	2,500	(4,000)
3	2,500	(1,500)
4	5,500	– Payback at 3 plus 1,500/5,500 years = 3.27 years

This will then be compared to the business's hurdle period for payback. If it is later than the hurdle period, the project will be rejected. When cash flow is important, for example when the cost of capital is high, or when the risks in a project increase significantly the longer it runs, payback provides a measure of how quickly the investment in the project will be repaid, any subsequent cash flows being viewed as a bonus. However, it can result in a project being selected that is considerably less profitable than another that happens to take longer to repay the investment in it. It also ignores the time value of money. ('Real' payback will always be later than revealed by calculation as later receipts are not worth so much in today's money as early ones due to inflation.)

Closer inspection of the approach reveals that payback ignores everything after the (first) breakeven point. Applied blindly, it is not concerned about whether a project breaks even overall – only that the amount invested in a project is reduced to zero at some stage. If a project breaks even in three years, but then requires more investment in year five, only finally breaking even in year six, this can easily be overlooked when calculating payback.

These deficiencies in the payback approach can be addressed by discounting all cash flows to their present values, and by ensuring that the calculation includes a check for there being multiple payback points. While the first is generally sensible, the second is essential if payback is to be effectively applied.

46.11 Taxation

One factor often overlooked in consideration of capital projects is taxation. Items of equipment acquired will give rise to tax allowances that can be used to reduce tax payable, and any incremental profits arising from a capital project will give rise to payments of tax. Once calculated, the impact of taxation on the incremental cash flows is taken into account in the same way as any other item of incremental income or expenditure.

Example

A new machine costing £10,000 has an estimated useful economic life of four years, after which it will be scrapped. During those four years, it is expected to generate sales of £5,000 per annum. Production costs are anticipated to be 40 per cent of sales revenue. Working capital of £3,000 will be required for this activity, all of which will be recovered when the machine is scrapped. Depreciation is by the straight line method, i.e. £2,500 per annum starting in year one. Corporation tax of 40 per cent is paid nine months after the end of each accounting period. A writing-down allowance of 25 per cent (reducing balance) will be available if the machine is acquired.

The expected annual profit is:

	£	£
Sales		5,000
Production costs	2,000	
Depreciation	2,500	
		(4,500)
		500
Corporation tax		(200)
Net profit after tax		£300

The expected cash flows that would be used for the capital project appraisal are:

Investment (£)	Year: 1	2	3	4	5
Machine	(10,000)				
Working capital	(3,000)			3,000	
Tax allowance		1,000	750	562.50	1,687.50
	(13,000)	1,000	750	3,562.50	1,687.50
Cash flows (£)					
Sales	5,000	5,000	5,000	5,000	
Production costs	(2,000)	(2,000)	(2,000)	(2,000)	
Tax (40% × £3,000)		(1,200)	(1,200)	(1,200)	(1,200)
	3,000	1,800	1,800	1,800	(1,200)
Net cash flows (£)	(10,000)	2,800	2,550	5,362.50	487.50

(The overall tax allowances are £4,000, which is 40 per cent of the cost of the equipment, for which it has been assumed that there will be no scrap proceeds. Also, the cost of the machine and additional working capital would be treated as having arisen in year zero for the purposes of the capital project appraisal techniques. They are shown in year one in the above table so as to clarify the timing of the tax and tax allowance cash flows.)

46.12 Annualised figures

It can be difficult comparing projects that have different lengths. To overcome this complication, it is possible to use annualised amounts. Notionally, this approach assumes that the comparison would then be made over a period that represented the lowest common multiple of the projects – a twelve-year cycle would be used for two projects, one of three years' duration, the other four. However, as will be seen, once the annualised amounts are calculated, the decision can be taken without reference to any particular length of time.

The first step is to calculate the present value of the projects and then identify the amount of the annuity for the period of each project that has the same present value as that project's NPV. For example, if a discount rate of 10 per cent is used and the NPV of the three-year project is £500, the annuity multiplier (from the table in Appendix II) is 2.487 and the three-year annuity with a present value of £500 is therefore £201 (i.e. £500 ÷ 2.487). If the four-year project has an NPV of £800, the four-year annuity is £252 (i.e. £800 ÷ 3.170). On the basis of these annualised amounts, the four-year project would be selected.

46.13 Leasing

Under a lease, the lessee agrees to pay a rental to the lessor for use of something for a period of time. Lease rental payments are treated as allowable expenses for tax, whereas assets that are purchased are only eligible for a partial deduction against tax in the form of a capital allowance. The lessor claims the capital allowances on the assets leased. The lessee charges all the lease rental payments against income.

Leasing exists because both lessee and lessor can benefit from the arrangement as a result of their differing tax positions and capital raising abilities. A small company may find it very expensive, possibly impossible, to borrow £200,000 for some new equipment, whereas a large leasing company would be able to raise the funds at a very competitive rate.

An organisation acquiring an asset will often consider whether leasing may be preferable to outright purchase. As the cost, expected useful economic life, anticipated scrap value, and leasing charges can all be identified, it is possible to identify the APR of the lease. That can then be used to assess whether it would be preferable to lease rather than buy the asset.

Example

A printing machine costing £200,000 has an expected useful economic life of ten years. Scrap value of the machine is expected to be zero, as the rate of obsolescence on machinery of this type is very high. The machine could be leased for £32,547 per annum. The APR is the interest rate that is found when the cost of the machine is equal to the present value of the annual rental payments. That is, it is the interest rate for which the ten-year multiplier will convert £32,547 into £200,000. £200,000 divided by £32,547 is 6.145. In the 10 year row of the annuity table in Appendix II, 6.145 is the multiplier for an interest rate of 10 per cent which is, therefore, the APR of the lease. If the multiplier being sought lay part-way between two values in the annuity table, the APR would be identified by interpolation, as in the calculation of IRR.

Normally, tax would be taken into account in identifying the APR of a lease. Ignoring the time lags inherent in the tax system, as the expense is charged directly against income, if the tax rate is 40 per cent, in the above example the net of tax cost of the lease would be 60 per cent of £32,547 (i.e. £19,528) and the APR would be 60 per cent of 10 per cent, i.e. 6 per cent. This could then be compared to the organisation's cost of capital after tax in order to assess whether to lease or purchase the machine.

So far as the option to purchase is concerned, an annualised cost approach can be used. The cost of £200,000 would be assumed to occur at year zero. If 100 per cent capital allowances were available on the machine, at a tax rate of 40 per cent, there would be a tax saving equivalent to 40 per cent of £200,000 in year one. If the organisation's net of tax cost of capital is 8 per cent, the £80,000 tax saving would be discounted to £74,080 (i.e. £80,000 × 0.926), leaving a net present value of £125,920. The annualised cost is, therefore, £125,920 ÷ 6.710 (which is the annuity multiplier for 10 years at 8 per cent), i.e. £18,766. When compared to the net of tax cost of the lease of £19,528, this suggests that it might be preferable to purchase the machine.

As an alternative, the £125,920 net present value of buying the machine (as derived in the annualised cost calculation) can be compared to the NPV of the lease payments. The net of tax NPV of leasing is the net of tax rental (£19,528) multiplied by the present value multiplier of a ten-year annuity at 8 per cent (6.710), i.e. £131,033.

46.14 Financial implications of leasing

Despite the existence of a legal obligation to continue paying rental on a lease, neither the extent of the obligation to the lessor, nor the benefits obtainable under the lease normally appear on the face of the lessee's balance sheet. However, a lease often represents the equivalent of a loan. The equivalent loan is the NPV of the outstanding lease payments discounted at the pre-tax rate of interest. For example, the NPV of a ten-year lease with rental of £32,547 and a pre-tax rate of interest of 10 per cent would be £32,547 × 6.145 = £200,000.

46.15 Accounting for leases

Leases are either finance leases or operating leases. SSAP 21: *Accounting for leases and hire purchase contracts* defines the difference between them. The principal characteristic of a finance lease is that substantially all the risks and rewards of ownership are transferred to the lessee. Various steps are described in SSAP 21 that should be followed in order to determine whether a finance lease exists. These involve determining whether the present value of the minimum lease payments amount to substantially all (normally 90 per cent) of the fair value of the asset.

However, if the substance of the lease is to have the opposite effect, then it should be categorised accordingly. At the end of the day, it is the substance (i.e. what is actually happening to the risks and rewards of ownership) rather than the form of the transaction that decides whether there exists a finance or an operating lease.

Hire purchase contracts will usually be of a financing nature and treated in the same way as finance leases.

When a lease is classified as 'operating', it is deemed to still be an asset of the lessor. Both lessor and lessee take the rentals to the profit and loss account. The lessor should also record the fixed asset and depreciate it over its useful life.

An asset held under a finance lease is deemed to 'belong' to the lessee, who should capitalise it and make a corresponding entry in creditors. The initial value used should be the present value of the minimum lease payments. Depreciation should then be provided over the shorter of the lease term and the asset's useful life, except in the case of a hire purchase contract, under which circumstances the asset should be depreciated over its useful life. As each payment is made, the proportion which relates to the creditor balance should be applied to reduce that balance. The rest of the payment should be treated as a lease charge in the profit and loss account for the period.

Lessors should initially record the amount due under a finance lease as a debtor using the amount of the net investment in the lease. As each payment is received, the proportion which relates to payment of the debtor balance should be applied to reduce that balance. The rest of the receipt should be treated as lease income in the profit and loss account for the period.

Operating leases are accounted for in the same way as most revenue expenditure and income. Finance leases, however, are much more complex. The rental payments comprise a mixture of capital and revenue, and they must be separated and recorded differently. An approach called the actuarial method is generally used. Under this approach, it is first necessary to calculate the real rate of interest implied in the lease. This requires that information is available concerning the rental payments, the lease period and the cash value of the asset at the start of the lease.

Example

Quarterly rental on a leased computer is £400, the lease period is 12 quarters from 1 January 19X4, and the cash value of the computer at 1 January 19X4 is £4,000. The interest rate implied in the lease is that which produces a present value for the 12 payments of £400 equal to £4,000. Note, the first payment is at the start of the lease, yet ordinary annuity calculations relate to payments at the end of periods. In order to bring the example into line with this assumption, the first payment is offset against the cash value, reducing it to £3,600, and the annuity is calculated over 11 periods rather than 12.

$$\text{The factor for 11 periods is } \frac{£3,600}{400} \quad = \quad 9$$

From the tables   3%   =   9.253

                 4%   =   8.760

By interpolation, the gap between 3 per cent and the rate is 253/493 = 0.513, therefore, the interest rate implied in the lease is 3.513 per cent. This can be verified by substituting the rate and other information into the formula given in section 46.9:

$$\text{Present value} \quad = \quad \text{Payment} \times \left[\frac{1 - \dfrac{1}{(1 + r)^n}}{r} \right]$$

$$3,600 \quad = \quad 400 \times \left[\frac{1 - \dfrac{1}{(1 + 0.03513)^{11}}}{0.03513} \right]$$

$$3,600 \quad = \quad £400 \times 9$$

Applying the rate of interest of 3.513 to the lease data produces the data in Exhibit 46.4.

Exhibit 46.4 Calculation of the periodic finance charge in the lease

Quarter	Capital sum at start of period £	Rental paid at start of period £	Capital sum during period £	Finance charge (3.513% per quarter) £	Capital sum at end of period £
19X4 – 1	4,000	400	3,600	126	3,726
2	3,726	400	3,326	117	3,443
3	3,443	400	3,043	107	3,150
4	3,150	400	2,750	96	2,846
19X5 – 1	2,846	400	2,446	86	2,532
2	2,532	400	2,132	75	2,207
3	2,207	400	1,807	63	1,870
4	1,870	400	1,470	51	1,521
19X6 – 1	1,521	400	1,121	39	1,160
2	1,160	400	760	27	787
3	787	400	387	13	400
4	400	400	–	–	–
		4,800		800	

The finance charges for each year of the lease are:

	£
19X4 (126 + 117 + 107 + 96)	= 446
19X5 (86 + 75 + 63 + 51)	= 275
19X6 (39 + 27 + 13)	= 79
	800

The overall picture in each of the three years is:

Year	Total rental £	less	Finance charge £	=	Capital repayment £
19X4	1,600		446		1,154
19X5	1,600		275		1,325
19X6	1,600		79		1,521

In the balance sheet of the lessee, the liability under the finance lease would be:

Year	Obligations under finance lease at start of year £	less	Capital repayment £	=	Obligations under finance lease at end of year £
19X4	4,000		1,154		2,846
19X5	2,846		1,325		1,521
19X6	1,521		1,521		–

46.16 The rule of 78

Before spreadsheets became commonplace, these actuarial method lease calculations were often considered too complex and, in their place, a simple rule-of-thumb approach was adopted: the rule of 78.

The '78' is the sum of the numbers 1 to 12, and is used because these calculations originally focused on twelve-month periods. Each month receives a proportion in reverse to its position. Thus, month 1 of 12 would be accorded $\frac{12}{78}$ of the total, and month 12 of 12, $\frac{1}{78}$.

Similarly to the actuarial method, under the rule of 78, earlier periods will carry the majority of the allocation. For the purpose of lease calculations, the proportion is applied to the difference between the total payments under the leasing agreement and the cash value of the asset at the start.

Using the example from Exhibit 46.4, the rule of 78 produces the following:

Quarter	Rental payment number	Rule of 78	Allocation × £800	Annual allocation £
19X4 – 1	1	11	11/66 × £800 =133	
2	2	10	121	
3	3	9	109	
4	4	8	97	460
19X5 – 1	5	7	85	
2	6	6	73	
3	7	5	61	
4	8	4	49	268
19X6 – 1	9	3	36	
2	10	2	24	
3	11	1	12	
4	–	–	–	72
		66	800	800

(There is no allocation to the final quarter as the payments are made at the start of each quarter.) Comparison of the two methods shows that the rule of 78 provides a general indication of the flows.

Year	Actuarial method £	Rule of 78 £
19X4	446	460
19X5	275	268
19X6	79	72
	800	800

46.17 Uncertainty

Many of the values used in the calculations and formulae described in this chapter are, at best, objectively based estimates of future cash flows and interest rates. It is, for example, virtually inconceivable that the figures forecast in a capital project appraisal will be confirmed to have been 100 per cent accurate when the project is completed.

Proposers of a course of action tend to be over-optimistic and, in order to avoid the risk of non-achievement of forecasted results, a number of measures have been adopted. The two most common are the adoption of a higher cost of capital rate than is actually required in practice, and reducing estimates of income by a fixed percentage and using the same percentage to increase all costs. However, such arbitrary adjustments can no more guarantee accuracy than the original estimates, and they will often cause the decision taken to be different from that which the original, possibly more meaningful, data would have produced.

A more rational adjustment that can be adopted is to change the amounts forecast according to their subjective probabilities. The probabilities would be provided by the proposers of a project.

Example

Estimated sales ×	Probability of occurrence =	Expected sales
£		£
2,000	0.2	400
4,000	0.5	2,000
6,000	0.2	1,200
8,000	0.1	800
	1.0	4,400

In this case, the expected value of £4,400 will be used, rather than the most likely value of £4,000. While this approach appears more rational than the other possible methods of dealing with uncertainty, it is dependent upon the probabilities used being soundly based.

46.18 Sensitivity analysis

One of the greatest benefits of spreadsheets is the facility to perform unlimited numbers of sensitivity analysis computations on a given set of data. Cash flows can be adjusted marginally to see if the change turns a positive NPV negative; interest rates can be altered to see if the same decision would be made; the timing of cash flows can be altered to see what the impact of doing so is upon NPV. Sensitivity analysis enables information generated using the formulae and methods described in this chapter to be manipulated in order to maximise the understanding of the flexibility and limits of that information.

The importance of discounting has been recognised by the Institute of Chartered Accountants in England and Wales, who have issued Technical Release 773, *The Use of Discounting in Financial Statements*. It is an excellent source of discussion on this topic, and on its application in practice.

Main points to remember

1   As time passes, money loses value and this loss of value must be allowed for when considering long-term investments.

2   Interest rates may be simple or compound, and interest may be paid at any appropriate frequency. Compound interest will generate significantly greater values than the same rate of simple interest the longer the time period involved and the greater the frequency of interest payments.

3   The real rate of interest often differs from the apparent rate and an annual percentage rate (APR) must be calculated in order to compare alternatives.

4   Annuity calculations are useful when considering rental agreements, hire purchase and leases.

5   Net present value (NPV) and internal rate of return (IRR) usually lead to the same selection being made between mutually exclusive projects. When they differ, it is the NPV selection that should be followed.

6   Accounting rate of return (ARR) is still used, but the rate it produces cannot be compared to the cost of capital and the technique is not recommended.

7   Where alternative projects are of unequal length, annualised amounts can be calculated to enable comparison.

8   Operating leases are accounted for differently from finance leases.

Review questions

46.1

(a) If you were lent £12,000 for 56 days at 9 per cent, how much interest would you pay?

(b) If a debt factor offered to discount a £6,000 bill of exchange at 15 per cent, and if the bill had an outstanding period of 80 days, how much would the debt factor pay for the bill?

46.2A

What is the real rate of interest of discounting the bill of exchange in question 46.1?

46.3

Interest of £1,000 is charged and included in a loan of £3,000. The loan has to be repaid at £750 per quarter over the next 12 months. What is the real rate of interest of the loan?

46.4

If £1,000 is invested for five years at 12 per cent compound per annum, how much interest is earned over the five years?

46.5A

If the interest on the investment in question 46.4 had been compounded every six months, how much interest would have been earned over the five years?

46.6A

Shares bought on 1 January 19X2 for £2,000 were sold on 31 December 19X5 for £3,158. What was the rate of annual compound interest on the investment?

46.7

Should you accept an offer of £15,000 for your rights over the next four years to the £4,000 annual rent from shop premises you own and have leased to a local company? You could invest the £15,000 at 10 per cent per annum.

46.8A

In relation to the rental income, what rate of interest does the offer made in question 46.7 represent?

46.9

A condition of a ten-year loan of £20,000 is that the borrower will pay equal annual amounts into a sinking fund so that it accumulates at the end of the ten years to the amount of the loan. The sinking fund will earn interest at 8 per cent per annum. How much should be paid into the sinking fund each year?

46.10A

If the interest on the sinking fund in question 46.9 were at 10 per cent, how much would the annual payments into it be?

46.11

The following project costs have been estimated relating to the upgrading of some equipment; all the costs are being incurred solely because of the project:

19X2			£
January	1	One year's rent on premises paid	6,000
	31	Equipment purchased	40,000
March	31	Installation of equipment completed and paid	12,000
December	31	Costs incurred in commissioning equipment	18,000
19X3			
January	1	One year's rent on premises paid	6,000
March	31	Additional commissioning costs paid	10,000
May	31	Training costs paid	4,000
June	30	Additional working capital provided	14,000
December	31	Cash proceeds from sale of old equipment	10,000

Ignoring tax, prepare a statement showing the outlays of cash on the project in 19X2 and 19X3. The new facility will be in full use from 1 July 19X3.

46.12 Assume the company in question 46.11 pays tax at 40 per cent, on 30 September each year, nine months after the end of its financial period. The company receives 25 per cent writing-down allowances on the cost of equipment and will receive the allowances for 19X2 expenditure to be offset against the tax payable on the profits for 19X2. 100 per cent capital allowances were received on the old equipment sold in 19X3 and the receipts from the sale of the old equipment must, therefore, be treated as taxable income of 19X3. Show the impact on the cash flows of these tax items.

46.13 Assuming an interest rate of 10 per cent, what is the net present value of the net of tax cash flows in question 46.12 for 19X2, 19X3, 19X4 and 19X5?

46.14A The annual profit from a project is forecasted as:

	£	£
Sales		110,000
Labour, materials, and overheads	30,000	
Depreciation	20,000	
		50,000
Net profit before tax		60,000
Tax at 40%		24,000
Net profit after tax		36,000

Equipment with a five-year useful economic life and no residual value will be purchased on 1 September for £30,000. £15,000 additional working capital, which will be recovered in full at the end of the five years, will be required from 1 September. A 25 per cent writing-down allowance will be available throughout the period of the project. Tax at 40 per cent will be payable on 1 June each year, nine months after the end of the company's financial period on 31 August. Prepare a cash flow budget for the project.

46.15A If the interest rate is 10 per cent, what is the net present value of the net cash flows arising from the project in question 46.14?

46.16A If retained, a machine would be depreciated at £2,500 for the next four years, at which point it would be fully written down and scrapped. The machine could be sold at any point in the next year for £15,000, the gain being subject to tax at 40 per cent, payable the following year. If it were sold, a new machine costing £80,000 would be bought. The new machine would receive 25 per cent writing-down allowances to be offset annually against profits. It is estimated that the new machine would save material costs of £25,000 per year. Profits are subject to tax at 40 per cent, payable nine months after the end of the company's financial period. The new machinery would have a four-year life, with a residual value of zero, and would be depreciated straight line over that period. Prepare a cash flow statement for the replacement option, and indicate how the profits reported in the financial statements would be altered were the existing machine to be replaced.

46.17 What is the payback period on the following project cash flows? (Brackets indicate expenditure.)

	Net cash flows £
Year 0	(10,000)
1	8,000
2	4,000
3	2,000
4	1,000

46.18 Using a discount rate of 12 per cent, what is the net present value of the project in question 46.17?

46.19 What is the internal rate of return on the project in question 46.17?

46.20 What is the annualised amount of the net benefits from the project in question 46.17?

46.21A What is the payback on a project requiring £60,000 initial investment that has a net cash inflow of £40,000 in year 1, £25,000 in year two, and £15,000 in year three?

46.22A Using a discount rate of 10 per cent, what is the net present value of the project in question 46.21?

46.23A What is the internal rate of return on the project in question 46.21A?

46.24A What is the annualised amount of the net benefits from the project in question 46.21A?

46.25A The annual profit from a project is forecasted as:

	£	£
Sales		80,000
Labour, materials, and overheads	20,000	
Depreciation	15,000	
		35,000
Net profit before tax		45,000

The project requires that a new machine be purchased for £65,000. It will be depreciated using the straight line method over four years to a residual value of £5,000. The project will cease when the machine is sold for £5,000 at the end of the fourth year. Ignoring taxation, what is the accounting rate of return? (No additional working capital is required for this project.)

46.26A Assuming that all sales are for cash, what is the internal rate of return on the project in question 46.25A?

46.27 Which of the following two mutually exclusive alternatives should be selected if a 10 per cent interest rate is used for the calculation of net present value?

	Net cash flow Year 0 £	Net cash flow Year 3 £
Machine A project	(12,000)	22,000
Machine B project	(38,000)	66,000

46.28 Using internal rate of return, which of the two projects in question 46.27 would be preferred?

46.29A Which of the following two mutually exclusive alternatives should be selected if a 12 per cent interest rate is used for the calculation of net present value?

	Net cash flow Year 0 £	Net cash flow Year 1 £	Net cash flow Year 3 £
Project A	(34,000)	16,000	26,000
Project B	(29,000)	22,000	12,000

46.30A Using internal rate of return, which of the two projects in question 46.29A would be preferred?

46.31 Equipment with an estimated useful economic life of five years has an NPV of £3,100 using a 10 per cent discount rate. What is the annualised equivalent of the £3,100 NPV?

46.32A Two mutually exclusive alternatives are available. Project A will require initial investment of £3,000 and run for two years at a cost of £500 per annum. Project B will require initial investment of £7,000 and last for four years at a cost of £800 for the first three years and £1,000 in the fourth. Calculate the annualised cost of both projects over a four-year period, assuming that reinvestment in project A would cost £2,500 at the end of year two and assuming an interest rate of 8 per cent. Which alternative should be selected?

46.33 What is the implied interest rate if equipment can be leased for four years at £20,000 per annum and the cash price is £64,800?

46.34 A machine with a five-year useful life could be purchased for £60,000. It would have zero residual value at the end of the five years. Alternatively, the machine could be rented at £14,633 per annum for five years. Assuming a tax rate of 40 per cent and that tax relief is obtained in the same period as the payments, what is the implicit interest rate in the lease?

46.35 The annual rental payments on a six-year lease are £4,000. If the rate of interest payable on borrowing for this purpose is 16 per cent, what is the capital value of the lease?

46.36 Roadwheelers Ltd were considering buying an additional lorry but the company had not yet decided which particular lorry to purchase. The lorries had broadly similar technical specifications and each was expected to have a working life of five years.

The following information was available on the lorries being considered:

1

	Lorries		
	BN	FX	VR
	Roadhog	Sprinter	Rocket
Purchase price	£40,000	£45,000	£50,000
Estimated scrap value after 5 years	£8,000	£9,000	£14,000
Fixed costs other than depreciation	£	£	£
Year 1	2,000	1,800	1,500
Year 2	2,000	1,800	1,500
Year 3	2,200	1,800	1,400
Year 4	2,400	2,000	1,400
Year 5	2,400	2,200	1,400
Variable costs per road mile	6p	8p	7p

2   The company charges 25p per mile for all journeys irrespective of the length of journey and the expected annual mileages over the five-year period are:

	Miles
Year 1	50,000
Year 2	60,000
Year 3	80,000
Year 4	80,000
Year 5	80,000

3   The company's cost of capital is 10 per cent per annum.

4   It should be assumed that all operating costs are paid and revenues received at the end of year.

5   Present value of £1 at interest rate of 10 per cent per annum:

Year 1	£0.909
Year 2	£0.826
Year 3	£0.751
Year 4	£0.683
Year 5	£0.621

Required:
(a) (i)   Appropriate computations using the net present value method for each of the lorries under consideration.
     (ii) A report to the directors of Roadwheelers Ltd advising them as to which specific lorry should be purchased.
(b) A brief outline of the problems encountered in evaluating capital projects.

(*Associated Examining Board: GCE A–Level*)

46.37A Hirwaun Pig Iron Co. operate a single blast furnace producing pig iron. The present blast furnace is obsolete and the company is considering its replacement. The alternatives the company is considering are:

(i) Blast furnace type Exco. Cost £2 million.

This furnace is of a standard size capable of a monthly output of 10,000 tonnes. The company expects to sell 80 per cent of its output annually at £150 per tonne on a fixed price contract. The remaining output will be sold on the open market at the following expected prices:

	19X5	19X6	19X7	19X8
Price per tonne	£150	£140	£140	£160

(ii) Blast furnace type Ohio. Cost £3.5 million.

This large furnace is capable of a monthly output of 20,000 tonnes. A single buyer has agreed to buy all the monthly output at a fixed price which is applicable from 1 January each year. The prices fixed for the next four years are as follows:

	Payments per tonne of output			
	19X5	19X6	19X7	19X8
Price per tonne	£130	£130	£140	£170

Additional information:

1 Blast furnaces operate continuously and the operating labour is regarded as a fixed cost. During the next four years the operating labour costs will be as follows:

Exco £1.2 million per annum
Ohio £2.5 million per annum

2 Other forecast operating payments (excluding labour) per tonne:

	19X5	19X6	19X7	19X8
Exco	£130	£130	£135	£135
Ohio	£120	£120	£125	£125

3 It can be assumed that both blast furnaces will have a life of 10 years.
4 The company's cost of capital is 12 per cent per annum.
5 It should be assumed that all costs are paid and revenues received at the end of each year.
6 The following is an extract from the present value table for £1:

	11%	12%	13%	14%
Year 1	£0.901	£0.893	£0.885	£0.877
Year 2	£0.812	£0.797	£0.783	£0.770
Year 3	£0.731	£0.712	£0.693	£0.675
Year 4	£0.659	£0.636	£0.613	£0.592

Required:

(a) The forecast budgets for each of the years 19X5–19X8 and for each of the blast furnaces being considered. Show the expected yearly net cash flows.

(b) Appropriate computations using the net present value method for each of the blast furnaces, Exco and Ohio, for the first four years.

(c) A report providing a recommendation to the management of Hirwaun Pig Iron Co as to which blast furnace should be purchased. Your report should include a critical evaluation of the method used to assess the capital project.

(*Associated Examining Board: GCE A–Level*)

46.38 Moray Ferries Ltd own a single ship which provides a short sea ferry service for passengers, private vehicles and commercial traffic. The present ship is nearing the end of its useful life and the company is considering the purchase of a new ship.

The forecast operating budgets using the present ship are as follows:

	19X5 £m	19X6 £m	19X7 £m	19X8 £m	19X9 £m
Estimated revenue receipts					
Private traffic	2	3	4.5	6	7
Commercial traffic	3	4	4.5	5	6
	5	7	9.0	11	13
Estimated operating payments	4	5	6.5	7.5	9
	1	2	2.5	3.5	4

The ships being considered as a replacement are as described below.

1   Ship A. Cost £10m
This ship is of similar capacity to the one being replaced, but being a more modern ship it is expected that extra business would be attracted from competitors. It is anticipated therefore that estimated revenue receipts would be 10 per cent higher in each year of the present forecast. There would be no change in operating payments.

2   Ship B. Cost £14m
This modern ship has a carrying capacity 30 per cent greater than the present ship. It is expected that private traffic receipts would increase by £½m a year in each year of the forecast. Commercial traffic receipts are expected to increase by 15 per cent in each of the first two years and by 30 per cent in each of the remaining years.
Operating payments would increase by 20 per cent in each year of the forecast.

Additional information:
3   The company's cost of capital is 15 per cent per annum.
4   It is company policy to assume that ships have a life of 20 years.
5   It should be assumed that all costs are paid and revenues received at the end of each year.
6   The following is an extract from the present value table for £1:

	12%	14%	15%	16%
Year 1	£0.893	£0.877	£0.870	£0.862
Year 2	£0.797	£0.769	£0.756	£0.743
Year 3	£0.712	£0.675	£0.658	£0.641
Year 4	£0.636	£0.592	£0.572	£0.552
Year 5	£0.567	£0.519	£0.497	£0.476

7   All calculations should be made correct to three places of decimals.

Required:
(a) Revised operating budgets for 19X5–19X9 for each of the alternatives being considered.
(b) Appropriate computations using the net present value method for each of the ships, A and B.
(c) A report providing a recommendation to the management of Moray Ferries Ltd as to which course of action should be followed. Your report should include any reservations that you may have.

(*Associated Examining Board: GCE A–Level*)

46.39A The Rovers Football Club are languishing in the middle of the Premier Division of the Football League. The Club have suffered a loss of £200,000 in their last financial year and whilst receipts from spectators have declined over the last five years, recently receipts have stabilised at approximately £1,000,000 per season. The Club is considering the purchase of the services of one of two new football players, Jimmy Jam or Johnny Star.

Jimmy Jam is 21 years old and considered to be a future international footballer. He is prepared to sign a five-year contract with Rovers for a salary of £50,000 per annum. His present club would require a transfer fee of £200,000 for the transfer of his existing contract. With J Jam in the team the Rovers Club would expect receipts to increase by 20 per cent.

Johnny Star is 32 years old and a leading international footballer who is prepared to sign for Rovers on a two-year contract before retiring completely from football. He would expect a salary of £200,000 per annum and his present club would require a transfer fee of £100,000 for the transfer of his existing contract. Rovers believe that as a result of signing Star receipts would increase by 40 per cent.

The rate of interest applicable to the transaction is 12 per cent and the following is an extract from the present value table for £1:

	12%
Year 1	0.893
Year 2	0.797
Year 3	0.712
Year 4	0.636
Year 5	0.567

It should be assumed that all costs are paid and revenues received at the end of each year.

Required:
A report, incorporating an evaluation of the financial result of engaging each player by the net present value method, providing the Rovers Football Club with information to assist it in deciding which alternative to adopt. Indicate any other factors that may be taken into consideration.

(*Associated Examining Board: GCE A–Level*)

Appendix I
Examination techniques

If you were completely devoid of examination technique you would probably not have advanced to this stage of the examinations. All of the advice given to you in *Business Accounting 1* is still applicable. If you have not already read that advice you should try to borrow a copy of the book from a friend, or read it in a library.

A lot of what follows was written in *Business Accounting 1*. Don't avoid reading it just because you used it. In your first examination you were competing with people who had probably never sat an accounting examination before. A lot of them will not get past Stage 1. In Stage 2 you are competing against people who have already proved they have a certain degree of competence in the subject. You might have got away with a certain amount of poor examination technique at Stage 1, but that will not be as easy at Stage 2.

Here we want to concentrate on the main deficiencies noted by examiners. These have never changed during the last 50 years. Students really should read examiners' reports – they will learn a lot from them.

Students do not read the questions properly

A large number of students do not answer the questions as set by the examiner, because they have not read the question properly. They answer what they think the examiner wants, not what he is asking for.

Let us take a simple example. Suppose the examiner sets the following question: 'Describe the use of accounting ratios in assessing the performance of businesses.'

A lot of students will immediately start to describe how to calculate various accounting ratios. Marks which will be obtained – nil. The question asked for the *use* of accounting ratios, not *how to calculate* them.

Many other students will have concentrated on the word *use*. They will then write their answer based on comparing this year's accounting ratios in a business with those of last year. They may well even mention trend ratios which will earn them some extra marks. If they keep their discussion to comparing ratios in a business in the year with other years, however, they cannot get top marks, no matter how well they have written their answers.

Why not? Well, they picked up the word *use*, but from then on they stopped reading properly. The question does not in any way limit itself to the ratios of one business only. First of all you can compare the performance of a business with its own performance in the past. Secondly, you may be able to compare one business with another business of a similar kind. In addition, if you miss out mentioning interfirm comparisons you will lose marks.

Therefore, (a) *read* the question carefully, (b) *underline* the *key* words to get to the meaning of the question, (c) *think carefully* about how widespread your answer should be.

On the other hand there is no point in widening the question more than is needed. It is for the *use* of *accounting* ratios, *not* the use of *all types* of ratios. Besides accounting ratios there are marketing ratios – e.g. size of share of market, how long it takes to supply orders, ratios of defective goods etc. The question does not ask for all of these. If you give them, you will not get any extra marks.

Poor time management

Using time well to gain the highest possible marks is essential. Examiners constantly report that examinees are very poor in this aspect of tackling an examination. How then can you avoid the usual pitfalls?

First of all read the *rubric* carefully. These are the instructions at the top of the paper, e.g. 'Attempt four questions only: the three questions in Section A and one from Section B. Begin each answer on a separate page.'

You would be surprised to know that a lot of students would try to answer more than one question from Section B. If you tackle two questions from Section B you will get marks for only one of your answers. No examiner will mark both and then give you the marks for your highest marked answer. They will mark the first of the optional questions answered and ignore the next unnecessary answer.

Secondly, don't annoy the examiner by not starting your answer on a separate page. It is your job to make the examiner's work as easy as possible. Examiners are only human, and it would not be surprising if their annoyance did not result in it influencing the marking of your paper.

You really must attempt each and every question to fulfil the examination requirements. If you have to answer five questions then you must avoid only attempting four questions.

Students often feel that they would be better off by handing in the complete answers to only four questions, instead of five incomplete answers. In accounting examinations this is not true. Why is this so?

1   Examiners use positive marking in accounting examinations. If you have done 80 per cent of an answer worth 20 marks in total, and you have got it absolutely correct, then you get 80% of 20 = 16 marks.
2   The first marks in a question are the easiest to obtain. Thus it is easier to get the first 10 marks out of 20 than it is to get the second lot of marks to get full marks. By ensuring that you get the easiest marks on every question it therefore makes your task easier.

To ensure that you tackle (not necessarily finish) each question you should mark the number of minutes to be allowed by *yourself* for each question. Thus a 20-mark question, in a 100-mark examination, should be given 20 per cent of the time, i.e. 20% of 3 hours = 36 minutes. When 36 minutes have passed, *stop answering the question* unless it is the last question to be attempted, and go on to the next question.

If you don't know the answer, or part of an answer, you should guess. You don't lose marks for guessing, and if you guess correctly you get the marks. Intuition will often give the correct answer. Very often if you don't guess on part of a computational question you will be unable to go on to the remainder of the question which you can answer.

Workings

You may wonder why we have put this under a separate heading. We cannot emphasise enough how important it is that you should:

(*a*) submit all your workings; and
(*b*) ensure that the workings are set out so that the examiner can follow them.

A very high percentage of candidates in an examination are near the pass mark, within either a few percentage points above it or below it. If you are one of these candidates, and, as we have said, there are a lot of them, handing in workings which can be understood by the examiner will often ensure you a pass mark. Conversely, no workings, or completely unintelligible workings may well ensure your failing the examination.

Tackle the easiest questions first

Never start off your examination by tackling a difficult question. You must be able to settle down properly, and not let your nerves get out of control. Starting off on the easiest question is the best way to enable you to get off to a good start. Much more about this was written in *Business Accounting 1*.

State your assumptions

It does happen that sometimes a question can contain ambiguities. Examination bodies try to prevent it happening, but it does occur occasionally. Unfortunately, questions do sometimes contain errors.

In both of these cases you must point out the ambiguity/error. You should then make an assumption, based on what you thought the examiner meant, and carry on with your answer. You must, however, state what your assumption is. Try to make your assumption as sensible as possible. The examiner will then mark your answer accordingly. If you make a ridiculous assumption, it is unlikely that he will give you any marks for that part of your answer. Don't be sarcastic in your comments or complain about inefficiency – there are other times and places for that.

Answering written questions

The problem

Unlike computational-type answers you will not know whether your written answers are up to the mark until you receive your examination result. Likewise, written questions lack the certainty and precision of accounting problems and it is often difficult to fathom out exactly what the examiners require of you. For this reason, sound examination technique is absolutely essential together with precise knowledge of relevant law and regulations.

There are several major aspects to success in written papers. *Plan* your answer, answer the question *as set*, pay attention to good *layout*, and explain in clear and simple terms what you are doing. Remember you can only be marked on what you write down. You have no opportunity to explain some ambiguity or other and if what you write is unclear you will *not* get the benefit of the doubt.

Plan

First read the question and jot down the key *verb*, i.e. your instructions; this may be to discuss, explain, advise, set out, list, draft an audit programme, write a letter, etc.

If the question requires a discussion or an explanation it should be written in proper paragraph form. Each paragraph should be self-contained and explain the point it makes. Sentences should be short and to the point. The ideal length for a paragraph is three sentences with four as a maximum. Over four and you are probably making more than one point and should have gone into two paragraphs.

Plan how many points you are going to make and what the answer is. This is essential as otherwise your answer will 'drift' as you struggle to come to some conclusion. The plan should consist of arrows connecting points to each other so that the answer will flow and be logical. The plan need not be too extensive; it is silly to waste time on a 'mini-answer'. It should consist of the *headings* you are going to use.

Layout

Whenever examiners meet to discuss results, or write down their commentary on students' performance, they all agree on the importance of good layout; yet students generally tend to take no notice. The range of marks between good papers and poor papers tends to be quite small. Anything you can do to put the examiner on your side will pay off in those few extra marks.

The main areas for good layout are:

1 *Tabulate* in numbered points, unless you are writing an essay-type question (as explained above).
2 Leave at least a clear line between each point or paragraph.
3 Use headings whenever possible to indicate what major point or series of points you are about to make. Make it easy for the examiner to read your work and follow what you are doing. A solid mass of material is difficult to read, provides no respite for the eye and shows a lack of discipline. Remember that you are taking a *professional* examination and there is no room for academic licence.
4 Take care with your *language*. Be objective and avoid the use of the words 'I' or 'we' at too frequent intervals. Be direct and concise, say what you mean, do not use pompous terminology and use technical words with their correct meaning.

    Short sentences are far more effective and punchy than long ones. An accounting programme or evaluation of an internal control system could well start with a series of *verbs*. Good ones are: test, examine, inspect, calculate, reconcile, compare, summarise, inquire, investigate. These key words will help you to make answers to these types of questions much more direct and to the point. If you start with them you are bound to avoid falling into the trap of being long-winded, or of padding out your answer. You only have a limited time and everything you write down must earn you marks.
5 *Think* while you are writing out your answer to make sure you are answering the question *as set*. Keep on reading the instructions and make sure you are following them. Use the question to help you to get the answer and, while this should be tackled at the planning stage, it is always possible that inspiration will strike while you are writing out your answer. In which case jot the point down on your plan, otherwise you might forget it and that can cause frustration. What you say should be relevant but if you are in doubt about the relevance but sure about the accuracy – give it to him! You cannot lose and it may be one of the key points he was looking for.

Key points

Do try to find a couple of key points to each question. These are points which you feel are vital to answer the question. You may well be right, and anyway jotting them down after you have read the question carefully can help to give your answer much needed direction.

Practice

You will need to practise the above routine. Written answers in fact need more practice than computational ones. Have a go at the question. Write out the answer as you would in the examination. Compare with the suggested answers.

Write out at the foot of your answer *what you left out* and *what you got wrong*.

Learn from the answers and from the work you do, so that when you see a similar question you will produce a better answer.

Time pressure

You will experience a lot of time pressure as you progress with written questions. Do not worry; this is a good sign.

In the examination spread your time sensibly. Start with the questions you like the look of most and if you have to go slightly over time do so. End with the question you think you cannot answer, but do give yourself time to have a reasonable go at it.

If a written question is included in a computational paper do not go over the time on it but do spend the allocated time. Examiners pay great attention to the written parts of computational papers, so do not skimp this part.

All this sounds formidable and, of course, it is. It requires skill and application and above all confidence. Practice makes perfect and once the skill is acquired then, like riding a bicycle, it will not be forgotten. Take pride in your work and be critical of your own efforts, but do not imagine your answers will have to be perfect to pass the examination. Suggested answers tend to be too long because tutors are afraid to reveal any signs of weakness or ignorance.

Go for the main points and make them well. That is the secret of success.

Appendix II
Interest tables

Table 1 Compound sum of £1

Year	1%	2%	3%	4%	5%	6%	7%	8%	9%	10%
1	1.010	1.020	1.030	1.040	1.050	1.060	1.070	1.080	1.090	1.100
2	1.020	1.040	1.061	1.082	1.103	1.124	1.145	1.166	1.188	1.210
3	1.030	1.061	1.093	1.125	1.158	1.191	1.225	1.260	1.295	1.210
4	1.041	1.082	1.126	1.170	1.216	1.262	1.311	1.360	1.295	1.331
5	1.051	1.104	1.159	1.217	1.276	1.338	1.403	1.469	1.412	1.464
6	1.062	1.126	1.194	1.265	1.340	1.419	1.501	1.587	1.539	1.611
7	1.072	1.149	1.230	1.316	1.407	1.504	1.606	1.714	1.677	1.772
8	1.083	1.172	1.267	1.369	1.477	1.594	1.718	1.851	1.828	1.949
9	1.094	1.195	1.305	1.423	1.551	1.689	1.838	1.999	1.993	2.144
10	1.105	1.219	1.344	1.480	1.629	1.791	1.967	2.159	2.172	2.358
11	1.116	1.243	1.384	1.539	1.710	1.898	2.105	2.332	2.367	2.594
12	1.127	1.268	1.426	1.601	1.796	2.012	2.252	2.518	2.580	2.853
13	1.138	1.294	1.469	1.665	1.886	2.133	2.410	2.720	2.813	3.138
14	1.149	1.319	1.513	1.732	1.980	2.261	2.579	2.937	3.066	3.452
15	1.161	1.346	1.558	1.801	2.079	2.397	2.759	3.172	3.342	3.797
									3.642	4.177

Year	12%	14%	15%	16%	18%	20%	24%	28%	32%
1	1.120	1.140	1.150	1.160	1.180	1.200	1.240	1.280	1.320
2	1.254	1.300	1.323	1.346	1.392	1.440	1.538	1.638	1.742
3	1.405	1.482	1.521	1.561	1.643	1.728	1.907	2.097	2.300
4	1.574	1.689	1.749	1.811	1.939	2.074	2.364	2.684	3.036
5	1.762	1.925	2.011	2.100	2.288	2.488	2.932	3.436	4.007
6	1.974	2.195	2.313	2.436	2.700	2.986	3.635	4.398	5.290
7	2.211	2.502	2.660	2.826	3.185	3.583	4.508	5.629	6.983
8	2.476	2.853	3.059	3.278	3.759	4.300	5.590	7.206	9.217
9	2.773	3.252	3.518	3.803	4.435	5.160	6.931	9.223	12.166
10	3.106	3.707	4.046	4.411	5.234	6.192	8.594	11.806	16.060
11	3.479	4.226	4.652	5.117	6.176	7.430	10.657	15.112	21.199
12	3.896	4.818	5.350	5.936	7.288	8.916	13.215	19.343	27.983
13	4.363	5.492	6.153	6.886	8.599	10.699	16.386	24.759	36.937
14	4.887	6.261	7.076	7.988	10.147	12.839	20.319	31.691	48.757
15	5.474	7.138	8.137	9.266	11.974	15.407	25.196	40.565	64.359

Year	36%	40%	50%	60%	70%	80%	90%
1	1.360	1.400	1.500	1.600	1.700	1.800	1.900
2	1.850	1.960	2.250	2.560	2.890	3.240	3.610
3	2.515	2.744	3.375	4.096	4.913	5.832	6.859
4	3.421	3.842	5.062	6.544	8.352	10.498	13.032
5	4.653	5.378	7.594	10.486	14.199	18.896	24.761
6	6.328	7.530	11.391	16.777	24.138	34.012	47.046
7	8.605	10.541	17.086	26.844	41.034	61.222	89.387
8	11.703	14.758	25.629	42.950	69.758	110.200	169.836
9	15.917	20.661	38.443	68.720	118.588	198.359	322.688
10	21.647	28.925	57.665	109.951	201.599	357.047	613.107
11	29.439	40.496	86.498	175.922	342.719	642.684	1164.902
12	40.037	56.694	129.746	281.475	582.622	1156.831	2213.314
13	54.451	79.372	194.619	450.360	990.457	2082.295	4205.297
14	74.053	111.120	291.929	720.576	1683.777	3748.131	7990.065
15	100.712	155.568	437.894	1152.921	2862.421	6746.636	15181.122

Table 2 Present value of £1

Year	1%	2%	3%	4%	5%	6%	7%	8%	9%	10%	12%	14%	15%
1	0.990	0.980	0.971	0.961	0.952	0.943	0.935	0.926	0.917	0.909	0.893	0.877	0.870
2	0.980	0.961	0.943	0.925	0.907	0.890	0.873	0.857	0.842	0.826	0.797	0.769	0.756
3	0.971	0.942	0.915	0.889	0.864	0.840	0.816	0.794	0.772	0.751	0.712	0.675	0.658
4	0.961	0.924	0.889	0.855	0.823	0.792	0.763	0.735	0.708	0.683	0.636	0.592	0.572
5	0.951	0.906	0.863	0.822	0.784	0.747	0.713	0.681	0.650	0.621	0.567	0.519	0.497
6	0.942	0.888	0.838	0.790	0.746	0.705	0.666	0.630	0.596	0.564	0.507	0.456	0.432
7	0.933	0.871	0.813	0.760	0.711	0.665	0.623	0.583	0.547	0.513	0.452	0.400	0.376
8	0.923	0.853	0.789	0.731	0.677	0.627	0.582	0.540	0.502	0.467	0.404	0.351	0.327
9	0.914	0.837	0.766	0.703	0.645	0.592	0.544	0.500	0.460	0.424	0.361	0.308	0.284
10	0.905	0.820	0.744	0.676	0.614	0.558	0.508	0.463	0.422	0.386	0.322	0.270	0.247
11	0.896	0.804	0.722	0.650	0.585	0.527	0.475	0.429	0.388	0.350	0.287	0.237	0.215
12	0.887	0.788	0.701	0.625	0.557	0.497	0.444	0.397	0.356	0.319	0.257	0.208	0.187
13	0.879	0.773	0.681	0.601	0.530	0.469	0.415	0.368	0.326	0.290	0.229	0.182	0.163
14	0.870	0.758	0.661	0.577	0.505	0.442	0.388	0.340	0.299	0.263	0.205	0.160	0.141
15	0.861	0.743	0.642	0.555	0.481	0.417	0.362	0.315	0.275	0.239	0.183	0.140	0.123
16	0.853	0.728	0.623	0.534	0.458	0.394	0.339	0.292	0.252	0.218	0.163	0.123	0.107
17	0.844	0.714	0.605	0.513	0.436	0.371	0.317	0.270	0.231	0.198	0.146	0.108	0.093
18	0.836	0.700	0.587	0.494	0.416	0.350	0.296	0.250	0.212	0.180	0.130	0.095	0.081
19	0.828	0.686	0.570	0.475	0.396	0.331	0.276	0.232	0.194	0.164	0.116	0.083	0.070
20	0.820	0.673	0.554	0.456	0.377	0.319	0.258	0.215	0.178	0.149	0.104	0.073	0.061
25	0.780	0.610	0.478	0.375	0.295	0.233	0.184	0.146	0.116	0.092	0.059	0.038	0.030
30	0.742	0.552	0.412	0.308	0.231	0.174	0.131	0.099	0.075	0.057	0.033	0.020	0.015

Year	16%	18%	20%	24%	28%	32%	36%	40%	50%	60%	70%	80%	90%
1	0.862	0.847	0.833	0.806	0.781	0.758	0.735	0.714	0.667	0.625	0.588	0.556	0.526
2	0.743	0.718	0.694	0.650	0.610	0.574	0.541	0.510	0.444	0.391	0.346	0.309	0.277
3	0.641	0.609	0.579	0.524	0.477	0.435	0.398	0.364	0.296	0.244	0.204	0.171	0.146
4	0.552	0.516	0.482	0.423	0.373	0.329	0.292	0.260	0.198	0.153	0.120	0.095	0.077
5	0.476	0.437	0.402	0.341	0.291	0.250	0.215	0.186	0.132	0.095	0.070	0.053	0.040
6	0.410	0.370	0.335	0.275	0.227	0.189	0.158	0.133	0.088	0.060	0.041	0.029	0.021
7	0.354	0.314	0.279	0.222	0.178	0.143	0.116	0.095	0.059	0.037	0.024	0.016	0.011
8	0.305	0.266	0.233	0.179	0.139	0.108	0.085	0.068	0.039	0.023	0.014	0.009	0.006
9	0.263	0.226	0.194	0.144	0.108	0.082	0.063	0.048	0.026	0.015	0.008	0.005	0.003
10	0.227	0.191	0.162	0.116	0.085	0.062	0.046	0.035	0.017	0.009	0.005	0.003	0.002
11	0.195	0.162	0.135	0.094	0.066	0.047	0.034	0.025	0.012	0.006	0.003	0.002	0.001
12	0.168	0.137	0.112	0.076	0.052	0.036	0.025	0.018	0.008	0.004	0.002	0.001	0.001
13	0.145	0.116	0.093	0.061	0.040	0.027	0.018	0.013	0.005	0.002	0.001	0.001	0.000
14	0.125	0.099	0.078	0.049	0.032	0.021	0.014	0.009	0.003	0.001	0.001	0.000	0.000
15	0.108	0.084	0.065	0.040	0.025	0.016	0.010	0.006	0.002	0.001	0.000	0.000	0.000
16	0.093	0.071	0.054	0.032	0.019	0.012	0.007	0.005	0.002	0.001	0.000	0.000	
17	0.080	0.060	0.045	0.026	0.015	0.009	0.005	0.003	0.001	0.000	0.000		
18	0.069	0.051	0.038	0.021	0.012	0.007	0.004	0.002	0.001	0.000	0.000		
19	0.060	0.043	0.031	0.017	0.009	0.005	0.003	0.002	0.000	0.000			
20	0.051	0.037	0.026	0.014	0.007	0.004	0.002	0.001	0.000	0.000			
25	0.024	0.016	0.010	0.005	0.002	0.001	0.000	0.000					
30	0.012	0.007	0.004	0.002	0.001	0.000	0.000						

Table 3 Sum of an annuity of £1 for *n* years

Year	1%	2%	3%	4%	5%	6%	7%	8%
1	1.000	1.000	1.000	1.000	1.000	1.000	1.000	1.000
2	2.010	2.020	2.030	2.040	2.050	2.060	2.070	2.080
3	3.030	3.060	3.091	3.122	3.152	3.184	3.215	3.246
4	4.060	4.122	4.184	4.246	4.310	4.375	4.440	4.506
5	5.101	5.204	5.309	5.416	5.526	5.637	5.751	5.867
6	6.152	6.308	6.468	6.633	6.802	6.975	7.153	7.336
7	7.214	7.434	7.662	7.898	8.142	8.394	8.654	8.923
8	8.286	8.583	8.892	9.214	9.549	9.897	10.260	10.637
9	9.369	9.755	10.159	10.583	11.027	11.491	11.978	12.488
10	10.462	10.950	11.464	12.006	12.578	13.181	13.816	41.487
11	11.567	12.169	12.808	13.486	14.207	14.972	15.784	16.645
12	12.683	13.412	14.192	15.026	15.917	16.870	17.888	18.977
13	13.809	14.680	15.618	16.627	17.713	18.882	20.141	21.495
14	14.947	15.974	17.086	18.292	19.599	21.051	22.550	24.215
15	16.097	17.293	18.599	20.024	21.579	23.276	25.129	27.152
16	17.258	18.639	20.157	21.825	23.657	25.673	27.888	30.324
17	18.430	20.012	21.762	23.698	25.840	28.213	30.840	33.750
18	19.615	21.412	23.414	25.645	28.132	30.906	33.999	37.450
19	20.811	22.841	25.117	27.671	30.539	33.760	37.379	41.446
20	22.019	24.297	26.870	29.778	33.066	36.786	40.995	45.762
25	28.243	32.030	36.459	41.646	47.727	54.865	63.249	73.106
30	34.785	40.568	47.575	56.085	66.439	79.058	94.461	113.283

Year	9%	10%	12%	14%	16%	18%	20%	24%
1	1.000	1.000	1.000	1.000	1.000	1.000	1.000	1.000
2	2.090	2.100	2.120	2.140	2.160	2.180	2.200	2.240
3	3.278	3.310	3.374	3.440	3.506	3.572	3.640	3.778
4	4.573	4.641	4.779	4.921	5.066	5.215	5.368	5.684
5	5.985	6.105	6.353	6.610	6.877	7.154	7.442	8.048
6	7.523	7.716	8.115	8.536	8.977	9.442	9.930	10.980
7	9.200	9.487	10.089	10.730	11.414	12.142	12.916	14.615
8	11.028	11.436	12.300	13.233	14.240	15.327	16.499	19.123
9	13.021	13.579	14.776	16.085	17.518	19.086	20.799	24.712
10	15.193	15.937	17.549	19.337	21.321	23.521	25.959	31.643
11	17.560	18.531	20.655	23.044	25.738	28.755	32.150	40.238
12	20.141	21.384	24.133	27.271	30.350	34.931	39.580	50.895
13	22.953	24.523	28.029	32.089	36.766	42.219	48.497	64.110
14	26.019	27.975	32.393	37.581	43.672	50.818	59.196	80.496
15	29.361	31.722	37.280	43.842	51.659	60.965	72.035	100.815

Year	28%	32%	36%	40%	50%	60%	70%	80%
1	1.000	1.000	1.000	1.000	1.000	1.000	1.000	1.000
2	2.280	2.320	2.360	2.400	2.500	2.600	2.700	2.800
3	3.918	4.062	4.210	4.360	4.750	5.160	5.590	6.040
4	6.016	6.326	6.725	7.104	8.125	9.256	10.503	11.872
5	8.700	9.398	10.146	10.846	13.188	15.810	18.855	22.370
6	12.136	13.406	14.799	16.324	20.781	26.295	33.054	41.265
7	16.534	18.696	21.126	23.853	32.172	43.073	57.191	75.278
8	22.163	25.678	29.732	34.395	49.258	69.916	98.225	136.500
9	29.369	34.895	41.435	49.153	74.887	112.866	167.983	246.699
10	38.592	47.062	57.352	69.814	113.330	181.585	286.570	445.058
11	50.399	63.122	78.998	98.739	170.995	291.536	488.170	802.105
12	65.510	84.320	108.437	139.235	257.493	467.458	830.888	1444.788
13	84.853	112.303	148.475	195.929	387.239	748.933	1413.510	2601.619
14	109.612	149.240	202.926	275.300	581.859	1199.293	2403.968	4683.914
15	141.303	197.997	276.979	386.420	873.788	1919.869	4087.745	8432.045

Table 4 Present value of annuity of £1 per period

Year	1%	2%	3%	4%	5%	6%	7%	8%	9%	10%
1	0.990	0.980	0.971	0.962	0.952	0.943	0.935	0.926	0.917	0.909
2	1.970	1.942	1.913	1.886	1.859	1.833	1.808	1.783	1.759	1.736
3	2.941	2.884	2.829	2.775	2.723	2.673	2.624	2.577	2.531	2.487
4	3.902	3.808	3.717	3.630	3.546	3.465	3.387	3.312	3.240	3.170
5	4.853	4.713	4.580	4.452	4.329	4.212	4.100	3.993	3.890	3.791
6	5.795	5.601	5.417	5.424	5.076	4.917	4.766	4.623	4.486	4.355
7	6.728	6.472	6.230	6.002	5.786	5.582	5.389	5.206	5.033	4.868
8	7.652	7.325	7.020	6.733	6.463	6.210	5.971	5.747	5.535	5.335
9	8.566	8.162	7.786	7.435	7.108	6.802	6.515	6.247	5.985	5.759
10	9.471	8.983	8.530	8.111	7.722	7.360	7.024	6.710	6.418	6.145
11	10.368	9.787	9.253	8.760	8.306	7.887	7.499	7.139	6.805	6.495
12	11.255	10.575	9.954	9.385	8.863	8.384	7.943	7.536	7.161	6.814
13	12.134	11.348	10.635	9.986	9.394	8.853	8.358	7.904	7.487	7.103
14	13.004	12.106	11.296	10.563	8.899	9.295	8.745	8.244	7.786	7.367
15	13.865	12.849	11.938	11.118	10.380	9.712	9.108	8.559	8.060	7.606
16	14.718	13.578	12.561	11.652	10.838	10.106	9.447	8.851	8.312	7.824
17	15.562	14.292	13.166	12.166	11.274	10.477	9.763	9.122	8.544	8.022
18	16.398	14.992	13.754	12.659	11.690	10.828	10.059	9.372	8.756	8.201
19	17.226	15.678	14.324	13.134	12.085	11.158	10.336	9.604	8.950	8.365
20	18.046	16.351	14.877	13.590	12.462	11.470	10.594	9.818	9.128	8.514
25	22.023	19.523	17.413	15.622	14.094	12.783	11.654	10.675	9.823	9.077
30	25.808	22.397	19.600	17.292	15.373	13.765	12.409	11.258	10.274	9.427

Year	12%	14%	16%	18%	20%	24%	28%	32%	36%
1	0.893	0.877	0.862	0.847	0.833	0.806	0.781	0.758	0.735
2	1.690	1.647	1.605	1.566	1.528	1.457	1.392	1.332	1.276
3	2.402	2.322	2.246	2.174	2.106	1.981	1.868	1.766	1.674
4	3.037	2.914	2.798	2.690	2.589	2.404	2.241	2.096	1.966
5	3.605	3.433	3.274	3.127	2.991	2.745	2.532	2.345	2.181
6	4.111	3.889	3.685	3.498	3.326	3.020	2.759	2.534	2.339
7	4.564	4.288	4.089	3.812	3.605	3.242	2.937	2.678	2.455
8	4.968	4.639	4.344	4.078	3.837	3.421	3.076	2.786	2.540
9	5.328	4.946	4.607	4.303	4.031	3.566	3.184	2.868	2.603
10	5.650	5.216	4.833	4.494	4.193	3.682	3.269	2.930	2.650
11	5.988	5.453	5.029	4.656	4.327	3.776	3.335	2.978	2.683
12	6.194	5.660	5.197	4.793	4.439	3.851	3.387	3.013	2.708
13	6.424	5.842	5.342	4.910	4.533	3.912	3.427	3.040	2.727
14	6.628	6.002	5.468	5.008	4.611	3.962	3.459	3.061	2.740
15	6.811	6.142	5.575	5.092	4.675	4.001	3.483	3.076	2.750
16	6.974	6.265	5.669	5.162	4.730	4.033	3.503	3.088	2.758
17	7.120	5.373	5.749	4.222	4.775	4.059	3.518	3.097	2.763
18	7.250	6.467	5.818	5.273	4.812	4.080	3.529	3.104	2.767
19	7.366	6.550	5.877	5.316	4.844	4.097	3.539	3.109	2.770
20	7.469	6.623	5.929	5.353	4.870	4.110	3.546	3.113	2.772
25	7.843	6.873	6.907	5.467	4.948	4.147	3.564	3.122	2.776
30	8.055	7.003	6.177	5.517	4.979	4.160	3.569	3.124	2.778

Appendix III Answers to review questions

Note : All the answers are the work of the author. None has been supplied by an examining body. The examining bodies accept no responsibility whatsoever for the accuracy or method of working in the answers given.

Note : In order to save space, £ signs have been omitted from columns of figures, except where the figures refer to £000, or where the denomination needs to be specified.

1.1

Branch Stock (dates omitted)

	Memo			Memo	
Balance b/d	4,400	3,300	Branch debtors	21,000	21,000
Goods from head office	24,800	18,600	Cash sales	2,400	2,400
Gross profit		5,850	Returns to HO	1,000	750
			Goods stolen	600	450
			Profit and loss:		
			Normal wastage	100	75
			Profit and loss:		
			Excess wastage	152	114
			Balance c/d	3,948	2,961
	29,200	27,750		29,200	27,750

Branch Debtors

Balances b/d	3,946	Bad debts	148
Branch stock: Sales	21,000	Discounts allowed	428
		Bank	22,400
		Balance c/d	1,970
	24,946		24,946

1.2

(a) (dates omitted)

Branch Current Account

Balance b/d	20,160	Cash	30,000
Goods sent	23,160	Goods returned	400
Expenses paid	6,000	Balance c/d	22,420
Net profit	3,500		
	52,820		52,820

(b) Proof:

Branch assets	xxx
Less Branch liabilities	xxx
= Balance of branch current account	xxx
Indicates: Amount of money invested in branch	

1.3

(a) (i)

Goods from head office		**Branch Stock (Selling Prices)**		
(82,400 + 10% 8,240 =		Cash sales	89,940
90,640 + 25%)	113,300	Sales: Branch debtors	1,870
		Goods to other branches	3,300
		Branch stock adjustment:	
		Reductions	2,250
		Balance c/d	15,940
	113,300		113,300

(ii)

		Branch Stock Adjustment *(profit margin)	
Goods to other branches	660	Branch stock	22,660
Branch stock: Reductions	2,250	(113,300 – 90,640)	
Profit and loss	16,562		
Balance c/d	3,188		
	22,660		22,660

*As cost to branch (original cost + 10%) is subject to further mark-up of 25%, therefore margin is 20%, and this is profit margin used in this account.

(b)

Book stock per branch stock account	15,940
Physical stock	14,850
	1,090

Four possible reasons for deficiency:
(i) thefts by customers;
(ii) thefts by staff;
(iii) wastages due to breakages, miscounting, etc.;
(iv) cash misappropriated.

(c) Figure to be taken for RST balance sheet:

Actual stock at selling price	14,850
Less 20% margin	2,970
Cost to branch	11,880
Less head office loading	
(+10%=1/11th of adjusted figure) 1/11th	1,080
Actual cost to company	10,800

Therefore (iii) 10,800 is correct answer.

1.5

Packer & Stringer

Trading & Profit & Loss Account for the year ended 31 December 19X4

	HO		Branch	
Sales		39,000		26,000
Less Cost of goods sold				
Opening stock	13,000		4,400	
Add Purchases	37,000			
	50,000			
Goods to branch	17,200		17,200	
	32,800		21,600	
Less Closing stock	17,560	15,240	6,570	15,030
				10,970
				20
				10,990
Bad debt provision not required				
Salaries	4,500		3,200	
Administrative expenses	1,440		960	
Carriage	2,200		960	
General expenses	3,200		1,800	
Provision for bad debts	50			
Depreciation	150		110	
Manager's commission			360	
	11,540		7,390	
Net profit	9,900		3,600	
				13,500
Packer: Commission			900	
Interest on capital: Packer	840			
Stringer	240		1,080	
			1,980	
Balance of profits: Packer ¾	8,640			
Stringer ¼	2,880		11,520	13,500
				13,500

Balance Sheet as at 31 December 19X4

Fixed assets		
Furniture	2,600	
Less Depreciation	1,110	1,490
Current assets		
Stock	21,810	
Debtors	10,000	
Less Provision for bad debts	830	9,170
Cash and bank		3,000
		33,980
Less Current liabilities		
Creditors		6,200

Bank overdraft		1,350	
Manager's commission		120	7,670
Working capital			26,310
			27,800

1.7

Nion

Trading and Profit and Loss Account for the year ended 31 October 19X1

	Head office £000		Branch £000	
Sales		850		437
Transfers to branch		380		
		1,230		
Less Cost of goods sold:				
Opening stock	8		20	
	914			
Add Purchases				
Add Goods from HO	922		375	
			395	
Less Closing stock	12	910	15	380
Gross profit		320		57
Less Expenses:				
Administrative	200		16.5	
Distribution	80.5		5	
Depreciation	35		10	
Changes in provision for bad debts	(6)	309.5	0.5	32
Net profit		10.5		25

Balance Sheet as at 31 October 19X1

	£000	£000
Fixed assets at cost		450
Less Depreciation to date		215
		235
Current assets		
Stocks (12 + 12 + 4*)	28	
Debtors	120	
Less Provision	6	
	114	
Cash and bank (15.5 + 13 + 50)	78.5	
	220.5	
Less Current liabilities		
Creditors	50	
		170.5
		405.5

Capital
Balance at 1.11.19X0 410
Add Net profit 35.5
445.5
Less Drawings 40
405.5

*5 × 4/5

Net profit		41,200	2,286
Add Balance from last year			43,486
Balance carried forward to next year			2,000
			45,486

Balance Sheet as at 30 June 19X8

	£	£
Fixed assets		
Freehold buildings at cost		23,000
Machinery at cost	24,000	
Less Depreciation	9,600	14,400
		37,400
Current assets		
Stock	30,040	
Debtors	13,360	
Bank	14,500	
Cash in transit	1,990	
	59,890	
Less Current liabilities		
Creditors*	9,809	
Working capital		50,081
		87,481
Financed by:		
Share capital: Authorised and issued		40,000
Reserves		
Difference on exchange	1,995	
Profit and loss	45,486	
		47,481
		87,481

*Creditors HO 9,500 + Branch 195 + Manager 114 = 9,809.

(HO Books) *Branch Account*

	£	Fl		£	Fl
Balance b/d	25,136	189,260	Cash from debtors	36	320
Components	35,000	315,000	Remittances	28,000	256,000
Net profit	2,286	*24,000	Cash in transit	1,990	16,000
Difference on exchange	1,995	—	Balance c/d	34,391	255,940
	64,417	528,260		64,417	528,260

*This represents the profit per branch profit and loss account if it had been drawn up using florins.

1.9

Conversion of Branch Trial Balance to Pounds Sterling

	Fl	Fl	Rate	£	£
Freehold buildings	63,000		7	9,000	
Debtors and creditors	36,000	1,560	8	4,460	195
Sales		432,000	9		48,000
Head office		504,260	Actual		60,100
Branch cost of sales	360,000		*below	40,400	
Depreciation: Machinery	56,700			8,100	
Administration costs	18,000		9	2,000	
Stock 30.6.19X8	11,520		8	1,440	
Machinery at cost	126,000		7	18,000	
Remittances	272,000		Actual	29,990	
Balances at bank	79,200		8	9,900	
Selling and distribution	28,800		9	3,200	
Profit on exchange		—			1,995
	994,520	994,520		118,390	118,390

*Cost of sales: Branch Fl 360,000
Less Depreciation Fl 12,600 ÷ 7 = £1,800
Fl 347,400 ÷ 9 = £38,600
£40,400

EG Company Ltd

Trading and Profit and Loss Accounts for the year ended 30 June 19X8

	Head office		Branch	
Sales		104,000		48,000
Less Cost of sales	58,400		38,600	
Depreciation	600		1,800	
	59,000		40,400	
Goods to branch	35,000			
		24,000		
		80,000		
Gross profit				7,600
Administration costs	15,200		2,000	
Selling and distribution	23,300		3,200	
Provison for unrealised profit on branch stock	300			
Manager's commission			114	
		38,800		5,314

1.10

(a)

Trial Balance as at 31 December 19X0

	Crowns	Crowns	Rate	£	£
Bank	66,000		4	16,500	
Creditors		92,400	4		23,100
Debtors	158,400		4	39,600	
Fixed assets	145,200		5	29,040	
Head office		316,800	Actual		65,280
Profit and Loss		79,200	4.4		18,000
Stocks	118,800		4	29,700	
Difference on exchange			4		8,460
	488,400	488,400		114,840	114,840

(b) (Books of head office) Highland Branch

	£		£
Balance b/d	65,280	Balance c/d	91,740
Difference on exchange	8,460		
Net profit	18,000		
	91,740		91,740

(c)

Balance Sheet as at 31 December 19X0

	£	£
Fixed assets		68,640
Current assets:		
Stocks	56,100	
Debtors	58,080	
Bank	27,060	
	141,240	
Less Current liabilities		
Creditors	44,220	
Working capital		97,020
		165,660
Financed by:		
Issued share capital		86,400
Reserves		
Profit and loss	70,800	
Difference on exchange	8,460	79,260
		165,660

2.1

Machinery

19X3		£
Jan 1	Vendor	6,000

Vendor's Account

19X3		£	19X3		£
Jan 1	Bank	846	Jan 1	Machinery	6,000
Dec 31	Bank	2,000	Dec 31	HP interest	412
,, 31	Balance c/d	3,566			
		6,412			6,412
19X4			19X4		
Dec 31	Bank	2,000	Jan 1	Balance b/d	3,566
,, 31	Balance c/d	1,851	Dec 31	HP interest	285
		3,851			3,851
19X5			19X5		
Dec 31	Bank	2,000	Jan 1	Balance b/d	1,851
			Dec 31	HP interest	149
		2,000			2,000

Provision for Depreciation: Machinery

19X3		£	19X3		£
Dec 31	Balance c/d	600	Dec 31	Profit and loss	600
19X4			19X4		
Dec 31	Balance c/d	1,140	Jan 1	Balance b/d	600
			Dec 31	Profit and loss	540
		1,140			1,140
19X5			19X5		
Dec 31	Balance c/d	1,626	Jan 1	Balance b/d	1,140
			Dec 31	Profit and loss	486
		1,626			1,626

Balance Sheet as at 31 December 19X3

	£
Machinery at cost	6,000
Less Depreciation	600
	5,400
(included in Liabilities) Owing on HP	3,566

2.3

(a) Bulwell's books

Motor Lorries

19X1		£
	Granby Garages	54,000

Hire Purchase Interest

19X1		£	19X1		£
	Granby	11,250		Profit and loss	11,250
19X2	Granby	8,063	19X2	Profit and loss	8,063
19X3	Granby	4,078	19X3	Profit and loss	4,078

Bank

19X1		£
	Granby (Jan 1)	9,000
	Granby (Dec 31)	24,000
19X2	Granby	24,000
19X3	Granby	20,391

Granby Garages

Motor lorries / HP interest

		£			£
19X1	Bank	9,000			
	Bank	24,000	19X1	HP interest	54,000
	Balance c/d	32,250			11,250
		65,250			65,250
19X2	Bank	24,000	19X2	Balance b/d	32,250
	Balance c/d	16,313		HP interest	8,063
		40,313			40,313
19X3	Bank	20,391	19X3	Balance b/d	16,313
				Interest	4,078
		20,391			20,391

Depreciation

		£			£
19X1	Balance c/d	12,500	19X1	Profit and loss	12,500
19X2	Balance c/d	25,000	19X2	Balance b/d	12,500
				Profit and loss	12,500
		25,000			25,000
19X3	Balance c/d	37,500	19X3	Balance b/d	25,000
				Profit and loss	12,500
		37,500			37,500
19X4	Balance c/d	50,000	19X4	Balance b/d	37,500
				Profit and loss	12,500
		50,000			50,000

Balance Sheet as at 31 December

	19X1	19X2	19X3	19X4
Motor lorries cost	54,000	54,000	54,000	54,000
Less Depreciation to date	12,500	25,000	37,500	50,000
	41,500	29,000	16,500	4,000
Liabilities:				
HP debt outstanding	32,250	16,313		–
Charge against profit:				
HP interest	11,250	8,063	4,078	
Depreciation	12,500	12,500	12,500	

NB: Calculation of interest
19X1 25% × £45,000 = £11,250
19X2 25% × £32,250 = £8,063
19X3 25% × £16,313 = £4,078

(b)

Granby's books

Bulwell Aggregates

		£			£
19X1	HP sales	54,000	19X1	Bank – deposit	9,000
	HP interest	11,250		– instalment	24,000
				Balance c/d	32,250
		65,250			65,250
19X2	Balance b/d	32,250	19X2	Bank – instalment	24,000
	HP interest	8,063		Balance c/d	16,313
		40,313			40,313
19X3	Balance b/d	16,313	19X3	Bank – instalment	20,391
	HP interest	4,078			
		20,391			20,391

Bank

		£
19X1	Bulwell	9,000
	Bulwell	24,000
19X2	Bulwell	24,000
19X3	Bulwell	20,391

HP Interest

		£			£
19X1	HP trading	11,250	19X1	Bulwell	11,250
19X2	HP trading	8,063	19X2	Bulwell	8,063
19X3	HP trading	4,078	19X3	Bulwell	4,078

Hire Purchase Trading

(19X1)

	£		£
Cost of lorries	43,200	HP sales	54,000
Provision for unrealised profit c/d	6,450	HP interest	11,250
Gross profit	15,600		
	49,650		65,250

(19X2)

	£		£
Less Provision for unrealised profit c/d	3,263	HP interest	8,063
Gross profit		Provision for unrealised profit b/d	6,450
	3,187		
	11,250		

(19X3)

	£		£
Gross profit	4,078	HP interest	4,078
	3,263	Provision for unrealised profit b/d	3,263
	7,341		

2.5

Working: Unrealised profit

Profit margin $\dfrac{10,800}{54,000} \times \dfrac{100}{1} = 20\%$

20% × £32,250 = £6,450
20% × £16,313 = £3,263

Vehicles & Finance Co Ltd

Motor lorry

19X7				19X7		
Dec 31	Cash	1,000		Dec 31	Motor lorry	3,081
Dec 31	Balance c/d	2,081				
		3,081				3,081
19X8				19X8		
Dec 31	Cash	1,199		Jan 1	Balance b/d	2,081
Dec 31	Balance c/d	1,090		Dec 31	HP interest 10% of 2,081	208
		2,289				2,289
19X9				19X9		
Dec 31	Cash	1,199		Jan 1	Balance b/d	1,090
				Dec 31	HP interest 10% of 1,090	109
		1,199				1,199

Motor Lorry

19X7			
Dec 31	Vehicles and finance	3,081	

Provision for Depreciation: Motor Lorry

19X7			
Dec 31	Profit and loss	770	
19X8			
Dec 31	Profit and loss	578	
19X9			
Dec 31	Profit and loss	433	

Hire Purchase Interest

19X8					
Dec 31	Vehicles and finance	208	Dec 31	Profit and loss	208
19X9					
Dec 31	Vehicles and finance	109	Dec 31	Profit and loss	109

Balance Sheet as at 31 December 19X8

Motor lorry at cost		3,081
Less Depreciation to date		1,348
		1,733
(Included in Liabilities) Owing on hire purchase		1,090

2.6

S Craven

Hire Purchase Trading Account for the year ended 30 September 19X6

Sales at hire purchase price (1,900 × 100)		190,000
Purchases	120,000	
Less Stock (100 × 60)	6,000	
	114,000	
Provision for unrealised profit and interest*	42,560	
		156,560
Gross profit		33,440
Less Rent	4,500	
Wages	8,600	
General expenses	10,270	
		23,370
Net profit		10,070

*Cash yet to be collected 190,000 − 83,600 = 106,400

Therefore provision $\dfrac{106,400}{190,000} \times 76,000 = 42,560$

Balance Sheet as at 30 September 19X6

Fixed assets		10,000
Current assets		
Stock	6,000	
HP debtors	106,400	
Less Provision: unrealised profit and interest	42,560	
	63,840	
Bank	10,630	
	80,470	
Less Current liabilities		
Creditors	8,400	
Working capital		72,070
		82,070
Financed by:		
Capital		
Balance at 1.10.19X5		76,000
Add Net profit		10,070
		86,070
Less Drawings		4,000
		82,070

2.7

RJ

Hire Purchase Trading and Profit and Loss Account for the year ended 31 December 19X8

Sales at hire purchase price (850 × 300)		255,000
Purchases	180,000	
Less Stock (50 × 200)	10,000	
Cost of goods sold	170,000	
Provision of unrealised profit	59,500	229,500
Gross profit		25,500
Less Wages and salaries	12,800	
General expenses	5,500	
Bank interest	400	18,700
Net profit		6,800

Balance Sheet as at 31 December 19X8

Fixed assets		10,000
Current assets		
Stock in warehouse	10,000	
Hire purchase debtors	178,500	
Less Provision for unrealised profit	59,500	
	119,000	
	129,000	
Less Current liabilities		
Creditors	16,600	
Bank overdraft	19,600	
	36,200	92,800
		102,800
Financed by:		
Capital		100,000
Cash introduced		6,800
Add Net profit		106,800
Less Drawings		4,000
		102,800

2.11

(a)(i)

Machine Hire Purchase

1. 1X8	Bank	2,000		1. 1X8	Machine	10,000
30. 6.X8	Bank	3,056		1. 1X8	HP interest	7,280
31.12.X8	Bank	3,056				
31.12.X8	Balance c/d	9,168				
		17,280				17,280
30. 6.X9	Bank	3,056		1. 1X9	Balance b/d	9,168
31.12.X9	Bank	3,056				
31.12.X9	Balance c/d	3,056				
		9,168				9,168
30. 6.X0	Bank	3,056		1. 1X0	Balance b/d	3,056

(ii)

Machine Hire Purchase (see workings)

		Machine HP				
1. 1X8	Machine HP	7,280		31.12.X8	Profit and loss	4,368
				31.12.X8	Balance c/d	2,912
		7,280				7,280
1. 1X9	Balance b/d	2,912		31.12.X9	Profit and loss	2,427
				31.12.X9	Balance c/d	485
		2,912				2,912
1. 1X0	Balance b/d	485		31.12.X0	Profit and loss	485

(b)

(Extracts) Balance Sheets as at 31 December

	19X8	19X9	19X0
Fixed assets			
Machinery at cost	10,000	10,000	10,000
Less Depreciation to date	1,800	3,600	5,400
	8,200	6,400	4,600
Creditors:			
Falling due within 1 year			
Hire purchase*	3,685	2,571	
Falling due after 1 year			
Hire purchase*	2,571		

(19X8 3,056 + 3,056 − 2,427)
(19X9 3,056 − 485)

Workings: Interest (sum of digits is 15)
To 31.12.19X8 (5/15 × 7,280) 2,427 + (4/15 × 7,280) = 4,368
To 31.12.19X9 (3/15 × 7,280) 1,456 + (2/15 × 7,280) 971 = 2,427
To 31.12.19X0 1/15 × 7,280 = 485
Depreciation (10,000 − 1,000) ÷ 5 = 1,800 p.a.

3.1

Cases Stock (dates omitted)

	Rate	Qty	£		Rate	Qty	£
Stocks b/d				Sales		450	100
In warehouse	1.5	600	900	Cases kept by			
At customers	1.5	4,000	6,000	customers	6	800	4,800
Purchases	2	5,000	10,000	Cases suspense:			
Profit on cases				Profit on hire			34,000
Service to				Stocks c/d			
profit and loss			34,525	Factory	1.5	2,150	3,225
				At customers	1.5	6,200	9,300
		9,600	51,425			9,600	51,425

3.2

Cases Suspense

	Rate	Qty	£		Rate	Qty	£
Customers cases returned	6	14,000	84,000	Deposits returnable b/d	6	4,000	24,000
Cases kept	6	800	4,800	Customers: Cases sent	8	17,000	136,000
Cases stock: Profit on hire			34,000				
Deposits returnable c/d	6	6,200	37,200				
		21,000	160,000			21,000	160,000

Cases Stock

	Rate	Qty	£		Rate	Qty	£
Stocks b/d:				Returned to supplier		4,000	11,610
In warehouse	£2	9,600	19,200	Cash: Scrapped		3,500	55
At customers	£2	6,100	12,200	Deficit		420	-
Purchases	£3	18,000	54,000	Kept by customers		5,800	23,200
Profit on cases Service to P/L			37,025	Profit on cases hire			47,600
				Stocks c/d			
				In warehouse	£2	15,180	30,360
				At customers	£2	4,800	9,600
		33,700	122,425			33,700	122,425

Cases Suspense

	Rate	Qty	£		Rate	Qty	£
Returns	£4	43,100	172,400	Deposits returnable	£4	6,100	24,400
Kept by customers	£4	5,800	23,200	Sent to customers	£5	47,600	238,000
Cases stock: Profit on hire			47,600				
Deposits Returnable c/d	£4	4,800	19,200				
		53,700	262,400			53,700	262,400

3.3

Containers Stock

(dates omitted)

	Rate	Qty	£		Rate	Qty	£
Stocks b/d:				Scrapped	-	120	-
Warehouse	10	2,000	20,000	Container suspense:			
At customers	10	5,500	55,000	Kept by customers (W1)	20	250	5,000
Bank: Purchases	10	1,250	12,500	Containers missing (W2)	-	40	-
Profit and loss				Stocks c/d			
Profit on containers			900	Warehouse	10	3,390	33,900
				At customers	10	4,950	49,500
		8,750	88,400			8,750	88,400

Containers Suspense

	Rate	Qty	£		Rate	Qty	£
Debtors	20	9,050	181,000	Deposits on crates returnable b/d	20	5,500	110,000
Container stock Kept by customers	20	250	5,000	Debtors: Charged out (W1)	20	8,750	175,000
Deposits on crate returnable c/d	20	4,950	99,000				
		14,250	285,000			14,250	285,000

Workings: (W1) Balancing item needed for container suspense, caused by customers keeping containers beyond the permitted time limit.
(W2) Balancing item – quantities only. 40 containers are missing. An investigation should be made into how this could have happened.

3.4

(balances not carried down)

Note: It would have been possible to have these records kept in only two accounts, a Containers Suspense Account and a Containers Stock Account. However, the examiner has asked for another method, using four accounts, now illustrated. The eventual answer is the same as per the shorter textbook method.

(a) **Cases Stock (at valuation £5 per case)**

	No	£		No	£
Balances b/d:			Cases profit and loss	-	2,000
In warehouse	1,000	5,000	(Purchases written down to £5 each)		
At customers	3,000	15,000	Retained by customers	1,500	7,500
Purchases	2,000	12,000	Cases damaged to p/l	100	500
			Cases sold	50	250
			Balances c/d:		
			In warehouse	850	4,250
			At customers	3,500	17,500
	6,000	32,000		6,000	32,000

(b) **Cases Suspense (at £8 returnable price each)**

	No	£		No	£
Returned by customers	23,000	184,000	Balances b/d with customers	3,000	24,000
Cases stock (Purchases)	1,500	12,000	Charged to customers	25,000	200,000
Balances c/d	3,500	28,000			
	28,000	224,000		28,000	224,000

(c) **Cases sent to Customers (at chargeable price £10)**

	No	£		No	£
Balances b/d	3,000	30,000	Cases returned	23,000	184,000
Cases charged out	25,000	200,000	Bank: Cases kept	1,500	15,000
Cases profit and loss		50,000	Bank: Cash from customers (23,000 × £2)		46,000
			Balances c/d	3,500	35,000
	28,000	280,000		28,000	280,000

5.1

(d)

Cases Profit and Loss Account

Dr	£	Cr	£
Cases stock: Purchases written down	50,450	Cases to customers (25,000 × £2)	50,000
Cases sold	2,000	Profit on cases retained	4,500
Cases damaged	250	Cash sales	100
Cash: Repairs	500		
Profit to main profit and loss	1,400		
	54,600		54,600

Bank

Dr	£	Cr	£
Application	20,000	Balance c/d	120,220
Allotment (30,000 less excess applications 5,000)	25,000		
First call (119,200 × 0.25)	29,800		
Second call (119,200 × 0.375)	44,700		
D Regan (800 × 0.9)	720		
	120,220		120,220

D Regan

Dr	£	Cr	£
Ordinary share capital	800	Bank	720
		Forfeited shares	80
	800		800

Application and Allotment

Dr	£	Cr	£
Ordinary share capital	45,000	Bank	20,000
		Bank	25,000
	45,000		45,000

Ordinary Share Capital

Dr	£	Cr	£
Forfeited shares	800	Application and allotment	45,000
Balance c/d	120,000	First call	30,000
		Second call	45,000
		D Regan	800
	120,800		120,800

First Call

Dr	£	Cr	£
Ordinary share capital	30,000	Bank	29,800
		Forfeited shares	200
	30,000		30,000

Second Call

Dr	£	Cr	£
Ordinary share capital	45,000	Bank	44,700
		Forfeited shares	300
	45,000		45,000

Forfeited Shares

Dr	£	Cr	£
First call	200	Ordinary share capital	800
Second call	300		
D Regan	80		
Transfer to share premium	220		
	800		800

Balance Sheet

	£		£
Bank	120,220	Ordinary share capital	120,000
		Share premium	220
	120,220		120,220

5.2

Bank

Dr	£	Cr	£
Application (32,600 × 0.50)	16,300	Application and allotment: Refund of application monies	1,300
Allotment (20,000 × 1.50 less excess application monies 5,000)	25,000	Balance c/d	100,160
First call (19,900 × 2)	39,800		
Second call (19,880 × 1)	19,880		
B Mills (120 × 4)	480		
	101,460		101,460

Application and Allotment

Dr	£	Cr	£
Bank: Refunds	1,300	Bank	16,300
Ordinary share capital	40,000	Bank	25,000
	41,300		41,300

First Call Account

Dr	£	Cr	£
Ordinary share capital	40,000	Bank	39,800
		Forfeited shares	200
	40,000		40,000

Second Call Account

Dr	£	Cr	£
Ordinary share capital	20,000	Bank	19,880
		Forfeited shares	120
	20,000		20,000

Ordinary Share Capital

Dr	£	Cr	£
Forfeited shares	600	Application and allotment	40,000
Balance c/d	100,000	First call	40,000
		Second call	20,000
		B Mills	600
	100,600		100,600

5.3

Forfeited Shares

First call	200	Ordinary share capital	600
Second call	120		
B Mills	120		
Transfer to share premium	160		
	600		600

B Mills

Ordinary share capital	600	Bank	480
		Forfeited shares	120
	600		600

Cosy Fires Ltd

Application and allotment

Cash: Return of unsuccessful applications 5,000 × 0.60	3,000	Cash application for 65,000 × 0.60	39,000
Share capital: Due on application 40,000 × 0.70	28,000	Cash: Balance due on allotment (see workings)*	1,975
and allotment 40,000 × 0.25	10,000	Balance c/d: Due from allottee in respect of 500 shares:	
		500 × 0.35 =	175
		Less o/paid on application	
		250 × 0.60 =	150
			25
	41,000		41,000
Balance b/d	25	Forfeited shares	25
			25

Share Capital

Forfeited shares: Amount called on shares forfeited: 500 × 0.70	350	Balance b/d	75,000
Balance c/d	115,000	Application and allotment	28,000
		Call	11,850
		Forfeited shares	500
	115,350		115,350

Share Premium

Balance c/d	10,375	Application and allotment	10,000
		Forfeited shares	375
	10,375		10,375

Forfeited Shares

Application and allotment	25	Share capital	350
Share capital	500	Cash: 500 × 1.10 per share	550
Share premium	375		
	900		900

Call

Share capital 39,500 × 0.30	11,850	Cash	11,850

Balance Sheet as at 31 May 19X7

Share capital
Authorised: 160,000 ordinary shares of 1 each ... 160,000

Issued and fully paid: 115,000 ordinary shares of 1 each ... 115,000
Capital reserve:
Share premium ... 10,375

*Workings:

Due on application 0.60 × 40,000	24,000	
Due on allotment 0.35 × 40,000	14,000	38,000
Received on application: 0.60 × 65,000	39,000	
Less Refunded 5,000 × 0.60	3,000	36,000
Balance due on allotment		2,000
Less Amount due on		
application and allotment 500 × 0.95	475	
Received on application 750 × 0.60	450	25
		1,975

5.5

M Ltd

Ledger Accounts (dates omitted)

Cash

Application and allotment (750,000 × 85p)	637,500	Application and allotment (Refund 125,000 × 85p)	106,250
Application and allotment 18,750 (500,000 × 25p – overpaid 125,000 × 85p)			
First and final call (495,000 × 50p)	247,500		
Forfeited shares (5,000 × 90p)	4,500		

Application and Allotment

Share capital	250,000	Cash	637,500
Share premium	300,000	Cash	18,750
Cash	106,250		
	656,250		656,250

Share Premium

Balance c/d	302,000	Application and allotment	300,000
		Forfeited shares	2,000
	302,000		302,000

6.1

Share Capital

Forfeited shares	5,000	Balance b/d	500,000
Balance c/d	1,000,000	Application and allotment	250,000
		First and final call	250,000
		Forfeited shares	5,000
	1,005,000		1,005,000

First and Final Call

Share capital	250,000	Cash	247,500
		Forfeited shares	2,500
	250,000		250,000

Forfeited Shares

First and final call	2,500	Share capital	5,000
Share capital	5,000	Cash	4,500
Share premium	2,000		
	9,500		9,500

Given format 1 of the Companies Act 1985, there are two places where uncalled capital can be shown. These are either place A or C II (5).

If C II(5) is chosen it becomes:

Current assets

II Debtors

(5) Called up share capital not paid ... 2,500

Issued share capital

1,000,000 ordinary shares of £1 each ... 1,000,000

Reserves

Share premium ... 302,000

The authorised share capital should be shown also as a note only.
The increase in share premium would also be shown as a note in the statement showing changes in reserves.

(a)

	Dr	Cr
(A1) Bank	5,000	
(A2) Ordinary share applicants		5,000

Cash received from applicants.

	Dr	Cr
(B1) Ordinary share applicants	5,000	
(B2) Ordinary share capital		5,000

Ordinary shares allotted.

	Dr	Cr
(C1) Preference share capital	5,000	
(C2) Preference share redemption		5,000

Shares to be redeeemed.

	Dr	Cr
(D1) Preference share redemption	5,000	
(D2) Bank		5,000

Payment made to redeem shares.

	Balances before	Effect Dr	Effect Cr	Balances after
Net assets (except bank)	20,000			20,000
Bank	13,000	(A1) 5,000	(D2) 5,000	13,000
	33,000			33,000
Preference share capital	5,000	(C1) 5,000		–
Preference share redemption	–	(D1) 5,000	(C2) 5,000	–
Ordinary share capital	15,000		(B2) 5,000	20,000
Ordinary share applicants	–	(B1) 5,000	(A2) 5,000	–
Share premium	2,000			2,000
	22,000			22,000
Profit and loss	11,000			11,000
	33,000			33,000

(b)

	Dr	Cr
(A1) Preference share capital	5,000	
(A2) Preference share redemption		5,000

Shares to be redeemed.

	Dr	Cr
(B1) Preference share redemption	5,000	
(B2) Bank		5,000

Cash paid on redemption.

	Dr	Cr
(C1) Profit and loss appropriation	5,000	
(C2) Capital redemption reserve		5,000

Transfer per Companies Act.

	Balances before	Effect Dr	Effect Cr	Balances after
Net assets (except bank)	20,000			20,000
Bank	13,000		(B2) 5,000	8,000
	33,000			28,000

	Balances before	Effect Dr	Effect Cr	Balances after
Preference share capital	5,000	(A1) 5,000		–
Preference share redemption	–	(B1) 5,000	(A2) 5,000	–
Ordinary share capital	15,000			15,000
Capital redemption reserve	–		(C2) 5,000	5,000
Share premium	2,000			2,000
	22,000			22,000
Profit and loss	11,000	(C1) 5,000		6,000
	33,000			28,000

(c)

	Dr	Cr
(A1) Bank	1,500	
(A2) Ordinary share applicants		1,500

Cash received from applicants.

	Dr	Cr
(B1) Ordinary share applicants	1,500	
(B2) Ordinary share capital		1,500

Ordinary shares allotted.

	Dr	Cr
(C1) Profit and loss appropriation	3,500	
(C2) Capital redemption reserve		3,500

Part of redemption not covered by new issue, to comply with Companies Act.

	Dr	Cr
(D1) Preference share capital	5,000	
(D2) Preference share redemption		5,000

Shares to be redeemed.

	Dr	Cr
(E1) Preference share redemption	5,000	
(E2) Bank		5,000

Payment made for redemption.

	Balances before	Effect Dr	Effect Cr	Balances after
Net assets (except bank)	20,000			20,000
Bank	13,000	(A1) 1,500	(E2) 5,000	9,500
	33,000			29,500
Preference share capital	5,000	(D1) 5,000		–
Preference share redemption	–	(E1) 5,000	(D2) 5,000	–
Ordinary share capital	15,000		(B2) 1,500	16,500
Ordinary share applicants	–	(B1) 1,500	(A2) 1,500	–
Capital redemption reserve	–		(C2) 3,500	3,500
Share premium	2,000			2,000
	22,000			22,000
Profit and loss	11,000	(C1) 3,500		7,500
	33,000			29,500

(d)

	Dr	Cr
(A1) Preference share capital	5,000	
(A2) Preference share redemption		5,000

Shares to be redeemed.

	Dr	Cr
(B1) Profit and loss appropriation	1,250	
(B2) Preference share redemption		1,250

Premium on redemption of shares not previously issued at premium.

	Dr	Cr
(C1) Profit and loss appropriation	5,000	
(C2) Capital redemption reserve		5,000

Transfer because shares redeemed out of distributable profits.

	Dr	Cr
(D1) Preference share redemption	6,250	
(D2) Bank		6,250

Payment on redemption.

	Balances before	Effect Dr	Effect Cr	Balances after
Net assets (except bank)	20,000			20,000
Bank	13,000		(D2) 6,250	6,750
	33,000			26,750
Preference share capital	5,000	(A1) 5,000		–
Preference share redemption	–	(D1) 6,250	(A2) 5,000 (B2) 1,250	–
Ordinary share capital	15,000			15,000
Capital redemption reserve	–		(C2) 5,000	5,000
Share premium	2,000			2,000
	22,000			22,000
Profit and loss	11,000	(C1) 5,000 (B1) 1,250		4,750
	33,000			26,750

(e)

	Dr	Cr
(A1) Bank	7,000	
(A2) Ordinary share applicants		7,000

Cash received from applicants.

	Dr	Cr
(B1) Ordinary share applicants	7,000	
(B2) Ordinary share capital		7,000

Ordinary shares allotted.

(C1) Preference share capital ... 5,000
(C2) Preference share redemption ... 5,000
Shares being redeemed.

(D1) Share premium account ... 1,500
(D2) Preference share redemption ... 1,500
Amount of share premium account used for redemption.

(E1) Profit and loss appropriation ... 500
(E2) Preference share redemption ... 500
Excess of premium payable over amount of share premium account usable for the purpose.

(F1) Preference share redemption ... 7,000
(F2) Bank ... 7,000
Amount payable on redemption.

	Balances before	Effect Dr	Effect Cr	Balances after
Net assets (except bank)	20,000			20,000
Bank	13,000	(A1) 7,000	(F2) 7,000	13,000
	33,000			33,000
Preference share capital	5,000	(C1) 5,000		–
Preference share redemption	–	(F1) 7,000	(C2) 5,000 (D2) 1,500 (E2) 500	–
Ordinary share capital	15,000		(B2) 7,000	22,000
Ordinary share applicants	–	(B1) 7,000	(A2) 7,000	–
Share premium account	2,000	(D1) 1,500		500
	22,000			22,500
Profit and loss	11,000	(E1) 500		10,500
	33,000			33,000

6.3

(a)
(A1) Ordinary share capital ... Dr 6,000
(A2) Ordinary share purchase ... Cr 6,000
Shares to be purchased.

(B1) Ordinary share purchase ... 6,000
(B2) Bank ... 6,000
Payment for shares purchased.

(C1) Profit and loss ... 4,500
(C2) Capital redemption reserve ... 4,500
Transfer of deficiency of permissible capital payment to comply with Companies Act.

	Balances before	Effect Dr	Effect Cr	Balances after
Net assets (except bank)	12,500			12,500
Bank	13,000		(B2) 6,000	7,000
	25,500			19,500
Preference share capital	5,000			5,000
Ordinary share capital	10,000	(A1) 6,000		4,000
Ordinary share purchase	–	(B1) 6,000	(A2) 6,000	–
Non-distributable reserves	6,000			6,000
Capital redemption reserve	–		(C2) 4,500	4,500
	21,000			19,500
Profit and loss	4,500	(C1) 4,500		–
	25,500			19,500

(b)
(A1) Ordinary share capital ... Dr 6,000
(A2) Ordinary share purchase ... Cr 6,000
Shares to be purchased.

(B1a) Profit and loss ... 4,500
(B1b) Non-distributable reserves ... 1,500
(B2) Ordinary share purchase ... 6,000
Transfers of profit and loss and non-distributable reserves per Companies Act.

(C1) Ordinary share purchase ... 12,000
(C2) Bank ... 12,000
Payment to shareholders.

	Balances before	Effect Dr	Effect Cr	Balances after
Net assets (except bank)	12,500			12,500
Bank	13,000		(C2) 12,000	1,000
	25,500			13,500
Preference share capital	5,000			5,000
Ordinary share capital	10,000	(A1) 6,000		4,000
Ordinary share purchase	–	(C1) 12,000	(A2) 6,000 (B2) 6,000	–
Non-distributable reserves	6,000	(B1b) 1,500		4,500
	21,000			13,500
Profit and loss	4,500	(B1a) 4,500		–
	25,500			13,500

6.5

Workings: Opening balance 10% debentures (a/c below)
Originally issued 375,000
Less Redeemed previously 150,000   225,000

10% Debentures

30/9	Debenture redemption	225,000	1/7 Balance b/d 225,000

Workings: Sinking fund investments (A/c below)

Appropriations to date 334,485
Interest invested (39,480 – 2,475) 37,005
371,490
Less Sold – at cost 144,915
226,575

Sinking Fund Investments

1/7	Balance b/d	226,575	2/8	Bank No 2 Sale 73,215
2/8	Sinking fund: Profit (73,215 – 69,322)	3,893	25/9	Bank No 2 Sale 160,238
25/9	Sinking fund: Profit (Cost 226,575 – 69,322 = 157,253. Sold for 160,238)	2,985		
		233,453		233,453

Workings: Sinking fund (A/c below)
Previous contributions 334,485
Interest on investments 39,480
Profit: Previous sales of investments (147,243 – 144,915) 2,328
Profit: Previous purchase debentures (150,000 – 147,243) 2,757
379,050
Less Transfer to general reserve sum equal to debentures redeemed 150,000
229,050

Sinking Fund A/c

30/9	Debentures redemption (Premium 1%)	2,250	1/7 Balance b/d 229,050
30/9	General reserve	236,889	7/7 No 2 Bank: Interest 1,756
			2/8 SF Investments: Profit 3,893
			13/9 No 2 Bank: Interest 1,455
			25/9 SF Investments: Profit 2,985
		239,139	239,139

No 2 Bank A/c

1/7	Balance b/d	2,475	30/9 W Bank plc (deposit) 15,150
7/7	Sinking fund: Interest	1,756	30/9 Debentures redemption 212,100
2/8	SF investments: Sale	73,215	30/9 No 1 Bank transfer of balance 11,889
13/9	Sinking fund: Interest	1,455	
25/9	SF investments: Sale	160,238	
		239,139	239,139

Debenture Redemption A/c

30/9	No 2 Bank (225,000 Debentures – 15,000 B Ltd = 210,000 at 1% premium)	212,100	30/9 10% Debentures 225,000
			30/9 Sinking fund (premium) 2,250
30/9	Balance c/d (15,000 outstanding at premium 1%)	15,150	
		227,250	227,250

W Bank plc

30/9	No 2 Bank	15,150
		15,150

6.7

(Dates omitted – all figures shown in £000)

Application and Allotment

Ordinary shares	80	Bank 60
Share premium	20	Bank 40
	100	100

Call Account

Ordinary shares	20	Bank 18
		Investments 2
	20	20

Investments (own shares)

Call	2	Bank 11
Share premium	9	
	11	11

6.9

(*Note*: some abbreviations are used)

10% Debentures

31.12.X8	Debenture redemption	12,000	1.4.X8 Balance b/d 100,000
31.3.X9	Balance c/d	88,000	
		100,000	100,000

7.1

Debenture Redemption Fund

31.12.X8	Reserve (equal to debentures redeemed)	12,000	1.4.X8	Balance b/d	20,000
			31.12.X8	DRFI (profit on redemption)	1,400
			31.12.X8	DR (profit on purchase)	900
			31.12.X9	Bank	1,600
			31.3.X9	Profit and loss (annual appropriation)	2,000
31.3.X9	Balance c/d	13,900			
		25,900			25,900

Debenture Redemption Fund Investment

1.4.X8	Balance b/d	20,000	31.12.X8	Bank (sale)	11,400
31.12.X8	DR Fund (profit on sale)	1,400			
31.3.X9	Bank (2,000 + 300 + 1,600)	3,900	31.3.X9	Balance c/d	13,900
		25,300			25,300

Debenture Redemption

31.12.X8	Bank (purchase)	11,400	31.12.X8	10% Debentures	12,000
31.12.X8	DR Fund (profit on redemption)	900	31.12.X8	Debenture interest accrued	300
		12,300			12,300

Debenture Interest

30.9.X8	Bank (100,000 × 10% ÷ 2)	5,000			
31.12.X8	Debenture redemption (interest included in price 12,000 × 10% × ¼)	300			
31.3.X9	Bank (88,000 × 10% ÷ 2)	4,400	31.3.X9	Profit and loss	9,700
		9,700			9,700

(a)

Checkers Ltd

Profit and Loss Account for the year ended 31 December 19X5

	Total	Basis of allocation	Pre-incorporation	Post-incorporation
Gross profit	28,000	Turnover	8,000	20,000
Less				
Salaries of vendors	1,695	Actual		1,695
Wages	8,640	Time	2,160	6,480
Rent	860	Time	215	645
Distribution	1,680	Turnover	480	1,200
Commission	700	Turnover	200	500
Bad debts	314	Actual	104	210
Interest	1,650	Time	990	660
Directors' remuneration	4,000	Actual		4,000
Directors' expenses	515	Actual		515
Depreciation*				
Motors	1,900	Actual	400	1,500
Machinery	575	Actual	125	450
Bank interest	168	Actual		168
	22,697		6,369	16,328
Net profit	5,303		1,631	3,672
	28,000		8,000	20,000

*Depreciation:

Motors to 31 March 19X5 $20\% \times 3$ months $\times 7,000 + 20\% \times 1$ month $\times 3,000 = 400$

After $20\% \times 9$ months $\times 7,000 + 20\% \times 9$ months $\times 3,000 = 1,500$

(b) Transfer to capital reserve

(c) Charge to a goodwill account

7.2

Adjusted Profits

Profit per accounts	16,400	23,920		19,650
Add Motor expenses saved	620	660		700
,, Depreciation overcharged	1,500	700		60
,, Wrapping expenses saved	420	480		510
,, Bank interest	180	590		740
,, Preliminary expenses		690		
	2,720	3,120		2,010
	19,120	27,040		21,660
Less Extra management remuneration	1,500	1,500		1,500
,, Investment income	290	340		480
,, Rents received	940	420		
,, Opening stock		1,900		
,, Profit on property		4,800		
	2,730	8,960		1,980
Profits as adjusted	16,390	18,080		19,680

Average profit

16,390
18,080
19,680
54,150 ÷ 3 = 18,050

If 18,050 is a return of 25% on investment, then

$\dfrac{18,050}{25} \times 100 = 72,200$ purchase price.

7.3

(a)

CK

Realisation

Freehold premises	8,000	CK Ltd: Value at which	27,200
Plant	4,000	assets taken over	
Stock	2,000	Discount on creditors	150
Debtors	5,000		
Profit on realisation	8,350		
	27,350		27,350

Capital

CK Ltd: Shares	24,150	Balance b/d	16,000
Cash	200	Profit on realisation	8,350
	24,350		24,350

CK Ltd (not asked for in question)

Realisation	27,200	Creditors	3,050
		Shares	24,150
	27,200		27,200

RP Ltd – Realisation

Freehold premises	4,500	CK Ltd: Value at which assets	13,000
Plant	2,000	taken over	
Stock	1,600		
Debtors	3,400		
Profit on realisation	1,500		
	13,000		13,000

Sundry Shareholders

CK Ltd	5,000	Share capital	4,000
Cash	3,000	Profit on realisation	1,500
		Revenue surplus	2,500
	8,000		8,000

CK Ltd (not asked for in question)

Realisation	13,000	Bank overdraft	3,500
		Creditors	1,500
		Sundry shareholders: Cash	5,000
		Shares	3,000
	13,000		13,000

(b) *Journal of CJK Ltd*

(Have omitted narratives)

Cash	5,000	
Share premium		3,000
Ordinary shares		2,000
Cash	7,840	
Discount on issue	160	
7 per cent debentures		8,000
Goodwill	7,000	
Freehold premises	10,000	
Plant	3,500	
Stock	2,000	
Debtors	5,000	
Provision for discounts receivable	150	
Creditors		3,200
Provision for bad debts		300
Ordinary shares		24,150
Goodwill	500	
Freehold premises	5,500	
Plant	2,000	
Stock	1,600	
Debtors	3,400	
Creditors		1,500
Bank overdraft		3,500
Cash		5,000
Ordinary share capital		3,000
Formation expenses	1,200	
Cash		1,200

(c)

CJK Ltd
Balance Sheet as at 1st January 19X0

		£
Fixed assets: at cost		
Freehold premises		15,500
Plant		5,500
Goodwill		7,500
		28,500
Current assets		
Stock		3,600
Debtors	8,400	
Less Provision for bad debts	300	8,100
Cash at bank		3,140
		14,840
Less Current liabilities		
Creditors	4,700	
Less Provision	150	4,550
Working capital		10,290
		38,790

8.1

Debenture Interest

		£			£
19X3			19X3		
Dec 31	Bank	9,600	Dec 31	Profit and loss	12,800
,, 31	Income tax	3,200			
		12,800			12,800

Income Tax

		£			£
19X3			19X3		
Dec 31	Balance c/d	3,200	Dec 31	Debenture interest	3,200

Ordinary Dividends

		£			£
19X3			19X3		
Jul 1	Bank	20,000	Dec 31	Profit and loss	50,000
Dec 31	Accrued c/d	30,000			
		50,000			50,000

Deferred Taxation

		£			£
19X3			19X3		
Dec 31	Balance c/d	14,000	Dec 31	Profit and loss*	14,000

*35% of (£90,000 − £50,000) = £14,000

Corporation Tax

		£			£
19X3			19X3		
Dec 31	Balance c/d	90,000	Dec 31	Profit and loss	90,000

Profit and Loss Account (extracts) year to 31 December 19X3

	£	£
Net trading profit		220,000
Less Debenture interest		12,800
Profit on ordinary activities before taxation		207,200
Corporation tax	90,000	
Deferred tax	14,000	104,000
Profit on ordinary activities after taxation		103,200
Less Ordinary dividends: Interim	20,000	
Final proposed	30,000	50,000

Balance Sheet (extracts) as at 31 December 19X3

	£
Creditors: Amounts falling due within one year	
Proposed ordinary dividend	30,000
Corporation tax	90,000
Deferred tax	14,000
Income tax	3,200

8.3

Workings:
(W1) Tax deducted from fixed interest income is $\frac{1}{3} \times £24,000 = £8,000$
(W2) Changes in deferred taxation account.

Timing difference:	£
Capital allowances allowable for tax (D)	90,000
Depreciation actually charged (D)	50,000
	40,000

Transferred to deferred tax account £40,000 × 35% = £14,000

Deferred Tax

		£				£
19X2			19X2			
Dec 31	Balance c/d	81,000	Jan 1	Balance b/d	(J)	67,000
			Dec 31	Tax on profit on ordinary activities (W2)		14,000
		81,000				81,000

Income Tax

		£				£
19X2			19X2			
Oct 31	Interest (C1) receivable	8,000	Nov 30	Debenture interest	(B)	20,000
Dec 15	Bank	12,000				
		20,000				20,000

Interest Receivable

19X2			£	19X2			£
Dec 31	Profit and loss		32,000	Oct 31	Bank	(C1)	24,000
				,, 31	Income tax	(C1)	8,000
			------				------
			32,000				32,000

Debenture Interest

19X2			£	19X2			£
Nov 30	Bank	(B)	60,000	Dec 31	Profit and loss		80,000
,, 30	Income tax	(B)	20,000				
			------				------
			80,000				80,000

Investment Income

19X2			£	19X2			£
Dec 31	Profit and loss		900	Sept 1	Bank	(C2)	900
			-----				-----
			900				900

Corporation Tax

19X2			£	19X2			£
Sept 30	Bank[1]		112,000	Jan 1	Balance b/d	(K)	115,000
,, 30	Tax on profit			Dec 31	Tax on profit		
	on ordinary				on ordinary		
	activities[2]	(K)	3,000		activities	(L)	154,000
Dec 31	Balance c/d	(L)	154,000				
			--------				--------
			269,000				269,000

Notes:
1. £115,000 owing – £3,000 reduction (K) = £112,000.
2. Adjustment for amendment in tax bill.

Tax on Profit on Ordinary Activities

19X2			£	19X2			£
Dec 31	Corporation			Sept 30	Corporation		
	tax		154,000		tax	(K)	3,000
Dec 31	Deferred			Dec 31	Profit and loss		165,000
	tax	(W2)	14,000				
			--------				--------
			168,000				168,000

Preference Dividends

19X2			£	19X2		£
Jun 30	Bank	(F)	18,000	Dec 31	Profit and loss	18,000

Ordinary Dividends

19X2			£	19X2			£
Mar 31	Bank	(I)	90,000	Jan 1	Accrued b/d	(I)	90,000
Jul 15	Bank	(G)	75,000	Dec 31	Profit and loss		195,000
Dec 31	Accrued c/d		120,000				
			--------				--------
			285,000				285,000

Barnet Ltd

Profit and Loss (extracts) for the year ended 31 December 19X2

		£
Net trading profit	(A)	560,000
Add Fixed rate interest (C1) (gross)	32,000	
Investment income (C2) (gross)	900	32,900

		592,900
Less Debenture interest (B) (gross)		80,000
Profit on ordinary activities before taxation		512,900
Tax on profit on ordinary activities[1]		165,000
Profit on ordinary activities after taxation		347,900
Less Dividends:		
Preference dividend	18,000	
Ordinary: Interim	75,000	
Final	120,000	213,000

Note:
1. Notes attached to accounts giving make-up of this figure.

Balance Sheet (extracts) as at 31 December 19X2

	£
Creditors amounts falling due within one year	
Proposed ordinary dividend	120,000
Corporation tax	154,000
Deferred tax	81,000

A final point concerns the difference in treatment of tax on investment income as compared with tax on other income, such as interest. It is only the tax on investment income which is treated as part of the final tax costs, while the tax on interest is simply deducted from charges paid by the company. You would have to study taxation in detail to understand why this happens.

8.5

BG Ltd
Profit and Loss Account for the year ended 31 December 19X7

Trading profit		50,000
Income from shares in related companies	3,000	
Other interest receivable and similar income	1,100	4,100
		54,100
Interest payable and similar charges		3,600
Profit on ordinary activities before taxation		50,500
Tax on profit on ordinary activities		24,000
Profit on ordinary activities after taxation		26,500
Undistributed profits from last year		9,870
		36,370
Transfers to reserves	5,000	
Dividends proposed	21,000	26,000
Undistributed profits carried to next year		10,370

Preference dividend 6% £9,000
Ordinary dividend £125,000

Research and development expenditure: assumed to have been carried forward in accordance with SSAP 13 and can be justified. Failing this it would have to be a realised loss.

For a plc no changes required, except that the payment should not reduce net assets below called-up share capital and undistributable reserves = 400 + 150 + 100 = 650. A further bad debt might change this position.

8.6

(All in £million)

Ordinary Dividends

31.8.X8	Bank (X7 final)	28	1.4.X8	Balance b/d	28
31.12.X8	Bank (X8 interim)	12	31.3.X9	Profit and loss	48
31.3.X9	Balance c/d	36			
		76			76

Deferred Taxation

31.3.X9	Balance c/d	8	1.4.X8	Balance b/d	3
			31.3.X9	Profit and loss	5
		8			8

9.1

Either Ltd

	+	£000
Profit per draft accounts		157
(i) Stock: reduce to net realisable value		—
(ii) Directors' remuneration		35
(iii) Bad debt		43
(iv) Corporation tax saved on (i) + (ii) + (iii) × 50% 54		30
(v) Depreciation adjustment (W1)		30
(vi) Revaluation reserve (realised on sale)	125	
(vii) General reserve	80	
(viii) Loss brought forward (W2)	144	
	259	282
	net −23	
Maximum possible dividend	−23	
	134	

(W1) *Reducing balance*

Cost 1.12.19X1		100,000
Depreciation 19X2		25,000
		75,000
Cost 1.6.19X3		25,000
		100,000
Depreciation 19X3		25,000
		75,000
Cost 29.2.X4		28,000
31.5.X4		45,000
		148,000
Depreciation 19X4		37,000
		111,000
Cost 1.12.19X4		50,000
		161,000
Depreciation 19X5		40,250
		120,750
		127,250

Total 25,000 + 25,000 + 37,000 + 40,250 =

Straight line

	19X2	19X3	19X4	19X5
Cost 1.12.19X2	100,000			
1.6.19X3	25,000			
29.2.19X4	28,000			
31.5.19X4	45,000			
1.12.19X4	50,000			
	25,000	25,000	25,000	25,000
		3,125	6,250	6,250
			5,250	7,000
			5,625	11,250
				12,500
	25,000	28,125	42,125	62,000

Total 157,250

Extra depreciation 157,250 − 127,250 = 30,000

(W2) As profits after tax were £157,000 but were shown in the balance sheet as £13,000, this means that a deficit of £144,000 had been brought forward from last year.

(W4)   See (W1) 7,500 + 25,000 + 12,500 + new shares issued for cash
30,000 = 75,000

(b) (Main points)

	Old shareholdings	New shareholdings
Expected profit	22,500	22,500
Less Interest 11½%	11,500	
,, 8%		12,000
Taxable profits	11,000	10,500
Less Corporation tax 33⅓%	3,667	3,500
Profits before dividends	7,333	7,000
Preference dividends – if profits sufficient	9,000	–

Before reconstruction

(Old) Preference shareholders

Before reconstruction it would have taken over 5 years at this rate before preference dividends payable, as probably deficit of 38,850 on the profit and loss account would have to be cleared off first.

(Old) Ordinary shares

Even forgetting the profit and loss account deficit, the preference dividends were bigger than available profits. This would leave nothing for the ordinary shareholder.

After reconstruction

The EPS (earnings per share) is £7,000 ÷ 150,000 = 4.67p
If all profits are distributed the following benefits will be gained:

By old preference shareholders
50,000 shares × 4.67p   2,335
£50,000 8% debentures   4,000
                      6,335

Plus any benefits from tax credits.

By old ordinary shareholders
15,000 shares × 4.67p   700

Plus any benefits from tax credits.

(c) Preference shareholders – points to be considered:

(i) What were prospects for income?

Based on projected earnings would have been no income for over 5 years, then earnings of 7,333 per annum if all profits distributed.

(ii) What are new prospects for income?

Total income of 6,333 per annum immediately.

(iii) Is it worth exchanging (i) for (ii)?

Obviously depends on whether forecasts are accurate or not. If the above are accurate would seem worthwhile.

10.1 (a)   **Merton Manufacturing Co Ltd**
Balance Sheet as at ...

Fixed tangible assets			
Freehold land and buildings at cost			95,000
Plant and equipment at written-down value	(W1)		104,350
			199,350
Current assets			
Stocks		25,000	
Debtors		50,000	
Bank	(W2)	14,150	
		89,150	
Creditors: Amounts falling due within one year			
Creditors		63,500	
Net current assets			25,650
Total assets *less* current liabilities			225,000
Long-term loans: 8 per cent debentures	(W3)		150,000
			75,000
Capital and reserves			
Called-up share capital			
150,000 50p ordinary shares	(W4)		75,000
			75,000

Workings:

(W1)   *Capital Reduction*

Ordinary shares 50p (new)	7,500	Ordinary shares £1 (old)	90,000
(1 for 6 = 15,000 × 50p)		6% preference shares (old)	150,000
Ordinary shares 50p (new)	25,000	11½% Debentures (old)	100,000
(1 for 3 – preference –		Share premium written off	25,000
50,000 × 50p)			
8% debentures	50,000		
(1 for 3 preference)			
8% debentures	100,000		
(exchange for 11½%)			
Ordinary shares 50p	12,500		
(1 for every £4 old debenture)			
Goodwill written off	50,000		
Profit and loss written off	38,850		
Plant and equipment*	81,150		
	365,000		365,000

*per (vii) of question – amount needed to balance.

(W2)   Shares issued 60,000 shares × 50p = 30,000
           Cash 30,000 – overdraft 15,850 = balance 14,150

(W3)   See capital reduction – debit side (W1) new debentures 50,000 +
           100,000 = 150,000

(iv) What have preference shareholders given up?

Some of exchange consists of ordinary shares which are more risky than preference shares, both in terms of dividends and of payments on liquidation.

(v) What have they gained?

Debenture interest payable whether profits made or not.

10.2

(a) (Narratives omitted)

	Dr	Cr
Preference share capital	37,500	
Ordinary share capital	175,000	
Capital reduction		212,500

Preference shares reduced 25p each (0.25 × 150,000) &
Ordinary shares reduced by 0.875 (200,000 × 0.875).

Capital reduction	3,375	
Ordinary share capital		3,375

Ordinary shares issued re preference dividend
arrears, 27,000 × 0.125.

Share premium	40,000	
Capital reduction		40,000

Share premium balance utilised.

Provision for depreciation	62,500	
Capital reduction	72,500	
Plant and machinery		135,000

Plant and machinery written down to 75,000.

Capital reduction	176,625	
Profit and loss		114,375
Preliminary expenses		7,250
Goodwill		55,000

Profit and loss account and intangible assets written off.

Cash	62,500	
Ordinary share applicants		62,500

Applications for shares 500,000 × 0.125.

Ordinary share applicants	62,500	
Ordinary share capital		62,500

500,000 ordinary shares issued.

(b) *Balance Sheet as at 31 December 19X5*

Fixed assets			
Leasehold property at cost		80,000	
Less Provision for depreciation		30,000	
			50,000
Plant and machinery at valuation			75,000
			125,000
Current assets			
Stock		79,175	
Debtors		31,200	
Bank		11,500	
		121,875	
Less Current liabilities			
Creditors		43,500	
Working capital			78,375
			203,375
Financed by:			
Share capital:			
Preference shares			112,500
150,000 shares £0.75			
Ordinary shares			
727,000 ordinary shares £0.125			90,875
			203,375

10.3

(i)	*The Journal (narratives omitted)*	Dr	Cr
	Preference share capital	37,500	
	Capital reduction		37,500
(ii)	Ordinary share capital	360,000	
	Capital reduction		360,000
(iii)	Capital reserve	48,000	
	Capital reduction		48,000
(iv)	Preference share capital	112,500	
	Ordinary share capital	240,000	
	New ordinary share capital		352,500
(v)	(a) Debenture holders	150,000	
	Debentures		150,000
	(b) Cash	150,000	
	Debenture holders		150,000
(vi)	Capital reduction	445,500	
	Goodwill etc.		210,000
	Plant		45,000
	Furniture		6,600
	Profit and loss		183,900

11.2

(i) The replacement cost is irrelevant. The stock should be shown at the cost of £26,500. This assumes historic cost accounts.

(ii) *Paramite*: Stock to be valued at direct costs £72,600 plus fixed factory overhead £15,300 = £87,900. Under no circumstances should selling expenses be included.

Paraton: As net realisable value is lower than the costs involved, this figure of £9,520 should be used (SSAP 9).

(iii) In this case there is a change of accounting policy. Accordingly a prior period adjustment will be made. On a straight line basis net book value would have been:

Cost 160,000 less 12½% × 2 years =	120,000
Value shown	90,000
Therefore prior period adjustment of	30,000

to be added to retained profit at 1 November 19X4.

For 19X5 and each of the following 5 years depreciation will be charged at the rate of £20,000 per annum (FRS 3).

(iv) The cost subject to depreciation is £250,000 less land £50,000 = £200,000. With a life of 40 years this is £5,000 per annum.

This also will result in a prior period adjustment, in this case 10 × £5,000 = £50,000. This will be debited to retained profits at 1 November 19X4. For 19X5 and each of the following 29 years the yearly charge of depreciation will be £5,000 (FRS 3).

(v) Write off £17,500 to profit and loss (SSAP 13).

(vi) As this development expenditure is almost definitely going to be recovered over next 4 years it can be written off over that period (SSAP 13).

(vii) As this is unlikely to happen often it is an exceptional item. Charge to profit and loss on ordinary activities under the appropriate statutory heading (FRS 3).

(viii) As this is over 20 per cent, it is material and appears to be long-term. This means that Litteshall Ltd is an associated company and accounts should be prepared accordingly. The post-acquisition profits to be brought in are 30% × £40,000 = £12,000.

11.5 The fact that this is a partnership does not mean that accounting standards are not applicable; they are just as applicable to a partnership as they are to a limited company.

(a) (i) These should be included as Sales £60,000 in the accounts for the year to 31 May 19X7. This is because the matching concept requires that revenue, and the costs used up in achieving it, should be matched up. Profits: increase of £60,000.

Finer Textiles Ltd
Balance Sheet as at 31 March 19X6

Fixed assets		
Intangible: Goodwill		15,000
Tangible: Plant		169,800
Furniture		6,000
		190,800
Current assets		
Stock	170,850	
Debtors	65,100	
Bank	107,400	
Cash	150	
	343,500	
Creditors: Amounts falling due within 1 year		
Creditors	31,800	
Net current assets		311,700
Total assets *less* current liabilities		502,500
Creditors: Amounts falling due after more than 1 year		
Debentures		150,000
		352,500
Capital and reserves		
Called-up share capital		352,500

11.1 (a) Following is a brief answer:

(i) Such closure costs should be treated as an exceptional item, because:
- it is (probably) a material item;
- these are costs not likely to recur regularly or frequently.

(ii) This should be adjusted in tax charge for 19X7. Because it is not material (probably) it does not need to be disclosed separately.

(iii) The excess should be credited to a reserve account, and a note attached to the balance sheet. Depreciation to be based on revalued amount and on new estimate of remaining life of the asset, to be disclosed in a note to the accounts.

(iv) Treat as bad debt and write off to profit and loss. Because it is a material item it should be disclosed as an exceptional item in the profit and loss account.

(v) This is a prior period adjustment. The retained profit brought forward should be amended to allow for the change in accounting policy in the current year. The reasons: (a) it is material, (b) relates to a previous year, (c) as a result of change in accounting policy. The adjustment should be disclosed in a note to the financial statements.

(b) *See* Section 11.25 and 11.39.

(ii) Stock values are normally based on the lower of cost or net realisable value. In this case it depends how certain it is that the stock can be sold for £40,000. If a firm order can definitely be anticipated, then the figure of £40,000 can be used as this then represents the lower figure of net realisable value. Profit: an increase of £15,000. However, should the sale not be expected, then the concept of prudence dictates that the scrap value of £1,000 be used. Profit: a reduction of £24,000.

(b) It is important to establish the probability of the payment of the debt of £80,000. If it is as certain as it possibly can be that payment will be made, even though it may be delayed then no provision is needed. Profit change: nil.

However, the effect on future profits can be substantial. A note to the accounts detailing the possibilities of such changes should be given.

(c) The concepts which are applicable here are (i) going concern, (ii) consistency, (iii) accruals, (iv) prudence.

Following on the revelations in (b) and the effect on sales so far of the advertising campaign, is the partnership still able to see itself as a going concern? This would obviously affect the treatment of valuations of all assets.

Given that it can be treated as a going concern, the next point to be considered is that of consistency. The treatment of the expense item should be treated consistently.

The accruals concept is concerned with matching up revenues and costs, and will affect the decision as to how much of the costs should be carried forward. Some revenue in future periods needs to be expected with a high degree of certainty before any of this expenditure should be carried forward. It does not seem highly likely that large revenues can be expected in future in this case. In any case 75 per cent is a very large proportion of such expenditure to be carried forward. There is no easy test of the validity of the partners' estimates. Granted that under SSAP 13 for development expenditure some of it, under very stringent conditions, can be carried forward. If the partners' estimates can be accepted under this, then profits would be increased by 75% × (50,000 + 60,000) = £82,500.

(d) The expected profit/loss is as follows:

	Project A	Project B	Project C
Direct costs to date	30,000	25,000	6,000
Overheads to date	4,000	2,000	500
Future expected direct costs	10,000	25,000	40,000
" " overheads	2,000	2,000	3,000
Total of expected costs	46,000	54,000	49,500
Sale price of project	55,000	50,000	57,500
Expected total profit/loss	9,000	(4,000)	8,000
% Complete	75%	50%	15%

When a project is sufficiently near completion then a proportion of the profits can be taken as being realised.

Project A is 75 per cent complete and this indicates profit being taken. Whether or not 75 per cent can be taken, i.e. £6,750, will depend on the facts of the case. If completion at the above figures can be taken for granted then it might be reasonable to do so. Prudence dictates that a lesser figure be taken.

With project B there is an expected loss. Following the prudence concept losses should always be accounted for in full as soon as they become known.

In project C it is too early in the project, 15 per cent completed, to be certain about the outcome. No profit should therefore be brought into account.

Profit, dependent on comments about project A, will therefore be increased by £6,750 – £4,000 = £2,750.

(e) This is a case where the examiner has dipped into topics from other subjects. What is needed here is a tree diagram to show the probabilities.

(i) Redundancy payments: £100,000.

The reorganisation satisfies the requirements of FRS3, that it had a material effect on the nature and focus of the reporting entity's operations. As a result, the costs should be shown separately on the face of the profit and loss account after operating profit and before interest, and included under the heading of continuing operations. Relevant information regarding its effect on the taxation charge should be shown in a note to the profit and loss account. If there are other exceptional items in the financial period, and where, where practicable, between them, further information should be given, to assist users in assessing the impact of the different items on the net profit or loss attributable to shareholders.

(ii) Closure costs of a factory

FRS 3 requires that material profits or losses on the termination of an operation should be treated as exceptional and shown separately on the face of the profit and loss account after operating profit and before interest, and included under the appropriate heading of continuing or discontinued operations. In calculating the profit or loss in respect of the termination, consideration should only be given to revenue and costs directly related to it. Clearly, the costs have been identified and are known and there is a loss on the termination. It should not have been deducted from reserves, it must go through the profit and loss account.

(iii) Change of basis of depreciation: £258,000

There should only be a change in the basis of depreciation if it brings about a fairer presentation of the accounting results and financial position of the company – *see* SSAP 12. This SSAP also requires that the depreciation should be shown as normal expenses, rather than as a prior period adjustment.

Because the item is a material one, and makes comparison difficult, a note as to the details should be appended to the accounts.

(iv) Additional expenses covered by fire: £350,000

These expenses are covered by SSAP 17 as post-balance sheet non-adjusting events. The fire happened after the balance sheet date, and therefore did not affect conditions as at that date. The figures in this year's accounts should not therefore be altered.

If the event was such as to call into question the continuation of the business, then there should be a note to the accounts on the going-concern basis. In this particular instance this does not seem to be the case, but good practice, although not necessary, would be to give details of the event in notes to the accounts.

(v) Bad debt: £125,000

The accounts have not yet been approved by the directors, and it does affect the valuation of assets at the year end. SSAP 17 would be to treat it as a post-balance sheet adjusting event. It should therefore be

There is a probability of 0.75 of achieving £50,000 sales. As this is greater than the specified figure of 0.70 then the stocks should not be written down. Effect on profits: nil.

(f) The opening stock should be shown as the revised figure. If error had not been found this year's profit would have been £7,000 greater.

The adjustment should be shown as a prior period adjustment in the current accounts.

(a)

The Chief Accountant

Uncertain Ltd

Dear Sir/Mr...,

Report on Draft Profit and Loss Account for the year ended 30 September 19X6

Further to your letter/our meeting of . . . I would like to offer my suggestions for the appropriate accounting treatment of items *(i)* to *(v)*.

Address

Date

11.6

written off as a bad debt.

Where it is considered to be a material and unusual event, there should also be a note attached to the accounts.

Should you like to have further discussions concerning any of the points raised, will you please contact me. I hope that you will find my comments to be of use.

Yours faithfully,

CACA

(b)

Uncertain Ltd

Draft profit and loss account for the year ended 30 September 19X6

Sales		5,450,490
Manufacturing cost of sales (W1)		2,834,500
		2,615,990
Administration expenses	785,420	
Selling expenses (W2)	1,013,600	
		1,799,020
Operating profit		816,970
Continuing operations – redundancy payments	100,000	
Discontinued operations – factory closure costs	575,000	
		675,000
Profit before tax		141,970
Corporation tax (50%) (W3)		70,985
		70,985
Proposed dividend on ordinary shares		125,000
Reduction in retained profits		(54,015)

(W1) £3,284,500 − £100,000 (i) − £350,000 (iv) = £2,834,500
(W2) £629,800 + £258,800 (iii) + £125,000 (v) = £1,013,600
(W3) 50% of profits before tax

11.7 (a) (i) Post-balance sheet events consists of those events, whether favourable or unfavourable, which take place between the date of the balance sheet and the date on which the financial accounts and notes are approved by the directors.

(ii) Adjusting events are post-balance sheet events which give extra evidence of what was happening at the balance sheet date. The events included may be included because they are either of a statutory nature or taken into account by convention.

(iii) Non-adjusting events are balance sheet events concerned with matters which did not exist at the balance sheet date.

(iv) Contingent gain/loss is concerned with something which seems to be apparent at the balance sheet date but can only be verified by future events which are uncertain.

(b) Adjusting entries: (i) debtor's inability to pay; (ii) subsequent discovery of frauds rendering accounts incorrect; (iii) when net realisable value is used for stock valuation later shown to be wrong when stock sold; (iv) subsequent discovery of errors rendering accounts incorrect.

Non-adjusting entries: (i) change in foreign exchange rates; (ii) strikes; (iii) nationalisation; (iv) share issues.

(c) (i) A material contingent loss should be accrued for where some future event will give evidence of the loss, subject to the fact that it should be able to be determined with reasonable accuracy when the accounts are agreed by the directors.

(ii) They should be disclosed in the financial statements if it is very probable that they will be realised.

12.1 (i) (for internal use) **Rogers plc**

Trading and Profit and Loss Account for the year ended 31 December 19X2

Sales			288,000
Less Returns inwards			11,500
			276,500
Less Cost of sales:			
Stock 1 January 19X2		57,500	
Add Purchases	164,000		
Less Returns outwards	2,000		
		162,000	
Carriage inwards		1,300	
		220,800	
Less Stock 31 December 19X2		64,000	
			156,800
Gross profit			119,700
Distribution costs:			
Salaries and wages		2,800	
Rent and rates		3,750	
General distribution expenses		4,860	
Motor expenses		3,600	
Depreciation: Motors		6,500	
Equipment		700	
			22,210
Administrative expenses:			
Salaries and wages		5,600	
Rent and rates		2,500	
General administrative expenses		3,320	
Motor expenses		3,600	
Auditors' remuneration		500	
Discounts allowed		3,940	
Bad debts		570	
Depreciation: Motors		3,500	
Equipment		1,100	
			24,630
			46,840

[12.1 (i) continued — internal use]

	(I)	(II)	(III)
Other operating income: Royalties receivable		1,800	72,860
			74,660
Income from shares in undertakings in which the company has a participating interest	660		
Interest on bank deposit	770	1,430	76,090
Interest payable: Debenture interest			2,400
Profit on ordinary activities before taxation			73,690
Tax on profit on ordinary activities			30,700
Profit on ordinary activities after taxation			42,990
Retained profits from last year		15,300	58,290
Transfer to general reserve		8,000	
Proposed ordinary dividend		30,000	38,000
Retained profits carried forward to next year			20,290

(ii) (published accounts) **Rogers plc**

Profit and Loss Account for the year ended 31 December 19X2

	(I)	(II)	(III)
Turnover			276,500
Cost of sales			156,800
Gross profit			119,700
Distribution costs	22,210		
Administrative expenses	24,630	46,840	72,860
Other operating income		1,800	74,660
Income from shares in undertakings in which the company has a participating interest	660		
Other interest receivable	770	1,430	76,090
Interest payable			2,400
Profit on ordinary activities before taxation			73,690
Tax on profit on ordinary activities			30,700
Profit for the year on ordinary activities after taxation			42,990
Transfer to general reserve		8,000	
Proposed ordinary dividend		30,000	38,000
Retained profits for the year			4,990

Notes to accounts on debenture interest.

12.2 *(i)* (for internal use)

Federal plc

Trading and Profit and Loss Account for the year ended 31 December 19X4

	(I)	(II)	(III)
Sales			849,000
Less Returns inwards		5,800	843,200
Less Cost of sales:			
Stock 1 January 19X4		64,500	
Add Purchases	510,600		
Less Returns outwards	3,300	507,300	
Carriage inwards		4,900	
		576,700	
Less Stock 31 December 19X4		82,800	
Cost of goods sold		493,900	
Wages		11,350	
Depreciation of plant and machinery		1,500	506,750
Gross profit			336,450
Distribution costs			
Salaries and wages	29,110		
Rent and rates	20,000		
Motor expenses	10,400		
General distribution expenses	8,220		
Haulage costs	2,070		
Depreciation: Motors	15,000		
Plant and machinery	8,000	92,800	
Administrative expenses			
Salaries and wages	20,920		
Rent and rates	5,000		
Motor expenses	5,200		
General administrative expenses	2,190		
Bad debts	840		
Discounts allowed	5,780		
Auditors' remuneration	2,000		
Directors' remuneration	5,000		
Depreciation: Motors	7,000		
Plant and machinery	5,000	58,930	
Less Discounts received		6,800	52,130
		144,930	
		191,520	
Income from shares in undertakings in which the company has a participating interest		3,500	
Interest from government securities		1,600	5,100
			196,620

Amount written off investment in related
companies 14,000
Debenture interest .... 3,800 → 17,800
Profit on ordinary activities before taxation 178,820
Tax on profit on ordinary activities 74,000
Profit on ordinary activities after taxation 104,820
Retained profits from last year .... 37,470 → 142,290

Transfer to debenture redemption reserve 20,000
Proposed ordinary dividend .... 50,000 → 70,000
Retained profits for the year 72,290

(ii) (published accounts)   Federal plc

Profit and Loss Account for the year ended 31 December 19X4

Turnover		843,200
Cost of sales		506,750
Gross profit		336,450
Distribution costs	92,800	
Administrative expenses	52,130	144,930
		191,520
Income from shares in undertakings in which the company has a participating interest	3,500	
Other interest receivable	1,600	5,100
		196,620
Amounts written off investments	14,000	
Interest payable	3,800	17,800
Profit on ordinary activities before taxation		178,820
Tax on profit on ordinary activities		74,000
Profit on ordinary activities after taxation		104,820
Transfer to reserves	20,000	
Proposed ordinary dividend	50,000	70,000
Retained profits for the year		34,820

12.3 (a)   Rufford plc

Profit and Loss Account for the year ended 31 March 19X6

	Notes	£000	£000
Turnover	(1)		642
Cost of sales (60 + 401 − 71)			390
Gross profit			252
Distribution costs (33 + 19)		52	
Administrative expenses (97 + 8)		105	157
Operating profit – continuing operations	(2)		95
Loss on disposal of discontinued operations	(3)		12
			83
Income from other fixed asset investments	(4)	14	
Other interest receivable		25	39
			122
Interest payable	(5)		6
Profit on ordinary activities before taxation			116
Tax on profit on ordinary activities	(6)		44
Profit for the year on ordinary activities after taxation			72
Dividends (21 + 42)	(7)		63
Retained profits for the period			9

Notes to the accounts:

1 Turnover is net of VAT.

2 Operating profit is shown after charging the following:

	£000	£000
Depreciation: distribution costs	19	
administrative expenses	8	27
Auditor's remuneration		20
Directors' emoluments		45
Hire of plant		12

3 Factory closure expenses.

4 Income from fixed asset investment is in respect of a listed company.

5 Interest payable is on a bank overdraft, repayable within 5 years.

6 Tax on profit on ordinary activities:

	£000
Corporation tax at 50% on profits	38
Transfer to deferred taxation	9
Overprovision in 19X5	(3)
	44

7 Dividends:

	£000
Interim 5p per share	21
Final: proposed 10p per share	42
	63

8 Earnings per share:

EPS of 17.1p per share based on earnings of £72,000 and on average 420,000 shares in issue throughout the year (*see* FRS 3 amendment).

(b)   *Balance Sheet extracts as at 31 March 19X6*

	£000	£000
Creditors: Amounts falling due within one year		
Other creditors including taxation and social security (W1)		77
Provisions for liabilities and charges		
Taxation, including deferred taxation (W2)		33

Workings:

(W1) Corporation tax for year to 31 March 19X6

	£000
Corporation tax for year to 31 March 19X6	35
Proposed dividend	42
	77

(W2)

Deferred tax as given	24
Transfered from profit and loss	9
	33

13.1

Owen Ltd
Balance Sheet as at 31 December 19X1

Called-up share capital net paid			150
Fixed assets			
Intangible assets			
Development costs	3,070		
Goodwill	21,000	24,070	
Tangible assets			
Land and buildings	32,000		
Plant and machinery	7,100	39,100	
Investments			
Shares in undertakings in which the company has a participating interest		35,750	98,920
Current assets			
Stock			
Raw materials and consumables	3,470		
Finished goods and goods for resale	18,590	22,060	
Debtors			
Trade debtors	17,400		
Amounts owed by undertakings in which the company has a participating interest	3,000		
Prepayments	1,250	21,650	
		43,710	
Creditors: amounts falling due within one year			
Debentures	6,000		
Bank overdrafts	4,370		
Trade creditors	12,410		
Bills of exchange payable	1,600	24,380	
Net current assets			19,330
Total assets less current liabilities			118,400
Creditors: amounts falling due after one year			
Debentures	4,000		
Bills of exchange payable	2,000	6,000	
			112,400
Capital and reserves			
Called-up share capital		75,000	
Share premium account		20,000	
Other reserves:			
Capital redemption reserve	5,000		
General reserve	4,000	9,000	
Profit and loss account		8,400	
		112,400	

Notes:

(i) Called-up share capital consists of:

	£
50,000 £1 ordinary shares	50,000
50,000 preference shares of 50p each	25,000
	75,000

(ii) Land and buildings:

	£	£
Cost		48,000
Depreciation to 31 December 19X0	12,000	
Depreciation for year to 31 December 19X1	4,000	16,000
		32,000

(iii) Plant and machinery:

	£	£
Cost		12,500
Depreciation to 31 December 19X0	3,600	
Depreciation for year to 31 December 19X1	1,800	5,400
		7,100

13.2

Belle Works plc
Balance Sheet as at 30 September 19X4

Fixed assets			
Intangible assets			
Concessions, patents, licences, trade marks and similar rights and assets		1,500	
Goodwill		17,500	19,000
Tangible assets			
Land and buildings		72,500	
Plant and machinery		19,400	91,900	110,900

Current assets
Stock

Raw materials and consumables	14,320	
Work in progress	5,640	
Finished goods and goods for resale	13,290	33,250

Debtors

Trade debtors	11,260	
Other debtors	1,050	
Prepayments and accrued income	505	12,815
		46,065

Creditors: amounts falling due within one year

Debenture loans	6,000	
Bank loans and overdrafts	3,893	
Trade creditors	11,340	
Bills of exchange payable	4,000	
Other creditors including taxation and social security	14,675	39,908
Net current assets		6,157
Total assets less current liabilities		117,057

Creditors: amounts falling due after more than one year

Debenture loans	12,000	
Trade creditors	1,260	13,260

Provisions for liabilities and charges

Pensions and similar obligations	1,860	
Taxation, including deferred taxation	640	2,500
		15,760
		101,297

Capital and reserves

Called-up share capital	70,000
Share premium account	5,000
Revaluation reserve	10,500

Other reserves

General reserve	6,000	
Foreign exchange reserve	3,500	9,500
Profit and loss account		6,297
		101,297

Notes appended to the accounts on the details of Tangible assets and Depreciation, also exact details of items lumped under group descriptions.

13.3

Baganza plc
Profit and Loss Account for the year ended 30 September 19X7 (£000s)

Turnover		19,500
Cost of sales (W1)		14,700
Gross profit		4,800
Distribution costs	600	
Administrative expenses (W2)	1,390	1,990
		2,810
Other operating income (W3)		249
		3,059
Profit on ordinary activities before taxation		
Tax on profit on ordinary activities (W4)		870
Profit on ordinary activities after taxation		2,189
Extraordinary item		1,500
Profit for the financial year		3,689
Dividends (W5)		756
Retained profits for the year		2,933

Earnings per share (W6)	182.4p

Workings (in £000s):
(W1) Opening stock 2,300 + Purchases 16,000 – Closing stock 3,600 = 14,700
(W2) Per trial balance 400 + Research 75 + Depreciation: Property (5% × 2,700) 135 + Plant (15% × 5,200) 780 = 1,390
(W3) Dividends received 249
(W4) Corporation tax 850 + Deferred tax 40 – Overpayment last year 20 = 870
(W5) Dividends: Interim 36 + Final 720 = 756
(W6) EPS = Profit 3,689,000 ÷ Shares 1,200,000 = 307.4p

Baganza plc
Balance Sheet as at 30 September 19X7

	£000	£000	£000
Fixed assets			
Tangible assets			
Land and buildings		2,305	
Plant and machinery		820	
			3,125
Investments			2,000
			5,125
Current assets			
Stocks		3,600	
Debtors		2,700	
Cash at bank		60	
			6,360

	£000	£000
Creditors: amounts falling due within one year		
Trade creditors	2,900	
Corporation tax (850 + 360)	1,210	
Proposed dividend	720	
		4,830
Net current assets		1,530
Total assets less current liabilities		6,655
Taxation, including deferred taxation (460 + 40)		500
		6,155
Capital and reserves		
Called-up share capital		1,200
Profit and loss account (2,022 + 2,933)		4,955
		6,155

14.1

X Limited
Balance Sheet at 31 March 19X7

	Notes	£000	£000	£000
Fixed assets				
Intangible assets				
Development costs	(1)		35	
Tangible assets	(2)			
Freehold properties		1,040		
Plant and machinery		850		
Vehicles		285		
			2,175	
Investments				
Investments in listed shares	(3)		200	2,410
Current assets				
Stock	(4)	500		
Debtors and prepayments (see workings)		654		
Cash at bank		439		
		1,593		
Creditors: amounts falling due within 1 year				
Trade creditors and accrual		878		
Other creditors (see workings)		550		
		1,428		
Net current assets				165
Total assets less current liabilities				2,575
Creditors: amounts falling due after more than 1 year				
12% debentures 19X6			500	
Provisions for liabilities and charges				
Deferred taxation	(5)		128	
				628
				1,947
Capital and reserves				
Called-up share capital	(6)			1,000
Share premium				150
Revaluation reserve				612
Profit and loss account (see workings)	(7)			185
				1,947

Workings:

	£000	£000
Profit and loss	356	
Less Bad debt (225,000 × 76%)	171	
		185
Debtors	825	
Less Bad debt (225,000 × 76%)	171	
		654
Other creditors: Proposed dividend	280	
Corporation tax	270	
		550

Notes to the balance sheet

1 Research and development

Research costs are written off immediately. Development costs are carried forward when there is a reasonable certainty of profitable outcome of the project and amortised over the useful life of the project.

2 Tangible assets

	Freehold property £000	Plant and machinery £000	Vehicles £000
Cost on 1 April 19X6*	800	1,500	220
Disposal at cost	(320)		
Addition			200
Revaluation adjustment	612		
On 31 March 19X7	1,092	1,500	420
Depreciation at 1 April 19X6*	80	500	80
Depreciation on disposals	(40)		
Provision in year	12	150	55
On 31 March 19X7	52	650	135
Net book values	1,040	850	285

*Exam note only. Found by working backwards, leaving these figures as difference.

Note: Freehold property was valued by Messrs V & Co, Chartered Surveyors, at a market value of £1,040,000 as compared with net book value of £428,000. The valuation figure has been included in balance sheet, and £612,000 has been credited to a revaluation reserve. Depreciation for 19X7 has been based on the revalued figure.

Billinge plc
Balance Sheet as at 30 June 19X6

	Notes	£000	£000	£000
Fixed assets				
Tangible assets	(7)			187
Fixtures and fittings				
Current assets				
Stocks: Finished goods and goods for resale		100		
Debtors		500		
Cash at bank		157		
		757		
Creditors: Amounts falling due within one year				
Trade creditors		64		
Other creditors, taxation and social security	(W4)	100		
Proposed dividend		100	264	
Net current assets				493
Total assets less current liabilities				680
Provisions for liabilities and charges				
Taxation including deferred taxation	(8)			100
				580
Capital and reserves	(9)			
Called-up share capital				500
Profit and loss account (40+40)				80
				580

Workings:

(W1)	Opening stock	70	
	Purchases	855	
		925	
	Less Closing stock	100	
		825	

(W2)	Depreciation	340	
	Less disposals	20	
		320	
	Additions	60	
		380	

(W3)	C/T for year	100		20% × 380	76
	Deferred taxation	40		Loss on disposals	20
		140		Less Depreciation	(15)
	Less Previous overprovision	10		Less Cash	(3)
		130			2
					78

(W4)	Other creditors, taxation and social security:		Administrative expenses	242
	Corporation tax	100		320

Notes to the accounts:
1 Accounting policies
(a) The financial statements have been drawn up using the historical cost

---

3 Investments

These had a market value of £180,000 on 31 March 19X7, but as this is not considered by the directors to be a permanent fall in value, the cost figure has been retained.

4 Stock

	£000
Finished goods	250
Raw materials	200
Work in progress	50
	500

The current replacement cost of goods is £342,000.

5 Deferred taxation

Provision as at 1 April 19X6	78	
Add Provision during year	50	
	128	
Less ACT recoverable	70	
		58

6 Share capital

1,000,000 ordinary shares of £1 each is the authorised capital, which has been fully issued and called up.

7 Reserves

	Profit and loss account	Share premium	Revaluation reserve
Balance at 1 April 19X6	?	150	–
Change during the year			612
	215	150	612

14.2

Billinge plc
Profit and Loss Account for the year to 30 June 19X6

	Notes	£000	£000
Turnover – continuing operations			1,500
Cost of sales (W1)			825
Gross profit			675
Distribution costs	(2)	55	
Administrative expenses (W2)		320	375
			300
Loss on disposal of discontinued operations	(3)		30
			270
Tax on profit on ordinary activities	(4)		130
			140
Profit from ordinary activities after taxation			140
Dividends paid and proposed	(5)		100
Retained profits for the year			40
Earnings per share	(6)		28.0p

convention.

(b) Turnover consists of sales to external customers less VAT.

(c) Stocks are valued at lower of cost or net realisable value.

(d) Depreciation of fixed assets is based on cost, using the straight-line method over 5 years, salvage values being ignored.

(e) Deferred taxation is at the anticipated rate, taking into account the differing periods and the probability that a liability will occur.

2 Administrative expenses include depreciation £78,000.

3 Exceptional charges have arisen of £30,000 on the closure of a factory.

4 Taxation

	£000
Corporation tax at 35% on profit for the period	100
Deferred taxation	40
	140
Less Adjustment re last year's corporation tax	10
	130

5 Proposed ordinary dividend of 20p per share.

6 EPS calculated by dividing profit after taxation by number of ordinary shares on issue during the period.

7 Tangible fixed assets:

	£000	£000	£000
Fixtures etc. at 1.7.19X5		340	
Additions		60	
		400	
Less Disposals		20	
		380	
Depreciation at 1.7.19X5	132		
For the period	76		
	208		
Less Disposals	15		
	193		
		187	

8 Deferred taxation at 1.7.19X5 | | 60 |

	£000
Deferred taxation at 1.7.19X5	60
Profit and loss charge	40
	100

9 Authorised, issued × fully paid ordinary £1 shares 500

14.6

Scampion plc
Profit and Loss Account for the year ended 31 May 19X7

	£000	£000
Turnover (3,489 − VAT 259)		3,232
Cost of sales (1,929 + 330 + 51)		2,310
Gross profit		922
Administrative expenses (595 + 25 + 45)		665
Operating profit		257
Income from shares in related companies	5	
Other interest receivable (note 2)	10	15
		272
Interest payable (note 3)	18	
Written off investments (note 7)	4	22
Profit on ordinary activities before taxation		250
Tax on profit on ordinary activities (note 4)		100
Profit on ordinary activities after taxation		150
Proposed ordinary dividend		66
Retained profits for the year		84
Earnings per share (note 5)		22.73p

Scampion plc
Balance Sheet as at 31 May 19X7

	£000	£000
Fixed assets		
Tangible assets (note 6)		1,372
Investments (note 7)		60
		1,432
Current assets		
Stock	230	
Debtors (67 − 45)	22	
Investments (market value £115,000)	103	
Cash at bank and in hand	84	
	439	
Creditors: amounts falling due within one year (note 8)	553	
Net current liabilities		(114)
Total assets less current liabilities		1,318
Creditors: amounts falling due after more than one year (note 9)		50
		1,268
Capital and reserves		
Called-up share capital		660
Share premium account		225
Profit and loss account (note 10)		383
		1,268

Notes:

1 Accounting policies
The historical cost convention has been used.
Provisions for depreciation are to write off the cost or valuation over the expected useful lives of the assets, by equal instalments, as follows:

Freehold buildings 40 years
Fixtures, fittings or equipment 10 years
Motor vehicles 5 years

Depreciation provisions have not been made on freehold land. The basis of the valuation of stock is the lower of cost or net realisable value.

2 Other interest receivable
This is income from government securities £10,000.

3 Interest payable

Interest on loans repayable within 1 year	12,000
Interest on loans repayable in more than 5 years' time	6,000
	£18,000

4 Taxation
(It has been assumed that 'tax charge based on the accounts for the year' means that the profit shown of £250 is same as the taxable profits.)
Corporation tax at the rate of 40 per cent on profits has been provided for.

5 Earnings per share $= \dfrac{150}{660} = 22.73\text{p}$

6 Tangible assets (£000)

	Valuation or cost at 31.5.X6	Additions at cost	Less disposals	Depreciation to: 31.5.X6	31.5.X7	Net
Freehold land and buildings	1,562	50	400	29	5	1,178
Fittings, fixtures and equipment	141	40		38	18	125
Motor vehicles	117	20		40	28	69
	1,820	110	400	107	51	1,372

7 Investments

Valuation by directors of shares in related companies	64,000
Less Written off during the year	4,000
	60,000

8 Creditors

Trade creditors (487,000 – Tax 120,000)	367,000
Corporation tax	100,000
Proposed dividend	66,000
Bank loan	20,000
	553,000

9 Creditors – amounts falling due after more than one year £50,000 12% debentures repayable in X years' time.

10 Reserves

	Revaluation	Profit and loss
Balance 31.5.19X6	150	149
Transfer to profit and loss	(150)	150
Retained profits for year to 31.5.X7	–	84
	–	383

15.1 See text of Chapter 15, section 15.2.

15.3 *Cash Flow Statement (using the direct method) for Lee Ltd for the year ended 31 December 19X4*

Operating activities		
Cash received from customers	6,550	
Cash paid to suppliers	(2,875)	
Cash paid to employees	(2,025)	
Other cash payments	(600)	
Net cash inflow from operating activities		1,050
Returns on investment and servicing of finance		
Interest paid		(100)
Taxation		–
Capital expenditure and financial investment		
Payments to acquire tangible assets	(700)	
Acquisitions and disposals	–	
Equity dividend paid		(50)
Management of liquid resources		–
Financing		
Repurchase of debentures	(100)	
Increase in cash in the period		100

Notes to the cash flow statement
1 Reconciliation of operating profit to net cash inflow from operating activities:

Operating profit	400
Depreciation charges	500
Decrease in stocks	100
Decrease in debtors	50
Net cash inflow from operating activities	1,050

Working:
Operating profit = profit for the year (300) + interest (100) = 400

15.5 See text of Chapter 15, section 15.2.

15.6

Nimmo Limited

Cash Flow Statement (using the indirect method) for the year ended 31 December 19X9 (£000s)

Net cash inflow from operating activities		2,150
Returns on investments and servicing of finance		
Taxation		(3,200)
Capital expenditure and financial investment		
Purchase of fixed assets	(11,800)	
Sale of fixed assets	1,000	
Net cash outflow for capital expenditure		(10,800)
Acquisitions and disposals		–
Equity dividend paid		(5,100)
Management of liquid resources		–
Financing		
Issue of debenture stock		150
Decrease in cash in the period		(16,800)

Notes to the cash flow statement

1 Reconciliation of operating profit to net cash inflow from operating activities:

Operating profit	20,400
Depreciation charges	5,050
Loss on sale of fixed assets	700
Increase in stocks	(10,000)
Increase in trade debtors	(18,100)
Increase in prepayments	(100)
Increase in trade creditors	4,000
Increase in accruals	200
Net cash inflow from operating activities	2,150

Working:

Loss on sale of fixed assets = 1,000 – (5,500 – 3,800) = (700)

15.7

Track Limited

Cash Flow Statement (using the indirect method) for the year ended 30 June 19X1 (£000s)

Net cash outflow from operating activities		(75)
Returns on investments and servicing of finance		–
Taxation		(230)
Capital expenditure and financial investment		
Purchase of fixed assets	(175)	
Sale of investments	150	
Sale of fixed assets	20	
Net cash outflow for capital expenditure		(5)
Acquisitions and disposals		–

Equity dividend paid		(150)
Management of liquid resources		–
Financing		
Issue of share capital		300
Net cash outflow for period		(160)

Notes to the cash flow statement

1 Reconciliation of operating profit to net cash inflow from operating activities:

Operating profit	180
Depreciation charges	110
Profit on sale of fixed assets	(5)
Increase in stocks	(300)
Increase in trade debtors	(200)
Increase in trade creditors	140
Net cash inflow from operating activities	(75)

Workings:

Profit before tax: 670 – 530 = retained loss of 140 + tax (190) + dividends (130) = 180

Profit on sale of fixed assets = 20 – (25 – 10) = (5)

15.10

Baker Limited

(a) Forecasted net cash position for the three quarters ended 30 Sept 19X7

	Quarter to		
	31 March 19X7 £000	30 June 19X7 £000	30 Sept 19X7 £000
Receipts			
Trade debtors (W1)	235	290	345
Tangible fixed assets	12	–	–
Investments	10	–	–
Debentures	–	–	50
	257	290	395
Payments			
Trade creditors (W2)	150	230	285
Administration, selling and distribution expenses	37	40	42
Tangible fixed assets	–	240	–
Investments	–	–	5
Taxation	8	–	–
Dividend	15	–	–
	210	510	332
Forecasted net cash flow	47	(220)	63
Add Opening cash	80	127	(93)
Forecasted closing cash	127	(93)	(30)

(b)

Baker Limited

Forecasted cash flow statement (using the direct method)
for the nine months ended 30 September 19X7 (£000s)

Operating activities		
Cash received from customers (W1)	870	
Cash paid to creditors (W2)	(665)	
Other cash payments (admin, selling & distribution)	(119)	
Net cash outflow from operating activities		86
Returns on investments and servicing of finance		–
Taxation		(8)
Capital expenditure and financial investment		
Purchase of fixed assets	(240)	
Sale of fixed assets	12	
Net cash outflow for capital expenditure		(228)
Acquisitions and disposals		–
Equity dividend paid		(15)
Management of liquid resources		
Addition to 90 day deposit	(5)	
Realisation of 90 day deposit	10	
Net cash inflow from management of liquid resources		5
Financing		
Issue of debentures		50
Net cash outflow for period		(110)

Notes to the cash flow statement

1 Reconciliation of operating profit to net cash inflow
from operating activities:

Operating profit	34
Depreciation charges	27
Increase in stocks	(15)
Increase in trade debtors	(30)
Increase in trade creditors	70
Net cash outflow from operating activities	86

Workings:

1 Trade debtors: forecasted cash receivable:

	31 March 19X7 £000	30 June 19X7 £000	30 Sept 19X7 £000
Sales	250	300	350
Less Closing trade debtors	65	75	80
	185	225	270
Add Opening trade debtors	50	65	75
Forecasted cash receipts from trade debtors	235	290	345

2 Trade creditors: forecasted cash payable

	31 March 19X7 £000	30 June 19X7 £000	30 Sept 19X7 £000
Opening stock	40	30	40
Purchases (by deduction)	190	250	295
	230	280	335
Less Closing stock	30	40	55
Cost of sales	200	240	280
Purchases (as above)	190	250	295
Less Closing trade creditors	120	140	150
	70	110	145
Add Opening trade creditors	80	110	120
Forecasted cash payments to trade creditors	150	230	285

16.1

Contract

Year 1:				
Plant	16,250	Work certified	58,000	
Materials	25,490	Plant c/d	10,250	
Wages	28,384	Stock and work in progress c/d	12,200	
Direct expenses	2,126			
Gross profit to profit and loss	8,200			
	80,450		80,450	
Year 2:				
Plant b/d	10,250	Work certified	116,000	
Stock and work-in-progress b/d	12,200	Sale of plant	4,100	
Materials	33,226			
Wages	45,432			
Direct expenses	2,902			
Penalty	700			
Gross profit to profit and loss	15,390			
	120,100		120,100	

Workings:

Computation profit of Year 1:

Contract price	174,000
Less Actual expenditure	
25,490 + 28,384 + 2,126	56,000

Estimated cost of plant (16,250 − 4,250)   12,000
Estimated expenses Year 2   81,400   149,400
Estimated total contract profit: estimate made at end of year 1   24,600

Using formula given by question:

$$\frac{\text{Work certified}}{\text{Total contract price}} \times \text{Total estimated profit} = \text{Profit for Year 1}$$

$$= \frac{52,200 + 5,800}{174,000} \times 24,600 = 8,200$$

16.2

Stannard and Sykes Ltd
Pier Contract Account
Contract for Seafront Development Corporation valued at £300,000

Materials: direct	58,966	Materials on site c/d	11,660
from store	10,180	Work in progress c/d	151,167
	69,146		
Wages	41,260		
Hire of plant	21,030		
Direct expenditure	3,065		
Overheads	8,330		
Wages accrued c/d	2,826		
	145,657		
Profit and loss account (proportion of profit to date)	17,170		
	162,827		162,827
Materials on site b/d	11,660	Wages accrued b/d	2,826
Work in progress b/d	151,167		

A suggested method for prudently estimating the amount of profit to be taken to November 30 is:

$$\frac{2}{3} \times \frac{\text{Cash received}}{\text{Value of work certified}} \times \text{Estimated profit (Value of work certified less cost of work certified)}$$

Total expenditure to date   145,657
Less Materials on site at November 30 19X8   11,660
Cost of work not yet certified   12,613   24,273
Cost of work certified (a)   121,384
Value of work certified (b)   150,000
Total profit to date (b) − (a)   28,616

17.1 (a) Board of Directors
Manvers Ltd
Report on advantages of value added statement
Such statements were recommended for use in the *Corporate Report* as published by the professional accountancy bodies in 1975.
The advantages can be listed as:

1 It avoids using profit as the important factor. This is useful, as 'profit' is something misunderstood by many people.

2 Clarity. As it is concerned with linking revenue to the inputs and services paid for, it gives a clear picture of the operation of the business.

3 It illustrates interdependence between the various factors in a business.

4 Value added can also be related to capital employed.

The profit and loss account is legally necessary. The value added statement may use the same information, but it is used to demonstrate different factors and sheds light on matters which might have escaped attention otherwise.

The source and application funds statement is quite different. It is concerned with all items of a capital nature, whereas value added deals with performance on a revenue basis.

(b)

Manvers Ltd
Profit and Loss Account for the year ended 31 May 19X6

Turnover (204,052 − 30,608)		173,444
Less Expenses		
Materials and services	146,928	
Depreciation	1,835	
Pension scheme	2,810	
Salaries	16,468	
Profit sharing schemes	525	
Welfare and staff amenities	806	
Rates	325	
Bank interest	250	
Loan interest	1,600	171,547
Profits before taxation		1,897
Corporation tax		985
Profits after taxation		912
Dividends		500
Retained profits		412

(c)

Profits before tax	1,897
Add back non-cash item – depreciation	1,835
Operating profits	3,732

18.1

Consolidated Loan 4%

Date	Detail	Nominal	Income	Capital	Date	Detail	Nominal	Income	Capital
19X6								240	
Jul 1	Bank	12,000	200	7,060	19X6				
19X7					Aug 1	Bank		240	
Jan 2	Adjustment for 1 month's interest on sale		10		19X7				
Jun 30	Investment income account		420		Jan 2	Bank: Sale at 61 ex div	3,000		1,830
„ 30	Profit and loss: Profit on sale			75	„ 2	Adjustment contra		10	
					Feb 1	Bank		240	
					Jun 30	Balances c/d	9,000	150	5,295
		12,000	**630**	**7,135**			**12,000**	**630**	**7,135**

Abee Ltd: Ordinary Shares

Date	Detail	Nominal	Income	Capital	Date	Detail	Nominal	Income	Capital
19X6					19X6				
Jul 12	Bank	2,000		4,000	Aug 15	Bank: Sale	2,500		2,000
Aug 15	Bonus issue	3,000		–	Mar 1	Bank: Dividend		225	
Jun 30	Investment income		225		Jun 30	Balances c/d	2,500		2,500
Jun 30	Profit on sale to: Profit and loss			500					
		5,000	**225**	**4,500**			**5,000**	**225**	**4,500**

Ceedee Ltd: Ordinary Shares

Date	Detail	Nominal	Income	Capital	Date	Detail	Nominal	Income	Capital
19X6					19X7				
Oct 1	Bank	5,000		3,875	Apl 1	Bank: Sale of rights	2,500		625
19X7					Jun 1	Bank: Dividend		625	
Apl 1	Rights issue	2,500		–	Jun 30	Balance c/d	5,000		3,250
Jun 30	Investment income		625						
		7,500	**625**	**3,875**			**7,500**	**625**	**3,875**

18.2

Shares in Composite Interest Ltd

Date	Detail	Nominal	Income	Capital	Date	Detail	Nominal	Income	Capital
19X5					19X5				
Apl 1	Bal b/d	6,000		7,200	Apl 1	Bank: Sale of shares	1,000		1,965
	Bonus issue	3,000				Bank: Sale of rights			210
	Bank	1,800		1,890		Bank: Dividend		1,000	
	Profit and loss			765		Bank: Dividend 5%		490	
	Investment income		1,490			Balance at cost c/d	9,800		7,680
		10,800	**1,490**	**9,855**			**10,800**	**1,490**	**9,855**

19.1 See text section 19.6.
19.2 See text section 19.8.
19.3 See text section 19.4.
19.4 See text section 19.9.

20.1

P & S Consolidated Balance Sheet

Goodwill	10
Stock	140
Bank	50
	200
Share capital	200
	200

20.2

P & S Consolidated Balance Sheet (SSAP 22)

Fixed assets	3,800
Stock	1,500
Debtors	700
Bank	300
	6,300
Share capital	6,000
Capital reserve	300
	6,300

P & S Consolidated Balance Sheet (FRS 10)

Fixed assets	3,800
Goodwill: negative goodwill	(300)
Stock	1,500
Debtors	700
Bank	300
	6,000
Share capital	6,000
	6,000

20.3

P & S Consolidated Balance Sheet

Fixed assets	62,000
Stock	27,000
Debtors	8,000
Bank	3,000
	100,000
Share capital	100,000
	100,000

20.6

P & S Consolidated Balance Sheet

Goodwill	300
Fixed assets	2,000
Stock	1,300
Debtors	900
Bank	300
	4,800
Share capital	4,000
Minority interest	800
	4,800

20.7

P & S Consolidated Balance Sheet (SSAP 22)

Fixed assets	3,325
Stock	3,000
Debtors	2,000
Bank	200
	8,525
Share capital	8,000
Capital reserve	375
Minority interest	150
	8,525

P & S Consolidated Balance Sheet (FRS 10)

Fixed assets	3,325
Goodwill: negative goodwill	(375)
Stock	3,000
Debtors	2,000
Bank	200
	8,150
Share capital	8,000
Minority interest	150
	8,150

20.10

P, S1 & S2 Consolidated Balance Sheet (SSAP 22)

Fixed assets	12,600
Current assets	5,900
	18,500
Share capital	10,000
Profit and loss	6,500
Capital reserve*	600
Minority interest	1,400
	18,500

*Goodwill S1 300, Capital reserve 900 = Net capital reserve 600.

P, S1 & S2 Consolidated Balance Sheet (FRS 10)

Fixed assets	12,600
Goodwill	300
Negative goodwill	(900)
Current assets	5,900
	17,900
Share capital	10,000
Profit and loss	6,500
Minority interest	1,400
	17,900

20.11

P, S1 & S2 Consolidated Balance Sheet (SSAP 22)

Goodwill*	350
Fixed assets	9,450
Current assets	6,000
	15,800
Share capital	10,000
Profit and loss	2,000
General reserve	1,400
Minority interest	2,400
	15,800

*Goodwill (S1) 600, Capital reserve (S2) 250 = Net goodwill 350.

P, S1 & S2 Consolidated Balance Sheet (FRS 10)

Goodwill	600
Negative goodwill	(250)
Fixed assets	9,450
Current assets	6,000
	15,800

Share capital 10,000
Profit and loss 2,000
General reserve 1,400
Minority interest 2,400
15,800

21.1
P & S Consolidated Balance Sheet as at 31 December 19X6
Goodwill 950
Fixed assets 10,950
Current assets 3,900
15,800

Share capital 10,000
Profit and loss (P 4,000 + S 1,800) 5,800
15,800

21.2
P & S Consolidated Balance Sheet as at 31 December 19X9 (SSAP 22)
Fixed assets 47,400
Current assets 27,100
74,500

Share capital 50,000
Profit and loss (14,000 – (400 of 70% = 280)) 13,720
General reserve 5,000
Capital reserve 1,790
Minority interest (3,000 + 600 + 390) 3,990
74,500

P & S Consolidated Balance Sheet as at 31 December 19X9 (FRS 10)
Fixed assets 47,400
Goodwill: negative goodwill (1,790)
Current assets 27,100
72,710

Share capital 50,000
Profit and loss (14,000 – (400 of 70% = 280)) 13,720
General reserve 5,000
Minority interest (3,000 + 600 + 390) 3,990
72,710

21.4
P, S1 & S2 Consolidated Balance Sheet as at 31 December 19X5
Goodwill 1,390
Fixed assets 36,900
Current assets 20,900
59,190

Share capital 40,000
Profit and loss 8,270
General reserve 5,000
Minority interest 5,920
59,190

Minority interest 40% of (10,000 + 2,800 + 2,000) = 5,920.
Goodwill S1 cost 8,150 – 60% of 10,000 + 1,800) = 1,100.
11,400 – (8,000 + 500 + 1,800) = 1,100 + 2,000 = 290, S2 cost
Profit and loss P 7,550 + S1 1,020 – S2 300 = 8,270.

22.1
P & S Consolidated Balance Sheet as at 31 December 19X9
Goodwill 850
Fixed assets 2,300
Current assets
Stock (1,200 + 900 – 90) 2,010
Debtors (2,100 + 1,400 – 220) 3,280
Bank 500
5,790
Less Current liabilities
Creditors (900 + 700 – 220) 1,380
Net current assets 4,410
7,560

Financed by
Share capital 2,000
Profit and loss
(P 3,700 – 90 + S 1,150) 4,760
General reserve 800
7,560

22.2
P & S Consolidated Balance Sheet as at 31 December 19X4
Goodwill 1,600
Fixed assets 14,200
Current assets
Stock (3,100 + 7,200 – 50) 10,250
Debtors (4,900 – 600 + 3,800) 8,100
Bank 2,500
20,850
Less Current liabilities
Creditors (3,800 + 2,100 – 600) 5,300
Net current assets 15,550
31,350

Financed by

Share capital		20,000
Profit and loss (P 4,000 − 50 + S 60% of 2,000)		5,150
Minority interest (40% of 10,000 + 5,500)		6,200
		31,350

22.3

P, S1 & S2 Consolidated Balance Sheet as at 31 December 19X8

Fixed assets		65,000
Current assets		
Stock (£46,000 − £640)	45,360	
Debtors (£28,000 − £1,400)	26,600	
Bank	9,000	
	80,960	
Less Current liabilities		
Creditors (21,000 − 1,400)	19,600	
Net current assets		61,360
		126,360

Financed by:

Share capital		100,000
Profit and loss account:		
(£23,000 − £400 − £240 − S1 £5,000 + S2 ⅖ths of £1,800)		18,860
General reserve		2,000
Minority interest (⅙th of (£30,000 + £3,000))		5,500
		126,360

S1 Capital reserve: Cost £39,000 − £30,000 − £8,000 − £4,000 = £3,000.
S2 Goodwill: Cost £29,000 − ⅗ths of £30,000 + £1,200 = £2,800.
Net goodwill = £3,000 − £3,000 = Nil.

22.6

Pagg Group of Companies
Consolidated Balance Sheet as at 31 March 19X0

			£000
Fixed assets			
Intangible assets (Note 1)			1,898
Tangible assets			3,500
			5,398
Current assets			
Stocks (1,300 + 350 + 100 − 10)		1,740	
Debtors (3,000 + 300 + 200 − 200 − 35)		3,265	
Cash at bank and in hand		270	
		5,275	
Creditors falling due within 1 year			
(270 + 400 + 4,000 − 200 − 35)		4,435	
Net current assets			840
Total assets less current liabilities			6,238

Minority interests (Note 2)		500
		5,738
Capital and reserves		
Called-up share capital		5,500
Profit and loss		238
		5,738

Notes:

1 Cost of control

		Ragg		Tagg
Consideration		3,000		1,000
Less Shares	(80%) 800		(60%) 300	
Profit and loss	(80% × 600) 480		(60% × 100) 60	
		1,280		360
Goodwill		1,720		640
Total amount written off to 31.3.19X0	(5 years)		(1 year)	
		430		32
Amount not yet written off		1,290		608
				1,898

2 Minority interests

		Ragg		Tagg
Share capital called up		1,000		500
Profit and loss		200		150
		1,200		650
	(20%)	240	(40%)	260
				500

3 Profit and loss:

Pagg	1,000
Ragg 80% of (200 − 600)	(320)
Tagg 60% of (150 − 100)	30
Goodwill (Note 1) 430 + 32	(462)
Inter-company profit on stock (⅚ of 60)	(10)
	238

23.1

60% Share capital and reserves 31.12.19X6			56,400
Shares bought 31.12.19X4	10,000	23,500	
Shares bought 31.12.19X6	14,000	31,000	
	24,000		54,500
Negative goodwill			1,900

23.3

Shares bought		50,000
Profit and loss balance 31.12.19X7	36,000	
Add proportion 19X8 profits before acquisition		
8/12 × 42,000	28,000	
	64,000	

Creditors: amounts falling due within 1 year

Trade creditors	212,000	
Preference dividend proposed	8,000	220,000
Net current assets		120,000
Total assets *less* current liabilities		855,000

Capital and reserves

Called-up share capital: ordinary shares £1 fully paid	500,000
Reserves	185,000
Minority interest	170,000
	855,000

Note 1 Tangible fixed assets

	Cost	Depreciation to date	Net
Buildings	420,000	110,000	310,000
Plant and machinery	320,000	70,000	250,000
Motor vehicles	210,000	90,000	120,000
	950,000	270,000	680,000

Workings:

(a) *Goodwill*

Cost of investment		250,000
Less Ordinary shares (75%)	150,000	
Reserves (75%)	37,500	187,500
		62,500
Less Dividend from pre-acquisition profits		7,500
		55,000

(b) *Minority interest*

Preference shares	100,000
Reserves 25% × 80,000	20,000
Ordinary shares 25%	50,000
	170,000

The proposed preference dividend could be shown as part of the minority interest.

(c) *Reserves*

P Ltd	170,000
S Ltd 75% of extra reserves since acquisition 80,000 − 50,000 = 30,000	22,500
	192,500
Less Dividends received by P Ltd which were from pre-acquisition profits	7,500
	185,000

Proportion of pre-acquisition profit:

$$\frac{50,000}{80,000} \times 64,000 = 40,000$$

	90,000

Paid for shares 158,000

Therefore goodwill is 158,000 − 90,000 = 68,000.

24.1 *P & S Consolidated Balance Sheet as at 31 December 19X7*

Goodwill	1,000
Fixed assets	57,000
Current assets	15,000
	73,000
Share capital	50,000
Profit and loss account (H 19,000 + S 4,000)	23,000
	73,000

Workings: Goodwill: Cost 29,000 − 20,000 − 3,000 − Dividend 5,000 = 1,000.

24.3 *P & S Consolidated Balance Sheet as at 31 December 19X9*

Goodwill		14,000
Fixed assets		80,000
Current assets	33,000	
Less Current liabilities		
Proposed dividend	1,500	
Net current assets		31,500
		125,500
Share capital		80,000
Profit and loss account: (P 23,000 + S ¾ of 6,000 + ¾ of 7,000))		32,750
Minority interest (¼ of (40,000 + 11,000))		12,750
		125,500

Workings: Goodwill: Cost 47,000 − ¾ of (40,000 + 4,000) = 14,000.

24.5 *Consolidated Balance Sheet of P Ltd & S Ltd as at 31 December 19X6*

Fixed assets

Intangible assets		
Goodwill (*see* Workings)		55,000
Tangible assets (Note 1)		680,000
Current assets		
Stocks	160,000	
Debtors	140,000	
Bank	40,000	
	340,000	

24.6 Reconciliation of current accounts

X		Y	
Balance b/d	19	Balance b/d	14
		In transit	2
Balance c/d	19	Bank (1)	3
	19	Stock (2)	19
			19

Reserves

X		220
19X6 retained profits		20
Proposed dividend Y 80%		8
80% Y profits for 19X6 × 18		14.4
		262.4
− Cost of control (above) written off	108	
− Profit in goods in transit	0.4	
− Profit in Y's stock	2	110.4
		152

Consolidated Balance Sheet for X plc & subsidiary Y plc as at 31 December 19X6

	Cost £000	Depreciation to date £000	Net £000
Tangible fixed assets			
Freehold property	280	18	262
Plant and machinery	245	52	193
	525	70	455
Current assets			
Stock (see Workings)		150.6	
Debtors		250	
Bank		24	
		424.6	
Less Current liabilities			
Trade creditors (130 + 80 + 2)	212		
Taxation	44		
Proposed dividends	20	276	148.8
			603.6
Called-up share capital			
400,000 ordinary shares £1			400
Reserves (see Workings)			152
			552
Minority interest (see Workings)			51.6
			603.6

Workings:

Cost of control (remember to calculate it as on 1.1.X6) £000

Cost of investment		300
Less Nominal value shares bought 80%	120	
Reserves 80% × 90	72	192
		108

Minority interest

20% of reserves at 1.1.X6 × 90	18	
20% of 19X6 retained profit × 18	3.6	
20% of shares × 150	30	51.6

Stock

X	80	
Y	70	
In transit	3	153
Less Profit element in Y's stock	2	
,, ,, ,, goods in transit	0.4	2.4
		150.6

Bank 24

X 10 + Y 12 + in transit 2

25.1 P & S Consolidated Balance Sheet as at 31 December 19X8

Goodwill		100,000
Fixed assets	500,000	
Less Depreciation	138,000	362,000
Current assets		205,000
		667,000
Share capital		500,000
Profit and loss account:		
(P 143,000 − 10,000 + S 32,000 + 2,000)		167,000
		667,000

25.3 P & S Consolidated Balance Sheet as at 31 December 19X7

Goodwill		19,000
Fixed assets	185,000	
Less Depreciation	33,500	151,500
Current assets		68,000
		238,500
Share capital		150,000
Profit and loss (P 77,000 + 14,000 − 2,500)		88,500
		238,500

26.1

P, S1 & S2 Consolidated Balance Sheet as at 31 December 19X7

Goodwill		9,320
Fixed assets		127,000
Current assets		33,000
		169,320
Share capital		100,000
Profit and loss account		53,290
(P 37,000 + S1 90% of 16,000 + S2 63% of 3,000)		
General reserve		10,000
Minority interest		6,030
		169,320

Minority interest:

Shares in S1	1,000	
Shares in S2 37% of 5,000	1,850	
		2,850
Profit and loss S1 10% of 23,000	2,300	
S2 37% of 4,000	1,480	
		3,780
		6,630
Less Cost of shares in S2 for minority interest of S1 10% of 6,000		600
		6,030

Goodwill:

Cost of shares to group in S1		23,000	
in S2 90% of 6,000		5,400	
			28,400
Less Shares: In S1		9,000	
In S2 63% of 5,000		3,150	
Profit and loss S1 90% of 7,000		6,300	
S2 63% of 1,000		630	
			19,080
			9,320

26.3

Sales Ltd & subsidiaries
Balance sheet as at 31 October 19X5

	Cost	Depreciation	Net
Fixed assets	184,000	–	184,000
Buildings	260,000	92,400	167,600
Plant (W1)	362,900	203,700	159,200
	806,900	296,100	510,800
Current assets			
Stock (W2)		247,400	
Debtors (W3)		275,200	
Bank		50,600	
		573,200	
Less Current liabilities			
Creditors (W4)	297,400		
Bank overdraft (W5)	26,100		
Corporation tax	129,100		
Proposed dividends	80,000		
Proposed dividends relating to minority interests (W6)	16,000	548,600	
Net current assets			24,600
			535,400
Ordinary share capital			200,000
Revenue reserves (W7)			189,390
Capital reserve (W8)			9,000
			398,390
Minority interest (W9)			137,010
			535,400

Workings:

Note: S Ltd owns 75% of M Ltd & 75% × 80% = 60% of C Ltd

(W1) Plant 102,900 + 170,000 + 92,000 = 364,900
Less (Note (g)) inter-company profit 2,000
362,900

Depreciation 69,900 + 86,000 + 48,200 = 204,100
Less 2 years on inter-company profit element 10% × 2,000 × 2 = 400
203,700

(W2) Stock 108,500 + 75,500 + 68,400 = 252,400
– Unrealised profit (Note (f)) 20% × 25,000 = 5,000
247,400

(W3) Debtors 196,700 + 124,800 + 83,500 = 405,000
– Inter-indebtedness (Note (h)) 56,900
(Note (h)) 28,900
– Dividends: 80% of 10,000 = 8,000
75% of 48,000 = 36,000
129,800
275,200

(W4) Creditors 160,000 + 152,700 + 59,200 = 371,900
– Inter-indebtedness (Note (h)) 28,900
45,600
74,500
297,400

(W5) Overdraft 37,400
– cheque in transit (Note (i)) 11,300
26,100

(W6) Minority interests: Shares of proposed dividends

Components Ltd: Ordinary 20% × 10,000	2,000	
Preference	2,000	
Machinery Ltd: Ordinary 25% × 48,000	12,000	
	16,000	

(W7)

Reserves S Ltd	154,000	
M Ltd	85,000	
C Ltd	74,000	313,000
Add Reduction in depreciation of components		
2,000 × 10% × 2 years = 400 × 60%		
ownership of components		240
		313,240
Less Profit on machinery	2,000	
Unrealised profit on stock	5,000	
Cost of control of C Ltd on 1.4.X3		
60% × 60,000	36,000	
Minority interest in C Ltd		
40% × 74,000	29,600	
Cost of control of M Ltd on 1.4.X3		
75% × 40,000	30,000	
Minority interest in M Ltd		
25% × 85,000	21,250	123,850
		189,390

(W8) Cost of control

C Ltd at date of purchase. Capital:		
Ordinary shares	100,000	
Reserves	60,000	
	160,000	
M Ltd had owned 80% =	128,000	
Then had paid	96,000	
Bringing about a capital reserve	32,000	
Of this 25% is owned by minority		
interest of M Ltd	8,000	
M Ltd at date of purchase: Capital	120,000	
Reserve	40,000	
	160,000	24,000
S Ltd owns 75%	120,000	
S Ltd paid	135,000	
Cost of control	15,000	
Net figure for capital reserve	9,000	

(W9) Minority interest

Ordinary shares: 25% M Ltd	30,000	
40% C Ltd	40,000	
	40,000	
Preference shares	160	
Increase in profit because of		
depreciation change 40% × 400		
25% revenue reserves M Ltd × 85,000	21,250	
40% „ C „ × 74,000	29,600	
	161,010	
Less 25% payment made by M Ltd		
for investment in C Ltd × 96,000	24,000	137,010

27.1

Brodick plc & subsidiaries
Consolidated Profit and Loss Account for the year ended 30 April 19X7

	£000	£000
Turnover (1,100 + 500 + 130)		1,730
Cost of sales (630 + 300 + 70)		1,000
Gross profit		730
Administrative expenses (105 + 150 + 20)		275
Profit on ordinary activities before taxation		455
Tax on profit on ordinary activities (65 + 10 + 20)		95
Profit on ordinary activities after taxation		360
Minority interests (20% × 40 + 40% × 20)		16
Profit for the financial year		344
Retained profits from last year (W1)		506
		850
Dividends paid and proposed		200
Retained profits carried to next year (Note 1)		650

Note 1

Retained profits carried to next year comprise:		
Brodick plc (*see* W1)		590
Subsidiaries (*see* W1)		60
		650

Norbreck plc & its subsidiary Bispham Ltd
Consolidated Balance Sheet as at 30 September 19X7

	£000	£000	£000	£000
Fixed assets				
Tangible assets				1,720
Current assets				
Stocks		550		
Debtors (280 + 150 – 80 dividend)		350		
Cash and Bank		50		
			950	
Creditors: amounts falling due within one year				
Trade creditors		240		
Other creditors, taxation and social security		230		
Proposed dividends (270 + 20% × 100)		290		
			760	
Net current assets				190
Total assets less current liabilities				1,910
Provisions for liabilities and charges				
Taxation, including deferred taxation				480
				1,430
Capital and reserves				
Called-up share capital				900
Profit and loss account				430
				1,330
Minority interest (20% × £500)				100
				1,430

Workings:

Goodwill	£000	£000
Investment		400
Nominal value of shares (80% of 400)	320	
Profit and loss (80% of 40)	32	
		352
Goodwill on acquisition		48
Retained profits b/d		
Norbreck		220
Bispham	70	
– Pre-acquisition	40	
	30	
– Minority interest (20%)	6	
		24
		244
– Goodwill on acquisition (see above)		48
Retained profits of Group b/d		196
For the year (per consolidated P/L 594 – 360)		234
		430

Workings:

(W1) Retained profits b/d

Brodick			460
Lamlash			40
Less Minority (20%)		106	
Less Pre-acquisition (80% × 56)		(21.2)	
		(44.8)	
		30	
Corrie		12	
Less Minority (40%)	12		
Less Pre-acquisition			
(60% × 20)	12		
		24	
		6	
Retained profits for year (344 – 200)		506	
		144	
		650	

27.2 Norbreck plc & its subsidiary Bispham Ltd
Consolidated Profit and Loss Account for the year ended 30 September 19X7

	£000
Turnover	2,150
Cost of sales	995
Gross profit	1,155
Administrative expenses	475
Profit on ordinary activities before taxation	680
Tax on profit on ordinary activities	50
Profit on ordinary activities after taxation	630
Minority interest (20% × 180)	36
Profit for the financial year	594
Retained profits from last year	196
	790
Dividends	360
Retained profits carried to next year	430
Earnings per share (594/900)	66p

28.1

(a)

Large Ltd & its subsidiary Small Ltd
Consolidated Profit and Loss Account for the year ended 30 September 19X6

	£000	£000
Turnover (10,830 + 2,000 – 108)		12,722
Cost of sales and production (3,570 + 1,100 – (⅔ of 108))		4,598
		8,124
Administrative and marketing expenses	2,772	
Unpurchased goodwill written off (per Companies Act 1985)	50	
Research costs written off (*see* SSAP 13)	50	2,872
Profit on ordinary activities before taxation		5,252
Tax on profit on ordinary activities		2,504
Profit on ordinary activities after taxation		2,748
Minority interests		121
		2,627
Retained profits from last year		1,290
		3,917
Dividend		2,400
Retained profits carried to next year		1,517

(b)

Large Ltd & its subsidiary Small Ltd
Consolidated Balance Sheet as at 30 September 19X6

	£000	£000	£000
Fixed assets			
Intangible assets			
Development costs	180		
Goodwill	48		
Negative goodwill (W1)	(129)	99	
Tangible assets			
At cost less depreciation		4,648	4,747
Current assets			
Stock (594 + 231 – 27)	798		
Debtors	2,620		
Bank	123	3,541	
Creditors: amounts falling due within one year			
Trade creditors		453	
Net current assets			3,088
			7,835
Capital and reserves			
Called-up share capital			6,000
Profit and loss account			1,517
Minority interest (W2)			318
			7,835

Workings:

	£000	£000
(W1) Investment in Small cost		525
Less Share capital	600	
75% Retained earnings of 72	54	654
Negative goodwill on acquisition		129
(W2) Share capital		200
25% Retained earnings of 472		118
		318

(c) In this case merger accounting is not permitted. It can only be used when 90 per cent of the consideration is given as equity share capital, and here Large obtained 75 per cent for cash.

If merger treatment had been used the profits made before the merger could be distributed as dividends.

Note: This answer is per SSAP 22, under FRS 10, below the Goodwill line, there will be a line for negative goodwill of (129), the capital reserve line will disappear and the totals will be 7,835 rather than 7,964.

29.1 If Q plc is unable to exercise significant influence over N Ltd, the group comprises the parent undertaking (Q) and two subsidiaries (L and M). N Ltd should be excluded from consolidation (the grounds would be 'severe long-term restrictions') and treated as a fixed asset investment at cost. However, if Q plc is able to exercise significant influence over N Ltd, it should treat it as an associated undertaking using the equity method.

29.2 (a) There are two acquisition points. Any dividends received from the pre-acquisition (of the first investment) profits should be applied to reduce the initial investment of £80,000. Similar treatment should be applied to the £110,000 investment. The investment should be shown in the P's company balance sheet at cost of £190,000 less any such dividends received (or it could be shown at valuation). Dividends received and receivable should be shown in the profit and loss account after adjustment for any pre-acquisition element.

(b) At the time the investment became 21 per cent, the net assets of the clothing company were £840,000. The company's share of this is £176,400. The premium paid on acquisition, subject to adjustment for pre-acquisition reserves distributed, is £13,600 (£80,000 + £110,000 – £176,400) and, after any such adjustment required, it should either be written off to the reserves, or capitalised and amortised. Disclosure in the company's own financial statements is as for trade investments. The group profit and loss should show the company's share of the publishing company's pre-tax profits/losses and its attributable share of the associated undertaking's tax charge on those profits/losses. The group balance sheet carrying value in respect of this investment will comprise the cost of the investment plus the company's share of post-acquisition retained profits, less any amounts written-off either of these.

30.1 Solvency, profitability, efficiency, capital structure and shareholder.

30.3

Solvency	– see text sections 30.2 and 30.7.
Profitability	– see text sections 30.3 and 30.7.
Efficiency	– see text sections 30.4 and 30.7.
Capital structure	– see text sections 30.5 and 30.7.
Shareholder	– see text sections 30.6 and 30.7.

30.5 (a) Stock turnover.

30.7
(i) (b) and (d).
(ii) (b) and (d).
(iii) (d).
(iv) If current liabilities greater than current assets, (b) and (d); if current assets greater than current liabilities, (a) and (c).
(v) (b) and (d) but only after a customer takes up the offer.

30.9 (a)

(i) Gross profit as % of sales:
$$\frac{20,000}{80,000} \times \frac{100}{1} = 25\% \qquad \frac{24,000}{120,000} \times \frac{100}{1} = 20\%$$

(ii) Net profit as % of sales:
$$\frac{10,000}{80,000} \times \frac{100}{1} = 12.5\% \qquad \frac{15,000}{120,000} \times \frac{100}{1} = 12.5\%$$

(iii) Expenses as % of sales:
$$\frac{10,000}{80,000} \times \frac{100}{1} = 12.5\% \qquad \frac{9,000}{120,000} \times \frac{100}{1} = 7.5\%$$

(iv) Stockturn:
$$\frac{60,000}{(25,000 + 15,000) \div 2} = 3 \text{ times} \qquad \frac{96,000}{(22,500 + 17,500) \div 2} = 4.8 \text{ times}$$

(v) Rate of return:
$$\frac{10,000}{(38,000 + 42,000) \div 2} \times \frac{100}{1} = 25 \qquad \frac{15,000}{(36,000 + 44,000) \div 2} \times \frac{100}{1} = 37.5\%$$

(vi) Current ratio:
$$\frac{45,000}{5,000} = 9 \qquad \frac{40,000}{10,000} = 4$$

(vii) Acid test ratio:
$$\frac{30,000}{5,000} = 6 \qquad \frac{22,500}{10,000} = 2.25$$

(viii) Debtor/sales ratio:
$$\frac{25,000}{80,000} \times 12 = 3.75 \text{ months} \qquad \frac{20,000}{120,000} \times 12 = 2 \text{ months}$$

(ix) Creditor/purchases ratio:
$$\frac{5,000}{50,000} \times 12 = 1.2 \text{ months} \qquad \frac{10,000}{91,000} \times 12 = 1.3 \text{ months}$$

(b) Business B is the most profitable: both in terms of actual net profits £15,000 compared to £10,000, but also in terms of capital employed, B has managed to achieve a return of £37.50 for every £100 invested, i.e. 37.5 per cent. A has managed a lower return of 25 per cent. Reasons – possibly only – as not until you know more about the business could you give a definite answer.

(i) Possibly managed to sell far more merchandise because of lower prices, i.e. took only 20 per cent margin as compared with A's 25 per cent margin.
(ii) Maybe more efficient use of mechanised means in the business. Note that B has more equipment, and perhaps as a consequence kept other expenses down to £6,000 as compared with A's £9,000.
(iii) Did not have as much stock lying idle. Turned over stock 4.8 times in the year as compared with 3 for A.
(iv) A's current ratio of 9 far greater than normally needed. B kept it down to 4. A therefore had too much money lying idle and not doing anything.
(v) Following on from (iv) the acid test ratio for A also higher than necessary.
(vi) Part of the reason for (iv) and (v) is that A waited (on average) 3.75 months to be paid by customers. B managed to collect in 2 months on average. Money represented by debts is money lying idle.
(vii) A also paid creditors more quickly than did B, but not by much.

Put all these factors together, and it is obvious that business B is run far more efficiently, and is more profitable as a consequence.

30.11 (a) The ratios reveal that L Ltd's relative profitability has fallen between the two years. The gross and net profit margins have both fallen, but this may be due to the new sales manager's price-cutting policy, rather than because of any change in costs.

The fall in return on capital employed is not what was hoped for from the new sales price policy. A drop from 31 per cent to 18 per cent is very significant and suggests that the change in sales price policy and the investment in new machinery, although with the related increased borrowings, have led to short-term depressed returns. If the increased market resulting from the new sales policy can be retained, it would be worthwhile considering an increase in sales price to a point where a higher rate of return would be achieved.

The company appears solvent – there is no shortage of liquid assets. However, it has taken on considerably more long-term debt in order to fund the market expansion. This will have to be serviced and the level of profit should be monitored to ensure that margins do not fall further, raising the current level of risk to unacceptable levels. As 38.2

per cent (£192,000) of net profits before interest (£502,000) are already being used to meet debt interest payments, compared to only 3.8 per cent in 19X2, it would not take very large changes in costs or selling price to cause this to become a major problem. The current level of gearing will also inhibit the company's ability to raise additional loan funding in future.

Profitability	19X2	19X3
Gross profit:sales	$\frac{540}{900} \times 100 = 60\%$	$\frac{1,120}{2,800} \times 100 = 40\%$
Net profit:sales	$\frac{302}{900} \times 100 = 34\%$	$\frac{310}{2,800} \times 100 = 11\%$
ROCE	$\frac{302 + 12}{929 + 100} = 31\%$	$\frac{310 + 192}{1,267 + 1,600} = 18\%$

Solvency

Current ratio	$\frac{125}{36} = 3.47:1$	$\frac{821}{186} = 4.41:1$
Acid test ratio	$\frac{125 - 30}{36} = 2.63:1$	$\frac{821 - 238}{186} = 3.13:1$

Capital structure

Capital gearing	$\frac{100}{100 + 929} = 10\%$	$\frac{1,600}{1,600 + 1,267} = 56\%$

(b) Current debtor collection period (i.e. debtor days) $= \frac{583}{2,800} \times 365 = 76$ days.

If the collection period were 45 days, the new debtors amount would be:

$$\frac{45}{76} \times 583,000 = 345,200$$

The amount released if a 45-day debtors collection period could be imposed would be £237,800.

31.1 (a)   *Trading and Profit and Loss Accounts for the year ended 31 December 19X9*

	X	Y
Sales	480,000	762,500*
Less Cost of goods sold	400,000	(+10,000) 610,000
Gross profit	80,000	152,500

		X		Y
Less Admin. expenses (–10,000)	40,000		(–2,500) 57,500	
Selling expenses	15,000	55,000	35,000	92,500
Net profit		25,000		60,000

* Assumed 25 per cent mark-up despite wrong stock valuation.

(b)   *Profitability:*

	X	Y
Gross profit %	20%	25%
Net profit %	$\frac{25}{480} \times \frac{100}{1} = 5.2\%$	$\frac{60}{762.5} \times \frac{100}{1} = 7.87\%$
Stockturn	$\frac{400,000}{40,000} = 10$ times	$\frac{610,000}{45,000^*} = 13.6$ times

* Adjusted to take into account inaccurate valuation.

Return on Capital Employed (ROCE) (previous owners)

X	Y
$\frac{25,000}{200,000} \times \frac{100}{1} = 12.5\%$	$\frac{60,000}{350,000} \times \frac{100}{1} = 17.14\%$

Based on purchase price of business the ROCE for Adrian Frampton would be:

X	Y
$\frac{25,000}{190,000} \times \frac{100}{1} = 13.15\%$	$\frac{60,000}{400,000} \times \frac{100}{1} = 15\%$

All ratios are favourable for Y. If gross profit ratios remained the same in future together with other expenses then Y business is best value.

However:

(i) Can gross profit ratios of X be improved as compared to those of Y?

(ii) Can stockturn be improved?

If so, then X could be cheapest business to buy as it gives a better ROCE.

(c) (i) Need to know current assets and current liabilities in detail.

(ii) Are these similar businesses?

Type of business

Areas in which situated

Competition

Prefer several years' accounts to gauge trends

Quality of staff and whether they would continue.

31.2

(a) 19X4

	A £000		B £000		C £000	
Return on capital of 20% = Profit*		120.0		120.0		120.0
Interest less tax		—	24.0		66.0	
			13.2	10.8	36.3	29.7
Profit for ordinary shares		120.0		109.2		90.3
Ordinary share capital		600		400		50
Profit return (%)		20		27.3		180.6

19X5

	A £000		B £000		C £000	
Return on capital of 10% = Profit		60.0		60.0		60.0
Interest less tax		—	24.0		66.0	
			13.2	10.8	36.3	29.7
Profit for ordinary shares		60.0		49.2		30.3
Ordinary share capital		600		400		50
Profit return (%)		10		12.3		60.6

*Profit is assumed to be after tax but before interest.

(b) High gearing accentuates the rate of return to the ordinary shareholder. In the zero-geared position of A the return to the shareholder supply reflects the change in profits earned on trading. In the high-geared position of Company C the return to the shareholder decreases from 180.6 per cent to 60.6 per cent, i.e. to a reduction of 66.5 per cent as profits reduce by only 50 per cent. Company B reflects an intermediate position with a relatively moderate level of gearing.

High gearing increases risk to shareholders for two reasons. First if the profits earned are not sufficiently high to meet interest charges then the company may find itself failing since the lenders may seek a winding up order. Second the risk is increased simply because of exaggerated fluctuations in the returns which are accentuated in the high-geared situation.

However, it can be seen that if profits earned are higher than the interest rate, this will produce a significantly higher return to the shareholder in a high-geared company. The fact that interest is allowed as a deduction for tax purposes indicates that gearing may give an overall advantage. The market's assessment of the risk position will counter this, and will be based on the nature of the business and management.

31.4

(a) Refer to the text.

(b)

	Company A £000	%	Company B £000	%
Ordinary shares	300		800	
Revenue: Share premium	300		400	
Retained profit	400		200	
	1,000	62.5	1,400	87.5
8% preference shares	200		—	
10% loan – debentures	—		200	
12% loan – debentures	400		—	
	600	37.5	200	12.5
Total share capital and loan	1,600	100.0	1,600	100.0

$$\text{Company A Debt/Equity} = \frac{37.5}{62.5} = 60\%$$

$$\text{B} \qquad\text{,,}\qquad = \frac{12.5}{87.5} = 14.3\%$$

(c) Company A is more highly geared than B since it is committed to paying a higher proportion of fixed dividend and interest payments for its profits. A higher level of gearing increases risk. (Note the answer in 35.2 (b) is appropriate.)

(d)

	A	B
Trading profit before interest	200,000	200,000
Less Interest charges	48,000	20,000
Net profit after interest charge	152,000	180,000
Preference dividend	16,000	–
Ordinary dividend	45,000	120,000
	61,000	120,000
Retained profit	91,000	60,000

31.6

(a)

	19X4	19X5
Equity shares	100,000	150,000
Reserves	150,000	220,000
Total equity capital	250,000	370,000
Loans	40,000	40,000
Total capital employed	290,000	410,000
Profits (net after tax)	60,000	70,000
Return on total equity	24%	18.9%

(b) **To Mr C. Black**

The reduction in profits from 24 per cent to 18.9 per cent of total equity needs to be analysed into its causal factors. During the year the net profits have increased but not as fast as the equity capital which has gone up by £120,000 over the year. If the increase reflected an investment late in 19X5 it would reduce returns because a full year's profit could not be earned.

It is therefore essential to examine the nature of the investment and the future. Before shares are bought it is essential to examine future prospects. If these are good the historic analysis may not be important. However, if the new funds were used – clearly prospects may not be good and shares should not be bought.

(c) Reserves are profits retained within the business. The profits may be from revenue, i.e. from profits which could be distributed as dividends to shareholders or capital – for example where fixed amounts are revalued upwards to reflect current market value.

The creation of reserves reflects an increase in capital in the organisation which would normally not normally be to reflect an increasing scale of operation. In this sense reserves reflect an alternative to issuing new shares. In the case of capital reserves from revaluation – these are simply 'paper adjustments' to value which do not in themselves indicate more resources in the organisation.

Revenue reserves may in fact be distributed as dividends whereas capital reserves would not normally be available for this purpose and are more akin to share capital.

31.8 *(a) Profit and Loss Accounts for the year to 31 March 19X8*

	Chan plc £000	Ling plc £000	Wong plc £000
Operating profit	300	300	300
Interest payable	—	—	(10)
	300	300	290
Profit on ordinary activities before tax			
Taxation (30%)	(90)	(90)	(87)
Profit on ordinary activities after tax	210	210	203
Dividends: Preference	—	(20)	(30)
Ordinary	(100)	(60)	(40)
	(100)	(80)	(70)
Retained profit for the year	£110	£130	£133

(b) (i) Earnings per share

$$\text{Earnings per share} = \frac{\text{Net profit after tax and preference dividend}}{\text{Number of ordinary shares in issue}}$$

	Chan plc	Ling plc	Wong plc
	$\dfrac{210}{500} = 42\text{p}$	$\dfrac{210-20}{300} = 63.3\text{p}$	$\dfrac{203-30}{200} = 86.5\text{p}$

(ii) Price/earnings ratio

$$= \frac{\text{Market price of ordinary shares}}{\text{Earnings per share}}$$

	Chan plc	Ling plc	Wong plc
Market price of ordinary shares	840	950	1038
Earnings per share	42	63.3	86.5
	20	15	12

(iii) Gearing ratio

$$= \frac{\text{Loan capital} + \text{preference shares} \times 100}{\text{Shareholders' funds}}$$

Chan plc $=$ Nil

Ling plc $= \dfrac{200}{300 + 100 + 130} \times 100 = 37.7\%$

Wong plc $= \dfrac{300 + 100}{200 + 100 + 133} \times 100 = 92.4\%$

(c) A gearing ratio expresses the relationship that exists between total borrowings (that is, preference share capital and long-term loans), and the total amount of ordinary shareholders' funds. It should be noted that other definitions of gearing are possible and are sometimes used.

Any company with a gearing ratio of, say, 70 per cent would be considered to be high geared, whilst a company with a gearing ratio of, say, 20 per cent would be low geared.

Gearing is an important matter to consider when investing in ordinary shares in a particular company. A *high-geared company* means that a high proportion of the company's earnings are committed to paying either interest on any debenture stock and/or dividends on any preference share capital *before* an ordinary dividend can be declared. If a company is low geared, then a high proportion of the company's earnings can be paid out as ordinary dividends.

Chan plc has not issued any long-term loans or any preference share capital. Gearing does not, therefore apply to this company, and all of the earnings may be paid out to the ordinary shareholders.

Ling plc is a relatively low-geared company. It has no debenture stock, and only a small proportion of its earnings are committed to paying its preference shareholders. The balance may then all be declared as an ordinary dividend.

Wong plc is an extremely high-geared company. A high proportion of borrowings (in this case consisting of both debenture stock and preference share capital) means that a high proportion of its earnings has to be set aside for both its debenture holders and its preference shareholders before any ordinary dividend can be declared. As a result, if the profits of the company are low, no ordinary dividend may be payable.

If profits are rising a high geared company may not be a particularly risky company in which to purchase some ordinary shares, but the reverse may apply if profits are falling.

For the year to 31 March 19X8, Chan, Ling and Wong's operating profit is identical. Wong is committed to paying interest on its debenture stock (which is allowable against tax), and both Ling and Wong have to pay a preference dividend (which is *not* allowable against tax).

In deciding whether to invest in any of the three companies, there are a great many other factors to be considered, including future prospects of all three companies. However, when profits are fluctuating an ordinary shareholder is more likely to receive a higher return by investing in Chan rather than by investing in either Ling or Wong. Similarly, an ordinary shareholder can expect a higher return by investing in Wong.

Based on the limited amount of information given in the question, therefore, an investor considering purchasing ordinary shares in only one of these three companies would be recommended to buy shares in Chan plc.

It should be noted that if profits were *increasing*, an investor would be recommended to buy shares first in Wong, then in Ling and finally in Chan. The earnings per share in both Ling and Wong are far higher than in Chan, so there is a much greater chance of an increase in the ordinary dividend, but this is not necessarily the case if profits are falling or fluctuating.

31.10 (a) (i) *Forecast Profit and Loss Appropriation Accounts*

	19X6	19X7	19X8
	£000	£000	£000
Forecast profits	1,800	500	2,200
Less Corporation tax (30%)	540	150	660
	1,260	350	1,540
Less Dividends proposed	1,260	350	1,540

Balance sheet extracts

Shareholders' equity

	19X6	19X7	19X8
Issued ordinary shares of £1 each fully paid	6,000	6,000	6,000
Share premium account	1,000	1,000	1,000
Retained profits	1,650	1,650	1,650
	8,650	8,650	8,650

Current liabilities

	19X6	19X7	19X8
Dividends proposed	1,260	350	1,540

(ii) *Forecast Profit and Loss Appropriation Accounts*

	19X6	19X7	19X8
	£000	£000	£000
Forecast profits	1,800	500	2,200
Less interest (12% × £2m)	240	240	240
	1,560	260	1,960
Less Corporation tax (30%)	468	78	588
	1,092	182	1,372
Less Dividends proposed	1,092	182	1,372

Balance sheet extracts

Shareholders' equity

	19X6	19X7	19X8
Issued ordinary shares of £1, each fully paid	5,000	5,000	5,000
Retained profits	1,650	1,650	1,650
	6,650	6,650	6,650

Deferred liabilities

	19X6	19X7	19X8
12% debentures	2,000	2,000	2,000

Current liabilities

	19X6	19X7	19X8
Dividend proposed	1,092	182	1,372

(b) (i) If planned expansion is financed by share issue, the forecast return on shareholders' equity for the next three years will be:

19X6 $1,260/8,650 \times 100$ = 14.6%
19X7 $350/8,650 \times 100$ = 4.0%
19X8 $1,540/8,650 \times 100$ = 17.8%

(ii) If planned expansion is financed by debenture issue, the forecast return on shareholders' equity for the next three years will be:

19X6 $1,092/6,650 \times 100$ = 16.4%
19X7 $182/6,650 \times 100$ = 2.7%
19X8 $1,372/6,650 \times 100$ = 20.6%

Note: All the above figures are, of course, net of tax and should be grossed up by a factor of 100/70 if comparison with gross interest rates is to be made (on the assumption of 30 per cent tax rate).

(c) The return on shareholders' equity for the year ended 30 September 19X5 was $600/6,620 \times 100$ = 9.1 per cent, and it could have been 9.5 per cent if full distribution of the year's profit had been made. To have the return fluctuate between 2.7 per cent and 20.6 per cent, as it will do if the planned expansion is financed by the debenture issue, will surely unnerve all but the most sturdy shareholders. Such a violent swing from year to year will confuse, confound and alarm anyone looking at the shares as an investment.

To finance the planned expansion by a share issue does not improve matters greatly, as it will be seen that the return will still fluctuate between 4.0 per cent and 17.8 per cent. But since we are told that the industry is 'subject to marked variations in consumer demand' it does seem more appropriate to use share capital (by definition risk-bearing) rather than a debenture. The poor profits forecast for 19X7 suggest that it would not take much of a variation from the expected results to show no profit at all, and were this to occur, is there not a possibility that the debenture holders could not be paid their due interest? Failure to pay debenture interest on time would bring in a receiver (assuming the debentures were secured); his function would then be to collect not only the unpaid interest but the capital as well, as failure to pay interest would be a breach of the conditions under which the debenture was issued.

If shareholders are to miss a year's dividends as a result of there being no profits for distribution, the directors can expect a stormy annual general meeting, but that is far less dangerous than the entry of a receiver.

In practice, of course, it is unusual for a company to pay out all profits as dividends, and since shareholders will pay more attention usually to the level of dividends paid than to profits earned, it would make better financial sense if the 19X6 dividend were maintained at or slightly above the 19X5 level, enabling an addition to be made to retained profits. This in turn would enable a fund to be built up to supplement current profits for dividends and/or to redeem the debentures.

The all-shares or all-debentures choice is also an unrealistic one. Although there is much to be said for a broad share base to support what is obviously a risky business, it could make better sense to raise part of the required £2,000,000 by shares and part by debentures. A restrained dividend policy coupled with the use of the (probably enlarged) depreciation charge arising after the expansion had taken place could enable a debenture redemption programme to be established over the course of the next few years.

31.12 (a) (i) Shareholders

Earnings per share (EPS)

$$19X6 \quad \frac{9,520}{39,680} = 24p \qquad 19X7 \quad \frac{11,660}{39,680} = 29.4p$$

Dividend cover
(= EPS ÷ dividend per share)

$$\frac{24p}{(2,240 \div 39,680)} \qquad \frac{29.4p}{(2,400 \div 39,680)}$$

$$= \frac{24p}{5.6p} = 4.3 \text{ times} \qquad = \frac{29.4p}{6p} = 4.9 \text{ times}$$

(ii) Trade creditors

Current ratio $\quad \frac{92,447}{36,862} = 2.5 \qquad \frac{99,615}{42,475} = 2.3$

Acid test $\quad \frac{40,210 + 12,092}{36,862} = 1.4:1 \qquad \frac{43,370 + 5790}{42,475} = 1.2:1$

(iii) Internal management

Debtor ratio/Sales*

*assumed credit sales $\quad \frac{40,210}{486,300} \times 52 = 4.3 \text{ weeks} \qquad \frac{43,370}{583,900} \times 52 = 3.9$

Return on capital employed
(before tax) $\quad \frac{15,254}{40,740} = 37.4\% \qquad \frac{18,686}{50,000} = 37.4\%$

(b) Shareholders

EPS. An increase of 5.4p per share has occurred. This was due to an increase in profit without any increase in share capital.

Dividend cover. Increased by 0.6 times because increase in profit not fully reflected in dividends.

Trade creditors

Current ratio. This has fallen but only marginally and it still appears to be quite sound.

Acid test. This has also fallen, but still seems to be quite reasonable.

Internal management

Debtor ratio. There appears to have been an increase in the efficiency of our credit control.

Return on capital employed. This has stayed the same for each of the two years. The increase in capital employed has seen a proportional increase in profits.

31.14 To the Board of G plc

From AN Other, Accountant

Subject: *Potential acquisition of either of companies A Ltd and B Ltd as subsidiaries in the machine tool manufacturing sector. Financial performances assessed.*

As instructed by you I have investigated the financial performances of these two companies to assist in the evaluation of them as potential acquisitions.

It should be borne in mind that financial ratio analysis is only partial information. There are many other factors which will need to be borne in mind before a decision can be taken.

The calculations of the various ratios are given as an appendix.

Profitability

While the main interest to the board is what G plc could obtain in profitability from A Ltd and B Ltd, all I can comment on at present is the current profitability enjoyed by these two companies.

Here the most important ratio is that of ROCE (Return on Capital Employed). A's ROCE is 27.2 per cent as compared with B's 15.6 per cent.

The great difference in ROCE can be explained by reference to the secondary ratios of profit and asset utilisation. Both ratios are in A's favour. The profit ratios are A 34 per cent: B 20 per cent. The asset utilisation ratios are A 0.9 per cent: B 0.6, showing that A is utilising its assets 50 per cent better than B. It is the effect of these two ratios that give the ROCE for each company.

The very low working capital employed by A Ltd very much affects the asset utilisation ratio. How far such a low working capital is representative of that throughout the whole year is impossible to say.

Liquidity

It would not be sensible to draw a final conclusion as to the liquidity positions of the two companies based on the balance sheet figures. As a balance sheet is based at one point in time it can sometimes be misleading, as a reading of figures over a period would be more appropriate.

A Ltd does appear to have a short-term liquidity problem, as the current assets only just cover current liabilities. The 'quick' or 'acid test ratio' on the face of it appears to be very inadequate at 0.6.

By contrast, B Ltd with a current ratio of 1.4 and a 'quick ratio' of 1.0 would appear to be reasonably liquid.

However, much more light is shed on the position of the companies when the debtor collection period is examined. A collects its debts with a credit period of 9 weeks. In the case of B Ltd this rises to an astonishing 36.7 weeks. Why is this so? It could be due simply to very poor credit control by B Ltd. Such a long credit period casts considerable doubt on the real worth of the debtors. There is a high probability that many of the debts may prove difficult to collect. It might be that B Ltd, in order to maintain sales, has lowered its requirements as to the creditworthiness of its customers. If the credit period were reduced to a normal one for the industry it might be found that many of the customers might go elsewhere.

The problem with debtors in the case of B Ltd is also carried on to stock. In the case of A Ltd the stock turnover is 4.3 falling to 2.8 in B Ltd. There could be a danger that B Ltd has stock increasing simply because it is finding it difficult to sell its products.

Capital gearing

A Ltd is far more highly geared than B Ltd: 93.6 per cent as compared with 14.1 per cent. A comparison with this particular industry by means of interfirm comparison should be undertaken.

Limitations of ratio analysis

You should bear in mind the following limitations of the analysis undertaken:

(i) One year's accounts are insufficient for proper analysis to be undertaken. The analysis of trends, taken from, say, five years' accounts would give a better insight.

(ii) Differences in accounting policies between A Ltd and B Ltd will affect comparisons.

(iii) The use of historical costs brings about many distortions.

(iv) The use of industry interfirm comparisons would make the ratios more capable of being interpreted.

(v) The plans of the companies for the future expressed in their budgets would be of more interest than past figures.

Conclusions

Depending on the price which would have to be paid for acquisition, I would suggest that A Ltd is the company most suitable for takeover.

A N Other
Accountant

Appendix

(i) Return on capital employed

	A Ltd	B Ltd
$\dfrac{\text{Profits before interest and tax}}{\text{Capital employed}}$	$\dfrac{211}{775} \times 100 = 27.2\%$	$\dfrac{88}{565} \times 100 = 15.6\%$

(ii) Assets utilisation ratios

	A Ltd	B Ltd
Total assets turnover: $\dfrac{\text{Turnover}}{\text{Total assets}}$	$\dfrac{985}{1,140} = 0.9$	$\dfrac{560}{990} = 0.6$
Fixed assets turnover: $\dfrac{\text{Turnover}}{\text{Fixed assets}}$	$\dfrac{985}{765} = 1.3$	$\dfrac{560}{410} = 1.4$
Working capital turnover: $\dfrac{\text{Turnover}}{\text{Working capital}}$	$\dfrac{985}{10} = 98.5$	$\dfrac{560}{150} = 3.6$

(iii) Profitability ratios

	A Ltd	B Ltd
Gross profit % $\dfrac{\text{Gross profit}}{\text{Turnover}}$	$\dfrac{335}{985} \times 100 = 34\%$	$\dfrac{163}{560} \times 100 = 29\%$

Profit before taxation and
interest as % turnover $\frac{211}{985} \times 100 = 21\%$ $\quad \frac{88}{560} \times 100 = 16\%$

(iv) Liquidity ratios

Current ratio: $\dfrac{\text{Current assets}}{\text{Current liabilities}}$ $\quad \dfrac{375}{365} = 1.0 \qquad \dfrac{580}{425} = 1.4$

Acid test or
Quick ratio: $\dfrac{\text{Current assets} - \text{stock}}{\text{Current liabilities}}$ $\quad \dfrac{220}{365} = 0.6 \qquad \dfrac{440}{425} = 1.0$

Debtor ratio: $\dfrac{\text{Trade debtors} \times 52}{\text{Credit sales}}$ $\quad \dfrac{170}{985} \times 52 = 9 \text{ weeks} \qquad \dfrac{395}{560} \times 52 = 36.7 \text{ weeks}$

(v) Capital structure

Gearing ratio: $\dfrac{\text{Long-term borrowing}}{\text{Shareholders' funds}}$ $\quad \dfrac{220}{555} \times 100 = 39.6\% \qquad \dfrac{70}{495} \times 100 = 14\%$

Proprietary ratio: $\dfrac{\text{Shareholders' funds}}{\text{Tangible assets}}$ $\quad \dfrac{555}{1,140} = 0.5 \qquad \dfrac{495}{990} = 0.5$

33.1 (a) T (b) F (c) T (d) F (e) T

33.4 £40,000

33.6

At 31 December 19X5, accumulated depreciation is:

$30\% \times 30,000 \times \dfrac{160}{90} = 16,000$

At 31 December 19X4, accumulated depreciation is:

$20\% \times 30,000 \times \dfrac{120}{90} = 8,000$

Depreciation charge for the year ended 31 December 19X5 is:

$10\% \times 30,000 \times \dfrac{160}{90} = 5,333$

Hence, depreciation provision at 31 December 19X5 is:
$8,000 + 5,333 = 13,333$

Backlog depreciation is $16,000 - 13,333 = 2,667$

33.8

Opening stock at average prices = $50,000 \times \dfrac{100}{80}$ = 62,500

Purchases = 450,000

Closing stock at average prices = $70,000 \times \dfrac{100}{120}$ = 58,333

Current cost of sales = 454,167
Historic cost of sales = 430,000
Cost of sales adjustment = 24,167

33.10

Opening working capital = 7,000
Closing working capital = 10,000
Change in the year = 3,000

At average values:

Opening working capital = $7,000 \times \dfrac{240}{200}$ = 8,400

Closing working capital = $10,000 \times \dfrac{240}{280}$ = 8,571

Change in the year = 171

The monetary working capital adjustment is $£3,000 - £171 = £2,829$

33.12

	19X3 £000	19X2 £000
Loan stock	200	200
Cash	145	50
Net borrowings	55	150

Average net borrowings = $\dfrac{55,000 + 150,000}{2}$ = 102,500

	19X3 £000	19X2 £000
Ordinary shares	250	250
Reserves	370	340
Current cost reserve	35	30
Shareholder interest	655	620

Average shareholder interest = $\dfrac{655,000 + 620,000}{2}$ = 637,500

Gearing adjustment percentage is: $\dfrac{102,500}{102,500 + 637,500}$ = 13.85%

33.14 Many accountants believe that during a period of inflation financial reports prepared under the historical cost convention are subject to a number of severe limitations. The question lists five such limitations, and a brief explanation of each one is as follows:

1 Stocks are undervalued.

Stock values are normally based on historical costs. This means that the historic closing stock will usually have cost less than its current economic value. Hence the cost of sales will tend to be higher than it would be if the closing stock was revalued at its current cost. As a result, the gross profit will be higher, and the entity may then pay out a higher level of net profit.

If the entity pays out a high level of profit and at the same time it has to pay more for its stocks (because prices are rising), it may be left with insufficient funds for it to be able to replace its stocks with the same *quantity* of goods that it had sold during the previous period. Hence it will not be able to operate at the same level of activity as it had previously experienced.

2 Depreciation is understated.

Depreciation is usually based on the historic cost of fixed assets. Such assets will normally increase in price during a period of inflation. The annual depreciation charge, therefore, may not reflect the amount needed to be able to replace the assets at their increased cost. Consequently, the accounting profit tends to be overstated, and this may mean that too much profit is withdrawn from the business. The cash resources may then prove insufficient to replace the assets at the end of their useful life. Like the stock valuation problem, therefore, the business may not be able to operate at the same level of activity that it has previously experienced.

3 Gains or losses on net monetary assets are undisclosed.

Net monetary assets include both long and short-term loans made to and by the entity, for example, debentures, and trade debtors and trade creditors. During a period of inflation, an entity gains on both long and short-term borrowings. The gain arises because although the amount originally borrowed will eventually be repaid at its face value, its purchasing power will have been reduced; for example, £5,000 borrowed in 19X1 will not purchase the same quantity of goods in 19X5 as it did in 19X1. In 19X5 the borrower may have to pay (say) £8,000 to purchase the same quantity of goods as he might have done in 19X1. Hence the entity will have, in effect, gained £3,000 by borrowing during an inflationary period, because it is effectively having to pay back less in purchasing power (or in real terms, as it is known) than it borrowed.

By contrast, if the entity has *loaned* money during a similar period (perhaps by allowing its customers to buy goods on credit), it loses money because the purchasing power of the respective debts (which are fixed in monetary terms) will purchase fewer goods when they are eventually settled

than they would have done when they were first incurred.

In financial reports prepared under the historical cost system, neither the gross nor the net effect of these types of transactions is disclosed.

4 Balance sheet values are unrealistic.

Fixed assets are normally recorded in the balance sheet at their original cost, that is, at their historic cost. During a period of inflation, the historic cost of the assets may be far less than their *current cost*, that is, at the value the entity places on them at the time that the financial reports are prepared. Hence the financial reports give a misleading impression of the entity's net worth as at the time that they are prepared.

5 Meaningful periodic comparisons are difficult to make.

A meaningful comparison of financial reports prepared under the historic cost convention over several accounting periods may be misleading since such accounts will normally have been prepared using, say, pounds sterling in one period and pounds sterling in all subsequent periods.

Financial reports prepared in such a way are not, however, strictly comparable. For example, £100 in 19X1 is not the same as £100 in 19X5, because £100 would not purchase the same amount of goods in 19X5 as it did in 19X1. In fact the comparison is just as meaningless as comparing financial reports prepared, say, in dollars with, say, reports prepared in marks. It is obvious to most users of such reports that 100 dollars are not the same as 100 marks, but it is less obvious that £19X1 are not the same as £19X5.

In order to be able to make a meaningful comparison between financial reports prepared in different time periods, therefore, it is desirable to translate them into the same currency, that is, to use the same price base. The argument behind this point is similar in principle to that used in translating dollars into marks or marks into dollars.

34.1 See text section 34.6.

34.2 See text section 34.6. Difficulties lie in trying to give these measures a value in money that would get universal acceptance. How can you place a money value on living conditions, for example?

34.3 See text section 34.7.

34.4 Basically, there are many things that could be done to improve the various parts of 'social well-being'. However, (a) benefits cost a lot of money in the short term, and (b) beneficial effects are felt only in the long term. Examples are better education, and better housing.

34.5 See text section 34.10, social programme measurement.

34.7 The accountant's model of income measurement, with its reliance upon data that can be expressed in financial terms, can be said to be too narrow and fails to consider wider social and environmental issues. The air we breathe does not have a 'price' in financial terms. Yet, what businesses do may cause costs to be incurred by others as a result of their abuse of the air in their environment. Similarly, the true cost of a natural resource may never be accounted for – the rainforests being a very well known example: they are being removed upon payment of a financially stated price, but the price only satisfies the seller, it does little to replace the environment being destroyed. Thus the price being added into the cost of manufacturing paper from the trees in the rainforests does not include the social and environmental cost of their destruction.

Thus, in the income model, it could be argued only in a narrow sense of the term that 'capital' is being maintained. In reality, the destruction of natural resources that are not or cannot be replaced means that the 'capital' is being consumed and future consumption impaired as a result.

It is for reasons of this type that it can be argued that accountants ought to be involved in disclosing the effects of a company's business activities upon its environment, for only by doing so will a true view of a company's activities be revealed.

35.1 See text sections 35.1 and 35.2.
35.2 See text sections 35.1 and 35.2.
35.3 See text section 35.2.
35.4 See text section 35.3.
35.5 See text section 35.4.
35.6 See text section 35.7

36.1 (i) f, b. (ii) m. (iii) a, c, e, g, j, $4/5$ of $n.t.v.$ $\frac{3}{4}$ of w, x. (iv) b, d, i, $\frac{1}{5}$ of n, p, q, part of $\frac{1}{4}$ of w. (v) l, r, s, z, part of $\frac{1}{4}$ of w. (vi) o, k, v, y.

36.3

Raw materials consumed (120,000 + 400,000 – 160,000)		360,000
Haulage costs		4,000
Direct labour 70% × 220,000		154,000
Royalties		1,600
		519,600

(a) **Prime cost**

Factory overhead

Factory indirect labour	66,000	
Other factory indirect expenses	58,000	
Travelling expenses	100	
Depreciation: Factory machinery	38,000	
Firms canteen expenses	4,000	
		166,100
		685,700

(b) **Production cost**

Administration expenses

Salaries	72,000

Travelling expenses	200	
Firm's canteen expenses	2,000	
Depreciation: Acctg. & office machinery	2,000	
Cars of admin. staff	1,600	
Other administrative expenses	42,000	
		119,800

Selling and distribution expenses

Salaries	8,000	
Commission	1,400	
Travelling expenses	2,900	
Depreciation: Equipment	300	
Salesmen's cars	3,800	
Other selling expenses	65,000	
Carriage costs on sales	7,800	
		89,200

Finance costs

Interest on loans and overdrafts		3,800
(c) **Total cost**		898,500

37.1 (a) Answers to be drafted by students in proper memo form.

Introduction:

Marginal cost is:	
Direct labour	3.00
Direct materials	3.50
Variable expenses	2.25
	8.75

As selling price £9.00 exceeds marginal cost £8.75 we should accept (but see below)*

Proof

	Without new order	With new order
Direct labour	6,000	6,300
Direct materials	7,000	7,350
Factory indirect expenses		
Variable	4,500	4,725
Fixed	500	500
Administration expenses	1,200	1,200
Selling and distribution expenses	600	600
Finance expenses	200	200
	20,000	20,875
	22,000	22,900
Sales	22,000	
Sales 22,000 + 900		22,900
Profit	2,000	2,025

*Depends on how other things affected besides simple accounting calculation.

(b) For extra order:

Marginal costs per unit (see (a))	8.75
Depreciation £300 p.a. ÷ 150	2.00
Running costs £600 p.a. ÷ 150	4.00
Marginal costs per unit	14.75

As £14.75 is greater than selling price £10 do NOT accept.

37.3

	(A) Magellan Ltd (Marginal)		(B) Frobisher Ltd (Absorption)	
Year 1				
Sales £29 × 900		26,100		26,100
Less Variable costs				
Direct labour £3 × 1,200	3,600		3,600	
Direct materials £5 × 1,200	6,000		6,000	
Variable overheads £2 × 1,200	2,400		2,400	
Total variable cost	12,000		12,000	
Less in (A) Valuation closing stock				
(300/1,200 × £12,000)	3,000			
		9,000		
Less in (B) Valuation closing stock				
(300/1,200 × £21,000)			5,250	
			6,750	
Fixed overhead	9,000		9,000	
Total costs		18,000		15,750
Gross profit		8,100		10,350

	(A)		(B)	
Year 2				
Sales £29 × 1,200		34,800		34,800
Less Variable costs				
Direct labour £3 × 1,300	3,900		3,900	
Direct materials £5 × 1,300	6,500		6,500	
Variable overheads £2×1,300	2,600		2,600	
Total variable cost	13,000		13,000	
Add in (A) Opening stock b/d	3,000			
Add in (B) Opening stock b/d			5,250	
	16,000		18,250	
Less in (A) Valuation closing stock				
(400/1,300 × 13,000)	4,000			
		12,000		
Less in (B) Valuation of closing stock				
(400/1,300 × £22,000)			6,769	
			11,481	
Fixed overhead		9,000		9,000
Total costs		21,000		20,481
Gross profit		13,800		14,319

	(A)		(B)	
Year 3				
Sales £29 × 1,100		31,900		31,900
Less Variable costs				
Direct labour £3 × 1,250	3,750		3,750	
Direct materials £5 × 1,250	6,250		6,250	
Var. overheads £2 × 1,250	2,500		2,500	
Total variable cost	12,500		12,500	
Add in (A) Op. stock b/d	4,000			
Add in (B) Op. stock b/d			6,769	
	16,500		19,269	
Less in (A) Valuation of closing stock				
(550/1,250 × £12,500)	5,500			
		11,000		
Less in (B) Valuation of closing stock				
(550/1,250 × £21,500)			9,460	
			9,809	
Fixed overhead		9,000		9,000
Total costs		20,000		18,809
Gross profit		11,900		13,091

37.5

(a) Subject to points raised in (c) the extra production should be taken on, as this results in greater profits amounting to £1,562,000. Proof is as follows:

Extra revenue 60,000 × £150   9,000,000

Less Extra costs
Direct materials (W1)	3,141,600	
Direct labour 60,000 × 18.70 × 120% =	1,346,400	
Variable overhead 60,000 × 7.50	450,000	
Fixed costs	2,500,000	7,438,000
		1,562,000

Extra profit 4,488,000

(W1) 60,000 × 74.80   4,488,000
Less saving 10% on extra materials
saving 10% on materials
used on day shift
10% × 120,000 × 74.80   897,600   1,346,400
       3,141,600

(b) Break-even point to justify night shift

Sale price per unit		150.00
Less Costs per unit		
Material	74.80	
Direct labour 18.70 + 20%	22.44	
Variable overhead	7.50	104.74
Contribution per unit		45.26

Total fixed costs $\frac{2,500,000}{4526}$

= Break-even at 55,236 units.

Note: No 10% reduction on materials because demand less than extra 60,000 units.

(c) (i) Would firm be able to maintain selling price of £187 on first 120,000 units per year?
(ii) Would it have been more profitable to subcontract extra units needed?
(iii) Could we diversify into a more profitable alternative product?
(iv) Could extra day facilities have been more profitable?

37.7 (a)

Arncliffe Ltd
Revenue Statement for the year ended ...

	Crowns		Kings		Total
Sales		60,000		25,000	85,000
Direct costs:					
Raw mats	8,000		2,000		
Labour	20,000		10,000		
M/c running costs	12,000	40,000	3,000	15,000	55,000
Contribution		20,000		10,000	30,000
Rate of contribution to sales		33.3%		40%	35.3%

(b) Best product mix for next year:
Crowns manufactured per hour = 20,000/8,000 = 2.5 per hour
Kings manufactured per hour = 10,000/2,000 = 5 per hour
Kings gives best contribution rate, so produce Kings up to maximum requirements.

	Crowns		Kings	
	Units	Hours	Units	Hours
Minimum required	6,000 ÷ 2.5	2,400	6,000 ÷ 5	1,200
Produce up to maximum of 36,000 Kings			30,000 ÷ 5	6,000
				7,200
Still (10,000 − 7,200 − 2,400) = 400 hours left, so now produce Crown	1,000 ÷ 25	400		
		2,800		7,200

Best mix is therefore: Crowns (6,000 + 1,000) = 7,000
         Kings (6,000 + 30,000) = 36,000

Sales therefore   7,000 × £3   21,000   36,000   × £2.5 = 90,000

Contributions:	Crowns (33.3%)	7,000
	Kings (40%)	36,000
		43,000
Floorspace costs		15,000
Insurances		15,600
Profit		600
		27,400

(c) Product mix with extra machine

As maximum requirements for Kings have already been met in (b), all new output will be of Crowns.

	Crowns	Kings
Sales (as before) in £s	21,000	90,000
Extra (10,000 hours × 2.5) = 25,000 × £3 =	75,000	
	96,000	90,000
Contributions: Crowns (33.3%)	32,000	
Kings (40%)	36,000	68,000
Hire of extra machine	20,000	
Floorspace costs	15,000	
Insurance	600	
	35,600	
	32,400	

(d) Briefly:

(i) Market demand maintained.
(ii) Flexibility of return of extra machine if demand falls.
(iii) To see if wholesaler will guarantee minimum orders.
(iv) Are there outlets possible other than wholesaler?
(v) Selling price to wholesaler.

37.9 (a)

Paul Wagtail
Manufacturing Trading and Profit and Loss Account
for the year ended 30 April 19X9

	Marginal method		Absorption method	
Purchases of raw mats (125,000 – 2,100)		122,900		122,900
Carriage of raw materials		1,500		1,500
		124,400		124,400
Less Stock raw materials		8,900		8,900
Cost of raw materials consumed		115,500		115,500
Production wages		105,270		105,270
Prime cost		220,770		220,770
Factory overhead expenses:				
Factory power	12,430			
Factory supervisors' wages	29,600			
Factory repairs	19,360			
Factory insurance (40%)	1,920			
Factory heating & light (40%)	1,440			
Depreciation of plant	17,600	82,350		82,350
		303,120		303,120
Less Work in progress (W1)		11,038		15,156
Production cost of goods completed c/d		292,082		287,964

Sales		464,360		464,360
Production cost b/d	292,082		287,964	
Less Stock finished goods (W2)	18,447	273,635	18,187	269,777
Gross profit		190,725		194,583
Less Expenses:				
Administration expenses	46,700		46,700	
Distribution expenses	25,400		25,400	
Selling expenses	23,800		23,800	
Insurance (60%)	2,880		2,880	
Heating and lighting (60%)	2,160		2,160	
Depn: delivery vehicles	35,200	136,140	35,200	136,140
Net profit		54,585		58,443

Workings

(W1) 625 × 80% = 500 equivalent making total 9,500 + 500 = 10,000

Valuations: *Marginal*

$$\frac{500}{10,000} \times 220,770 = 11,038$$

Absorption

$$\frac{500}{10,000} \times 303,120 = 15,156$$

(W2) *Marginal* $\frac{600}{9,500} \times 292,082 = 18,447$

Absorption $\frac{600}{9,500} \times 287,964 = 18,187$

(b) *See text.*

37.13 (a)

	Q	R	S	T
Direct labour and materials	14	28	60	32
Variable overheads	4	8	13	12
Fixed overhead	2	4	7	6
Total cost per unit	20	40	80	50
Add Profit 10 per cent	2	4	8	5
Selling price	22	44	88	55

(b) Discontinue S. All other items are above marginal cost.

(c)

Sales	(i) Followed our advice	(ii) Produced all items
Q 100 × £33	3,300	3,300
R 100 × £39	3,900	3,900
S 100 × £7	–	7,000
T 100 × £49	4,900	4,900
	12,100	19,100

Less Costs
Direct labour and materials

	(i)	(ii)
(i) 14 + 28 + 32 × 100	7,400	
(ii) 14 + 28 + 60 + 32 × 100		13,400
Variable overhead		
(i) 4 + 8 + 12 × 100	2,400	
(ii) 4 + 8 + 13 + 12 × 100		3,700
Fixed overhead	1,900	1,900
	11,700	19,000
Net profit	400	100

Note: The net profit or loss could have been worked out using contributions per items e.g. (i) Contributions per unit (i.e. Selling price *less* Marginal cost).

Q 33 – (14 + 4) = 15
R 39 – (28 + 8) = 3
R 49 – (32 + 12) = 5   23 × 100 of each = 2,300
Less Fixed costs 1,900
Net profit (same as using method shown) 400

In (ii) the contribution from S would be a negative one.

(d) Discontinue Q and T. All other items are above marginal cost.

(e)

Sales	(i) Followed our advice	(ii) Produced all items
Q 100 × £17	–	1,700
R 100 × £48	4,800	4,800
S 100 × £140	14,000	14,000
T 100 × £39	–	3,900
	18,800	24,400

Less Costs
Direct labour and materials

	(i)	(ii)
(i) 28 + 60 × 100	8,800	
(ii) 14 + 28 + 60 + 32 × 100		13,400
Variable costs		
(i) 8 + 13 × 100	2,100	
(ii) 4 + 8 + 13 + 12 × 100		1,900
Fixed overhead	1,900	1,900
	12,800	19,000
Net profit	6,000	5,400

38.1

	Production Departments				Service Departments		
	A	B	C	D	K	L	M
Indirect lab.	4,000	6,000	8,000	2,000	1,500	3,000	4,100
Other exp.	2,700	3,100	3,600	1,500	4,500	2,000	2,000
	6,700	9,100	11,600	3,500	6,000	5,000	6,100
Apportionment of costs:							
Dept K	1,500	1,800	1,200	600	(6,000)		900
Dept L	3,000		1,500	500		(5,000)	
Dept M		2,100	3,500	1,400			7,000 / (7,000)
	11,200	13,000	17,800	6,000	–	–	–

(a) Overhead rates per direct labour hour

Department A $\frac{£11,200}{2,000} = £5.6$

Department C $\frac{£17,800}{4,450} = £4.0$

(b) Overhead rates per machine hour

Department B $\frac{£13,000}{2,600} = £5.0$

Department D $\frac{£6,000}{2,400} = £2.5$

38.2

Job Cost Sheet Job 351 Dept. A

Direct materials	190
Direct labour	56 × £2.1 = 117.6
Factory overhead	56 × £5.6 = 313.6
	621.2

(b) Because the figures belong to the future and therefore cannot be known precisely.

(c) (i) and (ii). Note that parts (i) and (ii) illustrate two different methods in use. The method in (iii) is not in the text.

Continuous apportionment (repeated distribution) method:

Line	Production departments A	B	C	Service departments X	Y
1 Allocation per analysis	14,000	12,000	8,000	4,000	3,000
2 Allocation of X(4,000)	(35%) 1,400	(30%) 1,200	(20%) 800	(4,000)	(15%) 600
3 Allocation of Y(3,600)	(30%) 1,080	(40%) 1,440	(25%) 900	(5%) 180	3,600
4 Allocation of X (180)	(35%) 63	(30%) 54	(20%) 36	(180)	(15%) 27
5 Allocation of Y (27)	(40%) 8	(25%) 12*	(5%) 7	0	(27)
Rounded off	16,551	14,706	9,743		(= total 41,000)

*Rounded off.

Explanation:
Steps:
(1) Allocate X overheads to others by % shown.
(2) Allocate Y overheads to others by % shown.
Keep repeating (1) and (2) until the figures left under X and Y are insignificant.

(iii) Elimination method:

Line	Production departments A	B	C	Service departments X	Y
1 Allocation per analysis	14,000	12,000	8,000	4,000	3,000
2 Allocate service dept X	(35%) 1,400	(30%) 1,200	(20%) 800	(4,000)	(15%) 600
3 Allocate service dept Y (30/95)	(40/95) 1,137	(25/95) 1,516	947	—	(3,600)
	16,537	14,716	9,747		(total 41,000)

Explanation:
Steps:
(1) Allocate service department overheads which does largest proportion of work for other departments, i.e. department X.
(2) Allocate next service department per (1), in this case is only Y.
(3) When doing (2) nothing is charged to service departments already allocated, i.e. in this case X.
(4) Note that since (3) happens the ratios in the next allocation change. As X 5% of Y is not returned then A gets 30/95 of Y, not 30% and so on.

(iv) The answer will depend on whichever approach is adopted. No one can categorically state which method is the most accurate; there is no 'ideal' method.

Job Cost Sheet Job 352 Dept. B

Direct materials		1,199
Direct labour	178 × £1.7	302.6
Factory overhead	176 × £5.0	880
		2,381.6

Job Cost Sheet Job 353 Dept. C

Direct materials		500
Direct labour	130 × £2.4	312
Factory overhead	130 × £4.0	520
		1,332

Job Cost Sheet Job 354 Dept. D

Direct materials		666
Direct labour	90 × £2.3	207
Direct overhead	64 × £2.5	160
		1,033

Job Cost Sheet Job 355 Depts. C and B

Dept C	Direct materials		560
	Direct labour	160 × £2.4	384
	Factory overhead	160 × £4.0	640
Dept B	Direct materials		68
	Direct labour	30 × £1.7	51
	Factory overhead	20 × £5.0	100
			1,803

38.5(a) See text Section 38.5

(b)(i)

	Materials	Labour	Overhead
Finished items	4,000 (90%)	4,000 (75%)	4,000 (55%)
W-I-P (600)	540	450	330
Total units	4,540	4,450	4,330

(ii)
Cost per complete unit

Material	£8,172 + 4,540 =	1.80
Labour	£7,120 + 4,450 =	1.60
Overhead	£5,196 + 4,330 =	1.20
		£4.60

(iii)
Value of work in progress

Material	540 × 1.80 =	972
Labour	450 × 1.60 =	720
Overhead	330 × 1.20 =	396
		£2,088

38.7(a) Allotment: where overheads traced directly to units.

Apportionment: where overheads not directly traceable and have to be apportioned between units.

Absorption rates: the total amount of overheads calculated as being charged to each unit.

38.9

(a) and (b) See text.

(c)(i) *Batch No. 23*

Raw materials 300 × 1.60	480
Direct labour 4.20 × 20 hours	84
Setting up of machine	21
Overheads 3.60 × 20 hours	72
Total cost	657

Cost per unit 657 ÷ 300 = £2.19

(ii) *Batch No. 23*

Raw materials 300 × 1.60	480.00	
Less Received for scrap 20 × 0.86	17.20	462.80
Direct labour:		
Normal 20 × 4.20	84.00	
Rectification 9 × 4.20	37.80	121.80
Setting up:		
Normal	21.00	
Rectification	18.00	39.00
Overheads: Running time 3.60 × 20	72.00	
Rectification 3.60 × 9	32.40	104.40
		728.00

Per usable unit £728 ÷ 280 = 2.60

(iii)

Loss because of extra costs 728 − 657 =		71.00
Loss because of faulty products 657 × 20/300 =		43.80
		114.80

39.1

	Jan	Feb	Mar	Apr	May	Jun
Opening stock	740	690	780	1,100	1,400	1,160
Add Production	750	1,010	1,410	1,620	1,240	800
	1,490	1,700	2,190	2,720	2,640	1,960
Less Sales	800	920	1,090	1,320	1,480	1,020
Closing stock	690	780	1,100	1,400	1,160	940

39.2

(a)

Opening stock		140
Add Production	?	(C)
		(B)
Less Sales total – see question		1,550
Closing stock		150

Missing figure (B) must be 1,700
Missing figure (C) must then be 1,560
Equal production per month 1,560 ÷ 12 = 130 units.

(b) Given figures per (a).

	(J)	(F)	(M)	(A)	(M)	(J)	(J)	(A)	(S)	(O)	(N)	(D)
Opening stock	140	160	110	70	50	60	90	150	250	210	230	210
Add Production	130	130	130	130	130	130	130	130	130	130	130	130
	270	290	240	200	180	190	220	280	380	340	360	340
Less Sales	110	180	170	150	120	100	70	30	170	110	150	190
Closing stock	160	110	70	50	60	90	150	250	210	230	210	150

Lowest closing figure is April 50 units.
If stock is not to fall below 80 units an extra 80 − 50 = 30 units will have to be produced in January making production for that month of 160 units.

40.1

(a) *B Ukridge: Cash Budget*

	May	Jun	Jul	Aug	Sep	Oct
Balance b/d		5,305	4,305	1,305		
Overdraft b/d					6,695	9,695
Receipts from debtors	400	4,000	8,000	12,000	9,000	5,000
Capital	5,005					
	5,405	9,305	12,305	13,305	2,305	(4,695)
Payments	100	5,000	11,000	20,000	12,000	7,000
Balance c/d	5,305	4,305	1,305			
Overdraft c/d				6,695	9,695	11,695

(b) There are the possibilities of delaying payments to creditors, delaying purchases or somehow getting debtors to pay up more quickly. Apart from these it is possible that a credit factoring firm could help in 'buying' the amounts of debtors from Ukridge.

If none of these is possible only a really fantastic product could warrant interest at 100 per cent per annum. This would rarely be the case, although there are many people whose optimism about their products exceeds the true profitability.

40.2

N Morris: Cash Budget

	Jul	Aug	Sep	Oct	Nov	Dec
Balance b/d	1,200	260	250	160		
Overdraft b/d					540	420
Receipts	4,000	6,400	5,800	8,000	6,000	9,500*
	5,200	6,660	6,050	8,160	5,460	9,080
Payments (see schedule)	4,940	6,410	5,890	8,700	5,880	5,410
Balance c/d	260	250	160			3,670
Overdraft c/d				540	420	

*Includes £2,500 legacy

Payments schedule

Jul
Raw materials 320 (Jul) × £4	1,280
300 (Jun) × £1	300
Direct labour 320 × £8	2,560
Variable 300 × £1 + 320 × £1	620
Fixed expenses	400
Drawings	300
	5,460

Aug
Raw materials 350 (Aug) × £4	1,400
320 (July) × £1	320
Direct labour 350 × £8	2,800
Variable 350 × £1 + 320 × £1	670
Fixed expenses	400
Drawings	300
	5,890

Sep
Raw materials 370 (Sep) × £4	1,480
350 (Aug) × £1	350
Direct labour 370 × £8	2,960
Variable 370 × £1 + 350 × £1	720
Fixed expenses	400
Drawings	300
	6,210

Oct
Raw materials 380 (Oct) × £4	1,520
370 (Sep) × £1	370
Direct labour 380 × £8	3,040
Variable 380 × £1 + 370 × £1	750
Fixed expenses	400
Drawings	300
Machinery	2,000
	8,380

Nov
Raw materials 340 (Nov) × £4	1,360
380 (Oct) × £1	380
Direct labour 340 × £8	2,720
Variable 340 × £1 + 380 × £1	720
Fixed expenses	400
Drawings	300
	5,880

Dec
Raw materials 310 (Dec) × £4	1,240
340 (Nov) × £1	340
Direct labour 310 × £8	2,480
Variable 310 × £1 + 340 × £1	650
Fixed expenses	400
Drawings	300
	5,410

40.3

(a) Cash Budget

	Jul	Aug	Sep
Receipts			
Cash sales (W1)	9,600	4,800	7,200
Credit sales (W2)	17,640	14,112	7,056
	27,240	18,912	14,256
Payments			
Purchases	3,600	5,400	8,100
Direct labour	1,600	2,400	3,600
Direct production expenses	4,800	2,400	3,600
Variable selling expenses	4,000	3,200	1,600
Fixed expenses	1,820	1,820	1,820
	15,820	15,220	18,720
Balance start of month	+3,900	+15,320	+19,012
Balance at end of month	+15,320	+19,012	+14,548

(W1) July   800 × 40% × £30 = 9,600
     August   400 × 40% × £30 = 4,800
     September 600 × 40% × £30 = 7,200

(W2) July   1,000 × 60% × £30 =
     August   800 × 60% × £30 =
     September   400 × 60% × £30 =
     July   18,000 – 2% = 17,640
     August   14,400 – 2% = 14,112
     September 7,200 – 2% = 7,056

(b) (i) Can forecast when and if money needs to be borrowed.
(ii) Can forecast when surplus funds are available so that they can be invested elsewhere.
(iii) To use as basis when dealing with supplier as to creditworthiness or bank for borrowing powers.

40.5

	Jul	Aug	Sept	Oct
Receipts				
Sales this month 20%		9,000	9,000	9,000
Sales last month 70%		32,000	31,500	31,500
Sales 2 months ago 10%			4,000	4,500
Other receipts from drs	40,000			
	40,000	41,000	44,500	45,000
Payments				
Wages	2,000	2,000	2,000	2,000
Bank loan and interest	242	242	242	242
Drawings	500	500	500	500
Purchases	34,000	38,250	38,250	45,750
PAYE tax	500	500	500	500
Rent	1,250			1,250
Rates				2,250
Value added tax	5,000	8,150		
Motor van				3,950
	43,492	49,642	41,492	56,442
Current account balances				
Start of month	5,000	1,508	(7,134)	(4,126)
End of month	1,508	(7,134)	(4,126)	(15,568)

40.6

(a) In brief:

Current ratio of 210,000 : 150,000 = 1.4 : 1

Acid test ratio not known. Very dangerous situation because if bank manager asks for repayment of overdraft it is unlikely it can be repaid in the short term.

Profits get ploughed back into the company in all sorts of ways, e.g. extra fixed assets, more stock. It has no direct connection with the balance at the bank. (Use cash flow statements as an illustration.)

(b)

Cash Budget

	Apr	May	Jun	Jul
Receipts				
Cash sales	40,000	40,000	40,000	40,000
Credit sales	65,000	70,000	70,000	70,000
	105,000	110,000	110,000	110,000
Payments				
Purchases	60,000	58,000	61,000	55,000
Selling and administration	5,700	6,600	6,600	6,600
Administration charges	10,000	10,000	10,000	13,500
Final dividend 19X9/X0		7,500		
Interim dividend 19X0/X1				4,000
	75,700	82,100	77,600	79,100
Balance overdraft start of month	(150,000)	(120,700)	(92,800)	(60,400)
Balance overdraft end of month	(120,700)	(92,800)	(60,400)	(29,500)

(c) Would seem to be proceeding satisfactorily to eliminate overdraft.
Could be further reduced by:
(i) Issuing new shares
(ii) Getting debtors to pay more quickly
(iii) Delaying payment of creditors
(iv) Selling off fixed assets
(v) Issuing debentures.

41.1 (a) Stock Budget 19X7

		Aug	Sep	Oct	Nov
Opening stock	(A)	5,000*	7,000	8,000	7,000
Add Purchases	(B)	20,000	23,500	21,500	31,000
	(C)	25,000	30,500	29,500	38,000
Less Cost of sales	(D)	18,000	22,500	22,500	27,000
Closing stock	(E)	7,000	8,000	7,000	11,000

* After special sale of £8,000 goods at cost.
To work out missing figures:
August (A) is known. (D) is 24,000 – 25%

Therefore, as stockturn is 3, $\dfrac{\text{(D) }18{,}000}{[\text{(A) }5{,}000 + \text{(E) question}] \div 2} = 3$

Therefore bottom line is 6,000 so (E) must be 7,000.
Repeat following months.

(b) *Cash Budget 19X7*

	Aug	Sep	Oct	Nov
Receipts:				
Capital	10,000			
Soul's debtors	20,250	–		
Debtors		–	24,000	30,000
Special sale	8,000			
	38,250	–	24,000	30,000
Payments:				
Creditors	10,000	20,000	23,500	21,500
General expenses	700	700	700	700
	10,700	20,700	24,200	22,200
Bank: Opening	(20,000)	7,550	(13,150)	(13,350)
Closing	7,550	(13,150)	(13,350)	(5,550)

41.3

Cash Budget

	Jan	Feb	Mar	Apr	May	Jun
Opening balance	25,000					
Opening overdraft		+890	–370	–600	–740	–600
Received (*see schedule*)	400	600	1,750	2,200	2,900	3,550
	25,400	1,490	1,380	1,600	2,160	2,950
Payments (*see schedule*)	24,510	1,860	1,980	2,340	2,760	3,460
Closing balance	+890					
Closing overdraft		–370	–600	–740	–600	–510

Cash Receipts Schedule

	Jan	Feb	Mar	Apr	May	Jun
Cash sales	400	600	800	1,000	1,300	1,400
Credit sales		–	800	1,200	1,600	2,000
Rent received			150			150
	400	600	1,750	2,200	2,900	3,550

Cash Payments Schedule

	Jan	Feb	Mar	Apr	May	Jun
Drawings	250	250	250	250	250	250
Premises	20,000					
Shop fixtures	3,000					
Motor van	1,000					
Salaries of assistants	260	260	260	260	260	260
Payments to creditors		1,200	1,320	1,680	2,100	2,800
Other expenses		150	150	150	150	150
	24,510	1,860	1,980	2,340	2,760	3,460

D Smith

Forecast Trading and Profit and Loss Accounts for the six months ended 30 June 19X4

Sales		16,500
Less Cost of goods sold:		
Purchases	11,410	
Less Closing stock (130 × £7)	910	
		10,500
Gross profit		6,000
Add Rent received		300
		6,300
Less Expenses:		
Assistants' salaries	1,560	
Other expenses	900	
Depreciation: Shop fixtures	150	
Motor van	100	
		2,710
Net profit		3,590

Balance Sheet as at 30 June 19X4

Fixed assets	Cost	Depn	Net
Premises	20,000	–	20,000
Shop fixtures	3,000	150	2,850
Motor van	1,000	100	900
	24,000	250	23,750

Current assets			
Stock-in-trade		910	
Debtors		5,400	
		6,310	
Less Current liabilities			
Creditors	2,310		
Other expenses owing	150		
Bank overdraft	510		
		2,970	
Working capital			3,340
			27,090

Financed by:		
Capital		25,000
Cash introduced		3,590
		28,590
Add Net profit		1,500
		27,090
Less Drawings		

41.6

(a)

Issa Ltd

Trading & Profit & Loss Account for the year ended 31 December 19X1

		£000s
Sales		900.0
Less Cost of goods sold		
Opening stock	80.0	
Purchases (difference)	570.0	
	650.0	
Less Closing stock	65.0	
		585.0
Gross profit		315.0
Less Expenses		
Administration expenses	63.6	
Selling and distribution expenses (54 + 15)	69.0	
Financial charges	20.8	
Provision for doubtful debts	2.5	
Depreciation	60.0	
		215.9
Net profit		99.1
Profit on sale of land and buildings		150.0
Retained earnings from last year		350.0
		599.1
Less Appropriations		
Bonus share issue	50.0	
Preference share dividends	9.0	
Ordinary dividend	7.5	
		66.5
Retained earnings carried to next year		532.6

(b)   *Balance Sheet as at 31 December 19X1*

	£000s	£000s	£000s
Fixed assets at cost (750 – 50)		700.0	
Less Depreciation to date		204.0	496.0
Investment in Yates Ltd at cost			100.0
Current assets			
Stock		65.0	
Trade debtors	100.0		
Less Provision	7.5	92.5	
Bank		350.1	
		507.6	
Less Current liabilities			
Trade creditors	56.0		
Expense creditors	15.0	71.0	
			436.6
			1,032.6
Financed by			
Ordinary share capital (200 + 100)			300.0
Share premium (150 – 50)			100.0
9% Preference shares			100.0
Retained earnings			532.6
			1,032.6

(c) Advantages:

(i) Business can establish desired profit in advance. It can then take necessary action to try to achieve it.

Desired ROCE can be set as target.

Also helps in forecasting dividends/planning for taxation purposes/organising necessary finance/for use with financial backers.

(ii) Manage working capital to ensure its sufficiency when needed.

Managing cash balances to seek overdrafts/loans from bank when needed. Ensure creditors paid on time to gain discounts. Invest surpluses as and when they may occur.

41.7

Cash Payments Schedule

	Jul	Aug	Sep	Oct	Nov	Dec
Direct materials	240	140	160	220	200	160
Direct labour	450	450	450	450	450	450
Variable overhead	210	270	270	270	270	270
Fixed overhead	90	90	90	90	90	90
Machine	500					
Motor vehicle			2,000			
	1,490	950	2,970	1,030	1,010	970

Cash Receipts Schedule

	Jul	Aug	Sep	Oct	Nov	Dec
Debenture					5,000	
Receipts from debtors	990	900	1,080	1,440	1,800	1,850
	990	900	1,080	1,440	6,800	1,850

(a) Cash Budget (in £s)

	Jul	Aug	Sep	Oct	Nov	Dec
Opening balance	7,100	6,600	6,550	4,660	5,070	10,860
Add Receipts	990	900	1,080	1,440	6,800	1,850
	8,090	7,500	7,630	6,100	11,870	12,710
Less Payments	1,490	950	2,970	1,030	1,010	970
	6,600	6,550	4,660	5,070	10,860	11,740

(b) Debtors Budget (in £s)

	Jul	Aug	Sep	Oct	Nov	Dec
Opening balance	1,890	1,980	2,520	3,240	3,650	3,515
Add Sales	1,080	1,440	1,800	1,850	1,665	1,295
	2,970	3,420	4,320	5,090	5,315	4,810
Less Receipts	990	900	1,080	1,440	1,800	1,850
Closing balance	1,980	2,520	3,240	3,650	3,515	2,960

(c) Creditors Budget (in £s)

	Jul	Aug	Sep	Oct	Nov	Dec
Opening balance	540	520	580	580	500	440
Add Purchases	220	200	160	140	140	180
	760	720	740	720	640	620
Less Payments	240	140	160	220	200	160
Closing balance	520	580	580	500	440	460

(d) Raw Materials Budget (in £s)

	Jul	Aug	Sep	Oct	Nov	Dec
Opening stock	300	340	360	340	300	260
Add Purchases	220	200	160	140	140	180
	520	540	520	480	440	440
Less Used in production	180	180	180	180	180	180
Closing stock	340	360	340	300	260	260

(e)

Gregg Ltd
Forecast Operating Statement for the six months ended
31 December 19X6

Sales		9,130
Less Cost of goods sold		
Operating stock finished goods	1,800	
Add Cost of goods completed (£10 × 540)	5,400	
	7,200	
Less Closing stock finished goods (220 × £10)	2,200	
		5,000
Gross profit		4,130
Less Expenses:		
Fixed overhead		540
Depreciation: Machinery	700	
Motor vehicles	600	
Office fixtures	30	
		1,330
		1,870
Net profit		2,260

(f)   *Forecast Balance Sheet as at 31 December 19X6*

Fixed assets	Cost	Depreciation to date	Net
Tangible assets			
Land and buildings	40,000	—	40,000
Plant and machinery	10,500	6,700	3,800
Motor vehicles	8,000	3,400	4,600
Office fixtures	500	250	250
	59,000	10,350	48,650

Current assets		
Stocks: Finished goods	2,200	
Raw materials	260	
Debtors	2,960	
Cash and bank	11,740	
	17,160	
Creditors: amounts falling due within 1 year		
Creditors for raw materials	460	
Creditors for variable overhead	270	
	730	
Net current assets		16,430
Total assets less current liabilities		65,080

Creditors: amounts falling due after more than 1 year	
Debentures	5,000
	60,080

Capital and reserves	
Called-up share capital	50,000
Profit and loss account (7,820 + 2,260)	10,080
	60,080

41.8 **A** (a) *Debtor budget*

	Jul	Aug	Sep	Oct
Balances from last month	52,250	52,250	49,500	51,750
Add Credit sales	24,750	24,750	27,000	33,000
	77,000	77,000	76,500	84,750
Less Paid by debtors	24,750	27,500	24,750	24,750
Balances at end of month	52,250	49,500	51,750	60,000

Note: Sales are Jul 900, Aug 900, Sep 900, Oct 1,100. October is taken to be June figure + 10%.

(b) *Raw material budget* (in kgs)

	Jul	Aug	Sep	Oct
Stock from last month	1,800	1,800	1,800	2,200
Add purchases	1,800	1,800	2,200	2,200
	3,600	3,600	4,000	4,400
Less Used	1,800	1,800	1,800	2,200
Stock at end of month	1,800	1,800	2,200	2,200

B *See text Section 39.8*

$$EOQ = \sqrt{\frac{2 \times 12,000 \times £10}{£6}} = 200 \text{ units}$$

(i) Based on estimates which obviously can vary a lot from actual.
(ii) Consumption may be uneven at times, EOQ assumes even usage.
(iii) Such things as strikes, catastrophes, etc. can render it useless.

41.9 **A** *Workings:*
1 Raw materials 294,400 ÷ 64,000 = 4.6 per unit
2 Direct labour 236,800 ÷ 64,000 = 3.7 per unit
3 Power 38,400 ÷ 64,000 = 0.60 per unit
4 Repairs are 51,200 − 25%(12,800) = 38,400 fixed. Variable 12,800 + 64,000 = 0.20
5 Indirect wages 64,000 − 15%(9,600) = 54,400 fixed. Variable 9,600 ÷ 64,000 = 0.15.

Bedford Ltd

Flexible Budget at varying levels of production

Level of Production

	60%	70%	75%	90%	85%	Actual	Variance +(–)
Units	48,000	56,000	60,000	72,000	68,000	68,000	
Variable costs £							
Raw materials	220,800	257,600	276,000	331,200	312,800	310,750	2,050
Direct labour	177,600	207,200	222,000	266,400	251,600	249,100	2,500
Power	28,800	33,600	36,000	43,200	40,800	39,800	1,000
Repairs and Maintenance	9,600	11,200	12,000	14,400	13,600	14,650	(1,050)
Indirect wages	7,200	8,400	9,000	10,800	10,200	10,850	(650)
	444,000	518,000	555,000	666,000	629,000	625,150	3,850
Fixed costs							
Repairs and Maintenance	38,400	38,400	38,400	38,400	38,400	38,400	–
Insurance	1,300	1,300	1,300	1,300	1,350	1,350	(50)
Heating/lighting	1,250	1,250	1,250	1,250	1,200	1,200	50
Indirect wages	54,400	54,400	54,400	54,400	54,400	54,400	–
	95,350	95,350	95,350	95,350	95,350	95,350	–
Total costs	539,350	613,350	650,350	761,350	724,350	720,500	3,850

Briefly: generally efficient as most variances are favourable. Comment in detail on each variance.

B *See text.*

42.1 (a) *Standard cost per unit*

	X	Y	Z
Material 1	0.6	1.8	2.4
Material 2	3.0	2.1	
Material 3	0.4	2.5	1.5
Material 4	0.4		0.9
	4.0	6.4	4.8
Labour: Dept A	4.0	2.4	4.8
Dept B	3.0	1.8	3.6
	7.0	4.2	8.4
Production cost	11.0	10.6	13.2
Overheads			
Production (1.8 per hour)	9.0	5.4	10.8
	20.0	16.0	24.0
Administration (50%)	10.0	8.0	12.0
Selling	5.0	4.0	6.0
Standard cost	35.0	28.0	42.0
Profit (⅐ of standard cost)	5.0	4.0	6.0
Standard selling price	40.0	32.0	48.0

(b) *Sales budget in units*

	X	Y	Z
Budgeted at std price	800,000	1,280,000	2,400,000
Unit selling price	40.0	32.0	48.0
Sales budget in units	20,000	40,000	50,000

(c) *Production budget in units*

	X	Y	Z
Needed for sales	20,000	40,000	50,000
For stock purposes	5,000	10,000	10,000
To produce	25,000	50,000	60,000

(d) *Direct materials purchases budget*

Materials	1	2	3	4
Product X	–	100,000	360,000	
Product Y kg	900,000		300,000	1,080,000
Product Z	1,440,000	700,000	500,000	480,000
	2,340,000	800,000	1,160,000	1,560,000
Cost in £	£234,000	£120,000	£290,000	£78,000

43.1

(i) Net variance:

Actual cost per unit	37 × £18	666
Standard cost per unit	34 × £20	680
Net variance (favourable)		£14

Made up of:

Favourable price variance	£2 × 34	68
Adverse usage variance	3 × £18	54
Net variance (favourable)		£14

(ii) Net variance:

Actual cost per unit	46 × £19	874
Standard cost per unit	50 × £17	850
Net variance (adverse)		£24

Made up of:

Favourable usage variance	4 × £17	68
Adverse price variance	46 × £2	92
Net variance (adverse)		£24

(iii) Total variance:

Actual cost per unit	18 × £14	252
Standard cost per unit	15 × £12	180
Variance (adverse)		£72

Made up of:

Adverse price variance	15 × £2 (+ £6 common)	36
Adverse usage variance	3 × £12	36
Total variance (adverse)		£72

(iv) Total variance:

Actual cost per unit	$27 \times £37$	999
Standard cost per unit	$29 \times £40$	1,160
Total variance (favourable)		£161

Made up of:

Favourable price variance	$27 \times £3$	81
Favourable usage var.	$2 \times £37 (+ £6$ common$)$	80
		£161

(v) Total variance:

Actual cost per unit	$154 \times £8$	1,232
Standard cost per unit	$145 \times £7$	1,015
Total variance (adverse)		£ 217

Made up of:

Adverse price var.	$145 \times £1 (+ £9$ common$)$	154
Adverse usage variance	$9 \times £7$	63
		£ 217

(vi) Total variance:

Actual cost per unit	$9,850 \times £22$	216,700
Standard cost per unit	$10,000 \times £25$	250,000
Total variance (favourable)		£33,000

Made up of:

Favourable price variance	$£3 \times 9,850$	29,550
Favourable usage variance	$150 \times £22 (+ £450$ common$)$	3,750
		£33,300

43.3

(i)

Actual cost per unit	$218 \times £2.1$	457.8
Standard cost per unit	$220 \times £2.1$	462
Favourable labour efficiency variance		£ 4.2

(ii)

Actual cost per unit	$115 \times £1.9$	218.5
Standard cost per unit	$115 \times £1.7$	195.5
Adverse wage rate variance		£23.0

(iii)

Actual cost per unit	$240 \times £1.8$	432
Standard cost per unit	$200 \times £1.8$	360
Adverse labour efficiency variance		£72

(iv)

Actual cost per unit	$104 \times £2.0$	208
Standard cost per unit	$120 \times £2.0$	240
Favourable labour efficiency variance		£32

(v)

Actual cost per unit	$68 \times £1.5$	102
Standard cost per unit	$68 \times £1.8$	122.4
Favourable wage rate variance		£ 20.4

(vi)

Actual cost per unit	$34 \times £1.7$	57.8
Standard cost per unit	$30 \times £1.7$	51
Adverse labour efficiency variance		£ 6.8

(vii)

Actual cost per unit	$77 \times £1.6$	123.2
Standard cost per unit	$70 \times £1.6$	112
Adverse labour efficiency variance		£11.2

(viii)

Actual cost per unit	$100 \times £2.0$	200
Standard cost per unit	$100 \times £1.9$	190
Adverse wage rate variance		£10

43.5 **(a)** *See text*

(b)
Standard hours produced in March

Dishwashers	150×10	1,500
Washing machines	100×12	1,200
Refrigerators	90×14	1,260
Total standard hours		3,960

(c)
(i) Standard hours × standard hourly rate

$3,960 \times £4$		15,840
Actual wages		18,450
Total direct labour variance		2,610 (Adverse)

(ii) Standard pay $4,100 \times £4$ 16,400
Actual pay 18,450
Direct labour rate variance 2,050 (Adverse)

(iii) Direct labour efficiency variance
Standard hours − actual hours × standard rate
$3,960 − 4,100 \times £4 = 560$ (Adverse)

(d) Labour rate variance:
1 Higher grade labour used than necessary.
2 Job running behind time so extra people brought in to help.

Direct labour efficiency variance:
1 Using unsuitable machinery.
2 Workers slowing up work so as to get overtime rates paid.

43.7

(a)

Profit Statement for the month of July 19X1

	Budgeted	Actual
Sales	1,000,000	1,071,200
Less Manufacturing costs		
Direct materials	200,000	201,285
Direct labour	313,625	337,500
Variable overheads	141,400	143,000
Fixed overheads	75,000	71,000
	730,025	752,785
Gross profit	269,975	318,415
Less: Variable sales o/h	64,400	69,500
Admin costs	150,000	148,650
	214,400	218,150
	55,575	100,265

(b)
(i) Material price variance =
(Standard price – actual price per unit) × quantity purchased
= 10.00 – 10.65 = 0.65 × 18,900 = 12,285 Adverse

Material usage = (Standard quantity – actual quantity used) × standard price
= (20,000 – 18,900) × 10 = 11,000 Favourable

Summary: Material price variance 12,285 (A)
Material usage variance 11,000 (F)
Material cost variance 1,285 (A)

(ii) Labour rate variance =
(Standard rate per hour – actual wage rate) × actual hours worked
= (6.50 – 6.75) × 50,000 = 12,500 (A)

Labour efficiency variance =
(Standard labour hours – actual hours) × standard rate per hour
= (48,250 – 50,000) × 6.50 = 11,375 (A)

Summary: Labour rate variance 12,500 (A)
Labour efficiency variance 11,375 (A)
Labour cost variance 23,875 (A)

(c) In each case find out why the variance has occurred. Then it must be established whether the variances were outside the control of anyone in the firm or whether they were caused by the actions, or lack of action, by people in our organisation. Any necessary corrective action can then be taken.

44.1

(a) Actual overhead 5,840
Overhead applied to production × £6 6,000
Favourable budget (or spending) variance £ 160

(b) Actual overhead 21,230
Overhead applied to production 5,000 × £4 20,000
Adverse budget (or spending) variance £ 1,230

(c) Actual fixed overhead 11,770
Budgeted fixed overhead 12,000
Favourable fixed overhead spending variance £ 230

(d) Actual fixed overhead 41,390
Budgeted fixed overhead 40,000
Adverse fixed overhead spending variance £ 1,390

(e) Actual hours × standard rate (7,940 × £3) 23,820
Budgeted hours × standard rate (8,000 × £3) 24,000
Favourable efficiency variance £ 180

(f) Actual hours × standard rate (15,000 × £4) 60,000
Budgeted hours (4,860 × 3) × standard rate (14,580 × £4) 58,320
Adverse efficiency variance £ 1,680

44.3

The standard variable overhead rate is:

$\frac{£400,000}{80,000} = £5$ per direct labour hour and £10 per unit

The standard fixed overhead rate is:

$\frac{£160,000}{80,000} = £2$ per direct labour hour and £4 per unit

The variances are:
Variable overhead
(i) Budget or spending variance
Actual overhead 403,600
Overhead applied to production 78,500 × £5 392,500
Adverse budget (or spending) variance £11,100

(ii) Efficiency variance
Actual hours × standard rate 78,500 × £5 392,500
Budgeted hours × standard rate (42,000 units which
should be produced in 42,000 × 2 hours = 84,000 hours × £5 420,000
Favourable efficiency variance £27,500

Fixed overhead

(i) Efficiency variance

	£
Actual units produced × std rate 42,000 × 2 hrs per unit × £2	168,000
Actual Labour hours × standard rate 78,500 × £2	157,000
Favourable efficiency variance	£11,000

(ii) Spending (or budget) variance

	£
Actual overhead	157,200
Budgeted overhead	160,000
Favourable spending variance	£2,800

(iii) Volume variance

	£
Actual hours × standard rate 78,500 × £2	157,000
Budgeted hours × standard rate 80,000 × £2	160,000
Adverse volume variance	£3,000

The variances can be explained further:

Variable overhead

	£
Actual overhead	403,600
Budgeted overhead for actual production 42,000 units × £10	420,000
Net favourable variance (made up of favourable efficiency variances £27,500 *less* Adverse budget variance 11,100)	£16,400

Fixed overhead

	£
Actual overhead	157,200
Overhead based on units of production 42,000 × £4	168,000
Net favourable variance (made up of favourable efficiency variance £11,000 *plus* favourable spending variance £2,800 *less* Adverse volume variance £3,000)	£10,800

44.5

			£
Actual units sold 150,000 × Budget price	£2.50	=	375,000
150,000 × Actual price	£2.375	=	356,250
Adverse price variance	£0.125		18,750

	£
Actual units sold 150,000 × Budget gross profit £1.00 =	150,000
Budgets units sold 125,000 × Budget gross profit £1.00 =	125,000
Favourable volume variance	25,000

44.7

	Actual units sold £	Budget price £	Actual price	Unit price variance £	Total price variance £
M	840	5	5.10	+0.10	+84
N	1,680	8	7.90	-0.10	-168
P	280	7	7.30	+0.30	+84
	2,800		Total price variance		0

	Actual units sold	Actual units in budget %	Budget sales	Variance in units	Budget gross profit per unit £	Total variance £
M	840	700	800	-100	1.00	-100
N	1,680	1,400	1,600	-200	1.50	-300
P	280	700	800	-100	1.20	-120
	2,800	2,800	3,200	-400		-520

	Actual units in budget %	Actual units sold	Variance in units	Budget gross profit per unit £	Total variance £
M	700	840	+140	1.00	+140
N	1,400	1,680	+280	1.50	+420
P	700	280	-420	1.20	-504
	2,800	2,800	—		+56

Summary of Sales Variance

Price variance	0
Volume variance adverse	520
Mix variance favourable	56
Net adverse variance	464

44.9

(a) See text Section 43.1.

(b)

(i) *Manufacturing Account for the year ended 31 August 19X9*

Singleton Ltd

	Actual £	Budget £	Variance £
Raw material consumed	90,000	80,000	(10,000)
Direct labour wages	115,600	120,000	4,400
Direct expenses	6,000	5,800	(200)
Prime cost	211,600	205,800	(5,800)
Factory overhead expenses:			
Factory rent	10,000	10,000	–
Factory maintenance	6,100	6,700	600
Heating and lighting	3,900	2,900	(1,000)
Depreciation	10,500	8,900	(1,600)
Wages, maintenance labour	24,000	18,000	(6,000)
Other factory overhead	10,000	12,700	2,700
Production cost of goods completed	276,100	265,000	(11,100)

(ii) *Trading Account for the year ended 31 August 19X9*

	£	£
Sales		405,000
Stock of finished goods 1 Sep X8	28,900	
Production cost	276,100	
	305,000	
Less Stock of fin. goods 31 Aug X9	35,000	
Cost of sales		270,000
Gross profit		135,000

(c) See text.

Note to Exercises on Break-Even Analysis

The general idea of the questions is to get you to draw up the schedules of costs and revenues and then to draw them carefully on graph paper. It will be a waste of time if you do not use graph paper. It illustrates that accounting data can be represented in diagram form for some users in a more effective way than just using figures. It also puts over the idea that businesses exist to make a profit, and that until sufficient volume is achieved then the business will incur losses. The impact of fixed costs on firms can be revealed quite sharply by this sort of analysis.

45.1

(i)

No. of units	Fixed cost	Variable cost	Total cost	Revenue	Profit	Loss
0	8,000	–	8,000	–	–	8,000
1,000	8,000	4,000	12,000	6,000		6,000
2,000	8,000	8,000	16,000	12,000		4,000
3,000	8,000	12,000	20,000	18,000		2,000
4,000	8,000	16,000	24,000	24,000	nil	nil
5,000	8,000	20,000	28,000	30,000	2,000	
6,000	8,000	24,000	32,000	36,000	4,000	
7,000	8,000	28,000	36,000	42,000	6,000	
8,000	8,000	32,000	40,000	48,000	8,000	
9,000	8,000	36,000	44,000	54,000	10,000	
10,000	8,000	40,000	48,000	60,000	12,000	

(ii) Similar in style to Exhibit 45.2 in the textbook. As it really needs graph paper we regret that the graph cannot be provided in this answer section.

45.2 (a) (i) £24,000 (ii) £36,000 (iii) £44,000 (iv) £30,000.
(b) (i) £18,000 (ii) £48,000 (iii) £33,000.

45.4 (i) Loss £2,000 (ii) Profit £12,000 (iii) Nil (iv) Profit £6,000 (v) Profit £9,000.

45.6

(a)

(i) $\text{Break-even point} = \dfrac{\text{Total fixed costs}}{\text{Selling price per unit} - \text{Variable cost per unit}}$

For 19X1 = $\dfrac{250,000}{130 - 110}$ = 12,500 units

= sales of 12,500 units × £130 = £1,625,000 sales

For 19X2 = $\dfrac{275,000}{129 - 118\cdot5}$ = sales of 26,190 units × £129

= £3,378,510 sales

For 19X3 = $\dfrac{275,000}{128.5 - 122}$ = sales of 42,308 units × £128.5 = £5,436,578 sales

(ii)

Polemic Ltd
Actual & Forecast Profit & Loss Accounts for years to 30 September (£000s)

	Actual 19X1	Forecast 19X2	Forecast 19X3
Sales	6,500	6,708	6,810.5
Direct materials	2,500	2,860	2,915
Direct labour	1,500	1,638	1,749
Variable production	500	572	636
Direct expenses	250	260	318
Variable sales overhead	750	832	848
	5,500	6,162	6,466
Contribution	1,000	546	344.5
Fixed costs			
Production	50	55	55
Overhead	200	220	220
	250	275	275
	750	271	69.5

(b) Should best be on graph paper. General idea follows:

Total sales

Total costs

Not exactly to scale

Break-even point

Cost in £m — (axis: 7, 6, 5, 4, 3, 2, 1)

Sales units in 000s — (axis: 0 1 2 3 4 5 6)

(c) The management of Polemic should be explaining to the union that their demand is unreasonable. As it is, profits have fallen dramatically and the break-even point in 19X3 will be over three times higher than in 19X1.

It is therefore almost impossible for the company to raise prices still further and maintain their level of sales. To try to do so would almost certainly mean a fall in demand and a shedding of a large part of the workforce.

(d) See text.

45.8 A

Hampshire plc
Profit Statement for first and second quarters

	First quarter		Second quarter	
Sales		126,000		143,640
Materials	32,850		39,420	
Labour	18,900		22,680	
Variable factory o/h	12,600		15,120	
Variable selling costs	7,650	72,000	9,180	86,400
Contribution		54,000		57,240
Fixed costs:				
Factory overhead	21,375		21,375	
Selling & admin	16,125	37,500	16,125	37,500
Net profit		16,500		19,740

Contribution per unit $\frac{54,000}{9,000} = 6.00$ $\qquad \frac{57,240}{10,800} = 5.30$

B Draw on graph paper. Break-even points are at:

First quarter $= \frac{37,500}{14.00 - 8.00} = 6,250$ units

Second quarter $= \frac{37,500}{13.30 - 8.00} = 7,075$ units

Margins of safety above these points.

C Profit statements incorporating suggestions

No. of units sold	(i)	(ii)	(iii)	(iv)	(v)
	11,880	11,556	12,960	10,800	10,800
Sales (W1)	158,004	158,317	155,131	143,640	143,640
Materials	46,926	43,913	47,304	39,420	
Labour	24,948	27,734	27,216	22,680	see (W2)
Variable factory o/h	16,632	16,178	18,144	15,120	87,900
Variable selling o/h	10,098	9,823	11,016	11,340	
Total variable costs	98,604	97,648	103,680	88,560	87,900
Contribution	59,400	60,669	51,451	55,080	55,740
Fixed costs					
Factory	21,375	21,375	21,375	21,375	see (W3)
Selling, etc.	16,125	16,125	16,125	12,025	35,000
	37,500	37,500	37,500	33,400	35,000
Net profit	21,900	23,169	13,951	21,680	20,740
Redundancy					12,000

Workings

(W1) Selling price per unit (i) 13.30 (ii) 13.70 (iii) 11.97 (iv) 13.30 (v) 13.30.

(W2) Per accounts of second quarter in A 86,400 + extra costs 5p per component, 30,000 × 0.5p = 1,500. Total 87,900.

(W3) Fixed costs 37,500 – saving 2,500 = 35,000. Assumed that the 20 per cent of the firm's fixed costs would still continue as they would have to be paid anyway. Question not too clear on this point.

D Briefly:

(i) Would increase profit by 21,900 – 19,740 = 2,160. Seems to be a sensible opportunity which should be considered.

(ii) Apparently increases profit by 23,169 – 19,740 = 3,429. No mention as to what the cost of maintaining the guarantee is likely to be. Until this is known it is impossible to come to a conclusion.

(iii) Fall in profit of 19,740 – 13,951 = 5,789. Should not be considered.

(iv) Increases profit by 21,680 – 19,740 = 1,940. Have to renegotiate terms of employment with sales staff. Worth considering.

(v) Firm

(a) If we stop making components how can we be certain that suppliers will not later raise prices?

(b) Would we have to keep larger stocks of components in case of breakdown of supply?

(c) Possible that newly established firm has got its prices wrong and will be unable to maintain at this price for long.

(d) Effect on morale of other employees. Local community: write generally about effects of unemployment and knock-on effects.

E *See text Section 27.4.*

45.10 (a) Magwitch Ltd

Summarised Profit and Loss Account for the year to 31 May 19X1

Sales volume: units	20,000

	£
Sales £1.50 + 10% = 1.65 per unit	33,000
Variable costs (20–10) × 0.50 + 10% = 55p per unit	11,000
Contribution	22,000
Fixed costs 0.50 + 10% = 55p per unit	11,000
Profit	11,000

(b) Compeyson plc

Balance sheet as at 31 May 19X1

Fixed assets (40 + 160)		200
Current assets (65 + 340 – 24 *see* W2)	381	
Short-term liabilities (26 +110)	136	
		245
		445
Share capital (200 + 60 *see* W2)		260
Share premium (60 × 0.80)		48
Reserves (190 – 53)		137
		445

Workings

(W1) Purchase price 12 × 11 = | 132

Net assets taken over	71
+ revalued property	8
	79
Goodwill written off to reserves	53

46.9

$$\text{Paid in per year} = \frac{\text{Value} \times (r)}{(1+r)^n - 1}$$

$$= \frac{£20{,}000 \times 0.08}{(1.08)^{10} - 1}$$

$$= £1{,}380 \text{ per year}$$

46.11

		19X2	19X3
Equipment purchased		40,000	
Sale of old equipment			(10,000)
Installation of equipment completed and paid		12,000	10,000
Costs incurred in commissioning equipment		18,000	
Rent on premises up to completion date		6,000	(6 months)
Training costs			3,000
Working capital			4,000
Net cash outlay		76,000	14,000
			21,000

46.12

Capital cost 19X2	76,000			
19X2 25% WDA	19,000	@ 40% tax £7,600 received 19X3		
balance c/d	57,000			
New expenditure	17,000	excluding scrap value and		
	74,000	additional working capital		
19X3 25% WDA	18,500	@ 40% tax £7,400 received 19X4		
balance c/d	55,500			
19X4 25% WDA	13,875	@ 40% tax £5,550 received 19X5		
balance c/d	41,625			
19X5 25% WDA	10,406	@ 40% tax £4,162 received 19X6		
balance c/d	31,219			

This will continue over the life of the equipment. In 19X4 the cash received from the sale of old equipment will be taxed at 40 per cent, resulting in a tax outflow of £4,000.

	19X2	19X3	19X4	19X5	
Capital cash flow	(76,000)	(7,000)			
Tax relief		7,600	7,400	5,550	etc
Tax on sale			(4,000)		
Net cash flow	(76,000)	600	3,400	5,550	etc

(W2) Method of payment of purchase price

Shares 40 × 3/2 = 60 × 1.80	108	
Cash (balance)	24	132

(c) Shares 6,000 × 3/2 = 9,000 shares

Cash 6,000/40,000 × 24,000 = £3,600

46.1 (a) $12{,}000 \times 0.09 \times \frac{56}{365} = 165.70$

(b) $6{,}000 \times 0.15 \times \frac{80}{365} = 197.26$ Discount,

therefore amount paid = £5,802.74

46.3 The amount borrowed is:

$3{,}000 \times \frac{1}{4}$ =	750.00	
$2{,}250 \times \frac{1}{4}$ =	562.50	
$1{,}500 \times \frac{1}{4}$ =	375.00	
$750 \times \frac{1}{4}$ =	187.50	
Equivalent loan for 1 year	1,875.00	

$$r = \frac{1000}{1875} = 0.533 \text{ or } 53.3\%$$

46.4 £1,000 will accumulate to $£1{,}000 \times (1 + 0.12)^5 = £1{,}762$

Interest is £1,762 − £1,000 = £762

46.7 The present value of an annuity of £4,000 p.a. for four years at 10%

= £4,000 × 3.170 = £12,680 or:

$$\text{Present value} = £4{,}000 \times \left[\frac{1 - \dfrac{1}{(1+0.1)^4}}{0.1} \right] = £12{,}680$$

As it exceeds the present value of the rent, you should accept the offer of £15,000.

46.13

	Net cash flow	Discount factor (10%)	Present value
19X2	(76,000)	0.909	(69,084)
19X3	600	0.826	496
19X4	3,400	0.751	2,553
19X5	5,550	0.683	3,791
		NPV at start	(62,244)

46.17

Period	Amount	Balance	
0	(10,000)	(10,000)	
1	8,000	(2,000)	–
2	4,000		–
3	2,000		–
4	1,000		–

payback at 1 plus 2,000/4,000 years = 1.5 years

46.18

Period	Amount	Discount factor 12%	Present value
0	(10,000)	1.000	(10,000)
1	8,000	0.893	7,144
2	4,000	0.797	3,188
3	2,000	0.712	1,424
4	1,000	0.636	636
	Overall net present value of cash flows		2,392

46.19

Period	Amount	Discount factor (28%)	Present value	Discount factor (32%)	Present value
0	(10,000)	1.000	(10,000)	1.000	(10,000)
1	8,000	0.781	6,248	0.758	6,064
2	4,000	0.610	2,440	0.574	2,296
3	2,000	0.477	954	0.435	870
4	1,000	0.373	373	0.329	329
			15		(441)
			456		

28% discount rate gives NPV of 15
32% discount rate gives negative NPV of 441
456

The IRR is $\frac{15}{456}$ × 4% = 0.13% + 28% = 28.13%

46.20 The present value of an annuity of £1 for four years at 12% is 3.037. The NPV according to 46.18 is £2,392, therefore the annualised amount = 2,392/3.037 = 787.62

46.27

	Net present value (10%)
Machine A project	4,522
Machine B project	11,566

The Machine B project should be selected.

46.28

	Internal rate of return
Machine A project	22.4%
Machine B project	20.2%

The Machine A project would be preferred. However, comparing the NPV and IRR results, and remembering the rule of thumb that NPV should be followed when the two methods disagree, the Machine B project should be selected.

46.31 The present value of an annuity of £1 for five years at 10% is 3.791. Therefore the annualised amount = 3,100/3.791 = 817.73

46.33 £20,000 × present value factor of an annuity = £64,800. Therefore the present value factor = 64,800/20,000 = 3.24, which is 9% according to the tables.

46.34
Cost of machine £60,000 × (1 – 0.4) = 36,000
Cost of leasing £14,633 × (1 – 0.4) = 8,780

Present value for five years = $\frac{36,000}{8,780}$ = 4.1

which is 7% according to the tables.

46.35 Factor present value of an annuity of £1 for six years at 16% = 3.685
£4,000 × 3.685 = £14,740 capital value of the lease.

To the Directors of Road Wheelers Ltd
The NPV anticipated for the three vehicles is as follows:

BN Roadhog	£6,002	Positive
FX Sprinter	£2,519	Negative
VR Rocket	£ 92	Negative

On the basis of NPV assessment using a discount rate of 10 per cent the BN Roadhog appears to be the best option.

The payback position on the three vehicles is as follows:

BN Roadhog	3 years	9.3 months
FX Sprinter	4 years	3.8 months
VR Rocket	4 years	3.2 months

This indicates that the BX Roadhog recovers the cash outlay faster than the other two options which is in its favour.

Since the capital outlay on the BX Roadhog is also significantly lower than the other options this indicates a lower risk and will enhance the ROC on the balance sheet figures.

The BN Roadhog appears to be the best choice.

(b) The problems in evaluating capital projects are essentially related to the estimates involved in forecasting the revenues and costs associated with the project. In this evaluation the relative performance of the three alternatives may be more reliable than overall estimates of the environment. In some situations important factors in the decision may not be readily quantified especially in areas of new technology where many factors are unknown.

The techniques of evaluating the cash flow data are well understood but care must be taken that an appropriate 'cost of capital' is chosen and that risk is taken into account.

46.36 (a)

BN Roadhog

	0	1	2	3	4	5
Cash inflow		12,500	15,000	20,000	20,000	20,000
Cash outflow						
fixed		2,000	2,000	2,200	2,400	2,400
variable		3,000	3,600	4,800	4,800	4,800
Operating cash flow		7,500	9,400	13,000	12,800	12,800
Capital	40,000					8,000
	40,000	7,500	9,400	13,000	12,800	20,800
	1.00	0.909	0.826	0.751	0.683	0.621
	40,000	6,817	7,764	9,763	8,742	12,916

NPV = 6,002 positive

FX Sprinter

	0	1	2	3	4	5
Cash inflow		12,500	15,000	20,000	20,000	20,000
Cash outflow						
fixed		1,800	1,800	1,800	2,000	2,200
variable		4,000	4,800	6,400	6,400	6,400
Operating cash flow		6,700	8,400	11,800	11,600	11,400
Capital	45,000					9,000
	45,000	6,700	8,400	11,800	11,600	20,400
	1.00	0.909	0.826	0.751	0.683	0.621
	45,000	6,090	6,938	8,862	7,923	12,668

NPV = 2,519 negative

VR Rocket

	0	1	2	3	4	5
Cash inflow		12,500	15,000	20,000	20,000	20,000
Cash outflow						
fixed		1,500	1,500	1,400	1,400	1,400
variable		3,500	4,200	5,600	5,600	5,600
		7,500	9,300	13,000	13,000	13,000
Capital	50,000					14,000
	50,000	7,500	9,300	13,000	13,000	27,000
	1.00	0.909	0.826	0.751	0.683	0.621
	50,000	6,817	7,682	9,763	8,879	16,767

NPV = 92 negative

noting, however, that Ship B does have much higher capacity. If operating revenues were to expand more than forecast over the five years and thereafter, this ship might provide much higher returns. This operating forecast and the likely market values of the two vessels should therefore be closely examined.

46.38 (a) *Revised Operating Budget*

Ship A	19X5	19X6	19X7	19X8	19X9
Estimated revenue receipts	5	7	9	11	13
Extra revenue 10%	0.5	0.7	0.9	1.1	1.3
	5.5	7.7	9.9	12.1	14.3
Operating payments	4.0	5.0	6.5	7.5	9.0
Net cash flow Ship A	1.5	2.7	3.4	4.6	5.3

Ship B	19X5	19X6	19X7	19X8	19X9
Estimated revenue receipts:					
Private	2.5	3.5	5.0	6.5	7.5
Commercial	3.45	4.6	5.85	6.5	7.8
	5.95	8.1	10.85	13.0	15.3
Operating payments	4.8	6.0	7.9	9.0	10.8
Net cash flow Ship B	1.15	2.1	2.95	4.0	4.5

(b) *Cash flows*

	Ship A	Factor 15%		Ship B	Factor 15%	
0	(10.0)	1.0	(10.0)	(14.0)	1.0	(14.0)
19X6	1.5	0.870	1.3	1.15	0.87	1.0
19X7	2.7	0.756	2.0	2.1	0.756	1.6
19X8	3.4	0.658	2.2	2.95	0.658	1.9
19X9	4.6	0.572	2.6	4.0	0.572	2.3
19X0	5.3	0.497	2.6	4.5	0.497	2.2
			0.7			5.0
NPV	7.5	0.497	3.7	10.5	0.497	5.2

Assumed value of ship on market $^{15}/_{20}$ × cost: 4.4 | 0.2

Note: The calculation has been done with a zero assumption about cash value of ships at the end of year 5 and then with an assumed value equal to the unexplained cost value based on a 20-year life.

(c) The evaluation assumes an interest rate of 15 per cent and evaluates cash flows over the first five years' life of the ships. If the assumption is that at the end of five years the ships will have no value then Ship A has a positive NPV of £0.7m whilst B has a negative NPV of £5.0m. However, it is unlikely that the ships would be valueless at the end of year 5 and if an assumption is made to take 15/20 of the cost as the realisable value then both NPVs become positive at £4.4m and £0.2m respectively.

From this evaluation Ship A looks to give a better return. It is worth

Index

WEBSITE

A new feature of the Frank Wood range of accounting texts is a Website. This will support the many users of the books all over the world with valuable information and advice, including the teachers and lecturers who recommend Frank Wood's books and the many hundreds of thousands of students who learn about accounting from them.

The Website is contactable at **www.ftmanagement.com**

Main features are:

Welcome message from Frank Wood

Biographical information on Frank Wood and the history of his books
- information on Frank Wood's writing partners
- a list of current publications

Site map

Special area for students
- Which book? – matches your course to the books you require
- Updates on recent accounting standards
- Exam tips
- Tutorial support books
- Multiple-choice questions

Special password-protected area for lecturers
- Which book? feature – matches your course to the books and support material
- Updates on recent accounting standards
- Inspection copy ordering information
- On-line query service
- Additional questions and answers
- Case studies taken from *Financial Times*
- Overhead transparency masters
- *Solutions Manual*
- Order form
- Catalogue
- Links to other useful websites